THE NEW INTERNATIONAL COMMENTARY ON
THE NEW TESTAMENT

F. F. Bruce, *General Editor*

THE GOSPEL ACCORDING TO MARK

THE ENGLISH TEXT
WITH INTRODUCTION, EXPOSITION AND NOTES

by

WILLIAM L. LANE, TH. D.

Professor of New Testament and Judaic Studies in the Gordon-Conwell Theological Seminary

WILLIAM B. EERDMANS PUBLISHING COMPANY
GRAND RAPIDS, MICHIGAN

Printed in the United States of America

Reprinted, November 1975

Library of Congress Cataloging in Publication Data

Bible. N.T. Mark. English. 1974.
The Gospel according to Mark.

(The New international commentary on the New Testament, v. 2)

1. Bible. N.T. Mark–Commentaries.
I. Lane, William L., 1931- II. Title. III. Series.

BS2585.3.L36 226'.3'066 73-76529

ISBN 0-8028-2340-8

To

DR. BURTON L. GODDARD

Dean Colleague Friend

whose entire life and ministry

has exemplified

evangelical theological stewardship

CONTENTS

EDITOR'S FOREWORD

This is the third volume on the Gospels in the New International Commentary on the New Testament. The volume on the Gospel of Luke, by the late Norval Geldenhuys, was published as long ago as 1950 – it was in fact the first volume to appear in the series as a whole – and then we had to wait for over twenty years for the next Gospel commentary, Dr. Leon Morris's comprehensive exposition of the Gospel of John. Hard on its heels comes the present volume, and Professor Herman Ridderbos is currently at work on the exposition of Matthew's Gospel, which will complete the quartet.

The late General Editor of the series, Dr. N. B. Stonehouse, invited Dr. Lane to undertake the commentary on the Gospel of Mark shortly before his death in 1961. How sound Dr. Stonehouse's judgment was in extending this invitation the reader of the commentary may judge for himself.

Dr. Lane is known in scholarly circles as a member of the international Society for New Testament Studies and as a contributor to its journal, *New Testament Studies*. At a less specialist level he is known as joint-author (along with two of his colleagues at Gordon-Conwell Theological Seminary) of the volume *The New Testament Speaks* (New York: Harper & Row, 1969). But the writing of this commentary has provided him with an opportunity to deploy his scholarly and exegetical power to its full extent. In his Author's Preface he tells us, in greater detail than most of the contributors to this series, something of the scope and character of the commentary as he at first envisaged it and then carried it towards its conclusion. It is unnecessary for me to repeat what he has said, but much of the success of his enterprise is due to his early realizing that a commentator's primary task is "to listen to the text". Only if he has learned this lesson will a commentator effectively expound the text to others.

Mark did something which no one had done before: he wrote a Gospel. He was, in Laurence Housman's words,

> *The saint who first found grace to pen*
> *The life which was the Life of men.*

Dr. Lane (rightly, as I think) inclines to the view that the situation which called forth the writing of his Gospel was the crisis which broke upon the Christians of Rome in the reign of Nero, and repeatedly he shows how aptly the Gospel reflects its life-setting and speaks to the condition of its first readers. Jesus' warning that those who would follow him could do so only by denying themselves and taking up the cross must have come home with power to those first readers. The fiery ordeal which had come upon them was no "strange thing"; it was consistent with their Master's words, and as they underwent it they were drinking his cup and sharing his baptism. "Truly", said the centurion at the cross, "this man was the Son of God"; but it was the death of the cross that made this truth plain to men. As we see from the Caesarea Philippi incident and its sequel, the verbal recognition of our Lord's identity is meaningless unless it is given content by the declaration that "the Son of Man must suffer".

We are sometimes asked why, at this time of day, we persist in using the American Standard Version of 1901 as the basic text for the New International Commentary. The principal reason for our persistence is that its excessively literal style of translation, however unsuitable it may be for other purposes, is admirably suited to serve as the basis of a commentary which endeavors to pay careful attention to the details of the text.

F. F. Bruce

AUTHOR'S PREFACE

The invitation to prepare a full-length commentary on the Gospel of Mark came from Dr. Ned B. Stonehouse in the fall of 1961. At that time I had not yet completed my doctoral studies and I felt very inadequate to the task. I was encouraged to accept this responsibility only by the prospect of working closely with Dr. Stonehouse, who had been my mentor. He felt certain that in preparing his volume on Matthew he would encounter many of the problems which surface in a detailed study of Mark, and that we could meet periodically for an exchange of thoughts concerning the commentary. But before our first scheduled meeting it pleased the Lord to call his servant to himself. Since then, more than ten years have elapsed, during which I and the commentary have gradually matured together.

My conviction from the beginning has been that the kind of commentary which is needed is one which will reflect the wealth of contemporary scholarship and insight found in journal articles and monographs. Frequently aspects of the Marcan text that have been explored in depth have been lost for practical purposes with the binding and shelving of the volumes in which they were published. I have tried to review this vast reservoir of critical opinion and to make the best material accessible to the man who is not a specialist. My indebtedness to those who have labored in Gospel research, Roman law, Rabbinics and Marcan studies is evident on every page. Without the assistance offered by a multitude of men and women who became my teachers through their articles the present commentary could not have been prepared.

My research and writing of the commentary has been controlled by several goals. (1) In the interpretation of the Gospel I have sought for a new and primary faithfulness to the biblical text. My desire was to allow Mark to speak as a distinctive witness to the fact that Jesus is the Messiah, the Son of God. It was imperative that his voice not be drowned out by a concern for the harmonization of Mark's record with the other Synoptic Gospels. In the commentary there is a narrow concentration upon Mark's distinctive point of view, and only rarely is attention drawn to the Matthean or Lucan witness. This critical decision reflects the conviction that Mark is the oldest written Gospel. Since there was a formative period in which it was the only Gospel in circulation, it is imperative that the work as a whole and its several sections be seen in Marcan perspective. This approach has made possible a contribution to the interpretation of certain aspects of the mission and message of Jesus as well as an advance upon the historical and theological interpretation of Mark. (2) In attempting to reconstruct the life situation which called forth the Gospel and to fill in the gaps which make it intelligible, I have sought to indicate how the text was heard by Mark's contemporaries. Two impressions emerge: the material of the Gospel frequently presupposes the supportive activity of a charismatic teacher; and Mark's pastoral concern for his readers in Rome seems to account for the particular emphases and arrangement of the Gospel. (3) It has been important to place the study of Mark within the frame of reference offered by contemporary Gospel research. I have especially used the notes to interact with this research, as well as to advance the material support for a given position. I regard the notes to the commentary as an essential component in the total presentation of Mark's distinctive witness.

Only gradually did I come to understand that my primary task as a commentator was to listen to the text, and to the discussion it has prompted over the course of centuries, as a child who needed to be made wise. The responsibility to discern truth from error has been onerous at times. When a critical or theological decision has been demanded by the text before I was prepared to commit myself, I have adopted the practice of the Puritan commentators in laying the material before the Lord and asking for his guidance. This had made the preparation of the commentary a spiritual as well as an intellectual pilgrimage through the text of the Gospel. In learning to be sensitive to all that the evangelist was pleased to share with me I have been immeasurably enriched by the discipline of responsible listening.

It is a pleasant task to acknowledge the many persons who have encouraged me in the course of my research and writing. I am deeply grateful to Dr. Stonehouse for the confidence he expressed in me when he extended the invitation to contribute the volume on Mark to the New International Commentary. In my work I have sought to reflect the high standards of scholarship which he exemplified. I have appreciated the encouragement of his successor as General Editor, Dr. F. F. Bruce, who has been a model of patience in waiting for me to complete my work. My colleagues Glenn W. Barker and J. Ramsey Michaels read a first draft of the initial chapters and helped me to perceive the nature of my task. I have relied upon them for counsel and criticism at numerous points. Dr. Burton L. Goddard, to whom this volume is respectfully dedicated, has continually called to my attention items in the growing bibliography on Mark and has graciously secured for the library the volumes necessary to my research. The teaching of a course on Mark the past six years has allowed me to test my proposals with able students, whose questions and responses have served to sharpen my understanding of the text. The Senate and Administration of Gordon-Conwell Theological Seminary granted me a sabbatical year 1969-70 which permitted me to draft the major portion of the manuscript, while a faculty grant from the American Association of Theological Schools made possible travel to Lund, Sweden, where I was able to expose myself to Scandinavian Gospel research and was free to write without interruption. Thanks are due to my typists, Mrs. Lucilla Haynes, Mrs. Margaret Anderson and Mrs. Sylvia Lloyd, for the care with which they have prepared the manuscript. Many friends have expressed keen interest in the progress of the work whom I remember with thanksgiving. Special gratitude must be expressed to my wife, Lillian, and to our four children, Bill, Kristine, Mark and David, to whom this volume belongs in a real sense, for they have sacrificed much to assure its completion. Without their love, support and understanding the work would have been severely retarded. Finally, it is necessary to acknowledge the sustaining strength granted by the Lord, whose faithfulness to his servant is reflected in any excellence this volume may display. The commentary is sent forth with the prayer that it may strengthen the Church and call many others to a knowledge of Jesus the Messiah, the Son of God.

WILLIAM L. LANE

PRINCIPAL ABBREVIATIONS

A-G	[Walter Bauer's] *Greek-English Lexicon of the New Testament and Other Early Christian Literature,* translated and adapted by W. F. Arndt and F. W. Gingrich (Chicago, 1957)
ASV	*American Standard Version*
AThR	*Anglican Theological Review*
AV	*The Authorized Version*
BA	*Biblical Archaeologist*
BC	*The Beginnings of Christianity. Part 1: The Acts of the Apostles,* ed. K. Lake and F. J. Foakes-Jackson (London, 1922-33)
Bib Leb	*Bibel und Leben*
BJRL	*Bulletin of the John Rylands Library*
Bl-D-F	F. Blass & A. Debrunner, *A Greek Grammar of the New Testament & Other Early Christian Literature,* tr. and ed. by R. W. Funk (Chicago, 1961)
BZ	*Biblische Zeitschrift*
BZNW	*Beiheft zur Zeitschrift für die neutestamentliche Wissenschaft*
CBQ	*Catholic Biblical Quarterly*
CD	The Covenant of Damascus
ConThMon	*Concordia Theological Monthly*
DB	*Dictionnaire de la Bible*
DB Suppl	*Dictionnaire de la Bible, Supplement*
EC	*Encyclopedia of Christianity*
Eng. Tr.	English Translation
EphThLov	*Ephemerides Theologicae Lovanienses*
Est Bíb	*Estudios Bíblicos*
Ev Th	*Evangelische Theologie*
Exp	*Expositor*
ExT	*Expository Times*
HTR	*Harvard Theological Review*
HUCA	*Hebrew Union College Annual*
it	*Itala* (Old Latin Translation)
JBL	*Journal of Biblical Literature*
JE	*Jewish Encyclopedia*
JJS	*Journal of Jewish Studies*
JPOS	*Journal of the Palestine Oriental Society*
JQR	*Jewish Quarterly Review*

JRel	*Journal of Religion*
J Sem S	*Journal of Semitic Studies*
JThS	*Journal of Theological Studies*
LXX	The Septuagint
M	The Mishnah
MGWJ	*Monatschrift für die Geschichte und Wissenschaft des Jüdenthums*
M-M	*The Vocabulary of the Greek Testament,* by J. H. Moulton and G. Milligan (London, 1930)
MS (S)	Manuscript(s)
MT	The Massoretic Text
NEB	*The New English Bible, New Testament* (Oxford and Cambridge, 1961)
Nov Test	*Novum Testamentum*
n.s.	New Series
NT	New Testament
NTS	*New Testament Studies*
Or Syr	*l'Orient Syrien*
OT	Old Testament
RB	*Revue Biblique*
Rev Qum	*Revue de Qumran*
Rev Sci Ph Th	*Revue des Sciences Philosophiques et Théologiques*
Rev Théol Phil	*Revue de Théologie et de Philosophie*
RIDA	*Revue Internationale des Droits de l'Antiquité*
RSR	*Revue des Sciences Religieuses*
RSV	*The Revised Standard Version*
S-B*K*	(H. L. Strack and) P. Billerbeck, *Kommentar zum Neuen Testament aus Talmud und Midrasch*
ScJTh	*Scottish Journal of Theology*
Stud Theol	*Studia Theologica*
SvExÅrs	*Svensk Exegetisk Årsbok*
Targ. Onk.	Targum Onkelos
TB	The Babylonian Talmud
Theol Quart	*Theologisches Quartalschrift*
ThStKr	*Theologische Studien und Kritiken*
ThZ	*Theologisches Zeitschrift*
TJ	The Jerusalem Talmud

TLZ	*Theologische Literaturzeitung*
TrierThZ	*Trierer Theologisches Zeitschrift*
Tos	The Tosephta
TWNT	*Theologisches Wörterbuch zum Neuen Testament* (ed. G. Kittel and G. Friedrich)
Verb Dom	*Verbum Domini*
vg	The Vulgate
VS (S)	Version(s)
ZAW	*Zeitschrift für die Alttestamentliche Wissenschaft*
ZDPV	*Zeitschrift des Deutschen Palästina-Vereins*
ZNW	*Zeitschrift für die Neutestamentliche Wissenschaft*
ZThK	*Zeitschrift für Theologie und Kirche*

Quotations from the Bible are normally from the ASV, those from the Mishnah from the translation by H. Danby, from the Midrash and the Talmud from the Soncino translation, from the Qumran material from the translation of A. Dupont-Sommer, from Josephus, Philo and the Apostolic Fathers from the Loeb translation, from the Pseudepigrapha from the edition of R. H. Charles.

INTRODUCTION

It is generally recognized that Mark represents the earliest attempt to reduce the apostolic tradition to a written form. Synoptic criticism has in the last century and a half produced detailed evidence that Matthew and Luke had before them a document virtually identical with our Gospel of Mark. The remarkable agreements of both Matthew and Luke with Mark in regard to content, order and wording found a convincing explanation on the hypothesis of Marcan priority.[1]

If Mark is indeed the first Gospel, it merits the most careful consideration. Its author introduced to the Roman world a type of popular literature previously unknown. The form of the Gospel appears to have been shaped by the mission proclamation of the early Christian community. Here for the first time the words and deeds of Jesus were remembered and proclaimed in a written form. It is therefore appropriate to label Mark a *witness document* that found its creative impulse in the early apostolic preaching of salvation through Jesus Christ. It is intended to be neither a formal historical treatise nor a biography of Jesus, but proclamation. The evangelist's intention is grasped when the opening line of the Gospel is paraphrased, "The beginning of the preaching of the joyful tidings." What follows is an historical narrative oriented around a crisis – the death of Jesus the Messiah. There are valid reasons for believing that the Gospel was written for people who themselves confronted a crisis not dissimilar to the one faced by Jesus.

Throughout his entire Gospel Mark bears witness to the word of revelation that Jesus is the Messiah, the Son of God (Ch. 1:1). The initial verse of the Gospel dictates the structure of the account which follows. Mark's witness in the first half of the document reaches a point of climax with the confession of Peter at Caesarea Philippi that Jesus is the Messiah (Ch. 8:29). All that has preceded has prepared for this moment of recognition. All that follows, as Jesus directs his way to Jerusalem and the Passion, clarifies what messiahship entails. The climax to the second half of the Gospel is provided in the confession

1 A standard statement of the evidence for the priority of Mark is presented by B. H. Streeter, *The Four Gospels* (London, 1953), pp. 151-198; cf. D. Guthrie, *New Testament Introduction, The Gospels and Acts* (Chicago, 1965), pp. 114-211. For recent challenges to this position see William R. Farmer, *The Synoptic Problem* (New York, 1964), who argues for Matthean priority; and R. L. Lindsey, "A Modified Two-Document Theory of the Synoptic Dependence and Interdependence," *Nov Test* 6 (1963), pp. 239-263, who argues for Lucan priority.

of the centurion in charge of the crucifixion that Jesus is the Son of God (Ch. 15:39). Through the vehicle of these two confessions, one uttered by a representative of Israel and the other by a spokesman for the Gentile world, Mark bears witness to the faith which undergirds his document.

Mark's Gospel has been described as "a passion-narrative with an extended introduction."[2] The reason that almost half of Mark's sixteen chapters describe the final period of Jesus' ministry is that it is in his suffering, death and resurrection that the revelation of God in Christ is most clearly seen. Throughout the Gospel Mark has prepared for the acceleration of tension and movement which characterizes the Passion-narrative.[3] The task and destiny of the Son is sharply presented in a series of mission-sayings which reflect on the purpose for which Jesus was sent into the world by the Father (cf. Chs. 2:17; 8:31; 9:31; 10:33f., 45). These statements involve Mark's readers in the offense of the cross, and prepare them to be left before the witness of the empty tomb as interpreted by the word of an angel:

> "You seek Jesus of Nazareth, who was crucified. He has risen, He is not here. See the place where they laid him" (Ch. 16:6).

Mark records this tradition in order to call men to faith. It is this characteristic of the Gospel which sets it off as a witness-document.

Mark's work was widely circulated and became the model for two other evangelists, Matthew and Luke, who not only appropriated much of the Marcan material but adopted the structure of his Gospel as well. Thus the first Gospel became a literary influence, stimulating a new form of popular literature, the "Gospel" or book of witness.

The sections of the introduction which follow attempt to place the Gospel in the larger context of contemporary discussion. They are necessarily brief and introductory in character, rather than exhaustive. Nevertheless, the issues posed have bearing on the interpretation to the text and are foundational to the exposition presented in the commentary.

---

[2] The phrase is Martin Kähler's and was applied by him to all the Gospels. See *The So-called Historical Jesus and the Historic Biblical Christ* (Chicago, 1964, transl. of 1896 edition), p. 80.

[3] The increasing clarity with which Jesus and his opponents speak may be noted in the sequence Chs. 2:20; 3:5f.; 8:31; 9:12, 31; 10:33f., 38, 45; 12:6-8; 14:1-2, 8, 10f., 17-21, 22-25, 27, 34, 36, 37f., 41f., 48f.

1. A New Direction for Marcan Studies

Prior to the emergence of modern criticism the Gospel of Mark was almost totally neglected. In the patristic period it was so thoroughly overshadowed by the Gospel of Matthew that in the late fifth century Victor of Antioch complained of the total absence of commentaries on Mark. To supply what was lacking Victor made a compilation from earlier exegetical writings of Origen, Titus of Bostra, Theodore of Mopsuestia, Chrysostom and Cyril of Alexandria, who had commented incidentally on Mark in their expositions of Matthew, Luke and John. [4] The rarity of ancient commentaries on the Gospel is due to the commonly received opinion that Mark was only an abstract of Matthew. This persuasion was scarcely challenged until the nineteenth century, when the conviction that Mark provided the key for solving the Synoptic problem introduced the period of modern criticism.

The early emphasis upon literary and source criticism of the Gospels was followed by the dominance of form criticism under the influence of men like K. L. Schmidt, Martin Dibelius and R. Bultmann. [5] Paradoxically, it was the interruption in literary publications during the second World War that opened the way for fresh questions and a re-thinking of Synoptic studies. Among the new names whose appearance signaled a shift in emphasis in the approach to the Gospels were G. Bornkamm (Matthew), H. Conzelmann (Luke) and W. Marxsen (Mark). [6]

With the publication in 1956 of Willi Marxsen's *Der Evangelist Markus – Studien zur Redaktionsgeschichte des Evangeliums,* a new direction was given to Marcan studies. [7] Marxsen's concern was the evangelist Mark who first created the distinctive literary form designated "the Gospel." His basic presupposition was that the well-planned, particular character of the Gospel of Mark – in contrast to the anonymous char-

---

4 H. Smith, "The Sources of Victor of Antioch's Commentary on Mark," *JThS* 19 (1918), pp. 350-370. See further the patristic material in J. A. Cramer, *Catenae Graecorum Patrum in Novum Testamentum* I (Oxford, 1840), pp. 263-447, and the discussion of R. Devreesse, "Chaînes exégétiques grecques. Les chaînes sur S. Marc," *DB Suppl* I (1928), cols. 1175-1181.

5 A convenient summary of the presuppositions, emphases and insights of these men is provided by J. Rohde, *Rediscovering the Teaching of the Evangelists* (Philadelphia, 1968), pp. 1-8, 31-46.

6 *Ibid.,* pp. 47-54, 113-140, 154-178.

7 Eng. Tr., *Mark the Evangelist. Studies on the Redaction History of the Gospel,* transl. by R. A. Harrisville *et al.* (Nashville, 1969). The numbers in parenthesis in the discussion of Marxsen refer to the English edition of this work.

acter of individual passages derived from the oral tradition – demands "an individual, an author-personality who pursues a definite goal with his work" (p. 18). He reasoned that the individual impetus exerted in fashioning the oldest Gospel could be estimated from the fact that, unlike Matthew and Luke, who possessed Mark's structured account, the first evangelist had at his disposal only a passion narrative, certain collections of material and anonymous individual units of tradition. By transmitting this tradition according to a planned editing, Mark succeeded in structuring, and even restructuring, the tradition in terms of a personal formation. In Gospel research, Marxsen contended, primary consideration must be given to this formation, i.e. to the tradition as laid down within the totality of the Gospel. While form criticism had been oriented toward individual fragments of the tradition, what was distinctive of Marxsen's approach was its orientation toward the total work, in the conviction that the evangelist-redactor who edited the tradition was himself a creative person (pp. 21 f.).

Marxsen labelled his approach "redaction criticism." To the extent that form-critical analysis was assumed to determine the limits of the redactor's work, redaction criticism is the child of form criticism. But it was clear that the child was engaged in open revolt against the parent. Form criticism, with its interest in small units of tradition within the text, traced their development back to earlier stages in the tradition in order to account for their form in terms of the presumed life situation in which they arose. The decisive question concerned the life situation out of which a given unit of tradition emerged. The redactors or editors of the Gospels were considered essentially "collectors" of developed traditions who contributed almost nothing to the formation and shaping of the material. In opposition to this critical reconstruction, the proponents of redaction criticism consider the evangelist-redactors to be the crucial figures in the formation of the Synoptic Gospels. In the construction of the framework of the Gospel and in the use of techniques of style, they were guided by a conscious theological purpose. Marxsen urged that it was necessary for NT research to move beyond the formation of individual units of tradition to the form and shaping of the canonical Gospels themselves. In pursuance of this quest, he defined as the essential question the determination of the life situation out of which a particular Gospel emerged.

In order to grasp Mark's achievement Marxsen investigated the framework of the Gospel, broadly conceived. By framework Marxsen meant the "seams," interpretive comments, summaries, modifications of material, the selection of material, the omission of material, the arrangement, the introductions and conclusions to sections, i.e. all "textual transformations, to the extent we can recognize them" (p. 22). On the basis of an examination of this framework Marxsen insisted that it was necessary to distinguish three different levels of life situation within the Gospel: the first level is found in the non-recurring situation of Jesus' activity; the second is provided by the situation of the church in which units of tradition circulate; the third level relates to the situation of the primitive community in which the Gospel originated. This third level is the particular concern of redaction criticism, on the assumption that "a literary work or fragment of tradition is a primary source for the historical situation out of which it arose, and is only a secondary source for the historical details concerning which it gives information" (p. 24).[8] Marxsen, therefore, inquires into the situation of the community in which the Gospel came into being – its point of view, its time, and even its composition. This sociological concern, however, is narrowly related to the specific interest and basic conceptions of the evangelist himself. Marxsen believes that each community developed a distinct "form" from its own problems and for its own ends (p. 25). In spite of the fact that the three Synoptic Gospels contain extensively similar subject matter, their individual "form" is distinct. This is already suggested by the statements with which each of the Gospels begins. While Mark created the "gospel-form," Matthew intended to produce a chronicle while Luke's purpose was to write a life of Jesus (pp. 25, 207-213).

In the pursuit of his research Marxsen used both the analytical and the constructive approach. He pointed to the circular character in which the work of redaction criticism participates. From (1) the form of the Gospel one can make (2) conclusions about the author and the situation in his community, which in turn provides (3) insight into the form of the Gospel. His method was to approach Mark from two vantage-points. First, he sought to go back beyond Mark and to separate the tradition from the final redaction in order to construct a reasonable explanation for the manner in which the Gospel is composed. Then, second, he brings to the investigation Matthew and Luke, emphasizing their altered conception in an attempt to achieve a clear understanding of that which is typically Marcan. Matthean and Lucan developments

[8] Cited by Marxsen from R. Bultmann, "The New Approach to the Synoptic Problem," *JRel* 6 (1926), p. 341.

which go beyond Mark are important for the conclusions which may be drawn from them for Mark's distinctive point of view.[9]

Without considering the conclusions to which Marxsen was led by his critical methodology,[10] it is important to appreciate the positive contributions that his approach has made to the study of the Gospels and of Mark. (1) In contrast to the emphases of form criticism which viewed the evangelists primarily as editors of pre-formed units of tradition, redaction criticism emphasizes their creative role in shaping the tradition and in exercising a conscious theological purpose in writing the Gospels. (2) While form criticism focused upon the formation of the *oral* tradition, redaction criticism focuses upon the completed *written* Gospels. Since oral tradition exists in the shadowy pre-history of the Gospels and is therefore ultimately irretrievable, the concentration upon the written form of the Gospel in redaction criticism affords the possibility of a somewhat greater objectivity with respect to the text. (3) Because redaction criticism takes seriously the unity of the Gospels, it provides guidelines for detecting the theological intention behind the selection and arrangement of the material by the evangelists. (4) As a discipline it serves to caution the interpreter of the danger latent in the harmonization of two similar accounts and in the exegesis of small independent units without consideration of the Gospel as a total work. (5) The recognition of the distinct theological perspective of each evangelist has encouraged a greater concern to reconstruct the life situation which called forth the Gospels.

Marxsen's own redaction-critical study of Mark is flawed by a number of questionable assumptions that he shares with form criticism. He incorrectly assumed (1) that units of Synoptic tradition are basically anonymous in origin (p. 19); (2) that the Gospels are not primary sources for the historical details they report (p. 24); and (3) that proclamation, rather than history *per se,* is the locus of divine self-disclosure. These deficiencies reflect a defective view of the relationship of history to revelation. God appears to act not in space-time history, but only in Church proclamation. This de-historicizing hermeneutic ob-

---

[9] This two-pronged approach was applied in four studies: (1) John the Baptist and the wilderness tradition; (2) the geographical statements of the Gospel; (3) Mark's use of the term εὐαγγέλιον; (4) the speech complex in Ch. 13. A final summary correlated the major results of these independent studies.

[10] See W. L. Lane, "*Redaktionsgeschichte* and the De-historicizing of the New Testament Gospel," *Bulletin of the Evangelical Theological Society* 11 (1968), pp. 27-33.

scures both the OT witness to God's mighty acts *in history* and the central truth of God's Incarnation in human life and affairs. The result is a new gnosticizing of the Christian faith.

There is no necessary reason why redaction criticism should lead to the de-historicizing of the NT Gospel. Marxsen's conclusions in this regard are due not to the method he uses but to his faulty presupposition that a literary work is a primary source for the historical situation out of which it arose, and is only a secondary source for the historical details concerning which it gives information. Historical questions are inherent in the content of early Church proclamation, while the existence of the four Gospels testifies to the Church's interest in the earthly life of Jesus. The assertion that Mark made historical events subservient to his theological purpose demands the affirmation that there were *historical events*. The theological import of these events is dependent upon the activity of God. While the theological significance of the historical facts must not be denied, it must also be maintained that their theological meaning is dependent upon their historical occurrence. Ultimately it is the creative life of Jesus Christ, not the evangelists or the Church, that originates, controls and gives essential unity to the documents through which witness is borne to his achievement as the Messiah, the Son of God.

Nevertheless, Marxsen's critical studies were programmatic for all future Marcan research. While his own conclusions have been sifted and his critical methodology refined by subsequent studies, his achievement remains a permanent contribution to the study of the Gospel of Mark. That redaction criticism is a valid hermeneutical approach to understanding the text of Mark and the intention of the evangelist has been assumed in the commentary.

2. The Tradition Concerning the Gospel

The central question in inquiring about the tradition concerning the origin of Mark is whether the witness of the Gospel is essentially apostolic. An unbroken tradition affirms that the evangelist was intimately associated with the apostle Peter and that the contents of this Gospel depend significantly upon the message he proclaimed. The nature of the second century tradition may be exhibited in summary fashion before examining the Gospel record for supportive evidence that the tradition is credible.

The earliest statement concerning the Gospel of Mark is that of Papias, Bishop of Hierapolis, who wrote a book now lost, *Exegesis of the Lord's Oracles* (*ca.* A.D. 140), but known to us through quotations made by Eusebius. At one point he cited the testimony of an elder, who was evidently an older contemporary:

> And the Elder said this also: "Mark, having become the interpreter of Peter, wrote down accurately whatever he remembered of the things said and done by the Lord, but not however in order." For neither did he hear the Lord, nor did he follow him, but afterwards, as I said, Peter, who adapted his teachings to the needs of his hearers, but not as though he were drawing up a connected account of the Lord's oracles. So then Mark made no mistake in thus recording some things just as he remembered them. For he took forethought for one thing, not to omit any of the things that he had heard nor to state any of them falsely. [11]

The testimony that the author of the Gospel was intimately associated with the ministry of the apostle Peter is presented not as Papias's opinion but as the word of an earlier authority. It is therefore probable that Papias has preserved a tradition that can be traced at least as far as the beginnings of the second century. The passage as a whole appears to be intended to explain the character and authority of Mark's Gospel. It affirms that it is based upon proclamation and catechesis, and that its authority is apostolic since Peter was both an apostle and an eyewitness to the events of which he spoke. While the content of Mark's Gospel is viewed as derived substantially from Peter, there is a recognition of the initiative and independence of Mark as an evangelist, who did what Peter failed to do when he prepared a composition consisting of the sayings and deeds of the Lord. [12] By placing in the foreground

---

[11] Cited by Eusebius, *Hist. Eccl.* III. xxxix. 15. The passage has been often discussed and its terminology debated. See H. A. Riggs, "Papias on Mark," *Nov Test* 1 (1956), pp. 160-183; J. Kürzinger, "Das Papiaszeugnis und die Erstgestalt des Matthäusevangeliums," *BZ* 4 (1960), pp. 19-38; H. E. W. Turner, "Modern Issues in Biblical Studies: The Tradition of Mark's Dependence upon Peter," *ExT* 71 (1960), pp. 260-263; T. Y. Mullins, "Papias on Mark's Gospel," *Vigiliae Christianae* 14 (1960), pp. 216-224; W. C. van Unnik, "Zur Papias-Notiz über Markus (Eusebius, *H. E.* III. 39, 15)," *ZNW* 54 (1963), pp. 276 f.; N. B. Stonehouse, *Origins of the Synoptic Gospels* (Grand Rapids, 1963), pp. 10-15.

[12] On the comprehensive character of τὰ λογία in Papias see R. Gryson, "A propos du témoignage de Papias sur Matthieu. Le sens du mot λογίον chez les Pères du second siècle," *EphThLov* 41 (1965), pp. 530-547.

the statement that Mark wrote "accurately," and by concluding with an attestation to the trustworthiness of the Gospel, Papias displays a high regard for Mark's achievement.

An independent witness appears to be provided by the Anti-Marcionite Prologue attached to the Gospels in many Old Latin MSS (*ca.* 160-180 A.D.).[13] Although the preface to Mark is fragmentary, it provides the new information that Mark wrote his Gospel in Italy after the death of Peter:

> ... Mark declared, who is called "stump-fingered", because he had rather small fingers in comparison with the stature of the rest of his body. He was the interpreter of Peter. After the death of Peter himself he wrote down this same gospel in the regions of Italy.

This tradition provides the earliest testimony in support of the Roman origin of Mark, and takes its place as a significant witness from the period between Papias and Irenaeus.

The testimony of Irenaeus (*ca.* A.D. 175) is recorded in a section in which he speaks of all the Gospels.[14] After stating that Matthew wrote while Peter and Paul were preaching the gospel in Rome and establishing the church, he adds:

> And after the death of these Mark, the disciple and interpreter of Peter, also transmitted to us in writing the things preached by Peter.

Irenaeus thus adds his voice to the tradition that the specific background for the publication of the Gospel was the apostolic preaching of Peter, and affirms with the Anti-Marcionite Prologue that Mark undertook to transmit the proclamation in writing only after the apostle's death.

The Muratorian Canon, which contains a list of the books recognized as authoritive by the Church of Rome in the period A.D. 170-190, is a badly mutilated fragment. The initial sentence is a broken phrase which clearly refers to Mark since it is followed by a reference to Luke as the third of the Gospels. The sentence reads:

> "... at some things he was present, and so he recorded them."

---

13 See D. de Bruyne, "Les plus anciens prologues latines des Évangiles," *Revue Bénédictine* 40 (1928), pp. 193-214; R. G. Heard, "The Old Gospel Prologues," *JThS* n.s. 6 (1955), pp. 1-16.

14 *Adv. Haer.* III. i. 2. See on this passage N. B. Stonehouse, *op. cit.,* pp. 4-7.

A reasonable conjecture is that the preceding clause had made reference to Peter's preaching and teaching.[15]

These four citations, together with the superscription to the Gospel which has bearing on the question of authorship, may be regarded as representative of the received tradition in the second century. The witnesses may be associated with church centers in Asia (Papias), Rome (Anti-Marcionite Prologue, the Muratorian Canon) and Lyon (Irenaeus).[16] To these voices Tertullian (North Africa) and Clement (Alexandria) add their concurrence *ca.* A.D. 200.[17] The self-witness of the Gospel of Mark must be examined to determine the degree of confidence which may be placed in the early Church tradition.

The repeated statements that the background for Mark's Gospel was provided by Peter's preaching is supported by the striking fact that the outline of the Gospel is already suggested in the sermon summarized in Acts 10:36-41. The degree of parallelism may be exhibited in a table:

	Mark	Acts 10:36-41
Ch. 1:1	"The beginning of the joyful tidings concerning Jesus the Messiah, the Son of God.	"You know the word which he [God] sent to Israel, preaching joyful tidings of peace by the Messiah Jesus (he is Lord of all)
Ch. 1:2	As it is written in Isaiah the prophet . . . 'Prepare the way of the Lord.'	
Ch. 1:14	"Now after John was arrested, Jesus came into Galilee, preaching the joyful tidings of God . . .	which was proclaimed throughout all Judea, beginning from Galilee
Cf. Ch. 1:4-8		after the baptism which John preached:
Ch. 1:10	"And when he came up out of the water, immediately he saw the heavens opened and the Spirit descending upon him like a dove . . ."	how God anointed Jesus of Nazareth with the Holy Spirit and power;

15 See A. Ehrhardt, "The Gospels in the Muratorian Fragment," in *The Framework of the New Testament Stories* (Cambridge, Mass., 1964), pp. 11-14.

16 See N. B. Stonehouse, *op. cit.*, pp. 15-18.

17 Tertullian, *Against Marcion* IV. 2; Clement of Alexandria, *apud* Eusebius, *Hist. Eccl.* II. xv. 2; VI. xiv. 6 f.; *Adumbr. in I Peter* 5:13.

Cf. Ch. 1:16-10:52	dominated by narratives describing healing and exorcism, demonstrating the power of God at work in Jesus' ministry.	how he went about doing good and healing all that were oppressed by the devil, for God was with him.
Cf. Chs. 11-14	where Mark presents the Jerusalem ministry and activity of Jesus.	And we are witnesses of all that he did . . . in Jerusalem.
Cf. Ch. 15:1-39,	which focuses on the crucifixion of Jesus.	They put him to death by hanging him on a tree;
Cf. Ch. 16:1-8,	with its witness: "He is not here. He is risen, as he said."	but God raised him up on the third day."

While Peter's preaching has been epitomized for inclusion in the Acts, it is clear that its structural development and emphases are accurately reflected in the Marcan outline.

The content of Mark's Gospel is as kerygmatic as the outline, and provides added support to the tradition linking the written account with the apostolic preaching. Behind the Marcan form of the narrative it is sometimes possible to detect Peter's voice. Two illustrations of this occur early in the Gospel, in narratives which are told from Peter's perspective. In a natural way the accounts can be recast into the first person of experiential preaching:

Ch. 1:29 f.	"And he immediately left the synagogue, and entered the house of Simon and Andrew, with James and John. Now Simon's mother-in-law lay sick with a fever and in due course they spoke to him concerning her."	The Account Recast: "We immediately left the synagogue and entered into our house, and James and John also accompanied us within. Now my wife's mother was lying sick with a fever, and in due course we spoke to him concerning her."
Ch. 1:35-37	"And in the morning, a great while before day, he rose and went out to a lonely place, and there he prayed. And Simon and those who were with him followed him, and they found him and said to him, 'Every one is searching for you.'"	The Account Recast: "And in the morning, a great while before day, he rose and went out to a lonely place, and there he prayed. And we followed him and we found him and said to him, 'Every one is searching for you.'"

In other instances an incident is structured so that it displays an apparent sermonic introduction, and a conclusion appealing for men to consider some aspect of the dignity of Jesus (e.g. Chs. 2:1-12; 4:35-41; 7:31-37). The self-witness of the Gospel tends to validate the witness of the tradition and challenges the common critical presupposition that Mark was heir to an anonymous tradition, except for certain complexes and the Passion narrative. [18] If this were the case, then indeed a creative redactor would be needed to give the stamp of individuality to a faceless tradition. The personal stamp already impressed on the tradition by the apostles and first generation of teachers, however, must not be obscured. The Gospel tradition originated not with anonymous congregations but with eyewitnesses to the activity of Jesus from the time of his baptism to the moment of his ascension (cf. Acts 1:22; 2:32; I Cor. 15:5). Mark was not the inheritor of a completely faceless tradition, but one which already bore the impress of Peter's experience.

The tradition handed down by Papias, however, also stressed Mark's initiative and independence from Peter in the composition of the Gospel. Although Mark is a witness document prompted by the apostolic preaching and intended to serve the proclamation, the evangelist was ultimately responsible for the selection, arrangement and structuring of the tradition. The framework of the Gospel and its theological development demonstrate that Mark was a historian and theologian in his own right. The Church leaders responsible for attaching the superscription "according to Mark" to the Gospel early in the second century rightly displayed an awareness of the individuality which has been impressed upon the corporate witness of the church to Jesus the Messiah, the Son of God.

3. The Life Situation That Occasioned the Gospel

The clear tradition of the Church both in the west and the east toward the end of the second century and the beginning of the third is that Mark prepared his Gospel primarily for the Christians in Rome and Italy. [19] If it appeared in the second half of the decade A.D. 60-70 it

---

[18] E.g. W. Marxsen, *op. cit.*, p. 19.

[19] The Anti-Marcionite Prologues to Mark and Luke; Irenaeus, *Adv. Haer.* III. i. 1; cf. III. x. 6; Clement of Alexandria, *Hypotyposes apud* Eusebius, *Hist. Eccl.* VI. xiv. 6 f.

was called forth by a crisis confronting the Christian community. An appreciation of the life situation will indicate how the Christians in Rome could be informed by the tract read in their meetings.

The emperor at this time was Nero. After five years of responsible rule (A.D. 54-59) he had shown himself recklessly despotic in his relations with the aristocracy of Rome. By heavy taxation on the estates of childless couples, false accusations followed by confiscation of wealth, invitations to suicide at public banquets, he had reduced the Senate to abject servility and made of life a reign of terror for men of wealth. Relatively little attention, however, had been given by imperial authorities to the gatherings of Christians for worship. Their assemblies undoubtedly appeared indistinguishable from the vast number of religious societies and guilds found throughout Rome. Christians were occasionally accused of heinous offences by segments of the population. Especially were they accused of the hatred of men,[20] a charge based on the reluctance of Christians to participate in pagan guild feasts and other social affairs where idolatrous practices and immorality were common. No evidence exists, however, that the authorities regarded these charges seriously, or that there had been police investigation of the Christian gatherings.

The situation was radically altered by the disastrous fire that swept Rome in the summer of A.D. 64. The fire began among the cluttered shops near the Circus Maximus, but fanned by a strong wind it quickly spread to other wards of the city. After raging unchecked for more than a week it was brought under control, only to break out a second time from the estates of Tigellinus, head of the Praetorian guard. Of the fourteen wards of the city, only four were spared. Three wards were reduced to ash and rubble; in seven others many of the oldest buildings and monuments were destroyed or seriously damaged.

After the initial shock, popular resentment was fanned by widespread rumors that the fire had been officially ordered. Suetonius charges that Nero "set fire to the city so openly that several former consuls did not venture to lay hands on his chamberlains although they caught them on their estates with tow and firebrands."[21] Tacitus is more cautious. He states tersely, "Disaster followed. Whether it was accidental or

---

20 E.g. Tacitus, *Annals* XV. 44; cf. Athenagoras, *Legatio pro Christianis* iii; "Letter of the Churches of Lyons and Vienne" in Eusebius, *Hist. Eccl.* V. 1.

21 *The Lives of the Caesars* Bk. VI, *Nero* 38.

caused by the emperor's criminal act is uncertain – both versions have supporters." He reports that "no one dared fight the flames; attempts to do so were prevented by menacing gangs. Torches, too, were openly thrown in, by men crying that they acted under orders," but adds, "perhaps they had received orders; or they may just have wanted to plunder unhampered."[22] Nero did his utmost to aid the homeless and the injured, levying a tax for relief and lowering the price of grain to provide food for the impoverished. In a program of urban renewal he cleared the slums, widened the streets, provided new parks, and insisted that all new construction consist of fireproof material such as brick or stone. When none of these measures succeeded in allaying suspicion and resentment a scapegoat had to be found. Blame for the fire was placed squarely upon the Christians. Tacitus, writing a generation removed from these events, expressed himself with strong feeling:

> Neither human resources, nor imperial munificence, nor appeasement of the gods, eliminated sinister suspicions that the fire had been instigated. To suppress this rumor, Nero fabricated[23] scapegoats – and punished with every refinement the notoriously depraved Christians (as they were popularly called)... First, Nero had self-acknowledged Christians arrested. Then, on their information, large numbers of others were condemned – not so much for incendiarism as for their anti-social tendencies. Their deaths were made farcical. Dressed in wild animals' skins, they were torn to pieces by dogs, or crucified, or made into torches to be ignited after dark as substitutes for daylight. Nero provided his Gardens for the spectacle, and exhibited displays in the Circus, at which he mingled in the crowd – or stood in a chariot, dressed as a charioteer. Despite their guilt as Christians, and the ruthless punishment it deserved, the victims were pitied. For it was felt that they were being sacrificed to one man's brutality rather than to the national interest.[24]

Such erratic behavior by the central government meant that life became precarious for the Christians in Rome and Italy. While mass arrests and capital punishment upon admission to membership in a Christian group were presumably short-lived and localized excesses, they introduced the

[22] *Annals* XV. 36-38.

[23] Latin, *subdidit,* used of fraudulent substitution, or false suggestion. Tacitus did not believe the Christians were guilty of arson.

[24] *Annals* XV. 44.

Church to martyrdom. The self-awareness of the Christian community in this critical situation is reflected in I Peter, with its message of trial by fire addressed to the Asian churches. In I Peter 5:13 "Babylon" is a cryptogram for Rome, the city where the new Israel now found itself exiled and captive.

On this understanding, Mark's task was the projection of Christian faith in a context of suffering and martyrdom. If Christians were to be strengthened and the gospel effectively proclaimed it would be necessary to exhibit the similarity of situation faced by Jesus and the Christians of Rome. The Gospel of Mark is a pastoral response to this critical demand.

When Roman believers received the Gospel of Mark they found that it spoke to the situation of the Christian community in Nero's Rome. Reduced to a catacomb existence, they read of the Lord who was driven deep into the wilderness (Ch. 1:12 f.). The detail, recorded only by Mark, that in the wilderness Jesus was with the wild beasts (Ch. 1:13) was filled with special significance for those called to enter the arena where they stood helpless in the presence of wild beasts. In Mark's Gospel they found that nothing they could suffer from Nero was alien to the experience of Jesus. Like them, he had been misrepresented to the people and falsely labelled (Ch. 3:21 f., 30). And if they knew the experience of betrayal from within the circle of intimate friends it was sobering to recollect that one of the Twelve had been "Judas Iscariot, who betrayed him" (Ch. 3:19).

When Mark was read in Christian gatherings there were notes peculiarly appropriate to the Roman situation. Jesus had spoken openly of the persecution that could be expected in the Christian life. In the interpretation of a parable he had referred to "those who have no root in themselves, but endure for awhile; then, when affliction or persecution arises on account of the word, immediately they fall away" (Ch. 4:17). He had foreseen that there would be others who had heard the word, "but the cares of the world, and the delight in riches, and the desire for other things" would prevent the gospel from becoming effective in their lives (Ch. 4:19). Mark recorded the fulfilment of these sober sayings in the experience of Jesus when a man of great wealth turned from him when he learned of the cost of discipleship (Ch. 10:17-22), and later Jesus' own disciples fled from him (Ch. 14:41-52, 66-72). In a critical situation unfaithfulness and denial always threaten the life of the community from within. While Jesus promised his followers "houses and brothers and sisters and mothers and children and lands," Mark noted that he had added the qualification, "with persecutions" (Ch. 10:30). He had warned of the day when those who followed him would be handed over to councils to be beaten because of their association with him. Jesus had not withheld the cruel truth that brother would betray to death brother, and the father his child, and children their parents, and that his followers would be hated by all men because they represented him. Precisely in this situation they would bear their witness for him (Ch. 13:1-13). In crucial statements on discipleship brought together by Mark, Jesus had made it clear that what he demanded was a radical abandonment of life in response to a call to martyrdom (Ch. 8:34-38). He had spoken of cross-bearing, which Tacitus affirms was a literal reality for Mark's readers in Rome. It had been the literal experience of Jesus as well, preceded by trial before a Roman magistrate, scourging with the bone-tipped *flagellum,* and the cruel mockery of the Roman guard (Ch. 15:15-20). It was the threat of such treatment that could move a man to deny Jesus, displaying shame for his association with the Lord. In the pages of the Gospel he learned that he could save his life through denial only to experience rejection by Jesus when he returned at the last day as the sovereign Judge of all men (Ch. 8:38). This kind of language was charged with relevance for men and women upon whom was heaped derision and humiliation because they bore the name of Jesus.

Mark's Gospel left no doubt concerning the sovereign authority of Jesus. In response to the call to discipleship men had left family, home and profession (Chs. 1:17, 20; 2:14; 10:28). The issue of Caesar's authority had been raised pointedly when Jesus was questioned concerning the payment of taxes to Rome. His response, "Render to Caesar the things that are Caesar's and to God the things that are God's" (Ch. 12:17) imposed significant limits to the authority and the dignity of the emperor. There could be no acclamation that Caesar is Lord from one who rendered to God "the things that are God's." When Jesus finally stood before Caesar's representative at a Roman tribunal Pilate marvelled at his dignity. He delivered him to be scourged and crucified to satisfy the demand of the crowd, but when his centurion saw how Jesus died he exclaimed, "Truly this man was the Son of God!" (Ch. 15:39). This acknowledgment of Jesus' dignity by a Roman was validated by Jesus' resurrection on the third day (Ch. 16:6-7).

Jesus' vindication by resurrection provided the Christians in Rome with the pledge of their own vindication. In the command to share these joyful tidings with the disciples (Ch. 16:7) they found the encouragement to continue their mission activity, in spite of imperial opposition. The explicit reference to Peter meant that the way was open for restoration for one who had denied his Lord (cf. Ch. 14:66-72). Here was a basis for forgiveness for those who had denied they were Christians when brought before the tribunals of Rome. The situation of the Christians in Rome was too intensely critical for them not to read the Gospel in this way.

4. The Date of the Gospel

The Gospel of Mark is generally dated within the decade A.D. 60-70. According to the early tradition preserved in the Anti-Marcionite Prologue to the Gospel and in Irenaeus, Mark wrote subsequent to the death of Peter, who was martyred in Rome during this period.[25] Another early strand of tradition, found in Clement of Alexandria, asserts that Mark produced his Gospel while Peter was yet alive.[26] Various attempts have been made to show that both of these lines of tradition are correct. It has been argued that Mark began his Gospel during Peter's lifetime but completed it after his death,[27] or that Irenaeus did not mean to imply Peter's death but only his departure from the place where Mark was.[28] While the first proposal is possible, the second is disallowed by the earliest witness that has been preserved, the Anti-Marcionite Prologue (*ca.* 160 A.D.). It clearly dates the origin of Mark after the death of Peter (*post excessionem*). The period in view would seem to be the second half of the seventh decade.

This conclusion finds support in the internal evidence provided by the Gospel itself. The production of the Gospel of Mark must have an effective cause. The emphasis placed by the evangelist upon suffering

---

25 See above, p. 9. The key statement in the Anti-Marcionite Prologue is "Mark... was the interpreter of Peter. After the death of Peter himself he wrote down this same Gospel in the regions of Italy." Irenaeus, *Adv. Haer.* III. i. 2: "And after the death of these [Peter and Paul] Mark, the disciple and interpreter of Peter, also transmitted to us in writing the things preached by Peter."

26 Eusebius, *Eccl. Hist.* II. xv. 2; VI. xiv. 6 f.; *Adumbr. in I Peter* 5:13.

27 H. A. Riggs, *op. cit.*, pp. 176-180.

28 T. W. Manson, "The Foundation of the Synoptic Tradition: The Gospel of Mark," in *Studies in the Gospels and Epistles* (Manchester, 1962), pp. 38-40.

and persecution suggests that it was the Neronian persecution following the great fire of Rome (A.D. 64) that called forth the Gospel.[29] What was required by the situation was a substantial tract which would sustain Christians who were exposed to suffering and death for Jesus and the gospel (see on Ch. 8:36; 10:29; 13:9, 13). In response to this need Mark brought together a witness document designed to preserve the apostolic tradition and to strengthen the Church in this critical situation.

The question of the date of the Gospel has been reopened by the claim that fragments of Mark have been found which can be dated paleographically to A.D. 50.[30] The papyrologist José O'Callaghan has identified 7Q5 as a fragment of Ch. 6:52-53; 7Q6, 1 as Ch. 4:28; 7Q7 as Ch. 12:17 and 7Q15 as possibly Ch. 6:48. The claim to have identified Marcan fragments which can be dated more or less to the first half of the first century is based on a study of infra-red and normal photographs of fragments of papyrus from Cave 7 at Qumran. If substantiated, O'Callaghan's discovery calls into question the traditional date of the Gospel and raises important questions concerning the origin and character of Mark.

The fragments of Cave 7 at Qumran consist of 19 tiny scraps of papyrus, some containing nothing more than a part of a letter.[31] Unlike the other caves at Qumran, all the fragments consist of papyrus and are inscribed in Greek. The fact that only Greek fragments have been found in the cave suggests that it did not serve as a cache for the Essene community at Qumran. One proposal is that it was used as a hiding place by an early Christian community in the territory of Jericho.[32] The first editors of the fragments identified 7Q1 as Exodus 28:4-7, to which C. H. Roberts assigned a date of 100 B.C. paleographically. 7Q2, consisting of five fragmentary lines, could be identified as the Epistle of Jeremiah 43-44. The remaining fragments were unidentified, but they

---

[29] E.g. Chs. 4:17; 8:34-38; 9:49; 10:29 f.; 13:9-13.

[30] José O'Callaghan, "Papiros neotestamentarios en la cueva 7 de Qumran?" *Biblica* 53 (1972), pp. 91-100. Cf. the United Press International release "St. Mark's gospel text discovered," *The Boston Globe* (March 11, 1972), p. 2; "Scrap of Dead Sea Scrolls Said to Show that Gospel was Written Earlier than Believed," *New York Times* (March 19, 1972), p. 13.

[31] The fragments were edited by M. Baillet, J. T. Milik, and R. de Vaux, in *Discoveries in the Judaean Desert of Jordan* III (Oxford, 1962), pp. 142-146. For photographs of the fragments see Plate XXX.

[32] Carlo M. Martini, "Note sui papiri della grotta 7 di Qumran," *Biblica* 53 (1972), pp. 101-104.

were dated paleographically 50 B.C.-A.D. 50. For 7Q5, which O'Callaghan identified as Mk. 6:52-53, the upper limit is accepted, i.e., a date approximately at the middle of the first century.[33] The state of this fragment, and the methodology employed by O'Callaghan, deserve careful consideration.

The fragment contained 20 letters, in five lines of Greek text, but the first editors were able to decipher only 17. They offered the following transcriptions, placing a dot under any letter which to them seemed uncertain:

] · [
] . τῳ α̣ . [
] η̣ και τω̣ [
] ν̣νησ̣ [
] θ̣ηε̣σ̣ [

O'Callaghan, after detailed study of the photographs, proposed that the transcription could read as follows:

] ε̣ [
] υ̣τω . η̣ [
] η̣ και τι̣ [
] ν̣νησ̣ [
] θ̣ησα̣ [

He then estimated the number of letters the MS can have to a line from the only two fragments of papyrus previously identified. For 7Q1 lines 10-13 were not intact, but the eleven lines that were fully preserved averaged 20 letters per line. The four full lines of text in 7Q2 averaged 21 letters. Working with this model O'Callaghan recognized in 7Q5

---

[33] This conclusion is based on examples from R. Seider, *Paläographie der griechischen Papyri,* II. *Literarische Papyri* (Stuttgart, 1970), 64-67.

the stichometry of Mk. 6:52-53.[34] The same procedure is followed in identifying 7Q6, 1 as Ch. 4:28 and 7Q7 as Ch. 12:17, only in each of these instances only four letters are completely certain in three lines of text.[35] The basis for O'Callaghan's suggestion that 7Q15 may contain Ch. 6:48 is five letters in two lines of text.[36]

On the basis of the photographs of the fragments, Father O'Callaghan's thesis seems very tenuous. The size of the fragments, and the number of letters which are visible, do not allow a certain identification.[37] The

---

[34] J. O'Callaghan, *op. cit.*, p. 97:

[συνηκαν]ε̣[πιτοισαρτοισ]	20 letters
[αλληνα]υ̣τω̣ν̣η[καρδιαπεπωρω]	23 letters
[μεν]η̣ καιτι̣[απερασαντεσ]	20 letters
[ηλθονεισΓε]ν̣νη̣σ[αρετκαι]	21 letters
[προσωρμισ]θ̣ησα̣[νκαιεξελ]	21 letters

This proposal assumes the omission of ἐπὶ τὴν γῆν after διαπεράσαντες, a textual variant previously known only from Bohairic MSS.

[35] *7Q6, 1* — *7Q7*

7Q6, 1	7Q7
].[	].[
]ε̣ι̣τ..[	]κ̄α.[
].λη..[	]θα.[

[36] *7Q15:*]ντῳε.[

]....[

[37] The methodological problem inherent in the material may be illustrated with reference to 7Q7, which O'Callaghan holds is very probably Ch. 12:17. His confidence is based on the clear evidence for the scribal sign for an abbreviation over the kappa (κ̄), and he proposes that κ̄α represents Κ(αίσαρος) ἀ[πόδοτε. The second line of the text appears to contain a θα, which would fit the word εξε]θα[υμαζον. However, even if the words Καίσαρι, θεοῦ and θεῷ are also abbreviated, the length of the line demanded exceeds what O'Callaghan had stated to be normal for the fragments:

Κ̄ α[πόδοτε Κ̄ καὶ τὰ τοῦ θ̄ τῷ θ̄ καὶ ἐξε] 27 letters
θα[ύμαζον ἐπ' αὐτῷ.

If θεοῦ and θεῷ were written in full, or if any other letters preceded the kappa and the theta, the line is lengthened even more.

fragments are not necessarily biblical in character. The fact that the two which have been identified with certainty are from Exodus and the apocryphal Epistle of Jeremiah may provide presumptive evidence that the remaining fragments belonged to biblical or post-biblical Jewish texts. But this is not to say that they represent NT texts.[38] Even should the identifications proposed by O'Callaghan prove precise, the question would inevitably have been raised whether these fragments put us in touch with Mark or with a pre-Marcan source. The scraps are too small to assert that they stem from the Gospel itself. Moreover, although paleography is a highly developed science, according to Gerald Brown, a leading papyrologist at Harvard University, the dating of a MS by paleography is precise *within 25 years*. This means that even if O'Callaghan is correct in his general estimate of the date and content of the fragments, the dating of Mark's Gospel within the decade 60-70 is by no means disproven. In short, a substantial basis for revising our estimate of the date of Mark has not been offered.

5. The Author of the Gospel

The Gospel which bears Mark's name is actually anonymous, but an unbroken tradition puts forth as its author John Mark, who would have been in Rome with Peter at the time of the crisis under Nero (cf. I Peter 5:13). He was a Jewish Christian whose mother Mary owned a home in Jerusalem where the nucleus of the original Christian community met; it was to this house that Peter came after his miraculous release from prison (Acts 12:12). When Barnabas and Saul of Tarsus returned to Antioch after a visit to Jerusalem on a mission of famine relief they added to their party "John, whose other name was Mark" (Acts 12:25). Since Barnabas was the cousin of Mark (Col. 4:10), it is probable that he persuaded the apostle to take along the younger man. Mark travelled to Cyprus with Barnabas and Paul on a preaching mission to the diaspora synagogues (Acts 13:4), but when they turned to go inland to Asia, Mark returned to Jerusalem (Acts 13:13). Paul evidently regarded his action as irresponsible, for he refused to take him along on

[38] J. O'Callaghan, *op. cit.*, p. 92, n. 2 suggests that 7Q4 = I Tim. 3:16; 4:1, 3, and lists as "very probable" the following identifications: 7Q6, 2 = Acts 27:38; 7Q9 = Rom. 5:11, 12; and as "possible" 7Q10 = 2 Peter 1:15. On pp. 99 f. he identifies 7Q8 as James 1:23, 24.

a projected second journey. A bitter quarrel over this issue disrupted the relationship between the veteran missionaries. Barnabas and Mark returned to Cyprus to strengthen the young churches while Paul and Silas gave oversight to the churches in Syria and Cilicia (Acts 15:36-41).

Though details are lacking, Paul was later reconciled with Mark, who was with the apostle during an imprisonment in Rome, and served as the apostle's delegate on an important mission to Asia Minor (Philemon 24; Col. 4:10). Some years later, when Paul was again in prison and sentence had been passed upon him he instructed Timothy in Ephesus to bring Mark to Rome, since he would be useful to him (II Tim. 4:11). When I Peter was written Mark was in Rome laboring with Peter, who regarded him affectionately as his son (I Peter 5:13).

To this brief sketch two notes may be added. In Acts 13:5 Luke designates Mark by a term which can usually be rendered "servant," "helper," or "assistant."[39] The RSV states simply, "And they [Barnabas and Paul] had John [Mark] to assist them." It is not at all certain, however, that this is an accurate indication of the office he filled. In first and second century Greek texts Luke's term frequently designates a man who handles documents and delivers their content to men (cf. Lk. 4:20).[40] Two other instances of the term in Luke-Acts, however, suggest that more than the services of a temple clerk are implied in the office. (1) In Acts 26:16 Paul states that the risen Lord appointed him a *servant* and a witness to the truth. The same term appears as a self-designation in I Cor. 4:1, where it is associated with the ministry of the word of God. (2) In Luke 1:1-2 the evangelist links the *servants* of the word with those who were the eyewitnesses and guarantors of apostolic tradition. He states:

> "Inasmuch as many have undertaken to compile a narrative of the things which have been accomplished among us, just as they were delivered to us by those who from the beginning were eyewitnesses and servants of the word . . . "

Here the term *servants* is qualified by the sphere in which their service was rendered, the ministry of the word of God, and an intimate relation-

[39] Gr. ὑπηρέτης.

[40] See B. T. Holmes, "Luke's Description of John Mark," *JBL* 54 (1935), pp. 63-72; R. O. P. Taylor, "The Ministry of Mark," *ExT* 54 (1942-43), pp. 136-138.

ship is established between the tradition delivered by the primary witnesses to the events and the narrative accounts which had begun to be compiled. One narrative which may reasonably be said to have been before Luke when he undertook his own work was the Gospel of Mark. Presumably the third evangelist intended to include Mark among the "servants of the word" who reduced the tradition to a written form. But on any reading of these verses, the term descriptive of Mark in Acts 13:5 is associated in Luke-Acts with the ministry of the gospel. This recognition sheds light on Mark's function with Peter in Rome, where the close relationship between the eyewitness and the minister of the word acknowledged in Lk. 1:2 was exemplified in the ministry of the apostle and his younger companion.

Finally, it is possible to sketch an intellectual portrait of Mark the evangelist from the form and content of the Gospel. It is evident that he was a charismatically endowed teacher and evangelist. His use of the wilderness motif in the prologue and throughout the Gospel displays a significant grasp of OT revelation and its relevance for the Church (see e.g. Chs. 1:1-13, 35-39; 6:30-34).[41] The employment of the allusive qualities of rare vocabulary (e.g. Chs. 7:32; 8:3) and of parenthetical clauses introduced by the conjunction "for" to evoke the biblical background which informs an event (e.g. Chs. 1:16; 11:13)[42] exhibits an agile mind. The recognition that events which transpire on the historical plane ultimately possess cosmic significance in regard to the battle between God and Satan (e.g. Chs. 1:4-13; 3:7-12; 4:35-41; 8:34-38; 11:27-33) indicates an ability to perceive the character of reality.[43] At the same time Mark's profound pastoral concern for the Christians of Rome is evident in his willingness to underscore the significance of a particular incident for his readers (e.g. Chs. 2:10, 28; 7:19) as much as in his selection of material which would address itself pointedly to their needs (e.g. Ch. 13:9-13, 32-37). A careful reading of the Gospel will serve to introduce the author as a theologian of the first rank who never forgot that his primary intention was the strengthening of the people of God in a time of fiery ordeal.

---

41 U. Mauser, *Christ in the Wilderness. The Wilderness Theme in the Second Gospel and its Basis in the Biblical Tradition* (Naperville, Ill., 1963).

42 Cf. C. H. Bird, "Some γάρ clauses in St. Mark's Gospel," *JThS* n.s. 4 (1953), pp. 171-187.

43 Cf. J. M. Robinson, *The Problem of History in Mark* (London, 1957).

6. The Place of Composition

Early Church tradition associates the composition of the Gospel with Rome or Italy.[44] Although the content of Mark's Gospel does not prove Roman origin, it is highly consistent with it. Among the words of Jesus which Mark alone records was the statement, "Everyone will be salted by fire" (Ch. 9:49). Jesus' enigmatic statement had found fulfilment in the trial and persecution of Roman Christians under Nero. It has already been urged that their needs provided the major incentive for the preparation of the Gospel.

In language, Mark shows a distinct preference for Latin technical terms, particularly terms connected with the army (e.g. *legion,* Ch. 5:9; *praetorium,* Ch. 15:16; *centurion,* Ch. 15:39), the courts (e.g. *speculator,* Ch. 6:27; *flagellare,* Ch. 15:15) and commerce (e.g. *denarius,* Ch. 12:15; *quadrans,* Ch. 12:42). Although such terms were in use throughout the empire, it is particularly significant that twice common Greek expressions in the Gospel are explained by Latin ones (Ch. 12:42, "two copper coins [*lepta*], which make a *quadrans*"; Ch. 15:16, "the palace, that is the *praetorium*"). The first of these examples is particularly instructive, for the *quadrans* was not in circulation in the east.[45] The presence of latinisms and of technical terminology confined to the west is harmonious with the tradition that Mark was written in Rome.

In agreement with the Roman method of reckoning time Mark speaks of four watches of the night, rather than of the three which were traditional in Jewish reckoning (Chs. 6:48; 13:35). It is even possible that Mark has structured his Passion narrative in accordance with the four Roman night watches, since Jesus enters Jerusalem to share the Passover with his disciples *in the evening* (Ch. 14:17); the hour of betrayal in the Garden of Gethsemane is very probably *midnight* (Ch. 14:41); the denial of Peter occurs in connection with *cock-crow* (Ch. 14:72); and the time

---

44 The sole exception is the late (second half of the fourth century) witness of John Chrysostom that Mark wrote his Gospel in Egypt at the request of hearers there (*Homily 1 on Matthew*). For a discussion of the origin of this tradition and of the later tradition connecting the beginnings of Alexandrian Christianity with the activity of John Mark see B. W. Bacon, *Is Mark a Roman Gospel?* (Cambridge, Mass., 1919), pp. 21 f.; L. W. Barnard, "St. Mark and Alexandria," *HTR* 52 (1964), pp. 145-150.

45 See W. M. Ramsay, "On Mark xii. 42," *ExT* 10 (1898/99), pp. 232, 336; cf. O. Roller, *Münzen, Geld und Vermögensverhältnisse in den Evangelien* (Leipzig, 1929).

when Jesus is brought to Pilate is early *morning* (Ch. 15:1).[46] If it was Mark's intention to structure his narrative in this fashion, it was in Rome that the significance of this would be especially appreciated.

It is apparent, moreover, that Mark prepared his Gospel for Gentile Christians who were familiar with the OT in the Greek VS, and who needed an explanation of Palestinian customs and practices (e.g. Chs. 7:3; 14:12; 15:42). The evangelist regularly translates for his readers the Aramaic words and phrases preserved in the tradition (e.g. Chs. 3:17; 5:41; 7:11, 34; 9:43; 10:46; 14:36; 15:22, 34), including the simple *Abba* which Paul had used when writing to the Church at Rome (Rom. 8:15).

Finally, it is noteworthy that the Gospel of Mark reaches its climax in the confession of Jesus' deity by a Roman centurion (Ch. 15:39). Roman Christianity found in the Gospel an account peculiarly appropriate to its life and problems.[47]

7. Some Considerations on Style and Literary Method

A clear conception of Mark's intention in the Gospel sheds light on the distinctive character of his style. Mark's task was to project Christian faith in a climate of uncertainty where martyrdom had been a reality. He selected and arranged the tradition to present the Christ who continues to speak and act meaningfully in the context of crisis. What was demanded by the situation was not a past word, descriptive of what Jesus had said and done, but a word from the present through which

---

46 Cf. R. H. Lightfoot, *The Gospel Message of St. Mark* (Oxford, 1950), p. 53.

47 W. Marxsen, *op. cit.*, pp. 54-95 argues that Mark originated in Galilee and was intended for Galilee near the close of the decade A.D. 60-70 when the Palestinian Christians were expecting the parousia of the Lord there. Stressing the contemporary situation of the Church presumed to be in Galilee he neglects certain elements in the text which might have influenced his conclusions concerning the life situation of the Marcan framework. Thus no consideration is given to features of the text which are particularly intelligible in terms of a Roman provenance for the Gospel. In assigning the emphasis upon Galilee in the Gospel to Mark's creative activity Marxsen has failed to take into account the geographical data, including Galilee, in the kerygmatic outline received by Mark (cf. Acts 10:37). In seeking to account for the interest in Galilee in Mark's Gospel, it would seem simpler and more accurate to posit that Mark had access primarily to sources that concerned Jesus in Galilee. If Mark was indeed Peter's associate, this is understandable since Peter was a Galilean.

the living Lord could be heard and known. The account Mark drew up is characterized by simplicity and straightforwardness. His language and style are less elaborate and more popular than that adopted by Matthew or Luke. Mark's sentences are simply constructed and commonly are strung together by the conjunction "and" (parataxis). Frequent use of the word "immediately" lends a sense of vividness and excitement to the action. Within a narrative the evangelist shows a preference for direct speech. He is especially fond of using the present tense to relay past happenings. Mark employs this "historical present" over 150 times when other writers would have used the simple past tense.

Mark's literary style has frequently been described as "barbarous" or "unrefined." It is better to understand it as supporting a conscious literary or even theological intention. Simple sentence construction, parataxis, direct speech and the historical present serve to make Jesus the contemporary of those who hear or read the account. Through the Gospel, Jesus continues to manifest his presence and his authority among his people.

The vividness of Mark's narrative style calls for comment. While the evangelist is capable of summary report (e.g. Chs. 1:14 f.; 3:7-12), more usually the Marcan narrative is vivid and concrete. Several incidents are narrated at greater length and in fuller detail than the parallel accounts in the other synoptic Gospels (e.g. Chs. 2:1-12; 5:1-20). The graphic details that are found in Mark alone may reflect eyewitness report. But it is ultimately Mark who was responsible for preserving such details as the presence of the wild beasts in the wilderness (Ch. 1:13), the nicknaming of James and John (Ch. 3:17), the use of the fisherman's pillow in the stern of the boat (Ch. 4:38), or the name of a blind man who received his sight (Ch. 10:46). This concern for detail is reflected in Mark's frequent reference to the emotional response of the participants in the drama of salvation. He notes not only the stunned reaction of the people (e.g. Chs. 1:27 f.; 2:12) or the fear and amazement of the disciples (e.g. Chs. 9:5 f.; 10:24, 32), but the indignation, stern anger, godly sorrow or exasperation experienced by Jesus as well (e.g. Chs. 1:41, 43; 3:5; 7:34). The resultant account is marked by color and movement. But the important consideration is that Mark's literary style succeeds in putting his listeners on the scene where they may visualize and feel what the evangelist has described.

Mark did not hesitate to address his readers even more directly. At several points in the Gospel he has used the literary device of a parenthetical statement to underscore the significance of a particular action or pronouncement. This seems clearly to be the case in the account of the healing of a paralytic (Ch. 2:1-12) where the crucial issue of the authority to forgive sins is introduced: "Know that the Son of Man has authority to forgive sins on the earth" (Ch. 2:10a). The public use of "Son of Man" as a self-designation so early in Jesus' ministry, in the presence of blatant unbelief, is in conflict with Mark's witness to the reserve with which Jesus spoke of himself. The evangelist clearly understands that it is in the context of faith (cf. Ch. 8:29-31), especially after Easter (Ch. 9:9), that men are appointed to receive the revelation that Jesus is the Son of Man. It is necessary, therefore, to understand the statement of Ch. 2:10a as a parenthetical remark addressed by Mark to the Christian readers of the Gospel. These words explain the significance of the event for them. Jesus' command for the paralytic to pick up his mat and walk was not ultimately to satisfy the demand of the antagonistic scribes but to assure the people of God that the Lord has authority to exercise forgiveness on earth (see on Ch. 2:10; cf. Ch. 2:28). In a controversy with Jerusalem scribes over ritual defilement Mark's audience required the explanatory note that "the Pharisees, and all the Jews, do not eat before washing their hands" (Ch. 7:3 f.). But the theological point of the preserved tradition is expressed in a parenthetical statement again directed by Mark to the Christian: "Thus he declared all foods clean" (Ch. 7:19; cf. Acts 10:5-10). When Mark does not himself speak directly to his readers (cf. Ch. 13:14), he terminates a long discourse in such a way that Jesus addresses them: "And what I say to you, I say to all, watch!" (Ch. 13:37). The account of the stilling of the storm (Ch. 4:35-41) is terminated abruptly by a rhetorical question: "Who then is this, that even wind and sea obey him?" (Ch. 4:41). The reader is invited to provide the appropriate answer: he is the Messiah, the Son of God (cf. Ch. 1:1). The use of such literary devices as the parenthetical statement or the rhetorical question was designed to keep men from a spectator-relationship to what Jesus said or did. They are called by the evangelist to stand where Jesus stood, and where he stands.

Mark's concern to involve men in the crisis of decision prompted by Jesus' presence is reflected in the care with which he has structured the material of the Gospel. His literary method may be illustrated by reference to three other devices. (1) By juxtaposing two contrasting accounts Mark sharpens the issues at stake. E.g.:

Ch. 3:7-19	*Ch. 3:20-35*
1. The scene is the sea, then a mountain.	1. The scene is set in a house.
2. People gather from several regions, and Jesus chooses twelve.	2. Jesus' family comes from their home and scribes come from Jerusalem.
3. Demons acknowledge Jesus' divine sonship.	3. It is alleged that Jesus is the agent of Beelzebul.
4. Jesus frees the possessed.	4. Jesus is said to be possessed.

The contrast achieved forces the recognition that a decision has to be made. Either Jesus is the divine Son who liberates the possessed or he is the agent of Satan. (2) Ch. 3:20-35 may illustrate a different device, the intercalation of one account within another. Ch. 3:20-21 reports that Jesus' family left their village to seize him and bring him home. Their arrival at a house where Jesus was teaching is reported in Ch. 3:31-35. By inserting the account of the scribes from Jerusalem between the two parts of the report concerning Jesus' family Mark suggests a significant parallel between those who say that Jesus is deranged (verse 21) and those who ascribe his extraordinary powers to possession (verse 30). At other times this literary device is used to indicate a lapse of time or to sharpen a contrast (see on Chs. 5:21-43; 6:7-30; 11:12-21; 14:1-11). (3) The development of two independent cycles of tradition in parallel fashion is evident in Mark's arrangement of Ch. 6:35-8:30. The focus upon the two feedings of the multitude (Chs. 6:35-44, 52; 8:1-10, 19 f.) and the repeated use of the word "bread" (cf. Chs. 6:52; 7:2, 28; 8:14) serve to underscore the crucial importance of this tradition for perceiving the identity of Jesus. Significantly, each of the two parallel cycles concludes with a note of confession: "He has done all things well" (Ch. 7:37), and "You are the Messiah" (Ch. 8:29). By balanced arrangement Mark encourages the reader to take his place within the confessing Church as one who has recognized the truth.

These examples are sufficient to demonstrate Mark's use of style and literary method to involve his audience in the witness he has given to Jesus Christ. The consummate skill with which he has prepared his Gospel is exhibited throughout the commentary.

8. Analysis of the Gospel According to Mark

I. Prologue to the Gospel, Ch. 1:1-13

1. The Herald in the Wilderness, Ch. 1:1-8
2. The Lord in the Wilderness, Ch. 1:9-11
3. Temptation in the Wilderness, Ch. 1:12-13

II. The Initial Phase of the Galilean Ministry, Ch. 1:14-3:6

1. Entrance into Galilee, Ch. 1:14-15
2. The Call to Become Fishers of Men, Ch. 1:16-20
3. A New Teaching–with Authority, Ch. 1:21-28
4. The Healing of Peter's Mother-in-Law, Ch. 1:29-31
5. The Sick Healed at Evening, Ch. 1:32-34
6. The Decision to Leave Capernaum, Ch. 1:35-39
7. The Cleansing of a Leper, Ch. 1:40-45
8. Conflict in Galilee, Ch. 2:1-3:6
   - *(a) The authority to forgive sins,* Ch. 2:1-12
   - *(b) The call of a tax farmer,* Ch. 2:13-14
   - *(c) Messiah eats with sinners,* Ch. 2:15-17
   - *(d) The new situation,* Ch. 2:18-22
   - *(e) Sabbath infringement and the Lord of the Sabbath,* Ch. 2:23-28
   - *(f) The decision that Jesus must be destroyed,* Ch. 3:1-6

III. Later Phases of the Ministry in Galilee, Ch. 3:7-6:13

1. Withdrawal to the Sea, Ch. 3:7-12
2. The Choice of the Twelve, Ch. 3:13-19a
3. The Character of Jesus' Family, Ch. 3:19b-35
   - *(a) The charge that Jesus is deranged,* Ch. 3:19b-21
   - *(b) The charge that Jesus is possessed,* Ch. 3:22-30
   - *(c) Jesus' true family,* Ch. 3:31-35
4. Parables concerning the Kingdom of God, Ch. 4:1-34
   - *(a) The parable of the Sower,* Ch. 4:1-9
   - *(b) The fulfilment of the purpose of God,* Ch. 4:10-12
   - *(c) The interpretation of the parable of the Sower,* Ch. 4:13-20
   - *(d) Exhortation to true hearing,* Ch. 4:21-25
   - *(e) The parable of the Growth of the Seed,* Ch. 4:26-29
   - *(f) The parable of the Mustard Seed,* Ch. 4:30-32
   - *(g) Parabolic utterance and private interpretation,* Ch. 4:33-34

5. The Vanquishing of Powers Hostile to God, Ch. 4:35-5:43
   (a) *The subduing of the sea,* Ch. 4:35-41
   (b) *The Gerasene demoniac: the subduing of the demonic,* Ch. 5:1-20
   (c) *The plea of Jairus,* Ch. 5:21-24
   (d) *The woman with the hemorrhage,* Ch. 5:25-34
   (e) *The raising of Jairus' daughter: the subduing of death,* Ch. 5:35-43
6. Rejection at Nazareth, Ch. 6:1-6a
7. The Mission of the Twelve in Galilee, Ch. 6:6b-13

IV. Withdrawal Beyond Galilee, Ch. 6:14-8:30

1. Popular Estimates of the Identity of Jesus, Ch. 6:14-16
2. The Imprisonment and Death of John, Ch. 6:17-29
3. The Provision of Rest in the Wilderness, Ch. 6:30-34
4. The Provision of Bread in the Wilderness, Ch. 6:35-44
5. The Lord of the Sea, Ch. 6:45-52
6. Healing in the Region of Gennesaret, Ch. 6:53-56
7. Defilement According to the Tradition, Ch. 7:1-8
8. The Conflict between Commandment and Tradition, Ch. 7:9-13
9. True Defilement, Ch. 7:14-23
10. The Faith of a Gentile, Ch. 7:24-30
11. Healing in the Decapolis, Ch. 7:31-37
12. The Provision of Bread in the Decapolis, Ch. 8:1-10
13. The Request for a Sign, Ch. 8:11-13
14. The Failure to Understand, Ch. 8:14-21
15. The Opening of Blind Eyes, Ch. 8:22-26
16. The Recognition of the Messiah, Ch. 8:27-30

V. The Journey to Jerusalem, Ch. 8:31-10:52

1. The Sufferings of the Messiah: the first Major Prophecy of the Passion, Ch. 8:31-33
2. The Requirements for Following Jesus, Chs. 8:34-9:1
3. The Transfiguration: the Glory of the Son of Man, Ch. 9:2-8
4. The Coming of Elijah, Ch. 9:9-13
5. The Healing of a Possessed Boy, Ch. 9:14-29
6. The Second Major Prophecy of the Passion, Ch. 9:30-32
7. True Greatness, Ch. 9:33-37
8. Exorcism through Jesus' Name, Ch. 9:38-42

9. The Demanding Requirements of Discipleship, Ch. 9:43-50
10. The Question of Divorce, Ch. 10:1-12
11. The Blessing of the Children, Ch. 10:13-16
12. Riches and the Kingdom of God, Ch. 10:17-27
13. The Rewards of Discipleship, Ch. 10:28-31
14. The Third Major Prophecy of the Passion, Ch. 10:32-34
15. Rank, Precedence and Service, Ch. 10:35-45
16. The Faith of Blind Bartimaeus, Ch. 10:46-52

VI. MINISTRY IN JERUSALEM, Ch. 11:1-13:37

1. The Entry into Jerusalem, Ch. 11:1-11
2. The Unproductive Fig Tree, Ch. 11:12-14
3. The Expulsion of the Merchants from the Temple Precincts, Ch. 11:15-19
4. The Withered Fig Tree, Faith and Prayer, Ch. 11:20-25
5. The Authority of Jesus, Ch. 11:27-33
6. The Parable of the Defiant Tenants, Ch. 12:1-12
7. The Question Concerning Tribute, Ch. 12:13-17
8. The Question Concerning the Resurrection, Ch. 12:18-27
9. The Question Concerning the Great Commandment, Ch. 12:28-34
10. The Question Concerning David's Son, Ch. 12:35-37
11. The Warning Concerning the Scribes, Ch. 12:38-40
12. The Widow Who Gave Everything, Ch. 12:41-44
13. The Olivet Discourse, Ch. 13:1-37
    - *(a) Jesus' prophecy of impending destruction,* Ch. 13:1-4
    - *(b) Warning against deception,* Ch. 13:5-8
    - *(c) A call to steadfastness under persecution,* Ch. 13:9-13
    - *(d) The appalling sacrilege and the necessity for flight,* Ch. 13:14-23
    - *(e) The triumph of the Son of Man,* Ch. 13:24-27
    - *(f) The lesson of the fig tree,* Ch. 13:28-31
    - *(g) The call to vigilance,* Ch. 13:32-37

VII. THE PASSION NARRATIVE, Ch. 14:1-15:47

1. The Plot to Seize Jesus, Ch. 14:1-2
2. The Anointing in Bethany, Ch. 14:3-9
3. The Betrayal by Judas, Ch. 14:10-11
4. The Preparation of the Meal, Ch. 14:12-16

9. Select Bibliography

1. *Editions and Commentaries*

Aland, K., *Synopsis Quattuor Evangeliorum, Locis parallelis evangeliorum apocryphorum et patrum adhibitis* (Stuttgart, 1964).

Allen, W. C., *The Gospel according to Saint Mark* (London, 1915).

Bartlet, J. V., *St. Mark.* Century Bible (Edinburgh, 1922).

Bede, *In Marci Evangelium Expositio* (in J. P. Migne, *Patrologia Latina,* XCII, columns 131-302).

Bengel, J. A., *Gnomon Novi Testamenti* (Tübingen, 1742). Eng. Tr. Vol. I (Edinburgh, 1877).

Berkelbach von der Sprenkel, S. F. H. J., *Het evangelie van Markus* (Amsterdam, 1937).

Black, M., Metzger, B. M., Wikgren, A., *The Greek New Testament* (Stuttgart, 1966).

Blunt, A. W. F., *The Gospel according to Saint Mark,* Clarendon Bible (Oxford, 1929).

Bowman, J., *The Gospel of Mark. The New Christian Jewish Passover Haggada* (Leiden, 1965).

Branscomb, B. H., *The Gospel of Mark* (London, 1937).

Calvin, J., *Commentary on a Harmony of the Evangelists, Matthew, Mark, and Luke* (Grand Rapids, 1949).

Carrington, P., *According to Mark. A Running Commentary on the Oldest Gospel* (Cambridge, 1960).

Cole, A., *The Gospel According to Mark.* Tyndale Bible Commentary (London, 1960).

Cranfield, C. E. B., *The Gospel according to St. Mark.*[2] Cambridge Greek Testament (Cambridge, 1963).

Dehn, G., *Jesus Christus der Gottessohn. Das Evangelium des Marcus*[3] (Berlin, 1932).

Dillersberger, J., *Das Evangelium des hl. Markus theologisch und heilsgeschichtlich erklärt.* 5 vols (Salzburg, 1937-38).

Gould, E. P., *The Gospel according to Saint Mark.*[7] International Critical Commentary (Edinburgh, 1932).

Grant, F. C., *The Gospel according to St. Mark. Interpreter's Bible* Vol. VII, pp. 627-917 (New York, 1951).

Grob, R., *Einführung in das Markus-Evangelium* (Zürich, 1965).

Grundmann, W., *Das Evangelium nach Markus.* Theologischer Handkommentar zum Neuen Testament (Berlin, 1959).

Haenchen, E., *Der Weg Jesu. Erklärung des Markusevangeliums und der kanonischen Parallelen* (Berlin, 1966).

Hauck, F., *Das Evangelium des Markus.* Theologischer Handkommentar zum Neuen Testament (Leipzig, 1931).

Hermann, I., *Das Markusevangelium* 2 vols (Düsseldorf, 1965, 1967).

Hunter, A. M., *The Gospel according to Saint Mark,*[8] Torch Bible Commentary (London, 1967).

Jeremias, J., *Das Evangelium nach Markus*[3] (Chemnitz, 1928).

Johnson, S. E., *The Gospel according to St. Mark.* Harper's NT Commentary (New York, 1960).

Jones, A., *The Gospel according to St. Mark. Text and Commentary* (London, 1963).

Keulers, J., *De Evangelien volgens Marcus en Lucas.* De boeken van het Nieuwe Testament (Roermond, 1951).

Klostermann, E., *Das Markusevangelium.*[4] Handbuch zum Neuen Testament (Tübingen, 1950).

Lagrange, M.-J., *Évangile selon Saint Marc.*[8] Études Bibliques (Paris, 1947).

Legg, S. C. E., *Novum Testamentum graecum secundum textum Westcotto-Hortianum. Evangelium secundum Marcum* (Oxford, 1935).

Lohmeyer, E., *Das Evangelium des Markus.*[16] Kritisch-Exegetischer Kommentar über das Neue Testament (Göttingen, 1963).

Loisy, A., *Les évangiles synoptiques,* 2 vols (Ceffonds, Paris, 1907).

———, *L'évangile selon Marc* (Paris, 1912).

Lowrie, W., *Jesus according to St. Mark* (London, 1929).

Mitton, C. L., *The Gospel according to St. Mark* (London, 1957).

Moule, C. F. D., *The Gospel according to Mark* (Cambridge, 1965).

Nestle, E., *Novum Testamentum Graece cum apparatu critico*[25] (Stuttgart, 1963).

Nineham, D. E., *Saint Mark.* Pelican Gospel Commentary (Baltimore, 1963).

Osty, E., *Évangile selon saint Marc* (Paris, 1949).

Pirot, L. & Leconte, T., *Évangile selon saint Marc.*[2] La Sainte Bible (Paris, 1950).

Rawlinson, A. E. J., *The Gospel according to St. Mark.*[7] Westminster Commentary (London, 1949).

Schlatter, A., *Die Evangelien nach Markus und Lukas* (Stuttgart, 1947).

———, *Markus, der Evangelist für die Griechen* (Stuttgart, 1935).

Schmid, J., *Das Evangelium nach Markus*[4] (Regensburg, 1958).

Schnackenburg, R., *Das Evangelium nach Markus.* 2 vols (Düsseldorf, 1966).

Schniewind, J., *Das Evangelium nach Markus.*[9] Das Neue Testament Deutsch (Göttingen, 1960).

Schweizer, E., *Das Evangelium nach Markus.* Das Neue Testament Deutsch (Göttingen, 1967).

Staab, K., *Das Evangelium nach Markus und Lukas.* Echter-Bibel (Würzburg, 1956).

Strack, H. L. & Billerbeck, P., *Kommentar zum Neuen Testament aus Talmud und Midrasch,* Vol. I and II (München, 1922, 1924).

Swete, H. B., *The Gospel according to St. Mark.*[3] Macmillan NT Commentaries (London, 1927).

Taylor, V., *The Gospel according to St. Mark.* Macmillan NT Commentaries (London, 1952).

Turner, C. H., *The Gospel according to St. Mark* (London, 1928).

Urichio, F. M., & Stana, G. M., *Vangelo secondo San Marco.* La Sacra Biblia (Torino, 1966).

Victor of Antioch, in P. Possinus, *Catena Graecorum Patrum in Evangelium secundum Marcum* (Rome, 1673).

Weiss, J., *Das älteste Evangelium* (Göttingen, 1903).

———, *Das Markusevangelium* in *Die Schriften des Neuen Testaments* Vol. I, 3 (Göttingen, 1917).

Wellhausen, J., *Das Evangelium Marci*[2] (Berlin, 1909).

2. *Special Studies*

Barker, G. W., Lane, W. L., Michaels, J. R., *The New Testament Speaks* (New York, 1969).

Barrett, C. K., *Jesus and the Gospel Tradition* (London, 1967).

Bauer, W., *A Greek-English Lexicon of the New Testament and Other Early Christian Literature,* tr. W. F. Arndt & F. W. Gingrich (Chicago, 1957).

Bauernfeind, O., *Die Worte der Dämonen im Markusevangelium* (Stuttgart, 1927).

Beasley-Murray, G. R., *A Commentary on Mark Thirteen* (London, 1957).

Best, E., *The Temptation and the Passion. The Marcan Soteriology* (Cambridge, 1965).

Bieneck, J., *Sohn Gottes als Christusbezeichnung der Synoptiker* (Zürich, 1952).

Black, M., *An Aramaic Approach to the Gospels and Acts*[3] (Oxford, 1967).

Blass, F. & Debrunner, A., *A Greek Grammar of the New Testament and Other Early Christian Literature,* tr. and ed. by R. W. Funk (Chicago, 1961).

Blinzler, J., *The Trial of Jesus*[2] (New York, 1959).

Boobyer, G. H., *St. Mark and the Transfiguration Story* (Edinburgh, 1942).

Bornkamm, G., *Jesus of Nazareth* (New York, 1960).

Bratcher, R. G. & Nida, E. A., *A Translator's Handbook on the Gospel of Mark* (Leiden, 1961).

Bultmann, R., *The History of the Synoptic Tradition* (Oxford, 1963).

Burkill, T. A., *Mysterious Revelation. An Examination of the Philosophy of St. Mark's Gospel* (Ithaca, N.Y., 1963).

Carrington, P., *The Primitive Christian Calendar. A Study in the Making of the Marcan Gospel* (Cambridge, 1952).

Colon, J. B., "Marc" in *Dictionnaire de la Bible, Supplement* V (Paris, 1954), columns 835-862.

Coppens, J. & Dequeker, L., *Le Fils de l'Homme et les Saints du Très-Haut en Daniel VII, dans les Apocryphes et dans le Nouveau Testament* (Louvain, 1961).

Cullmann, O., *The Christology of the New Testament*[2] (Philadelphia, 1959).

————, *Peter: Disciple, Apostle, Martyr* (New York, 1958).

Dalman, G., *Orte und Wege Jesu*[3] (Leipzig, 1924).

Daube, D., *The New Testament and Rabbinic Judaism* (London, 1956).

Deissmann, A., *Light from the Ancient East*[4] (Grand Rapids, 1965).

Denis, A. M., *Christus de verlosser en het leven der Christenen. Theologische schets van het Marcus-evangelie* (Antwerpen, 1963).

Dibelius, M., *From Tradition to Gospel*[2] (London, 1934).

Dodd, C. H., *The Parables of the Kingdom*[2] (London, 1961).

Doeve, J. W., *Jewish Hermeneutics in the Synoptic Gospels and Acts* (Assen, 1953).

Doudna, J. C., *The Greek of the Gospel of Mark* (Philadelphia, 1961).

Dupont-Sommer, A., *The Essene Writings from Qumran* (Cleveland, 1962).

Ebeling, H. J., *Das Messiasgeheimnis und die Botschaft des Marcus-Evangelisten* (Berlin, 1939).

Eitrem, S., *Some Notes on the Demonology in the New Testament* (Oslo, 1950).

Farrer, A., *A Study in St. Mark* (London, 1951).

————, *St. Matthew and St. Mark* (London, 1954).

Fuller, R. H., *Interpreting the Miracles* (London, 1963).

Funk, R. W., *Language, Hermeneutic, and Word of God. The Problem of Language in the New Testament and Contemporary Theology* (New York, 1966).

Geslin, G., *La prédication de Saint Pierre à Rome, laquelle est l'évangile de saint Marc* (Sees, 1959).

Grässer, E., *Das Problem der Parusieverzögerung in den synoptischen Evangelien und in der Apostelgeschichte* (Berlin, 1960).

Guthrie, D., *New Testament Introduction* I. *The Gospels and Acts* (Chicago, 1965).

Guy, H. A., *The Origin of the Gospel of Mark* (New York, 1954).

Hartmann, L., *Prophecy Interpreted. The Formation of Some Jewish Apocalyptic and of the Eschatological Discourse Mark 13 Par* (Lund, 1966).

Hooker, M. D., *The Son of Man in Mark* (London, 1967).

Jaubert, A., *La date de la cène: calendrier biblique et liturgie chrétienne* (Paris, 1957). Eng. Tr. *The Date of the Last Supper* (Staten Island, N.Y., 1965).

Jeremias, J., *The Eucharistic Words of Jesus*[2] (Oxford, 1955).

————, *The Parables of Jesus*[6] (New York, 1963).

Jonsson, J., *Humour and Irony in the New Testament Illuminated by Parallels in Talmud and Midrash* (Reykjavik, 1965).

Kittel, G. & Friedrich, G., *Theologisches Wörterbuch zum Neuen Testament* 9 vols (Stuttgart, 1933-1973), Eng. Tr. by G. W. Bromiley, *Theological Dictionary of the New Testament* Vol. I-VIII (Grand Rapids, 1964-1972).

Knox, W. L., *The Sources of the Synoptic Gospels,* I. *St. Mark,* ed. H. Chadwick (Cambridge, 1953).

Kopp, C., *Die heiligen Stätten der Evangelien* (Regensburg, 1959).

Kümmel, W. G., *Introduction to the New Testament* (Nashville, 1966).

Ladd, G. E., *Jesus and the Kingdom* (New York, 1964).

Lambrechts, J., *Die Redaktion der Markus-Apokalypse. Literarische Analyse und Strukturuntersuchung* (Rome, 1967).

Lightfoot, R. H., *The Gospel Message of St. Mark* (Oxford, 1950).

Lindsey, R. L., *A Hebrew Translation of the Gospel of Mark* (Jerusalem, 1969).

Lohmeyer, E., *Galiläa und Jerusalem* (Göttingen, 1936).

Lohse, E., *Mark's Witness to Jesus Christ* (London, 1960).

Loos, H. van der, *The Miracles of Jesus* (Leiden, 1965).

Lövestam, E., *Son and Saviour* (Lund, 1961).

Marxsen, W., *Der Evangelist Markus. Studien zur Redaktionsgeschichte des Evangeliums*[2] (Göttingen, 1959).

Mauser, U. W., *Christ in the Wilderness. The Wilderness Theme in the Second Gospel and its Basis in the Biblical Tradition* (London, 1963).

McGinley, L. J., *Form Criticism of the Synoptic Healing Narratives* (Woodstock, Md., 1944).

Meye, R. P., *Jesus and the Twelve. Discipleship and Revelation in Mark's Gospel* (Grand Rapids, 1968).

Metzger, B. M., *Index to Periodical Literature on Christ and the Gospels* (Leiden, 1962).

———, *The Text of the New Testament* (Oxford, 1964).

Moore, A. L., *The Parousia in the New Testament* (Leiden, 1966).

Moule, C. F. D., *An Idiom-Book of New Testament Greek*[2] (Cambridge, 1960).

Newman, R. G., *Tradition and Interpretation in Mark* (Ann Arbor, 1966).

Parker, P., *The Gospel before Mark* (Chicago, 1953).

Pesch, R., *Naherwartungen. Tradition und Redaktion in Mk 13* (Düsseldorf, 1968).

Peter, J. F., *Finding the Historical Jesus. A Statement of the Principles Involved* (New York, 1966).

Potterie, I. de la, *Exegeses Synopticorum, "Sectio Panum" in Evangelio Marci (6, 6-8, 35)* (Rome, 1965-1966).

Richardson, A., *The Miracle-stories of the Gospels*[6] (London, 1959).

Ridderbos, H. N., *The Coming of the Kingdom* (Philadelphia, 1962).

Riesenfeld, H., *Jésus transfiguré. L'arrière-plan du récit évangelique de la transfiguration de Nôtre Seigneur* (Lund, 1947).

Rigaux, B., *Témoignage de l'évangile de Marc* (Bruges, 1965).

Robertson, A. T., *Studies in Mark's Gospel* (Nashville, 1958).

Robinson, J. M., *The Problem of History in Mark* (London, 1957).

Ruckstuhl, E., *Chronology of the Last Days of Jesus* (New York, 1965).

Schmidt, K. L., *Der Rahmen der Geschichte Jesu. Literarische Untersuchungen zur ältesten Jesusüberlieferung* (Berlin, 1919).

Schreiber, J., *Der Kreuzigungsbericht des Markusevangeliums. Ein traditionsgeschichtliche Untersuchung von Mk. 15, 20b-41* (Dissertation Bonn, 1959).

Schürer, E., *Geschichte des jüdischen Volkes im Zeitalter Jesu Christi,*[4] 3 vols (Leipzig, 1909).

Sherwin-White, A. W., *Roman Society and Roman Law in the New Testament* (Oxford, 1963).

Smith, M., *Tannaitic Parallels to the Gospels* (Philadelphia, 1951).

Stauffer, E., *Jesus and His Story* (New York, 1960).

———, *New Testament Theology*[5] (New York, 1955).

Stonehouse, N. B., *Origins of the Synoptic Gospels* (Grand Rapids, 1963).

———, *The Witness of Matthew and Mark to Christ* (Philadelphia, 1944).

Suhl, A., *Die Funktion der alttestamentlichen Zitate und Anspielungen im Markusevangelium* (Gütersloh, 1965).

Sundwall, J., *Die Zusammensetzung des Markus-Evangeliums* (Åbo, 1934).

Tagawa, K., *Miracles et évangile. La pensée personnelle de l'évangéliste Marc* (Paris, 1966).

Tillesse, G. Minette de, *Le secret messianique dans l'évangile de Marc* (Paris, 1968).

Tödt, H. E., *The Son of Man in the Synoptic Tradition* (Philadelphia, 1965).

Trilling, W., *Christusgeheimnis–Glaubensgeheimnis. Eine Einführung in das Markus-Evangelium* (Leipzig, 1957).

Trocmé, E., *La formation de l'évangile selon Marc* (Paris, 1963).

Wenger, L., *Die Quellen des römischen Rechts* (Vienna, 1953).

Wink, W., *John the Baptist in the Gospel Tradition* (Cambridge, 1968).

Winter, P., *On the Trial of Jesus* (Berlin, 1961).

Wrede, W., *Das Messiasgeheimnis in den Evangelien, zugleich ein Beitrag zum Verständnis des Markusevangeliums*[3] (Göttingen, 1963).

CHAPTER 1

I. PROLOGUE TO THE GOSPEL. Ch. 1:1-13

The reason for designating as prologue Ch. 1:1-13 is that these verses supply the key to the entire Gospel by introducing the central figure of the account. In accordance with the prophetic word, Jesus appears in the wilderness of Judea, summoned by the call of John the Baptist. His baptism and sojourn there constitute his first public acts and provide the foundation for his subsequent ministry. The Gospel of Mark will be the account of Jesus' trial, throughout which he decisively encounters Satan and receives help from God. This is what it means for Jesus to go out to the wilderness.[1]

The motif of the wilderness dominates the prologue. The prophetic note of the voice of one crying in the wilderness (Ch. 1:3) serves to introduce John the Baptist, whose ministry in the Jordan valley attracts Jesus of Nazareth (Ch. 1:4-8). The situating of John "in the wilderness" (Ch. 1:4) binds the account of his ministry to the prophetic announcement of Ch. 1:2-3. Mark relates the baptisms in the Jordan to the wilderness, for the lower Jordan valley is part of the wilderness scene and was called "desert" in both the Old and New Testament periods.[2] Subsequent to the baptism of Jesus the wilderness remains prominent as the arena where he was tempted (Ch. 1:12-13). Thus in Ch. 1:1-13 the wilderness is the location common to the several events related, and serves to underline the unity of the initial section.[3] In Ch. 1:14 the locality changes: Jesus leaves the wilderness and returns to Galilee to begin his ministry following the imprisonment of John.

Theological and literary considerations confirm this analysis of Ch. 1:1-13. In the building of his Gospel Mark frequently groups together

---

[1] See especially U. Mauser, *Christ in the Wilderness* (Naperville, Ill., 1963), pp. 77-102; J. M. Robinson, *The Problem of History in Mark*[2] (London, 1962), pp. 21-32. The argument that the prologue should be extended to Ch. 1:15 can be seen in O. J. F. Seitz, "*Preparatio Evangelica* in the Markan Prologue," *JBL* 82 (1963), pp. 201-206; *idem,* "Gospel Prologues: A Common Pattern?" *JBL* 83 (1964), pp. 262-268; L. E. Keck, "The Introduction to Mark's Gospel," *NTS* 12 (1966), pp. 352-370.

[2] Cf. C. C. McCown, "The Scene of John's Ministry," *JBL* 59 (1940), pp. 113-131; and especially R. W. Funk, "The Wilderness," *JBL* 78 (1959), pp. 205-214, where the biblical material is supplemented by the relevant texts from Qumran.

[3] U. Mauser, *op. cit.,* pp. 77-79.

traditions by the use of key-word association.[4] As a result, larger sections in Mark can be identified by the recurrence of basic words and phrases. In Ch. 1:1-13 the primary unifying term is "wilderness." But there is also repeated reference to the person of the Spirit within this section (Ch. 1:8, 10, 12). The allusion to the one who baptizes with the Spirit in the summary of John's message (Ch. 1:8) prepares for the reference to the Spirit at Jesus' baptism, and binds Ch. 1:4-8 to Ch. 1:9-11, while the role of the Spirit in the temptation (Ch. 1:12-13) associates this unit with the previous ones. The fact that the Spirit is introduced into the record only rarely beyond the prologue suggests that Mark has consciously unified his opening statement by a threefold reference to the Spirit.[5]

The most striking characteristics of the Marcan prologue are its abruptness and its silences. This is surprising because the one introduced is not an ordinary person but the Son of God, acknowledged by the heavenly voice, who in the initial phases of his public ministry provokes wonder and astonishment by the authority of his teaching and the power of his mighty acts. The evangelist makes no attempt to provide an historical explanation for John's presence in the wilderness or for Jesus' appearance before John. The prophetic voice and the Son of God appear, veiled in mystery from the very beginning. Yet their appearance in the wilderness is full of meaning for men precisely because the veil has been removed and the significance which it has in the divine plan of redemption has been disclosed. This Mark declares in the opening verse of his account. Accordingly, with a few broad strokes the prologue associates Jesus with the preaching and baptizing activity of John, and with trial in the wilderness. It indicates that the Messiah, who is divinely chosen and qualified for his ministry, has come. The accent falls upon the disclosure that Jesus is the Messiah, the very Son of God, whose mission is to affirm his sonship in the wilderness. His encounter with Satan provides the background for the delineation of the conflict between the Son of God and the forces of Satan which is so prominent an element in the Marcan narrative of Jesus' ministry.[6]

---

[4] See especially J. Sundwall, *Die Zusammensetzung des Markus-Evangeliums* (Åbo, 1934).

[5] Apart from the prologue "Spirit" occurs only in Chs. 3:29; 12:36; 13:11. See J. M. Robinson, *op. cit.*, pp. 28 f.; U. Mauser, *op. cit.*, p. 79.

[6] So N. B. Stonehouse, *The Witness of Matthew and Mark to Christ* (Philadelphia, 1944), pp. 6-21; cf. R. H. Lightfoot, *The Gospel Message of St. Mark* (Oxford, 1950), pp. 15-20; T. A. Burkill, *Mysterious Revelation. An Examination of the Philosophy of St. Mark's Gospel* (Ithaca, N.Y., 1963), pp. 9-23.

1. The Herald in the Wilderness. Ch. 1:1-8

1 The beginning of the gospel of Jesus Christ, the Son of God.[7]
2 Even as it is written in Isaiah the prophet,[8]
Behold, I send my messenger before thy face,
Who shall prepare thy way;
3 The voice of one crying in the wilderness,
Make ye ready the way of the Lord,
Make his paths straight;
4 John came, who baptized in the wilderness[9] and preached the
baptism of repentance unto remission of sins.[10]
5 And there went out unto him all the country of Judea, and all
they of Jerusalem; and they were baptized of him in the river
Jordan, confessing their sins.
6 And John was clothed with camel's hair, and *had* a leathern
girdle about his loins, and did eat locusts and wild honey.
7 And he preached, saying, There cometh after me he that is

---

[7] While the words "the Son of God" are included by most modern translations (ASV, RSV, NEB, Jerus. Bible) they are reduced to the apparatus of the critical editions of the Greek text [Westcott and Hort, Nestle, S. C. E. Legg, *Novum Testamentum Graece: Evangelium secundum Marcum* (Oxford, 1935), K. Aland, *Synopsis Quattuor Evangeliorum* (Stuttgart, 1964)]. The reading υἱοῦ θεοῦ is supported by B D W *pc* (latt), υἱοῦ τοῦ θεοῦ by 𝔎 A λ φ *pm* (latt) sy^{p} sa bo, together constituting the vast majority of manuscripts. The words are missing from א Θ 28 255 1555* sy^{pal} geo^{1} arm^{pt} Iren^{pt} Or. N. B. Stonehouse well remarks: "if these words are a gloss, they represent the action of a scribe who enjoyed a measure of real insight into the distinctiveness of Mark's portrayal of Christ" (*op. cit.,* p. 12). In six other instances in Mark Jesus is designated Son of God. There is good presumptive reason for judging that "Son of God" in Ch. 1:1 is an integral part of the text since Mark's superscription affords an indication of the general plan of his work: Peter's acknowledgment of the messiahship of Jesus in Ch. 8:29 has its Gentile counterpart in Ch. 15:39, where the centurion confesses that Jesus is the Son of God. Moreover, since the text of Codex Sinaiticus may be based upon that of papyri which Origen took with him from Alexandria to Palestine, the two chief witnesses for the omission (א and Origen) are, perhaps, reduced to one. It is better, accordingly, to suppose that "Son of God" was omitted unintentionally in manuscript transmission.

[8] The reading of the AV, "as it is written in the prophets," supported by 𝔎 A W φ *pm,* represents an alteration of the earlier reading (𝔋 D *pc*) in recognition that only Ch. 1:3 is a citation from Isaiah.

[9] RSV "John the Baptizer appeared in the wilderness."

[10] RSV "for the forgiveness of sins"; NEB "a baptism in token of repentance, for the forgiveness of sins."

mightier than I, the latchet of whose shoes[11] I am not worthy to stoop down and unloose.

8 I baptized you in water; but he shall baptize you in the Holy Spirit.

1 The opening words of Mark's Gospel form a superscription which indicates the character of that which follows in Ch. 1:1-13.[12] They emphasize that the good news concerning Jesus the Christ was inseparably bound up with the preparation provided by John the Baptist, whose ministry served to summon Jesus to the wilderness. Mark's intention is grasped by reading verses 1-4 as a single sentence: the good news *concerns* Jesus the Christ, but it *begins* with the wilderness prophet John. The word "beginning" has biblical overtones which lend an awesome ring to the opening phrase, and serves to recall that it is God who initiates redemption on behalf of men.[13] What Mark celebrates is not merely the prophetic activity of John the Baptist but the redemptive activity of God in providing salvation for men. The prophetic testimony cited in Ch. 1:2-3 finds its fulfilment both in the ministry of John and in the coming of Jesus into the wilderness. The emphasis thus falls upon the unity of God's action in its historical unfolding; the whole complex of events from the appearance of John to the beginning of Jesus' ministry is a single movement, the beginning of the gospel.

The term "gospel" or "evangel" was not a word first coined among the Christians. On the contrary, the concept was significant both in pagan and Jewish culture.[14] Among the Romans it meant "joyful tidings" and was associated with the cult of the emperor, whose birthday, attainment to majority and accession to power were celebrated as festival occasions for the whole world. The reports of such festivals were called "evangels" in the inscriptions and papyri of the Imperial

---

[11] RSV "the thong of whose sandals."

[12] Cf. N. B. Stonehouse, *op. cit.*, pp. 7-10. C. E. B. Cranfield, *The Gospel according to St. Mark*[2] (Cambridge, 1963), pp. 34 f. surveys ten different interpretations of verse 1, which indicates the complexity of the question, but lends his support to the position adopted here.

[13] Cf. E. Lohmeyer, *Das Evangelium des Markus*[16] (Göttingen, 1963), p. 10 who recalls not only Gen. 1:1 and John 1:1 but Hos. 1:2 LXX, ἀρχὴ λόγου κυρίου πρὸς 'Ωσῆε; Prov. 1:1; Eccl. 1:1; Cant. 1:1.

[14] On the concept "gospel" see J. Schniewind, *Euangelion. Ursprung und erste Gestalt des Begriffs Evangelium* (Gütersloh, 1927-31); G. Friedrich, *TWNT* II (Eng. Tr. 1964), pp. 707-737; R. Asting, *Die Verkündigung des Wortes im Urchristentum* (Stuttgart, 1939), pp. 300-457.

Age. A calendar inscription from about 9 B.C., found in Priene in Asia Minor, says of the emperor Octavian (Augustus): "the birthday of the god was for the world *the beginning of joyful tidings* which have been proclaimed on his account" (*Inscr. Priene,* 105, 40).[15] This inscription is remarkably similar to Mark's initial line and it clarifies the essential content of an evangel in the ancient world: *an historical event which introduces a new situation for the world.* In this perspective the Roman would understand Mark's proclamation of Jesus the Messiah. Beginning with the inauguration of Jesus' public ministry, Mark announces Jesus' coming as an event that brings about a radically new state of affairs for mankind.[16]

There is, however, another aspect to the meaning of "gospel." Mark's own understanding of what constituted "joyful tidings" drew heavily on the prophetic tradition of the Old Testament, as the twofold citation of Ch. 1:2-3 makes clear. The explicit reference to Isaiah indicates that the gospel receives its proper interpretation only in the light of the coming salvation promised in the prophetic word. Especially in Isaiah the Hebrew terms signifying "good news" concern the announcement of future salvation, or of the time of salvation.[17] In this context to proclaim salvation on God's authority is itself a creative act; in a sense it inaugurates the reality of which it speaks.[18] This fact points up the difference between the biblical concept of joyful tidings and that found in the imperial cult. For the Roman an evangel was retrospective, a

---

[15] For this and related texts see G. Friedrich, *op. cit.*, pp. 724 f. Bibliography on the Priene inscription is listed in n. 35 to Friedrich's discussion.

[16] Cf. E. Stauffer, *New Testament Theology* (New York, 1956), pp. 157-159. G. Friedrich, *op. cit.,* p. 725 rightly comments on the parallel between "evangel" in the imperial cult and the Bible: "Caesar and Christ, the emperor on the throne and the despised rabbi on the cross, confront one another. Both are evangel to men. They have much in common. But they belong to different worlds."

[17] Cf. G. Friedrich, *op. cit.,* pp. 707-710, 714-717, 721, 726 f. The connection between בִּשֵּׂר and בְּשֹׂרָה in the OT and εὐαγγελίζομαι and εὐαγγέλιον in the NT has been found in the preservation of the Semitic terminology of the OT in the Galilean Aramaic of the Palestinian Syriac Version of the Gospels. See J. W. Bowman, "The term *Gospel* and its cognates in Palestinian Syriac," in *New Testament Essays. Studies in Memory of T. W. Manson,* ed. A. J. B. Higgins (Manchester, 1959), pp. 54-67.

[18] This has important implications for the ministry of John and Jesus, both of whom proclaim "the gospel." Cf. A. Schlatter, *Das Evangelium nach Matthäus* (Stuttgart, 1929), p. 175: "John did not only prophesy; he was himself prophesied. He gave the people not simply hope for the future; with him began the fulfillment of this hope."

reflection of the joyous event which has already taken place. In the prophetic word there is a distinctively forward-looking eschatological perspective. The messenger of joy will announce the beginning of the time of salvation and thereby introduce it (cf. Isa. 52:7-10).

In keeping with this usage in Isaiah, Mark's opening verses center attention both on the earliest apostolic preaching about "Jesus the Messiah, the Son of God," and on the joyful tidings announced by Jesus himself (Ch. 1:14 f.).[19] In the initial phrase of Mark's Gospel and the summary of Jesus' Galilean proclamation, the word "gospel" has not yet come to mean a written document. It refers to a living word of hope from the lips of an appointed messenger.[20]

In Ch. 1:1 "gospel" is the technical term for Christian preaching, and the words which qualify it should be understood objectively, "the good news *concerning* Jesus the Messiah, the Son of God."[21] Mark's Gospel as a whole gives an interpretive account of the historical appearance of Jesus; it is concerned with his teaching far less than the other Gospels. Consistent with this "Jesus the Messiah,[22] the Son of God"[23]

---

19 G. Friedrich, *op. cit.*, p. 728 tends to disbelieve that Jesus actually used the term "gospel" in Chs. 1:15; 8:35; 10:29; 13:10; 14:9; it is the evangelist who is responsible for the term. Against this opinion see J. W. Bowman, *Prophetic Realism and the Gospel* (London, 1955), pp. 64-68, who rightly notes that these references reflect an early period when the gospel was something which Jesus heralded, rather than something that he was himself.

20 Not until the second century did the term "gospel" come to designate a particular kind of document. The transition from the one usage to the other reflects the second century evaluation of the canonical Gospels as authoritative proclamations of the one gospel concerning Jesus Christ.

21 Rather than "the good news *which Jesus* the Messiah *proclaimed*." Cf. N. B. Stonehouse, *op. cit.*, p. 12.

22 Mark's usage of the designation "Messiah" in Chs. 8:29; 12:35; 14:61 and 15:32 show that he is presupposing in Ch. 1:1 the traditional connotations of the term. Accordingly, Χριστοῦ in Ch. 1:1 is not a proper name but a titular designation, parallel to υἱοῦ θεοῦ.

23 For "Son of God" in Mark see below on Chs. 1:11; 3:11; 8:38; 9:7; 12:6; 13:32; 14:36, 61; 15:39. It is widely recognized that the figure of Jesus in Mark's Gospel is altogether supernatural. Cf. E. Lohmeyer, *op. cit.*, p. 4: "The Son of God is not primarily a human but a divine figure . . . He is not merely endowed with the power of God, but is himself divine as to his nature; not only are his word and his work divine, but his essence also." Cf. J. Bieneck, *Sohn Gottes als Christusbezeichnung der Synoptiker* (Zürich, 1951); W. Grundmann, "Sohn Gottes," *ZNW* 47 (1956), pp. 113-133. In the ultimate sense "Son of God" is a mysterious term which Jesus alone can clarify. What Son means is determined by what Jesus is, by what he does, by what he says, and it is this revelation which dominates Mark's Gospel.

in verse 1 should be understood as the content of Christian proclamation. The superscription indicates that Mark's primary concern is to delineate the historical content of the primitive Christian message of salvation. It also suggests the general plan of his work by anticipating the crucial points in the history he relates. The recognition that Jesus is the Messiah in Ch. 8:29 is the point of transition to the second half of the Gospel where Mark clarifies what it means for Jesus to be the Messiah. The climax is reached in Ch. 15:39 with the affirmation that Jesus is the Son of God. It is evident that the first line of Mark's Gospel invites the reader to consider every aspect of the Gospel from a distinctly Christological perspective.[24]

The primary reference in Ch. 1:1 is to the ministry of John and the fulfilment of the hope of Israel. This hope is distinctly eschatological in character; the forerunner announces the coming of the Messiah who introduces the new age of redemption promised through the prophets. For this reason the transition from Mark's initial verse to the day of the Lord is not as abrupt as is sometimes supposed. The coming of John signaled both the beginning of the joyful tidings of salvation and the intrusion of the rule of God.

2-3 The citation formula, "even as it is written in Isaiah the prophet," indicates that the proper context for understanding the gospel is the promise of future salvation found in the latter half of Isaiah. The citation which follows is a composite quotation from Ex. 23:20; Mal. 3:1 and Isa. 40:3, passages which evoke the image of the forerunner Elijah. In the exegetical tradition of the rabbis these texts had already been combined, in the conviction that the "messenger of the covenant" (Ex. 23:20) is Elijah (Mal. 3:1; 4:5).[25] Mark's first statement is from the Law, and agrees verbatim with the text of Ex. 23:20 in the Septuagint. It is enriched by a formulation originating in the Hebrew text of Mal. 3:1, although the first person has been altered to the second in the interest of the messianic interpretation of the passage. This fused text may have been selected from a testimony-collection in which the con-

---

[24] Cf. R. P. Meye, *Jesus and the Twelve. Discipleship and Revelation in Mark's Gospel* (Grand Rapids, 1968), p. 30: "Mark and the community in which his work originated worshipped Jesus as the Son of God. The narrative of Mark's Gospel and its origin with the worshipping Church, as well as its continual use by the worshipping Church, makes this abundantly clear."

[25] Cf. Exodus Rabba 23:20. The identical words, "Behold I send my messenger," in Ex. 23:20 and Mal. 3:1 furnished the exegetical ground of the conflation.

flation had already taken place.[26] The second statement introduces a word from the Prophets, and agrees with Isa. 40:3 LXX, with the single alteration of "the paths of God" to "his paths." By this change the text becomes applicable to Jesus, who was known in the early church as "the Lord."

The integrity of the mixed citation in Ch. 1:2 has often been questioned. It fails to satisfy the formula of citation which specifies "the prophet Isaiah" but agrees in form with a quotation introduced in a different context by Matthew and Luke. For these reasons it is commonly regarded as a very ancient gloss, interpolated into the text at so early a stage that it has left its mark upon the entire manuscript tradition.[27] Opposed to this conjecture is not merely the consistent witness of the manuscript tradition, which lends no textual support to the omission of verse 2, but the important fact that the three OT passages, blended in this fashion, are all related to the wilderness tradition and have a significant function in the prologue itself. Ex. 23:20 contains God's promise to send his messenger before the people on a first exodus through the wilderness to Canaan. In Isa. 40:3 the messenger announces the second exodus through the wilderness to the final deliverance prepared for God's people. In both the citation from the Law and from the Prophets the theme of an exodus through the wilderness is dominant and appropriate to Mark's conception and purpose. The blended citation functions to draw attention to three factors which are significant to the evangelist in the prologue: the herald, the Lord and the wilderness. In the verses which immediately follow, the significance of each of these elements is emphasized by Mark,[28] who sees in the coming of John and Jesus to

---

[26] Pre-Christian testimony texts were provided for the first time by the discoveries in Cave Four at Qumran. For 4QFlorilegium and 4QTestimonia see A. Dupont-Sommer, *The Essene Writings from Qumran* (Cleveland, 1962), pp. 310-317.

[27] E.g. M. J. Lagrange, *L'Évangile selon Saint Marc*[9] (Paris, 1947), p. 4; J. B. Colon, "Marc (Évangile selon Saint)," *DB Suppl* V (1957), col. 838; J. A. T. Robinson, "Elijah, John and Jesus. An Essay in Detection" in *Twelve New Testament Studies* (London, 1962), p. 34 n. 14. This surmise is due to the fact that Mt. 3:3 and Lk. 3:4 cite only the text of Isaiah in the context of the Baptist's activities, while the mixed quotation occurs in a different context, Mt. 11:10 and Lk. 7:27. That a citation from a testimony collection would be introduced by a reference to Isaiah is also felt to be questionable.

[28] E. Lohmeyer, *op. cit.,* p. 10 sees verses 4-8 as a line by line commentary on the biblical citation. By restricting the interpretation to the account of John's activity, however, Lohmeyer fails to consider adequately the reflection upon the Lord in the wilderness which is central to the citation. Cf. U. Mauser, *op. cit.,*

the wilderness the fulfilment of the promised salvation of which the prophet Isaiah had spoken. In stressing the element of fulfilment at the beginning of his account Mark conforms the narrative to the apostolic preaching, in which the theme of fulfilment was of strategic importance.[29] The authenticity of verse 2 should be accepted.[30]

4-5 John the Baptist is a crucial figure in the history of revelation and redemption. In retrospect, his appearance in the wilderness was the most important event in the life of Israel for more than three hundred years. The absence of a prophet throughout this period had been interpreted to signify that the prophetic task was accomplished. Yet men clung to the hope that the "faithful prophet" would appear, the Prophet like Moses, whose coming would signal the events of the "last days" (Deut. 18:15-19; I Macc. 4:42-46; 14:41; 1QS ix. 11). The very fact of John's appearance was an eschatological event of the first magnitude, and signified that the decisive turning point in the history of salvation was at hand. It was John, the preacher of radical repentance, who initiated the messianic crisis. To speak of the gospel of Jesus is to speak of the good news which began with John.[31]

Precisely because the Baptist belongs so intimately to the gospel, it is difficult to recover John as a person. The discovery of an Essene center at Khirbet Qumran in the Judean wilderness has led to the conjecture that John may have spent a period of time there.[32] The

---

p. 82: "The wilderness in Mark 1:3 carries with it the full weight of a great religious tradition embracing high hopes and promises as well as the deep shadows of judgment and despair, and this is imposed upon the succeeding verses, moulding them as counterparts of Israel's experience in the desert." Mauser explores this old biblical tradition on pp. 15-52.

29 E.g. Acts 2:16-21, 25-31, 34-36; 3:18, 21-26; 8:30-35; 10:43 *et passim*. Cf. C. H. Dodd, *According to the Scriptures. The Substructure of New Testament Theology* (London, 1952).

30 It is possible that the reference to "Isaiah the prophet" in Mk. 1:2 is not intended to introduce the quotation which follows but indicates the context in terms of which John's own self-understanding may be grasped. John knows that he has been called by God, and his fundamental primer for understanding what this means is the prophecy of Isaiah. John needed no instruction apart from the words of Isaiah; his message was constantly found as he reflected on Chs. 1:10 ff.; 2:9 ff.; 4:1; 6:10 f.; *et passim*.

31 On the theological interpretation of John in the Gospels see W. Wink, *John the Baptist in the Gospel Tradition* (Cambridge, 1968), especially pp. 1-17 for a treatment of Mark.

32 Cf. W. H. Brownlee, "John the Baptist in the New Light of Ancient Scrolls,"

documents from Qumran indicate that John shared many ideas in common with the Covenanters, among them an appreciation of the biblical traditions centering in the wilderness, a vivid sense of crisis heightened by messianic expectations, and a strong anticipation of the Holy Spirit. Both the Baptist and the men of Qumran appealed to Isa. 40:3 to explain their presence in the wilderness. [33] A careful comparison of the Qumran Covenanters with John the Baptist, however, reveals differences so extensive as to make the possibility of contact unimportant. If the Baptist was ever associated with the community he broke with its tradition and found his destiny along wholly different lines. His mission was shaped by the summons of God which came to him in the wilderness.

From Mark's perspective, John is important not for his own sake but as the beginning of the unfolding drama of redemption which centers in Jesus of Nazareth. The brevity of his presentation of John serves to project into sharp relief two features of the Baptist's ministry which were of special significance to him: (1) John's career was the result of divine appointment in fulfilment of prophecy; (2) John bore witness to the supreme dignity and power of the Messiah, whose coming was near.

The citation of Isa. 40:3 in verse 3 explains John's advent: the herald of the Lord will cry in the wilderness. From the point of view of transition Ch. 1:4 is tied to Ch. 1:3 by means of the identical phrase "in the wilderness" in both verses. Mark's interest in the wilderness is not primarily geographical; the reference to the lower Jordan River valley fails to provide any specific information about the locale in which the Baptist ministered. But the evangelist has preserved the emphasis upon the wilderness which he found in his sources and has allowed it to shape his own theological understanding of the gospel. The historical tradition that John appeared in the wilderness establishes the relevance of the citation from Isaiah and provides the key to Mark's concentration upon wilderness motifs throughout the prologue.

---

in *The Scrolls and the New Testament,* ed. K. Stendahl (New York, 1957), pp. 33-53; H. H. Rowley, "The Baptism of John and the Qumran Sect," in *New Testament Essays,* ed. A. J. B. Higgins (Manchester, 1959), pp. 218-229; J. Pryke, "John the Baptist and the Qumran Community," *Rev Qum* 4 (1964), pp. 483-496.

[33] On the citation of Isa. 40:3 in 1QS viii. 12-16 see the commentary of P. Wernberg-Møller, *The Manual of Discipline* (Leiden, 1957), pp. 34, 129; U. Mauser, *op. cit.,* pp. 58-61. The interpretation of Isa. 40:3 at Qumran relates to the study of the Law and obedience to its mandates.

Briefly and concisely verses 4-8 describe the Baptist's ministry. Mark focuses attention on three elements in John's ministry, each of which is related to the OT prophecies with which he has prefaced his Gospel: (1) John was a man of the wilderness; (2) he performed his ministry of baptism in the wilderness, and so prepared the way of the Lord; (3) he announced one greater than himself who was to come after him. Each detail of the five verses is related to one or more of these three emphases.

Those who heard John would not have failed to recognize the familiar prophetic call to repentance. But in response to his preaching John called for an action which was wholly novel – baptism in the Jordan River. It has been conjectured that John's baptism was derived from the Jewish practice of baptizing proselytes,[34] or from the rites of initiation practiced at Qumran.[35] No clear line of dependence can be shown in support of these theories. Baptism appears rather as a unique activity of this prophet, a prophetic sign so striking that John became known simply as "the Baptizer."

The absence of qualifying clauses makes it difficult to ascertain the exact nuance in the phrase, "a baptism of repentance for the forgiveness of sins."[36] The biblical concept of repentance, however, is deeply rooted in the wilderness tradition.[37] In the earliest stratum of OT prophecy, the summons to "turn" basically connotes a return to the original relationship with the Lord. This means a return to the beginning of God's history with his people, a return to the wilderness. Essential to the prophetic concern with repentance in Hosea, Amos and Isaiah is the concept of Israel's time in the wilderness as the period of true sonship

---

34 For a discussion of this position see J. Jeremias, "Der Ursprung der Johannestaufe," *ZNW* 28 (1929), pp. 312-320; T. M. Taylor, "The Beginnings of Jewish Proselyte Baptism," *NTS* 2 (1956), pp. 193-198.

35 Cf. J. A. T. Robinson, "The Baptism of John and the Qumran Community," *HTR* 50 (1957), pp. 175-191. For an opposing point of view see H. H. Rowley, *op. cit.*, pp. 218-229.

36 Cf. U. Mauser, *op. cit.*, pp. 84-89 for a brief summary of several points of view and a more extensive analysis of the interpretations of E. Lohmeyer (John's baptism was a sacramental act which conferred forgiveness) and of C. H. Kraeling (John's baptism was an act symbolic of repentance which could mediate forgiveness without conferring it). See E. Lohmeyer, "Zur evangelischen Überlieferung von Johannes dem Taufer," *JBL* 51 (1932), pp. 300-319 and his commentary, pp. 13-19; C. H. Kraeling, *John the Baptist* (New Haven, 1951), pp. 69-122.

37 Cf. E. Würthwein, *TWNT* IV (1942), pp. 976-985; U. Mauser, *op. cit.*, pp. 46-52; and especially H. W. Wolff, "Das Thema 'Umkehr' in der Alttestamentlichen Theologie," *ZThK* 48 (1951), pp. 129-148.

to God, a status into which the Lord is going to lead his people once again in a future time. Although there is no trace of this understanding in orthodox Jewish circles in the first century,[38] the theology of the Qumran Community indicates that this strand of the prophetic tradition was kept alive in sectarian Judaism.[39] The correlation between the wilderness and repentance was not John's innovation and must have been understood by his contemporaries. John's call to repentance and his call to come out to him in the wilderness to be baptized are two aspects of the same reality. It is a call to renew sonship in the wilderness. The peculiar urgency in the call lies in the fact that the crisis of God's final act is close at hand.

The same correlation should be seen between baptism and the wilderness. The summons to be baptized in the Jordan meant that Israel must come once more to the wilderness. As Israel long ago had been separated from Egypt by a pilgrimage through the waters of the Red Sea, the nation is exhorted again to experience separation; the people are called to a second exodus in preparation for a new covenant with God. Both John's call to repentance and his baptism are intelligible as aspects of the prophetic tradition which expected the final salvation of God to be unveiled in the wilderness.

Repentance in John's proclamation is conditioned by the action of God, who is about to enter history in a definitive fashion. The opportunity[40] and urgency for repentance lie in the fact that the one who will baptize with the Holy Spirit is close at hand. As the people heed John's call and go out to him in the desert far more is involved than contrition and confession. They return to a place of judgment, the wilderness, where the status of Israel as God's beloved son must be re-established in the exchange of pride for humility. The willingness to return to the wilderness signifies the acknowledgment of Israel's history as one of

---

38 Cf. J. Behm, *TWNT* IV (1942), pp. 991-994, where the evidence is analyzed.

39 Cf. K. G. Kuhn, *Konkordanz zu den Qumrantexten* (Göttingen, 1960), pp. 217 f. s.v. שׁוּב. The texts are gathered and discussed by U. Mauser, *op. cit.*, pp. 58-61.

40 H. W. Wolff, *op. cit.*, pp. 138-143 points out that in Amos, Hosea and Isaiah "return" is never used in prophetic admonitions, but exclusively in proclamations of rebuke because the people will not return, or of the promise of a future time when opportunity to return will again be provided by God. Israel has forfeited the opportunity of returning (e.g. Hos. 5:4), but that possibility will be restored by a future divine action (e.g. Hos. 3:4 f.). The nation does not have the opportunity to repent and return to God at any time, according to these prophets. Only God can provide the situation of judgment and grace in which repentance is possible.

disobedience and rebellion, and a desire to begin once more. John's proclamation of the forgiveness of sins provides the assurance that God extends grace as well as judgment.[41] It is in the context of judgment and grace that the people of Jerusalem and Judea go out to the wilderness to be baptized by John.

6 The reference to John's clothing and diet serves to emphasize that he is a man of the wilderness. Both his garb and his food are those familiar to the wilderness nomad, and characterize life in the desert.[42] The reference to the leather girdle about the Baptist's waist recalls a characteristic feature of another man of the wilderness, the prophet Elijah (II Kings 1:8). The explicit identification of John with Elijah, however, is not made until Ch. 9:9-13.

7-8 John's message is telescoped to focus upon a single theme, the proclamation of a person still to come who will baptize the people with the Holy Spirit. In referring to this new Baptizer, whose dignity overshadowed his own, John avoided traditional messianic terms. The announcement is framed in accordance with Israel's expectation either of the eschatological coming of God himself or of his appointed representative. The formulation, "the Coming One," echoes Mal. 3:1f.; 4:5f. with its warning concerning the Lord who comes suddenly in sifting judgment, or Ps. 118:26 with its ascription of praise to "him who comes in the name of the Lord."[43] The precise identity of the Coming One remained hidden, apparently, even from John. "To come after some-

---

41 Cf. U. Mauser, *op. cit.,* p. 89: "This reduction to nothing is a divine judgment, acknowledged by the people of Judea and Jerusalem in the confession of their sin, but it is also the starting point for a new history of grace." On this response of the people see below on Ch. 1:9.

42 Cf. C. H. Kraeling, *op. cit.,* pp. 10f., 14f. The desert nomad does not hesitate to eat small insects, including locusts. Locusts are listed among clean foods in Lev. 11:21 f.

An interesting parallel is offered by the first century A.D. Martyrdom of Isaiah 2:8-12. Isaiah withdraws from Jerusalem to Bethlehem because of the lawlessness of the people, but the men of Bethlehem are also wicked. With a company of men he withdraws further south into the Judean desert, settling "on a mountain in a solitary place" (Ch. 2:8). Isaiah and his companions are "clothed with garments of hair" (Ch. 2:9) because they are all prophets. Their food consists of wild herbs (Ch. 2:11). They spent two years in the wilderness lamenting over the sins of the people (Ch. 2:12). For the hairy mantle as the garb of a prophet see Zech. 13:4.

43 Cf. J. Schneider, *TWNT* II (Eng. Tr. 1964), pp. 668-671; S-B*K* IV. 2 (1928), pp. 872ff.

one" is technical terminology for discipleship among the scribes and rabbis of the first century, and this usage is reflected in Jesus' summons to men *to come,* or *follow after* him (cf. Ch. 1:17). It is possible, therefore, that John is saying, "He who is coming is a follower of mine."[44] Yet he affirms that he is not worthy of performing the most menial task, from which even the Hebrew slave was released, the removal of the master's sandals.[45] In no stronger manner could the mystery and the dignity of the Coming One be emphasized.

The reference to the bestowal of the Spirit is appropriate to the wilderness context of John's proclamation.[46] Isaiah describes Israel's trek in the wilderness as a march under the guidance of the Spirit of God (Isa. 63:11); it was the Spirit who gave the people rest in the wilderness (Ch. 63:14). As the first exodus had been a going forth into the wilderness under the leadership of God's Spirit, the prophet announces the second exodus as a time when there will be a fresh outpouring of the Spirit (Chs. 32:15; 44:3). With this concept in mind John calls the people to the wilderness in anticipation of the fulfilment of the prophetic promise. It is this note of anticipation[47] which Mark emphasizes by reducing John's message to two statements, both of which point forward to something to come. They affirm that John is the forerunner of the Messiah (Ch. 1:7) and that his baptism is a preparation for the messianic baptism to come (Ch. 1:8).

By introducing his Gospel with an account of the ministry of John, the evangelist re-creates for his own contemporaries the crisis of decision

---

[44] Cf. K. Grobel, "He that cometh after me," *JBL* 60 (1941), pp. 397-401; O. Cullmann, "ὁ ὀπίσω μου ἐρχόμενος," *Coniectanea Neotestamentica* (Zürich, 1947), pp. 26-32. H. Seesemann, *TWNT* IV (Eng. Tr. 1967), p. 290 dissents, finding in ὀπίσω simply an indication of time.

[45] E.g. Mekilta to Ex. 21:2 (ed. Lauterbach, Vol. III, pp. 5 f.): "A Hebrew slave must not wash the feet of his master, nor put his shoes on him, nor carry his things before him . . . But one's son or pupil may do so." TB *Ketuboth* 96a: "All services which a slave does for his master a pupil should do for his teacher, with the exception of undoing his shoes."

[46] Isa. 32:15; 44:3; 63:10-14. On these passages see E. Schweizer, *TWNT* VI (1959), pp. 363, 368, 382 f. On the function of Spirit-baptism see J. E. Yates, "The Form of Mark i. 8b. 'I baptized you with water; he will baptize you with the Holy Spirit,'" *NTS* 4 (1958), pp. 334-338.

[47] Cf. W. Wink, *op. cit.,* p. 6: "John does not fully belong to the time of fulfilment, for his message as recorded by Mark is entirely prophetic. John is distinguished from the time of the Old Testament in terms of fulfilment (1:2 ff.) but from that of Jesus in terms of anticipation (1:7 f.). The messenger of victory is not the victor."

with which John had confronted all Israel. It is not enough to know who John was, historically. What is required is an encounter, through the medium of history, with that summons to judgment and repentance which John issued. Because the church recognized John's role in redemptive history as the pioneer of the kingdom of God, it accorded him a prominent place in the Gospel tradition. It refused to allow his memory to slip uninterpreted into the past, but made his witness a part of the continuing Christian proclamation. John was the first preacher of the good news concerning Jesus.

2. The Lord in the Wilderness. Ch. 1:9-11

9 And it came to pass in those days, that Jesus came from Nazareth of Galilee, and was baptized of John in the Jordan.
10 And straightway [48] coming up out of the water, he saw the heavens rent asunder, and the Spirit as a dove descending upon him:
11 And a voice came out of the heavens,
Thou art my beloved Son, in thee I am well pleased.

9 The prophetic word announced not only the herald in the wilderness but also the Lord. In Ch. 1:4-8 the Lord was introduced only indirectly, as the greater one who is coming. He is introduced directly in Ch. 1:9-11; Jesus comes from Nazareth [49] in Galilee to be baptized by John. The explicit reference to the River Jordan [50] in Ch. 1:9 links this moment with John's prior activity (Ch. 1:5). Parallel to the treatment of the

---

[48] This is the first instance of a Marcan term which occurs between forty and fifty times in the Gospel (the number depends on textual variations). It is appropriate to translate "at once," but the meaning can be determined only from the context and varies from the sense of immediacy (as here) to that of logical order, "in due course" (as in Ch. 1:14). For an analysis of Marcan usage see D. Daube, *The Sudden in the Scripture* (Leiden, 1964), pp. 46-60.

[49] On Nazareth see especially C. Kopp, "Beiträge zur Geschichte Nazareths," *JPOS* 18 (1938), pp. 187-228; 19 (1939), pp. 82-119, 253-285; 20 (1940), pp. 29-42; 21 (1948), pp. 148-164; B. Bagatti, "Nazareth," *DB Suppl* VI (1960), cols. 318-333 and see below on Ch. 6:1-6a.

[50] Early rabbinic tradition explicitly disqualifies the River Jordan for purification, M. *Parah* VIII. 10. Only Josephus, *Ant.* XVIII. v. 2 explicitly associates John's baptism with purification (cf. Jn. 3:25), but he makes no reference to the Jordan. On the association of the Jordan with Israel's heritage cf. O. J. F. Seitz, "What Do These Stones Mean?" *JBL* 79 (1960), pp. 247-254.

Baptist, the appearance of Jesus is abruptly introduced. The sole key to his identity provided by Mark is John's word concerning "the coming one."

By skilfully placing verses 8 and 9 next to each other Mark portrays the enormous contrast between the baptism which the Lord is to perform and that to which he himself submits. Central in verse 8 is the giver of life, actively creating the people of God; in verse 9 it is the same one in the role of the lowly penitent, passively receiving the sign of repentance on behalf of the people of God. [51] In submitting to John's baptism Jesus acknowledges the judgment of God upon Israel. At the same time his baptism signifies that his mission will be to endure the judgment of God. Jesus comes to John as the true Israelite whose repentance is perfect. He *is* the beloved Son, but he comes to the wilderness because sonship must be reaffirmed in the wilderness. John's appearance in the wilderness, his call to repentance and his baptism signify that the time has come when God will execute a decisive judgment from which a new Israel will emerge. Jesus acknowledges this conviction which has roots in the prophetic tradition. He comes to John as one willing to assume the brunt of this judgment. The bearing of its burden constitutes his mission.

This becomes clearer when it is observed with E. Lohmeyer that Ch. 1:5 and Ch. 1:9 stand in relationship to each other. Both sentences are built in exactly the same way, so that the verses correspond, [52] but they exhibit a deep contrast in two respects. (1) In Ch. 1:5 Judea and Jerusalem are in view, the central province and the holy city; in Ch. 1:9 Nazareth of Galilee is in view, an unpromising region associated with

---

[51] So U. Mauser, *op. cit.*, p. 91, who comments, "There is no passage in the Second Gospel which exposes the so-called Messianic secret in a more forceful manner than verses 8 and 9 of the first chapter read together."

[52] *Comm. cit.*, p. 20. The parallelism may be exhibited by translating according to word order:

Ch. 1:5	"And there went out – all of the region of Judea and all those from Jerusalem and they were baptized by him in the river Jordan."	Ch. 1:9	"And there came – Jesus from Nazareth in Galilee and he was baptized in the Jordan."

It should be noted, however, that the concluding phrase of verse 5, "confessing their sins," has no parallel in verse 9.

disinterest in the Law.[53] (2) In Ch. 1:5 *all* of the people come forth to be baptized by John; in Ch. 1:9 *one* single representative is introduced, the only Galilean mentioned by Mark who heeded John's call to the wilderness. By this correspondence and contrast Mark suggests that all of those from Judea and Jerusalem who came out to John prove to be yet rebellious and insensitive to the purpose of God. Contrary to expectation, only the one from Galilee proves to be the unique Son who genuinely responds to the prophetic call to the wilderness. In doing so he identified himself with a rebellious generation in need of redemption. Mark is concerned to indicate from the very beginning that Jesus is not an isolated individual who is responsible only for his own righteousness. From the point of introduction Jesus shares the heritage and predicament of the people, and like Moses in the first exodus (Ex. 32:23), he does not set himself apart from their sins. This is the startling emphasis of verse 9, that the bestower of the baptism with the Spirit humbles himself to receive the baptism of repentance. With a company of others, he heeds John's call to the wilderness as the place where Israel's sonship to God must be renewed.[54]

10-11 Many had come to the Jordan to be baptized by John, but only in the instance of Jesus, in whom true submission to God was perfectly embodied, was the "coming up" from the water answered by a "coming down" from above.[55] The cosmic significance of this event is indicated by the vision of the rending of the heavens, the descent of the Spirit and the testimony of the voice from heaven. Mark's distinctive language echoes Isa. 64:1, where the prophet prays, "Oh that thou wouldst *rend the heavens,* that thou wouldst *come down,* that the mountains might quake at thy presence..."[56] The pattern had been established already

---

[53] Cf. L. E. Elliott-Binns, *Galilean Christianity* (London, 1956), pp. 13, 25. Johanan ben Zakkai († A.D. 90) struggled for eighteen years to establish a rabbinic academy in Galilee; his failure is reflected in the lament, "Galilee, Galilee, you hate the Torah; your end will be seizure by the Romans" (TJ *Shabbath* 16 end, 15d). On this rabbinic passage see A. Schlatter, *Johanan ben Zakkai der Zeitgenosse der Apostel* (Stuttgart, 1899), pp. 14 f.

[54] U. Mauser, *op. cit.*, pp. 90-95.

[55] Cf. E. Lohmeyer, *op. cit.*, p. 22.

[56] Mark's formulation σχιζομένους τοὺς οὐρανούς echoes the LXX of Isa. 63:19 (M.T. 64:1); Ezek. 1:1; but see also Test. Levi 2:6; 5:1 and especially 18:6 and II Bar. 22:1, where the rending of the heavens is associated with the hearing of a voice. In Test. Levi 18:6 f. and Test. Judah 24:2 f. it is associated with the bestowal of the Holy Spirit. Cf. C. Maurer, *TWNT* VII (1964), p. 962, who associates

in the first exodus that God could not come down until the people had been consecrated (Ex. 19:10 f.). For this reason Jesus expressed a vicarious confession of sin on behalf of the many. He walked into the waters of baptism in obedience to the Father's will. He had consecrated himself in faith, even as every other man must do. But in this instance God came down, and there was striking attestation that sonship has been re-established through the one true Israelite whose repentance was perfect.

The divine response to Jesus' acknowledgment of the judgment of God was the descent of the Spirit as a dove and the voice from heaven. Both of these elements are to be associated with the new exodus in the wilderness prophesied by Isaiah (Chs. 32:15; 44:3; 63:10-14).[57] This prophecy is fulfilled in proleptic fashion in the descent of the Spirit upon Jesus. It was in the wilderness that Israel was first designated as son by God, and particularly the prophet Hosea pointed forward to a time when God would renew Israel's sonship in the wilderness.[58] In Jesus this ancient promise finds fulfilment precisely because his pilgrimage into the wilderness was the only true exodus. Many went out to John but only Jesus understood that a return to the wilderness involved the determination to live under the judgment of God.

The analogy between the Holy Spirit and a dove must be understood within a frame of reference provided by the OT or post-biblical Judaism.[59] Two interpretations commend themselves more than others. (1) The reference contains a veiled allusion to Gen. 1:2, where the brooding of the Spirit over the waters at creation suggested to Ben Zoma (*ca.* A.D. 90) the action of a dove. The descent of the Spirit signifies new creation, corresponding to the cosmic overtones in the rending of

---

Mark's formulation with Isa. 64:3 f.: "Jesus is the Bringer of the Act of God, which was not expected from eternity and which no eye perceived and no ear heard."

[57] Cf. I. Buse, "The Markan Account of the Baptism of Jesus and Isaiah LXIII," *JThS* n.s. 7 (1956), pp. 74 f.

[58] Ex. 4:22 f.; Jer. 2:2; Hos. 11:1-3.

[59] Several points of view are surveyed by R. Bultmann, *The History of the Synoptic Tradition* (Oxford, 1963), pp. 248-250; T. A. Burkill, *op. cit.,* pp. 17-19, but for none of them is there strong Jewish support. They believe that the dove symbolizes the divine power which takes possession of the messianic king, but primary support is drawn from Persian and Egyptian texts. H. Greeven, *TWNT* VI (1959), pp. 64-68, interprets the term "dove" in terms of a larger Near Eastern tradition. Of special interest is the association of the dove with the heavenly voice in Judaism (TB *Berachoth* 3a). For a review of early patristic and modern interpretations see W. Telfer, "The Form of a Dove," *JThS* 29 (1928), pp. 238-242.

the heavens. A later tradition identified the Spirit in Gen. 1:2 as the Spirit of the Messiah, which would be withheld from Israel until the nation was prepared through repentance.[60] Only rarely, however, did the rabbis identify the dove as a symbol of the Holy Spirit. (2) More frequently the rabbis refer to the dove as a symbol of the community of Israel,[61] and this association may have been in Mark's mind. At the moment of his baptism Jesus is the one true Israelite, in whom the election of God is concentrated. The descent of the Spirit "as a dove" indicates that he is the unique representative of the new Israel created through the Spirit.

In the voice from heaven[62] God addresses Jesus as his unique Son, the object of his elective love. In this expression of unqualified divine approval there is recognition of Jesus' competence to fulfill the messianic task for which he has been set apart. It is common to find in the pronouncement a reflection of Ps. 2:7 and Isa. 42:1, but it is not a quotation and it is legitimate to hear within it other echoes.[63]

The declaration provides a unique appraisal of Jesus. The designation "Son" is enriched by the concept of the Servant of the Lord of Isa. 42:1, but the primary emphasis is upon sonship. In this context "Son" is not a messianic title, but is to be understood in the highest sense, transcending messiahship. It signifies the unique relationship which Jesus sustains to the Father, which exists apart from any thought of official function in

---

60 The texts are TB *Hagigah* 15a; Gen. Rabba 2; Yalqut to Gen. 1:2. Cf. J. Jeremias, *Jesus als Weltvollender* (Gütersloh, 1930), p. 17, who speaks of the "cosmic significance of Jesus' baptism; the barren time is past and a new creation has dawned."

61 Cf. the texts discussed in S-B*K* I (1922), pp. 123 f.; T. A. Burkill, *op. cit.*, pp. 18 f.; A. Feuillet, "Le Symbolisme de la Colombe dans les récits évangéliques du baptême," *RSR* 46 (1958), 524-544; J. de Cock, "Het symbolisme van de duif bij het doopsel van Christus," *Bijdragen* 21 (1960), 363-376.

62 On the concept of the voice from heaven (בַּת קוֹל, see S-B*K* I (1922), pp. 125-132; II (1924), p. 128; J. Kosnetter, *Die Taufe Jesu* (Freiburg, 1936), pp. 140-190; H. Traub, *TWNT* V (1954), pp. 530-532.

63 E.g. G. Vermes, *Scripture and Tradition in Judaism* (Leiden, 1961), p. 233 finds in the pronouncement an allusion to Isa. 42:1 and Gen. 22:2, "Take your son, your only son Isaac whom you love." On pp. 193-227 he has shown that Isaac was viewed in Judaism as the type of the beloved son and willing sacrifice. The thought of the passage would then be that Jesus fulfills all that is implied in the offering of Isaac. P. G. Bretscher, "Exodus 4:22-23 and the Voice from Heaven," *JBL* 87 (1968), pp. 301-311, points to the description of Israel as God's son in Ex. 4:22 f.

history:[64] Jesus is God's unique[65] Son. The first clause of the declaration (with the verb in the present tense of the indicative mood) expresses an eternal and essential relationship. The second clause (the verb is in the aorist indicative) implies a past choice for the performance of a particular function in history. The thought may be expressed in the formulation, Because you are my unique Son, I have chosen you for the task upon which you are about to enter.[66] The relationship between the two clauses is exactly paralleled in the declaration of Ch. 9:7, where the pronouncement of the first clause, "This is my beloved Son," furnishes the ground for the second, "listen to him." Jesus did not *become* the Son of God, at baptism or at the transfiguration; he *is* the Son of God, the one qualified to bestow the Holy Spirit. The rending of the heavens, the descent of the Spirit and the declaration of God do not alter Jesus' essential status, but serve to indicate the cosmic significance of Jesus' submission to the Servant-vocation and affirm God's good pleasure in his Son. As such, the passage marks the high point of revelation in the prologue to Mark's Gospel and provides the indispensable background for all that follows.

Jesus' baptism must be seen from the aspect of his self-concealment. He was baptized as any other person who came to John. There is no indication in Mark that anyone other than Jesus understood the significance of that event. Only from the perspective of the resurrection, and the revelation that event made possible, is the reader of the Gospel able to enter into its meaning. A. Schlatter well expresses its theological significance: "He associates himself with sinners and ranges himself in the ranks of the guilty, not to find salvation for himself, not on account of his own guilt in his flight from the approaching wrath, but because he is at one with the Church and the bearer of divine mercy."[67]

---

[64] Cf. N. B. Stonehouse, *op. cit.*, pp. 16-21; J. Bieneck, *op. cit.*, *passim.*

[65] Mark's term ἀγαπητός can signify "only" or "unique" (e.g. Gen. 22:2, 12, 16 LXX), and this thought may be present in Mark's mind. See C. H. Turner, "Ο ΥΙΟϹ ΜΟΥ Ο ΑΓΑΠΗΤΟϹ," *JThS* 27 (1926), pp. 113-129, 362.

[66] Cf. N. B. Stonehouse, *op. cit.*, pp. 18-20; T. A. Burkill, *op. cit.*, pp. 19 f.; M. D. Hooker, *Jesus and the Servant* (London, 1959), pp. 68-73.

[67] *Der Evangelist Matthäus* (Stuttgart, 1933), p. 89. See further, A. Feuillet, "Le Baptême de Jésus d'après l'Évangile selon Saint Marc," *CBQ* 21 (1959), pp. 468-490.

3. Temptation in the Wilderness. Ch. 1:12-13

12 And straightway the Spirit driveth him forth into the wilderness.
13 And he was in the wilderness forty days tempted of Satan; and he was with the wild beasts; and the angels ministered unto him.

12-13 The account of the baptism is followed by that of Jesus' trial in the wilderness. The intimate connection between the two events is established by the introductory phrase "and at once." [68] Jesus' expulsion into the desert is the necessary consequence of his baptism; it is the same Spirit who descended upon Jesus at his baptism who now forces him to penetrate more deeply into the wilderness.

The most striking characteristic of the Marcan temptation account is its brevity. In comparison with Matthew or Luke, Mark appears to have preserved no more than a fragment of the tradition. [69] This impression points up the fallacy of reading Mark through the eyes of any other evangelist. It is imperative to view the account in Marcan perspective. [70] These brief verses describe what it means for Jesus to heed John's summons to the wilderness; the several details are subservient to this description. The evangelist seizes upon the fact that the Lord, who was announced and baptized in the wilderness, continues there for forty days. This signifies that the aspect of humiliation in Jesus' mission is not yet terminated in spite of the declaration that he is the beloved Son. Jesus must remain submissive: the Spirit does not allow him to abandon the wilderness after his baptism. The function of verse 13 is to clarify

---

[68] D. Daube, *op. cit.*, p. 47 suggests that in Mark's phrase "and at once" there is a trace of "in due course," "as had to happen after what preceded." It is less purely temporal and more theological.

[69] The brevity of the account and the absence of any explanation of its elements have led interpreters to assume that Ch. 1:12-13 is an incipient tradition of an expanded story. Cf. J. Schniewind, *Das Evangelium nach Markus*[7/8] (Göttingen, 1958), p. 48; J. Dupont, "L'arrière-fond biblique du récit des tentations de Jésus," *NTS* 3 (1956-57), pp. 294 f. The treatment of the temptation of Jesus by H. Seesemann, *TWNT* VI (1959), pp. 34 f. is dominated by the Matthean and Lucan narratives; A. Feuillet, "L'épisode de la tentation d'après l'Évangile selon Saint Marc (I. 12-13)," *Est Bíb* 19 (1960), pp. 49-73, argues that the Marcan account is a deliberate abridgment of the fuller account preserved in Matthew and Luke.

[70] So M. Dibelius, *Die Formgeschichte des Evangeliums*[3] (Tübingen, 1959), p. 129.

the consequences of this submission: confrontation by Satan and temptation, exposure to the wild beasts, and reception of the ministry of the angels. These verses explain the primary theme of the prologue and constitute its climax. As U. Mauser has correctly seen, "each detail is rooted in the wilderness tradition of the Old Testament and serves to clarify the significance of the desert" to Mark. [71]

Jesus stays in the wilderness for forty days, a fixed time of symbolic significance. [72] The reference to the forty days recalls Moses' stay on Mount Sinai and Elijah's wandering through the wilderness to Mount Horeb. [73] In their case the time of the forty days concentrates into one crucial period the innermost quality of their mission. Moses and Elijah are men of the wilderness, both prior to this period as well as after it. There is evidence that the same perspective is true of Jesus in Mark. The forty days do not describe a period whose significance is exhausted once Jesus begins his public ministry but sound the dominant note of his entire ministry. [74]

Temptation is the inevitable concomitant phenomenon of remaining in the wilderness. This motif is frequently associated with the wilderness tradition in both the OT and NT. [75] The fact that Jesus is tempted by Satan, who attempts to frustrate the work of God, serves to emphasize the radical character of the issue. Jesus' determination to repent, to remain in the wilderness, inevitably results in a clash with the adversary of God. In this connection the cosmic language of Mk. 1:9-12 is important; it indicates that what happens on the plane of human decision in terms of John's call and Jesus' response is an aspect of the struggle between God and Satan. [76]

It is significant that Mark does not report the victory of Jesus over Satan, nor the end of the temptation. [77] It is the evangelist's distinctive

---

[71] *Op. cit.*, p. 98. The interpretation which follows is indebted to Mauser's exposition (pp. 98-101).

[72] On "forty" as a round and symbolic number see J. Bergmann, "Die runden und hyperbolischen Zahlen in der Agada," *MGWJ* 82 (1938), pp. 370-375.

[73] Ex. 24:18; I Kings 19:8, 15. G. Kittel, *TWNT* II (Eng. Tr. 1964), p. 658 tends to deny any association with OT tradition here, but see W. Schmauch, *Orte der Offenbarung und der Offenbarungsort im Neuen Testament* (Göttingen, 1956), p. 38.

[74] Cf. U. Mauser, *op. cit.*, p. 99.

[75] For passages and analysis cf. H. Seesemann, *op. cit.*, pp. 27, 32 f.

[76] Cf. J. M. Robinson, *op. cit.*, pp. 26-28.

[77] In contrast to Mt. 4:11; Lk. 4:13. A common opinion is that the triumph of Jesus over Satan is a matter of course, and could for that reason be simply implied.

understanding that Jesus did not win the decisive victory during the forty days nor did he cease to be tempted. Jesus is thrust into the wilderness in order to be confronted with Satan and temptation. It is this confrontation which is itself important, since it is sustained throughout Jesus' ministry. This explains why Mark does not say anything about the content of the temptation: his whole Gospel constitutes the explanation of the manner in which Jesus was tempted.[78]

A detail recorded only by Mark is that Jesus was with the wild beasts in the wilderness. Since Ch. 1:12-13 is usually understood as a report of Jesus' triumph over Satan the reference to the wild beasts has been interpreted as an element in the paradise motif. Jesus in the midst of the wild beasts signifies the victory of the New Adam over Satan and temptation so that paradise is restored in which man is at peace with the animals.[79] But as soon as it is recognized that the dominant motif of the prologue is the wilderness, Mark's distinctive reference to the wild beasts becomes intelligible. In the OT blessing is associated with inhabited and cultivated land; the wilderness is the place of the curse.[80] In the wilderness there is neither seed nor fruit, water nor growth. Man cannot live there. Only frightening and unwanted kinds of animals dwell there. Significantly, when the wilderness is transformed into a paradise no ravenous beast will be in it (Isa. 35:9; Ezek. 34:23-28). Mark's reference to the wild beasts in Ch. 1:13 serves to stress the character of the wilderness. Jesus confronts the horror, the loneliness and the danger with which the wilderness is fraught when he meets the wild beasts. Their affinity in this context is not with paradise, but with the realm of Satan.[81]

Mark also refers to the ministering angels. The motif of the angel

---

Cf. E. Lohmeyer, *op. cit.*, p. 28; J. Schniewind, *op. cit.*, p. 49; T. A. Burkill, *op. cit.*, p. 21.

78 U. Mauser, *op. cit.*, p. 100 remarks, "What is paramount at this stage of the drama is simply the statement that in Jesus' response to the Baptist's call and consequently in his decision to return to the wilderness, the confrontation of the Son of God with the power of Satan takes place."

79 So J. Jeremias, *TWNT* I (Eng. Tr. 1964), p. 141; L. Goppelt, *Typos. Die Typologische Deutung des Alten Testaments im Neuen* (Gütersloh, 1939), p. 118; J. Schniewind, *op. cit.*, p. 48; E. Fascher, "Jesus und die Tiere," *TLZ* 90 (1965), pp. 561-570.

80 See J. Pedersen, *Israel, Its Life and Culture* I-II (London-Copenhagen, 1926), pp. 453-470. U. Mauser, *op. cit.*, p. 37, n. 2 gives a list of passages where animals are said to occupy the wilderness.

81 U. Mauser, *op. cit.*, pp. 100 f.

who guides and helps Israel through the wilderness is prominent in many of the narratives of the first exodus.[82] The closest parallel to the Marcan account, however, is provided by I Kings 19:5-7 where an angel supplies nourishment for Elijah in the barren wilderness. Mark's reference to a plurality of angels indicates that Jesus is sustained by the servants of God. There is no indication in Mark that the service of the angels is withdrawn nor that it serves to mark the termination of the temptation. As Mauser remarks, "Mark thinks of the temptation, the being with the animals and the service of the angels as continuous events in the course of which all the forces of God and Satan are simultaneously present."[83] This is an appropriate description, for the Marcan account of the ministry of Jesus is dominated by his confrontation with demonic forces and the sustaining of temptation. Jesus' obedience to God is affirmed and sustained *in the wilderness,* the precise place where Israel's rebellion had brought death and alienation, in order that the new Israel of God may be constituted.

II. THE INITIAL PHASE OF THE MINISTRY. Ch. 1:14-3:6

The first major section of Mark's Gospel extends from Ch. 1:14 to Ch. 3:6, and describes the initial phase of the Galilean ministry. Within this section the evangelist records the calling of the first disciples (Chs. 1:16-20; 2:14), Jesus' ministry in and around Capernaum (Ch. 1:21-34), and a series of controversies (Ch. 2:1 - 3:6) which are climaxed by the decision to seek Jesus' death (Ch. 3:6). A new section begins with Ch. 3:7 and extends to Ch. 6:13. There appears to be a conscious parallel between the opening paragraphs of these first two sections of the Gospel. They begin with a summary statement of the ministry of Jesus (Ch. 1:14 f.; Ch. 3:7-12) and continue with the calling of the disciples as Jesus' first act: Ch. 1:16-20 reports the calling of the two pairs of brothers; Ch. 3:13-19, the election of the Twelve. The scene of these two incidents is a place of withdrawal, the sea (Ch. 1:16) and the mountain (Ch. 3:13). Within Mark's larger context these elements are intimately related to the wilderness motif developed in the prologue to the Gospel.[84]

---

[82] E.g. Ex. 14:19; 23:20 (cited in Mk. 1:2), 23; 32:34; 33:2.

[83] *Op. cit.,* p. 101. A helpful summary statement on Jesus' ministry as an incessant temptation is found on pp. 128-132.

[84] Cf. U. Mauser, *op. cit.,* pp. 108-119, 124-128.

1. ENTRANCE INTO GALILEE. Ch. 1:14-15

14 Now after John was delivered up,[85] Jesus came into Galilee, preaching the gospel of God,[86]
15 and saying, The time is fulfilled, and the kingdom of God is at hand:[87] repent ye, and believe in the gospel.

14-15 It is significant that Jesus does not enter upon his own distinctive ministry until after John has been arrested.[88] Mark's formulation suggests that Jesus is restrained by God from his ministry of proclamation until the Baptist is removed from the scene.[89] His arrest indicates that the time has come for Jesus to act. Jesus enters into Galilee proclaiming the gospel of God.

What is meant by "the gospel of God" is defined by the summary

---

85 RSV, NEB, "arrested." It is normal in Greek usage to clarify the particular sense in which παραδοθῆναι is employed by a qualifying clause, e.g. "delivered up *into prison*." That here it means "after John was arrested" is clear. The lack of a qualifying clause may be intentional to suggest a parallel between John's experience and the passion of Jesus: he too was "delivered up." Cf. Ch. 9:31; 14:10; 15:1, 15. See M-M, p. 483 s.v. παραδίδωμι 3 for examples from papyri and inscriptions where the unqualified use of the term means "to deliver up" to prison or judgment.

86 "The gospel of the kingdom of God," found in the AV, is supported by 𝔎 A D W *pm* latt sy^p, but is not as well attested as "the gospel of God," a phrase found also in Rom. 1:1; 15:16; II Cor. 11:7; I Thess. 2:2, 8 f.

87 The NEB rendering "the kingdom of God is upon you," represents the point of view of realized eschatology as defined by C. H. Dodd, *The Parables of the Kingdom* (London, 1935), pp. 43 ff.; *idem*, "The Kingdom of God Has Come," *ExT* 48 (1936-37), pp. 138-172. For a review of the linguistic and theological arguments involved see R. F. Berkey, "ΕΓΓΙΖΕΙΝ, ΦΘΑΝΕΙΝ, and Realized Eschatology," *JBL* 82 (1963), pp. 177-187.

88 According to W. Marxsen, *Der Evangelist Markus* (Göttingen, 1956), pp. 22-24, an impression of successiveness has been deliberately created by Mark where none existed before; historically John's arrest belongs later. Ch. 6:14 shows conclusively, however, that the activities of Jesus and John were both chronologically and spatially separated. Those who judged that Jesus is John raised from the dead could not have seen the two men working together, or known of Jesus' baptism by John. The public activity which brought Jesus to the attention of the people could only have begun after John had been removed from the scene through his arrest. "The people have an impression of successiveness, not contemporaneousness." See W. Wink, *op. cit.*, pp. 8-10.

89 Cf. C. E. B. Cranfield, *op. cit.*, p. 62 who finds in the general term παραδοθῆναι, particularly in the passive, the suggestion that "behind the schemes and actions of men in relation to John *God's* purpose and doing were to be recognized."

of Jesus' proclamation in Ch. 1:15; each element clarifies God's decisive action in sending forth his Son at this particular moment in history. The emphasis upon the fulness of time grounds Jesus' proclamation securely in the history of revelation and redemption. It focuses attention upon the God who acts, whose past election and redemption of Israel provided the pledge of his activity in the future. Jesus declares that the critical moment has come: God begins to act in a new and decisive way, bringing his promise of ultimate redemption to the point of fulfilment.[90] By sovereign decision God makes this point in time the critical one in which all the moments of promise and fulfilment in the past find their significance in one awesome moment. In comparison with John's preaching, the distinctive note sounded by Jesus is the emphasis upon fulfilment.[91] Its exact nuance is clarified by the phrase which follows.

What Jesus meant when he affirmed that the kingdom of God had drawn near is nowhere explicitly defined. The emphasis upon the "kingdom," however, links his proclamation to the self-revelation of God in the OT and stresses the continuity between the new and older revelation. In announcing "the kingdom *of God*," the accent falls upon God's initiative and action. The kingdom of God is a distinctive component of redemptive history. It belongs to the God who comes and invades history in order to secure man's redemption. The emphasis falls upon God who *is* doing something and who will do something that radically affects men in their alienation and rebellion against himself.[92]

The kingdom may be proclaimed as near, if God's decisive action in its realization has already begun. John's ministry had centered upon the

---

[90] Cf. G. Delling, *TWNT* III (1938), pp. 459-461 on the element of decisiveness in καιρός; and on the full phrase, which is distinctly eschatological in orientation, *idem, TWNT* VI (1959), p. 293.

[91] Cf. H. Ridderbos, *The Coming of the Kingdom* (Philadelphia, 1962), p. 48: "'The time is fulfilled' indicates that the threshold of the great future has been reached, that the door has been opened, and the prerequisites for the realization of the divine work of consummation are present, so that now the concluding drama can start. Owing to this, Jesus' initial proclamation of the nearness of the kingdom seems to speak of a more advanced point of time than that of John who had not yet mentioned the beginning of fulfilment."

[92] It is not possible to give an adequate exposition of the kingdom of God within the limits imposed by the commentary, but there are a number of valuable articles and books which may be consulted. Particularly helpful are K. L. Schmidt, *TWNT* I (Eng. Tr. 1964), pp. 565-593 (for the linguistic and theological background); H. Ridderbos, *op. cit.;* G. E. Ladd, *Jesus and the Kingdom* (New York, 1964), with extensive bibliography, pp. 337-351. The primary meaning of the Aramaic term used by Jesus is not properly "kingdom" but "sovereign author-

urgent demand for repentance because God was about to act decisively in bringing among the people "the Coming One." Jesus then proclaims that the kingdom has drawn near, and while his proclamation is veiled, Mark clearly understands that it is Jesus' own appearance which is the decisive event in the redemptive plan of God. The coming of the kingdom remains future, but it is certain precisely because God has begun to bring it to pass in the coming of his Son. The announcement that the consummation is at hand affirms that the decisive events in its approach are under way. The Anointed One is already present among the covenant people, and through him the royal act of God in redeeming his people has begun. The kingdom has drawn near, *spatially* in the person of Jesus who embodied the kingdom in a veiled way,[93] *and temporally* because it is the only event which takes place prior to the end. In the person of Jesus men are confronted by the kingdom of God in its nearness. A faithful response to the proclamation of the gospel is imperative.

The summons to "repent and believe in the gospel" is not new, but a fresh reiteration of the word addressed to men through the prophets.[94]

ity." Whenever the biblical texts speak of God becoming king the Targumim speak of God's exercise of sovereign authority, and render the Hebrew verb by an Aramaic noun. E.g.:

Ex. 15:18	"The Lord *shall reign* forever and ever."
Targ. Onkelos	"The *sovereignty* of the Lord endures forever and ever."
Isa. 40:10	"Behold, the Lord will come as a mighty man, and his arm *will rule* for him."
Targum	"The *sovereignty* of your God will be revealed."

Particularly this second example illustrates the interpretation of the Targum: for the Lord to come as a mighty man and for his arm to rule for him signifies the revelation of God's sovereignty through a saving action. This indicates well the *dynamic* character in the concept of the kingdom: God is he who comes and exercises his sovereign authority in the redemption of men. The contrary opinion, that the expression "kingdom of God" must be understood as God's house or community, is defended by S. Aalen, "'Reign' and 'House' in the Kingdom of God in the Gospels," *NTS* 8 (1962), pp. 215-240, and is challenged by G. E. Ladd, "The Kingdom of God–Reign or Realm," *JBL* 81 (1962), pp. 230-238.

93 C. E. B. Cranfield, *op. cit.*, p. 66 calls attention to Marcion's statement, as recorded by Tertullian, *Adversus Marcionem* IV. 33: "In the Gospel the Kingdom of God is Christ himself." The debate concerning the lexical background and meaning of ἤγγικεν is summarized by R. F. Berkey, *op. cit.*, pp. 177-187. The linguistic objections to the proposed rendering "has come" are weighty, and it is better to translate "has come near," understanding the phrase as defined above.

94 See above on Ch. 1:4 and the treatments of H. W. Wolff, *op. cit.*, pp. 129-148; E. Würthwein, *op. cit.*, pp. 976-985. For the treatment of repentance in the exegetical tradition of the rabbis see below, "Additional Note on Repentance in the Rabbinic Literature."

But the note of urgency in the summons to repent is sharpened, for now the nature of the gospel is clearer than ever before. The brief parable of the fig tree preserved by Mark in Ch. 13:28 echoes Jesus' proclamation that the kingdom *has come near* and clarifies why the nearness of the kingdom imposes radical demands upon men: "When the branch becomes tender and the leaves are about to sprout, you know that the summer *has come near"*; i.e., the summer is *the next thing* that comes. Jesus' action in confronting Satan, sin, disease and death, and subduing nature is the sign that the end stands as the next act of God in man's future. Provision has been made for men to repent, but there is no time for delay. Only through repentance can a man participate with joy in the kingdom when it does break forth. Jesus accordingly calls men to radical decision. In Jesus men are confronted by the word and act of God; he himself is the crucial term by which belief and unbelief come to fruition. Jesus proclaims the kingdom not to give content but to convey a summons. He stands as God's final word of address to man in man's last hour. *Either* a man submits to the summons of God *or* he chooses this world and its riches and honor. The either/or character of this decision is of immense importance and permits of no postponement. That is what repentance is all about. The radicalness of Jesus' kingdom proclamation is well caught in the agraphon, "He who is near me is near to the fire; he who is far from me is far from the kingdom":[95] Jesus himself, though veiled in the midst of men, becomes the crucial term by which men enter the kingdom of God, or exclude themselves from it. What he does is the work of God.

2. The Call to Become Fishers of Men. Ch. 1:16-20

16 And passing along by the sea of Galilee, he saw Simon and Andrew the brother of Simon casting a net in the sea; for they were fishers.
17 And Jesus said unto them, Come ye after me, and I will make you to become fishers of men.
18 And straightway they left the nets, and followed him.
19 And going on a little further, he saw James the *son* of Zebedee, and John his brother, who also were in the boat mending the nets.

---

[95] The Coptic Gospel of Thomas, Logion 82; Origen, *Homily in Jer.* XX. 3; Didymus the Blind, *in Ps.* lxxxviii. 8. On this saying see W. L. Lane, "Agrapha," *EC* I (1964), pp. 110 f.

20 And straightway he called them: and they left their father Zebedee in the boat with the hired servants, and went after him.

16-18 As the first act of the Galilean mission Mark reports the calling of Simon and Andrew to be fishers of men. Jesus found these brothers working as fishermen on the shores of the Sea of Galilee, elsewhere designated the Lake of Gennesaret or the Sea of Tiberias. The inland sea, which was twelve miles in length and six miles across at its widest point, provided a point of access between Galilee and Perea. There were many towns and fishing villages especially on the western and northern shores. The waters teemed with life,[96] and when Jesus summoned the brothers they were casting their nets into the sea.[97]

Jesus' word to Simon and Andrew was remembered for its vividness and urgency: "Come after me, and I will make you fishers of men." The call to come after someone implies discipleship because it is the disciple who breaks all other ties to follow his master as a servant.[98] Yet far more than this was involved in the call to become "fishers of men." To interpret this phrase only as a play on words appropriate to the situation is to fail to appreciate its biblical background and its relevance to the context, which has focused attention on God's eschatological act in sending Jesus. In the OT prophetic tradition it is God who is the fisher of men. The passages in which the image is developed are distinctly ominous in tone, stressing the divine judgment.[99] The fishing meta-

---

96 Josephus, *War* III. x..7 specifically states that various kinds of fish are taken there which are not found elsewhere. See for a description of the kinds of fish F. Dunkel, "Die Fischerei am See Genesareth und das Neue Testament," *Biblica* 5 (1924), pp. 383-386; G. Dalman, *Orte und Wege Jesu*[3] (Gütersloh, 1924), pp. 143-145.

97 Cf. F. Dunkel, *op. cit.,* p. 387: Mark employs the technical term for the throwing out of the circular casting net, which had a diameter varying from ten to fifteen feet. The outer edge was weighted to allow the net to sink rapidly, imprisoning fish under it; in the middle of the net was a rope by means of which it could be pulled up. With such a net, usually only a few fish were taken with each cast. Dunkel distinguishes between five types of nets used in fishing these waters (pp. 376-380).

98 Cf. G. Kittel, *TWNT* I (Eng. Tr. 1964), pp. 212-215 and H. Seesemann, *TWNT* V (1954), pp. 290 f. where the significance of an exclusive following after Jesus is developed.

99 E.g. Jer. 16:16; Ezek. 29:4 f.; 38:4; Amos 4:2; Hab. 1:14-17. While the canonical tradition nowhere identifies Jesus as the Fisher of men, the Coptic Gospel of Thomas, Logion 8, appears to do so: "And he said: The Man is like a wise fisher-

phor was kept alive at Qumran, and it is striking that it is the judgment aspect of the metaphor which is stressed, as when the Legitimate Teacher expresses his awareness of being commissioned to execute God's fishing among his contemporaries.[100] The Teacher continues what God has done, in the company of others who are fishers. It is this understanding which provides the key both to the urgency in Jesus' summons of Simon and Andrew and to the radical obedience they displayed in responding to his call. The summons to be fishers of men is a call to the eschatological task of gathering men in view of the forthcoming judgment of God. It extends the demand for repentance in Jesus' preaching. Precisely because Jesus has come fishing becomes necessary. Between Ch. 1:15 and Ch. 1:17 there is a most intimate connection; fishing is the evidence of the fulfilment which Jesus proclaimed, the corollary of the in-breaking kingdom.[101]

The immediate function of those called to be fishers of men is to accompany Jesus as witnesses to the proclamation of the nearness of the kingdom and the necessity for men to turn to God through radical repentance. Their ultimate function will be to confront men with God's decisive action, which to faith has the character of salvation, but to unbelief has the character of judgment. In specifically calling Simon and Andrew to be fishers, there is reflection upon the unpreparedness of the people for the critical moment which has come. In time the fishers will

---

man who cast his net into the sea, he drew it up from the sea full of small fish; among them he found a large (and) good fish; that wise fisherman, he threw all the small fish down into the sea; he chose the large fish without regret."

100 1QH v. 7-8, "And Thou hast set me in a place of exile among many fishers that stretch a net upon the face of the waters, and (among) hunters (sent) against the sons of perversity" (translation of A. Dupont-Sommer, *op. cit,* p. 214). On this and related texts from Qumran see especially O. Betz, "Donnersöhne, Menschenfischer und der Davidische Messias," *Rev Qum* 3 (1961), pp. 53-61. The formulation reflects esp. Jer. 16:16.

101 Cf. W. Wuellner, "Early Christian Traditions about the Fishers of Men," *The Hartford Quarterly* 54 (1965), pp. 50-60; *idem, The Meaning of "Fishers of Men"* (Philadelphia, 1967). For the stress on the ominous note in the fishing metaphor see C. W. F. Smith, "Fishers of Men," *HTR* 52 (1959), pp. 187-203. On the relationship of Ch. 1:17 to Ch. 1:15, Smith rightly remarks: "The call is rather a promise of fulfilment, another indication of the maturing of the eschatological time, a discreet application of the general announcement of the time fulfilled, the Kingdom at hand, a promise that the judgment anticipated will begin and that men may be selected to share in the gathering of the people for this purpose. They are, by these words, chosen at the call of him who, by this call, is announced implicitly to be the principal Agent of the judgment" (p. 196).

go where Jesus has not gone and they themselves will proclaim the message by which men are gathered. At this point, however, it is the eschatological urgency in Jesus' mission which is expressed in the sudden call, and the immediate response of the fishermen who abandon their nets to follow Jesus.

19-20 On this same occasion Jesus saw the sons of Zebedee, James and John, in their boat preparing the nets for another night's fishing.[102] The terms in which they were called are not explicitly stated, but the intimate relationship of these two incidents indicates that they also are summoned to be fishers of men. The stress in Mark's brief report falls upon the sovereign authority in Jesus' call, and the radical obedience of James and John. So compelling is the claim of Jesus upon them that all prior claims lose their validity.[103] Their father, the hired servants, the boat and the nets are left behind as they commit themselves in an exclusive sense to follow Jesus. The urgency in Jesus' call and the radical obedience of the fishermen pose the question, "Who, then, is this who calls?" The use of the fisher image in proximity to Jesus' proclamation summarized in Ch. 1:15 provides the answer; it is the eschatological Lord who calls. He summons men by an act of grace to serve as agents of the kingdom drawn near, who shall gather a people for judgment.[104]

R. P. Meye has called attention to the programmatic character of this pericope in Mark's total plan.[105] It is a crucial text for the interpretation of the Gospel by virtue of its primary position. It anticipates the call of the Twelve in Ch. 3:13-19 and their subsequent mission in Ch. 6:7-13, 30, but looks beyond this point to the conclusion of the Gospel. Jesus affirms his relationship to those called in terms of a program for the future: he *will* make them *become* fishers of men. What they will become

---

102 Mark's term means properly to put in order, or to make ready, and so includes cleansing, mending and folding the nets in preparation for the next evening's fishing in the deeper waters. Presumably the heavier drag nets are in view, on which see F. Dunkel, *op. cit.*, pp. 377-380.

103 Cf. E. Lohmeyer, *op. cit.*, p. 32: "He commands as God commands... He makes of the fishermen something new, that which he wills." Lohmeyer likens the words of Jesus to the compelling nature of "a sharp military command" which made possible only one response: obedience. See further K. L. Schmidt, *TWNT* III (1938), pp. 489 f.

104 Cf. C. W. F. Smith, *op. cit.*, pp. 191, 193-195, 201 f. On pp. 195 f. Smith calls attention to elements in Ch. 1:24, 27 f., 38 which convey a continuing impression of urgency, consistent with the eschatological interpretation of the fisher image.

105 *Op. cit.*, pp. 83 f., 99-110.

depends upon their following him. The initial command to follow Jesus receives a final and dramatic extension in the concluding resurrection story. Mark implies that the promise to be made fishers of men finds its fulfilment in the meeting in Galilee promised in Ch. 16:7.

3. A New Teaching – with Authority. Ch. 1:21-28

21 And they go into Capernaum; and straightway on the sabbath day he entered into the synagogue and taught.
22 And they were astonished at his teaching: for he taught them as having authority, and not as the scribes.
23 And straightway there was in their synagogue a man with an unclean spirit; and he cried out,
24 saying, What have we to do with thee, Jesus thou Nazarene? art thou come to destroy us? I know thee who thou art, the Holy One of God.
25 And Jesus rebuked him, saying, Hold thy peace, and come out of him.
26 And the unclean spirit, tearing him and crying with a loud voice, came out of him.
27 And they were all amazed, insomuch that they questioned among themselves, saying, What is this? A new teaching! with authority[106] he commandeth even the unclean spirits, and they obey him.
28 And the report of him went out straightway everywhere into all the region of Galilee round about.

Ch. 1:21-34 appear to be intended by Mark to represent the activity of a single day, or of two days if judged by the Jewish perspective that a new day begins with sunset. Jesus' sabbath activity includes teaching,

---

106 K. Aland, *op. cit.*, p. 54 punctuates the text differently, so that it reads "What is this? a new teaching with authority. He commands even the unclean spirits and they obey him." The NEB mediates between this punctuation and that presupposed in the ASV, RSV: "What is this? A new kind of teaching! He speaks with authority. When he gives orders, even the unclean spirits submit." The parallelism with Ch. 1:22 lends support to the punctuation adopted by K. Aland and the British and Foreign Bible Society text. For a fresh discussion of the text see G. D. Kilpatrick, "Some Problems in New Testament Text and Language" in *Neotestamentica et Semitica,* ed. E. E. Ellis and M. Wilcox (Edinburgh, 1969), pp. 198-201.

exorcism and healing. In comprehensive fashion the acts of God are initiated by Jesus, restoring men to wholeness, but in a manner which occasions both excitement and alarm.[107]

21-22 The continuation of the four fishermen with Jesus is indicated by the plural form "they went into Capernaum." This is confirmed by Ch. 1:29 where Jesus and the four enter the house of Simon and Andrew; it is probable that Capernaum was the town in which all four fishermen lived. Identified with the ruins at Tel Ḥûm on the northwestern shore of the Sea of Galilee, Capernaum is one of the few sites specified by Mark as a center of Jesus' preaching and healing activity.[108]

Mark concentrates upon a single sabbath[109] when Jesus' synagogue teaching provoked the astonishment of the congregation. The evangelist has no immediate interest in the precise content of Jesus' exposition; its general thrust is sufficiently indicated by Ch. 1:15 which summarizes

---

107 Cf. R. Pesch, "Ein Tag vollmächtigen Wirkens Jesu im Kapharnaum (Mk. 1, 21-34. 35-39)," *Bib Leb* 9 (1968), pp. 114-128, 177-195 for a detailed analysis of the passages according to literary, form- and redaction-criticism. Mark has edited his sources by putting at the beginning of the first main section of his Gospel two pericopes which portray Jesus as appearing in full power.

108 Capernaum is mentioned specifically in Chs. 1:21; 2:1; 9:33, but is probably in view also in 5:21ff. On the city see C. Kopp, "Christian Sites around the Sea of Galilee: I Capernaum," *Dominican Studies* 2 (1949), pp. 215-235; *idem, Die heiligen Stätten der Evangelien* (Regensburg, 1959), pp. 215-230; E. F. F. Bishop, "Jesus and Capernaum," *CBQ* 15 (1953), pp. 427-437. On the second century synagogue at Tel Ḥûm see E. R. Goodenough, "The Synagogues of Palestine: Capernaum (Tell Ḥum)," *Jewish Symbols in the Graeco-Roman Period* I (New York, 1952), pp. 181-192; E. L. Sukenik, "The Present State of Synagogue Studies," *Louis M. Rabinowitz Fund for Synagogue Research Bulletin* 1 (1949), pp. 8-23. B. Schwank, "Qualis erat forma synagogarum Novi Testamenti," *Verb Dom* 33 (1955), 267-279 argues that the synagogue with which Jesus was familiar was of a simple house style, an assembly hall without columns or gallery, such as those at Dura on the Euphrates and Hamman Lif in North Africa.

109 T. A. Burkill, *op. cit.*, p. 34 points to the plural form "on the sabbaths" (σάββασιν) and the imperfect tenses of the verbs and suggests that Mark, in Ch. 1:21-22, 27-28, is seeking to characterize Jesus' ministry in a general way. This appears to be incorrect, for in the NT "sabbath" regularly has a third declension form in the dative plural which is used with a singular meaning, while the imperfects denote not repeated activity but an inceptive sense, as in Ch. 1:21, ἐδίδασκεν = "he began to teach." On the synagogue service and the opportunity for Jesus to give the exposition of the reading from the Law (the Torah) or the Prophets (the Haftarah) see P. Billerbeck, "Ein Synagogengottesdienst in Jesu Tagen," *ZNW* 55 (1964), pp. 143-161; K. Hruby, "La Synagogue dans la littérature rabbinique," *Or Syr* 9 (1964), pp. 473-514.

Jesus' proclamation during this initial phase of the Galilean ministry. His primary emphasis is on the authority of Jesus' teaching and the response of the people, whose astonishment conveys the impression of real alarm.[110] Jesus' word, presented with a sovereign authority which permitted neither debate nor theoretical reflection, confronted the congregation with the absolute claim of God upon their whole person. Jesus' teaching recalled the categorical demand of the prophets rather than scribal tradition.

It has been argued that the contrast expressed between authoritative and scribal teaching implies that Jesus "taught with Rabbinic authority, and not like those who were unordained."[111] On this understanding the authority of an ordained rabbi to proclaim decisions is opposed to that of inferior teachers who could appeal only to the chain of tradition passed on from one informant to another. This view fails to appreciate the more-than-prophetic note which is present in Mark's account where the accent falls upon the alarm occasioned by Jesus' teaching. The authority in view is not merely the power to decide, but to compel decision. In contrast with rabbinic exposition, with its reference to the tradition of the elders, here was prophecy. The authority with which Jesus spoke presupposes a commission and authorization from God

---

[110] Mark employs a variety of terms to express the astonishment of the multitude and the disciples at the word and deed of Jesus: ἐκπλήσσειν (Chs. 1:22; 6:2; 7:37; 10:26; 11:18); θαυμάζειν (Chs. 5:20; 15:5, 44); ἐκθαυμάζειν (Ch. 12:17); θαμβεῖσθαι (Chs. 1:27; 10:24, 32); ἐκθαμβεῖσθαι (Ch. 9:15); ἐξίστημι (Chs. 2:12; 5:42; 6:51); cf. φοβεῖσθαι (Chs. 4:41; 5:15, 33, 36; 6:50; 9:32; 10:32; 11:18) and ἔκφοβος (Ch. 9:6). The response to Jesus' words and deeds has overtones of fear and alarm; it reflects an awareness of the disturbing character of his presence. Cf. G. Bertram, *TWNT* III (1938), p. 6: "The expressions of fear and astonishment therefore serve to emphasize the revelational content and thus the Christological meaning of numerous Synoptic scenes of Jesus."

[111] See D. Daube, "ἐξουσία in Mk. i. 22 and 27," *JThS* 39 (1938), pp. 45-59; *idem,* "Rabbinic Authority," in *The New Testament and Rabbinic Judaism* (London, 1956), pp. 205-233; the people were surprised that Jesus taught as one ordained. The amazement and fear which Jesus' teaching called forth is poorly explained, however, unless the people sense an implicit claim to an authority superior to rabbinic ordination. Moreover, as J. Jeremias has shown, "scribes" is the correct term for ordained theologians in the oldest strata of the rabbinic tradition and in the N.T. See *TWNT* I (Eng. Tr. 1964), pp. 740 f.; *idem, Jerusalem zu Zeit Jesu* (Göttingen, 1924-29), II A, pp. 27-32; II B, pp. 101-140; S. Légasse, "Scribes et disciples de Jésus," *RB* 68 (1961), 497-502; A. W. Argyle, "The Meaning of ἐξουσία in Mark I. 22, 27," *ExT* 80 (1969), p. 343. On the didactic motif in the pericope see R. P. Meye, *op. cit.,* pp. 45-47.

inseparable from the proclamation of the kingdom drawn near.[112] In the presence of Jesus men are disturbed, and this disturbance is the precise act of fishing to which Jesus had called the four fishermen.

23-24 Within the synagogue there was a man possessed by an unclean spirit.[113] His personality had been damaged to the point that the demonic power had usurped the center of his self, and spoke through him. The disturbance which Jesus brings was expressed in the excited response of this man, who sensed in Jesus a threat to his very existence. His cry of terror, expressed in verse 24, is laden with the language of defense and resistance. The demoniac does not confess the dignity of Jesus, but uses the accepted terms of opposition in the attempt to disarm him. The initial expression is a common formula in the OT within the context of combat or judgment,[114] and is roughly equivalent to "you have no business with us – yet." It is probable that the following statement is not a question but a declaration: "You have come to destroy us." The note of conflict implied is important, for the demonic power understands more clearly than the people the decisive significance of the presence of Jesus. In the question "What have *we* to do with you?" it is natural to find a reference to all of the demonic powers who shall be destroyed by Jesus. But it is also distinctly possible that the demoniac identifies himself with the congregation and speaks from their perspective: Jesus' presence entails the danger of judgment for all present.[115]

That the demonic powers possess a certain knowledge of Jesus' identity is clear from the cry of recognition, "I know who you are, the

---

112 Cf. W. Foerster, *TWNT* II (Eng. Tr. 1964), pp. 566-569. K. H. Rengstorf, *TWNT* I (Eng. Tr. 1964), p. 140 adds "the gap between Jesus and the Rabbis in respect of the subject of teaching is to be found not in the matter itself, but in His own person, i.e., in the fact of His self-awareness as the Son. This is why His teaching, whether in the form of exposition or otherwise, causes astonishment among His hearers."

113 On demonic possession see below on Ch. 5:1-20 and the literature cited there.

114 E.g. Judg. 11:12; II Sam. 16:10; 19:22; I Kings 17:18; II Kings 3:13; II Chron. 35:21; Isa. 3:15; 22:1; Jer. 2:18; Hos. 14:9. See especially O. Bauernfeind, *Die Worte der Dämonen im Markusevangelium* (Stuttgart, 1927), pp. 3-10, 14 f., 28-31, 68 f.

115 So H. van der Loos, *The Miracles of Jesus* (Leiden, 1965), p. 380; when the agitation of the demoniac is regarded in the light of the dismay and turmoil in the synagogue, "this is even the obvious interpretation." Van der Loos' interpretation is consistent with the fisher image as developed in the OT, at Qumran and in Ch. 1:17.

Holy One of God." The unclean spirit recognizes Jesus as the Holy One of God, the Bearer of the Holy Spirit, and between the Holy Spirit and an unclean spirit "there exists a deadly antithesis that the demons know."[116] This formula of recognition, however, does not stand alone. It is part of a larger complex of material exhibiting a striking difference between the forms of address employed by the demoniacs and the titles used by ordinary sick individuals. The latter group appeal to Jesus as "Lord" (Ch. 7:8), "Teacher" (Ch. 9:17), "Son of David" (Ch. 10:47-48) or "Master" (Ch. 10:51). The demoniacs, however, address Jesus as "the Holy One of God" (Ch. 1:24), "the Son of God" (Ch. 3:11) or "the Son of the Most High God" (Ch. 5:7), formulations which identify Jesus as the divine Son of God.[117] The contrast in address is an important characteristic distinguishing ordinary sickness from demonic possession, and reflects the superior knowledge of the demons. The recognition-formula is not a confession, but a defensive attempt to gain control of Jesus in accordance with the common concept of that day, that the use of the precise name of an individual or spirit would secure mastery over him.[118]

25-26 Jesus rebuked the unclean spirit with the words, "Be silenced! Come out of him." The defensive address of the demon was powerless before the sovereign command of Jesus. In contrast to contemporary

---

116 O. Procksch, *TWNT* I (Eng. Tr. 1964), p. 102.

117 Rightly stressed by J. Bieneck, *op. cit.*, pp. 46-48. E. Schweizer, "'Er wird Nazoräer heissen' (zu Mc. 1:24 Mt. 2:23)" in *Judentum, Urchristentum, Kirche*, ed. W. Eltester (Berlin, 1960), pp. 90-93 finds an intimate connection between the designation "Jesus thou Nazarene" and "the Holy One of God" on the basis of the LXX tradition of Judg. 13:7 and 16:17: in LXX^B Samson is designated "the holy one of God" (ὁ ἅγιος θεοῦ) while in LXX^A he is designated a Nazirite (ναζιραῖος θεοῦ). He argues that Jesus was first designated a Nazirite and Holy One of God, and the later Greek tradition evoked the relation with Nazareth. See, however, the full discussion of H. H. Schaeder, *TWNT* IV (1942), pp. 879-884, where it is argued that Mark's term Ναζαρηνός means "of Nazareth." So RSV "Jesus of Nazareth."

118 O. Bauernfeind, *op. cit.*, pp. 14 f. calls attention to the formulations in a magical papyrus of the fourth or fifth century, now in the British Museum: "I know your name which was received in heaven, I know your forms . . . I know your foreign names and your true name . . . I know you, Hermes, who you are and from whence you are . . . " Cf. T. A. Burkill, *op. cit.*, p. 76: "The demon knows the divine purpose of Jesus' coming and the divine character of his status; and by giving full expression to its knowledge it seeks to ward off the threatened offensive of its dangerous opponent."

exorcists, who identified themselves by name or by relationship to some deity or power, who pronounced some spell or performed some magical action, Jesus utters only a few direct words, through which his absolute authority over the demonic power that had held the man captive was demonstrated.[119] The unclean spirit convulsed the possessed man, and with a loud shriek left him.

The climax of the encounter was reached in Jesus' powerful command "Be silenced!" W. Wrede called attention to this passage and related injunctions to silence, and found in them the significant key to the Marcan theology.[120] His hypothesis of a Marcan construction at this point is untenable, for the injunction is an integral element in the account. Jesus' silencing of the demon was an aspect of a conflict which has cosmic dimensions – the sustained encounter of the Son of God with Satan. The silencing and expulsion of the demon is the proof of that judgment which Jesus has come to initiate. To have allowed the defensive utterance of the demon to go unrebuked would have been to compromise the purpose for which Jesus came into the world, to confront Satan and strip him of his power. As such, this initial act of exorcism in the ministry of Jesus is programmatic of the sustained conflict with the demons which is a marked characteristic in the Marcan presentation of the gospel.[121]

---

119 E.g. Josephus, *Ant.* VIII. ii. 5 reports of the exorcist Eleazar who demonstrated his ability before Vespasian: "he put to the nose of the possessed man a ring which had under its seal one of the roots prescribed by Solomon, and then, as the man smelled it, drew out the demon through his nostrils, and, when the man at once fell down, adjured the demon never to come back into him, speaking Solomon's name and reciting the incantations which he had composed. Then, wishing to convince the bystanders and prove to them that he had this power, Eleazar placed a cup or foot-basin full of water a little way off and commanded the demon, as it went out of the man, to overturn it and make known to the spectators that he had left the man" (Loeb translation). Cf. S. Eitrem, *Some Notes on the Demonology in the New Testament* (Oslo, 1950), pp. 6-8, 24; H. van der Loos, *op. cit.*, pp. 321-325, 380 f., who rightly stress the distinction between Jesus and contemporary exorcists. The similarities in form are stressed by T. A. Burkill, *op. cit.*, pp. 72 f., 86-89. That there is no parallel to Jesus in authority is indicated by the alarmed response of the people.

120 *Das Messiasgeheimnis in den Evangelien. Zugleich ein Beitrag zum Verständnis des Markusevangeliums* (Göttingen, 1901), pp. 9-149.

121 See further J. M. Robinson, *op. cit.*, pp. 33-42; and esp. H. C. Kee, "The Terminology of Mark's Exorcism Stories," *NTS* 14 (1968), pp. 232-246. Kee demonstrates that ἐπιτιμᾶν in Ch. 1:25 is the equivalent of the Semitic root גער, which in the documents of Qumran is a technical term designating the com-

27-28 The people were utterly astonished and alarmed at Jesus' word. The same measure of authority with which they had been confronted in his teaching was demonstrated in the word of command to the demon. There had been no technique, no spells or incantations, no symbolic act. There had been only the word. There was no category familiar to them which explained the sovereign authority with which Jesus spoke and acted. Their astonishment is reflected in the question, "What is this? A new teaching with authority! He commands even the unclean spirits and they obey him." The incident is generalized in their thinking from the single instance they have observed to the repeated instances they sense intuitively will take place. They do not fully understand who Jesus is or what his presence means, but they cannot evade the impression of having been confronted by a word invested with power to which there were no analogies in their experience. Here was a teaching qualitatively new in the authority with which it laid hold of men. And the people were alarmed.[122]

The report concerning the enigmatic bearer of the authoritative word went forth at once into the surrounding region.[123] The disturbance of men by God had begun.

4. The Healing of Peter's Mother-in-Law. Ch. 1:29-31

29 And straightway, when they were come out of the synagogue, they came into the house of Simon and Andrew, with James and John.
30 Now Simon's wife's mother lay sick of a fever; and straightway they tell him of her:

---

manding word uttered by God or his spokesman by which evil powers are brought into submission and the way is prepared for the establishment of God's rule. This is appropriate to the present context, where ἐπιτιμᾶν denotes the command that brought the hostile power under God's control. Jesus' exorcisms must be understood against a cosmic background; they affirm that God is gaining control over an estranged and hostile creation which was subject to Satan's invasion and rule.

122 Cf. C. W. F. Smith, *op. cit.*, p. 196 who notes that the reaction of the people is not one of unmixed joy, but of alarm.

123 It is not possible to ascertain Mark's intention in the phrase τὴν περίχωρον τῆς Γαλιλαίας. If the genitive is epexegetic it means "the whole region around, that is Galilee"; cf. NEB "he was soon spoken of all over the district of Galilee." The genitive may, however, indicate "the region around Galilee" and indicate a wider area than the district or "all that part of Galilee which is around (Capernaum)," designating an area less than the entire district.

31 and he came and took her by the hand, and raised her up; and the fever left her, and she ministered unto them.

29-31 The brief narrative of the healing of Peter's mother-in-law conveys the impression of unpretentiousness; the few details contained are told from Peter's point of view, and not once is the name of Jesus introduced into the account.[124] The connection with the preceding incident is explicit, indicating that the healing occurred upon the Sabbath. It is possible that the house shared by Simon and Andrew was not far from the synagogue at Capernaum.[125] The meaning is brought out by rendering "and in due course they left the synagogue and came straight to the house of Simon and Andrew." James and John were in the company as well. It is not possible to know what disease had caused the illness of Peter's mother-in-law, for in the ancient world fever was regarded as an independent disease and not as a distress accompanying a variety of illnesses.[126]

In response to the disciples' request, Jesus stood beside the bed, seized the woman's hand and lifted her up.[127] The fever was removed and there was no trace of the weakness which could be expected under normal circumstances. The woman immediately stood up and ministered

---

124 Cf. E. Lohmeyer, *op. cit.*, p. 40: "Already in this unpretentiousness, without a special word of Jesus, without the character of a miraculous deed, lies the uniqueness of this narrative. It is related as a chronicler would report things he had experienced after a long time before trusted hearers; he uses only the exterior sequence of movement to report the particular incidents; it is left to the hearers to open up and claim the meaning they contained. Not once is the name of Jesus indicated in the story; what is reported of him is scarcely distinguishable in the narration from what could be reported, now as later, of a pious Rabbi on his circuit. Only one thing is characteristic of the narrative, that in all of Mark's Gospel there is no other narrative in which there is this distant and yet near sound of recollection." Cf. P. Lamarche, "La guérison de la belle-mère de Pierre et les genres littéraires des évangiles," *Nouvelle Revue Théologique* 87 (1965), pp. 515-526.

125 G. Dalman, *op. cit.*, p. 163 makes this suggestion.

126 Fever was described as a fire, and this thought is expressed in several of the names given to it; cf. M. *Berachoth* V. 1 where fever is "a fire in the bones." S-B*K* I (1922), p. 479 lists fifteen Hebrew and Aramaic names for fever and lists the several remedies used with it; J. Preuss, *Biblisch-talmudische Medizin* (Berlin, 1911), pp. 182-187 devotes a chapter to fever. See further K. Weiss, *TWNT* VI (1959), pp. 956-959.

127 H. van der Loos, *op. cit.*, pp. 551 f. S-B*K* IV. 1 (1926), pp. 573 ff. treats the rabbinic rules for visiting with the sick. Visitors were not permitted to sit on the bed or on a chair, but were to stand or sit upon the floor.

to her guests, which is to be understood particularly of the preparation of the evening meal.[128] The notice that the woman "ministered to them" confirms the mercy and compassion extended toward her by Jesus and indicates that the figures in the background of the gospel narrative are affected by the power of this mysterious Galilean.[129]

The reference to Peter's mother-in-law serves to clarify what it meant for Peter to be confronted by Jesus' summons to follow him. He had a family and a home for which provision had to be made; the call to be a fisher of men demanded total commitment to Jesus. The healing accomplished within Peter's home indicates that salvation had come to his house in response to the radical obedience he had manifested.

5. The Sick Healed at Evening. Ch. 1:32-34

32 And at even, when the sun did set, they brought unto him all that were sick, and them that were possessed by demons.
33 And all the city was gathered together at the door.
34 And he healed many that were sick with divers diseases, and cast out many demons; and he suffered not the demons to speak, because they knew him.

32-33 This summary report reflects the point of view of a narrator who was excited with what he witnessed: "they brought all that were sick"; "all the city was gathered at the door." The incident is intimately connected with the previous narratives by the time sequence, the reference to the door of the home of Peter and Andrew, and the detail of the silencing of the demons. The time indicated is early evening, following the sunset which brought the Sabbath to a close. In response to the report from those present in the synagogue earlier in the day the people were bringing the sick or possessed to the house where Jesus was. In time it seemed as if the whole city was gathered at the door. In this connection verse 33 is particularly vivid, the tense of the verb suggesting the growing crowds. Apparently the people delayed their coming until

[128] Cf. H. W. Beyer, *TWNT* II (Eng. Tr. 1964), p. 85. There is little doubt but that a non-technical sense of καὶ διηκόνει αὐτοῖς is intended here. Yet in Chs. 9:33-37 and 10:43-45 the essence of discipleship is described in terms of service, and this may be anticipated in the present narrative. Do these later passages, which focus on service and expose the attitudes of James and John, shed any light on the explicit mention of these two brothers in Ch. 1:29?

[129] H. van der Loos, *op. cit.,* p. 555.

the close of the Sabbath lest the day be infringed by the carrying of the sick or acts of healing when there was no immediate peril to life.[130] Twice in this passage (Ch. 1:32, 34) and in Ch. 6:13 a clear distinction is observed between general sickness and demonic possession. It is unwarranted to obscure such distinctions with the hypothesis that what was described in antiquity as possession by demons is identical with various forms of psychoses recognized today by the medical profession.[131]

34 Jesus responded to the expectations of those who came, healing the sick and expelling the demons. The term "many," in the statement that Jesus healed "many that were sick," is used inclusively and is equivalent to the "all" of verse 32;[132] it reflects upon the large number of those who came for healing. The reference to the demons who knew Jesus is general, but intelligible in the light of the encounter with demonic possession reported in Ch. 1:23-26. In that instance Jesus was recognized as the divine Son, the Bearer of the Holy Spirit. As earlier he had muzzled the defensive cry of the unclean spirit, here he silences their shrieks of recognition,[133] for they are powerless before him.

---

130 In this connection Jer. 17:21 f., which prohibits the bearing of a burden on the Sabbath, may have been important in popular thinking. For the rabbinic regulations see E. Lohse, *TWNT* VII (1964), pp. 14 f., 20 and the discussion of Ch. 3:1-5 below.

131 Typical of an unwarranted approach is F. Fenner, *Die Krankheit im Neuen Testament* (Leipzig, 1930), who is strikingly confident that he can explain the healings in the Gospel tradition in the light of modern psychopathology. He identifies various types of hysteria and explains the overcoming of the damage to personality in terms of the powerful personality of Jesus. H. van der Loos is far more satisfying; however, when he treats belief in demons (*op. cit.*, pp. 204-211, 339-361) he is unequivocal that "we are concerned with the mentally ill as they are encountered everywhere and at all times" (p. 210). Against these assertions see the important work of C. Balducci, *Gli Indemoniati* (Rome, 1959), who compares authentic demonic possession with abnormal psychic phenomena. His investigation indicates that (1) the symptoms of possession are arbitrary, whereas psychotic syndromes are fixed; (2) the possessed react to religious matters but are indifferent to profane matters; (3) in the case of the possessed exorcism may be expected to produce psychic phenomena (such as knowledge of hidden things) which are not necessarily evident in possession itself, but these phenomena cease immediately after the exorcism. Cf. A. Rodewyck, "De Daemoniacis," *Verb Dom* 38 (1960), pp. 301-306.

132 For this use, which reflects a Semitism, see J. Jeremias, *TWNT* VI (1959), pp. 540-542 (Mk. 1:34 is noted on p. 541).

133 A harmonizing addition emanating from Lk. 4:41, χριστὸν εἶναι, is found in

It is not adequate to read this narrative as a report of success in the initial phase of the Galilean mission. The people come to Jesus, not because they recognized his dignity and function but because it is rumored that a miracle worker has come in their midst. Jesus had come to preach repentance and the nearness of the kingdom but the people think only of relief from pain and affliction. They fail to perceive the significance of Jesus' conflict with demonic power. In compassion and grace Jesus extends to them authentic healing, but it is not primarily for this purpose that he has come. In the morning he withdraws from the village and the clamoring crowds.

6. The Decision to Leave Capernaum. Ch. 1:35-39

35 And in the morning, a great while before day, he rose up and went out, and departed into a desert place, and there prayed.
36 And Simon and they that were with him followed after him;
37 and they found him and say unto him, All are seeking thee.
38 And he saith unto them, Let us go elsewhere into the next towns, that I may preach there also; for to this end came I forth.
39 And he went into their synagogues throughout all Galilee, preaching and casting out demons.

35 This narrative, which like the preceding two is told from Peter's perspective (note verse 36 "Simon and those that were with him"), is intended by Mark to be associated with the report of the crowds that came to Jesus for healing the previous evening. This is indicated both by the time sequence in verse 35 and the reference to the fresh gathering of a multitude seeking Jesus' benefactions in verse 37. The vivid phrase "a very great while before day" may reflect the perspective of Simon, who discovered that Jesus was gone, and initiated the search for him.

The fact that Jesus left the village while it was yet dark and sought

---

ℵ^{corr} B C L W Θ λ φ *pm*. On this understanding, Jesus did not allow the demons "to say that they know he is the Messiah." The addition should be rejected with ℵ* A D Δ 157 579 1071 *al a b c d e f ff q* vg sy$^{sin\ p}$. The prohibiting is general and discreet. Jesus forbids the demons to speak, for they know who he is; they recognize him as their adversary in a conflict which has cosmic proportions. See further on Ch. 1:25-26 above.

a solitary place where he prayed is interesting from two points of view. (1) To describe the site of prayer Mark uses a double term meaning literally "wilderness place." The description is inappropriate geographically, for the land about Capernaum was cultivated during this period. Its reference is to a place of solitude which in some sense recalls the wilderness. This is confirmed from the other two passages where this terminology occurs (Chs. 1:45; 6:31-33). These passages share certain formal characteristics with Ch. 1:35: in each instance reference to the wilderness-place is preceded by an account of Jesus' preaching and power; he then withdraws from the multitude which seeks his gifts, with the result that the people (in Ch. 1:35-37 their representatives) pursue him to the solitary place to which he has gone.[134] These texts suggest that Jesus deliberately withdraws from the people to return to an area which has the character of the wilderness where he encountered Satan and sustained temptation. The nature of the temptation in each instance may be related to the clamor of the crowds, who are willing to find in Jesus a divine-man who meets their needs and so wins their following. The people, however, have no conception of what it means to go out to the wilderness to bear the burden of judgment, as Jesus has done. He turns from their acclaim, returning to a place which recalls his determination to fulfill the mission for which he has come into the world. The passages which speak of "a wilderness place" thus refer back to the prologue to the Gospel, with its distinctive wilderness-theology.

(2) The second point of interest is the reference to Jesus' praying. In Mark's Gospel Jesus is seen in prayer only three times: at the beginning of the account, when his ministry is being defined (Ch. 1:35), in the middle after the feeding of the five thousand (Ch. 6:46), and near the conclusion when Jesus is in Gethsemane (Ch. 14:32-42). These three occasions have the character of a critical moment. The setting for Jesus' prayer in each instance is night and solitude, for even in Gethsemane Jesus is quite alone in spite of the three disciples who are separated a short distance from him.[135] The situation again recalls the wilderness when Jesus confronts the temptation of Satan, and is sustained by help

---

134 Cf. H. J. Ebeling, *Das Messiasgeheimnis und die Botschaft des Marcus-Evangelisten* (Berlin, 1939), pp. 116-120; U. Mauser, *op. cit.*, pp. 104-108. Mauser shows that the phrase ἔρημος τόπος is typically Marcan, for while Matthew and Luke include it where there is a Marcan parallel they consistently avoid it elsewhere, preferring ἔρημος alone. In Ch. 1:45 the RSV badly obscures this significant phrase by the rendering [he] "was out in the country."

135 U. Mauser, *op. cit.*, pp. 107 f.

from God. His strength is in prayer through which he affirms his intention to fulfill the will of God, which means his submission to the judgment of God on behalf of the many who return to the wilderness without understanding.

36-39 When the crowds returned to the house in the expectation of finding Jesus, Simon and those with him, presumably Andrew, James and John, sought for him. There is a note of reproach in the statement, "All are seeking for you," which means, What are you doing here when you should be in the midst of the multitude who are clamoring for you? A very considerable impression had been made in Capernaum, and in the mistaken thinking of the fishermen it was this response which Jesus had sought to elicit.

Jesus' answer indicates their failure to understand him or his mission. Acts of healing and expulsion of demons, as much as proclamation, entailed a disclosure of the nature of the kingdom of God and constituted a demand for decision. By his decision a person was qualified for participation in the kingdom or marked for judgment. The crowds that gathered in Capernaum had made their decision, but it could not be the appropriate one because it involved not repentance but attraction to Jesus as a performer of miracles. That is why Jesus interrupts the miracles to go elsewhere to proclaim "the gospel of God." His purpose is not to heal as many people as possible as a manifestation of the kingdom of God drawn near in his person, but to confront men with the demand for decision in the perspective of God's absolute claim upon their person. [136]

The word of explanation, "for this reason I came forth" may be deliberately ambiguous. It can suggest that Jesus left Capernaum in order to extend his preaching mission elsewhere in Galilee, or that he "came forth" from God to proclaim the word over an extended area. [137]

---

[136] Cf. H. Ridderbos, *op. cit.*, pp. 70, 117. Note that verse 38 exalts the ministry of the word; this emphasis is substantial throughout Mark's Gospel (e.g. Ch. 4; 8:35, 38), although R. P. Meye, *op. cit.*, pp. 52-60 is accurate in observing a shift from the kerygmatic terminology of Ch. 1 to a persistent use of didactic terminology in the remainder of the Gospel.

[137] The use in verse 38 of the verb which described Jesus' departure from Capernaum in verse 35 lends support to this first level of understanding; Lk. 4:43 indicates, however, that very early a deeper significance was seen in Jesus' words, which were understood in the context of his mission as determined by God. Cf. J. Schniewind, *op. cit.*, pp. 52 f.

In pursuance of his mission Jesus went throughout all Galilee, using the synagogue as a point of contact with the people. Preaching and the expulsion of demons are related facets of this ministry, the means by which the power of Satan is overcome. In this connection it may be significant that there is no reference to acts of healing in the summary statement. Healing is an aspect of the redemption but it demonstrates Jesus' confrontation with Satan less graphically than the restoration to wholeness of those who had been possessed by demons.

The reference to "all Galilee" serves to recall Mark's statement that the report concerning Jesus circulated all about Galilee (Ch. 1:28).[138] Josephus described Galilee as a land of great villages: "The cities lie very thick and the very many villages that are here are everywhere so full of people, because of the richness of their soil, that the very least of them contained more than fifteen thousand inhabitants."[139] In Ch. 1:38 Mark has used a precise term to designate these large agricultural villages which had the size of a city but the structure of a village.[140] His reference, apparently, is to the capital of a toparchy and its subordinate villages. The several tetrarchies were administered by the Herods under the Ptolemaic system of villages grouped into toparchies, with the largest of the villages serving as the capital of each district. Jesus, accordingly, went throughout Galilee concentrating his preaching mission in the synagogues located in toparchic capitals, confronting the several congregations with the absolute claim of God.

7. The Cleansing of a Leper. Ch. 1:40-45.

40 And there cometh to him a leper, beseeching him, and kneeling down to him, and saying unto him, If thou wilt, thou canst make me clean.

---

138 Ch. 1:28 εἰς ὅλην τὴν περίχωρον τῆς Γαλιλαίας; Ch. 1:39 εἰς ὅλην τὴν Γαλιλαίαν. On Galilee and its human geography see A. H. M. Jones, *Cities of the Eastern Roman Empire* (Oxford, 1937), Ch. 10 and A. N. Sherwin-White, "The Galilean Narrative and the Graeco-Roman World" in *Roman Society and Roman Law in the New Testament* (Oxford, 1963), pp. 120-143.

139 *War* III. iii. 2, on which see A. N. Sherwin-White, *op. cit.*, pp. 129-131.

140 Gr. κωμόπολις, a term occurring only here in the NT. Sherwin-White, *loc. cit.*, calls attention to Strabo, xii. 2. 5 where the term is applied to a great native town in the heart of Cappadocia and is equated with the phrase "having the establishment of a city."

41 And being moved with compassion,[141] he stretched forth his hand, and touched him, and saith unto him, I will; be thou made clean.
42 And straightway the leprosy departed from him, and he was made clean.
43 And he strictly charged him,[142] and straightway sent him out,
44 and saith unto him, See thou say nothing to any man: but go show thyself to the priest, and offer for thy cleansing the things which Moses commanded, for a testimony unto them.
45 But he went out, and began to publish it much, and to spread abroad the matter, insomuch that Jesus could no more openly enter a city, but was without in desert places: and they came to him from every quarter.

40 The identification of the man who came to Jesus as "a leper" is not as precise as at first glance it may seem. Leprologists who have examined the biblical data in Lev. 13-14 feel certain that the biblical term "leprosy" is a collective noun designating a wide variety of chronic skin diseases, one of which may have been interpreted in the modern

---

[141] NEB "in warm indignation," adopting the *v. l.* ὀργισθείς supported by D *a, d* ff^2 r^1 Ephraem. All other witnesses (except the Old Latin MS. *b* which omits either term) have σπλαγχνισθείς, which is reflected in the ASV, RSV. In spite of its slight manuscript support, ὀργισθείς should be read. It is scarcely conceivable that if σπλαγχνισθείς were original any scribe should have substituted the offensive ὀργισθείς. Moreover, ὀργισθείς in verse 41 is appropriate to ἐμβριμησάμενος in verse 43, which indicates that there was indignation on Jesus' part. The parallel sustained with Mark by Mt. 8:1-4; Lk. 5:12-16 is very close with the exception of these two harsh terms. Similarly, the Marcan depiction of Jesus as filled "with anger" (μετ' ὀργῆς) in Ch. 3:5 has no parallel in Mt. 12:3; Lk. 6:10. The absence of σπλαγχνισθείς from the parallel passages further supports the contention that it was not present originally in the Marcan text. For the suggestion that the variant arose in a Semitic context through the change of a single guttural (אתרחם־אתרעם corresponding to ὀργισθείς – σπλαγχνισθείς) see J. R. Harris, "Artificial Variants in the Text of the New Testament," *Exp* 24 (1922), pp. 259-261. It is more probable that ὀργισθείς was found offensive or was not understood and was accordingly altered. See further, K. Lake, "ΕΜΒΡΙΜΗΣΑΜΕΝΟΣ and ΟΡΓΙΣΘΕΙΣ, Mark 1, 40-43," *HTR* 16 (1923), pp. 197 f. (where the offense is removed by attributing the anger to the leper, translating "and he [the leper] put out his hand in a passion of rage and touched him"); C. H. Turner, "A Textual Commentary on Mark 1," *JThS* 28 (1926-27), pp. 147, 157; G. Stählin, *TWNT* V (1954), pp. 428 f.

[142] There is a note of harshness in the term ἐμβριμησάμενος which is better expressed by the RSV, "he sternly charged him."

sense of the word.[143] Nevertheless, any man who was identified as a leper was reduced to a most pitiful state of existence. In addition to the physical ravages of the disease, his cultic impurity was graphically described in the Levitical provision: "The leper who has the disease shall wear torn clothes and let the hair of his head hang loose, and he shall cover his upper lip and cry, 'Unclean, unclean'. He shall remain unclean as long as he has the disease; he is unclean; he shall dwell alone in a habitation without the camp" (Lev. 13:45 f.).[144] Rabbinic refinement of the biblical legislation imposed many practical difficulties upon the leper, for even a chance encounter between the leper and the non-leper could render the latter unclean.[145] Lepers were allowed to live unhampered wherever they chose, except in Jerusalem and cities which had been walled from antiquity. They could even attend the synagogue services if a screen was provided to isolate them from the rest of the congregation.[146] In spite of these two provisions, however, leprosy brought deep physical and mental anguish for both the afflicted individual and the community in which or near which he lived. It is against this background that the significance of the cleansing of a leper by Jesus can be appreciated, whether the man in Mark's account had true leprosy or some other frightful skin disease.

The leper, who had either seen Jesus' mighty works or had heard about them, came beseeching Jesus to remove from him the ravages and stigma of this dreadful disease. In the firm conviction, "If you will you can make me clean," he is asking for healing, not for the pronouncement that he is clean ritually, which only a priest could declare.[147] It

---

143 Cf. J. Preuss, *op. cit.*, pp. 369-373, and the survey of medical opinion in H. van der Loos, *op. cit.*, pp. 465-468. That the disease was not only serious but greatly feared is indicated by the rabbinic opinion that it is as difficult to cleanse a leper as to raise the dead. See S-B*K* IV. 2 (1928), p. 745.

144 Cf. R. Meyer, "Cultic Uncleanness," *TWNT* III (Eng. Tr. 1965), pp. 418-421.

145 The leper was not permitted to enter any house, for his presence conveyed uncleanness to both men and vessels in the house (M. *Kelim* I. 4; M. *Nega'im* XIII. 11. On the chance encounter see M. *Nega'im* XIII. 7: "If an unclean man [afflicted with leprosy] stood under a tree and a clean man passed by, the latter becomes unclean. If a clean man stood under a tree and an unclean one passed by, the former remains clean. If the latter stood still, the former becomes unclean.").

146 M. *Nega'im* XIII. 12. K. L. Schmidt, *Der Rahmen der Geschichte Jesu* (Berlin, 1919), pp. 63 f., questioned whether this pericope could possibly begin with Ch. 1:39, since it would have been possible for Jesus to have met the leper in a synagogue.

147 Cf. M. *Nega'im* III. 1 "Only a priest may declare them unclean or clean."

may be assumed that the man had shown himself to a priest once or several times already. His appeal was for Jesus to do what was believed impossible by human means, to cure him of his disease.[148] It is impossible to tell whether he regarded Jesus as an itinerant miracle-worker, or perceived more deeply that he was one through whom the power of God was directed.

41-42 Adopting the reading of the so-called Western text, "moved with indignation," it is necessary to determine the subject of the phrase. The proposal that the subject is the leper, who became so overwhelmed with his virtually hopeless plight that in blind rage he touched Jesus, is grammatically possible. The admonition in Ch. 1:43 would then have specific reference to this act after the leper had been made whole and was in a frame of mind to receive the rebuke.[149] This would remove the difficulties posed by the strong words in Ch. 1:41 and 43. It is not likely, however, that this interpretation is correct, for it too easily removes the offense that later scribes clearly sensed in the text, and which gave rise to the predominantly attested reading, "moved with compassion." Assuming that Jesus is the subject, the anger can be understood as an expression of righteous indignation at the ravages of sin, disease and death which take their toll even upon the living, a toll particularly evident in a leper. As such, Jesus' encounter with the leper brings him once more into the sphere of the demonic. It is, perhaps, in this perspective that elements in the narrative which seem more appropriate to an exorcism narrative than to an account of healing are to be explained.[150]

The treatment of Jesus consisted of a gesture and a pronouncement. The touch of Jesus was significant from two points of view. From the

---

148 In Papyrus Egerton 2 (fragment 1 recto) the tradition is found in an embellished form: "And behold, a leper came to him saying, Teacher, Jesus, I was travelling with lepers and eating with them in an inn, and I myself also became leprous. If therefore you wish, I shall be made clean. The Lord said to him, I will, be made clean. And immediately his leprosy departed from him. And the Lord said to him, Go, show yourself to the priests ..." For text see K. Aland, *op. cit.*, p. 60.

149 Cf. K. Lake, *op. cit.*, pp. 197 f.; S. Eitrem, *op. cit.*, pp. 42 f.

150 This interpretation is suggested by E. Bevan, "Note on Mark i. 41 and John xi. 33, 38," *JThS* 33 (1932), pp. 186-188; G. Stählin, *TWNT* V (1954), p. 428; J. M. Robinson, *op. cit.*, p. 40. The term ἐκβάλλειν in Ch. 1:43 occurs in exorcism narratives in Chs. 1:34, 39; 3:15, 22 f.; 6:13; 7:26; 9:18, 28. A spirit of leprosy is mentioned in TB *Horayoth* 10a.

perspective of the leper it was an unheard-of act of compassion which must have moved him deeply and strengthened him in his conviction he had not asked for help in vain. From the perspective of Jesus' relationship to the cultic and ritual system, it indicated that he did not hesitate to act in violation of its regulations when the situation demanded: "the ceremonial law gives place to the law of love when the two come into collision." [151] Jesus' touch and his sovereign pronouncement mean the same thing: "I will, be clean." [152] This was not a priestly pronouncement, as is made clear in verses 43-44, but a declaration that healing would follow immediately and completely. The text describes an instantaneous radical healing which was visible to all who met the man.

43-44 The difficulty confronting the interpreter in the reference to anger in Ch. 1:41 recurs in verse 43. The language is very strong, and seems more appropriate in an address to a demon than to a man whom Jesus has just healed: "he inveighed against him and drove him away." While it is possible to give a milder translation of the terms used, the statement is intelligible as an expression of Jesus' exasperation because he foresaw the disobedience of the man. [153] It is explicitly stated in verse 45 that Jesus was hindered from entering any further towns as a result of the man's failure to heed Jesus' injunction. As a consequence, the preaching mission within the synagogues of Galilee, reported in Ch. 1:39, was interrupted.

Jesus commanded the former leper to be silent concerning his healing, and instructed him to show himself to the priests, who alone could declare him clean, and to offer the sacrifices prescribed in the Mosaic Law. The procedure to be followed was set forth in Lev. 14:2-31, and involved different offerings depending on whether the man was poor or prosperous. In the first century the man had first to show himself to a priest in his place of residence, after which he must go to Jerusalem to be pronounced clean and to make the prescribed sacrifices. [154]

Jesus' demand that the man comply with Mosaic regulation is qualified by the words "for a testimony to them." This phrase may be interpreted differently depending on whether the testimony is considered to

---

[151] H. van der Loos, *op. cit.*, p. 484.

[152] Cf. G. Schrenk, "The θέλειν of Jesus," *TWNT* III (Eng. Tr. 1965), pp. 48 f. who speaks of "Jesus' decision and action in unique omnipotence."

[153] So G. Stählin, *op. cit.*, p. 428. For other suggestions see H. van der Loos, *op. cit.*, pp. 485 f.

[154] Tos. *Nega'im* VIII. 2.

be positive or negative in character, and whether the people or the priests are in view.[155] In keeping with the somber tone of the narrative it seems necessary to interpret the phrase in the negative sense demanded in the second instance where it occurs (Ch. 13:9): "as a testimony *against them.*" H. Strathmann's investigation has shown that the concept "testimony" or "witness" here, as in many passages, has the meaning of incriminating testimony which may serve as evidence for the prosecution. "Testimony" means a piece of proof which may be recalled and which can become an accusation.[156] It is better to understand "them" as the priests, for it is they who must examine the man to determine whether the leprosy has been removed. Jesus' statement then means that if the priests establish that healing has taken place and accept the sacrifice for cleansing but fail to recognize the person and power through whom healing has come, they will stand condemned by the very evidence which they have supplied. The healing of the leper demonstrated that God had done something new. If they neglect this sign or deliberately refer this gracious act to an evil origin, the accomplished sacrifice will testify against them on the day of judgment.[157] It was, therefore, imperative that the man comply with Jesus' instruction. It was necessary on his own behalf, but more important, he was to provide the evidence of the new thing God was doing, which if met with unbelief would serve as incriminating evidence against the priests.

45 It is not known whether the man obeyed the injunction to show himself to a priest. He blatantly disregarded the injunction to silence, and assumed the posture of a missionary, declaring publicly over an extended area what he had experienced from Jesus.[158] The result was

---

[155] Cf. H. van der Loos, *op. cit.*, pp. 487-489 where a number of varying interpretations are reviewed: the offerings which Moses prescribed will serve to authenticate the recovery to the people, or will indicate that Jesus does not subvert the Law, or that he who makes lepers clean has appeared.

[156] *TWNT* IV (1942), pp. 488 f., 508-510. On p. 509 Strathmann interprets Ch. 1:44 to mean, if the priest should presently establish that the healing has taken place this will form *for the people* highly incriminating evidence against the unbelief in which they persist. It will militate against them and accuse them on the day of judgment.

[157] Cf. G. Schrenk, *TWNT* III (1938), p. 264; H. van der Loos, *op. cit.*, p. 489.

[158] NEB "But the man went out and made the whole story public; he spread it far and wide." "To proclaim" (κηρύσσειν) and "to spread the word" (διαφημίζειν τὸν λόγον) are technical terms signifying the Christian mission in Acts 8:4 f.; 9:20; 10:42; II Tim. 4:2.

that Jesus' ministry in the synagogue was hampered, for he was no longer able to enter any town without encountering crowds of people waiting to throng one who could heal a leper, claiming benefactions for themselves. This was not the mission Jesus had come to fulfill. When he withdrew to places of solitude the people pursued him, but they understood neither Jesus nor the significance of his withdrawal to a place which recalled the wilderness in which his submission to the Father had been affirmed.[159]

This incident has an important position in the Marcan outline. It serves to terminate the preaching tour of the Galilean villages and provides the point of transition to the five accounts of controversy which follow (Ch. 2:1-3:6). The pericope establishes the surpassing nature of the salvation which Jesus brings, for while the Law of Moses provided for the ritual purification of a leper it was powerless to actually purge a man of the disease. In all of the OT only twice is it recorded that God had healed a leper (Num. 12:10 ff.; II Kings 5:1 ff.), and the rabbis affirmed that it was as difficult to heal the leper as to raise the dead. The cleansing of the leper indicates the new character of God's action in bringing Jesus among men. Salvation transcends cultic and ritual regulations, which were powerless to arrest the hold that death had upon the living, and issues in radical healing.

---

159 See above on Ch. 1:35.

CHAPTER 2

8. Conflict in Galilee. Chs. 2:1-3:6

The five narratives found in Chs. 2:1-3:6 share in common the element of controversy. Jesus and his disciples are covertly (Chs. 2:6-7; 3:2) or openly (Ch. 2:16, 18, 24) challenged by the Pharisees and the scribal interpreters of their tradition. They are offended by Jesus' actions; their indignation is expressed in the categorical statement, "he blasphemes" (Ch. 2:7) or in the demanding question, "Why does he eat with publicans and sinners?" (Ch. 2:16). The reaction of the scribes and Pharisees calls forth a crucial pronouncement of Jesus which sheds light on the new situation his coming has introduced. In recounting these incidents Mark makes no attempt to tell the story for its own sake. There is no dwelling on details which might create narrative interest or sustain suspense. In faithfulness to the tradition, he re-creates the events in order to make intelligible the words of Jesus which informed the Church and silenced his adversaries.

It is unlikely that these five incidents happened consecutively or even at the same period in Jesus' ministry. Mark introduces them in a most general way: "Now John's disciples and the Pharisees were fasting..."; "One sabbath he was going through the grain fields..."; "Again he entered the synagogue..." These was probably brought together in the tradition to which Mark was heir by the common element of conflict in Galilee. The incidents were remembered because they illumined aspects of the messianic mission: Ch. 2:1-17 concerns sin and sinners, and the forgiveness of God; Chs. 2:18-3:6 concern fasting and the observance of the sabbath, and the intention of God. This Galilean unit occupies an important position early in the Marcan outline and is balanced in the latter half of the Gospel by a series of five controversies in Jerusalem (Chs. 11:27-12:37). Together they indicate that the intrusion of the radically new situation provoked sustained conflict with the old and was the historical occasion for the decision that Jesus must be put to death.

(a) The Authority to Forgive Sins. Ch. 2:1-12

1 And when he entered again into Capernaum after some days,
it was noised that he was in the house. [1]
2 And many were gathered together, so that there was no longer
room *for them,* no, not even about the door: and he spake
the word unto them.
3 And they come, [2] bringing unto him a man sick of the palsy, [3]
borne of four.
4 And when they could not come nigh unto him for the crowd,
they uncovered the roof where he was: and when they had
broken it up, [4] they let down the bed [5] whereon the sick of
the palsy lay.
5 And Jesus seeing their faith saith unto the sick of the palsy,
Son, thy sins are forgiven.
6 But there were certain of the scribes sitting there, and reasoning in their hearts,
7 Why doth this man thus speak? he blasphemeth: who can forgive sins but one, *even* God?
8 And straightway Jesus, perceiving in his spirit that they so
reasoned within themselves, saith unto them, Why reason
ye these things in your heart?
9 Which is easier, to say to the sick of the palsy, Thy sins are
forgiven; or to say, Arise, and take up thy bed, and walk?
10 But that you may know that the Son of man hath authority
to forgive sins (he saith to the sick of the palsy), [6]
11 I say unto thee, Arise, take up thy bed, and go unto thy house.
12 And he arose, and straightway took up the bed, and went
forth before them all; insomuch that they were all amazed,
and glorified God, saying, We never saw it on this fashion.

---

[1] ASVmg RSV "at home."

[2] The indefinite plural occurs 21 times in Mark. It is identified as an Aramaism by C. H. Turner, "Marcan Usage, Notes Critical and Exegetical on the Second Gospel," *JThS* 25 (1924), pp. 378 ff.

[3] RSV "a paralytic." On the nature of paralysis and lameness and the attitude toward these afflictions in the Jewish world see J. Preuss, *Biblisch-talmudische Medizin* (Berlin, 1911), pp. 266-270, 351-355.

[4] RSV "and when they had made an opening." The roof was made of a light material like straw covered with mud. See G. Dalman, *Orte und Wege Jesu*[3] (Leipzig, 1924), p. 78.

[5] ASVmg RSV "pallet." The term refers to a mattress, which was the common bed of a poor man.

[6] On this verse and the correct placement of the parenthesis see the commentary below.

The first account centers in the healing of a paralyzed man and raises the question of Jesus' authority to forgive sins. The pericope sheds light on the relation of sin and sickness to healing and forgiveness and affirms that the authority to forgive sins on earth is the unique prerogative of the Son of Man.

1-2 The movement of Jesus in the early phase of the Galilean ministry seems to alternate between "the wilderness" and the city. From Capernaum (Ch. 1:21-34) he had departed to a "wilderness place" (Ch. 1:35) before going to other towns and villages proclaiming the Kingdom of God. When his preaching tour was disrupted by the presence of crowds at the city gates clamoring for some benefaction he again returned to "wilderness places" (Ch. 1:45). His entrance into Capernaum marks a return to the city. The house in which he stayed is not identified, but it is natural to think of the home belonging to Peter and Andrew (Ch. 1:29). His presence could not be concealed for more than a few days, and a large crowd gathered within the house and about the doorway. Jesus spoke to them "the word," i.e., the word of God concerning the nearness of the kingdom and the necessity for repentance and faith (cf. Ch. 1:14 f.).[7]

3-5 Jesus' preaching was interrupted by the arrival of a small party of men who carried a paralyzed man on a mattress. It is impossible to say anything definite about the nature of the man's affliction beyond the fact that he was unable to walk. The determination of those who brought him to Jesus suggests that his condition was wretched. When they were unable to break through the crowd they ascended a stairway on the side of the house to the flat roof which they broke open in order to lower the man before Jesus.[8] Jesus recognized this bold expedient as an expression of faith: the four clearly believed that he had the power to heal this man.

---

[7] Mark uses "the word" without qualification again in Ch. 4:14-20, 33, where the context is explicit that the word concerns the secret of the Kingdom (Ch. 4:11).

[8] The opening of a roof is mentioned elsewhere in contemporary literature, e.g. Midrash Rabba to Leviticus, XIX. 6 end (in a story about Jeconiah's wife): "They opened the ceiling and let him down to him." Cicero, *In M. Antonium oratio Philippica* II. 18. 45, speaks of letting a man down through the tiles. On these and related passages see D. Daube, *The New Testament and Rabbinic Judaism* (London, 1956), pp. 385-387; H. van der Loos, *The Miracles of Jesus* (Leiden, 1965), pp. 440-442.

Jesus' response to their faith was the unexpected statement, "Son, your sins are forgiven!"[9] The pronouncement was startling because it seemed inappropriate and even irrelevant to the immediate situation. It is intelligible, however, against the background provided by the OT where sin and disease, forgiveness and healing are frequently interrelated concepts.[10] Healing is conditioned by the forgiveness of God and is often the demonstration of that forgiveness (cf. II Chron. 7:14; Ps. 103:3; 147:3; Isa. 19:22; 38:17; 57:18 f.). In a number of texts "healing" and "forgiveness" are interchangeable terms (Ps. 41:4, "heal me, for I have sinned against thee"; Jer. 3:22 and Hos. 14:4, God will "heal" his people's backsliding).[11] Healing is a gracious movement of God into the sphere of withering and decay which are the tokens of death at work in a man's life. It was not God's intention that man should live with the pressure of death upon him. Sickness, disease and death are the consequence of the sinful condition of all men. Consequently every healing is a driving back of death and an invasion of the province of sin. That is why it is appropriate for Jesus to proclaim the remission of sins. It is unnecessary to think of a corresponding sin for each instance of sickness; there is no suggestion in the narrative that the paralytic's physical suffering was related to a specific sin or was due to hysteria induced by guilt. Jesus' pronouncement of pardon is the recognition that man can be genuinely whole only when the breach occasioned by sin has been healed through God's forgiveness of sins.[12]

---

[9] The passive expression was a customary Jewish way of making a pronouncement about God's action while avoiding the divine name. Cf. II Sam. 12:13, "David said to Nathan, 'I have sinned against the Lord.' And Nathan said to David, 'The Lord has pardoned your sin.'" When transposed to the passive, in keeping with first-century usage, Nathan's statement becomes: "your sin is pardoned." Jesus' word to the paralytic would be understood as the pronouncement, "God forgives you." On this construction see Bl-D-F, § 130. 1 (p. 72). On the aoristic present ἀφίενται, which signifies "Your sins are forgiven *at this moment,*" see Bl-D-F, § 320 (p. 167).

[10] See especially H. A. Brongers, "Enkele opmerkingen over het verband tussen zonde en ziekte enerzijds en vergeving en genezing anderzijds in het Oude Testament," *Nederlands Theologisch Tijdschrift* 6 (1952), pp. 129-142.

[11] *Ibid.,* pp. 137 f.; H. van der Loos, *op. cit.,* pp. 255-263. Variant traditions of the OT text current in the first century show the same interchange of terms, e.g., Isa. 6:10 in Mk. 4:12 agrees with the Targum " . . . lest they should turn again and it should be *forgiven* them"; cf. Matt. 13:15 which agrees with the M.T. " . . . and should turn again and I should *heal* them."

[12] H. A. Brongers, *op. cit.,* p. 141.

6-7 The scribes, who are introduced into the Marcan record at this point, were men who were schooled in the written Law of God and its oral interpretation. They were admitted to a closed order of legal specialists only after they were deemed fully qualified and had been set apart through the laying on of hands.[13] They are mentioned frequently in Mark's Gospel but only once is the reference favorable (Ch. 12:28-34). As guardians of the teaching office they challenged Jesus concerning both his message and his refusal to submit to the *halakha,* the oral law, which the scribes regarded as binding in its authority.

The scribes who were present on this occasion were offended by Jesus' declaration. In the OT God alone can forgive sins, and later Judaism adhered scrupulously to this understanding.[14] The Messiah would exterminate the godless in Israel, crush demonic power and protect his people from the reign of sin, but the forgiveness of sins was never attributed to him. Jesus proclaimed the remission of sins like a prophet (II Sam. 12:13, "And Nathan said to David, 'The Lord has pardoned your sins'"). The scribes rejected this pretension to the prophetic office as so much arrogance. They sensed in Jesus' declaration of forgiveness an affront to the majesty and authority of God, which is the essence of blasphemy. The punishment for blasphemy was death by stoning, but the evidence of guilt had to be incontrovertible.[15] The significance of the suspicion of blasphemy so early in the Galilean ministry is that it becomes the basis of a formal accusation and condemnation before the Sanhedrin at the close of the ministry (Ch. 14:61-64).

Jesus' pronouncement was clearly ambiguous. This ambiguity was consistent with the indirectness of revelation which characterized his ministry; there was both a revealing and a veiling of his dignity. In the declaration of verse 5 there was nothing which suggested his *personal* power over sin. The reaction of the scribes does not imply that they have understood otherwise. They object to Jesus' conviction that he can

---

[13] See J. Jeremias, *TWNT* I (Eng. Tr. 1964), pp. 740-742; *idem, Jerusalem zu Zeit Jesu* (Göttingen, 1924-29), II B, pp. 101-140; S. Légasse, "Scribes et disciples de Jésus," *RB* 68 (1961), pp. 497-506; J. Bowman, "Scribes, Pharisees and Haberim," *The Gospel of Mark* (Leiden, 1965), pp. 337-341. A fine passage on the office of scribe is found in Ecclus. 38:24-39:11; cf. 33:16-18.

[14] See Ex. 34:6 f.; Ps. 103:3; 130:4; Isa. 43:25; 44:22; 48:11; Dan. 9:9; 1 QS ii. 9; CD iii. 18; xx. 34. Cf. S-B*K* I (1922), pp. 421 f., 424 ff., 495, 795 f.; II (1924), pp. 585 f.

[15] Lev. 24:10-16; Num. 15:30 f. For a discussion of the earliest rabbinic references see H. W. Beyer, *TWNT* I (Eng. Tr. 1964), pp. 622 f. See below on Ch. 14:63-64.

speak for God. Jesus did exercise the divine prerogative but in a veiled way that could be recognized unambiguously only after the resurrection.

8-9 Jesus sensed the sharp disapproval of the scribes and drew the attention of those present to it by addressing them with the pointed question, "Is it easier to say to a paralysed man 'Your sins are forgiven' or to say 'Arise, pick up your mattress and walk'?" Jesus' use of a counter-question in situations of debate recurs in other narratives (Chs. 3:4; 11:30; 12:37), and appears to be characteristic of his response to conflict.[16] It is important to appreciate its significance here. The scribes might think that a declaration of forgiveness is easier than one of healing, the efficacy of which would be open to immediate verification. This judgment seems to lie behind their contemptuous question, "Why does this fellow speak like this?" (verse 7). By use of a counter-question Jesus challenges their facile assumption that he has acted irresponsibly as a dispenser of cheap grace. It also prepares for the word of healing which demonstrates that forgiveness has actually been realized in the experience of the afflicted man. It is the declaration of forgiveness which is the more essential – and the more difficult – of the two actions.

10-11 Verse 10 constitutes a well-known *crux* in the interpretation of this pericope. Structurally, there is an awkward change of addressee in the middle of the verse. Jesus *appears* to be addressing the scribes: "But that you may know that the Son of Man has authority on earth to forgive sins"; the text, however, proceeds with the abrupt transition, "he says to the paralytic, 'I say unto you . . .'" A more significant problem arises from the public use of "Son of Man" so early in Jesus' ministry. In the presence of unbelieving scribes Jesus appears to make an open and unreserved claim to be the Son of Man with authority to forgive sins. "Son of Man" is a designation of transcendent dignity. With the exception of Ch. 2:10 and 28, it does not enter the Marcan record until after the acknowledgment that Jesus is the Messiah in Ch. 8:29. Then it occurs twelve times and provides the key to Jesus' self-disclosure *to his disciples.*[17] Basic to Mark's theology of the cross and resurrection is

[16] This rhetorical device is paralleled in rabbinic debate. On Ch. 2:9 see T. A. Burkill, *Mysterious Revelation* (Ithaca, N.Y., 1963), pp. 130-132.

[17] Chs. 8:31; 9:12, 31; 10:33; 14:21 (twice); 14:41 refer to the necessity of suffering for the Son of Man; Chs. 8:38; 13:26; 14:62 focus upon the *parousia* glory of the Son of Man; Ch. 9:9 anticipates the resurrection of the Son of Man while Ch. 10:45 defines the redemptive purpose of his incarnate life.

the conviction that there was no unreserved disclosure of the Son of Man until after the resurrection; prior to that time there was a veiled disclosure to men of faith, not unbelief (see on Ch. 9:9). The thought that the Lord affirmed his dignity and function before the scribes during his Galilean ministry is in conflict both with general probability and more particularly with Mark's testimony concerning Jesus' consistent refusal to reveal himself to the scribes, priests and elders who challenged his authority (cf. Ch. 11:33). To hold that he did so in Galilee contradicts the posture he assumed before unbelief throughout his earthly ministry.[18]

A common approach to these difficulties is to treat verses 5b-10 as an interpolation into a healing narrative in which verse 11 originally followed verse 5a: "And when Jesus saw their faith he said to the paralytic, 'I say to you, Arise, take up your mattress and go home.'"[19] There is no support for this radical expedient other than the disjointed construction in verses 10 and 11. If verse 10 is momentarily left out of consideration, the narrative is concerned with a single question of fact: is the declaration of pardon uttered by Jesus true and effective? The fact of pardon is announced in verse 5, questioned in verses 6-9, validated by the healing in verse 11, and recognized by the crowd in verse 12. This homogeneous development demonstrates the literary unity of the pericope. It also puts in clear relief the "commentary" character of verse 10.

It is necessary to recognize that Mark is responsible for verse 10 in its entirety. The awkward syntactical structure is deliberate and functional. It has been shown that in Hellenistic and Byzantine Greek a purpose clause is used to introduce an independent proposition expressing a decision or, more often, a weakened commandment, prayer or desire.[20] The Marcan clause should be translated, "Know that the Son

---

18 This is confirmed by the so-called "secrecy phenomena" in Mark; cf. G. H. Boobyer, "Mark II, 10a and the Interpretation of the Healing of the Paralytic," *HTR* 47 (1954), p. 115.

19 Cf. M. Dibelius, *From Tradition to Gospel* (London, 1934), pp. 66-68; V. Taylor, *The Gospel According to St. Mark* (London, 1952), pp. 191f.; H. Tödt, *Der Menschensohn in der synoptischen Überlieferung* (Gütersloh, 1959), pp. 118-121; R. T. Mead, "The Healing of the Paralytic–A Unit?" *JBL* 80 (1961), pp. 348-354; R. Bultmann, *The History of the Synoptic Tradition* (London, 1963), pp. 14-16, among others. This conjecture fails to explain the text as it now stands in Mark, and this is mandatory.

20 J. Duplacy, "Marc II, 10, note de syntax," in *Mélanges A. Robert* (Paris, 1957), pp. 424-426. The article exposes the significance of ἵνα followed by the subjunctive in Ch. 2:10.

of Man has authority . . . , " rather than "in order that you may know that the Son of Man has authority . . . " Verse 10a is a parenthetical statement[21] addressed by the evangelist to the *Christian* readers of the Gospel to explain the significance of the closing phase of the healing *for them.* In verse 5 nothing necessarily affirms the personal power of Jesus over sin. But this is precisely the crucial point of verse 10a. *They* may be assured that Jesus has both the right and the authority to forgive sins.[22] The significance of Jesus' action remained veiled for the scribes and the multitude. They were startled and recognized that Jesus had proved that the sins of the paralytic had really been pardoned. Nevertheless, they did not recognize the authority of Jesus to remit sins. The function of verse 10b ("he said to the paralytic . . . ") is to indicate the end of Mark's "commentary" and the return to the incident itself.[23]

This is the only place in the Gospel where the pardon of sins is associated with the Son of Man. Nowhere else in the Synoptic or apocalyptic tradition is it suggested that the Son of Man can forgive sins. It was only in the light of the resurrection that the primitive Church recognized unequivocally the full extent of Jesus' authority. Jesus demonstrated in this incident that he was more than a prophet; the power manifested in the remission of sins and the healing of the paralyzed man belonged properly to him. The risen Christ still exercises the remission of sins on earth. The purpose of Mark's commentary is to make the community of believers aware that they have experienced the messianic forgiveness of the Son of Man.

12 When Jesus caused the paralytic to walk before the eyes of his critics, they were forced to recognize that this declaration of forgiveness had been effective. The inter-relationship of forgiveness and healing is emphasized by the conclusion to the narrative: having received the

---

[21] Other instances of Marcan parenthetical statements to his Christian readers include Chs. 2:15, 28; 7:3 f., 19; 13:14.

[22] On the important term "authority" see A. Feuillet, "L'ἐξουσία du fils de l'Homme d'après Mark 2, 10-28 et parr," *RSR* 42 (1954), pp. 161-192.

[23] This interpretation was proposed by M. Dibelius, *op. cit.,* p. 67 and was developed by G. H. Boobyer, *op. cit.,* pp. 115-120; J. Duplacy, *op. cit.,* pp. 424-426; C. P. Ceroke, "Is Mk. 2, 10 a Saying of Jesus?" *CBQ* 22 (1960), pp. 369-390; and J. Murphy-O'Connor, "Péché et Communauté dans le Nouveau Testament," *RB* 74 (1967), pp. 181-185. This interpretation demands the removal of the parenthesis from Ch. 2:10b (where it stands in the ASV) to Ch. 2:10a.

forgiveness of God, the afflicted man receives healing. This is the nature of the salvation which Jesus brings. The healing of the paralytic was more than a display of mercy to a wretched man. The announcement and presentation of radical healing to a man in his entire person was a sign of the Kingdom of God drawn near.[24] The paralytic experienced the fulfilment of God's promise that the lame would share in the joy of the coming salvation (Isa. 35:6; Jer. 31:8). The demonstration that God had come near to his people was startling. All present glorified God because he redeemed men from every distress. It has been objected that Mark's "all" is too comprehensive, "an excusable and fairly obvious overstatement" which was not intended to include the scribes.[25] The objection is unfounded. They too were thoroughly shaken by the extraordinary event which had occurred. Their glorification of God does not mean that they thanked him for sending Jesus, or even that they recognized the relationship between Jesus' declaration of forgiveness and the actual restoration to health of the paralytic. It consisted rather in the statement "we have never seen anything like this." In the eyes of the evangelist, this amounted to an acknowledgment of the dignity of Jesus in spite of their intentions.

(b) The Call of a Tax-farmer. Ch. 2:13-14

13 And he went forth again by the sea side; and all the multitude resorted unto him, and he taught them.
14 And as he passed by, he saw Levi the *son* of Alphaeus sitting at the place of toll, and he saith unto him, Follow me. And he arose and followed him.

13 The report that Jesus withdrew to the sea and there taught a multitude appears at first sight fragmentary and abrupt. In Ch. 2:1-12 he is in Capernaum, and in Ch. 2:14 he is again within the city since the toll booth was not situated at some isolated point on the shore. Why should Jesus momentarily leave the city only to return there in pursuit of his

[24] H. van der Loos, *op. cit.*, p. 262 comments: "In His announcement and granting of remission of sins, Jesus indicates what man's essential distress is. This does not consist in his transient lot in life, with its many vicissitudes, but in his alienation from the living God, in his life in sin and guilt. It is from this that man must be redeemed, and it is from this that Jesus does in fact redeem him!"

[25] G. H. Boobyer, *op. cit.*, p. 119.

mission? This action becomes meaningful when it is seen as part of a recurring pattern in Mark's Gospel. After a demonstration of the saving power of God, Jesus withdraws from the populace to a lonely region, whether the wilderness, the mountain or the sea.[26] In Ch. 2:13 the sea provides a place of withdrawal. The preceding account concluded with the people praising God; Jesus' withdrawal follows an episode of distinct victory. Yet the sea-side has none of the associations of a peaceful retreat. Mark makes that clear through his reference to the pursuing multitude and Jesus' teaching ministry.[27] Its significance is deeper and more ominous. The withdrawal to the sea should be viewed as an approach to a realm which discloses its real nature in the raging of the sea at the height of a squall, as twice reported by Mark (Chs. 4:37 f.; 6:47 f.). Like the return to the wilderness, the move to the sea entails a deliberate entrance into the sphere of forces which manifest their hostility to God.[28] Jesus returns to the place where he confronts Satan and renews his vow to perform the will of God. The consequences of this withdrawal are the calling of a disciple (Ch. 2:14), the mediation of messianic forgiveness and the renewal of conflict (Ch. 2:15-17).

14 The call of Levi is presented in its barest essentials. Mark records his name, his occupation, the word addressed to him and his response. No attempt is made to identify him further. Moreover, when the evangelist records the names of those whom Jesus chose to be with him (Ch. 3:13-19), there is no reference to "Levi the son of Alphaeus."[29]

---

[26] E.g. Chs. 1:40-44, followed by verse 45; 2:1-12, followed by verse 13; 3:1-6, followed by verse 7; 3:9-12, followed by verse 13; 3:31-35, followed by 4:1; 5:1-20, followed by verse 21, *et al.*

[27] M. J. Lagrange, *Évangile selon Saint Marc*[9] (Paris, 1947), p. 40, suggests that the imperfects may express the coming and going of groups to which Jesus successively addresses the word.

[28] U. Mauser, *Christ in the Wilderness* (Naperville, Ill., 1963), pp. 124-128.

[29] Cf. R. Pesch, "Levi-Matthäus (Mc 2, 14 / Mt 9, 9; 10, 3) ein Beitrag zur Lösung eines alten Problems," *ZNW* 59 (1968), pp. 40-56. While "Levi" occurs in the parallel passage, Lk. 5:27 (Codex D: "Levi the son of Alphaeus"), the name found in Mt. 9:9 is "Matthew" and the identity of this man with the apostle is stressed in the Matthean list of the Twelve (Mt. 10:3, "Matthew the tax-collector"). M. J. Lagrange, *op. cit.*, p. 42 has called attention to Nabatean inscriptions where one finds the term מתקרא, "surnamed," between two Semitic names. He suggests that Levi had Matthew as a second Semitic name. Because the evidence is rare and the texts not easily accessible it will be convenient to set them forth here (adding a third example to the two cited by Lagrange). *Corpus Inscriptionum Semiticarum* I:2 (Aramaic Inscriptions):

These facts indicate that in Ch. 2:14 Mark is concerned to illustrate the radical character of Jesus' call, and that it is the nature of the call, rather than the name of the one called, which is of primary importance.

Levi's seat of customs was located at Capernaum, the first site of importance around the northern end of the Sea encountered by travellers from the territory of Herod Philip and from the Decapolis. Levi would be a Jewish tax official in the service of Herod Antipas. [30] Such officials were detested everywhere and were classed with the vilest of men. [31] The practice of leasing the customs duty of a district at a fixed sum encouraged gross oppression by tax officers anxious to secure as large a profit as possible. When a Jew entered the customs service he was regarded as an outcast from society: he was disqualified as a judge or

---

No. 158 line 2 (p. 185): חנינו בר אבא די מתקרא עבדאלהי "Honainu son of Aba who is surnamed 'Abdallahi"

No. 486 lines 1-2 (p. 346): ומרתי די מתקרא זבדת "And Martai who is surnamed Zabdath"

No. 488 lines 1-2 (p. 347): מלכו די יתקרא בשמה "Malku who is surnamed Bashamah"

On the variant reading "James the son of Alphaeus," supported by Western and Caesarean texts in Mk. 2:14, see F. C. Burkitt, "Levi Son of Alphaeus," *JThS* 28 (1927), pp. 273 f.; B. Lindars, "Matthew, Levi, Lebbaeus and the Value of the Western Text," *NTS* 4 (1958), pp. 220-222.

30 The customs officers were not "publicans," who were usually Romans of equestrian rank, but subordinate officials, most of whom were Jewish. In Ch. 2:15-16 Mark uses the ordinary Greek term, τελώνης. δημοσιώνης, which ordinarily renders the Latin term *publicanus,* never occurs in the Gospels. Except at Jerusalem, and perhaps Jericho, the tax-farmers must be collecting either for the tetrarch or for the municipality. It is questionable whether there were any municipal taxes in Jewish communes except at the very few cities upon which the Herods had bestowed Hellenistic city organization. Capernaum, where the toll-booth was located, was not one of these. See further A. N. Sherwin-White, *Roman Society and Roman Law in the New Testament* (Oxford, 1963), pp. 125 f.

31 TB *Baba Qama* 113a lists customs officials together with "murderers and robbers." Jewish sources distinguish two classes of tax officials, those responsible for the income-tax and the poll-tax, and the customs officers who were placed at bridges, canals and on state roads. The latter were especially despised because they had greater opportunities for vexatious exactions. See the articles on τελώνης in M-M, A-G and S-B*K* I (1922), pp. 377-380, 498.

The enemies of the Church who wished to discredit Jesus seized upon this incident. Celsus remarks that Jesus gathered around him ten or eleven persons of notorious character, the very wickedest of tax-farmers and sailors (Origen, *Contra Celsum* i. 62; in ii. 46 Celsus claimed that Jesus chose ten publicans and sailors to be his disciples).

a witness in a court session, was excommunicated from the synagogue, and in the eyes of the community his disgrace extended to his family.[32]

In two inscriptions from Magnesia and Ephesus reference is made to "those who are concerned with the toll on fish."[33] Apparently fish were taxed in these Asian cities, and it is possible that a toll on incoming fish was collected in Capernaum as well. It is probable that Levi knew the fishermen who accompanied Jesus. He may have also known Jesus, who spent considerable time in Capernaum. This would do much to explain his response to Jesus when he was called to discipleship. Be this as it may, what was remembered about this incident in the early Church was the brevity and urgency of Jesus' summons and the radical obedience demonstrated in Levi's dramatic response. Abandoning all other concerns, he arose and followed Jesus. The call of Levi has its sequel in the following pericope where grace is extended to yet other despised men in Capernaum.

(c) Messiah Eats with Sinners. Ch. 2:15-17

15 And it came to pass, that he was sitting at meat in his house, and many publicans[34] and sinners sat down with Jesus and his disciples: for there were many, and they followed him.[35]
16 And the scribes of the Pharisees, when they saw that he was eating with the sinners and publicans, said unto his disciples,

---

[32] TB *Sanhedrin* 25b, the commentary on M. *Sanhedrin* III. 3 which lists "notorious sinners."

[33] *IMM* 116. 42; *OGIS* 469. 9, cited by A. Schlatter, *Der Evangelist Matthäus* (Stuttgart, 1929), p. 302.

[34] See above n. 30. ASVmg clarifies "collectors or renters of Roman taxes." In the territory of Herod Antipas, however, they would be collecting taxes for the tetrarch. RSV "tax collectors."

[35] The question of the punctuation has bearing on the interpretation. Codex Sinaiticus and Codex Vaticanus (א, B) require a period after "disciples." They make the scribes the subject of the verb "follow": "and the scribes of the Pharisees also followed him." The textual tradition behind the ASV, RSV, however, is stronger and should be retained. The clause "for they were many, and they followed him," appears to be an explanatory note for Mark's Roman audience explaining the historical circumstance that there were many tax officers and sinners who followed Jesus. The term "follow" is here used untechnically. The meal brings on the scene a large number of officials to whom Jesus addresses a call to repentance. See R. P. Meye, *Jesus and the Twelve* (Grand Rapids, 1968), pp. 142-145.

How is it[36] that he eateth and drinketh[37] with publicans and sinners?
17 And when Jesus heard it, he saith unto them, They that are whole have no need of a physician, but they that are sick: I came not to call the righteous, but sinners.

15-16 As a spontaneous expression of his joy Levi[38] gave a banquet for Jesus and his disciples to which he invited his fellow tax officers and a group of men who are designated "sinners." This term cannot be understood in the generally accepted sense of "transgressors of the moral law of God" since Mark would then have written "tax officers and *other* sinners." The term is technical in this context for a class of people who were regarded by the Pharisees as inferior because they showed no interest in the scribal tradition. With the derisive epithet "the people of the land," the scribes often dismissed as inconsequential the common people who possessed neither time nor inclination to regulate their conduct by Pharisaic standards. They were particularly despised because they did not eat their food in a state of ceremonial cleanness and because they failed to separate the tithe.[39] The designation "sinners" as used by the scribes is roughly equivalent to "outcasts."

---

[36] Ὅτι is here like τί or διότι, as Matthew and Luke have understood. The same construction occurs in Mk. 9:11, 28 and elsewhere. See Bl-D-F § 300, pp. 157 f. RSV "Why does he eat with tax collectors and sinners?"

[37] The words "and drinks" are supported by a large number of MSS (C 𝔎 A λ φ *pl c f l q* vg syp sa bo) but should be omitted with B ℵ D W Θ 235 271 *a b e ff r*1.

[38] It is natural to see a clear connection between Ch. 2:15-17 and Ch. 2:14, as in the earliest commentary on Mark: "And Levi made him a great feast in his house" (Lk. 5:29).

[39] Cf. K. Rengstorf, *TWNT* I (Eng. tr. 1964), p. 328: "For the Pharisee, however, a ἁμαρτωλός is one who does not subject himself to the Pharisaic ordinances, i.e., the so-called *'am ha-areṣ*. He is not a sinner because he violates the Law, but because he does not endorse the Pharisaic interpretation." In the OT the term is far from technical, as is shown by E. W. Nicholson, "The Meaning of the Expression עם הארץ in the Old Testament," *JSemS* 10 (1965), pp. 59-66. The situation, however, is different by the time of the composition of the early Pharisaic document, the Psalms of Solomon (*ca.* 40 B.C.). For the group distinction between righteous and sinners see Ps. Sol. 2:37-41; 3:3-15; 12:7. See further I. Abrahams, "Publicans and Sinners," in *Studies in Pharisaism and the Gospels,* I (Philadelphia, 1917), pp. 54-61; and especially J. Jeremias, "Zöllner und Sünder," *ZNW* 30 (1931), pp. 293-300. Helpful (but undocumented) is W. H. Raney, "Who Were the 'Sinners'?" *JRel* 10 (1930), pp. 578-591.

The joint expression "publicans and sinners" denotes well-known and despised classes among the people.

The Pharisees and their scribes[40] were the spiritual descendants of the *Ḥasidim* who had distinguished themselves by zeal for observance of the Law in spite of the repressive measures of Antiochus IV Epiphanes.[41] They were deeply devoted to the Law and strictly governed their own life by the interpretation passed down in the scribal tradition. They criticized Jesus because he failed to observe the distinction between "the righteous" and "the sinners" which was an essential component of their piety. As a teacher of the Law he should have recognized that it was inappropriate for him to recline at table with the men gathered in Levi's house. In their banquets the Pharisees attempted to maintain an exclusive fellowship in order to avoid ritual impurity from contact with others who maintained the traditions less strictly. They considered it disgraceful for one of their teachers to recline at table with those unversed in the Law, and Jesus' disregard of time-honored custom offended them.[42]

17 Jesus silenced their protest with a traditional proverb: "the healthy have no need of a physician, but rather the sick."[43] With this maxim, which the Pharisees recognized as valid, Jesus implied that it was his responsibility to sit at table fellowship with excisemen and the despised common people. He is willing to adopt the scribal distinction between the righteous and sinners, but limits his own activity to the outcasts.

---

[40] On "the scribes of the Pharisees" see E. Schürer, *Geschichte des jüdischen Volkes im Zeitalter Jesu Christi*[4] II (Leipzig, 1909), p. 320. The material collected in S-B*K* IV (1928), pp. 339-352 indicates that the Sadducees also had their interpreters of the Law.

[41] I Macc. 1:62 f.; 2:29 f., 42; 7:13-16; II Macc. 14:6.

[42] The Mishnah provides the background for understanding their protest: M. *Demai* II. 2 "He that undertakes to be trustworthy (i.e. a Pharisee) may not be the guest of one of the people of the land"; II. 3 "He who undertakes to be an Associate... may not be the guest of one of the people of the land nor may he receive him as a guest in his own raiment." TB *Berachoth* 43b lists among six things inappropriate to a scholar "he should not recline at table in the company of ignorant persons," while TJ *Shabbath* 3c states clearly "Let not a Pharisee eat the sacrifice with the people of the land."

[43] Forms of this commonplace occur both in Jewish and non-Jewish sources: e.g., Mekilta to Ex. 15:26 "If they are not sick, why do they need a physician?"; Pausanias *apud* Plutarch, *Apophthegmata Laconica* 230 f. "The physicians, he said, are not to be found among the well but customarily spend their time among the sick."

The refusal to call the righteous is open to alternative interpretations. (1) Because the scribes were confident in their own righteousness they were incapable of perceiving the call to repentance. "Righteous" is used ironically or *ad hominem,* while the "sinners" are the humble who hear and respond to the call of God. [44] (2) Jesus recognized the true zeal for righteousness which distinguished the Pharisees. He shared the common conviction in Judaism that the sins of the righteous did not seriously jeopardize their relationship with God. If he does not occupy himself with the righteous it is not because of disdain. As a sensitive pastor he reserves all of his solicitude for the sinners. It is the impoverishment of this latter group, not their good disposition, which Jesus stresses. [45]

There are several elements which suggest that there is at least an implied condemnation of the scribes in this statement. The pericope demands the identification of "the righteous" with the Pharisees, and the tax collectors and outcasts with "the sinners." If Jesus at times spoke generously about the Pharisees, he was untiring in condemning their interpretation of the Law which had blurred God's intention (Chs. 2:23-27; 3:1-5; 7:1-15). This point is clear when the pericope is seen in the context of the hostility of the scribes of the Pharisees (Chs. 2:6, 16; 3:6, 22). It is accordingly better to see in the use of "righteous" in Ch. 2:17 a point of irony against those who believe themselves to be righteous. Jesus had not come to call for the Kingdom of God men like the scribes who considered themselves to be righteous, but outcasts who knew they needed to be made whole.

David Daube has called attention to the tripartite form of this pericope, a form which it shares with at least six other Synoptic incidents. [46] (1) Jesus performs a revolutionary action; (2) the Pharisees or their scribes remonstrate with him; and (3) he makes a pronouncement by which they are silenced. This form, with its direct, dramatic presentation, was well suited to emphasize the startling character of the Kingdom of God which broke in, step by step, as Jesus and those around him performed their task. The first part of the form described an action

---

44 A. Descamps, *Les Justes et la Justice dans les évangiles et le Christianisme* (Louvain, 1950), pp. 98-110; J. Mouson, "Non veni vocare justos, sed peccatores (Mt IX, 13- Mc II, 17- Lc V, 32)," *Collectanea Mechliniensia* 43 (1958), pp. 134-139.

45 M. J. Lagrange, *op. cit.,* p. 45; A. Schlatter, *op. cit.,* pp. 194, 309; G. Schrenk, *TWNT* II (Eng. tr. 1964), p. 189 and H. Ridderbos, *The Coming of the Kingdom* (Philadelphia, 1962), p. 220.

46 *Op. cit.,* pp. 171-175. The pattern also occurs in Mk. 2:1ff., 23 ff.; Mt. 12:22 ff.; 21:15 ff.; Lk. 11:37 ff.; 13:10 ff.

performed on some definite occasion: Jesus ate with tax officials and outcasts. The middle part of the form, the protest issued in the form of a challenge, assumes that Jesus and his disciples ought to behave as the scribes do. Because Jesus is judged as essentially belonging to the same camp as his remonstrants, his actions appear offensive to them. The third member of the form, the silencing of the remonstrants, confirms this observation. Jesus justifies his action by adducing a traditional proverb which his opponents recognize as valid ("the healthy have no need of a physician . . . "). Jesus starts from the same basis as do his antagonists; if he did not, he would be unable to silence them. Where he differs from them is in his interpretation of the teaching adduced. The third member of the form describes the defeat of the scribes by an argument resting upon a basis they acknowledge.

It is the first part of this form, Jesus' radical action, which brings into focus the theologically significant elements in this incident. To the scribes Jesus' conduct was offensive because it was improper for a teacher of the Law to share meal fellowship with outcast and ignorant common people. Jesus' action was actually more revolutionary than they could imagine. When Jesus shared meal fellowship with the tax officials and the common people, it was Messiah who was sitting with sinners. The expression used in Ch. 2:15, "they reclined at table together with Jesus,"[47] suggests that Jesus–the Messiah–and not Levi, was the host at this festive meal. When this is understood, the interest of the entire pericope centers on the significance of Messiah eating with sinners.[48] The specific reference in verse 17 to Jesus' call of sinners to the Kingdom suggests that the basis of table-fellowship was *messianic forgiveness,* and the meal itself was an anticipation of the messianic banquet.[49] When Jesus broke bread with the outcasts, Messiah ate with them at his table and extended to them fellowship with God. Mark's interest in

---

47 Gr. συνανέκειντο τῷ 'Ιησοῦ.

48 This has been correctly seen by A. Schlatter, *op. cit.,* p. 304; E. Lohmeyer, *Das Evangelium des Markus*[16] (Göttingen, 1963), pp. 56-58; D. M. Mackinnon, "Sacrament and Common Meal," in *Studies in the Gospels,* ed. D. E. Nineham (Oxford, 1955), pp. 201-207.

49 The exalted Messiah describes the relationship which exists between himself and the messianic community in the terms of meal fellowship: Rev. 3:20; 19:6-9; cf. Mt. 8:10-11. This concept of the "messianic banquet" was also known to the scribes. An early Tannaitic saying compares the Age to Come to a banquet hall: "This age is like a vestibule before the Age to Come. Prepare yourself in the vestibule that you may enter the banquet hall" (M. *Aboth* IV. 16). See further J. Jeremias, *Jesus' Promise to the Nations* (Naperville, Ill., 1958), pp. 55-65.

recording this incident lies precisely in the demonstration of forgiveness which it affords. It takes its place very naturally with the two preceding sections of the Gospel (Ch. 2:1-12, 13-14) as a sovereign demonstration of the forgiveness of sins. The meal was an extension of the grace of God and an anticipation of the consummation when Messiah will sit down with sinners in the Kingdom of God.

(d) The New Situation. Ch. 2:18-22

18 And John's disciples and the Pharisees were fasting: and they come and say unto him, Why do John's disciples and the disciples of the Pharisees fast, but thy disciples fast not?
19 And Jesus said unto them, Can the sons of the bride-chamber fast,[50] while the bridegroom is with them? as long as they have the bridegroom with them, they cannot fast.
20 But the days will come, when the bridegroom shall be taken away from them, and then will they fast in that day.
21 No man seweth a piece of undressed[51] cloth on an old garment: else that which should fill it up taketh from it, the new from the old, and a worse rent is made.[52]
22 And no man putteth new wine into old wineskins; else the wine will burst the skins, and the wine perisheth, and the skins: but *they put* new wine into fresh wine-skins.[53]

Having exhibited Jesus' relationship to sin and sinners, Mark turns to the issues of fasting and observance of the Sabbath. In these next narratives it is evident that opposition to Jesus has become heightened and outspoken (Ch. 2:18, 24). It reaches a point of culmination in the decision to seek his death (Ch. 3:6). The issue of fasting may have been important to the community within which Mark wrote since he brings

---

50 ASVmg "companions of the bridegroom"; RSV "wedding guests." The expression is a Semitism for all those who participate in the wedding, e.g. I Macc. 9:39, "and the bridegroom came out with his friends and his brothers to meet them with tamborines and musicians . . . "

51 Gr. ἄγναφος meaning "unbleached," "unsized," "unshrunken" and so is equivalent to "new." W. Bauer renders "a patch of new cloth" (A-G, p. 10); RSV "unshrunk."

52 RSV is clearer: "No one sews a piece of unshrunk cloth on an old garment; if he does, the patch tears away from it, the new from the old and a worse tear is made."

53 RSV "but new wine is for fresh skins."

together three statements of the Lord which have a bearing upon it. The introduction lacks detail, but is sufficient to indicate to a non-Palestinian community the historical circumstances in which the question of fasting arose during Jesus' ministry.

18 The reference to "the disciples of the Pharisees" is not technical since the Pharisees as such did not have disciples (although individual scribes among them did).[54] The designation indicates that larger group of people who were influenced by Pharisaic ideals and practice. This may be the proper nuance of "the disciples of John" as well.[55] They had submitted to the baptism of repentance and continued to pattern their lives in accordance with John's prophetic word. It is probable that John's disciples and the Pharisees were fasting for quite different reasons, and that it is the fast observed by the disciples of John which particularly interested Mark, who mentions this group first.

The OT specified only one day when fasting was mandatory upon all Israel. This was the Day of Atonement, designated as a day for cleansing from sin and affliction of the soul (Ex. 20:10; Lev. 16:1-34; 23:26-32; 35:9; Num. 29:9-11). In this context fasting is an act of repentance in preparation for expiation.[56] By the close of the prophetic period other occasions of fasting had become traditional,[57] and these

---

[54] K. Rengstorf, *TWNT* IV (1942), pp. 428-432, 434-446 (pp. 445 f. on Mk. 2:18).

[55] In Ch. 6:29 the disciples of John are mentioned again in connection with the burial of the Baptist. See K. Rengstorf, *TWNT* IV (1942), pp. 460-462.

[56] Cf. J. Behm, *TWNT* IV (1942), p. 929. The observance of this day during the first century is described in the Mishnah, tractate *Yoma*. Among the men of Qumran the Day of Atonement was designated "the Day of Fasting" (CD vi. 19; 1QpHab. vii. 8).

[57] Zech. 7:5; 8:19 refer to fasts in the fourth, fifth, seventh and tenth months. A rabbinic commentary on these texts (TJ *Ta'anith* 68a-d) identifies the fasts as follows:

17th of Tammuz (fourth month):	commemorated the breaking of the tables of the Law (Ex. 22:19).
9th of Ab (fifth month):	commemorated the destruction of the temple by Nebuchadnezzar (and later by Titus).
3rd of Tishri (seventh month):	commemorated the murder of Gedaliah (II Kings 25:25 f.).
10th of Tebeth (tenth month):	commemorated the siege and taking of Jerusalem by the Babylonians (Jer. 52:14).

For a slightly different arrangement see Jerome, *In Zach.* II. 8 (MPL XXV, col. 1475).

observances continued into the first century.[58] At this time it was customary for the Pharisees to fast voluntarily on Monday and Thursday of each week.[59] While the origins of this practice are obscure, it appears to have been an expression of piety and self-consecration. It is probably to this voluntary fast that reference is made in the statement "the Pharisees were fasting."

In the OT fasting may be an expression of mourning,[60] and it has been suggested that John's disciples were fasting because of the death of their master.[61] While this is possible the proposal lacks support from any detail in the text. It seems better to understand their fast as an expression of repentance designed specifically to hasten the coming of the time of redemption. This understanding gives point to Jesus' use of the wedding image (which implies a contrast between John's premessianic travail and Jesus' messianic feast), and appears to be assumed in the two brief parables appended to this initial metaphor. The demand to know why Jesus' disciples do not fast is critical in intention; the unidentified questioners wish to expose the disciples of Jesus to their disadvantage. In all probability many of them had been disciples of John who were expected to maintain the discipline encouraged by their master.

19-20 Jesus, in typical debate fashion, poses a counter-question designed to center attention on the new situation created by his presence with the disciples. He replies: "Can the bridal guests mourn during the bridal celebrations?"[62] The statement may be proverbial for any inappropriate

---

58 The term תַּעֲנִית occurs only once in the Hebrew Bible (Ezra 9:5; cf. 8:21) but had become a technical term for fasting by the time of the codification of the rabbinic material. Jewish practice in the first century is known especially through the Aramaic "Fast Scroll," *Megillat Ta'anith*. There is also a Mishnaic tractate entitled *Ta'anith*, with commentary in TB and TJ. See further, A. Lesêtre, "Jeûne," *DB* III (1910), cols. 1528-1532; E. Schürer, *op. cit.* II (1907), pp. 489-491; L. A. Rosenthal, "Megillat Ta'anit," *Jüdisches Lexikon* (Berlin, 1930), IV:1, p. 50; J. Behm, *op. cit.*, pp. 929-31; S. Lowy, "The Motivation of Fasting in Talmudic Literature," *JJS* 9 (1958), 19-38.

59 Cf. Luke 18:12 ("I fast twice in the week"); Didache 8:1: M. *Ta'anith* I. 4-5; TB *Ta'anith* 10a. See S-B*K* II (1924), p. 243; J. Winter, "Tanchuma," *Jüdisches Lexikon* IV:2 (1930), pp. 863 f.

60 E.g. I Sam. 31:13; cf. Judith 8:6; I Macc. 1:25-28.

61 A. E. J. Rawlinson, *St. Mark*[4] (London, 1936), p. 31; cf. V. Taylor, *op. cit.*, p. 209; C. E. B. Cranfield, *op. cit.*, pp. 108 f.

62 Translation of J. Jeremias, *The Parables of Jesus*[6] (New York, 1963), p. 52 n. 15. On the imagery see *idem*, *TWNT* IV (1942), pp. 1092-1099.

action, since a wedding was a time of great joy and festivity, heralded by music and gala processions.[63] To fast in the presence of the groom would be unthinkable. Although the image of the wedding feast was sometimes used by the rabbis to express the joy of the messianic era, neither in the OT nor in later Jewish literature was the Messiah represented as the bridegroom.[64] It is important to stress this fact, for it indicates that Jesus' statement would not have been recognized by his disciples or his adversaries as an explicitly messianic assertion. Jesus speaks of himself in an implicit, veiled manner because he has not yet spoken openly and in detail to his disciples about his distinctive mission (see Ch. 8:32).[65] The messianic significance of this use of the bridal image was understood only later.[66] The central comparison between the wedding festivities and Jesus' disciples lies in *the joy which they possess in their master*. Jesus emphasizes this with his answer to the critical question. The reason for the fundamentally different position of his disciples is that "the bridegroom is with them," and in his presence they experience joy. Even on this veiled level of parabolic speech something significant is said: an expression of sorrow is inappropriate to the new situation which has come with Jesus' presence.

Jesus is both the center and the cause of the joy that his disciples experience. Yet this condition will not remain undisturbed. Jesus referred to a period when the bridegroom would be taken away and then his disciples would understand the meaning of sorrow.[67] These words have

---

[63] Cf. I Macc. 9:37, 39: "It was reported to Jonathan and Simon his brother, 'The sons of Jambri are celebrating a great wedding and are conducting the bride . . . from Nadabath with a large escort . . . They raised their eyes and looked, and saw a tumultuous procession with much baggage; and the bridegroom came out with his friends and his brothers to meet them with tamborines and musicians . . . "

[64] Cf. J. Jeremias, *TWNT* IV (1942), pp. 1094 f. In *The Parables of Jesus*[6] (1963), p. 52 n. 13, Jeremias is able to offer only one passage, occurring in a relatively late rabbinic cycle of festival sermons: "The garment in which God will one day clothe the Messiah will shine ever more brightly from one end of the world to the other, for it is said (Isa. 61:10), 'Like a bridegroom who puts on a priestly mitre'" (*Pesiqta Rabbati* 149a). On the reading of 1QIsa.[a] 61:10 see J. Gnilka, "Bräutigam–spätjüdisches Messiasprädikat?" *TrierThZ* 69 (1960), pp. 298-301.

[65] H. N. Ridderbos, *The Coming of the Kingdom* (Philadelphia, 1962), pp. 50 f., 160.

[66] Note Jn. 3:29; II Cor. 11:2; Eph. 5:23; Rev. 19:7; 21:2.

[67] There are interesting variations on this saying in the Coptic Gospel of Thomas, which appears to be Enkratite in character. It appears most fully in Logion 104: "They said to him, Come and let us pray today and let us fast. Jesus

been judged to be alien to the context with its stress on the joy in the bridal celebrations; here, it is urged, the early Church reflects on Jesus' passion.[68] This inference is unwarranted. The language is cryptic in its reference to the bridegroom. Jesus speaks only of a time in which he will be taken away from his friends; there is no definite allusion to a violent death. The inner connection between Ch. 2:19a and Ch. 2:20 demands only that the phrase "because he is with them" be placed in opposition to "when he shall be taken away."[69] When the primitive Christian community reflected upon this word *after* Jesus' suffering and death it is natural that they should understand it in the light of that event. But in its original setting the word was veiled and spoke only of a time when joy would be exchanged for sorrow because Jesus would be with them no longer. It is especially important to notice that the specific formulation which Mark has recorded finds no explicit echo in the passion narrative of his Gospel.[70]

The final phrase of Jesus' statement ("and then they will fast on that day") has evoked the attention of interpreters of the Gospel from the

---

said, What then is the sin which I have committed, or in what have I been vanquished? But when the bridegroom comes out of the bridal chamber, then let them fast and let them pray." Entrance into the bridal chamber is mentioned in Logion 75 (which appears to be a brief formulation of Mt. 25:10). Similar in tenor to Mk. 2:20, without the bridal imagery, is Logion 38: "Jesus said, Many times have you desired to hear these words which I say unto you, and you have no other from whom to hear them. There will be days when you will seek me and you will not find me."

[68] So Jeremias, *TWNT* IV (1942), pp. 1094-1096; *idem, The Parables of Jesus*[6] (1963), p. 52.

[69] Rightly stressed by F. G. Cremer, *Die Fastenansage Jesu* (Bonn, 1965), pp. 5, 126, who points out that there is no underlying prophecy of the passion here. Between the futures ἐλεύσονται and νηστεύσουσιν the aorist subjunctive ἀπαρθῇ has the meaning of an exact future. Accordingly one should interpret ὅταν ἀπαρθῇ as similar in meaning to ὅτε ἀπηρμένος ἔσται, so that Jesus speaks only of a time in which he will be taken away from his own. There is no mention of a violent death.

For instances of wedding feast joy turned into occasions of sorrow, because the bridegroom was taken away, see Tobit 3:5-14; I Macc. 9:37-41 (verse 41, "Thus the wedding was turned into mourning and the voice of their musicians into a funeral dirge").

[70] That it would have been possible to do so is indicated by Isa. 53:8 LXX: "his life was taken away (αἴρεται) from the earth," which recalls ἀπαίρεσθαι in Mk. 2:20.

earliest period up to the present.[71] Jesus had spoken initially of "the *days* which are coming" (plural) but now he speaks of "that *day*" (singular). The veiled character of the phrase is appropriate to the context with its other cryptic elements and scarcely permits an allusion which is precise.[72] A common suggestion is that the reference is to Good Friday, and that the formulation reflects the practice of the Church of Rome which early observed a fast on this occasion.[73] In view of the pervading contrast between joy and sorrow in the developed image it is better to understand "fasting" in the broader sense of experiencing sorrow.[74]

21-22 The twin parables appended to Jesus' initial statements may have been delivered on some other occasion.[75] They possess a relevance which is broader than the narrow issue of fasting, and Mark makes no attempt to link them narrowly to the preceding verses. Their appropriateness to the issue at hand lies in the commentary they provide on the significance of Jesus' presence with his disciples.[76] These brief

---

[71] The material from the second century through the fifteenth has been adequately examined by F. G. Cremer, *op. cit.,* who sub-titles his book *Mk 2, 20 und Parallelen in der Sicht der patristischen und scholastischen Exegese* (pp. 7-146, the literal understanding of the words; pp. 147-175, the allegorical understanding). For more modern treatments see esp. K. T. Schafer, "... und dann werden sie fasten, an jenem Tage (Mk 2, 20 und Parallelen)," in *Synoptische Studien,* Alfred Wikenhauser ... dargebracht (München, 1953), pp. 124-147.

[72] Cf. Lagrange, *op. cit.,* p. 48. A similar alternation between "the days" and "the day" of the Son of Man occurs in Lk. 17:22-24, where the phrase ἐλεύσονται ἡμέραι echoes Mk. 2:20.

[73] Cf. M. H. Shepherd, Jr., *The Paschal Liturgy and the Apocalypse* (London, 1960), p. 35; G. Braumann, "'An jenem Tag' (Mk. ii. 20)," *Nov. Test.* 6 (1963), pp. 264-267. See the references in Cremer, *op. cit.,* pp. 10, 20, 25, 29, 30, 102, 104.

[74] So E. Lohmeyer, *op. cit.,* p. 60; J. Jeremias, *TWNT* IV (1942), p. 1096 n. 41; J. O'Hara, "Christian Fasting, Mk 2, 18-22," *Scripture* 19 (1967), pp. 82-95. The Aramaic אתענִי means both "to be sad" and "to fast" (see the Targum on I Kings 2:26 and Zech. 7:5 respectively). Cf. Ch. 14:20 where the joy of the disciples is broken by the explicit pronouncement that one of them will betray Jesus.

[75] Cf. Cremer, *op. cit.,* pp. 4 f. This common understanding finds new support in the Coptic Gospel of Thomas, Logion 47. A variant form of the new wine saying precedes the reference to the patching of the garment (where the formulation is the reverse to that in Mk. 2:21: "They do not sew an old patch on a new garment, because there would come a rent"), and both are independent of the wedding imagery in Logion 75 and 104.

[76] J. Jeremias, *The Parables of Jesus*[6] (1963), pp. 117 f.

parables directly answer the challenge implied in the question, Why do your disciples not fast?

Like the bridal metaphor, the sayings about the new garment and the new wine describe inappropriate actions (using valuable new cloth to mend a tattered garment; pouring fermenting new wine into worn-out damaged wineskins). In this context the meaning of these sayings is quite specific. If Jesus' disciples were to pursue the Pharisaic practice or continue to emulate the Baptist, they would be like people who put a new piece of cloth on an old garment, or who pour new wine into old skins. The practice of John's disciples was oriented to preparation for the coming of the Kingdom, especially in its aspect of judgment. That is why they fast. Jesus, on the other hand, came proclaiming that the time was fulfilled, and it is his presence which is the decisive element of fulfilment. The behavior of his disciples reflects the joyful certainty of the breaking in of the time of salvation. They experience the joy of the Kingdom because they belong to him. The time of the bridegroom signals the passing of the old and the coming of "the new."[77] Here "new" means that which is totally different; it is a characteristic which belongs to the final age.[78] The new disrupts the old and bursts its mold. That is why maintaining what is old (fasting as an expression of repentance in preparation for the judgment to come) represents a misunderstanding and a basic ignorance that the time of salvation has already come with Jesus. The Pharisaic practice of fasting perpetuated the old in an unbelieving mechanical fashion blind to the new moment which God had introduced. The presence of Jesus inaugurates the messianic time of joy when fasting is rendered superfluous, so long as he is in the midst of his people. The images of the wedding, the new cloth and the new wine are distinctly eschatological in character, like that of the messianic banquet in Ch. 2:15-17. It may be this factor which has caused them to be closely associated by the evangelist. They stress the element of fulfilment which is marked by the presence of Jesus. His person is both the sign that the old situation has been radically altered and the pledge that the reality described by these images shall be experienced in the appropriate time.

---

77 H. Ridderbos, *op. cit.*, pp. 50 f., 305-308.

78 Cf. J. Behm, *TWNT* III (1938), pp. 451 ff. There is no real basis for distinguishing between νέος and καινός, as if the first signified "new" in terms of recent while the second means qualitatively new. Mark speaks of οἶνος νέος, but there is an ostraca reference to οἶνος καινός and the expressions are equivalent. See M-M, pp. 314 f.; M. J. Lagrange, *op. cit.*, p. 48.

(e) *Sabbath Infringement and the Lord of the Sabbath. Ch. 2:23-28*

23 And it came to pass, that he was going on the sabbath day through the grainfields; and his disciples began, as they went, to pluck the ears.
24 And the Pharisees said unto him, Behold, why do they on the sabbath day that which is not lawful?
25 And he said unto them, Did you never read what David did, when he had need, and was hungry, he and they that were with him?
26 How he entered into the house of God when Abiathar was high priest, and ate the show-bread, which it is not lawful to eat save for the priests, and gave also to them that were with him?
27 And he said unto them, The sabbath was made for man, and not man for the sabbath:
28 so that the Son of man is lord even of the sabbath.

23-24 The action of the disciples in plucking heads of grain as they passed through a field on a Sabbath walk [79] provoked the fourth controversy recorded by Mark. The action in itself was wholly legitimate. The Mosaic Law provided explicitly that "when you come into your neighbor's standing grain, then you may pluck the ears with your hands, but you shall not bring a sickle into your neighbor's standing grain" (Deut. 23:25). The disciples' conduct came under the critical scrutiny of the Pharisees only because it occurred on the Sabbath. The action of plucking grain was interpreted as reaping, an act of work in violation of the Sabbath rest. Reaping on the Sabbath was formally prohibited by the Mosaic Law (Ex. 34:21), and of the 39 main categories of work

[79] The reference to the ripe grain is frequently taken as a chronological datum: the incident must have occurred after Passover, from April to June, and provides "the only clear indication in the Synoptic Gospels that the Ministry covered at least a year," according to V. Taylor, *op. cit.,* p. 216; cf. M. J. Lagrange, *op. cit.,* p. 52; C. E. B. Cranfield, *op. cit.,* p. 115. It is unwise, however, to base a chronological judgment on a detail which is incidental to the pericope. There is no indication that Mark has placed the account at this point for chronological reasons. Moreover, the caution that the incident is not chronologically precise is rightly urged by M. Smith, "Comments on Taylor's Commentary on Mark," *HTR* 48 (1955), p. 28: "While Passover marks the official beginning of harvest, grain is ripe sometimes earlier in sheltered places, not to mention the Jordan Valley."

forbidden on the Sabbath in the Mishnah, the third is reaping.[80]

Among the scribes it was assumed that a teacher was responsible for the behavior of his disciples. For this reason the Pharisees address their protest directly to Jesus. They raise a question of *halakha,* of what is legally permitted or prohibited,[81] perhaps with the intention of satisfying the legal requirement of a warning prior to prosecution for Sabbath violation.[82]

25-26 Jesus answered their protest with an appeal to Scripture, calling attention to the incident recorded in I Sam. 21:1-6. The formulation, "Have you not read . . . ," followed by a counter-question reflects the language of debate, and is appropriate to the context. Nevertheless, there are difficult questions raised by verses 25-26 which relate to the form of the allusion itself, the appropriateness of the reference to a question which centered *in the Sabbath,* and the relative value such an appeal would have in technical debate.

The chief problem in the allusion to David's act is the reference to Abiathar the high priest. If the meaning is that David received the five loaves of holy bread *at the time when*[83] Abiathar was high priest the reference is incorrect. The incident occurred when Ahimelech was high priest, and it was he who gave David the bread. Abiathar was a son of Ahimelech who escaped the massacre of the high priestly family, and who enters the record for the first time a chapter later (I Sam. 22:20). Because he served as high priest and was better known in association with David than his father, it is commonly assumed a primitive error entered the tradition before it came into Mark's hands or an early marginal gloss which was in error moved into the text.[84] The difficulty

---

80 M. *Shabbath* VII. 2; TJ *Shabbath* VII. 2, 9c (the plucking of grain is an act of reaping). See S-B*K* I (1922), pp. 615-618, 623-629; E. Lohse, *TWNT* VII (1964), pp. 11-14; B. Cohen, "The Rabbinic Law Presupposed by Mt. 12:1 and Lk. 6:1," *HTR* 23 (1930), pp. 91 f.; S. T. Kembrough, "The Concept of Sabbath at Qumran," *Rev Qum* 5 (1966), pp. 483-502.

81 ὃ οὐκ ἔξεστιν (= אסור), "not permitted." See E. Lohse, "Jesu Worte über den Sabbat," in *Judentum, Urchristentum, Kirche,* Festschrift für J. Jeremias, ed. W. Eltester (Berlin, 1960), p. 86 n. 27.

82 M. *Sanhedrin* VII. 8.

83 Gr. ἐπί *cum* genitive, on which see Bl-D-F § 234. 8 (p. 123). This is the most common understanding of the phrase in this context, and finds support from the idiom in I Macc. 13:42; Lk. 3:2; Acts 11:28.

84 Cf. M. J. Lagrange, *op. cit.,* pp. 53-55; A. D. Rogers, "Mark 2, 26," *JThS* n.s. 2 (1951), pp. 46 f.

was early felt and is reflected in the manuscript tradition.[85] An attractive proposal is that Mark's intention has been misunderstood in the translation of the passage. The same grammatical construction occurs in Ch. 12:26, where it must be translated "have you not read in the book of Moses, *in the passage concerning the Bush,* how God spoke unto him . . . ? " The construction is designed to call attention to the section of a biblical book where the reference is found, in the above instance Ex. 3:1 ff. In Ch. 2:26 Mark may have inserted the reference to Abiathar to indicate the section of the Samuel scroll in which the incident could be located.[86]

The allusion to David and his men receiving the showbread has often been felt to be inappropriate since there is no explicit reference to the Sabbath in the I Samuel account. Why is this particular incident relevant to the situation at hand? Jesus' reference to this occasion in David's life was not an isolated phenomenon in early Jewish exposition, for it attracted the attention of the rabbis as well. From details in the text, and especially from David's words, "how much more then today," they concluded that the incident occurred upon the Sabbath.[87] This interpretation may have been current already at the time of Jesus' ministry. There is, however, no reflection of this exegetical tradition in Mark's narrative. The emphasis rather falls on the association of David and his men, because this is the detail that provides the parallel to Jesus and his company of men. Twice in the text inferences are drawn from I Sam. 21:3-6 to underscore this fact ("when he had need and was hungry, *he*

---

85 The words ἐπὶ 'Αβιαθαρ ἀρχιερέως are absent from D W 271 *a b e ff i r*[1] sys[in] and the parallel passages in Matthew and Luke. In A C Θ λ φ and other MSS the article τοῦ is inserted before ἀρχιερέως. By this change the phrase could mean "in the days of Abiathar (who later became) the High Priest." Both variants may be due to a sense of historical difficulty in the text as it stands.

86 J. W. Wenham, "Mark 2, 26," *JThS* n.s. 1 (1950), p. 156. The objections which may be raised against this proposal are that ἐπὶ 'Αβιάθαρ is considerably separated from "have you not read," unlike Ch. 12:26; that Abiathar is by no means the central element in this section of I Samuel; that the introduction of Abiathar first in Ch. 22 constitutes it unlikely that his name would be given to the section; and that numerous instances in Tannaitic documents indicate that a section was usually designated by a term which occurs early, not late, in the section. The strongest argument for this proposal is the undoubted use of ἐπί *cum* genitive in Ch. 12:26 to indicate a section of Scripture.

87 B. Murmelstein, "Jesu Gang durch die Saatfelder," *Angelos* 3 (1930), pp. 111-120 calls attention to TB *Menaḥoth* 95b and *Yalquṭ Shim'oni* to I Sam. 21:5 (§ 130), where Rabbi Shim'on (*ca.* 150 A.D.) interprets the text of the Sabbath.

and they that were with him... he gave also to *them that were with him*"). David's conduct included that of his men. The relationship between the OT incident and the infringement of the Sabbath by the disciples lies in the fact that on both occasions pious men did something forbidden.[88] The fact that God does not condemn David for his action indicates that the narrowness with which the scribes interpreted the Law was not in accordance with the tenor of Scripture. Jesus argues that the tradition of the Pharisees is unduly stringent and exceeds the intention of the Law.

The relative value of an appeal to an historical argument like this has been questioned in the light of what is known of rabbinic debate.[89] It was of the essence of the scribal approach to *halakha* that any detailed rule must rest, directly or indirectly, on an actual precept promulgated in the Scriptures. An appeal to an example from history belongs to the realm of *haggadha;* it may be helpful to illumine a point of *halakha* which has been already established or to define the character of the amenities of life, but it would be without force in technical debate. These considerations are certainly true for the end of the first century, and may have been in effect much earlier. In the absence of any reference to the scribes, however, it is unwarranted to speak of "technical debate" to establish a point of *halakha.* The argument was of a popular kind designed for the Pharisees. If there was any attempt to debate in formal fashion, Mark shows no interest in preserving it for his readers. What was important to them was Jesus' attitude toward the Sabbath and the pronouncement he made upon it. The reference to David and his men was appropriate because it offered an analogy to Jesus and his disciples; but what is preserved is merely a fragment of the conversation indicating the direction in which the argument moved. Of crucial importance in the argument was the phrase "which *it is not permitted* to eat, except for the priests," for these words resume the legal terminology with which the Pharisees had couched their question.[90]

27-28 The relationship of verses 27-28 to those which immediately precede, and to the larger question of Sabbath observance, continues

---

88 E. Lohse, *TWNT* VII (1964), p. 22.

89 D. Daube, *op. cit.*, pp. 67-71. Daube points out that the argument from temple practice in Mt. 12:5 conforms to the technical demands of the situation if it was Jesus' intention to establish a point of *halakha.*

90 See above, n. 81.

to provoke discussion and conjecture.[91] The problems of the text that have encouraged conjecture arise from the MS tradition of verse 27,[92] the apparent lack of cohesion between verses 27 and 28,[93] the divergences between Mark and Matthew,[94] and the interpretation of the title "Son of Man" in verse 28.[95] These problems justify asking whether verse 27 or verse 28, or both united, existed in isolated fashion in the tradition, or whether from the beginning they were joined to the controversy recorded in Ch. 2:23-26. Moreover, the formulation of verse 27 has been understood as an expression of universalism introduced by Mark or some early glossator, but inconceivable as an authentic word of Jesus.[96]

In the face of such problems and objections it is mandatory to understand the text in its Marcan intention. With the introduction to verse 27 ("and he was saying to them") Mark indicates that the statement which follows has no direct relationship to the immediately preceding verses. This literary device recurs several times[97] and in each instance it signals that only a fragment of the conversation or teaching which took place

---

91 For a radical approach to the text see F. W. Beare, "The Sabbath was Made for Man?" *JBL* 79 (1960), pp. 130-136. A useful survey of contemporary approaches to these two verses is presented by F. Gils, "Le sabbat a été fait pour l'homme et non l'homme pour le sabbat (Mc, II, 27)," *RB* 69 (1962), pp. 506-513. His own proposal (pp. 513-523) will be discussed below.

92 Verse 27 is absent in D *a c e ff i*. These MSS read, "But I say unto you" followed by verse 28. W and sy^sin omit the latter part of verse 27 ("and not man for the sake of the Sabbath").

93 The problem arises from the initial particle ὥστε in verse 28. This particle can introduce an absolute proposition (so Bl-D-F § 391.2, pp. 197 f.), but more normally it establishes a link of consequence between two propositions. It is this more usual function of ὥστε that seems awkward since in verse 27 "man" is in view while in verse 28 "the Son of Man" is in view. For several possible exegetical approaches to this difficulty see F. Gils, *op. cit.*, pp. 509-513.

94 The Matthean parallel attests verse 28, but not verse 27. It may be under the influence of the Matthean text that verse 27 is omitted in D and the itala.

95 This is a large problem in itself and has called forth an enormous bibliography: cf. J. Coppens - L. Dequeker, *Le Fils de l'homme et les Saints du Très-Haut en Daniel VII, dans les Apocryphes et dans le Nouveau Testament* (Louvain, 1961), pp. 5-14, 54-55, 85-86. H. Tödt, *op. cit.*, pp. 121-123 is certainly correct in asserting that in Mk. 2:10 and 28 "Son of Man" is a title of the highest dignity.

96 E.g. F. W. Beare, *op. cit.*, p. 32, "the sentiment that 'the sabbath was made for man, not man for the sabbath,' and that 'man is master of the sabbath' is wholly inconceivable in any Jewish teacher, including Jesus; it sounds more like Protagoras of Abdera." Similarly, F. Gils, *op. cit.*, pp. 516-521.

97 Gr. καὶ ἔλεγεν αὐτοῖς: Chs. 2:27a; 4:2b, 11, 21, 24, 26; 6:10; 7:9; 8:21; 9:1.

has been recorded. Jesus' initial response to the Pharisees was broken off after verse 26. The pronouncement in Ch. 2:27 stands on its own as the conclusion to a larger discourse, of which only the most salient point has been preserved. The pronouncement was remembered and transmitted for its assertion that the Sabbath was instituted by God to benefit man. Its relevance to the question of verse 24 lay in the re-affirmation of the original intention of the Sabbath which the extensions of the Law in the Pharisaic tradition had obscured.[98]

There is no reason to deny the authenticity of verse 27 on the ground that it expresses a radical interpretation of the Sabbath unparalleled in Judaism and inappropriate to Jesus. There is twice recorded in the Mekilta, the Tannaitic commentary on Exodus, the dictum of Rabbi Simeon ben Menasya (*ca.* 180 A.D.) that "the Sabbath is delivered over for your sake, but you are not delivered over to the Sabbath."[99] Apart from its exegetical basis, the larger discussion in which this conclusion was reached is not recorded; like the pronouncement in Mk. 2:27, only a fragment of discourse is preserved. The Mekilta indicates that Rabbi Simeon was remembered especially because of this striking pronouncement,[100] but no more than the statement and its ground in Scripture is given. The fact that this statement is twice recorded, and that no attempt is made to deny or challenge its validity, is sufficient indication that there is nothing specifically "un-Jewish" about Jesus' pronouncement on the Sabbath. Verse 27 should be recognized, in the absence of clear evidence to the contrary, as an authentic pronouncement of Jesus expressing God's purpose in establishing the seventh day as a period of

---

98 Cf. Ch. 10:6-9, where Jesus again displays his concern to recover the original intention of a creation ordinance.

99 Mekilta, *Shabbata* I to Ex. 31:14 (ed. Lauterbach III, pp. 198, 199). R. Simeon b. Menasya is impressed by the fact that Ex. 31:14 reads "You shall keep the Sabbath, therefore; for it is holy unto you (לכם)." He reads this last term, apparently, "for your sake," and so deduces "for your sake the sabbath is delivered" and not "you are delivered for the sake of the Sabbath" (לכם שבת מסורה ואין אתם מסורין לשבת). In TB *Yoma* 85b this word is attributed to Jonathan ben Joseph, a pupil of R. Ishmael.

100 Ex. 13:14 is cited, followed by the comment, "This is the verse which R. Simeon the son of Menasya interpreted as saying: The Sabbath is given to you but you are not surrendered to the Sabbath." J. Z. Lauterbach, "Simeon ben Menasya," *JE* XI (1905), pp. 355 f. called attention to the parallel which this passage affords to Mk. 2:27; cf. also C. G. Montefiore, *The Synoptic Gospels*[2] (London, 1927) I, p. 64 and E. Lohse, *TWNT* VII (1964), pp. 15, 22 *et al.* A similar pronouncement on the Temple occurs in II Macc. 5:19.

joy and refreshment. The divine intention was in no way infringed by the plucking of heads of grain on the part of Jesus' disciples. The pronouncement of verse 27 rounds off the pericope and constitutes its key point: the Sabbath was made for man's enjoyment.[101]

On this understanding verse 28, with its reference to "the Son of Man," should be interpreted after the analogy of Ch. 2:10.[102] It represents the comment of Mark himself on the larger meaning of the total incident for the Christian Community. The function of the introductory particle[103] is not to link verse 28 narrowly to verse 27, as if the pronouncement that the Son of Man is Lord of the Sabbath is somehow being deduced from the more general principle that God instituted the Sabbath for the sake of man. Its function is rather to introduce a declaration which follows from the incident as a whole. Its significance can be expressed by translating "So then (in the light of verses 23-27) the Son of Man is Lord of the Sabbath." Reflection on Jesus' act and word, through which he established the true intention of the Sabbath and exposed the weakness of a human system of fencing the Law with restrictions, revealed his sovereign authority over the Sabbath itself. With this word Mark drives home for his readers the theological point of the pericope. These things were written that they may understand Jesus' true dignity: he is the Lord of the Sabbath.[104]

---

101 This needs to be asserted in the presence of an increasing desire to reject verse 27 altogether or to regard it as a Marcan addition to a tradition which consisted of Ch. 2:23-26, 28. To cite only recent authors, F. Gils, *op. cit.*, pp. 513-523; G. Barth, "Das Gesetzverständnis des Evangelisten Matthäus" in G. Bornkamm, G. Barth, H. Held, *Überlieferung und Auslegung im Matthäusevangelium* (Neukirchen, 1960), p. 85, n. 1; E. Schweizer, "Der Menschensohn," *ZNW* 50 (1959), p. 199, n. 47a.

102 See above, pp. 96-98. The Gospel of Truth 32:22-25 offers an interesting parallel to the Marcan device of providing a word to the Christian reader. After an allusion to Mt. 12:11 ff. the text continues "that you may understand at heart what the Sabbath is–viz., that in which it is not appropriate that salvation be idle."

103 Gr. ὥστε, on which see n. 93. Ὥστε designates the conclusion which Mark draws from the act and word of Jesus.

104 Strangely enough M. J. Lagrange, *op. cit.*, pp. 55 f. argued that verse 28 was not originally found in Mark's Gospel; it was early introduced under the pressure of Mt. 12:8. Among those holding that verse 28 is a reflection of the Community, or better, of Mark himself, are E. Lohmeyer, *op. cit.*, p. 66; E. Lohse, *TWNT* VII (1964), pp. 22 f. and n. 178; *idem,* "Jesu Worte über den Sabbat," *BZNW* 26 (1960), pp. 82 f.; G. Iber, *Überlieferungsgeschichtliche Untersuchung zum Begriff des Menschensohns im Neuen Testament* (Heidelberg, 1955), p. 71. Iber argues that verse 28 furnishes the ultimate response to the question posed in verse 24.

CHAPTER 3

(f) The Decision that Jesus Must Be Destroyed. Ch. 3:1-6

1 And he entered again into the synagogue; and there was a man there who had his hand withered.[1]
2 And they watched him, whether he would heal him on the sabbath day; that they might accuse him.
3 And he saith unto the man that had his hand withered, Stand forth.[2]
4 And he saith unto them, Is it lawful on the sabbath day to do good, or to do harm? to save a life, or to kill? But they held their peace.
5 And when he had looked round about on them with anger, being grieved at the hardening of their heart, he saith unto the man, Stretch forth thy hand. And he stretched it forth; and his hand was restored.
6 And the Pharisees went out, and straightway with the Herodians took counsel[3] against him, how they might destroy him.

The healing of the man with the withered hand forms the last of this first series of five conflict narratives. It takes its place at this point naturally by topical association with the previous incident and demonstrates that Jesus is the Lord of the Sabbath. The high point of the incident lies less in the act of healing than in the conflict between Jesus and his adversaries, in which they are left silent before his sovereign word.[4] It is striking that Jesus takes the initiative in asking what is permitted on the Sabbath, and that his adversaries are silent before his question. This pattern recurs in the series of controversies which took place in Jerusalem: in Ch. 12:34 Mark notes that no one dared question Jesus further, while in Ch. 12:35 Jesus himself seizes the initiative in the concluding conflict narrative. This parallel in structural arrangement is undoubtedly due to the evangelist. It is Mark's way of indicating that Ch. 3:6, reporting the conspiracy of the Pharisees and the Herodians,

---

1 Gr. ἐξηραμμένην from ξηραίνειν meaning "to make dry, harden, cause to wither," and in the passive, "withered." The description is medically imprecise. Cf. J. Preuss, *Biblisch-talmudische Medizin* (Berlin, 1911), pp. 351-354.

2 ASVmg "Arise into the midst"; RSV "Come here."

3 The OT background to this expression is treated technically by P. Haupt, "The Hebrew Noun *Melkh,* Counsel," *JBL* 34 (1915), pp. 54-70.

4 Cf. E. Lohse, "Jesu Worte über den Sabbat" in *Judentum, Urchristentum, Kirche, BZNW* 26 (ed. W. Eltester. Berlin, 1960), p. 84. On pp. 83-85 Lohse insists that this account reflects an authentic incident in the ministry of Jesus.

points forward to the Passion narrative. The decision to seek Jesus' death is not the result of a single incident; it is the response to an accumulation of incidents. It is therefore appropriate to see in Ch. 3:6 the conclusion to the whole section on conflict in Galilee (Ch. 2:1-3:6).[5]

1-2 Mark gives nothing more than the unadorned fact that Jesus was again in the synagogue on a Sabbath. It is natural to think of Capernaum[6] since the evangelist appears to situate the first two encounters with opposition there (Ch. 2:1-17), but the incident could have taken place in any Galilean town. Conflict erupted over the healing of a man with a withered hand in which the man himself was little more than a silent participant in the unfolding situation.[7]

Jesus' adversaries were convinced that he was a violator of the Sabbath.[8] Their attitude was well expressed by a synagogue-ruler who was exasperated with the people who came to Jesus for healing on the Sabbath: "There are six days on which work ought to be done; come on those days and be healed, and not on the Sabbath day."[9] Like other aspects of Jewish life, the practice of medicine and healing on the Sabbath was regulated by legal tradition. It was an accepted principle that "any danger to life takes precedence over the Sabbath." The scribes, however, had determined precisely in which cases it was proper to speak of immediate danger to life, and to what extent aid could be granted.[10] In none of the recorded healings which Jesus performed on the Sabbath would the scribes have agreed that there was any immediate threat to life. The presence in the synagogue of opponents who were scrutinizing

---

5 *Ibid.*, p. 84, n. 19.

6 G. Dalman, *Orte und Wege Jesu*³ (Leipzig, 1924), pp. 162 f.

7 Jerome, *Comm. in Matth.* 12:13, reports that according to the Gospel used by the Nazarenes and Ebionites the man approached Jesus with the words: "I was a mason, who earned his bread with his hands. I beg you, Jesus, to restore to me my health, so that I need not beg for food in shameful fashion." This statement is discussed by W. Bauer, *Das Leben Jesu im Zeitalter der neutestamentlichen Apokryphen* (Tübingen, 1909), p. 367. The colorlessness and restraint of the Marcan tradition contrasts sharply with the apocryphal embellishment.

8 Ex. 31:14-17 provides that the violator of the Sabbath shall be killed, while M. *Sanhedrin* VII. 4 specifies death by stoning.

9 Lk. 13:14. For Jesus' attitude see Lk. 13:10-16; 14:1-6. In the latter narrative Jesus' question whether it is permitted to heal upon the Sabbath, together with the silence of the Pharisees who were watching him, offer a close parallel to Mk. 3:1-5.

10 H. van der Loos, *The Miracles of Jesus* (Leiden, 1965), pp. 212 f. See below, on verse 4.

Jesus' activity indicates that they were convinced of his ability to heal. They did not regard his capability as extraordinary but as a power he shared with others who did not exercise it on the Sabbath.

3-4 Jesus commanded the man with the withered hand to stand in the midst of the assembled congregation, and then posed to his adversaries a rhetorical question: "Is it permitted on the Sabbath to do good, or to do harm; to save a life or to kill?" Formulated in this way, the question demands an answer in terms of the *halakha* [11] as determined in scribal study of the Law. The tradition clearly asserted that the Law was not opposed to the saving of life on the Sabbath. [12] The Pharisees refused to debate the *halakha* with Jesus. [13] They were indignant because the healing of a paralyzed hand could wait until the next day. They understood that Jesus was not asking a theoretical question for the sake of halakhic refinement. The point at issue was "doing good" on the Sabbath now in the concrete instance of the man who stood in their midst. [14]

5 Jesus did not mistake the silence of his opponents for consent that the man should be healed. He regarded them with an anger which expressed the anger of God. [15] In their concern for legal detail they had forgotten the mercy and grace shown by God to man when he made provision for the Sabbath. [16] In the name of piety they had become

---

11 See above, pp. 115-117 and n. 81.

12 There are many points at which later Jewish halakhic discussion of this issue can be sampled: cf. Mekilta, Tractate *Shabbata I* (ed. Lauterbach III, pp. 198-205); Tractate *Nezikin* (ed. Lauterbach III, pp. 38-40); M. *Yoma* VIII. 6: "Whenever there is doubt whether life is in danger this takes precedence over the Sabbath." See further S-B*K* I (1922), pp. 623-629.

13 The silencing of his enemies suggests that Jesus overcame the powers of evil which are at work in his adversaries. See J. M. Robinson, *The Problem of History in Mark*² (London, 1962), p. 45, who calls attention to the significance of σιωπάω here and in Ch. 4:39.

14 Rightly stressed by Van der Loos, *op. cit.*, pp. 439 f. The Pharisees, presumably, would have answered that it is good to heal on the Sabbath only when an individual is dangerously ill. Cf. S-B*K* I (1922), p. 623.

15 On the anger of God see especially F. Fichtner, *TWNT* V (1954), pp. 395-410.

16 Cf. G. Stählin, *TWNT* V (1954), pp. 428 f., 443 f. On p. 429, n. 331 he calls attention to a striking parallel to the relationship between the Pharisees and Jesus in an incident between certain Romans and Caesar. Cf. E. Stauffer, "Clementia Caesaris," in *Schrift und Bekenntnis, Zeugnisse lutherischer Theologie* (Stuttgart, 1950), pp. 174-184.

insensitive both to the purposes of God and to the sufferings of men. Jesus' anger was tempered by a godly sorrow for men who could no longer rejoice in the tokens of God's goodness to men.[17] When Jesus restored the man's hand he demonstrated what it means "to do good" and "to preserve life" on the Sabbath. Moreover, he provided a sign of the true observance and joy of the Sabbath. As Lord of the Sabbath Jesus delivers both the Sabbath and man from a state of distress.

6 The decision of the Pharisees to conspire with the Herodians to destroy Jesus is indicative of the seriousness of the conflict with authority which erupted in Galilee. The Sabbath controversies reported by Mark did not originate in subordinate departures from the scribal tradition, but were symptomatic of Jesus' entire attitude toward the oral law. Jesus refused to observe the traditional rules; he moved in grace toward sick individuals and healed them without regard to the day of the week. From the Pharisaic point of view Jesus' word and action totally undermined their interpretation of the Law, their piety and their actions. Jesus was not simply another scribe who advocated an independent opinion; he constituted a threat to true religion and ancestral tradition.[18] When Jesus failed to submit to the scribal regulation of the Sabbath he broke the tradition, and authority confronted authority. It was inevitable that conflict should ensue, and that the Pharisees should seek to destroy Jesus.

In their opposition to Jesus they had the support of the Herodians, who are mentioned also in Ch. 12:13 in association with the Pharisees. Apart from one reference in Josephus,[19] the Herodians are not mentioned in any other ancient source, a fact which indicates that they were

---

[17] G. Stählin, *op. cit.*, p. 429. The preposition in the compound word συλλυπεῖσθαι intensifies its basic meaning, "being *deeply* grieved." R. Bultmann, *TWNT* IV (1942), p. 325 comments: "Since the opponents have no λύπη, it appears that συλλυπούμενος is only a very strengthened expression of grief."

[18] Cf. Van der Loos, *op. cit.*, pp. 214-215 and especially W. G. Kümmel, "Jesus und der jüdische Traditionsgedanke," *ZNW* 33 (1934), pp. 105-130. The Pharisees failed to recognize that Jesus acknowledged the Law in spite of his disregard for traditional concepts; to them disrespect for the tradition necessarily entailed disrespect for the Law. Yet "Jesus did not wish to put aside the Law; rather he wished, through his proclamation of the will of God, to exhibit the true meaning of the Law" (p. 128). On the historicity of Jesus' conflict with the Pharisees see H. Merkel, "Jesus und die Pharisäer," *NTS* 14 (1968), pp. 194-208.

[19] *War* I. xvi. 6 [319] οἱ Ἡρώδειοι; cf. *Ant.* XIV. xv. 10 [450] τοὺς τὰ Ἡρώδου φρονοῦντας.

not a sect or an organized party. The word is of Latin formation (*Herodiani*), designating "adherents" or "partisans" of Herod;[20] in Galilee this would mean Herod Antipas. Their name suggests a common attitude of allegiance to Herod in a country where large numbers of people chafed under his rule. In Josephus the term clearly denotes those who were sympathizers and supporters of the cause of Herod the Great. It is reasonable to understand Mark's term in the same light: in Ch. 3:6 and Ch. 12:13 the Herodians are, apparently, influential men of standing who loyally support Herod Antipas.[21] Their concern with tribute money in Ch. 12:13 indicates that they were also loyal to the Roman control of Palestine upon which the Herodian dynasty depended.[22] Undoubtedly they lent their support to the Pharisees because they saw Jesus as a threat to the peace and stability of the tetrarchy. The history of Herodian Galilee is marked by popular uprisings under the leadership of quasi-messianic figures, and they may have envisioned that Jesus posed this kind of peril to the land.

The decision to destroy Jesus climaxes the conflicts in Galilee. God's grace toward Israel, proclaimed and demonstrated through Jesus, will be rejected by the responsible leaders of the people.[23] Their considered intention is an ominous sign, both for Jesus and for Israel. For Jesus it means that the passion already impinges upon him. This was inevitable from the moment he decided to submit to the Father and bear the brunt of the judgment upon the people. But Jesus now feels the sting of that decision with a new reality. It was ominous for Israel because it entailed the rejection of the Bearer of salvation. Jesus answered the question of what is permitted on the Sabbath by healing the man with the withered hand. Ironically, the guardians of the Sabbath determine to do harm and to kill. The decision points forward to the Passion, but it also contains the seed of self-destruction. The rejection of Jesus entails the rejection of life and redemption and leaves men prey to distress and

---

20 H. S. von Carolsfeld, "Das lateinische Suffix *-anus*," *Archiv für lateinische Lexikographie* 1 (1884), pp. 177-194; especially pp. 183 ff.

21 There is a persistent desire to understand the Herodians as partisans of Herod Agrippa I (A.D. 41-44). See B. W. Bacon, "Pharisees and Herodians in Mark," *JBL* 39 (1920), pp. 102-112; H. G. Wood, "Interpreting This Time," *NTS* 2 (1956), p. 262; E. Lohmeyer, *Das Evangelium des Markus*[16] (Göttingen, 1963), p. 67.

22 H. H. Rowley, "The Herodians of the Gospels," *JThS* 41 (1940), pp. 14-27. For an attempt to identify the Herodians as Essenes see C. Daniel, "Les 'Hérodiens' du Nouveau Testament sont-ils des Esséniens?" *Rev Qum* 6 (1967), pp. 31-53.

23 Cf. T. A. Burkill, *Mysterious Revelation* (Ithaca, N.Y., 1963), pp. 117-139.

death. This is the bitter fruit of that hardness of heart which provoked in Jesus both anger and godly sorrow.

III. Later Phases of the Ministry in Galilee. Ch. 3:7-6:13

The clear note of rejection sounded in Ch. 3:6 terminates Mark's treatment of the initial phase of the Galilean ministry. The summary statement in Ch. 3:7-12 introduces a new division which is climaxed by the sending forth of the Twelve (Ch. 6:7-13). [24] An advanced stage in Jesus' ministry is indicated by the presence of scribes from Jerusalem in Galilee. The disturbance created by Jesus has by this time reached the ears of the Jerusalem authorities, who have dispatched their representatives to investigate the reports received. A developing situation is also implied by the election of the Twelve and their preparation for mission. Within this second larger unit Mark has placed the parables of the kingdom, which illustrate Jesus' teaching in the context of unbelief (Ch. 4:1-34), and the reports of miracles which display his power and dignity (Ch. 4:35-5:43). The motif of rejection is woven into the fabric of this material. It is voiced explicitly in the charge of insanity and collusion with Beelzebul (Ch. 3:20-30), in the firm request that Jesus leave Transjordan (Ch. 5:17), and in the offense of the townsmen of Nazareth (Ch. 6:2-6). In closing the division with the commissioning of the Twelve (Ch. 6:6b-13) Mark rounds off the unit with a report of the fulfilment of the program announced to the Twelve at the time of their election (Ch. 3:13-19). This correspondence between the beginning and conclusion of the unit indicates careful forethought by the evangelist in

---

[24] The divergence of opinion regarding the point of termination for the division is due primarily to uncertainty how best to regard the parenthetical account of the imprisonment and death of John (Ch. 6:17-29) and notice of Herod's fears with which it is introduced (Ch. 6:14-16). See E. Trocmé, *La Formation de l'Évangile selon Marc* (Paris, 1963), pp. 63-69. Trocmé himself prefers to find the first main section extending from Chs. 1:1-3:12, on the understanding that the report of the great multitudes which flock to Jesus in Ch. 3:7-12 corresponds to the report of all Judea flocking to John the Baptist in Ch. 1:4-5. The second main section extends from the choosing of the Twelve (Ch. 3:13-19) to the sending forth of the Twelve (Ch. 6:7-13). On the other hand, E. Lohmeyer, *Das Evangelium des Markus*[16] (Göttingen, 1963), pp. 70 f., designates Chs. 3:7-6:16 as the second main division. He finds the unifying factor in the arrangement of the material in terms of a geographical center, the Sea of Gennesaret.

structuring the Gospel. The fact that most of the action occurs in the vicinity of the Sea of Gennesaret gives to this division a geographical unity.

1. Withdrawal to the Sea. Ch. 3:7-12

7 And Jesus with his disciples withdrew to the sea; and a great
multitude from Galilee followed; and from Judea,
8 and from Jerusalem, and from Idumea, and beyond the Jordan,
and about Tyre and Sidon, a great multitude, hearing what
great things he did,[25] came unto him.
9 And he spake to his disciples, that a little boat should wait on
him because of the crowd, lest they should throng him:
10 for he had healed many; insomuch that as many as had
plagues[26] pressed upon him that they might touch him.
11 And the unclean spirits, whensoever they beheld him, fell
down before him, and cried, saying, Thou art the Son of God.
12 And he charged them much[27] that they should not make him
known.

The care with which Mark has structured his Gospel is evident in the corresponding manner in which the first two units are introduced. In Ch. 1:14-3:6 a summary statement of Jesus' ministry stands at the beginning of a larger division of the Gospel and is followed by the programmatic call to be fishers of men. This pattern is reproduced in Ch. 3:7-6:13. The initial summary statement (Ch. 3:7-12) corresponds to Ch. 1:14-15, while the election of the Twelve (Ch. 3:13-19) corresponds to Ch. 1:16-20 and is equally programmatic in character. The parallel is not sustained beyond the introductory sections, and the second unit reporting the later Galilean ministry is developed independently. The correspondence between Ch. 1:14-20 and Ch. 3:7-19, however, suggests that the summary statement which introduces the second unit has no

---

25 Gr. ἀκούοντες ὅσα ποιεῖ, ASVmg "all the things that he did"; RSV "all that he did".

26 Gr. μάστιγας, "scourges"; RSV "diseases." It is not necessary to see in the term, which recurs in Ch. 5:29, 34, the notion of divinely imposed affliction. In Ch. 3:10 it is the collective designation for the various sufferings which Jesus alleviated. It describes sickness and suffering, without specifying its source or origin. See C. Schneider, *TWNT* IV (1942), pp. 521-525.

27 RSV "And he strictly ordered them."

necessary connection with the material which immediately precedes.[28] It is designed to look forward, anticipating actions and motifs which are characteristic of this section. The withdrawal to the sea and the mountain, on Mark's understanding, represents a return to the wilderness where Jesus' mission began.[29]

7-10 The report of Jesus' withdrawal to the sea and the pursuit of the multitude invites comparison with Ch. 2:13. Beyond the common elements of retreat to the sea and the pursuing multitude, both statements occur at a similar point in the Marcan outline. In Ch. 2:1-12 and Ch. 3:1-5 a sick man is healed and the objections of opponents are silenced. Yet in the face of what appears to be a triumph over men hostile to his mission Jesus withdraws to the sea. The retreat to the sea is related to the return to the wilderness; in each instance it entails an affirmation of sonship and obedience.[30] That the region of the sea is the sphere of the demonic is suggested by two elements in the Marcan summary. (1) The people from the several regions are attracted to Jesus because they believe he is a miracle worker. It is because they have heard of all that Jesus had done that they follow after him. They press toward him, hoping merely to touch him and be relieved of their sufferings. In their actions they resemble the crowds who followed Apollonius of Tyana or others like him who paraded as "divine-men" in the ancient world.[31] They have no thought of an exodus into the wilderness that sonship may be affirmed, but openly seek physical healing from a man who

---

[28] Cf. C. E. B. Cranfield, *The Gospel according to St. Mark* (Cambridge, 1963), p. 124: the summary statement "looks forward, the references to the crowds and the boat, to the demon-possessed, and to the anxiety of the sick to touch Jesus anticipating iv. 1 ff., iii. 27, v. 1-20, v. 25-34, vi. 56." M. J. Lagrange, *L'Évangile selon Saint Marc*[9] (Paris, 1947), pp. 60 f. cautions that Mark may not have structured Chs. 3:7-4:1 according to a chronological order. The boat prepared in Ch. 3:9 is not used until Ch. 4:1 and during the interval Jesus has been upon the mountain where the Twelve were chosen. In a structural analysis of Ch. 3:7-35, T. A. Burkill shows that the evangelist juxtaposes the erroneous but enthusiastic opinion of the multitude to the hostility of the scribes from Jerusalem (*op. cit.*, p. 136 n. 41).

[29] Cf. U. Mauser, *Christ in the Wilderness* (Naperville, Ill., 1963), pp. 124-125, 138-140.

[30] See above on Ch. 2:13.

[31] See L. Bieler, ΘΕΙΟΣ ΑΝΗΡ. *Das Bild des "göttlichen Menschen" in Spätantike und Frühchristentum* (Wien, 1935-36), Vol. I – Hellenistic material; Vol. II – Jewish and Early Christian Material; G. Eder, *Der göttliche Wundertäter. Ein exegetischer und religionswissenschaftlicher Versuch* (Girching, 1957).

appears to be endowed with more than natural power. They do not understand Jesus or his mission. In the press of the crowd which fails to understand the character of a return to the wilderness Jesus encounters renewed temptation and the power of Satan to blind men's minds. (2) The second element is explicit. The presence of the demonic makes itself known in the cry of recognition on the part of the evil spirits. This aspect of Jesus' experience by the sea displays the contrast and irony in the situation: the demons know that Jesus is the Son of God (verse 11); the multitude think only in terms of a miracle worker to whom they turn for selfish reasons (verses 8-10).

The several regions mentioned in verses 7-8 furnish a comprehensive designation for Israel and its immediate neighbors. Galilee, Judea and Jerusalem represent Israel proper, while Idumea, [32] Transjordan and the region of the coastal cities Tyre and Sidon [33] constitute the southern, eastern and northwestern borders of the land. By twice referring to the "great multitude" (verses 7b, 8) the evangelist distinguishes between the Galileans who were native to the region and the crowds who had come from a distance. [34] The several districts enumerated are important in the general scheme of the Gospel. In the course of the narrative Jesus is active in all the places specified in Ch. 3:7f. with the exception of Idumea. His entrance into Galilee is reported in Ch. 1:14. He visits the Transjordan in Ch. 5:1, the regions of Tyre and Sidon in Ch. 7:24, 31, the territories of Judea and Transjordan in Ch. 10:1 and enters Jerusalem in Ch. 11:11. The summary statement in Ch. 3:7f. suggests that the Lord's astonishing authority awakened an active interest in his person over a wide area and that Jesus responded to this interest by

---

[32] The reference to Idumea is absent in some texts of Mark (א* W Θ *pc c* sy[s]) apparently under the influence of the parallel passage Mt. 4:25. Idumea is ancient Edom, Israel's enemy which was finally conquered and forcibly subjected to circumcision by John Hyrcanus I (134-104 B.C.). Ironically, through the family of Herod, Idumea now ruled Israel. See Josephus, *Ant.* XIII. ix. 1.

[33] A reference to the two cities, Tyre and Sidon, became virtually a formula for the northwestern portion of Palestine, e.g. Jer. 25:22; 27:3; 47:4; I Macc. 5:15; Judith 2:28.

[34] On the complicated question of text in Ch. 3:7-8 see V. Taylor, *The Gospel according to St. Mark* (London, 1952), pp. 226f. Taylor feels that the areas enumerated are intended to describe an extension of the ministry of Jesus. If the interpretation adopted above is correct, it is clear that an extension is not significant beyond confirming that the people fail to understand what is involved in a trek to the wilderness, whether they come from Jerusalem and Judea, Galilee or beyond these areas.

visiting the districts from which the multitude came. Jesus' own outreach within and beyond Palestine proper anticipates and authenticates the Church's mission to the world.[35]

Mark is the sole evangelist to report that Jesus asked his disciples to have a small boat ready in order to prevent the unruly crowds from pressing in upon him. In their eagerness to touch him they fell upon him. Nevertheless, he graciously healed a large number of persons afflicted with disease.

11-12 Among the crowd were demoniacs, unfortunate men possessed by unclean spirits whose behavior betrayed domination by a will alien to their own. The demons addressed Jesus as the divine Son of God in a futile attempt to render him harmless. These cries of recognition were designed to control him and strip him of his power, in accordance with the conception that knowledge of the precise name or quality of a person confers mastery over him.[36] In this context "Son of God" is not a messianic title,[37] but a recognition of the true status of their adversary.

Jesus did not allow them to continue their useless clamor. With sovereign authority he strictly ordered them not to make him known.[38] In this encounter authority confronted authority, and the unclean spirits were silenced.[39] At least two factors stand behind the rebuke of the

[35] L. Keck, "Mark 3:7-12 and Mark's Christology," *JBL* 84 (1965), pp. 353 f.

[36] See above on Ch. 1:23 f. Cf. O. Bauernfeind, *Die Worte der Dämonen im Markusevangelium* (Stuttgart, 1927), pp. 3 ff., 29-34, 68 f., 95-100; T. A. Burkill, *op. cit.*, pp. 62-85. W. Grundmann, *TWNT* III (1938), p. 901 describes the demonic cries as "magic adjuration formulas."

[37] According to Codex C, the cry of the demons in verse 11 is "You are the Messiah"; in verse 12 the reason given for Jesus' rebuke is "because they knew that he was the Messiah." This interpretative understanding has received modern support; cf. Burkill, *op. cit.*, pp. 18 n. 13, 284 f., 296.

[38] See above on Ch. 1:25. In the LXX ἐπιτιμᾶν translates the Hebrew root גער, which denotes the divine word of rebuke (e.g. II Sam. 22:16; Job 26:11; Ps. 80:16; 104:7; 106:9; Zech. 3:2). In Mark 1:25; 3:12; 4:39; 8:30, 33 the verb appears to signify divine authority. So H. C. Kee, "The Terminology of Mark's Exorcism Stories," *NTS* 14 (1968), pp. 232-246.

[39] Cf. J. Bieneck, *Sohn Gottes als Christusbezeichnung der Synoptiker* (Zürich, 1951), pp. 46-48. In connection with the secrecy phenomena and the demons Bieneck uses the term *Sohnesgeheimnis* ("Son [of God] secret") rather than Wrede's more familiar term, *Messiasgeheimnis* ("messianic secret"). W. Egger, "Die Verborgenheit Jesu in Mk 3, 7-12," *Biblica* 50 (1969), pp. 466-490 finds in Ch. 3:7-12 a picture of the suffering Son of God, and makes the important point that the dignity of the Son of God can be proclaimed and appreciated only within the framework of the cross. That is why Jesus silences the cries of the demons.

demonic cry. (1) Jesus *is* the Son of God, the Bearer of the Holy Spirit, and between the Holy Spirit and the unclean spirits there exists a categorical antithesis that the demons must recognize. The confession which Jesus wished to elicit was not one which a demonic personality could provide. (2) More important, the disclosure of Jesus' divine Sonship by the unclean spirits violated the character of his self-revelation, in which there were elements of restraint and veiledness as well as disclosure.[40]

Before Jesus' sovereign word of rebuke the demons were helpless; no formula of adjuration could strip him of his power. Nevertheless, the presence of the demons and their attempts to disarm Jesus confirm that the withdrawal to the sea provokes a confrontation with Satan. It is like a return to the wilderness where Jesus was tempted by the adversary of God. In the encounter with the demonic, Jesus affirms his Sonship and the decision to submit to the judgment of God.

2. The Choice of the Twelve. Ch. 3:13-19a

13 And he goeth up into the mountain, and calleth unto him whom he himself would; and they went unto him.
14 And he appointed twelve,[41] that they might be with him, and that he might send them forth to preach,[42]
15 and to have authority to cast out demons:
16 and Simon he surnamed Peter;
17 and James[43] the *son* of Zebedee, and John the brother of James; and them he surnamed Boanerges, which is, Sons of thunder;
18 and Andrew and Philip, and Bartholomew and Matthew, and Thomas, and James the *son* of Alphaeus, and Thaddaeus, and Simon the Cananaean,[44]
19 and Judas Iscariot, who also betrayed him.

---

40 See especially N. B. Stonehouse, *The Witness of Matthew and Mark to Christ* (Philadelphia, 1944), pp. 50-85.

41 Under the influence of Lk. 6:13 B ℵ C* Δ Θ (W) φ sa bo sy^{hmg} aeth geo^{1} add "whom also he named apostles." The text of the ASV is supported by C^{c} 𝔎 A D L λ *pl* latt sy$^{sin\ p\ h}$ geo^{2} arm. Mark uses the term "apostles" only in Ch. 6:30. See R. P. Meye, *Jesus and the Twelve* (Grand Rapids, 1968), pp. 189 f.

42 D W latt complete the formula, "to preach [the gospel, and he gave to them] authority to cast out demons . . ."

43 ASV^{mg} "Jacob," the Semitic name for James.

44 ASV^{mg} "Zealot," on which see below.

13-15 Jesus left the crowds which had pursued him to ascend "the mountain" where he appointed twelve men to be his disciples.[45] The evangelist shows no interest in the identification of the site; it is the withdrawal to the mountain which is itself significant for the interpretation of the narrative.[46] The mountain as a locus of revelation and redemptive action is familiar from the OT and is the essential background to the evangelist's understanding of significant moments in the mission and self-revelation of Jesus.[47] The appointment of the Twelve marks the formation of the messianic fellowship and anticipates the extension of Jesus' mission through them (Ch. 6:7-13).

The account appears to focus solely upon Jesus and the Twelve. While it is possible to think of a larger company of disciples from whom Jesus appointed twelve to remain with him, there is in the record no necessary thought of a selection of some from among others. It seems preferable to hold that only twelve disciples were involved from the beginning. The call of Jesus simply denotes a summons, as elsewhere in the Marcan narrative. In the synthetic parallelism of verses 13 and 14, the notice that Jesus summoned those whom he desired is itself a statement of election. The additional statement that "he appointed twelve" expresses officially the reality described as a summons and prepares for the qualifications which follow.[48] After this initial reference Mark's distinctive formulation for disciples of Jesus is "the Twelve."[49]

---

[45] Mark's phrase is unusual, ἐποίησεν δώδεκα, literally "he made" or "he created twelve." J. Schniewind, *Das Evangelium nach Markus*[7/8] (Göttingen, 1958), p. 65 takes this to mean that Jesus *creates* the new people of the twelve tribes. The verb, however, may have the meaning "appoint" as in I Sam. 12:6; I Kings 12:31; 13:33; II Chron. 2:18 LXX. Cf. Mk. 1:17, καὶ ποιήσω ὑμᾶς γενέσθαι ἁλεεῖς ἀνθρώπων, "and I *will appoint* you to become fishers of men." See R. P. Meye, *op. cit.*, pp. 106-108.

[46] Cf. Mauser, *op. cit.*, pp. 108-119 and W. Schmauch, *Orte der Offenbarung und der Offenbarungsort im Neuen Testament* (Göttingen, 1956), pp. 69-76 for the wilderness associations which cling to "the mountain."

[47] E.g. Chs. 6:46; 9:12; 13:3. On the significance of the mountain in the OT and in Mark see further W. Foerster, *TWNT* V (1954), pp. 479-485.

[48] G. Klein, *Die zwölf Apostel* (Göttingen, 1961), p. 203; R. P. Meye, *op. cit.*, pp. 146-148. Meye comments: "'Desired,' 'summoned' and 'appointed' are all terms that focus solely upon Jesus and the Twelve" (p. 147). His central thesis is that the Marcan concept of discipleship was limited to the Twelve.

[49] Mark refers to "the Twelve" (without the addition, "apostles") ten times: Chs. 3:14; 4:10; 6:7; 9:35; 10:32; 11:11; 14:10, 17, 20, 43. This designation occurs only six times each in Matthew and Luke, apparently in dependence upon Mark, four times in John, once in Acts and once in the Pauline corpus. For the significance of "the Twelve" to Mark see especially R. P. Meye, *op. cit.*, pp. 88-191.

The number twelve has a clear redemptive-historical significance.[50] The Twelve represent in a new form the people of the twelve tribes, Israel. Through the choice of twelve disciples Jesus made visible his claim upon the whole people in their several divisions. The Twelve reflect backward on the prior history of the people of God as the people of the twelve tribes. In proleptic fashion they represent the final form of the messianic community, the eschatological creation of God. In the calling of the Twelve Jesus orders his work and theirs in accordance with the structure of redemptive history and its goal, the creation of the community of God.[51]

Jesus chose these twelve men for the specific purpose that they might be with him and that he might extend his mission through them. The promise of a future ministry is fulfilled initially in the mission of the Twelve to the Galilean villages (Ch. 6:7-13), but finds its wider significance in the apostolic mission after the resurrection.[52] These two phases of mission were made possible through Jesus' free choice of these men and his preparation of them for their task. Their relationship to Jesus explains their existence and their authority.[53] Within the limits imposed by his structure, Mark devotes primary attention to the presence of the disciples with Jesus and their preparation for mission. Jesus' private instruction of the disciples is particularly prominent in the second half of the Gospel, but this facet of the mutual relationship between Jesus and the Twelve begins almost at once.[54] *Being with Jesus* qualified the Twelve to bear witness to him and to participate in his distinctive ministry of proclamation and the overthrow of demonic power. The promise given to the Twelve is that they will share in the power of the Kingdom of God which breaks through to men with the coming of Jesus.

On the historicity of the Marcan account of the appointment of the Twelve see K. Rengstorf, *TWNT* II (Eng. Tr. 1964), pp. 325-328; R. P. Meye, *op. cit.*, pp. 192-209.

50 This fact is obscured in the Talmudic statement that Jesus had *five* disciples: "Our rabbis taught (in a Baraitha): Yeshu had five disciples, Mattai, Nakkai, Netzer, Buni and Todah," TB *Sanhedrin* 43a (Baraitha). On this passage see M. Goldstein, *Jesus in the Jewish Tradition* (New York, 1950), pp. 31 f.

51 K. Rengstorf, *TWNT* II (Eng. Tr. 1964), pp. 322-328; H. Ridderbos, *The Coming of the Kingdom* (Philadelphia, 1962), pp. 198-200, 209.

52 Cf. I Cor. 15:5, where "the Twelve" are specifically mentioned as witnesses to the resurrection.

53 K. Rengstorf, *TWNT* II (Eng. Tr. 1964), p. 326.

54 Note Chs. 4:10-20, 33; 6:30; 7:17-23.

16-19a The traditional character of the list of the Twelve which Mark has adopted at this point is indicated by its awkward introduction ("and he surnamed Simon Peter"), by the presence of unexplained descriptive names ("Peter," "Boanerges"), and by the identification of Judas Iscariot as the betrayer of Jesus. The absence of an explicit reference to Levi is striking because Mark reported his call to discipleship in Ch. 2:14. Lists of the Twelve circulated independently in the churches and show slight variations in the manuscript tradition. [55] The Marcan list, unfortunately, raises some questions to which satisfactory answers cannot now be given.

The list is headed by Simon whose call to discipleship occurred early in the Galilean ministry (Ch. 1:16). Because he is designated by his Semitic name in subsequent mention (Ch. 1:29 f., 36), there is no clear Marcan context for interpreting the statement that Jesus surnamed him Peter. [56] The new name is the Greek equivalent of the Aramaic *Cephas,* which signifies "a stone" or "a rock." In this context it is not a proper name. Like "Boanerges," it may describe some quality or trait which Jesus recognized in Simon. In the OT and later Jewish literature, however, the giving of a surname frequently conferred a promise or designated appointment to a special task. [57] It is probable that the surname "Peter" conveys a promise which sets Simon apart as spokesman and representative of the Twelve during Jesus' ministry and as leader of the early church during its formative stage. Through his confession that Jesus is the Messiah (Ch. 8:29) and his proclamation in Jerusalem, Caesarea and elsewhere, Simon would become a foundation rock on which Jesus would build his Church. [58]

The introduction of the two sons of Zebedee next is appropriate to the importance which they assume in the subsequent narrative, where Peter, James and John constitute a privileged group within the Twelve. [59]

---

[55] For a convenient table setting forth several lists of the Twelve see *The Beginnings of Christianity, Part I,* ed. F. J. Foakes-Jackson and K. Lake, V (New York, 1933), p. 41. The variations consist primarily in the order of the names, although there are certain alterations in name also, e.g. Codex D and the itala read "Lebbaios" rather than "Thaddeus" in Mk. 3:18.

[56] With Mk. 3:16, which seems to imply that Simon received the name Peter at the time of the election of the Twelve, compare Mt. 16:17-19 and John 1:42. See further, O. Cullmann, *TWNT* VI (1959), pp. 100-109.

[57] O. Cullmann, *TWNT* VI (1959), pp. 102 f.; H. Bietenhard, *TWNT* V (1954), pp. 252 f.

[58] See further O. Cullmann, *Peter, Disciple, Apostle, Martyr*[2] (London, 1962).

[59] Cf. Chs. 5:37; 9:2; 13:3 (where Andrew is also mentioned); 14:33.

They are given the surname "Boanerges," which is interpreted to mean "sons of thunder." [60] Although no preparation for this characterization has been given by the evangelist, it is appropriate to the fiery outbursts which are attributed to the two brothers at later points in the narrative. [61]

Although Simon and Andrew were pressed into service together (Ch. 1:16), both here and in Ch. 13:3 Andrew is listed after James and John. He ranks high in the list as one who had followed Jesus from the beginning of the Galilean ministry.

The names which follow, with the exception of Judas, do not recur in the Marcan narrative and the men who bear them remain shadowy figures. "Philip" is an old Macedonian name, but Hebraized forms of this name occur in the Talmud. [62] "Bartholomew" is not a proper name but a patronymic meaning "Son of Talmai." [63] Presumably this disciple had a personal name as well. "Matthew" is a common Semitic name. It is probable that this man is identical with Levi whose call to discipleship was reported in Ch. 2:14, but Mark makes no attempt to underscore this fact. [64] "Thomas" is an Aramaic name meaning "twin." [65] "James the son of Alphaeus" is unknown apart from the apostolic lists. [66] If he is the brother of Levi, who is designated "the son of Alphaeus" in Ch.

---

60 Presumably the word should be divided Βοανη-ργες, i.e. בְּנֵי רֶגֶשׁ, but this is by no means certain. רגשׁ does not mean "thunder" in known Hebrew or Aramaic texts. A related word in Arabic, however, has this meaning and it is possible that the expression existed in the popular idiom of Jesus' day. For different proposals see C. C. Torrey, *The Four Gospels* (New York, 1933), p. 298; J. A. Montgomery, "Brief Communications," *JBL* 56 (1937), pp. 51 f.; A-G, p. 143.

61 See below on Chs. 9:38; 10:35-39; and cf. Lk. 9:54.

62 TJ *Ta'anith* IV, 68b top; *Megillah* IV 75a bottom; cf. *Yalquṭ* to Kings § 208. See M. Jastrow, *DTTML* II (1950), p. 1182.

63 Talmai is a biblical name, occurring in II Sam. 3:3; 13:37. Lagrange, *op. cit.*, p. 66 suggests that the proper name of the Son of Talmai was Nathanael, who is associated with Philip in Jn. 1:45. Nathanael is listed among the apostolic company in Jn. 21:2.

64 See above on Ch. 2:14. The identification is explicit in Mt. 10:3 and in the Caesarean text (Θ φ *pc*) of Mk. 3:18 where Matthew is designated "the tax collector."

65 Cf. Jn. 11:16; 20:24; 21:2: "who is called Twin." The plural form occurs in Targum Onkelos to Gen. 25:24. H. B. Swete, *The Gospel according to St. Mark*[2] (London, 1905), p. 61 has shown that the Syriac Church preserved a tradition that Thomas' proper name was Judas. See the Syriac Acts of Thomas 1:1 and Jn. 14:22 ("Judas, not Iscariot") where Sy[cur] reads "Judas Thomas" and sy[s] reads "Thomas."

66 Cf. F. Maier, "Zum Apostolizität des Jakobs und Judas," *BZ* 4 (1906), pp. 164-191; 255-266; K. Stendahl, "Alphäus," *RGG*[3] I (1957), p. 247 and the bibliography cited there.

2:14, there were three pairs of brothers among the Twelve. "Thaddeus'" standing among the Twelve is confirmed by both canonical and non-canonical sources, [67] but in Luke-Acts his place is taken by "Judas, the son of James." [68] It is possible that Judas is correct but that Thaddeus was this disciple's preferred name.

In contrast to these relatively colorless names the last two are of special interest. "Cananaean" is a transliteration of the Hebrew term *qannā'* signifying "jealous" or "zealous"; it is properly translated by the term "Zealot." The designation marks Simon as one who was jealous for the honor of God. He may have sought to pattern his life after the patriarch Phinehas whose indignation at Israelite idolatry turned aside God's wrath from Israel: "he was jealous with my jealousy among them . . . and made atonement for the people of God" (Num. 25:10-13). Phinehas' zeal for God had been honored in Scripture (Ps. 106:30 f.) and invited emulation. In Jesus' words and actions Simon found a zeal for the glory of God which exceeded his own. [69]

While Simon was remembered for his zeal for God a different distinction belonged to Judas, whose surname "Iscariot" identifies him as "the man from [the village of] Karioth." [70] The stigma of betrayal of the Lord is attached to his name. This notice presumes some knowledge of the passion narrative in which Judas plays a brief but significant part. [71] The preservation of the detail that one of the Twelve was the agent through whom Jesus was betrayed to his adversaries demonstrates the integrity of the early Christian tradition.

The importance of Ch. 3:13-19a in the total Marcan outline needs to be emphasized. The appointment of the Twelve provides the indispensable link between the program announced in Ch. 1:16f. and its proleptic fulfilment in Ch. 6:7-13. Beyond this, it clearly anticipates

---

[67] Mt. 10:3; Gospel of the Ebionites (*apud* Epiphanius, *Panarion haer.* XXX. xiii. 2-3).

[68] See Lk. 6:15; Acts 1:13. In Mk. 3:18 Codex D it read Λεββαῖον, a variant form of Levi. D 122 *k* Or have this reading in Mt. 10:3 also.

[69] When Jesus drove the money-changers from the Temple the disciples remembered the word "Zeal for thy house consumes me" (Ps. 69:9; Jn. 2:17), an association which may have first attracted Simon to Jesus. On Phinehas see W. R. Farmer, "The Patriarch Phinehas," *AThR* 34 (1952), pp. 26-30. To the references cited there add IV Macc. 18:12, where Phinehas is designated "the Zealot."

[70] M. Smith, *Tannaitic Parallels to the Gospels* (Philadelphia, 1951), pp. 1-2. This judgment is supported by the *v. l.* ἀπὸ Καρυώτου in Jn. 6:71 א* Θ φ; 12:4 D; 13:2 D; 14:22 D.

[71] See below on Ch. 14:10 f., 43-45.

the extension of Jesus' ministry through the apostles after their meeting with the Risen Lord promised in Ch. 14:28 and Ch. 16:7. In the narrative subsequent to Ch. 3:13-19 it is either the Twelve or a group within the Twelve who are visible and dominant. Mark assigns a central place to the Twelve as those in whom discipleship was concentrated. While the evangelist may have known of others who were also disciples of Jesus, this acquaintance has left almost no imprint upon the record. In the Gospel of Mark the disciples of Jesus are, apparently, "the Twelve."

3. The Character of Jesus' Family. Ch. 3:19b-35

Mark frequently inserts an event or narrative between two phases of some action of Jesus.[72] This literary device is effective for indicating a lapse of time, for dramatically heightening the tension, or for drawing attention to a significant parallel or contrast. The first instance of intercalation occurs in this section: the narrative dealing with Jesus' family (Ch. 3:20 f., 31-35) is divided by the account of the Beelzebul controversy (Ch. 3:22-30). The insertion of the incident involving the scribes from Jerusalem between the earlier and later phases of the family narrative is deliberate. It suggests that those in Jesus' family who declare that he is mad (Ch. 3:21) are not unlike the scribes who attribute his extraordinary powers to an alliance with Beelzebul, the prince of the demons (Ch. 3:22). The parallel is sharply emphasized by Mark's formulation of the charges against Jesus in verses 21 and 30:

verse 21 "for they [his family] said, He is beside himself."
verse 30 "for they [the scribes] said, He has an unclean spirit."

The charges are distinct, but parallel in their design to prevent Jesus from continuing his work. (Cf. Jn. 10:20, "many of them said, He has a demon, and he is mad; why listen to him?")

Against this common background of blindness and hostility Mark introduces the true family of Jesus. They are those who gather about Jesus and who perform the will of God (Ch. 3:33-35). In dramatic contrast, the mother and brothers of Jesus stand outside (Ch. 3:31),

---

[72] See below on Chs. 5:21-43; 6:7-30; 11:12-25; 14:1-11 and cf. Burkill, *op. cit.*, p. 121 n. 10.

while those who constitute the messianic family are seated within the house (Ch. 3:32, 34). This setting provides the occasion for the radical pronouncement of Jesus on the true family, in which the demands of the Kingdom of God are implied.

(a) The Charge that Jesus is Deranged. Ch. 3:19b-21

19b And he cometh into a house.[73]
20 And the multitude cometh together again, so that they could not so much as eat bread.[74]
21 And when his friends[75] heard it, they went out to lay hold on him: for they said, He is beside himself.

19b-21 Mark is the sole evangelist to report this incident of gross misjudgment. The alterations to verse 21 in the manuscript tradition indicate that in some quarters of the Church it was considered inconceivable that anyone should regard Jesus as insane.[76]

---

[73] RSV "Then he went home."

[74] "To eat bread" is a Semitic expression for taking food of any kind. Cf. J. Behm, *TWNT* I (Eng. Tr. 1964), p. 477; A-G, p. 110 and the references cited there.

[75] Gr. οἱ παρ' αὐτοῦ. Because the expression is clearly colloquial it is difficult to be certain of its exact nuance. The translation "his friends" or "associates" is adopted by the AV, ASV, RSV, and is supported by C. F. D. Moule, *An Idiom-Book of New Testament Greek* (Cambridge, 1953), p. 52. Moule argues that a less direct association than family may be inferred from a comparison of the prepositions παρά and ὑπό. The latter preposition expresses a more intimate relation, so that παρά would possibly mean a group of disciples or friends. Papyri support for the rendering "friends," "neighbors," "associates" is not lacking (see M-M, p. 479, col. 1, par. 1). On the other hand Mark's colloquial phrase for the disciples is οἱ περὶ αὐτόν (Ch. 4:10), while the context would seem to demand that the family of Jesus is in view. The translation "his family" is adopted by Moffatt, J. B. Phillips, NEB and is supported by the lexicographers M-M [p. 479, col. 1, par. 2; cf. J. H. Moulton, "Mark 3:21," *ExT* 20 (1909), p. 476] and W. Bauer (A-G, p. 61), who are able to muster abundant papyri support for the idiom. Thus in Papyrus Grenfell II. 36, 9 (*ca.* 95 B.C.) οἱ παρ' ἡμῶν πάντες means "all our family." For an extensive bibliography see A-G, p. 61 s.v. παρά I. 4. B. β.

[76] Codex D W it read "when the scribes and the rest heard concerning them," thus removing all possible reference to Jesus' family. The reason for seizing Jesus in D it is that "he escaped from them" (ἐξέσταται αὐτούς). Similarly in Codex W and 28 all reference to insanity is removed: "Because they said that they were adherents of his" or "dependent on him" (ἐξήρτηνται αὐτοῦ).

The home to which Jesus returned may have been the one owned by Simon and Andrew in Capernaum.[77] The presence of an enthusiastic multitude clamoring for attention evokes the description of Ch. 1:29-37 and Ch. 2:1-2. The absence of leisure in which to eat is mentioned again in Ch. 6:31, following the return of the disciples from their mission, and it may have been a frequent occurrence. When the report reached Jesus' family that he failed to care properly for his needs they came (presumably from Nazareth) to seize him and forcibly bring him home. The identity of those who came has been debated because Mark's colloquial expression could be translated "his family," "his relatives" or "his friends." It is natural, however, to find in Ch. 3:31-35 the proper sequel to Ch. 3:20 f.; the group of people described colloquially in verse 21 is further defined by verse 31 as including Jesus' mother and his brothers.[78]

The charge leveled against Jesus is that "he has lost his mind."[79] The Marcan term describes one who is ecstatic in the sense of psychic derangement. Reflection on Jesus' eschatological sense of mission, his urgent drive to minister, his failure properly to eat and sleep undoubtedly led the family to their conviction, but it reveals both misunderstanding and unbelief.[80] The entire incident calls to mind passages in which the man of God is despised by family and contemporaries who mistake his zeal for God as "madness."[81]

It is unnecessary to suppose that Mary also suspected that Jesus had lost his grasp upon reality. Her presence with Jesus' brothers in Ch. 3:31, however, indicates that her faith was insufficient to resist the determination of her sons to restrain Jesus and bring him home.

---

77 M. J. Lagrange, *op. cit.*, p. 69.

78 So also H. Riesenfeld, *TWNT* V (1954), p. 727.

79 The term is clarified by Paul's (ironical) use of the contrast "if we were out of our senses . . . if we were in our right mind" (II Cor. 5:13). See the references cited by A. Oepke, *TWNT* II (Eng. Tr. 1964), p. 459.

80 A. Oepke, *TWNT* II (Eng. Tr. 1964), pp. 456 f. The unbelief of Jesus' brothers is noted in Jn. 7:3-10.

81 Cf. Zech. 13:3-6, and esp. Wisd. Sol. 5:1-5: "Then will the righteous man stand with great confidence in the presence of those who have afflicted him, and those who make light of his labors... They will speak to one another in repentance, and in anguish of spirit they will groan, and say, 'This is the man whom we once held in derision and made a byword of reproach–we fools! We thought that his life was madness and that his end was without honor. Why has he been numbered among the sons of God?'"

(b) The Charge that Jesus is Possessed. Ch. 3:22-30

22 And the scribes that came down from Jerusalem said, He hath Beelzebub,[82] and, By the prince of the demons casteth he out demons.
23 And he called them unto him, and said unto them in parables, How can Satan cast out Satan?
24 And if a kingdom be divided against itself, that kingdom cannot stand.
25 And if a house be divided against itself, that house will not be able to stand.
26 And if Satan hath risen up against himself, and is divided, he cannot stand, but hath an end.[83]
27 But no one can enter into the house of the strong *man,* and spoil his goods, except he first bind the strong *man;* and then he will spoil his house.
28 Verily I say unto you, All their sins shall be forgiven unto the sons of men, and their blasphemies wherewith soever they shall blaspheme:[84]
29 but whosoever shall blaspheme against the Holy Spirit hath never forgiveness, but is guilty of an eternal sin:
30 because they said, He hath an unclean spirit.

This section follows naturally in the Marcan sequence through topical association – the listing of charges against Jesus. The conviction that he

---

[82] RSV "he is possessed by Beelzebul," which better prepares for verse 30 "for they had said, 'He has an unclean spirit'."

It seems best to adopt the reading Βεελζεβουλ, supported in Mark by ℵ C 𝔎 D W Θ λ *pl,* and to explain the reading of B (Βεεζεβουλ) by the fact that consonants are sometimes dropped in MS transmission, or due to the strangeness of λζ in Greek. The more familiar "Beelzebub," supported by the Latin and Syriac tradition, is due to assimilation to II Kings 1:2 ("Go, inquire of Baal-zebub, the god of Ekron ..."). W. E. M. Aitken, "Beelzebul," *JBL* 31 (1912), pp. 34-53 has brought together numerous texts which indicate that זבול means heaven or temple, and that the term was also a name for a foreign deity. The full term means "lord of heaven," a cacophemistic reference to Baalshamaim. By the time this term was applied to the prince of the demons its original meaning may have been forgotten, and what had originated as a descriptive term became a proper name. See further W. Foerster, *TWNT* I (Eng. Tr. 1964), pp. 605 f.; A-G, p. 138; H. van der Loos, *op. cit.,* pp. 407 f.; L. Gaston, "Beelzebul," *Theol Zeit* 18 (1962), pp. 247-255, where other explanations are discussed.

[83] RSV "but is coming to an end."

[84] RSV "and whatever blasphemies which they utter."

is deranged (verse 21) finds a more serious echo in the repeated accusation that he is possessed (verses 22 and 30). By framing the incident with the scribes in this way Mark announces his intention that Ch. 3:22-30 be understood as a self-contained unit.[85]

22 The arrival of a delegation of legal specialists from Jerusalem suggests that the Galilean mission of Jesus had attracted the critical attention of the Sanhedrin. The scribes know that Jesus has a considerable following and that he possesses the power to expel demons. It is possible that they were official emissaries from the Great Sanhedrin who came to examine Jesus' miracles and to determine whether Capernaum should be declared a "seduced city," the prey of an apostate preacher. Such a declaration required a thorough investigation made on the spot by official envoys in order to determine the extent of the defection and to distinguish between the instigators, the apostates and the innocent.[86]

The scribes bring two separate, but related accusations against Jesus: he is demon-possessed, and he casts out demons through collusion with the prince of the demons.[87] The first accusation is repeated in the concluding statement "they were saying he was possessed by an unclean spirit" (verse 30). Jesus answers the second charge directly with the parabolic language of verses 24-27; the pronouncement of verses 28-29 implies his answer to the first. These accusations were utterly serious and bordered on blasphemy.

The name "Beelzebul" occurs in no other Jewish writing, which may indicate that it was a passing colloquialism for a demon-prince. This is suggested both by the scribal reference to "the prince of demons" and by the general reference to possession by an unclean spirit in verse 30.

---

85 RSV regards Ch. 3:28-30 as a separate paragraph.

86 E. Stauffer, *Jesus and His Story* (New York, 1960), pp. 85, 207. Stauffer appeals to Deut. 13:15; Pseudo-Philo, *Liber Antiquitatum Biblicarum* 25:3-6, 8; M. *Sanh.* X. 4. Acts 5:27-40 verifies the interest and involvement of the Sanhedrin in such matters.

87 These separate accusations are indicated by the repeated ὅτι, which introduces direct speech: "They were saying, 'He is possessed by Beelzebul' and 'He casts out demons by the prince of demons'." The first charge is echoed in John four times: Chs. 7:20; 8:48, 52; 10:20. H. van der Loos, *op. cit.*, pp. 407 f. has suggested that the second charge entails an accusation that Jesus pronounced the name of Beelzebul, perhaps softly, in the exorcism of demons. For the veiled description of Jesus as "the Son of Satan" see W. Ziffer, "Two Epithets for Jesus of Nazareth in Talmud and Midrash," *JBL* 85 (1966), pp. 356 f.

By their accusations the scribes brand Jesus' work as unlawful, and consign him to the category of a magician. The related charge of sorcery became widespread and is attested both in the Talmud and early Patristic literature. [88]

23-27 Jesus addresses himself to the charge of collusion with Beelzebul through pithy proverbial sayings which expose the fallacy in the scribal accusation: Satan is not able to cast out Satan. [89] By tacitly substituting "Satan" for "Beelzebul" Jesus brings the controversy within the perspective of his mission as a direct confrontation with Satan. His argument is cumulative in its force: If what you say is true there exists the im-

---

[88] The key Tannaitic texts are TB *Sanhedrin* 43a (Baraitha): "Yeshu of Nazareth was hanged on the day of preparation for the Passover because he practiced sorcery and led the people astray"; 107b (Baraitha): "And a master has said, 'Yeshu the Nazarene practiced magic and led Israel astray'"; cf. *Soṭah* 47a; TJ *Ḥagiga* II. 2. Early Patristic texts include Justin Martyr, *Dialogue with Trypho,* ch. 69: Jews who witnessed Jesus' mighty works claimed that what they saw was magic "and they dared to say that he was a magician and seducer of the people" (καὶ γὰρ μάγον εἶναι αὐτὸν ἐτόλμων λέγειν καὶ λαοπλάνον); cf. Chs. 17, 108, 117; Origen, *Against Celsus* I:6, "Celsus says that Christians are strong through the names and the enchantments of certain demons... He further laid it to the Savior's charge that he had been enabled to perform the fancied miraculous feats by sorcery..." (γοητεία); cf. I. 28, 68, 71; II. 9, 14, 16, 44, 48, 49, 51; III. 1; V. 51. In VIII. 9, 39 Celsus calls Jesus a demon. Tertullian, *Against Marcion* III. 6 reports that the Jews persecuted Jesus "in the capacity of a man whom they took to be a magician with miraculous signs and a rival in teaching." On these several texts see H. van der Loos, *op. cit.,* pp. 158-167.

E. Stauffer, *op. cit.,* p. 10; *idem, Jerusalem und Rom im Zeitalter Jesu Christi* (Bern, 1957), pp. 113 ff., has argued that the Tannaitic formulation, "Jesus practiced sorcery and enticed Israel to apostasy" stems from the official records of the Great Sanhedrin of the year A.D. 32. There is, however, no evidence that the Sanhedrin adduced Jesus' "sorcery" as incriminating testimony against him in its official verdict at his trial. Contrast P. Winter, *On the Trial of Jesus* (Berlin, 1961), p. 144 who comments on TB *Sanhedrin* 43a: "The charge of magic is legendary and developed during the second century among Jews who had heard from Christians something of what the Gospels report of Jesus' miracles. Not disposed to deny the veracity of the miracle stories, Jews attributed Jesus' marvellous deeds to magical arts."

[89] Mark states in Ch. 3:23 that he spoke to them ἐν παραβολαῖς, which in this context means in the language of comparison and allegory, or through proverbial speech. There is, especially in what Jesus says in Ch. 3:27, the enigmatic, elusive character that is characteristic of parabolic language. With Ch. 3:27 cf. Gospel of Thomas, Logion 35: "Jesus said, It is impossible for anyone to enter a strong man's house and take him by violence, if he has not bound his hands. Then can he rob his house."

possible circumstance that Satan is destroying his own realm. For it is self-evident that a kingdom divided against itself will fall, while a household divided against itself cannot be established.[90] If your accusation is factual, then Satan has become divided in his allegiance. This should mean that he has become powerless. *Yet this is clearly not so.*[91] Satan remains strong, and this fact exposes the fallacy of your charge.

To this point Jesus has concentrated on the second charge. With verse 27 he directs himself also to the accusation that he is demon-possessed. Satan is the strong man whose strength is evidenced in the enslavement of men through sin, possession, disease and death; the demons are his servants in this destructive work. He is like a champion who exercises his sovereignty in the sphere of death. Only one who is stronger than he can enter into his realm, bind him and plunder his goods. This Jesus has done. The expulsion of demons is nothing less than a forceful attack on the lordship of Satan. Jesus' ability to cast out demons means that one stronger than Satan has come to restrain his activity and to release the enslaved.[92] The heart of Jesus' mission is to confront Satan and to crush him on all fields, and in the fulfilment of his task he is conscious of being the agent of irresistible power.[93]

Jesus' statement raises the pressing question of the source of his power. The pronouncement on blasphemy indicates that Jesus' works are accomplished through the power of the Holy Spirit. It is as the Bearer of the Spirit that he stands as the Champion of God in the battle with Satan.[94] In the face of the claim that he is possessed by an unclean spirit Jesus affirms that he possesses the Spirit of God.

---

90 Is there a reference here to the division in Jesus' own household, which is illustrated by Ch. 3:20 f., 31-35?

91 This is the force of εἰ with the indicative of reality. See Bl-D-F § 372. 1, p. 189.

92 The description of Satan as "the strong one" (ὁ ἰσχυρός) finds its counterpart in the description of the Bearer of the Holy Spirit as "the Stronger One" (ἰσχυρότερος) in Mk. 1:8.

93 Cf. W. Grundmann, *TWNT* III (1938), pp. 404 f. Grundmann insists that in Mk. 3:27 we have an authentic word of Jesus that is decisive for determining his self-understanding. He is the Stronger One, empowered with the Holy Spirit, whose mission is sustained in the confrontation and dethroning of Satan. Grundmann sees behind this logion Isa. 53:12. It is preferable to recall Isa. 49:24 f. "Shall the prey be taken from the mighty? . . . Even the captives of the mighty shall be taken away, . . . for I will contend with him that contends with you, and I will save your children." What God promises to do, Jesus has done!

94 Cf. G. Fitzer, "Die Sünde wider den Heiligen Geist," *ThZ* 13 (1957), pp. 173 f.

28-30 On the basis of the Gospel of Luke and the Coptic Gospel of Thomas it has been argued that verses 28-29 are separate sayings which circulated in the tradition unattached to this immediate context.[95] While this is possible, it is by no means a necessary conclusion. Mark clearly intends verses 28-29 to be interpreted from within the specific context provided by verses 22-27, since verse 30 repeats the substance of verse 22. When understood from the perspective of the controversy with the scribes these verses are appropriate and intelligible. When divorced from this context and viewed generally they raise insoluble questions, well illustrated in the history of the interpretation of this passage.[96]

Verse 28 provides the first instance of the recurring formula of introduction, "Amen, I say unto you . . . "[97], which in the NT is strictly limited to the sayings of Jesus. His use of "Amen" to introduce and endorse his own words is without analogy in the whole of Jewish literature and in the remainder of the NT. According to idiomatic Jewish usage "Amen" was regularly used to affirm, approve, or appropriate the words of another person, even in those few instances where it occurs at the head of a phrase (I Kings 1:36; Jer. 11:5; 28:6; M. *Soṭah* II. 5). Jesus' practice of prefacing his words with an "Amen" to strengthen the solemn affirmation which follows introduced a completely new manner of speaking. "Amen" denotes that his words are reliable and true because he is totally committed to do and speak the will of God. As such, the Amen-formulation is not only a highly significant characteristic of Jesus' speech, but a Christological affirmation: Jesus is the true witness of God.[98]

Jesus affirms that all the sins of men[99] are open to forgiveness, with

---

[95] Luke has placed the statement about blasphemy against the Holy Spirit in a different context (Lk. 12:10); in the Gospel of Thomas, Logion 44, it is found unattached to any context.

[96] For a brief survey of the history of interpretation see G. Fitzer, *op. cit.*, pp. 161-168.

[97] The formulation is found 13 times in Mk.: Chs. 3:28; 8:12; 9:1, 41; 10:15, 29; 11:23; 12:43; 13:30; 14:9, 18, 25, 30. See J. Jeremias, "Characteristics of the *ipsissima vox Jesu,*" in *The Prayers of Jesus* (London, 1967), pp. 112-115.

[98] Cf. H. Schlier, *TWNT* I (Eng. Tr. 1964), pp. 337 f. C. E. B. Cranfield, *op. cit.*, p. 140 aptly cites Jerome's comment on the "Amen" formula: "Christ swears: we ought to believe Christ swearing. For 'Amen, amen, I say unto you' in the NT is the equivalent of 'As I live, saith the Lord' in the OT."

[99] Mark's unusual employment of the double plural οἱ υἱοὶ τῶν ἀνθρώπων, "the sons of men," has led Fitzer (*op. cit.*, pp. 172-178) to propose that the text is corrupt and should read "the Son of Man." Jesus, for the sake of argument,

one fearful exception. Blasphemy against the Holy Spirit forever removes a man beyond the sphere where forgiveness is possible. This solemn warning must be interpreted in the light of the specific situation in which it was uttered. Blasphemy is an expression of defiant hostility toward God. The scribes were thoroughly familiar with this concept under the rubric "the profanation of the Name," which generally denoted speech which defies God's power and majesty. The scribal tradition considered blasphemy no less seriously than did Jesus. "The Holy One, blessed be he, pardons everything else, but on profanation of the Name [i.e. blasphemy] he takes vengeance immediately."[100] This is the danger to which the scribes exposed themselves when they attributed to the agency of Satan the redemption brought by Jesus. The expulsion of demons was a sign of the intrusion of the Kingdom of God. Yet the scribal accusations against Jesus amount to a denial of the power and greatness of the Spirit of God. By assigning the action of God to a demonic origin the scribes betray a perversion of spirit which, in defiance of the truth, chooses to call light darkness. In this historical context, blasphemy against the Holy Spirit denotes the conscious and deliberate rejection of the saving power and grace of God released through Jesus' word and act.[101] Jesus' action in releasing men from demonic posses-

---

grants that there could be sins of which he needs forgiveness, but for him to cast out demons by demonic means would entail blasphemy of the Holy Spirit and the loss of his power. His evident ability to cast out demons shows that the charge of possession is meaningless. This proposal is fruitless. It lacks any textual support and it fails to take account either of the seriousness with which the scribes make their allegation, or of the consequences that it entails for them.

[100] Sifré on Deut. 32:38 (end). On this passage see M. Smith, *op. cit.*, pp. 48 f. The scribal tradition recognized other "unforgiveable sins"; M. *Aboth* V. 18 = Tos. *Yom Hakkippurim* V. 11 (ed. Zuckermandel, p. 191): "One who causes many to sin is not given the opportunity to repent"; Tos. *Shebuoth* III. 4 (p. 449) excludes from God's forgiveness one who gives false witness in a capital trial. For a pattern of cursing against God in the OT Exodus accounts and in the Synoptics see E. Lövestam, *Spiritus Blasphemia. Eine Studie zu Mk 3, 28 f. par* (Lund, 1968).

[101] O. E. Evans, "The Unforgivable Sin," *ExT* 68 (1957), pp. 240-244. H. Beyer, *TWNT* I (Eng. Tr. 1964), p. 624 comments on Mk. 3:28 f.; "This can hardly refer to the mere utterance of a formula in which the word 'Spirit' appears. It denotes the conscious and wicked rejection of the saving power and grace of God towards man. Only the man who sets himself against forgiveness is excluded from it." Cf. K. Rengstorf, *TWNT* I (Eng. Tr. 1964), p. 304: "This sin is committed when a man recognizes the mission of Jesus by the Holy Spirit but defies and resists and curses it. The saying shows the seriousness of the situation. It is the last time, in which the lordship of God breaks in."

sion was a revelation of the Kingdom of God which called for decision. Yet his true dignity remained veiled, and the failure of the scribes to recognize him as the Bearer of the Spirit and the Conqueror of Satan could be forgiven. The considered judgment that his power was demonic, however, betrayed a defiant resistance to the Holy Spirit. This severe warning was not addressed to laymen but to carefully trained legal specialists whose task was to interpret the biblical Law to the people. It was their responsibility to be aware of God's redemptive action. Their insensitivity to the Spirit through whom Jesus was qualified for his mission exposed them to grave peril. Their own tradition condemned their gross callousness as sharply as Jesus' word. The admonition concerning blasphemy of the Holy Spirit is not to be divorced from this historical context and applied generally. Mark emphasizes this by terminating the incident with a reference to the specific accusation that Jesus was possessed by an unclean spirit. The use of the imperfect tense of the verb in the explanatory note, "because *they were saying* that he is possessed," implies repetition and a fixed attitude of mind, the tokens of callousness which brought the scribes to the brink of unforgivable blasphemy.[102]

(c) Jesus' True Family. Ch. 3:31-35

31 And then come his mother and his brethren; and standing without, they sent unto him, calling him.
32 And a multitude was sitting about him; and they say unto him, Behold, thy mother and thy brethren[103] without seek for thee.

---

[102] Cranfield, *op. cit.,* p. 142 rightly adds a pastoral note. "It is a matter of great importance pastorally that we can say with absolute confidence to anyone who is overwhelmed by the fear that he has committed this sin, that the fact that he is so troubled is itself a sure proof that he has not committed it." A person so insensitive to the Spirit that he attributes what is of God to demonic origin will not be conscious of having committed the ultimate transgression.

[103] K. Aland, *Synopsis Quattuor Evangeliorum* (Stuttgart, 1964), p. 123 adds καὶ αἱ ἀδελφαί σου, "and thy sisters," supported by 𝔎 A D *al.* The omission of these words from 𝔖 W Θ λ φ *pm* latt sys p sa bo, he feels, is due to harmonization of the text of Mark with that of Mt. 12:47 and Lk. 8:20. The inclusion of the words prepares for the reference to sisters in Mk. 3:35, which in the ASV, RSV appears abrupt. Jesus' sisters are mentioned again in Mk. 6:3.

33 And he answered them and saith, Who is my mother and my brethren?
34 And looking round on them that sat round about him, he saith, Behold, my mother and my brethren!
35 For whosoever shall do the will of God, the same is my brother, and sister, and mother.

31-32 The insertion of Ch. 3:22-30 within the narrative of the coming of Jesus' family to restrain him (Ch. 3:20f., 31-35) suggests a parallel between the insensitivity and unbelief of the scribes and the attitude of those who should have been closest to him. This is the requisite background to Jesus' pronouncement concerning his true family. The arrival of Jesus' mother and brothers on the scene resumes the account suspended in verse 21. Jesus was seated within a house surrounded by his disciples and certain others who had pressed in to listen to his teaching (cf. verses 19b-20). When the family were unable to penetrate the crowd they sent for him and stood outside calling. From the fact that those within the house knew that it was Jesus' immediate family it is natural to think of a message passed through the crowd from one to another until it reached the Lord. It is impossible to know whether Jesus was aware of the specific purpose behind the insistent call of his family. He was undoubtedly alert to the unbelief of his brothers.[104] He also knew from the Scriptures that there were occasions when pursuance of the will of God demanded severance of family ties.[105] This was his own experience and he had no hesitancy in calling men to abandon their homes and families in radical obedience to the gospel (Ch. 10:28-30). It is, therefore, not surprising that he failed to heed the call of his family. Those who sat before him felt compelled to call his attention to the persistent outcry, for in their thinking both the Law of God and common piety demanded that he respect the request of his mother.[106]

33-35 Jesus seized upon the interruption as an occasion for teaching. The rhetorical question, "Who are my mother and my brothers?" focus-

---

104 Only Jn. 7:3-10 speaks concretely of this.

105 Cf. Ex. 32:25-29; Deut. 33:8-9, *et al.*

106 Jesus was not insensitive to the demands of the Law on this point. In Mk. 7:10 he cites both the fifth commandment, "Honor thy father and thy mother" (Ex. 20:12) and the provision, "He that speaketh evil of father or mother, let him surely die" (Ex. 21:17). More is involved in his behavior and answer than compliance with the Law or filial custom.

es attention on the deeper issue involved in an authentic relationship to him. With a look which apparently took in those who sat closest to him, Jesus announced "Behold, my mother and my brothers." It is probable that the group indicated did not embrace more than the Twelve. The larger context stresses their special position as those who are with Jesus in obedience to his summons (Ch. 3:14). Their openness to God's action in sending Jesus bound them to him with ties more intimate than those achieved through physical relationship. By following Jesus the Twelve are marked off as those who do the will of God. Jesus' statement regarding the true family, however, looks beyond the Twelve to a larger company of men and women: *"whoever* shall do the will of God is my brother, and sister, and mother." It is the performance of the will of God which is decisive in determining kinship with Jesus. In the new family which Jesus calls into being there is demanded the radical obedience to God which he demonstrated in his submission to the Father and which the disciples manifested in their response to his call. The one context which makes Jesus' word intelligible is that provided by the demands of the Kingdom of God which has drawn near in his person.[107] Because the Kingdom is breaking in upon men there is a new urgency in the demand for obedience. At the same time this demand creates a fellowship in which the common pursuance of the will of God binds a man closely to Jesus and permits him to know another as brother, sister or mother.[108]

---

107 The form of the pronouncement in the Gospel of Thomas, Logion 99, makes this context explicit: "The disciples said to him: Thy brethren and thy mother are standing outside. He said to them: Those here who do the will of my Father, they are my brethren and my mother; these are they who shall enter the Kingdom of my Father."

108 Cf. Ps. 22:22, "I will declare thy name unto my brethren; in the midst of the assembly will I praise thee," which the author of the Epistle to the Hebrews rightly applies to Jesus (Heb. 2:11-12). See further H. von Soden, *TWNT* I (Eng. Tr. 1964), p. 145.

CHAPTER 4

4. Parables Concerning the Kingdom of God. Ch. 4:1-34

Apart from the Olivet Discourse in Ch. 13:3-37, Mark's grouping of parabolic material in Ch. 4:1-34 constitutes the largest unit in his Gospel devoted entirely to the teaching of Jesus. Included are three parables of growth: the sower (Ch. 4:3-8), the growth of the seed (Ch. 4:26-29) and the mustard seed (Ch. 4:30-32). It is not Mark's intention to present an exhaustive account of Jesus' parabolic teaching, [1] but to illustrate its form and content. Each of the three reflects upon sowing, growth and harvest—elements which illumine the character of the Kingdom of God. Mark appears to have selected these parables and placed them at this point in his presentation to illustrate the character of the coming of the Kingdom of God proclaimed by Jesus. [2] They indicate that the presence of Jesus signals the release of the mysterious forces of God which must culminate in the consummation and the recognition of the majesty and sovereignty of God. The failure of men generally to appreciate what the coming of Jesus means, the plan of the scribal authorities and responsible leaders of the people to destroy him (Ch. 3:6), the accusation that he has formed an alliance with Beelzebul (Ch. 3:22), define the climate of unbelief in which Jesus moves. The parables thus reflect significantly on the contemporary situation and look beyond it to the ultimate triumph of the Kingdom of God.

The parables are one of the most characteristic elements in the teaching of Jesus as recorded in the Synoptic Gospels. In a parable truth is expressed through concrete pictures rather than in abstractions. [3] The term "parable" is complex in meaning; it serves to designate all expressions which contain a comparison, whether direct or indirect. In the LXX, with two exceptions, the Greek term used by Mark translates a

---

1 Cf. Ch. 4:2, 10, 13, 33 where Mark implies that these three parables have been selected from a larger collection.

2 Cf. H. Ridderbos, *The Coming of the Kingdom* (Philadelphia, 1962), pp. 121-129; T. A. Burkill, *Mysterious Revelation* (Ithaca, N.Y., 1963), p. 97.

3 Cf. C. H. Dodd, *The Parables of the Kingdom*² (London, 1961), p. 16: "This concrete, pictorial mode of expression is thoroughly characteristic of the sayings of Jesus . . . At its simplest the parable is a metaphor or simile drawn from nature or common life, arresting the hearer by its vividness or strangeness, and leaving the mind in sufficient doubt about its precise application to tease it into active thought."

word meaning "to be similar or like something else." Within the OT this includes such diverse forms of speech as the proverb, taunt, similitude or wisdom oracle, the story, fable or allegory as well as dark enigmatic utterances.[4] The special characteristic of the OT parable is that it assumes such an understandable narrative form that its proper meaning can be concealed from its hearers (as in the parable of Nathan, II Sam. 12:5 f.). In apocalyptic literature of the intertestamental period the form assumes importance as the vehicle for the unfolding of revelatory secrets. In rabbinic literature the Word designates the extended simile, allegory and fable as well as proverbial maxims.[5]

The richly differentiated meanings of the Hebrew term passed over into Hellenistic Judaism and early Christianity through the LXX. As a result, the broad and varied nuances observed in the OT and rabbinic literature are found in the NT as well. In Mark "parable" may designate a brief utterance connected with a comparison or image (Ch. 7:17 which clarifies Ch. 7:11), a proverbial maxim (Ch. 3:24-25) or a similitude (Ch. 4:3-9, 26-29, 30-32). It is not possible to adopt a rigid definition of "parable"; the term can refer to figurative forms of speech of every kind. Moreover, the biblical and rabbinic evidence suggests that it is precarious to assert that a given element within a parable is an expansion, a late application or an allegorization of an original unit. The term "parable" is so broad and complex that it cannot be limited to any one type or application.

To a large extent the materials designated in Mark as "parables" are similar in nature. They may be classed generally as similitudes, i.e. expanded similes. The parables refer to a revelatory truth in the preaching of Jesus conveyed through the vehicle of a known relationship in nature or the daily life of men.[6] The central element is the similarity of situation between the vehicle and the tenor of Jesus' teaching.[7]

A distinction is made commonly between a "parable" and an "alle-

---

[4] Cf. F. Hauck, *TWNT* V (1954), pp. 744-746; J. Jeremias, *The Parables of Jesus*[6] (New York, 1963), p. 16 n. 22, for references.

[5] Cf. Hauck, *op. cit.*, pp. 746-748; Jeremias, *op. cit.*, p. 20; P. Fiebig, *Altjüdische Gleichnisse und die Gleichnisse Jesu* (Tübingen, 1909), *passim.*

[6] Cf. Hauck, *op. cit.*, pp. 753-755.

[7] Cf. Fiebig, *op. cit.*, pp. 95-98. In pointing out that the essential element in parables, as of the משלים, is the similarity of the situation, Fiebig adds that many details may appear which are not to be interpreted. They are merely part of the life-setting.

gory." Usually a parable stresses one main point, while an allegory introduces several points.[8] Broadly speaking, this distinction is well taken. Nevertheless, a parable may be somewhat complex. A parable is an organic unit; though it may possess a single central point, subordinate features bear on the understanding of the parable as a whole. The possibility of significant subordinate points or of supplementary points by way of expansion or application of the parable on the part of Jesus himself should not be denied. Parables which contain subordinate or supplementary features are not to be classified as allegories, nor are these features to be characterized as allegorizations. To deny to Jesus the freedom to modify traditional forms of teaching is to subordinate content and substance to form, and to impose the categories of form too rigidly upon the material.[9]

The parables make a direct appeal to the imagination and involve the hearers in the situation. This factor lends to the parable the character of an argument. It entices the hearers to judge the situation depicted, and then challenges them, directly or indirectly, to apply that judgment to themselves.[10] In Mark the parables focus upon the critical situation in which both Jesus and his hearers stand–a situation created by Jesus' presence.

Basic to parabolic utterance is the recognition of the two strata of creation: the natural and the redemptive. Through parables Jesus called attention to what had previously been hidden in the redemptive order. The realism of his parables arises from the certainty that no mere analogy exists between the natural and redemptive order, but an inner affinity, because both strata originate in the purpose of God. That is why the Kingdom of God is intrinsically *like* the daily natural order and the life of men. The createdness of the natural order thus becomes the vehicle for the tenor of the redemptive. A contemplation of the one order can reveal or illumine truths of the other, because both reflect God's intention.[11]

---

8 Cf. Dodd, *op. cit.*, pp. 18-20; Jeremias, *op. cit.*, pp. 18-21, 66-89; B. Mickelsen, *Interpreting the Bible* (Grand Rapids, 1963), pp. 212-235.

9 An example may be taken from Mk. 2:19-20. The application of verse 20 to Jesus himself represents a modification of pure form introduced by Jesus to teach something significant. He does not bind himself to the categories of form.

10 Cf. Dodd, *op. cit.*, p. 21.

11 *Ibid.*, pp. 20 f. For the relationship of parables to the fulfilment of God's purpose see below on Ch. 4:10-12.

(a) The Parable of the Sower. Ch. 4:1-9

1 And again he began to teach by the sea side. And there is gathered unto him a very great multitude, so that he entered into a boat, and sat in the sea; and all the multitude were by the sea on the land.
2 And he taught them many things in parables, and said unto them in his teaching,
3 Hearken: Behold, the sower went forth to sow:
4 and it came to pass, as he sowed, some *seed* fell by the way side, [12] and the birds came and devoured it.
5 And other fell on the rocky *ground,* where it had not much earth; and straightway it sprang up, because it had no deepness of earth:
6 and when the sun was risen, it was scorched; and because it had no root, it withered away.
7 And other fell among the thorns, and the thorns grew up, and choked it, and it yielded no fruit. [13]
8 And others fell into the good ground, and yielded fruit, growing up and increasing; and brought forth thirtyfold, and sixtyfold, and a hundredfold.
9 And he said, Who hath ears to hear, let him hear.

1-2 Mark's introduction to the discourse in which he has grouped Jesus' parables provides only the unadorned facts that Jesus is again by the sea and that a large multitude has assembled before him. Whether the boat into which Jesus enters before seating himself to teach the multitudes is the one prepared in Ch. 3:9 is uncertain. It is possible, however, that Ch. 4:1-34 summarizes the teaching given to the multitude on the occasion described in summary fashion in Ch. 3:7-12. The distinctive feature of Jesus' teaching was that he couched the truth in parabolic form. This was not the first occasion when he had made use of parables. While the word itself occurs only once before (Ch. 3:23), Mark has included several examples of Jesus' prior use of figurative speech (e.g. Chs. 2:17a, 19-20, 21, 22; 3:24, 25, 27). The three parables which follow are similitudes, and may be distinguished from the earlier figures by their form. While Mark does not indicate their theme until Ch. 4:11, his readers know from the initial summary of Jesus' proclama-

---

[12] RSV "some seed fell along the path"; NEB "along the footpath."

[13] Gr. καρπός, RSV consistently "grain," which is appropriate to the context; NEB interprets the seed as "corn" and here renders "it yielded no crop."

tion in Ch. 1:14-15 that the parables are illustrations bearing on the character of the Kingdom of God. Only a fragment of a larger discourse is given by Mark in the parables which follow, for he distinctly says that Jesus taught them "many things" (verse 2) in the course of his teaching.

3-9 The parable of the sower is framed at the beginning and end with a solemn call to attentive hearing.[14] With this call Jesus involves his hearers in the situation he describes and leads them to form a judgment upon it. He also warns them that there may be more to the parable than appears upon its surface; there can be a superficial hearing which misses the point. The introduction and conclusion to the parable of the sower set it apart as having special significance. It provides the key to the other parables of growth which follow, as indicated in Ch. 4:13, where Jesus makes understanding of this parable essential to the understanding of any other parable.

The parable of the sower is faithful to the life situation of Palestinian agriculture, in which plowing follows sowing.[15] The sower is not careless when he scatters the seed on the path or among the thorns or on ground which has no depth of soil. He does so intentionally, for the path on which the villagers have trodden over the stubble and the thorns which lie withered among the fallow ground will be plowed up to receive the seed. The seed that fell upon the rocky ground was scattered intentionally also, for the underlying limestone thinly covered with

---

14 V. Taylor, *The Gospel According to St. Mark* (London, 1952), p. 252 rightly remarks, "these expressions suggest that the parables were intended to provoke thought, and were *not* the transparent illustrations they are sometimes supposed to have been." In the Coptic Gospel of Thomas a call to hear and understand frequently follows a parable (Logia 8, 21, 63, 65, 96) but on only one occasion (Logion 24) does such a call precede the parable, as here. The parable of the sower occurs in a variant form in Logion 9, but lacks the call to hearing. See H. Montefiore, "A Comparison of the Parables of the Gospel according to Thomas and of the Synoptic Gospels," *NTS* 7 (1961), p. 229.

15 First pointed out by G. Dalman, "Viererlei Acker," *Palästina-Jahrbuch* 22 (1926), pp. 120-132; *idem, Arbeit und Sitte in Palästina* II (Gütersloh, 1932), pp. 179-194, citing TB *Shabbath* 73b, "In Palestine ploughing comes after sowing"; Tos. *Berachoth* VII. 2, "he sows, plows, reaps . . . " ; Tos. *Shabbath* VII. 2, "sowing, plowing . . . " W. G. Essame, "Sowing and Plowing," *ExT* 72 (1960), p. 54 calls attention to Jubilees 11:11, "And Prince Mastema sent ravens and birds to devour the seed which was sown in the land, in order to destroy the land and rob the children of men of their labors. Before they could plow in the seed, the ravens picked it from the surface of the ground."

topsoil does not show above the surface until the plowing exposes it.[16] The detail that plowing follows sowing is important for the correct interpretation of the parable; it serves to caution the interpreter that less attention is to be given to the various types of soils, and more to the central act of sowing. The feature of the parable which provides the key to its understanding is the act of sowing. This element is essential to the comparison being developed: the Kingdom of God breaks into the world even as seed which is sown upon the ground. In the details about the soils there is reflection on the diversity of response to the proclamation of the Word of God, but this is not the primary consideration. The central point concerns the coming of the Kingdom of God. God is in the center of the action.[17]

The climax of the parable strongly emphasizes the glorious character of the harvest, the thirtyfold, sixtyfold and hundredfold yield, the last of which would be an unusually large harvest.[18] Since this is seen against the background of many obstacles, it is clear that the emphasis does not fall on the enormity of the waste,[19] but on the enormity and splendor of the harvest. The harvest is a common figure for the consummation of the Kingdom of God[20] and in the parable there is a significant reflection on the future, eschatological aspect of the Kingdom: it shall be glorious in character. But in addition to this future aspect there is also significant reflection on the activity prior to harvest, the sowing of the seed and its growth. The action of God must be recognized in these phases as well as in the harvest. The coming of the Kingdom of God is thus presented in comprehensive terms which call

---

[16] Cf. J. Jeremias, *op. cit.*, pp. 11-12.

[17] See further below, on Ch. 4:13-20.

[18] Cf. Gen. 26:12, and the Coptic Gospel of Thomas, Logion 9, where the harvest is reported as sixtyfold and one hundred and twentyfold. Because of the enormity of the harvest C. H. Dodd (*op. cit.*, pp. 136 f.), J. Jeremias (*op. cit.*, pp. 149-151) and W. Michaelis, *Es ging ein Sämann aus, zu säen* (Berlin, 1938), pp. 34-39 agree that this is the focal point of the parable. While Dodd insists that the harvest has come ("realized eschatology"), Jeremias, following Michaelis, argues that it is still future.

[19] J. Schniewind, *Das Evangelium nach Markus*[7/8] (Göttingen, 1958), pp. 73 f. concludes that three-fourths of the seed was lost, and comments, "the normal success of the Word of God is failure." This is not said in the parable, however, which contains no reflection on the proportion of the seed which fell on the several types of soil.

[20] Cf. Jeremias, *op. cit.*, pp. 118-120 for a discussion of Joel 3:13 and its influence on several NT passages.

attention *both* to its present *and* to its future aspects. A common supposition–shared apparently by John the Baptist, Jesus' disciples and the multitude–was that the Kingdom of God meant harvest, judgment, consummation. What Jesus taught through the veiled means of the parable of the sower was the relationship between the coming of the Kingdom in his own person and proclamation, and the delay of the end, the harvest, the consummation. This tension is both the occasion and the "situation" of the parable. [21] If this is not clearly understood, the parable remains unintelligible and its interpretation is reduced to generalities. [22]

With the concluding admonition, "If you have ears to hear, then hear," Jesus indicates that there is more to this story than appears on the surface. That is why it is "a parable."

(b) The Fulfilment of the Purpose of God. Ch. 4:10-12

10 And when he was alone they that were about him with the twelve asked of him the parables.
11 And he said unto them, Unto you is given the mystery of the kingdom of God: but unto them that are without, all things are done in parables:
12 that seeing they may see, and not perceive; and hearing they may hear, and not understand; lest haply they should turn again, and it should be forgiven them.

10 The sequence of Jesus' parabolic teaching of the multitude is interrupted by Ch. 4:10-20. These verses illustrate the principle formulated in Ch. 4:33-34: Jesus spoke to the multitudes in parables, but he explained all things privately to his disciples. It must be assumed that the change of scene presupposed in verse 10 occurred on some later occasion, since Jesus is still in the boat in Ch. 4:36. At a time when the

---

21 Rightly observed by H. Ridderbos, *op. cit.,* pp. 121-134.

22 Thus W. Michaelis, *op. cit.,* pp. 34-39 finds only the future Kingdom of God in view. By the seed Jesus does not mean the presence of the Kingdom but only the announcement of the coming Kingdom. The purpose of the parable is to exhort the disciples to perseverance and to encourage them that in spite of all obstacles the Kingdom is certain to come in its appropriate time. On pp. 44 f. he argues that while this purpose is not made explicit in Jesus' explanation of the parable, the Synoptic Gospels preserve only a fragment of that explanation.

multitude had been left behind, a larger group of disciples[23] than the Twelve inquired concerning "the parables." It is not possible to discern the precise nature of their question(s), but from verse 13 it appears that they inquired specifically about the deeper significance of the parable of the sower. The disciples may also have asked Jesus why he did not express his thoughts to the multitude in a more direct way, without the use of parables, for this question seems to lie behind Jesus' word concerning the fulfilment of the sovereign purpose of God in verses 11-12. The plural form "parables" in verse 10 corresponds to the use of the plural in verse 2, and indicates that more lies behind their question than the meaning of the parable of the sower.

11-12 These verses are widely held to represent Mark's distinctive understanding of the purpose of parables, but to be inauthentic as an expression of the intention of Jesus. Support for this approach has been found in the presence of unusual language,[24] in the apparent interruption of the sequence of verses 10 and 13 by verses 11-12,[25] and in the incredibility of the thought that Jesus could have used parables to

---

[23] Mark's unusual expression for the disciples in Ch. 4:10 (οἱ περὶ αὐτόν) should be compared with Ch. 3:34 (τοὺς περὶ αὐτὸν κύκλῳ καθημένους), where the context makes it evident that true disciples are in view.

[24] C. H. Dodd, *op. cit.*, pp. 14 f. rests the weight of his case upon language. Grouping Ch. 4:11-12 with Ch. 4:13-20, he finds seven words which "are not proper to the rest of the Synoptic record. All seven are characteristic of the vocabulary of Paul, and most of them occur also in other apostolic writers. These facts create at once a presumption that we have here not a part of the primitive tradition of the words of Jesus, but a piece of apostolic teaching." As regards Ch. 4:13-20 Jeremias, *op. cit.*, pp. 77-79 adopts Dodd's linguistic argument. Two of Dodd's seven words, διωγμός and θλῖψις recur in Mk. 10:30; 13:19, 24; οἱ ἔξω as a phrase occurs only here, but in Mk. 3:32 ἔξω has been used of Jesus' mother and brothers in a passage which contrasts their unbelief with the true belief of those seated before Jesus within the house (τοὺς περὶ αὐτόν, corresponding to οἱ περὶ αὐτόν of the disciples in Mk. 4:10). A fourth term, μυστήριον, occurs nowhere else in the Synoptic Gospels, but is found no less than eight times in the translation of Daniel 2 where it means "eschatological secret," while in Wisdom 2:22 it connotes "the secret purposes of God." It is wholly appropriate to the context in Mk. 4:11-12, which reflects on the disclosure of God's purpose.

[25] J. Jeremias, *op. cit.*, pp. 13-18. Jeremias argues that the logion in Mk. 4:11-12 is the word of Jesus, but that it has been misplaced and is inappropriate to this context. It sheds no light on the parables, but is concerned with Jesus' preaching in general; moreover, it cannot be earlier than the confession of Peter, "the period of the secret teaching of Jesus." Its presence in Mark 4, where it interrupts the sequence of verses 10 and 13, is due to the evangelist, who was misled by the

veil the truth.[26] To answer these objections requires the formulation of sound principles of interpretation as well as the clarification of the meaning of the text itself. It is not possible to base on vocabulary a judgment concerning authenticity. The vocabulary of any given logion may be influenced by the audience and the situation to which it is addressed. The term "mystery" or "secret" in verse 11 illustrates this fact. The term belongs to the vocabulary of revelation. It occurs both in Daniel and in Tannaitic rabbinic literature with the meaning "secret things." In Daniel it carries the meaning of an eschatological secret, a veiled proclamation of future events appointed by God. The concept of revelation is sharply in view,[27] and is appropriate to the Marcan context. This provides strong reason for not allowing that this word reflects later ideas.

Mark 4:11-12 is properly understood only in the context of the contemporaneous situation set forth in Ch. 3, where unbelief and opposition to Jesus is blatant. In Ch. 3:6 Jesus' opponents conspire to secure his destruction, while in Ch. 3:22 they declare that his power is demonic. It is against this background that in Ch. 4:11-12 Jesus makes a sharp distinction between the disciples (to whom God entrusts the mystery of the Kingdom) and the unbelieving multitude (from whom the truth is concealed). Basic to this distinction is the fact that the revelation of God itself has its history of acceptance and rejection whenever it enters the

---

catchword "parable," which in this instance means not parable-proper but a riddle. Jeremias argues further that the connotation of "parable" in the logion is actually in conflict with the meaning of "parable" in Ch. 4 as a whole. The true purpose of a parable was not to obscure but to inform.

By way of brief response to Jeremias, it is arbitrary to separate a particular form of Jesus' preaching–the parables–from his preaching in general. If Mk. 4:11-12 describes Jesus' preaching, as Jeremias contends, it is a description appropriate to the parables as well. Moreover, it is not legitimate to oppose the two meanings of "parable," as if one form was designed to illumine, and the other to obscure the truth. A parable, in the nature of the case, is not as such perspicuous, especially when it relates to a concept as complex as the Kingdom of God. Finally, it is unwise to seek to restrict the question of Mk. 4:10 to the meaning of a particular parable. The twofold answer of Ch. 4:11-20 is appropriate to the context provided by the parable, which reflects upon the response to the word.

26 Cf. Jeremias, *op. cit.*, pp. 17 f.; Taylor, *op. cit.*, pp. 254-256; W. Manson, "The Purpose of the Parables: A Re-examination of St. Mark iv. 10-12," *ExT* 68 (1957), pp. 132-135, *et al.*

27 Cf. G. Bornkamm, *TWNT* IV (1942), pp. 820-825. Attention should also be called to the use of the term רז in the texts from Qumran. See K. G. Kuhn, *Konkordanz zu den Qumrantexten* (Göttingen, 1960), pp. 203 f.

human scene. The term "parable" in verse 11 expresses an aspect of revelation and of human understanding when confronted by revelation. This is the point stressed in the explanation of the parable of the sower in Ch. 4:14-20. To all who have no lasting adherence to the word of revelation, Jesus' whole mission partakes of the character of "a parable"; it is an enigma. Seen in this perspective, the term "parable" in verse 11 expresses an intensely theological idea; the word describes the fate of revelation faced with the understanding of the man whose heart is hardened. [28] The fundamental secret, which is common to all of the parables, concerns the one who spoke them. It is the secret that in Jesus the Kingdom of God has begun to penetrate the experience of men. Accordingly in Ch. 4:11 Jesus was not thinking of the Kingdom of God in any abstract sense, whether as a future or a present reality, but of the Kingdom as it is embodied in his own person. A greater appreciation of the historical situation of belief and unbelief in which Jesus spoke the parables will indicate the appropriateness of this logion to the context in which it is found.

Ch. 4:11-12 distinguishes two classes of people confronted with a single event, the significance of which is entirely different to each class. The one event which both experience is described as "all things" (Ch. 4:11, 34), i.e. the whole mission of Jesus. [29] The disciples are enabled by God to see in this mission "the secret of the Kingdom of God," while those whose eyes are blinded and whose ears are dulled see nothing but a disturbing enigma. The parables are, accordingly, an aspect of the mission of Jesus. Unbelief makes every phase of that mission a riddle, something wholly alien to the perspective of man. [30]

The distinctly Palestinian flavor of the logion contained in verses 11-12 has been demonstrated by T. W. Manson and J. Jeremias. [31] Of particular interest is the agreement of the citation of Isaiah 6:9 f. with the Targum against both the MT and the LXX. [32] This citation has proven

[28] Correctly seen by U. Mauser, *Christ in the Wilderness* (Naperville, 1963), p. 122.

[29] Cf. C. Masson, *Les paraboles de Marc IV* (Paris, 1945), p. 28.

[30] Cf. U. Mauser, *op. cit.*, pp. 120-122; H. Ridderbos, *op. cit.*, pp. 123-129.

[31] T. W. Manson, *The Teaching of Jesus* (Cambridge, 1935), pp. 75-80; J. Jeremias, *op. cit.*, pp. 13-18.

[32] This agreement extends to the use of the third instead of the second person plural in Isa. 6:9; the choice of the verb "forgive" instead of "heal" in Isa. 6:10; and the use of the passive "it should be forgiven" rather than the active voice in Isa. 6:10. On the function of the text in this context see J. Gnilka, *Die Verstockung Israels: Isaias 6. 9-10 in der Theologie der Synoptiker* (Munich, 1961).

offensive to many interpreters. Various proposals have been made for altering either the text itself or the usual translation of the passage [33] to circumvent the understanding that Jesus spoke in parables to guard the mystery of the Kingdom. It is not necessary to adopt these expedients. What must be seen is that the introductory term in verse 12 is intended to serve as a citation formula, meaning "that it might be fulfilled"; [34] what follows is essentially a quotation of Scripture which bears on the fulfilment of God's sovereign purpose. In verse 11 Jesus called attention to the contemporary situation of belief and unbelief, of revelation and veiledness; in verse 12 he cites the text from Isaiah, not to explain why he speaks in parables, but as a commentary on the contemporary situation in which the purpose of God was coming to fulfilment. In both verses the sovereignty of the divine disclosure and determination is clearly in view. [35]

The citation of Isa. 6:9 f. does not mean that "those outside" are denied the possibility of belief. It indicates that they are excluded from the opportunity of being further instructed in the secret of the Kingdom so long as unbelief continues. That the Kingdom has come in an initial phase in the presence of Jesus can be discerned only through faith, which is to say by the grace of God. Jesus' presence, therefore, means disclosure *and* veiling; it releases both grace *and* judgment.

---

33 A useful survey of these attempts to alter the translation or the Greek text is presented by Burkill, *op. cit.,* pp. 110-115.

34 Cf. Jeremias, *op. cit.,* p. 17, "In order to understand the ἵνα-clause of Mark 4:12 which follows it is imperative that the words coming after ἵνα should be regarded as a free quotation from Isa. 6:9 f., and as if in inverted commas. Hence the ἵνα is not expressing the purpose of Jesus but that of God; in fact it almost amounts to an abbreviation of ἵνα πληρωθῇ, and is therefore to be translated 'in order that.'" A parallel example of this construction occurs in Mt. 18:16. On this understanding Mk. 4:12 is parallel to Mt. 13:14 f., not to Mt. 13:13, and the Synopses of Huck-Lietzmann and K. Aland should be corrected accordingly.

35 Within the historical situation both the objective and subjective aspects of revelation must be considered. On the objective side, there is that which cannot be wholly grasped because of the nature of the content of the revelation; it is "a secret," or veiled. On the subjective side, men of faith display a genuine comprehension and appropriation of the truth, but not on such a scale as to exclude the need for further exposition, illumination and application. Those who hear the word of revelation in unbelief may have a general knowledge of the teaching; they lack a genuinely saving understanding of the truth, however, and the person of Jesus remains to them enigmatic.

(c) The Interpretation of the Parable of the Sower. Ch. 4:13-20

13 And he saith unto them, Know ye not this parable? And how shall ye know all the parables?
14 The sower soweth the word.
15 And these are they by the way side, where the word is sown; and when they have heard, straightway cometh Satan, and taketh away the word which hath been sown in them.
16 And these in like manner are they that are sown upon the rocky *places,* who, when they have heard the word, straightway receive it with joy;
17 and they have no root in themselves, but endure for a while; then, when tribulation or persecution ariseth because of the word, straightway they stumble.[36]
18 And others are they that are sown among the thorns; these are they that have heard the word,
19 and the cares of the world, and the deceitfulness of riches, and the lusts of other things[37] entering in, choke the word, and it becometh unfruitful.
20 And those are they that were sown upon the good ground; such as hear the word, and accept it, and bear fruit, thirtyfold, and sixtyfold, and a hundredfold.

13 The parable of the sower has the first position in Mark, not merely as the first in a series, but because of its meaning. It furnishes the starting-point and the ground for the understanding of the parables of growth which follow. This is indicated clearly in the question which Jesus addressed to the disciples, "Do you not know the meaning of this parable? How then will you know the meaning of any parables?"[38] The disciples' failure to grasp the meaning of this parable indicates that its point does not lie in generalities about the risks which attend the process of listening, but in a distinctly redemptive-historical element–the relationship between the events depicted in the parable and the revelation of the Kingdom of God. This relationship had remained obscure to the disciples, even though they had been privileged to understand the secret that in Jesus' person the Kingdom had entered into history. In

[36] Gr. σκανδαλίζονται; RSV "they fall away."

[37] RSV "the delight in riches, and the desire for other things."

[38] Cf. Bl-D-F § 275. 3 (p. 144), "πᾶς can come very close to the meaning 'anyone, someone'; thus Mk. 4:13 πάσας τὰς παραβολάς, 'any parables.'"

Jesus' explanation of the parable[39] the essential part is a clarification of this relationship.[40]

14-20 The parable of the sower reflected in comprehensive terms upon the coming of the Kingdom of God. The interpretation corresponds in complexity to the organic situation presented in the parable. The interpretation of details within the parable[41] must be understood in terms of their appropriateness to the historical situation in which the parable was spoken.

With the initial statement, "the sower sows the word," attention is focused on the word of proclamation containing the secret of the Kingdom of God. The word in view is Jesus' word as he proclaims the Kingdom; it is the decisive messianic word of power through which the Kingdom is disclosed and is demonstrated as having come.[42] What

---

39 There is wide agreement among interpreters of the parables that the explanation given to the parable in Ch. 4:14-20 is not authentic, but reflects the self-understanding of the early church. Cf. C. H. Dodd, *op. cit.*, pp. 14-15; J. Jeremias, *op. cit.*, pp. 77-79; F. Hauck, *op. cit.*, pp. 753-755. A convenient summary of the several interpretations of the parable of the sower and of the objections raised against the authenticity of the interpretation recorded by Mark is provided by C. E. B. Cranfield, "St. Mark 4:1-34," *ScJTh* 4 (1951), 398-414. This negative position has been challenged rightly by M. Black, "The Parables as Allegory," *BJRL* 42 (1960), pp. 273-287, R. E. Brown, "Parable and Allegory Reconsidered," *Nov Test* 5 (1962), pp. 36-45, and H. Ridderbos, *op. cit.*, pp. 132-136.

40 G. Bornkamm, *TWNT* IV (1942), pp. 824 f. comments that the mystery of the parable does not lie in its obscurity or complexity, but in its very simplicity. This holds for the interpretation as well. The sole spectacular fact is that in the parable, with its focus upon sowing, the real issue is the revelation of the Kingdom of God.

41 The interpretation of details within the parable has caused interpreters like Dodd, Jeremias and Hauck (see above, n. 39) to regard the interpretation as a whole as early church allegorization. The elements of allegory in the interpretation should not prove surprising when consideration is given to the organic situation presented in the parable itself. Dodd himself had commented that "if the parable is drawn out to any length, it is likely that details will be inserted which are suggested by their special appropriateness to the application intended, and if the application intended by the speaker is correctly made by the hearer, he will then see a secondary significance in these details" (p. 20). This statement is appropriate to the situation in Mk. 4:14-20. The chief emphasis in the interpretation falls upon the sowing of the seed. Interest in the diversity of response is also present, but it is not central. It should be further noted that no attempt is made to identify the sower nor to interpret the threefold harvest, yet these are elements which would have invited attention in early church allegorization.

42 Cf. Ridderbos, *op. cit.*, p. 30. G. Kittel, *TWNT* IV (1942), pp. 124, 127 com-

this implies concerning the meaning and manifestation of the Kingdom of God is elaborated in terms of the diversity of response to the word proclaimed. In keeping with the contemporary situation which Mark has reported in Chs. 2 and 3, Jesus calls attention to the negative response to the word. This response is contemplated in terms of the diversity of its various motives. While the unfruitfulness of the word is traced to a variety of circumstances, the interpretation does not force the details. The activity of Satan is not introduced artificially, but is a reflection on Satan's opposition consistent with Mark's prior presentation.[43] Similarly, the reference to superficial adherence to the word, and to the scandal and offense which the word occasions, is appropriate to the historical situation as Mark has set this forth. An unwillingness to endure tribulation and persecution, a desire for security in the world, an unwillingness to suffer characterize those to whom the word is presented. These elements indicate the way of the world; this is what men are like when confronted with the word of the Kingdom. Therefore the secret contained in the word remains veiled to them. Jesus' determination to submit to the judgment of God, to accept suffering and death, makes his word and his act an enigma which men cannot penetrate.[44] The event of revelation itself is what causes men to be offended and to turn away.

Jesus also reflects upon a positive response to the word, indicated as a receiving and understanding of the word on the part of genuine disciples. This feature has been in view as early as the contrast between unbelief and belief set forth in Ch. 3:20-34, where Jesus' true family is contrasted with his parental family; it is basic to the contrast set forth in Ch. 4:11-12. It is appropriate, therefore, that Jesus should call attention to the present, subjective response to the proclamation of the Kingdom of God. The assurance is given that those who have responded with an affirmation of faith shall be found bearing fruit according to

ments, "what the explanation of the parable of the seed with its application of the term 'the word' tries to assert about Jesus is nothing but that which constitutes the ultimate background to the entire tradition about Jesus"; "the explanation of the parable of the seed . . . derives its meaning and point from the conviction that the 'seed' which is explained as the 'word' is the Christ-event *(das Christus-Geschehen)* which has come to pass in Jesus."

[43] See on Chs. 1:13, 23-26, 32-33, 39; 3:11-12, 22-27.

[44] Cf. U. Mauser, *op. cit.*, p. 123. Mauser sees in the desire to avoid suffering the desire to evade "the wilderness." It is Jesus' determination to remain in the wilderness that constitutes the ultimate enigma.

the law of a wonderful multiplication at the time of harvest, that is, in the judgment that comes with the consummation. This is the eschatological note within the parable, and it is sustained in the interpretation as well. Accordingly in the parable Jesus draws attention *both* to the veiled manifestation of the Kingdom, hindered by many obstacles and Satanic opposition, *and* to the disclosure of the Kingdom, which manifests itself in fruitfulness, which is the more startling precisely because of the encountered opposition. To those who deny the authenticity of the interpretation given in Ch. 4:14-20, an answer may be given: when the total organic situation of the parable is recognized, the congruity of the interpretation with the parable and the historical situation is undeniable. The emphasis in this parable falls upon the central act of sowing; the emphasis in the interpretation falls upon the kind of reception which the proclamation of the Kingdom experienced. The succession of vivid images describing this reception is appropriate and significant.[45]

By way of summary it may be said that in this parable Jesus gives a fundamental insight into the coming of the Kingdom of God. The eschatological coming of God into the world goes the way of seed which is sown.[46] In the appropriate time there will come the harvest, the consummation. Whoever knows this understands that salvation has come with Jesus; he also knows that, in spite of his veiledness and the opposition encountered, the harvest is prepared by the sovereign word and act of God in Jesus the Christ. The interpretation, like the parable, thus stresses the comprehensive character of the Kingdom as *both* present in an incipient way in the person and mission of Jesus *and* future with a glory yet undisclosed.

It is natural that the Church, in reflecting on the parable and its interpretation, should find in it an exhortation to true hearing and appropriation of the word of proclamation. In the presence of persecution and affliction, the peril to discipleship could be appreciated in terms of the exposition Jesus had given. But Mark indicates by the placement of verses 11-12 before the explanation of the parable that the Church of his day had not forgotten that the parable concerned the coming of the Kingdom of God.

---

45 M. Black, *op. cit.*, pp. 278 f.

46 J. Schniewind, *op. cit.*, p. 73 comments on the simplicity which is the incomprehensible supposition of the coming of the Kingdom of God, "a sower went out to sow–and nothing further; and this means the new world of God."

(d) Exhortation to True Hearing. Ch. 4:21-25

21 And he said unto them, Is the lamp brought [47] to be put under the bushel, or under the bed, *and* not to be put on the stand?
22 For there is nothing hid, save that it should be manifested; neither was *anything* made secret, but that it should come to light.
23 And he said unto them, Take heed what you hear: with what measure you mete it shall be measured unto you; [48] and more shall be given unto you.
25 For he that hath, to him shall be given: and he that hath not, from him shall be taken away even that which he hath.

The aphorisms from which this section has been constructed are traditional in character and occur elsewhere unrelated to each other. [49] The evangelist has brought them together because of their relevance to Jesus' teaching through parables. Ch. 4:21-25 consists of two trilogies of sayings, which Mark appears to have understood as "the parable of the lamp" and "the parable of the measure." By inserting this block of material into the discourse on parables he sheds light on his distinctive understanding of these words of Jesus. It is not clear whether in his intention these words are to be understood as part of the private address to the disciples or as parabolic address to the multitude. The call to true hearing in verses 23-24, however, recalls Ch. 4:3 and 9, which suggests that the multitude is once again in view. This is clearly the case in Ch. 4:26, where the parable of the growth of the seed is introduced.

---

[47] Both the ASV ("is . . . brought") and the RSV ("is . . . brought in") fail to represent Mark's interesting ἔρχεται. NEB "Do you bring in the lamp" is closer, but appears still to fall short of what Mark understood by the phrase. See below on this term.

[48] RSV "the measure you give will be the measure you get."

[49] Cf. Lk. 8:16-18; Mt. 5:15 and Lk. 11:33; Mt. 10:26 and Lk. 12:2; Mt. 7:2 and Lk. 6:38; Mt. 13:12; Mt. 25:29 and Lk. 6:38b; Lk. 19:26. In the Coptic Gospel of Thomas Mk. 4:21 has a parallel in Logion 33; Mk. 4:22 in Logion 5 and the end of Logion 6, where it is attached to a variant of Mk. 2:18; Mk. 4:23 is echoed at the end of a variety of parables (Logia 8, 21, 63, 65, 96); Mk. 4:25 is a traditional formulation paralleled in Logion 41. For an analysis of how Mark grouped these statements to achieve two parables rather than a collection of sayings, see J. Jeremias, *op. cit.*, p. 91; E. Lohmeyer, *Das Evangelium des Markus*[16] (Göttingen, 1963), p. 80.

21-23 The parable of the lamp, which is not intended to be placed under a measure[50] or a bed[51] but upon a stand where it may illumine the whole room, has stimulated the imagination of modern interpreters.[52] It is necessary for the interpreter of Mark, however, to give special attention to the distinctively Marcan formulation of the logion and to the context in which it has been placed. The more interesting features of Mark's formulation are the use of the definite article before "lamp" and the choice of the verb "come": "Does *the lamp come* for the purpose of being placed under the measure or under the couch? Does it not *come* for the purpose of being placed on the lampstand?"[53] The use of "come"[54] is intriguing, precisely because lamps do not come but "are brought," and this more usual understanding is reflected in the rendering of the ASV and RSV. Mark's term at this point is wholly intelligible, however, if Jesus was speaking of himself as the lamp that has been kindled and that has come, in keeping with the mission pronouncements of Jesus which stress the purpose for his coming.[55] It seems reasonable that Mark understood the simile in this way. Assuming this to be the correct understanding, the use of the article with "lamp"

---

50 The term μόδιος means a bushel measure, and then a measure in general. Cf. S. Krauss, *Talmudische Archäologie* II (Leipzig, 1911), p. 395, n. 561.

51 Mark's term κλίνη probably designates a bench for dining. Cf. A-G, p. 437.

52 The fact that this saying occurs in contexts which differ from one another has encouraged quite different reconstructions of its original import. According to C. H. Dodd (*op. cit.*, pp. 106-108), the lamp is a figure for the Law, whose light had been hid from the people by the religious leaders of this day. In this context the parable is a biting comment on the behavior of those responsible for God's revelation. J. Jeremias (*op. cit.*, pp. 120 f.) states categorically "we do not know what meaning Jesus gave to the *simile of the Lamp whose Place is on the Lampstand*" (italics his). He finds in the simile a sharp contrast between kindling and extinguishing which is intelligible if the saying was uttered by Jesus in response to a warning of danger and an appeal to protect himself. The saying means that it was not for him to protect himself. "The lamp has been lit, the light is shining, but not in order to be put out again! No, in order to give light." See further *idem*, "Die Lampe unter dem Scheffel," *ZNW* 39 (1940), pp. 237-240. J. Jónsson, *Humour and Irony in the New Testament* (Reykjavik, 1965), p. 96 finds in the parable a reference to Jesus' gathering of disciples.

53 The thought of purpose is stressed both in verse 21 and 22; ἵνα (= "in order that") occurs twice in each verse.

54 Gr. ἔρχεται, on which see above, n. 47.

55 Cf. Chs. 1:24, 38; 2:17; 10:45. If Jesus is here speaking of his mission in a veiled way both the strong emphasis upon purpose and the use of ἔρχεται are intelligible.

indicates to those who have eyes to see "the lamp whose identity is known." Mark's placement of this parable after Ch. 4:11-20 suggests further that he has in view the secret of the Kingdom of God which is present in the person of Jesus, whose mission remains for many a veiled enigma. [56] The reference throughout is to the mission of Jesus. The contrast that is drawn in verse 21 is between hiddenness–"under the bushel" or "under the couch"–and open manifestation–"upon the stand." Verse 22, with its "secrecy" language, sustains this contrast and implies that there is something hidden now which shall later be unveiled; there is a secret which shall become known.

In the context of Jesus' mission the parable means that just as a man would not kindle a clay lamp to conceal its light under a bushel-measure or under a dining couch, it should not be thought that God has brought near the Kingdom in the person of Jesus for the ultimate purpose of concealing his dignity. No, there will come a day when the veil is taken away and He will be known as the Bearer of the Kingdom in a disclosure which all will see. The reference is to the parousia, when the one whose mission came the way of a sower scattering seed will appear in the dignity of the Harvester whose sovereign authority will be demonstrated to all. The solemn call to hear and perceive the deeper significance in the parable is a call to faith and to hope for the disciples to whom it is given to perceive the secret even in its veiledness. To those outside, it is a warning that there is a deeper significance to the enigma presented by the mission of Jesus. [57] It is as unnatural as kindling a lamp and concealing its light under a bushel. The day will surely come when its deeper purposes will be disclosed to all. The period of hiddenness is merely a prelude to the period of manifestation, when apparent obscurity and weakness will be exchanged for messianic glory and power. Like the

---

[56] Cf. Lohmeyer, *op. cit.*, p. 85. See further C. E. B. Cranfield, "Message of Hope. Mark 4:21-32," *Interpretation* 9 (1955), pp. 152-156.

[57] Cf. Cranfield, *op. cit.*, pp. 154-156: "If we are right in thinking that the secret of the kingdom of God (vs. 11) is the secret of the person of Jesus and also that the parable of the sower is in the last resort an appeal to men to penetrate beyond the present incognito of the Son of Man and to recognize him for what he is and to act accordingly, then the context in which Mark has placed the parable of the lamp is further support for the Christological interpretation of it." Vs. 23 "indicates the connection between the Messianic hiddenness and the fact that faith is only possible where there is room for personal decision. The kingdom is concealed, the revelation indirect, in order to give this room and to make faith possible. The challenge in vs. 23 seeks to elicit faith. At the same time it presupposes that the possession of the hearing ear is a divine gift."

parable of the sower, the parable of the lamp views the mission of Jesus in comprehensive terms and has a distinctly eschatological perspective from which the disciples were to find reassurance and insight concerning the nature of the coming of the Kingdom of God.

24-25 The sayings which follow may have been suggested to Mark by the reference to the bushel measure in verse 21. They constitute the parable of the measure.[58] They are introduced with the warning "take heed what you hear." If addressed to the multitude,[59] they are an appeal for spiritual perception and appropriation of the word which Jesus proclaims. Precisely because there is going to be an unveiling which unravels the enigma and reveals the mystery, hearing with true perception is important *now*. The reason for the urgency in the appeal is expressed through two words traditional to Judaism,[60] but which in this context have specific reference to the proclamation of the Kingdom of God. The first word indicates that hearing is now "the measure with which a man measures." If this measure is rich and profound, if the word of proclamation is appropriated with eagerness and joy, in like measure a rich share will be received in the eschatological revelation of the Kingdom, and "even more shall be given." The ultimate disclosure will result in a salvation far richer than a man can possibly anticipate even by faithful hearing and appropriation. The second word carries the thought one step further: what will ultimately be received in the Kingdom of God will depend upon that which a man possesses of it now. Present posses-

---

58 So Jeremias, *The Parables of Jesus*[6] (New York, 1963), pp. 91, 94.

59 F. Hauck, *Das Evangelium des Markus* (Leipzig, 1931), p. 57 and J. Schniewind, *op. cit.*, p. 77 understand these words and those which follow to be addressed to the disciples. The meaning is, Be careful to hear correctly for you must proclaim this message. If you proclaim faithfully you will receive a rich reward. This interpretation finds some support in the Coptic Gospel of Thomas, Logion 33: "Jesus said: What thou shalt hear in thine ear and in the other ear, that preach from your housetops; for no one lights a lamp and puts it under a bushel, nor does he put it in a hidden place, but he sets it on the lampstand, so that all who come in and go out may see its light." If this were the correct interpretation one would expect "Take care how (or what) you preach," rather than "Take care to what you hear." See further H. Ridderbos, *op. cit.*, pp. 134-136.

60 Cf. M. Smith, *Tannaitic Parallels to the Gospels* (Philadelphia, 1951), pp. 135 f., who calls attention to the completely parallel rabbinic formulation to Mk. 4:24 in Mekilta to Ex. 13:19 ff. M. *Soṭah* I. 7; Tos. *Soṭah* III. 1 (ed. Zuckermandel, p. 295); Sifré on Num. to 12:15 ff.; and to Mk. 4:25 in Mekilta to Ex. 15:26 and parallels.

sion depends upon hearing, upon appropriation or rejection of the word of the Kingdom that has been scattered like seed. With respect to the man who through faith appropriates that word the saying shall be true which declares "he that has, to him shall (even more) be given," where Mark's passive indicates the full thought "shall be given *by God.*"[61] But the man who, in hardness of heart, refuses the word shall experience that absolute loss described in the terms "and he that has not, even that (little) which he has shall be taken from him." In this sense the unity of the mission of Jesus and the unveiling of the Kingdom will be seen: what one receives from the Sower will be received from the Judge in double measure.[62] Only those who penetrate the mystery in the present will share in the glory which is yet to be revealed. Because God enters the world through the word of the Kingdom proclaimed by Jesus, the matter of one's response to Jesus is of ultimate seriousness. For this reason Mark introduces the parable of the measure with the solemn caution, Take heed what you hear![63]

(e) The Parable of the Growth of the Seed. Ch. 4:26-29

26 And he said, So is the kingdom of God, as if a man should cast seed upon the earth;
27 and should sleep and rise night and day, and the seed should spring up and grow, he knoweth not how.
28 The earth beareth fruit of herself; first the blade, then the ear, then the full grain in the ear.
29 But when the fruit is ripe, straightway he putteth forth the sickle, because the harvest is come.

26-29 Mark alone records the little parable of the growth of the seed.[64] With its reflection on sowing, growth and harvest it invites comparison with the parable of the sower. In that parable the meaning of the interim

---

61 Mark's passive δοθήσεται in Ch. 4:25 corresponds to the passive δέδοται in Ch. 4:11; in each instance the intention is "given by God."

62 The formulation is that of H. Ridderbos, *op. cit.*, p. 135.

63 A. Schlatter, *Die Evangelien nach Matthäus und Markus* (Stuttgart, 1935), p. 40 sees in the admonition a warning against hearing in this receptive manner other voices than Jesus'.

64 A convenient summary of five approaches to this parable is provided by C. E. B. Cranfield, "Message of Hope. Mark 4:21-32," *Interpretation* 9 (1955), pp. 158-162. Cranfield prefers to find the point of the parable in the contrast between sowing and harvest, thus bringing its pattern of thought into conformity

before the final manifestation of the Kingdom was clarified in a positive sense; the time of waiting is a time for sowing. The mystery of the Kingdom provides an opportunity for seed to be scattered in the field. In the parable of the sower significant attention was given also to the resistance and obstruction encountered by the seed. By contrast, the parable of the seed is oriented to the idea of the power released through the scattering of the seed. In this parable the identity between the sower and the harvester is emphasized. There can be no doubt that the harvest in view is the coming judgment of the world, for the concluding words of verse 29 reflect the Hebrew text of Joel 3:13. The stress in the parable thus falls upon the sowing of the seed as a messianic work which unleashes mysterious forces which operate of themselves in the achievement of the sovereign purposes of God.

The parable clarifies the relationship between what was then seen of Jesus within the context of his mission and what may still be expected of him.[65] His work was sowing; only after a certain lapse of time will there be the gathering of the harvest. The period between sowing and harvest, however, is not insignificant; for in that period *something happens.*[66] In this connection there occur some remarkable expressions. According to verse 27, the seed germinates and sprouts; it springs up and matures in a mysterious manner that goes almost unnoticed. This is the emphasis behind Mark's phrase "he knows not how." In verse 28 it is stressed that it is not by human intervention that the seed grows; the earth produces fruit "spontaneously."[67] This does not mean that the sower abandons his work, nor that he is uninterested in what takes place, for this is not the point in the reference to his sleeping and rising. It means that the seed must be allowed its appointed course, as the process of growth and ripening advances toward a harvest that is approaching. The sower takes account of the growth of the seed, but he cannot fully understand it. His ultimate interest is in the purpose for which the seed was sown–the harvest; when the grain is ripened, he

---

with Ch. 4:21, 22 and 30-32. On this understanding it is "the parable of seedtime and harvest," and teaches that as seedtime is followed by harvest, "so will the present hiddenness and ambiguousness of the kingdom of God be succeeded by its glorious manifestation" (p. 162). Additional bibliography is listed in A-G, p. 122.

65 Cf. H. Ridderbos, *op. cit.*, pp. 142-144.

66 This element is insufficiently appreciated in Cranfield's interpretation, as set forth in n. 64.

67 Mark's use of the rare word αὐτομάτη is deliberate, and reflects on the characteristics of growth. See A-G, p. 122; MM, p. 93.

immediately sends forth the sickle into the grain. These expressions exhibit aspects of the mysterious manifestation of the Kingdom of God in history. It comes mysteriously, by God's initiative and appointment, without human intervention.

Important elements in the parable are the certainty of the harvest in spite of the sower's temporary passivity [68] *and* the germinal power of the seed as the pledge and guarantee of its maturation. The certainty of the mature crop is indissolubly associated with the action of the seed within the soil. The total organic situation must be appreciated: emphasis falls not merely upon the harvest which is assured, [69] but upon the seed and its growth as well. The seed which is sown is the authoritative proclamation of Jesus, which does not prove barren. The proclamation of the gospel is the pledge of the ultimate manifestation of the Kingdom; it mysteriously, but irresistibly, brings it near. The parable thus depicts the coming of the Kingdom in comprehensive terms while emphasizing the sovereign initiative of God in the establishment of his rule.

(f) The Parable of the Mustard Seed. Ch. 4:30-32

30 And he said, How shall we liken the kingdom of God? Or in what parable shall we set it forth?
31 It is like a grain of mustard seed, which, when it is sown upon the earth, though it be less than all the seeds that are upon the earth, [70]
32 Yet when it is sown, groweth up, and becometh greater than all the herbs, [71] and putteth out great branches; so that the birds of the heaven can lodge under the shadow thereof. [72]

---

[68] J. Jeremias, *op. cit.*, pp. 151f. is much impressed with this detail, and so entitles Ch. 4:26-29 "the parable of the Patient Husbandman." There is, however, no reflection on the element of patience within the text; it has been imported from Jas. 5:7. Jeremias sees in the parable a reply to those of Zelotic persuasion who wished to bring in the Kingdom by force. This element is also stressed by B. T. D. Smith, *The Parables of the Synoptic Gospels* (Cambridge, 1937), p. 130.

[69] Cf. C. H. Dodd, *op. cit.*, pp. 131-134, who interprets "harvest" in the light of Mt. 9:37-38 and Lk. 10:2, and so finds support for the concept of realized eschatology. Jesus saw in the success of John the Baptist a sign that the power of God was at work; his parable suggests that the crisis of harvest is now at hand. The adoption of the eschatological language of Joel 3:13, however, resists Dodd's interpretation.

[70] RSV "is the smallest of all the seeds on earth."

[71] RSV "shrubs."

[72] RSV "the birds of the air can make nests in its shade."

30-32 Of the three parables of seed which is sown the last is most elaborately introduced in explicit parabolic formulation: [73] the Kingdom of God is like what happens to a grain of mustard. The mustard seed was proverbial in Jewish thinking as the smallest of all seeds. [74] Mark's explanatory phrase, "though it be the smallest of all the seeds upon the earth," may be understood as a gloss to inform his readers in the West of this underlying assumption. Unlike the previous parable, there is no real reflection upon the actual growth of the seed. All attention is focused upon the contrast [75] between the smallest of the seeds and the tallest of the shrubs. [76] The Kingdom is not likened to the mustard seed, but to what happens to the mustard seed. The whole life picture, in which there is significant reflection on the beginning and the end of an action, provides the basis of the comparison. [77] The reference to the birds of the air which find shelter in the branches of the mustard shrub may have a deeper significance, [78] but it seems more probable that they are part of the picture of the surprising character of the end when considered from the beginning. Though insignificant in its beginning, the matured result is the provision of strength and protection for those who come within its shade.

This parable is concerned with the enigmatic present manifestation of the Kingdom as embodied in Jesus' person. Its appearance may be characterized by weakness and apparent insignificance–but remember the mustard seed. The day will come when the Kingdom of God will

---

[73] The twofold introduction is paralleled in Isa. 41:18; for rabbinic parallels see S-B*K* II (1924), pp. 7 f.

[74] Cf. Mt. 17:20; Lk. 17:6 and the rabbinic references cited in S-B*K* I (1922), p. 699 and O. Michel, *TWNT* III (1938), p. 811, n. 1.

[75] Rightly stressed by J. Jeremias, *op. cit.*, pp. 147-149. Cf. Cranfield, *op. cit.*, p. 163, "We must surely recognize in this contrast the key feature of the parable."

[76] Cf. K. E. Wilken, *Biblisches Erleben im Heiligen Land* I (Lahr-Dinglingen, 1953), pp. 108 f. By the Lake of Gennesaret, the mustard shrub attains the height of eight to ten feet. The birds are attracted by the seed and the shade.

[77] Ridderbos, *op. cit.*, pp. 145 f. would find emphasis upon the growth as well. But it is not necessary to force the three main parables of Ch. 4 into the same mold. On the other hand, Ridderbos' discussion (pp. 345-347) with Lagrange (*op. cit.*, p. 122) and others who see in the parable a reference to the church is acute.

[78] The language reflects a number of passages in the OT which speak of the tree of God's planting, as a metaphor of a mighty kingdom, e.g. Ps. 104:12; Dan. 4:12, 21; Ezek. 17:23; 31:6. Jeremias, *op. cit.*, p. 147 finds in κατασκηνοῦν an eschatological technical term for the incorporation of the Gentiles into the people of God, and cites *Joseph and Aseneth* 15. This allusion *may* be present, but it would surely be lost on those who heard (or later read) the parable.

surpass in glory the mightiest kingdoms of the earth,[79] for it is the consequence of God's sovereign action. The mustard seed is the word of God proclaimed by Christ. This word possesses the power which one day will make all things new. When the glory of that manifestation breaks forth before men they will be as startled as the man who considers the tiny mustard seed and the mighty shrub.[80]

(g) Parabolic Utterance and Private Interpretation. Ch. 4:33-34

33 And with many such parables spake he the word unto them, as they were able to hear it;
34 And without a parable spake he not unto them: but privately to his own disciples he expounded all things.

33-34 Mark concludes his grouping of parables with a summary statement which indicates that he has selected illustrations of Jesus' teaching from a much larger cycle of tradition.[81] It was Jesus' habit to teach the multitude through parables like those which Mark has presented. Through the vehicle of parables Jesus was proclaiming "the word." The term is an echo of the explanation given to the parable of the sower, where it occurs eight times. It is appropriate to the vocabulary of revelation and means clearly "the word of God," or more concretely "the word of the Kingdom." The motive for Jesus' use of the parables is expressed in terms of his accommodation to that stage of preparation which was present in the crowd; he spoke the word "as they were able to hear it." This means that he adapted it to the level of understanding that he found in his listeners.[82] Had Jesus spoken to the crowds in a direct manner they would have been forced to make a decision immediately. That decision could have expressed only unbelief and rejection. Jesus' adoption of the indirect address of the parable was accordingly an ex-

[79] This seems to be the real import of the concluding words, which call to mind not one but several passages from the OT.

[80] Cf. O. Michel, *TWNT* III (1938), p. 811.

[81] Without appealing to those parables found in Matthew or Luke, attention may be called to Chs. 3:23-27; 12:1-9; 13:28, 34-35 where elements of this tradition are utilized by Mark.

[82] Cf. M. Smith, *op. cit.*, p. 155, who calls attention to the linguistic parallel in Mekilta of R. Simon to Ex. 19:18, where the point of the midrash is that God speaks to men in terms they can understand. See further T. F. Torrance, "A Study in New Testament Communication," *ScJTh* 3 (1950), pp. 298-313.

pression both of grace and of judgment. It was an expression of grace which allowed time for reflection on his appeal to penetrate beneath his words to "the word." It was an expression of judgment upon their lack of preparation to receive directly the word of the Kingdom of God.[83] For that reason "he did not speak to them without a parable," which in this context means enigmatic speech, not necessarily the kind of extended similitude illustrated by the parables of the seed.

With Jesus' utterance before the multitude the evangelist contrasts his private exposition of "all things" to his own disciples. "All things" within this context means more than parabolic utterance; it refers to the mission of Jesus in which the mystery of the Kingdom was veiled.[84] The summary, accordingly, points back to the contrast developed in Ch. 4:11-12 and exhibits the two aspects of the revelation of God in the mission of Jesus. There was *veiling* (or very partial disclosure) before the multitude and *disclosure* (but only partial understanding) to the disciples. This is the pattern illustrated in Ch. 4 and assumed throughout the Gospel of Mark. In the private instruction which Jesus gives to his disciples, the mystery of the Kingdom as present in his person is graciously unveiled. Only through revelation does the enigma become partially resolved; not until the consummation (to take the perspective of the parables) will it become resolved for all men.[85]

5. The Vanquishing of Powers Hostile to God. Ch. 4:35-5:43

The three[86] miracles reported in Ch. 4:35-5:43 reveal Jesus' sovereignty over sea and wind, demonic possession and death. They have been brought together as a unit, presumably by the evangelist, to illustrate the vanquishing of powers hostile to God. The cosmic dimensions of Jesus' encounter with Satan are emphasized in the first of these stories, where the sea is understood as a manifestation of the realm of death, with overtones of the demonic in its behavior. This in turn prepares for the account of Jesus' healing of the demoniac from Gerasa. Between

---

83 The element of judgment is more strongly emphasized in Ch. 4:12.

84 Cf. C. Masson, *op. cit.*, p. 28; U. Mauser, *op. cit.*, pp. 120-122.

85 See below on Ch. 9:9, where it becomes clear that the enigma will be resolved for the disciples more fully after Jesus' resurrection.

86 Or four, depending on whether Ch. 5:21-43 is understood as a single narrative or two.

the two narratives there are parallels too obvious to be incidental.[87] The narrative of the man who experienced self-destruction leads naturally to an encounter with death itself. In each event the presence of Jesus constitutes an affirmation of life and the defeat of death. Confronted with his word of power, the man of faith finds himself in the presence of the Lord of Life.

(a) The Subduing of the Sea. Ch. 4:35-41

35 And on that day, when even was come, he saith unto them, Let us go over unto the other side.
36 And leaving the multitude, they take him with them, even as he was, in the boat. And other boats were with him.
37 And there ariseth a great storm of wind, and the waves beat into the boat, insomuch that the boat was now filling.
38 And he himself was in the stern asleep, on the cushion: and they awake him, and say unto him, Teacher, carest thou not that we perish?
39 And he awoke, and rebuked the wind, and said unto the sea, Peace, be still. And the wind ceased, and there was a great calm.
40 And he said unto them, Why are ye fearful? have ye not yet faith?[88]
41 And they feared exceedingly, and said one to another, Who then is this, that even the wind and the sea obey him?

The Marcan account of the subduing of the wind and the sea bears the marks of the personal reminiscence of one who had experienced the

---

[87] U. Mauser, *op. cit.*, p. 126 calls attention to the howling sea, which corresponds to the raging fury of the demoniac who cannot be tamed by the strongest chains, while the stillness of the wind and the sea after Jesus' word finds its counterpart in the peace of the healed man who sits at the feet of Jesus clothed and sane.

[88] The text assumed in the translation is οὔπω ἔχετε πίστιν, supported by 𝔥 D Θ λ φ *al* latt sa bo, which is surely to be adopted as Marcan, for analogous formulae with οὔπω occur in Ch. 8:17, 21. K. Aland, *Synopsis Quattuor Evangeliorum* (Stuttgart, 1964), p. 186 adopts for his text πῶς οὐκ ἔχετε πίστιν, supported by C 𝔎 A *al* syp. Reading the stronger text, Jesus is not asking a question, but is expressing surprise at the lack of confidence and understanding in his disciples.

event. The precise notice of time, the unnecessary reference [89] to the other boats which were present, the vivid detail that "the boat was already filling," the precise location of Jesus' position ("in the stern, asleep on the cushion"), the harshness of the rebuke implied in the disciples' cry of indignation and terror as well as their subsequent bewilderment, combine to suggest an eyewitness report.

35-37 From a small boat Jesus had been teaching the multitude lined up on the shore (Ch. 4:2). Now that evening had come he determined to cross over to the eastern side of the lake (probably in keeping with the principle expressed in Ch. 1:38, that his mission must be extended elsewhere). The disciples included among their number fishermen who were experienced sailors, and the multitude was soon left behind as their boat, with others along the shore, moved out into deep water. The Sea of Galilee, surrounded by high mountains, is like a basin. Sudden violent storms on the sea are well known. Violent winds from the southwest enter the basin from the southern cleft and create a situation in which storm and calm succeed one another rapidly. Since the wind is nearly always stronger in the afternoon than in the morning or evening, fishing was done at night. But when a storm arises in the evening, it is all the more dangerous. [90] Such a storm struck as a fierce gust of wind came upon the lake, driving the waves over the sides of the boat, which was being swamped with water.

38-39 While the storm raged, Jesus lay sleeping [91] in the stern upon the pillow that was customarily kept under the coxswain's seat for

---

89 Unnecessary, unless the reference indicates the presence of witnesses to an epiphany-event. The absence of further reference to these boats, however, makes this unlikely.

90 Cf. G. Dalman, *Orte und Wege Jesu*³ (Gütersloh, 1924), pp. 128 ff., 197 f.; C. Kopp, *Die heiligen Stätten der Evangelien* (Regensburg, 1959), pp. 212 ff., 258 f. Mark's term, λαῖλαψ μεγάλη ἀνέμου, means "a fierce gust of wind" or "a gale."

91 The parallel with Jonah who slept in the midst of a raging storm has attracted attention. According to L. Goppelt, *Typos. Die typologische Deutung des Alten Testaments im Neuen* (Gütersloh, 1939), p. 84, the description of the situation and a number of verbal parallels indicate that Mark had the story of Jonah (1:1-17) clearly in mind (cf. Jonah 1:4 with Mk. 4:37; 1:5 with Mk. 4:38; 1:6 with Mk. 4:38; 1:11 with Mk. 4:39; 1:16 with Mk. 4:41). R. M. Grant, *Miracle and Natural Law in Graeco-Roman and Early Christian Thought* (Amsterdam, 1952), p. 169 says categorically, "... the framework of the stilling of the storm is based on the story

those who were not involved in the actual sailing or fishing.[92] The severity of the storm may be estimated from the fact that apparently even the experienced fishermen were terrified. They rudely awakened Jesus, and their cry carries a sharp tone of rebuke, "Teacher, are we to drown for all you care?"[93] Jesus rebuked the wind and the sea; the wind fell and there was a great calm. As suddenly as the storm had come it had subsided, subdued by Jesus' sovereign command, "Peace, be still."

The question of what was involved in the muzzling of the storm cannot be avoided.[94] The God of Israel is the Lord of history and nature. His sovereignty was demonstrated in the stilling of the roaring sea[95] and the silencing of the howling wind.[96] He is the personal, living God who intervenes in the experience of men with a revelation of his power and his will. He is the God who acts, not some pale abstraction. Through the expression of his word salvation is accomplished for men. When he chooses to reveal himself the forces of nature must submit to his will. This was never more evident than in the Exodus and the crossing of the Red Sea, but it is also evident in the subduing of the wind and the sea. In the same manner the Son of God threatened and subdued the forces which "spend themselves as forces of will in the elemental fury of

---

of Jonah." Yet in both form and content there are wide divergences between the two accounts. The parallels which have been suggested are those dictated by the circumstances of describing a severe storm, the fear it imposes, and the presence of one who sleeps undisturbed. Such parallels can be cited from elsewhere in the OT (cf. Ps. 107:23-32) and even from Virgil's *Aeneid* IV, 554-560. See further H. van der Loos, *The Miracles of Jesus* (Leiden, 1965), p. 646. This (with the parallel texts) is the only reference in the Gospels to Jesus sleeping.

92 Dalman, *op. cit.*, p. 198.

93 Moffatt's paraphrase. Other instances of impertinence on the part of the disciples occur in Chs. 5:31; 6:37; 8:4. These instances of rebuke indicate the extent of the veiledness of Jesus' person; the Son of God is subjected to the rudeness of men.

94 From a phenomenological point of view this pericope invites comparison with other accounts of the subduing of water and wind, for which see H. van der Loos, *op. cit.*, pp. 641-644. The Jewish attitude that only God can control the wind and waves finds expression not only in the OT (e.g. Ps. 65:7; 89:9; 107:23-32) but in II Macc. 9:8 (Antiochus Epiphanes believed "in supernatural arrogance that he could command the waves of the seas"). Rabbinic stories of the stilling of storms in answer to prayer are found in TB *Baba Mezia* 59b; TJ *Berachoth* 9, 13b on which see S-B*K* I (1922), p. 452.

95 Ps. 33:7; 65:7; 77:16; Job 12:15.

96 Ps. 107:25-30; 147:18; Prov. 30:4; Job 28:25; Amos 4:13; Nah. 1:3 f.

nature."[97] The cosmic overtones in the Gospel account must not be missed.[98] Mark has underlined them by a careful choice of terminology which recalls Jesus' encounter with the demons: Jesus rebuked the wind;[99] the sea is enjoined to obey with the command "Silence, be muzzled";[100] the wind subsides and the sea obeys with the result that great calmness ensues. Jesus addressed the raging storm as a "force" threatening him and his disciples. The force of the sea was muzzled as Jesus subdued it with his sovereign word of authority.

40-41 Jesus rebuked the disciples for the lack of faith expressed in their terror and fear. This is the first in a series of rebukes (cf. Chs. 7:18; 8:17 f., 21, 32 f.; 9:19) and its placement at this point is important. It indicates that in spite of Ch. 4:11, 34, the difference is one of degree, not of kind, between the disciples who have received through revelation some insight into the secret of the Kingdom of God as having come near in the person of Jesus and the multitude who see only a riddle. The disciples themselves are still quite blind and filled with misunderstanding. When Jesus asks, "Do you not yet have faith?" he means specifically faith in God's saving power as this is present and released through his own person.[101] The failure of the disciples to understand this is

---

97 E. Stauffer, *TWNT* II (Eng. Tr. 1964), pp. 624, 626. Stauffer adds, "The elements have found their Master... This man is more powerful than the forces of nature... Christ is the one who commands nature as its Lord and King. Thus the unconditional lordship of Jesus is powerfully revealed in this ἐπιτιμᾶν."

98 See the important chapter on "La Mer" in P. Reymond, *L'eau. Sa vie et sa signification dans l'Ancien Testament* (Leiden, 1958), pp. 163-196. On p. 195 Reymond comments "the account of the stilling of a sea which has not yet accepted its total submission since it attempts to rebel against the κύριος, ... and the conclusion, which sets forth as evidence the fact that Jesus commands even the winds and the waves, must be understood with all of its cosmic overtones."

99 Jesus rebuked the wind (ἐπετίμησεν, Ch. 4:39). The verb ἐπιτιμᾶν is used to express Jesus' rebuke to the demons in Chs. 1:25; 3:12 and 9:25. On the verb see Stauffer, *op. cit.*, pp. 623-627; H. C. Kee, "The Terminology in Mark's Exorcism Stories," *NTS* 14 (1968), pp. 232-246.

100 This detail (σιώπα, πεφίμωσο), found only in Mark, is reminiscent of the encounter with the demonic in Ch. 1:25 καὶ ἐπετίμησεν αὐτῷ ὁ Ἰησοῦς λέγων· φιμώθητι; Ch. 4:39 καὶ ... ἐπετίμησεν τῷ ἀνέμῳ καὶ εἶπεν ... πεφίμωσο. The parallel has been frequently pointed out. Cf. S. Eitrem, *Some Notes on the Demonology in the New Testament* (Oslo, 1950), p. 31; Burkill, *op. cit.*, pp. 54, 73; Lohmeyer, *op. cit.*, pp. 91 f.; Schniewind, *op. cit.*, p. 85 *et al.*

101 Cf. Ch. 2:5 where the same thought is in view. J. Schniewind, *op. cit.*, p. 86 is surely correct when he says, at this point "faith in God coincides with faith in Jesus."

expressed in their awe-inspired question, "Who then is this, that even the wind and the sea obey him?"

As the conclusion to Mark's paragraph the question is rhetorical, inviting the response of faith, "He is the Christ, the Son of God." In the account of the subduing of the sea we are told that Jesus is the living Lord. What is true of the God of Israel is true of him. At all times and in every sphere he exercises sovereign control over the situation. The subduing of the sea and the wind was not merely a demonstration of power; it was an epiphany, through which Jesus was unveiled to his disciples as the Savior in the midst of intense peril. Very early this incident was understood as a sign of Jesus' saving presence in the persecution which threatened to overwhelm the Church. It is not surprising that in early Christian art the Church was depicted as a boat driven upon a perilous sea; with Jesus in the midst, there was nothing to fear.[102]

[102] Cf. J. Allan, "The Gospel of the Son of God Crucified," *Interpretation* 9 (1955), p. 142; C. E. B. Cranfield, *St. Mark* (Cambridge, 1963), p. 175.

CHAPTER 5

(b) The Gerasene Demoniac: the Subduing of the Demonic. Ch. 5:1-20

1 And they came to the other side of the sea into the country of the Gerasenes.

2 And when he came out of the boat, straightway[1] there met him out of the tombs a man with an unclean spirit,

3 who had his dwelling in the tombs: and no man could any more bind him, no, not with a chain;

4 because that he had been often bound with fetters and chains, and the chains had been rent asunder by him, and the fetters broken in pieces: and no man had strength to tame him.

5 And always, night and day, in the tombs and in the mountains, he was crying out, and cutting himself with stones.

6 And when he saw Jesus from afar, he ran and worshipped him;[2]

7 and crying out with a loud voice he saith, What have I to do with thee, Jesus, thou Son of the Most High God? I adjure thee by God, torment me not.

8 For he said unto him, Come forth, thou unclean spirit, out of the man.

9 And he asked him, What is thy name? And he saith unto him, My name is Legion; for we are many.

10 And he besought him much that he would not send them away out of the country.

11 Now there was there on the mountain side a great herd of swine feeding.

12 And they besought him, saying, Send us into the swine, that we may enter into them.

13 And he gave them leave. And the unclean spirits came out, and entered into the swine: and the herd rushed down the steep into the sea, *in number* about two thousand; and they were drowned in the sea.

14 And they that fed them fled, and told it in the city, and in the country. And they came to see what it was that had come to pass.

---

[1] Perhaps εὐθύς should be omitted with B W it sys, p, h arm, as in the RSV.

[2] It would be better to translate "fell on his knees before him" in keeping with προσέπιπτον in Ch. 3:11 and γονυπετῶν in Ch. 1:40. There is no thought of adoration in the action, as is clear from the context.

15 And they come to Jesus, and behold him that was possessed with demons sitting, clothed and in his right mind, *even* him that had the legion: and they were afraid.
16 And they that saw it declared unto them how it befell him that was possessed with demons, and concerning the swine.
17 And they began to beseech him to depart from their borders.
18 And as he was entering into the boat, he that had been possessed with demons besought him that he might be with him.
19 And he suffered him not, but saith unto him, Go to thy house unto thy friends, and tell them how great things the Lord hath done for thee, and *how* he had mercy on thee.
20 And he went his way, and began to publish in Decapolis how great things Jesus had done for him: and all men marvelled.

The account of the Gerasene demoniac is elaborately told. The vivid details appear to reflect in part eyewitness report and in part the explanation supplied by townspeople long familiar with the history of the violent man of the tombs.[3] Mark has not included the narrative in his Gospel merely because he delights in a well-told story. This account, more graphically than any other in the Gospels, indicates that the function of demonic possession is to distort and destroy the image of God in man.[4] The subordinate detail of the destruction of the herd of swine has bearing upon this fact. For this very reason Jesus could not avoid a significant confrontation with demonic possession. His sovereign authority and the quality of the salvation that he brings finds graphic illustration in this historic account.

---

[3] E. Lohmeyer, *Das Evangelium des Markus*[16] (Göttingen, 1963), p. 94 sees in verses 3-5, where there are a string of perfect infinitives, the explanation given by townsfolk. In Ch. 5:15 the description τὸν δαιμονιζόμενον is no longer true, but reflects the point of view of the townsmen. The three participles καθήμενον, ἱματισμένον and σωφρονοῦντα describe features which they must have noticed immediately. For an interpretation of certain details of the text as a midrash on Isa. 65:1-5 see H. Sahlin, "Die Perikope vom gerasenischen Besessenen und der Plan des Markusevangeliums," *Stud Theol* 18 (1964), pp. 160-162.

[4] W. Foerster, *TWNT* II (Eng. Tr. 1964), pp. 18 f.: "In most of the stories of possession what is at issue is not merely sickness but a destruction and distortion of the divine likeness of man according to creation. The center of personality, the volitional and active ego, is impaired by alien powers which seek to ruin the man and sometimes drive him to self-destruction (Mk. 5:5). The ego is so impaired that the spirits speak through him. Jesus is conscious that He now breaks the power of the devil and his angels because He is the One in whom the dominion of God is present on behalf of humanity."

1 It would normally take two hours or so to cross the lake, but it is impossible to know whether Jesus and the disciples arrived in the evening or morning.[5] The point of arrival is indicated in a general way as the district of the Gerasenes, most probably in reference to a town whose name is preserved in the modern Kersa or Koursi.[6] At the site of Kersa the shore is level, and there are no tombs. But about a mile further south there is a fairly steep slope within forty yards from the shore, and about two miles from there cavern tombs are found which appear to have been used for dwellings.

2-5 The man who was demon-possessed is elaborately introduced, perhaps in a manner reflecting the excited report of townsmen who had long been familiar with his existence. His dwelling in the midst of the tombs and the inability of chains and fetters to bind him is especially

---

[5] M. J. Lagrange, *L'Évangile selon Saint Marc*[9] (Paris, 1947), p. 126 suggests "it would have been very astonishing if the disciples had not used the remainder of the night for fishing; accordingly, they debarked in the morning." There is, however, little evidence [Jn. 21:2-3 (?)] that the disciples continued to practice their vocation after having heeded Jesus' call.

[6] The problem of text and identification are well known. It is clear that Mark wrote Γερασηνῶν (supported by B ℵ* D latt sa Eus), apparently with reference to a town by the lake whose name may be preserved in the modern Kersa or Koursi on the eastern shore. Early readers of the Gospel found in this a reference to the well-known city of Gerasa, which unfortunately was located some thirty miles to the southeast of the lake. The strange variant "Gadara," supported by Mt. 8:28 and in Mark by C 𝔎 A φ 543 *pm* sy[p, h], may have arisen through a confusion between the place and the toparchy, for Gadara was the capital of a toparchy. The incident could have taken place at a suitable locality within the territory of the toparchy but remote from the town, so that in the tradition the name of the toparchic capital replaced that of the particular village concerned, according to A. N. Sherwin-White, *Roman Society and Roman Law in the New Testament* (Oxford, 1963), p. 128 n. 3. Origen, in his commentary on John (*In Ioan.* vi. 41), pointed out the difficulties in both the readings Gerasa (as commonly understood) and Gadara (the latter being six miles from the shore of the lake) and suggested that a more appropriate site would be Gergesa, near the lake, associated with the OT Girgashites. His reading Γεργεσηνῶν has left its mark on ℵ corr L Δ Θ λ 28 33 565 579 700 892 1071 Epiph, most of which are associated with the Caesarean tradition. On the question see esp. G. Dalman, *Orte und Wege Jesu*[3] (Gütersloh, 1924), pp. 190-192; C. Kopp, *Die heiligen Stätten der Evangelien* (Regensburg, 1959), pp. 282 ff.; M. J. Lagrange, *op. cit.*, pp. 132-136; F. M. Abel, "Koursi," *JPOS* 2 (1922), pp. 112 ff.; Tj. Baarda, "Gadarenes, Gerasenes, Gergesenes and the 'Diatessaron' Traditions," in *Neotestamentica et Semitica* (Edinburgh, 1969), pp. 181-197.

stressed, but every word emphasizes his pathetic condition. The people of the town undoubtedly felt that the man was mad, for his appearance and behavior conformed to the popular diagnosis of insanity.[7] In accordance with the practice of the day they had attempted to bind him by chains to protect themselves from his violence. When this proved to be futile, they had driven him off to wander restlessly in the wild hill country and to dwell in the subterranean caves which served as tombs and dwellings for the poorest people of the district.[8] At intervals during the night and the day he would be seen among the tombs or on the mountains, wildly shrieking, cutting his flesh with sharp stones,[9] attempting to destroy himself and bring to an end the torment of an unbearable existence. In the several features of the description the purpose of demonic possession to distort and destroy the divine likeness of man according to creation is made indelibly clear. The attitude and actions of the people of the town were an added cruelty based on popular misunderstanding. But ultimate responsibility for the wretchedness of the man and the brutal treatment he had endured rested with the demons who had taken possession of the center of his personality.

6-8 The movement of the story, which had been momentarily interrupted by verses 3-5, is now resumed. What had been summed up in Mark's phrase in verse 2 ("there met him . . . a man with an unclean spirit") is now related in more detail. The man had seen Jesus from a distance, and running he fell upon his knees before him. Shrieking with a loud voice the demoniac uttered an adjuration that was violent and fierce.[10] Its purpose is entirely defensive; sensing the identity of a

---

[7] According to the Talmud there were four characteristics of madness: walking abroad at night; spending the night on a grave; tearing one's clothes and destroying what one was given. This man demonstrated all four characteristics. See H. van der Loos, *The Miracles of Jesus* (Leiden, 1965), pp. 386 f.; S-B*K* I (1922), p. 491.

[8] For the use of tombs as dwellings see the LXX version of Ps. 68:6 (LXX 67:6); Job 30:5-6; Isa. 65:4. Tombs were frequently subterranean caves. See further E. Lohmeyer, *op. cit.*, p. 94 n. 3.

[9] Was this practice associated with worship of demonic deities? Cutting the flesh in frenzied worship is very ancient (cf. I Kings 18:28). In Ch. 5:7 Jesus is addressed by a title well attested in Gentile and Jewish syncretistic contexts appropriate to the Decapolis as a Hellenistic and pagan area. The suggestion lies close at hand that the possessed man was involved in a demonic form of worship contrary to his will.

[10] S. Eitrem, *Some Notes on the Demonology in the New Testament* (Oslo, 1950), p. 55 thinks that it is inconceivable that the man would have addressed

dangerous opponent, the unclean spirit raises its voice to defend itself against him.[11] The first phrase in this address to Jesus could be rendered "What have I and you in common?" or "Why do you interfere with me?"[12] It is surprising to find the demon addressing Jesus by his personal name, although it is possible that he had heard one of the disciples use this form of direct address. What is more noticeable is that the demon is fully aware of Jesus' divine origin and dignity. "Son of the Most High God" is not a messianic designation but a divine one,[13] in spite of the syncretistic associations that gather around the term "Most High."[14] The full address is not a confession of Jesus' dignity but a desperate attempt to gain control over him or to render him harmless, in accordance with the common assumption of the period that the use of

---

himself to Jesus at once with an adjuration so strong. He suggests the following reconstruction of the dialogue:

Demon: What have I to do with thee, Jesus, thou Son of the Most High God?
Jesus: What is thy name?
Demon: My name is Legion.
Jesus: Come out of the man, Legion.
Demon: I adjure thee by God, that thou torment us not and send us not away out of the country.

11 See on Ch. 1:24. T. A. Burkill, *Mysterious Revelation* (Ithaca, N.Y., 1963), pp. 88 f. points to the close parallel in formulation and function between Chs. 1:24 and 5:7. The first five words are the same in the two addresses, except that Ch. 1:24 has the first person plural ἡμῖν rather than the first person singular ἐμοί. On both occasions the demon is aware of Jesus' divine origin and nature. The designation "Son of the Most High God" in Ch. 5:7 corresponds to "the Holy One of God" in Ch. 1:24. In each instance the demon knows that the appearance of Jesus bodes ill for Satanic forces. The verb "torment" in Ch. 5:7 corresponds to the verb "destroy" in Ch. 1:24.

12 Similar expressions occur in the OT (e.g. Josh. 22:24; Judg. 11:12; II Sam. 16:10; 19:22; I Kings 17:18) and in classical Greek [cf. L & S s.v. εἰμί (*sum*) C. III. 2]. The expression may even convey a threat, "Mind your own business!"

13 Cf. J. Bieneck, *Sohn Gottes als Christusbezeichnung der Synoptiker* (Zürich, 1951), pp. 46-48.

14 Ὕψιστος is used in the OT mainly by non-Israelites to denote the God of Israel, e.g. Gen. 14:18 ff.; Num. 24:16; Isa. 14:14; Dan. 3:26; 4:2; cf. I Esdras 2:3. In the NT it appears only in passages with an OT coloring and in utterances of demons, e.g., Lk. 8:28 (D) τί ἐμοὶ καὶ σοὶ υἱὲ τοῦ ὑψίστου; and Acts 16:17. It is clearly syncretistic in first century A.D. inscriptions from the Black Sea, on which see H. J. Cadbury, *The Book of Acts in History* (New York, 1955), pp. 37, 54 n. 13, 91, 107 n. 14. O. Bauernfeind, *Die Worte der Dämonen im Markusevangelium* (Stuttgart, 1927), p. 24 finds definite polytheistic and magical associations in the use of the title here.

the precise name of an adversary gave one mastery over him. The very strong adjuration "by God" has a strange, ironic ring in the mouth of the demoniac. He senses that he is to be punished and employs the strongest adjuration that he knows. He invokes God's protection, but the adjuration is without force, for Jesus is the Son of God.[15] In the act of kneeling, the defensive use of the divine name and the violent invocation of God to strengthen the plea that Jesus would not torment him, there is the full recognition of Jesus' superior power on the part of the demon. On this understanding verse 8 is in its original position.[16] Jesus is sufficiently powerful that the demon at once understands that it must now leave its victim. An explicit command is scarcely necessary, and comes almost as an after-thought. It is put in the form of a subordinate clause, and Mark's historic imperfect may be translated "For *he had said* to him, Unclean spirit, come forth out of the man."

9-10 Jesus now demands to know the demon's name, and for the first time there is indicated the full degree of distortion to which the man was subjected: not one but a multitude of alien forces had taken possession of the volitional and active ego of the man ("My name is Legion, for we are many"). The term "Legion" is not strictly a Latinism *(legio);* like other military and governmental terms, it had entered the language and is found not only in Hellenistic Greek but in Aramaic as well. It is difficult to know what meaning to place upon the term.[17] The answer

---

15 Cf. J. Schneider, *TWNT* V (1954), pp. 463 f. When the demoniac begs not to be tormented Schneider feels that eternal punishment is in view. H. van der Loos, *op. cit.*, p. 387 argues that this is not necessarily so. "Nothing stands in the way of interpreting Mark ... as referring to the fear of the demons, i.e. to the crisis which the encounter with Jesus caused in the mind of the sick person." The punishment to which reference is made, however, is probably eschatological in nature, especially if it is correct to see βασανίσῃς ("torment") in Ch. 5:7 as the corresponding element to ἀπολέσαι ("destroy") in Ch. 1:24. On the adjuration formula see A. Deissmann, *Light from the Ancient East* (London, 1910), pp. 250-257.

16 Cf. E. Lohmeyer, *op. cit.*, pp. 95 f.; T. A. Burkill, *op. cit.*, p. 90. Other suggestions have been made concerning the position of verse 8, the most noteworthy conjecture being that the verse originally stood before verse 7, and perhaps in place of verse 6, a position defended by O. Bauernfeind, *op. cit.*, pp. 48 ff. Such conjectures, however, are unnecessary if verse 8 is seen as an explanatory insertion by Mark similar to Ch. 6:52.

17 H. Preisker, *TWNT* IV (1942), pp. 68 f. recognizes the military background of the term, pointing out that in the imperial period a legion consisted of 6000 foot soldiers, 120 horsemen and technical personnel. The entrance of the term into

may express the man's sense of being possessed by an aggregate of uncoordinated impulses and evil forces which have so impaired his ego that the spirits speak and act through him. If so, this response may be an appeal for compassion. It is a pathetic admission of the loss of all sense of identity. On the other hand, the answer may be evasive, the demons desiring to withhold their true names from Jesus in a desperate attempt to thwart his power.[18] It is also possible that the name may have been selected to invoke the fear of a powerful name. It is probable that the many demons can be referred to as a single being because they are in common possession of the same victim, but it is not possible to ascertain the exact nuance expressed in the term "Legion."[19] The demoniac made repeated requests that he not be sent out of the district, a conception which has parallels elsewhere.[20]

11-13 The reference to the herd of swine grazing on the mountainside is not strange in a narrative which takes place in the Decapolis, with its predominantly Gentile population. It is simply another indication of the pagan environment. The demons made a specific request to enter into the swine, and when Jesus complied, the demons left the man and entered their new hosts. In panic the herd rushed down the slope into the sea and drowned. This element in the narrative has invited special

---

colloquial speech indicates that the Roman occupation was a heavy burden. In this context, however, he insists that "legion" has nothing of its usual Roman military overtones, but is the designation of numinous powers which oppose themselves to Jesus as the embodiment of the power of God. The term, accordingly, does not display anti-Roman sentiment [cf. P. Winter, *The Trial of Jesus* (Berlin, 1961), p. 129; T. A. Burkill, *op. cit.*, p. 93 n. 12] but is to be understood in the context of the struggle between the forces of God and those of Satan.

18 Cf. M. J. Lagrange, *op. cit.*, p. 129. J. Jeremias, *Jesus' Promise to the Nations* (Naperville, Ill., 1958), pp. 30 f. n. 5, argues that the demon does give his name, and it is "Soldier, since we (the demons) are a great host (and resemble one another as soldiers do)." He further suggests that the military unit referred to was the τέλος, the strength of which was 2,048 men; hence Mark's reference to "about two thousand" swine.

19 S-B*K* II (1924), p. 9 and S. Eitrem, *op. cit.*, p. 56 explain the name to mean that the man was possessed by many demons who tormented him as one combined force, and this may be correct.

20 Assuming that the demons are the subject of παρεκάλει, O. Bauernfeind, *op. cit.*, pp. 38 f. cites parallels in which demons are sent to places like the desert, uninhabited mountains, the sea, the ends of the world, and into animals so that they may not harm men. Cf. Tobit 8:3. If the man is the subject, his pleas would be a pathetic appeal not to be driven off again as the townsmen had often done.

attention and varied conjectures, which need not be reviewed here.[21] What must be seen above all else is that the fate of the swine demonstrates the ultimate intention of the demons with respect to the man they had possessed. It is their purpose to destroy the creation of God, and halted in their destruction of a man, they fulfilled their purpose with the swine.

The drowning of the swine was not an unforeseen consequence in Jesus' concession; it was the express purpose which lay behind the request of the demons. Accordingly, the question why Jesus allowed them to enter the swine must be faced. The answer would seem to have two elements. First, Jesus recognized that the time of the ultimate vanquishment of the demons had not yet come; his encounter and triumph over the demonic does not yet put an end to Satan's power. It is the pledge and the symbol of that definitive triumph, but the time when that triumph will be fully realized is yet deferred. It must await the appointment of God.[22] Therefore, Jesus allows the demons to continue their destructive work, but not upon a man.[23] The second element is related to this: Jesus allowed the demons to enter the swine to indicate beyond question that their real purpose was the total destruction of their host. While this point may have been obscured in the case of the man, there was the blatant evidence in the instance of the swine. Their intention was no different with regard to the man whom they had possessed.

14-15 The herdsmen who had tended the swine fled the scene and hastened to the town and the small hamlets surrounding it[24] to report

---

[21] For a survey of seven principal interpretations see H. Ridderbos, *The Coming of the Kingdom* (Philadelphia, 1962), pp. 113-115. After a similar but less comprehensive survey Van der Loos, *op. cit.,* p. 392 rightly says, "These are all guesses, spotlighting now the one, and then the other party to the scene, and containing a search for a pedagogic motive in many cases."

[22] *Ibid.,* pp. 112 f., calling attention to Rev. 12:22.

[23] Cf. S. F. H. J. Berkelbach van der Sprenkel, *Het evangelie van Markus* (Amsterdam, 1937), *ad loc.,* who rightly places in the center of the discussion the two persons directly concerned in the healing, Jesus and the possessed man. Jesus does not appear to worry in the least about the loss of the swine, "not because, as a law-abiding Israelite, he regarded them as 'filthy lucre', but because at the moment of a 'liberation' everything must serve and must be available."

[24] With Mark's expression here, εἰς τὴν πόλιν καὶ εἰς τοὺς ἀγρούς, cf. Ch. 6:36 where the expression is εἰς τοὺς κύκλῳ ἀγρούς (where bread is to be bought).

the loss to the owners. As a result people came quickly together to see what had happened. By a series of three participles Mark emphasizes the features which must have gripped the attention of those who came: they saw Jesus and the man who had been possessed seated, clothed and restored to wholeness of mind. [25] Mark adds with emphasis, "the one who had been possessed by the legion." The man whom neither chains nor men could restrain was sitting in a docile manner before Jesus; he who had terrified others as he ran naked among the tombs was now clothed; the one who had shrieked wildly and behaved violently was now fully recovered. So radical was the transformation that the townspeople were stunned and frightened.

16-17 In the lively discussion which followed, the herdsmen told their story once again. To them the one who had been possessed was doubtless no stranger, and they made mention of him. But Mark indicates that they had not forgotten the swine, and the emphatic position of the phrase "and concerning the swine" suggests that this was foremost in their thought. The consequence was the pathetic request of the inhabitants that Jesus leave them. Their motive may well have been that they were afraid to have in their midst one whose power was as great as that which Jesus had demonstrated. [26]

18-20 In sharp contrast to the fear of the inhabitants is the devotion of the man who formerly had been possessed. As Jesus entered the boat the man begged Jesus that "he might be with him." Mark's formulation appears to be a technical one for discipleship. [27] The desire of the man

---

25 Ch. 5:15 καθήμενον ἱματισμένον καὶ σωφρονοῦντα. C. E. B. Cranfield, *The Gospel According to St. Mark* (Cambridge, 1963), p. 180 comments, "Previously even chains had not been able to control his demonic energy and restlessness; now he sits at rest. He had been naked like a beast; now his human characteristics are restored." A. Deissmann, *op. cit.,* p. 78 cites a papyrus where the statement "I have clothed him" occurs in a formula of adoption: to clothe a man is to adopt him. If this was a common understanding it would explain why the man asks to remain with Jesus in verse 18.

26 So H. van der Loos, *op. cit.,* p. 393. In support of this is the conclusion to verse 15: καὶ ἐφοβήθησαν, "and they were afraid." It is not likely that they understood what had happened after the discussion any more than they had before it took place. There is no mention of the loss of the swine in the request that Jesus depart.

27 With ἵνα μετ' αὐτοῦ ᾖ in Ch. 5:18 cf. ἵνα ὦσιν μετ' αὐτοῦ in Ch. 3:14, where the words describe the purpose for which Jesus called twelve disciples.

to accompany Jesus is the response of gratitude, and indicates that Jesus is not some strange divine-man who is to be feared. He is the one who bestows healing that is redemptive, and who calls forth the devotion of those who have received his benefactions. Jesus refused the man permission to accompany him, but instructed him to return to the circle of family[28] and friends from which he had been estranged and to declare[29] all that the Lord had done in extending mercy to him. In obedience[30] the man went his way and began to publish in the Decapolis[31] the outstanding things which Jesus had done for him, so that men marvelled. It was natural that he should have spoken openly of Jesus, for God had extended his mercy to him through Jesus.

It is striking that no restriction is placed upon the man by Jesus, in contrast to the injunctions to silence found in other instances of healing. The accent falls upon apprehension of the divine action and declaration in a manner which anticipates the primitive Christian mission rather than upon secrecy and silence. This may be due to the fact that the man was a Gentile and his proclamation is confined to a predominantly Gentile area. It is, nevertheless, an exception to the more usual pattern observed by Jesus in Galilee. It should also be observed that the object of the man's declaration was not the person of Jesus directly,

---

28 Mark's phrase τοὺς σοὺς may well include a circle wider than the man's family, but there can be no doubt that the family was at the center of that circle. A. Fridrichsen, *Le problème du miracle dans le Christianisme primitif* (Strasbourg, 1925), p. 82 rightly comments on the important part played by the family in the extension of the gospel; the largest influence was felt among the parents and those who lived in the same house with one who had received a benefaction from Jesus.

29 The *v.l.* διάγγειλον found in Caesarean texts (P^{45} D W λ φ *al*) is interesting because the word describes a missionary activity in Lk. 9:60; Acts 21:26; Rom. 9:17. The best supported text, however, reads ἀπάγγειλον (B ℵ C Θ).

30 The strained exegesis of W. Wrede, *Das Messiasgeheimnis in den Evangelien* (Göttingen, 1901), pp. 140 f., in which he attempted to draw a sharp contrast between Ch. 5:19 and Ch. 5:20 to show that the man was disobedient to Jesus' intention, has rightly been criticized by his opponents [e.g. N. B. Stonehouse, *The Witness of Matthew and Mark to Christ* (Philadelphia, 1944), p. 58] and pupils [e.g. R. H. Lightfoot, *History and Interpretation in the Gospels* (London, 1935), pp. 89 f.; T. A. Burkill, *op. cit.*, pp. 91 f.].

31 On the Decapolis see below on Ch. 7:31. A detailed description of the Decapolis is given by E. Schürer, *Die Geschichte des jüdischen Volkes im Zeitalter Jesu Christi* II[4] (Leipzig, 1907), pp. 115-148; H. Bietenhard, "Die Dekapolis von Pompeius bis Traian. Ein Kapitel aus der neutestamentlichen Zeitgeschichte," *ZDPV* 79 (1963), pp. 24-58.

but *what Jesus had done* in restoring him to wholeness. Thus in the midst of the Gentiles, the God of Israel was glorified through the proclamation of what Jesus had accomplished.

The story was remembered in the tradition because of the dramatic evidence it offered of the purpose of demonic possession and of the full deliverance brought by Jesus. It declared that the victory of Jesus over evil forces is a reality in which the liberating power of the Kingdom of God is manifested in an extension of the saving mercy of God.

(c) The Plea of Jairus. Ch. 5:21-24

21 And when Jesus had crossed over again in the boat[32] unto the other side, a great multitude was gathered unto him; and he was by the sea.
22 And there cometh one of the rulers of the synagogue, Jairus by name;[33] and seeing him, he falleth at his feet,
23 and beseecheth him much, saying, My little daughter is at the point of death: *I pray thee,* that thou come and lay thy hands on her, that she may be made whole and live.
24 And he went with him;[34] and a great multitude followed him, and they thronged him.

The narrative of the radical healing of Jairus' daughter is presented in two parts (Ch. 5:21-24, 35-43) which are separated by the account of the healing of the woman who had lived with a hemorrhage for twelve years. The two incidents may have become associated in this way merely because there was an interruption to the journey which proved disastrous for the young girl. But it is possible that Mark saw more in this association: the healing of a woman who has lived with the impingement of death anticipates the healing of a girl who has actually experienced death. The structural device of intercalating one incident within another is paralleled by other instances in which Mark uses the device of anticipation. The detail with which Mark recalls the woman with the

[32] The superfluous words "in the boat" are absent from P^{45} D Θ λ *pc* it sy^s, and should, perhaps, be omitted.

[33] The words "Jairus by name" are omitted from D it and in the Matthean parallel (Mt. 9:18). It is conceivable that they were added in Mark by a copyist who had Lk. 8:41 in mind. The Lucan formulation ᾧ ὄνομα Ἰάϊρος occurs in the Caesarean texts W Θ 565 *pc*.

[34] The RSV locates the paragraph division at this point, rightly judging that what follows prepares for the subsequent account.

hemorrhage indicates that his concern extends beyond the mere passage of time. The healing experienced by the woman is itself a reversal of death and a pledge of the raising of Jairus' daughter.[35]

21-24 Jesus returned to the western shore of the lake, perhaps to Capernaum,[36] and a multitude gathered around him while he was yet by the Sea. No indication is given whether the crowd came together as soon as he arrived or after an extended period of time; it is simply the first fact that Mark records, offering a contrast to Jesus' experience on the eastern shore where the inhabitants urged him to depart. All of the interest is focused upon Jairus[37] and his urgent appeal to Jesus. He may have had contact with Jesus previously, since as synagogue-ruler he was a lay official responsible for supervision of the building and arranging the service.[38] His request that Jesus should come and lay hands in healing upon his daughter reflects a common practice of the day.[39] What was unusual was his confidence that if Jesus would come, his daughter's life would be saved. Jesus went with him, followed by the crowd. Mark's reference to the fact that they were pressing all around him prepares for the following account of the woman who touched Jesus in order to be healed.

---

[35] A detail which may have contributed to the association of Ch. 5:21-43 with Ch. 5:1-20 is Jesus' contact with the unclean, since the man of the tombs (who is probably a Gentile), the flow of blood and the presence of death all involve Jesus in ceremonial uncleanness.

[36] Mark's phrase "the other side" generally means the eastern shore, which has led K. L. Schmidt, *Der Rahmen der Geschichte Jesu* (Berlin, 1919), p. 144 to write "just as well as in Capernaum we can seek the house of Jairus also in Bethsaida, on the north-eastern shore of the Sea." He has not been followed in this judgment, however. Cf. G. Dalman, *op. cit.,* pp. 149 ff.

[37] The name may reflect the biblical Jair, found in Num. 32:41; Judg. 10:3-5 and Esth. 2:5. For the Hellenized form found in Mark's text see Esth. 2:5 LXX.

[38] The title was also used sometimes in an honorary sense for distinguished members of the synagogue. For a review of the inscriptional evidence and of the functions of this office see B. Lifshitz, "Fonctions et titres honorifiques dans les communautés juives," *RB* 67 (1960), pp. 58-64; W. Schrage, *TWNT* VII (1964), pp. 842-845. Mark's peculiar formulation in Ch. 5:22 εἷς τῶν ἀρχισυναγώγων should be understood in the sense of one who belongs to the class of synagogue-rulers; for εἷς as equivalent of τις, see C. F. D. Moule, *An Idiom-Book of New Testament Greek*[2] (Cambridge, 1960), pp. 125, 174.

[39] While this is the first mention of the laying on of hands in Mark, other references occur in Chs. 6:5; 7:32; 8:23, 25. See H. van der Loos, *op. cit.,* pp. 313-321; D. Daube, *The New Testament and Rabbinic Judaism* (London, 1956), pp. 224-246.

(d) The Woman with the Hemorrhage. Ch. 5:25-34

25 And a woman, who had an issue of blood[40] twelve years,
26 and had suffered many things of many physicians, and had spent all that she had, and was nothing bettered, but rather grew worse,
27 having heard the things concerning Jesus, came in the crowd behind, and touched his garment.
28 For she said, If I touch but his garments, I shall be made whole.
29 And straightway the fountain of her blood was dried up;[41] and she felt in her body that she was healed of her plague.
30 And straightway Jesus, perceiving in himself that the power *proceeding* from him had gone forth, turned him about in the crowd, and said, Who touched my garments?
31 And his disciples said unto him, Thou seest the multitude thronging thee, and sayest thou, Who touched me?
32 And he looked round about to see her that had done this thing.
33 But the woman fearing and trembling, knowing what had been done to her, came and fell down before him, and told him all the truth.
34 And he said unto her, Daughter, thy faith hath made thee whole; go in peace, and be whole of thy plague.[42]

25-27 The woman who unobtrusively touched Jesus had experienced a flow of blood for a period of twelve years. It is common to think of chronic hemorrhaging from the womb,[43] but from Mark's description it is not possible to know the cause for her loss of blood.[44] She had consulted a number of physicians, had endured a wide variety of treatments, and had spent all of her money in a desperate attempt to better her condition. All this was in vain; in fact, her condition grew worse. Her existence was wretched because she was in a constant state of uncleanness and would be generally shunned by people since contact with

---

40 RSV "a flow of blood"; NEB "who had suffered from haemorrhages."

41 RSV "And immediately the hemorrhage ceased." The phrase ἡ πηγὴ τοῦ αἵματος αὐτῆς comes from Lev. 12:7.

42 RSV "be healed of your disease."

43 E.g. W. Ebstein, *Die Medizin im Neuen Testament und im Talmud* (Stuttgart, 1903), pp. 97 f.; S. Eitrem, *op. cit.*, p. 35.

44 Cf. J. Preuss, *Biblisch-talmudische Medizin* (Berlin, 1911), p. 439; H. van der Loos, *op. cit.*, pp. 509 f.

her rendered others unclean.[45] What she had experienced from the doctors may be estimated from the Talmud, which has preserved a record of the medicines and treatments applied to an illness of this nature.[46] None of these remedies had benefited the woman. Having heard reports of the healing power of Jesus, she determined her course of action. Despite her ritual uncleanness she entered the crowd behind him and reached out to his garment. The desire to touch Jesus' clothing probably reflects the popular belief that the dignity and power of a person are transferred to what he wears.[47] On this understanding, her touch combined faith with quasi-magical notions which were widespread in that day.

28-29 The intense conviction that if she could only touch Jesus' garments she would be made whole was undoubtedly part of "the whole truth" which the woman declared before Jesus (verse 33). She may have known that others had touched him and had been made well (cf. Ch. 3:10; 6:56). At the moment she had fulfilled her intention she experienced the cessation of her hemorrhage, and knew that she had been healed.

30-32 Concurrent with the moment of healing, Jesus knew that "power" had gone forth from him. This unusual expression, which occurs only here in Mark's Gospel, must be interpreted from the context of "the power of God" in the Scripture. Power is a constitutive element in the biblical concept of the personal God.[48] Jesus possesses

---

[45] A woman suffering from this complaint was called a *zabah,* and came under the restrictions of Lev. 15:25-33. So important was considered the regulation of life for such a person that the tractate *Zabim* of the Mishnah is devoted to this topic. Cf. F. Hauck, *TWNT* III (1938), pp. 419-432.

[46] Cf. J. Preuss, *op. cit.,* pp. 439 f.; S-B*K* I (1922), p. 520. One remedy consisted of drinking a goblet of wine containing a powder compounded from rubber, alum and garden crocuses. Another treatment consisted of a dose of Persian onions cooked in wine administered with the summons, "Arise out of your flow of blood!" Other physicians prescribed sudden shock, or the carrying of the ash of an ostrich's egg in a certain cloth.

[47] Cf. H. van der Loos, *op. cit.,* pp. 313-317; S-B*K* I (1922), p. 520. Similarly, ritual impurity is transferred from contact with the person to contact with his garments in Lev. 15:27; 17:15; M. *Ḥagiga* II. 7 distinguishes stages in which clothes become unclean.

[48] Cf. W. Grundmann, *Der Begriff der Kraft in der neutestamentlichen Gedankenwelt* (Stuttgart, 1932); *idem, TWNT* II (Eng. Tr. 1964), pp. 290-310; C. H. Powell, *The Biblical Concept of Power* (London, 1963), pp. 5-17, 71-116.

the power of God as the representative of the Father. Nevertheless, the Father remains in control of his own power. The healing of the woman occurred through God's free and gracious decision to bestow upon her the power which was active in Jesus. By an act of sovereign will God determined to honor the woman's faith in spite of the fact that it was tinged with ideas which bordered on magic.

Jesus' question "Who touched my garments?" seemed pointless to the disciples since he had been jostled and touched by a host of individuals. Their impatience with the Lord reflects an awareness that their immediate mission was to assist a girl who was dying, and delay could be fatal. It also betrays that they had no understanding of what had taken place. Certainly not every contact with the person of Jesus resulted in a transmission of power. Involved in the situation was not a unilateral event in which touch released power, but a mutual event in which the personal relationship between Jesus and the woman released power.[49] Jesus, therefore, could not allow the woman to recede into the crowd still entertaining ideas tinged with superstition and magic. He stopped and looked intently upon the people surrounding him in order to see who[50] had touched him with an expectation of salvation.

33-34 With fear and trembling the woman acknowledged all that had happened. Her action in making herself known indicates both courage and gratitude, and it is here that the accent should fall rather than upon her fear. Mark places all of the emphasis upon the fact that she knew she had experienced the healing of her person. With awe, and only partial understanding of what had taken place, she declared the truth to Jesus.

Jesus' insistence that the woman identify herself, together with his gentle correction of any erroneous ideas she may have had, calls attention to the essential aspect of her experience. It was *the grasp of her faith* rather than her hand that had secured the healing she sought. Her touch had brought together two elements – faith and Jesus – and that had made it effective.[51] Power had gone forth from Jesus to the woman for the precise reason that she sought healing *from him.*[52] The woman's

49 Rightly observed by H. van der Loos, *op. cit.*, pp. 513-516.

50 Mark uses a feminine relative pronoun at this point, but the gender is to be understood from the narrator's perspective. Jesus himself asked the question in all seriousness; he did not know who had touched him.

51 Cf. W. Foerster, *TWNT* VII (1964), p. 990.

52 See further H. van der Loos, *op. cit.*, pp. 264-270, who points to the importance of the intensity of faith *and* the personal relationship between Jesus and

faith that Jesus could make her well expressed an appropriate decision with respect to his person.

The final words spoken to the woman, "Go in peace," are a traditional valediction, [53] but here are informed by her entire experience. The peace with which she departed signified more than release from agitation over a wretched existence or from fear of recrimination for having touched Jesus. It was the profound experience of well-being which is related to salvation from God. When Jesus declares, "Be whole from your affliction," he confirms that her healing was permanent and affirms his active participation with the Father's will to honor the woman's faith.

Later tradition embellished the Gospel account, seeking to answer the questions asked by generations of people. In the Greek tradition the anonymous woman was given the name Berenice, while in the Coptic and Latin tradition she received the related name Veronica. [54] Eusebius states that she was from Caesarea Philippi, and that by the door of her home there was erected on a high stone a copper statue of a woman kneeling, her hands outstretched before her, entreating one purported to resemble Jesus. At the feet of the male figure a "strange sort of herb" is said to grow on the column which possessed medicinal powers against a wide variety of diseases. [55] In this way the evangelical tradition was embellished. What was not appreciated was that the woman had experienced an aspect of salvation in anticipation of the more radical healing to be experienced by the daughter of Jairus. From Mark's perspective, the entire incident is a call for radical faith.

(e) The Raising of Jairus' Daughter: the Subduing of Death. Ch. 5:35-43

35 While he yet spake, they came from the ruler of the synagogue's *house,* saying, Thy daughter is dead: why troublest thou the Teacher any further?

---

the sick individual. What is involved is nothing less than a "surrender from person to person, from the helpless man to the helping 'Lord,' and for *that* reason it is the 'saving' faith" (p. 270).

[53] E.g. Judg. 18:6; I Sam. 1:17; II Sam. 15:9; I Kings 22:17; Lk. 7:50; Acts 16:36; Jas. 2:16. Cf. W. Foerster, *TWNT* II (Eng. Tr. 1964), pp. 406-412.

[54] Acts of Pilate, ch. 7. For the text see K. Aland, *Synopsis Quattuor Evangeliorum* (Stuttgart, 1964), p. 193.

[55] *Eccl. Hist.* VII. xviii. 1-4. On the statue and its probable relationship to the cult of Aesculapius see H. van der Loos, *op. cit.*, pp. 518 f., n. 5.

36 But Jesus, not heeding the word spoken,[56] saith unto the ruler of the synagogue, Fear not, only believe.
37 And he suffered no man to follow with him, save Peter, and James, and John the brother of James.
38 And they come to the house of the ruler of the synagogue; and he beholdeth a tumult, and *many* weeping and wailing greatly.
39 And when he was entered in, he saith unto them, Why make ye a tumult, and weep? the child is not dead, but sleepeth.
40 And they laughed him to scorn. But he, having put them all forth, taketh the father of the child and her mother and them that were with him, and goeth in where the child was.
41 And taking the child by the hand, he saith unto her, Talitha cumi;[57] which is, being interpreted, Damsel, I say unto thee, Arise.
42 And straightway the damsel rose up, and walked; for she was twelve years old. And they were amazed straightway[58] with a great amazement.
43 And he charged them much that no man should know this: and he commanded that *something* should be given her to eat.

35-37 The healing of the woman with a chronic hemorrhage resulted in a delay which was catastrophic for the young girl. A party from the home informed the synagogue official that his daughter had died; any further disturbance of Jesus was futile. Jesus heard what they said but deliberately ignored its import. His response, "fear not, only believe," was a call for intense faith. Jairus had exercised faith when he came to Jesus in the confidence that he could save his daughter. He had witnessed the healing of the woman which demonstrated the relationship between faith and divine help. But he was now asked to believe that his child would live even as he stood in the presence of death. Such faith

---

56 The verb παρακούειν can mean "to overhear" or "to hear carelessly" and so "to ignore." Both the ASV and RSV understand the verb in Mark in this latter sense. To judge by the parallel passage, Lk. 8:50, it was early understood in the sense, "to overhear." Cf. C. E. B. Cranfield, *op. cit.*, p. 187.

57 The eastern Aramaic form ταλιθὰ κοῦμ is read by B ℵ C λ sa bo; the Palestinian feminine form κοῦμι, followed by the ASV and RSV, is supported by (D) 𝔎 A Θ φ *pm* vg. It is difficult to know which Mark wrote. K. Aland, *op. cit.*, p. 192, adopts κοῦμ. On the formula see S-B*K* II (1924), p. 10.

58 This second occurrence of εὐθύς in Ch. 5:42 is lacking in P^{45} 𝔎 A W Θ λ *pl* latt and should, perhaps, be omitted.

is radical trust in the ability of Jesus to confront a crisis situation with the power of God.[59]

Jesus would not allow any of those who had accompanied him to continue with him except the father and the three disciples who sustained a more intimate relationship to him, Peter, James and John. The seriousness of the situation demanded that only those whom Jesus chose as witnesses[60] should know what really took place.

38-39 Arriving at the house Jesus saw that preparations had been made already for the funeral. The minstrels and professional mourners were performing their duties as the first part of the mourning ceremony.[61] The wailing consisted of choral or antiphonal song accompanied by handclapping. Since even the poorest man was required by common custom to hire a minimum of two fluteplayers and one professional mourner in the event of his wife's death,[62] it is probable that one who held the rank of synagogue-ruler would be expected to hire a large number of professional mourners.[63] It was necessary to remove the mourners from the girl's room. Jesus rebuked their noisy tumult and declared, "the child is not dead, but is sleeping." His statement is ambiguous,[64] and could allow the interpretation that the girl was in a state of very deep unconsciousness that is to be distinguished from death itself. Jesus demonstrated his mercy to the girl at a highly critical moment when he healed her.[65] It is certain, however, that this is not

---

[59] Cf. R. Bultmann, *TWNT* VI (1959), pp. 203-218; H. van der Loos, *op. cit.*, pp. 264-270.

[60] The raising of the girl anticipated the resurrection of Jesus. It is to be noted that these three disciples were also privileged to witness an anticipation of Jesus' glory on the mountain of transfiguration.

[61] Cf. G. Stählin, *TWNT* III (1938), pp. 840-844, who discusses the mourning at Jairus' home in the light of Jewish practice.

[62] Cf. S-B*K* I (1922), pp. 521 f.

[63] A vivid description of the tumult is provided by L. Bauer, *Volksleben im Lande der Bibel* (Leipzig, 1903), pp. 211 ff. The women form a circle around the leader of the dance of death, and dance rhythmically from left to right with their hair hanging down. "Gradually they increase their mournful lament and the wild movement of hands and feet until their faces become flushed to a high degree and appear especially excited as the time of burial draws near. Jesus found such a tumult at the house of Jairus before his little daughter (Mk. 5:38)."

[64] Gr. καθεύδειν connotes literal sleep in Chs. 4:27, 38; 13:36; 14:37, 40, 41; it designates "sleep" in a figurative sense in I Thess. 5:6; and "sleep" as a euphemism for death in I Thess. 5:10.

[65] So H. van der Loos, *op. cit.*, p. 569.

Luke's understanding of what took place because he speaks of resuscitation.[66] It is probable that Mark intended his account to be understood in the same way.[67] Jesus' statement means that in spite of the girl's real death, she has not been delivered over to the realm of death with all of its consequences. Mourning is inappropriate because she experiences a sleep from which she will soon awake.

40-42 The mourners were absolutely certain that the girl was dead, and responded to Jesus' words with scornful laughter.[68] The fact that wailing and tears could be exchanged so quickly for laughter indicates how conventional and artificial the mourning customs had become.[69] Jesus cast the scoffers out of the house, and allowing only the parents of the girl and his three disciples to accompany him, entered the room where the young girl lay. Taking hold of her hand he spoke the Aramaic words *Talitha cumi,* "Little girl, arise." The girl rose up and walked about, for she was already a "young daughter" according to Jewish classification.[70]

The retention of Aramaic formulae in Marcan healing contexts (Chs. 5:41; 7:34) has led to the conjecture that, analogous to pagan custom, the early Christians commonly believed in the efficacy of esoteric utterances composed of foreign or incomprehensible words.[71] There is no

---

66 Cf. Lk. 8:55, "Little girl, Arise. And her spirit returned to her."

67 So A. Oepke, *TWNT* I (Eng. Tr. 1964), p. 370; *idem, TWNT* III (1938), pp. 439 f. In the second article, on καθεύδω, Oepke adds "it is questionable, however, whether this word of the Lord, if it is authentic, originally meant something else." He distinguishes, by this qualification, between the intention of Jesus and that of the evangelist. Cf. S-B*K* I (1922), p. 523.

68 K. Rengstorf, *TWNT* I (Eng. Tr. 1964), p. 660: "This obviously denotes scornful laughter on the basis of supposedly better information and therefore of a superiority which is not slow to make itself felt."

69 Cf. G. Stählin, *op. cit.*, pp. 843 f. H. van der Loos, *op. cit.*, pp. 569 f. cautions that too much weight should not be placed on the evidential value of the assertion that the girl was really dead by those who had often stood in the presence of death, for "medical knowledge was very imperfect, and mistakes were anything but out of the question."

70 S-B*K* II (1924), p. 10. Up to eleven years and one day a girl was regarded as "a child"; from eleven years and one day to twelve years and one day as "under age"; from twelve to twelve and a half years as "a young daughter"; and from twelve and a half years as "an adult." The distinctions were important in the determination of marriageable age.

71 Cf. R. Bultmann, *The History of the Synoptic Tradition* (Oxford, 1963), pp. 213 f.; T. A. Burkill, *op. cit.*, pp. 56 f. citing Lucian, *Philopseudes* 9, ῥῆσις βαρβαρική.

support for this proposal either in Mark or in the subsequent tradition. The evangelist retains Aramaic with translation in other contexts unrelated to healing. [72] Moreover, there is no evidence that "Talitha cumi" or "Ephphatha" were ever used by Christian healers as a magic spell. [73] Their presence in the narrative reflects a faithfulness to the tradition that Jesus had actually spoken these words on specific occasions. [74]

The unpreparedness of the parents and the disciples for what they had witnessed is expressed with emphatic language. There was, apparently, no doubt in their minds that they had stood in the presence of death. God had intervened so dramatically they were left speechless with utter amazement.

43 Mark records that Jesus strictly charged those present not to disclose to others what had happened. This injunction to silence has attracted particular attention, for it is alleged to be impracticable. It was widely known that the girl had died; it would be impossible to keep her in isolation for an extended period of time. Accordingly, William Wrede and others [75] have found in Ch. 5:43 strong confirmation that the secrecy phenomena in the Gospel is a theological construction for which Mark himself is responsible.

It is clear, however, that this context lends no support to the theory of secret messiahship, as Wrede conceived it. Fundamental to the narrative is the remarkable disclosure of Jesus' authority made to the parents of the girl and the disciples. These five received the privilege of a special revelation which they were not to share with others. The secret is, accordingly, "a witnessed secret" which is to be kept from others whom Jesus had excluded. The accent of the narrative alternates between disclosure of the messiahship and veiling. Special motivation for the injunction to silence may be found in the rank unbelief of those who had ridiculed Jesus with their scornful laughter. It is clear throughout Mark that Jesus revealed his messiahship only with reserve. It is appropriate

---

[72] E.g. Ch. 3:17 "Boanerges"; Ch. 7:11 "Corban"; Ch. 10:46 "Bartimaeus"; Ch. 14:36 "Abba."

[73] Pointed out by G. Kittel, *TWNT* IV (1942), p. 107.

[74] Cf. J. Schniewind, *op. cit.*, p. 86 who comments rightly that we are more likely to be concerned with Palestinian memoirs than with barbarisms; H. van der Loos, *op. cit.*, pp. 570 f.

[75] W. Wrede, *op. cit.*, pp. 48 f.; R. H. Lightfoot, *op. cit.*, p. 73; T. A. Burkill, *op. cit.*, pp. 79-82. Wrede found in this passage his most striking evidence that the secrecy phenomena was an arbitrary schematic construction of the evangelist.

to this consistent pattern of behavior that he was unwilling to make himself known to the raucous, unbelieving group that had gathered outside Jairus' house.[76] He did not permit them to witness the saving action by which the girl was restored to her parents, and he directed that it should continue to remain unknown to those outside. He recognized that the responsibility of the parents in this regard could not continue indefinitely. When the child appeared in public the facts would speak for themselves. The parents could, however, withhold what had happened and thus fulfill the intention of Jesus.[77] Before it was known that the girl was yet alive, the purpose for which the charge had been given would have been fulfilled; Jesus would have departed and could no longer be subject to ostentatious acclaim.[78]

There is a fine human touch in Mark's final note, that in the midst of the excitement and confusion Jesus realized that the girl would need food.

The resuscitation of Jairus' daughter is both a deed of compassion and a pledge of the conquering power of Jesus over the combined forces of death and unbelief, in which the Kingdom of God was disclosed as a saving reality. It is precisely in deliverance from death that the salvation which Jesus brings finds its most pointed expression.[79]

---

76 Cf. N. B. Stonehouse, *op. cit.*, pp. 62 f., who points to Jesus' inaction in the face of unbelief in his home city of Nazareth (Ch. 6:5 f.): "Jesus' passivity and reserve evidently were most conspicuous where unbelief was most blatant."

77 Cf. T. W. Manson, "Realized Eschatology and the Messianic Secret" in *Studies in the Gospels,* ed. D. E. Nineham (Oxford, 1955), p. 212, who distinguishes between the cure itself and the means by which it was effected. The latter could be kept secret, while the former could not for long. He calls attention to Acts 9:40, where there is no question of any messianic secret, and yet the same injunction is imposed.

78 So N. B. Stonehouse, *op. cit.*, pp. 63 f.

79 Cf. G. Sevenster, *De Christologie van het Nieuwe Testament* (Amsterdam, 1946), p. 32: "The dead are raised, because in Jesus' action that Kingdom is beginning to be realized in which there will be no more death (Rev. 21:4 and 20:14)"; H. D. Wendland, *Die Eschatologie des Reiches Gottes bei Jesus* (Göttingen, 1931), pp. 224-231, 238: "If Jesus stands in contrast to sin, disease, and the demons as the bearer of the living, purifying and renewing power of God, he can be no other in opposition to death."

CHAPTER 6

6. Rejection in Nazareth. Ch. 6:1-6a

1 And he went out from thence; and he cometh into his own country; and his disciples follow him.
2 And when the sabbath was come, he began to teach in the synagogue: and many hearing him were astonished, saying, Whence hath this man these things? and, What is the wisdom that is given unto this man, and *what mean* such mighty works wrought by his hands?
3 Is not this the carpenter, the son of Mary, and brother of James, and Joses, and Judas, and Simon? and are not his sisters here with us? And they were offended in him.
4 And Jesus said unto them, A prophet is not without honor, save in his own country, and among his own kin, and in his own house.
5 And he could there do no mighty work, save that he laid his hands on a few sick folk, and healed them.
6a And he marvelled because of their unbelief.

1 Jesus left Capernaum and travelled southward into the hill country until he came to the village where he had spent his youth and the early years of his maturity. While Mark does not name Nazareth, he has earlier indicated that this was the village from which Jesus came,[1] and it is undoubtedly in view under the phrase "his own country." Jesus returned to Nazareth as would a rabbi, accompanied by his disciples. The reference to the disciples is important, for during this period Jesus had been concerned with their training in preparation for the mission which Mark reports in Ch. 6:7-13.

2-3 On the sabbath day Jesus attended the synagogue and was given the opportunity to expound the reading from the Torah and the Haftarah,

---

[1] Ch. 1:9, 24. On Nazareth see G. Dalman, *Orte und Wege Jesu*[3] (Leipzig, 1924), pp. 61-88; C. Kopp, "Beiträge zur Geschichte Nazareths," *JPOS* 18 (1938), pp. 187-228; 19 (1939), pp. 82-119, 253-285; 20 (1940), pp. 29-42; 21 (1948), pp. 148-164; T. F. Meysels, "From the Home-town of Our Saviour: recent archeological discoveries at Nazareth," *Illustrated London News* 229 (1956), pp. 1074-75; B. Bagatti, "Nazareth," *DB Suppl* VI (1960), col. 318-333; *idem, Gli scavi di Nazaret,* Vol. I: Dalle origine al seculo XII (Jerusalem, 1967).

the Law and the prophetic portion.[2] The entire congregation[3] was astonished at his teaching, which prompted questions concerning the source of his doctrine and wisdom and of the power which had been exhibited elsewhere[4] in miracles of healing and exorcism. It is possible that the people entertained the dark suspicions voiced earlier by the Jerusalem scribes (Ch. 3:22). Jesus had not been schooled in rabbinic fashion but had been trained as a manual laborer. His immediate family were well known to the villagers, who judged that there was nothing extraordinary about them that would have led them to expect something unusual from Jesus. What was the source of his wisdom, and who had empowered him to speak and act with such authority? To these questions two answers lie close at hand: the source was God, or it was demonic. Their first impressions of astonishment shaded off to resentment when they recalled Jesus' earlier vocation and standing in Nazareth. Not knowing the source of his wisdom, they find his office as a teacher offensive. In spite of what they heard and saw they failed to penetrate the veil of ordinariness which characterized this one who had grown up in the village.

The rhetorical question, "Is not this the carpenter, the son of Mary?" deserves careful attention both to the text and its meaning. Significant strands of the Marcan textual tradition agree essentially with the Matthean formulation: "Is this not the son of the carpenter? Is not his

---

2 A wealth of information on the synagogue is now available in W. Schrage, *TWNT* VII (1964), pp. 810-826, 828-833 (with full bibliography, pp. 798 f.); P. Billerbeck, "Ein Synagogengottesdienst in Jesu Tagen," *ZNW* 55 (1965), pp. 1-17.

An examination of a synopsis [see K. Aland, *Synopsis Quattuor Evangeliorum* (Stuttgart, 1964), pp. 193-196] indicates that the parallel between Mk. 6:1-6a and Lk. 4:16-30 is extremely slight. The key point of parallelism is the traditional word (in different formulations) that "a prophet is not accepted in his own country." This is merely a traditional aphorism that can exist without context (as in the Oxyrhynchus Papyrus 1 No. 6 = the Coptic Gospel of Thomas, Logion 31) or in a different context (as John 4:44). The conclusion seems probable that Mk. 6:1-6a and Lk. 4:16-30 describe two distinct visits to Nazareth. They do not narrate the same visit from merely different points of view.

3 Gr. οἱ πολλοί, which the ASV, RSV translate as "many." It should probably be given an inclusive sense, as in the NEB, "the large congregation." For this use of οἱ πολλοί see J. Jeremias, *TWNT* VI (1959), pp. 540-542 specific reference is made to Mk. 6:2 on p. 541.

4 This seems a necessary deduction in the light of Ch. 6:5 f. The people may have been offended because Jesus failed to do any spectacular deeds in Nazareth. The phrase "wrought by his hands" is better understood as a Semitism meaning "wrought by him" rather than a reference to the laying on of hands.

mother called Miriam?" (Mt. 13:55).[5] Moreover, against the allegation of Celsus that Jesus was only a carpenter Origen answered forthrightly that in none of the Gospels accepted by the Church was Jesus himself designated a carpenter.[6] While the textual question is so complex that equally competent interpreters have adopted differing points of view,[7] it seems preferable to adopt the text of the uncials in which Jesus is designated "the carpenter, the son of Mary." The variant reading was apparently conformed to the text of Matthew in the interest of the virgin birth and perhaps to avoid the attribution of a menial trade to Jesus when to do so in the Graeco-Roman world would be to invite scorn.[8] The Marcan text as it stands is derogatory. "Is not this the carpenter?" means, Is he not a common worker with his hands even as the rest of us are?[9] The additional phrase "the son of Mary" is prob-

---

[5] The text translated in the ASV, RSV, NEB is supported by all uncials, many minuscules, some MSS of the Itala, the critical edition of the Vulgate, the Peshitta and Harclean Syriac and Coptic VSS. But P^{45} (which unfortunately is defective at this point), family 13, 33 and many other minuscules, the majority of Itala and some Vulgate MSS, and three MSS of the Bohairic support "the son of the carpenter."

[6] *Against Celsus* VI. 36, on which see H. Höpfl, "Nonne hic est fabri filius?" *Biblica* 4 (1923), pp. 42-43. Höpfl suggests that Origen's text had been colored by Matthew and had the reading supported by the important Ferrar group (family 13). E. Klostermann, *Das Markusevangelium*[4] (Tübingen, 1950), p. 63 argues that Origen was correct: the original reading was "the son of the carpenter and Mary." The Marcan text now found in most witnesses is a dogmatic correction in the interest of the virgin birth. See further H. E. W. Turner, "The Virgin Birth," *ExT* 68 (1956), pp. 12-17.

[7] E.g. V. Taylor, *The Gospel according to St. Mark* (London, 1952), pp. 299 f. supports the Caesarean text; C. E. B. Cranfield, *The Gospel according to St. Mark* (Cambridge, 1963), pp. 194 f. supports the text of the uncials. The discussion of these two men is instructive concerning the complexity of the question.

[8] Celsus' dismissal of Jesus with the remark that he was only a carpenter (see n. 6) reflects the low attitude toward the manual laborer common among Greeks and Romans.

[9] The term τέκτων commonly designates a worker in any hard material: wood, metal or stone, and so comes to mean a builder. While the Greek Fathers thought consistently of a worker with wood, the Latin Fathers generally thought of a worker with iron. The evidence is set forth fully by H. Höpfl, *op. cit.*, pp. 41-55; see further C. C. McCown, "ὁ τέκτων," in *Studies in Early Christology*, ed. S. J. Case (Chicago, 1928), pp. 173-189. Unfortunately the Sinaitic Syriac MS lacks Mk. 6:3 and failed to render τέκτων in Mt. 13:55. However, the Cureton MS and the Peshitta render τέκτων by נַגָּר, a term clarified in Tos. *Baba Ḳamma* X. 8 as one who makes chests, cupboards, stools and benches (i.e. a worker with wood).

ably disparaging. It was contrary to Jewish usage to describe a man as the son of his mother, even when she was a widow, except in insulting terms.[10] Rumors to the effect that Jesus was illegitimate appear to have circulated in his own lifetime and may lie behind this reference as well.[11] The rhetorical question of the people indicates that they know Jesus only in a superficial way. They find no reason to believe that he possesses the anointment of God.

4 Jesus responded with an aphorism to which there are numerous parallels in Jewish and Greek literature.[12] The comparison of his experience to that of the prophets who were dishonored among their own people is ironical.[13] It anticipates his ultimate rejection by Israel[14] and at the same time recalls Ch. 3:20-21, 31-35 when Jesus' family and kinsmen expressed the opinion that he was insane and attempted to halt his activities forcibly.

This understanding is supported in the Coptic, Ethiopic, Armenian and Gothic VSS as well.

G. W. Buchanan, "Jesus and the Upper Class," *Nov Test* 7 (1964), pp. 202-204 has suggested that τέκτων may have expanded in meaning from a simple craftsman to one who supervises craftsmen. There is, however, no support for this conjecture in the Marcan text.

10 Cf. Judg. 11:1 f.

11 E.g. Jn. 8:41; 9:29; the Jewish material collected in S-B*K* I (1922), pp. 39-43; Origen, *Against Celsus* I, 28. C. E. B. Cranfield, after a review of the evidence, writes, "it seems probable that what is after all the better attested reading in Mark reflects these rumours and accusations and so is an important piece of evidence in support of the historicity of the Virgin Birth, though of a sort that the Church would naturally tend to avoid" (*op. cit.*, p. 195). Cf. R. H. Lightfoot, *History and Interpretation in the Gospels* (London, 1935), pp. 182-188; E. Stauffer, "Jeschu ben Mirjam. Kontroversgeschichtliche Anmerkungen zu Mk 6:3" in *Neotestamentica et Semitica* (Edinburgh, 1969), pp. 119-128.

12 Cf. S-B*K* I (1922), p. 678; A-G, p. 642 s.v. πατρίς 2. The parallelism is not complete because the Jewish and pagan aphorisms do not speak of "a prophet," but the sense of rejection among those to whom one is well known is common to them all. The aphorism occurs in a different context in Jn. 4:44. Elsewhere it exists as an isolated word of Jesus (see n. 2 above; for texts see K. Aland, *op. cit.*, pp. 196, 521).

13 G. Friedrich, *TWNT* VI (1959), pp. 842 f. For the legendary account of the rejection and martyrdom of the prophets see the text edited by C. C. Torrey, *The Lives of the Prophets* (Philadelphia, 1946), and the discussion of H. A. Fischel, "Prophet and Martyr," *JQR* 37 (1947), pp. 265-280, 363-386.

14 In Mark's intention does it also point forward to the narrative of the martyrdom of John the Baptist in Ch. 6:17-29?

5-6a In the presence of gross unbelief Jesus restricted his activity to the healing of a few sick individuals.[15] It is not Mark's intention to stress Jesus' *inability* when he states that he could perform no miracles at Nazareth. His purpose is rather to indicate that Jesus was not free to exercise his power *in these circumstances.*[16] The performance of miracles in the absence of faith could have resulted only in the aggravation of human guilt and the hardening of men's hearts against God. The power of God which Jesus possessed could be materialized in a genuinely salutary fashion only when there was the receptivity of faith. Unbelief excluded the people of Nazareth from the dynamic disclosure of God's grace that others had experienced.

Apparently Jesus had not anticipated the reaction of the people. The statement that he "marvelled" is the sole instance when Mark uses this verb of Jesus. It vividly suggests the degree of resistance he encountered in Nazareth. In Ch. 6:5-6a Mark draws attention not to the limits of Jesus' power but rather to the privations which result from unbelief.[17]

In the Marcan outline the rejection at Nazareth is intimately related to the subsequent mission of the Twelve (Ch. 6:7-13). The tension between faith and unbelief permeates both accounts. Moreover in Ch. 6:11 there is a distinct indication that the disciples will also experience rejection. By situating these two incidents at this point in his Gospel the evangelist shows that unbelief is the context in which the Christian mission advances and that rejection is an experience common to the

---

[15] T. A. Burkill, *Mysterious Revelation* (Ithaca, N.Y., 1963), pp. 138 f. n. 48 calls attention to the logion "a prophet is not acceptable in his own country nor does a physician perform cures on those who know him," and suggests that Mk. 6:5a "may be a translation into dramatic form of the second part" of the logion. It is, however, more probable that the second part of the logion owes its origin to reflection on Mk. 6:5. See E. Lohmeyer, *Das Evangelium des Markus*[16] (Göttingen, 1963), pp. 110 f.

[16] Cf. L. Goppelt, *Typos. Die typologische Deutung des Alten Testaments im Neuen* (Gütersloh, 1939), p. 86, "By virtue of his communion with God, Jesus' power as Savior knows no bounds, but the use of it does"; H. Ridderbos, *The Coming of the Kingdom* (Philadelphia, 1962), p. 118, "Here the question is not whether Jesus possessed the power to work miracles, but whether he was free to exercise this power in all circumstances... There he could work no miracle because in such circumstances it would have the character of a deed of power and would lack the background from which they can only be understood. The expression 'he could not' in Mk. 6:5 must, therefore, be understood as an impossibility within the scope of Jesus' task and activity."

[17] Cf. A. Fridrichsen, *Le problème du miracle* (Strasbourg, 1925), pp. 51-54; H. van der Loos, *The Miracles of Jesus* (Leiden, 1965), pp. 190 f.

Lord and the Church. This point had immediate relevance for his own hard-pressed community. It is probable that he recognized in the juxtaposition of rejection and mission a pattern confirmed in the rejection of Jesus by the nation, climaxed by crucifixion and resurrection, which created the apostolic mission.

7. The Mission of the Twelve in Galilee. Ch. 6:6b-13

6b And he went round about the villages teaching.
7 And he calleth unto him the twelve, and began to send them forth by two and two; and he gave them authority over the unclean spirits;
8 and he charged them that they should take nothing for *their* journey, save a staff only; no bread, no wallet,[18] no money in their purse;[19]
9 but *to go* shod with sandals: and, *said he,* put not on two coats.[20]
10 And he said unto them, Wheresoever ye enter into a house, there abide till ye depart thence.
11 And whatsoever place shall not receive[21] you, and they hear you not, as ye go forth thence, shake off the dust that is under your feet for a testimony unto them.[22]
12 And they went out, and preached that *men* should repent.
13 And they cast out many demons, and anointed with oil many that were sick, and healed them.

---

18 Gr. πήρα, usually thought to be a travelling bag or bread-bag, e.g., W. Michaelis, *TWNT* VI (1959), p. 121; cf. RSV "no bag"; NEB "no pack." A. Deissmann, *Light from the Ancient East* (London, 1910), pp. 109 f. found here a special meaning suggested by a monument of the imperial period where πήρα means the beggar's collecting bag. Jesus' command would accordingly mean there is to be no begging of money.

19 RSV, NEB "no money in their belts."

20 RSV "two tunics."

21 On this term, which properly means "to welcome," see W. Grundmann, *TWNT* II (Eng. Tr. 1964), pp. 51 f.

22 RSV "for a testimony against them"; NEB "as a warning to them." Later texts have been brought into harmony with Mt. 10:15 at this point, reading, "Amen I say to you, it will be more tolerant for Sodom and Gomorrha in the day of judgment than for that city," as in the AV (ℜ A λ φ *pm a f q* sy^{p} bo^{pt}). The variant indicates that the figure of shaking off the dust of one's feet was understood as an act of judgment.

6b It is difficult to be certain whether Mark intended the reference to Jesus' itinerant ministry to be intimately associated with the rejection at Nazareth or the commissioning of the Twelve. As a succinct summary statement of the activity of Jesus, verse 6b is able to stand upon its own, without close association with either context. A connection with Ch. 6:1-6a would suggest that as a result of the rejection at Nazareth Jesus entered upon an extended tour of the Galilean villages. While the commissioning of the Twelve is the next event reported, that development has no necessary relationship to the village ministry. On the other hand, if verse 6b is tied to Ch. 6:7-13 it indicates that as a result of his tour Jesus determined to extend his ministry yet further through the direct commissioning of the Twelve. The text of Mark is intelligible on either reading, and both have found support.[23] This is the third tour of the Galilean villages reported by Mark (cf. Ch. 1:14, 39).

7-9 With the commissioning of the Twelve Mark reaches a point for which he has carefully prepared. The call to be fishers of men (Ch. 1:16-20) points forward to the election of Levi (Ch. 2:14), and then of the Twelve, who are set apart in terms of a specific promise (Ch. 3:13-19). They will be sent forth to preach and will be given authority to expel demons.[24] Since their election the disciples had been with Jesus and had shared his experiences. Private instruction (Ch. 4:11, 34) and exposure to his power over demonic possession, sickness and death (Ch. 5) had prepared them for more direct involvement in his ministry.

Jesus authorized the disciples to be his delegates with respect to both word and power. Their message and deeds were to be an extension of his own. The commissioning of the Twelve has a rich background in the juridical practice of Judaism, which recognized the official character of actions performed by authorized individuals. Reduced to its simplest form, the law acknowledged that "the sent one is as the man who com-

---

[23] E.g. K. L. Schmidt, *Der Rahmen der Geschichte Jesu* (Berlin, 1919), pp. 158-162 supports the connection with the rejection at Nazareth; V. Taylor, *op. cit.*, pp. 302 f. argues for the association with Ch. 6:7-13. Cf. the NEB: "On one of his teaching journeys round the villages he summoned the Twelve and sent them out in pairs on a mission." The RSV sets the half-verse off by itself, and perhaps this is wisest.

[24] The connection between Chs. 1:17; 3:13-15 and 6:7-13 is carefully established by R. P. Meye, *Jesus and the Twelve. Discipleship and Revelation in Mark's Gospel* (Grand Rapids, 1968), pp. 99-110.

missioned him."[25] This formulation lies behind the mission of the Twelve, who are sent forth as "appointed representatives" of Jesus in the legal sense of the term. Their return to Jesus and the report concerning all that they had taught and done in fulfilment of the commission (Ch. 6:30) is consistent with this legal background.[26] The fulfilment of a commission by pairs of messengers is attested elsewhere in Judaism.[27] The division of the Twelve into groups of two conforms their mission to the Mosaic provision that the truthfulness of a testimony is to be established "by the mouth of two witnesses."[28] There is in the context no thought of the creation at this time of a permanent office, but rather the fulfilment of a specific commission.[29] This is an important consideration; it signifies that the instructions which Jesus gave to the disciples do not have a general and permanent validity. They are relevant to this particular commission. The insistence that the disciples take neither food nor money, but depend wholly on hospitality, is a matter of special authorization within limits which were both local and temporary.[30]

The specific terms of the commission demanded of the disciples a rigorous commitment to total dependence upon God for food and shelter. While the minimum requirements for the journey–staff and sandals–were permitted,[31] they were to take nothing else. Bread, the

---

[25] See K. Rengstorf, *TWNT* I (Eng. Tr. 1964), pp. 400-430. The Jewish institution of the שָׁלִיחַ is discussed on pp. 419-420; the relationship of Jesus and the first circle of disciples to this institution on pp. 424-430. The formulation, "the one sent is as the man who commissioned him," is treated on pp. 415, 421, 425-427.

[26] *Ibid.*, p. 425; cf. H. Ridderbos, *op. cit.*, pp. 370 f.

[27] The OT and rabbinic evidence is assembled and discussed by J. Jeremias, "Paarweise Sendung im Neuen Testament," in *New Testament Essays* (Studies in Memory of T. W. Manson), ed. A. J. B. Higgins (Manchester, 1959), pp. 136-138. Mk. 6:7-13 is discussed briefly on pp. 138 f.

[28] *Ibid.*, p. 138, with reference to Deut. 17:6; Num. 35:30. A wealth of pertinent material is gathered by H. van Vliet, *No Single Testimony. A Study on the Adoption of the Law of Deut. 19:15 into the New Testament* (Utrecht, 1958).

[29] R. P. Meye, *op. cit.*, pp. 112 f.

[30] K. Rengstorf, *op. cit.*, pp. 426 f.

[31] The permission of staff and sandals over against their apparent exclusion in Mt. 10:9 f.; Lk. 9:3 poses a well-known problem of harmony. For a survey of ancient and modern proposals see E. Power, "The Staff of the Apostles, A Problem in Gospel Harmony," *Biblica* 4 (1923), pp. 241-266. Power's own conclusion is that the staff permitted in Mark is the walking stick or shepherd's crook which became the symbol of office, while the rod prohibited by Matthew and Luke was the shepherd's club designed for protection. M. J. Lagrange, *L'Évangile selon Saint*

beggar's bag, the smallest coin in the belt,[32] or a second tunic to keep out the night chill were all excluded.[33]

10-11 The disciples were instructed to accept the hospitality which was offered. Whenever a home was opened to them they were to stay there until they departed from the village.[34] They were not to dishonor the home by accepting more comfortable provisions offered by another host.

The clear intimation that the disciples would experience rejection injects an ominous note into the charge. There would be villages where no hospitality would be offered and where their word would not be tolerated. In this situation they were to shake the dust from their feet, as a testimony and warning to the villagers,[35] and go elsewhere. This instruction is intelligible in the light of Jewish practice. It was the custom of pious Jews who had travelled outside of Israel to remove carefully

---

Marc[9] (Paris, 1947), pp. 151-153 sees in the variation a different way of verbalizing the same truth, that the simplest of preparations alone was permitted. Especially attractive is the suggestion of U. Mauser, *Christ in the Wilderness* (Naperville, Ill., 1963), pp. 133 f.: Mk. 6:8 f. shows a striking similarity to Ex. 12:11 where the Israelites on the eve of the exodus from Egypt are commanded to eat the Passover in haste, "your loins girded, your sandals on your feet, and your staff in your hand." Mauser suggests that Mk. 6:8 f. represents a tradition independent of the other Synoptic Gospels, designed to recall the exodus tradition. On this assumption the missionary instruction given to the Twelve is patterned after the instruction given to Israel at the outset of the wilderness experience. The injunction to take neither bread nor bag can be understood in this same context. As Israel in the wilderness was nourished by the provision of God so the disciples are to be sustained by God's provision.

[32] Copper coins were those of lowest value. Cf. A-G, p. 883 where χαλκός is rendered "small change."

[33] Josephus, *Ant.* XVII. v. 7 mentions a messenger who wore two tunics, but the purpose was to conceal a secret message. It would seem better to see in the reference an insistence that the disciples depend upon God for the provision of shelter at night for them. E. Power, *op. cit.,* p. 245, suggests that the reference to two garments is intelligible if the shepherd is in view since the second garment was necessary as a covering at night. Because the disciples were to depend upon hospitality for shelter the second garment was excluded.

[34] The post-apostolic church limited the duration of hospitality to one or two days; a three-day stay was an indication of false intention, according to Didache 11:4-5.

[35] In a Semitic context it would be sufficient to say, "shake off the dust from your feet," but for the benefit of his western readers who would not understand the symbolism of this act Mark adds "as a testimony against them."

from their feet and clothing all dust of the alien lands in which they had travelled. By this action they dissociated themselves from the pollution of those lands and their ultimate judgment.[36] An analogous action on the part of the disciples would declare that a village was pagan in character. It would provide warning that the disciples had fulfilled their responsibility and that those who had rejected the mission would have to answer to God.[37] The removal of dust from the feet belongs to the category of symbolic realism; it is a prophetic act designed to provoke thought on the part of the rejecting villagers. The mission of the disciples has a selective character. Their presence in a town or village determines which of the inhabitants are open to the word of the Kingdom which they bear. Should they wipe the dust from their feet and break communication with a village they consign it to judgment.[38] This provision indicates that the coming of the disciples, like that of Jesus himself, had the character of sifting and gathering the true people of God.[39]

12-13 In obedience to their commission the Twelve proclaimed the gospel through their word and deed. Their message and the exercise of power confirm the representative character of their mission. They preach the message of repentance which Jesus had proclaimed; they cast out demons and heal the sick because these activities had characterized his ministry. Their coming to a village brought healing and salvation in the most comprehensive terms *because they were his representatives.* Jesus had commissioned them and they came in his name. What Jesus did in his own power as commissioned by God, the disciples did in his power.[40]

The essential element in the mission is the intrusion of the Kingdom of God "with power."[41] The expulsion of demons is clearly distinguished from the anointing of the sick,[42] but both actions were visible functions

---

36 Cf. Tos. *Baba Kamma* I. 5 (ed. Zuckermandel, p. 569), "The dust of Syria pollutes as does that of alien countries." See further S-B*K* I (1922), p. 571.

37 Cf. Acts 13:51; 18:6. In the latter passage the shaking of the dust from the feet is accompanied by the words, "Your blood be upon your own heads." They will be responsible at the Last Judgment for the consequences of their rejection.

38 Note how this has been understood in the variant reading discussed in n. 22.

39 See above on Ch. 1:14-15.

40 See below on Ch. 9:37.

41 H. van der Loos, *op. cit.*, p. 220.

42 The distinction between demonic possession and illness needs to be emphasized in the presence of the modern tendency to associate demonic possession

of the Kingdom. They declared that it was God's intention to apply salvation to man in his wholeness. The focus upon the words and works of Christ anticipates the character of the more permanent mission the disciples received by the appointment of the risen Christ.[43]

IV. Withdrawal Beyond Galilee. Ch. 6:14-8:30

The new section introduced by Ch. 6:14 and extending to Ch. 8:30 focuses upon a period during which Jesus was frequently in retirement beyond the borders of Galilee. During the mission of the Twelve, Mark calls attention to the reaction of Herod Antipas, who has heard of the mighty works of Jesus. Herod's suspicion that Jesus is John returned from the dead (Ch. 6:14-16) introduces the parenthetical account of the imprisonment and execution of the Baptist (Ch. 6:17-29). At the return of the Twelve Jesus withdraws to a solitary place, pursued by a multitude. In compassion he provides bread in the wilderness, and five thousand are fed (Ch. 6:35-44). A second feeding of four thousand is reported in the region of the Decapolis (Ch. 8:1-10), and the striking recurrence of the word "bread" throughout this section provides the pervading motif (Chs. 6:52; 7:2, 28; 8:14 ff.).[44] The importance of the two feeding miracles is emphasized when the disciples' own misunderstandings of Jesus are traced to their failure to understand the significance of the abundant provision of bread. While a single instance of public teaching occurs in Ch. 7:1-23, the accent falls on the instruction of the disciples, whose hardness of heart, unbelief and failure to understand is a prominent element in the record. A point of transition is provided by Ch. 8:22-26 where the restoring of sight to a man who was blind signals the opening of the eyes of the disciples as well. A climax in Mark's narrative is achieved in Ch. 8:27-29 when Jesus and his company approach Caesarea Philippi where Jesus' dignity as Messiah is acknowledged for the first time.

---

with mental illness. On oil as a medicine in the ancient world see the references collected by H. Schlier, *TWNT* I (Eng. Tr. 1964), p. 232; H. van der Loos, *op. cit.*, pp. 311 f.

[43] See R. P. Meye, *op. cit.*, pp. 108-113.

[44] This motif is carefully developed by L. Cerfaux, "La section des pains," *Recueil Lucien Cerfaux* I (Gembloux, 1954), pp. 471-485; I. de la Potterie, *Exegesis Synopticorum. "Sectio Panum" in Evangelio Marci (6, 6-8, 35)* (Rome, 1965-66).

1. Popular Estimates of the Identity of Jesus. Ch. 6:14-16

14 And king Herod heard thereof; for his name had become known: and he said, [45] John the Baptizer is risen from the dead, and therefore do these powers work in him.
15 But others said, It is Elijah. And others said, *It is* a prophet, *even* as one of the prophets. [46]
16 But Herod, when he heard *thereof,* said, John, whom I beheaded, he is risen.

14-15 If the connection with Ch. 6:6-13 may be pressed, it was the mission activity of Jesus and the Twelve throughout Galilee which brought to Herod's attention popular reports concerning Jesus. Herod Antipas, the son of Herod the Great and Malthace, was tetrarch of Galilee and Perea from his father's death in 4 B.C. to A.D. 39. [47] His total disregard for Jewish sensitivity was displayed not only in his marriage to Herodias, but in the selection of an ancient cemetery as the site for his capital, Tiberias. By this choice Herod virtually excluded Jewish settlers, for residence in the city would render them perpetually unclean in terms of the ritual law. The royal title had been denied to Antipas by Augustus. Goaded by the ambitious Herodias, it was Antipas' request for the title of "king" which officially led to his dismissal and exile in A.D. 39. [48] Mark's use of the royal title may reflect local custom, or it may be a point of irony. Herod had modeled his court after the imperial pattern, [49] and it is possible that the irony of designating him by a title he coveted, but failed to secure, would be appreciated in Rome where his sentence had been sealed.

---

[45] It is better to read the third person plural with B (D) W 6 271 *a b ff* vg[2] mss Aug[De cons.], in spite of the strong support for the third singular form, which may be accounted for by assimilation to the singular "he heard." RSV "Some said," NEB "and people were saying," interpreting ἔλεγον as an indefinite plural.

[46] It is possible that the original reading is preserved by D and the Itala, which reads "and others were saying that he is one of the prophets," which agrees in form with the text in Ch. 8:28. For a defense of this reading see O. Cullmann, *The Christology of the New Testament* (Philadelphia, 1959), pp. 34 f.

[47] On Antipas see A. W. Verrall, "Herod Antipas," *JThS* 10 (1909), pp. 322-353; A. H. M. Jones, *The Herods of Judaea* (Oxford, 1938), pp. 176 ff.; S. Perowne, *The Later Herods* (New York, 1958), pp. 43-58; H. W. Hoehner, *Herod Antipas* (Cambridge, 1972).

[48] Josephus, *Ant.* XVIII. i. 3; ix. 4.

[49] See below on Ch. 6:21, 27.

Accepting the indefinite plural as the original reading,[50] it was the people who recognized in Jesus' ministry the powers of the Age to Come released through resurrection. On this understanding, verses 14-15 refer to three popular estimates of the person of Jesus: he is John the Baptist, or he is Elijah, or he is one of the other prophets. The people view Jesus in the perspective of a prophet; their only question concerns his identity. Herod had been informed concerning the prophet who was exciting the aspirations of the people within his district, and had formed his own opinion.

The three popular estimates of Jesus constitute one of the earliest attempts to explain the enigma of his person and work. The conviction that Jesus is John risen from the dead comes from a group of people who had no direct experience with Jesus or the Baptist, since they did not know that Jesus was a contemporary of John and had been baptized by him. Because Jesus had not begun his ministry in Galilee until after the imprisonment of John (Ch. 1:4), the people had a distinct impression of succession rather than of contemporaneity. They understood the new proclaimer in terms of a more recent and, to them, better known figure, the prophet John. If they had even heard that Jesus was baptized by John they could not possibly have identified him with the Baptist.[51] John is not known to have performed any miracles during the course of his ministry (Jn. 10:41, "John did no sign"), and it was the element of power in Jesus' ministry which led them to believe that John had risen from the dead. The resurrection permitted the powers of the new age to be channeled through him. The opinion that John has returned from the dead in the same body he had possessed before his execution[52] sheds light on the popular conception of the resurrection and indicates that the people had no knowledge of Jesus prior to his ministry in Galilee. They think of him as one who appeared suddenly upon the earth a short time after the Baptist's death. The identification of Jesus with John, through whom the ancient gift of prophecy had been affirmed after so long a silence, appears to interpret Jesus as the promised eschatological Prophet whose word would herald the last days.[53]

---

[50] See above, n. 45.

[51] Cf. O. Cullmann, *op. cit.*, pp. 31-33; W. Wink, *John the Baptist in the Gospel Tradition* (Cambridge, 1968), pp. 8-10.

[52] For other examples of the sudden return of a prophet after his death see S-B*K* I (1922), p. 679.

[53] See O. Cullmann, *op. cit.*, pp. 13-30, 34, where the evidence is set forth.

The opinion that Jesus is Elijah identifies Jesus with "the Coming One" announced by John (Ch. 1:7). It probably reflects the conviction of the Baptist's followers. Although he left the identity of the one mightier than himself unnamed, John had defined his function in terms which pointed unmistakably to "the Messenger of the Covenant," the prophet Elijah, in the closing paragraphs of Malachi (Chs. 3:1 f.; 4:5 f.). John must have been responsible for communicating to his followers that Jesus was Elijah, as promised in the prophetic word. The identification of Jesus as the precursor to "the great and terrible day of the Lord" was a response of faith which stands in contrast to the popular opinion that Jesus was John risen from the dead. [54]

The third estimate is to be distinguished from the second by its reference to Jesus as an ordinary prophet, not one like Elijah whose coming is an ominous portent of the end. He is one more prophet in the succession of prophets who have spoken and acted for God in Israel's history. If the reading supported by the "Western" text ("he is one of the prophets") is correct, however, Jesus is identified with one of the ancient prophets who has returned for a new and final phase of ministry. This understanding is only a variant form of the previous two: Jesus is the eschatological prophet. The name of the returning prophet is not provided, since the people thought alternately of Elijah, Moses, Enoch or Jeremiah. [55]

16 Herod, disturbed by an uneasy conscience disposed to superstition, feared that John had come back to haunt him. This judgment presupposes that Jesus was unknown to the tetrarch until after John's death. He felt that in Jesus he was confronted with the Baptist once more, but now returned from the grave with the result that magical powers were at work in him. [56] The reference to Herod's execution of John serves to introduce the extended account of the Baptist's death in Ch. 6:17-29. It also indicates Herod's sense of his responsibility for John's death, which was brought home to him in a pointed way by the popular rumors stimulated by the activity of Jesus. In Jewish thinking resurrection is

---

[54] Cf. J. A. T. Robinson, "Elijah, John and Jesus, an Essay in Detection" in *Twelve New Testament Studies* (London, 1962), pp. 29-33.

[55] Cf. O. Cullmann, *op. cit.*, pp. 16-23, 34-35.

[56] Cf. W. Grundmann, *TWNT* II (Eng. Tr. 1964), p. 303 who sees behind Herod's statement a magical and superstitious statement aggravated by a guilty conscience.

the prelude to judgment, and the terror of judgment may be caught in Herod's statement, "John, whom I beheaded, is risen."

2. The Imprisonment and Death of John. Ch. 6:17-29

17 For Herod himself had sent forth and laid hold upon John, and bound him in prison for the sake of Herodias, his brother Philip's wife; for he had married her.
18 For John said unto Herod, It is not lawful for thee to have thy brother's wife.
19 And Herodias set herself against him, and desired to kill him; and she could not;
20 for Herod feared John, knowing that he was a righteous and holy man, and kept him safe. And when he heard him, he was much perplexed; [57] and he heard him gladly.
21 And when a convenient day was come, that Herod on his birthday made a supper to his lords, [58] and the high captains, and chief men of Galilee;
22 and when the daughter of Herodias herself came in and danced, she pleased Herod and them that sat at meat with him; and the king said unto the damsel, Ask of me whatsoever thou wilt, and I will give it thee.
23 And he sware unto her, Whatsoever thou shalt ask of me, I will give it to thee, unto the half of my kingdom.
24 And she went out, and said unto her mother, What shall I ask? And she said, The head of John the Baptizer.
25 And she came in straightway with haste unto the king, and asked, saying, I will that thou forthwith give me on a platter the head of John the Baptist.
26 And the king was exceeding sorry; but for the sake of his oaths, and of them that sat at meat, he would not reject her. [59]

---

[57] The reading behind the modern versions (ASV, RSV, NEB), πολλὰ ἠπόρει, is supported by P^{45} B ℵ L (W) Θ sa bo and corresponds perfectly to the character of Herod: he was very perplexed. The AV "he did many things" renders πολλὰ ἐποίει, supported by C 𝔎 A D N Π Σ Φ λ φ latt $sy^{s\,p}$, a reading which makes little sense in this context and which may reflect an error of hearing which originated in the dictation of the text to scribes who copied what they heard. The reading of the *textus receptus* is adopted without argument by J. Bowman, *The Gospel of Mark. The New Christian Jewish Passover Haggadah* (Leiden, 1965), p. 154.

[58] RSV "But an opportunity came when Herod on his birthday gave a banquet for his courtiers."

[59] RSV "he did not want to break his word to her."

27 And straightway the king sent forth a soldier of his guard, and commanded to bring his head: and he went and beheaded him in the prison,
28 and brought his head on a platter, and gave it to the damsel; and the damsel gave it to her mother.
29 And when his disciples heard *thereof,* they came and took up his corpse, and laid it in a tomb.

The Gospel of Mark contains two "passion narratives," the first of which reports the imprisonment and death of John the Baptist. The detailed narration of the circumstances resulting in the death of John stands in sharp contrast to the brief description of his mission in Ch. 1:4-8. It is probable that the present narrative reflects a special source [60] which circulated among the disciples of John. It is included here by Mark both to clarify the statements in Ch. 6:14, 16 and to point forward to the suffering and death of Jesus. [61]

The historical integrity of this narrative has been seriously challenged. [62] Alleged differences between Mark and Josephus, the presence of motifs which recall the conflict of Elijah with Jezebel or the story of Esther, and the improbability of a princess degrading herself by performing a sensuous solo dance at a royal banquet furnish the base for critical objection. On the other hand, between Mark and Josephus there are positive points of agreement. Both writers note the offensive adulterous union of Herod with Herodias, the fact of a daughter born of Herodias' first marriage who would have been of the age demanded

---

60 Cf. E. Lohmeyer, *op. cit.,* p. 118 who points to the accumulation of unusual words, the absence of the historical present, the numerous aorists and imperfects, the temporal distinctions, the free use of participles of the genitive absolute and the presence of a cultivated style which appears to reflect an Aramaic original.

61 Between Ch. 6:17-29 and Ch. 15:1-47 there are points of parallelism worth noting: Herod's respect for John as a righteous and holy man (Ch. 6:20) anticipates Pilate's attitude toward Jesus (Ch. 15:5, 14); Herodias' hatred for John and scheming to achieve his death finds its counterpart in the implacable hatred of the Jewish leaders towards Jesus; Herod's yielding to the pressure imposed by the circumstances (Ch. 6:26 f.) is the prelude to Pilate's yielding to the demands of the people (Ch. 15:15); the note of burial in a tomb with which the present narrative concludes (Ch. 6:29) anticipates the request for the body of Jesus and his burial (Ch. 15:43-46).

62 E.g. W. Wink, *op. cit.,* pp. 10 f. speaks of "this rambling, unedifying account of John's death" and adds, "the inaccuracies in the narrative are patent." On p. 28 he repeats earlier evaluations that "the account bears all the marks of bazaar-gossip."

by the Marcan narrative, the influence of Herodias on her weak husband, and the death of John by beheading. The differences which are alleged to exist between Mark and Josephus concern (1) the name of the first husband of Herodias, (2) the reason for John's execution and (3) the place of his imprisonment and execution.

(1) Josephus states that Herodias' first husband was Herod, the son of Herod the Great and Mariamne II, and half-brother to Antipas. Mark identifies this man as Philip.[63] There is no necessary discrepancy between the two accounts since nearly every son of Herod the Great bore the name "Herod" as a family designation (e.g. Herod Archelaus, Herod Philip, Herod Antipas, and the grandson Herod Agrippa). Josephus' failure to provide the personal name of this man should not obscure the fact that he was given a second name. It is common to suppose that "Philip" can only mean Herod Philip, the son of Herod the Great and Cleopatra, who was tetrarch of Iturea and Trachonitis. But the tetrarch and the husband of Herodias were the sons of different mothers and there is no firm reason why they could not have received the same name. The full name of Herodias' first husband is unknown, but no evidence exists that it was not Herod Philip. Moreover, no detail in Mark's narrative lends support to the supposition that his reference is to the tetrarch Philip.

(2) Josephus' report that Herod imprisoned and executed the Baptist because he feared a political uprising to which John might give leadership is thoroughly understandable. The territory of Antipas included the narrow strip designated Perea, which bordered on the Nabatean Kingdom. His marriage to Herodias had required the repudiation of a former wife, the daughter of Aretas IV of Nabatea. It is clear, therefore, that John's proclamation of the unlawfulness of Herod's adulterous union could be interpreted as a call to insurrection which threatened the tetrarch from within his province as seriously as did the incensed Nabateans to the east of his province.[64] It should be remembered that Josephus was writing some sixty years after the event for a Roman public who would find in Antipas' desire to suppress a potential public

---

[63] *Ant.* XVIII. v. 4. The name Philip is omitted in Mark by P^{45} and Codex 47; it is omitted in Mt. 14:3 by D *a c d ff k* vg Aug, and is absent in Lk. 3:19. Assuming that Mark wrote "Philip," the omission may be a scribal correction reflecting an alertness to the apparent conflict with Josephus. See the chart on the Herodian family.

[64] On the politically explosive nature of the denunciation in Mk. 6:18 see *Ant.* XVIII. v. 2; C. H. Kraeling, *John the Baptist* (New York, 1951), pp. 83-91.

disturbance merely the action of a Roman patriot. Mark, whose interests are very different from those of Josephus, stresses the scheming of Herodias. This emphasis is thoroughly consistent with what Josephus has reported at length concerning the active role played by women and their intrigues in the conduct of Herodian affairs. There is no sufficient reason for doubting the historical accuracy of the Marcan narrative on this account.

(3) Josephus states that Herod sent John to Machaerus, the southern tip of Perea tangent to the northeast corner of the Dead Sea.[65] The proximity of this area to the Judean wilderness where John seems to have concentrated his mission lends strong probability to the correctness of this detail. Mark does not say where John was imprisoned. Because "the first men of Galilee" were present at the banquet, and Jesus' presence in Galilee is the occasion for Herod's disturbed thoughts, it is natural to think of Tiberias in Galilee, the tetrarch's capital. There is nothing in Mark, however, which demands Galilee as the scene of John's imprisonment, and it is proper to read Mark through the eyes of Josephus at this point, placing the scene of the action in Machaerus.

It is possible that Mark incorporated details in the narrative which would call to mind the Elijah-Jezebel conflict, for it is clear that Jesus later identifies John as Elijah.[66] The parallels with Esther are those which are normal in the depiction of an oriental court scene. The final objection, that it is wholly improbable that a Herodian princess would debase herself by dancing before the company of men assembled by the tetrarch, loses its force when consideration is given to the moral depravity of Antipas and Herodias. It is clear from the Marcan narrative that there was calculation on Herodias' part to achieve her will; the dancing of her daughter was a crucial element in her plan, and was probably arranged by Herodias herself. The objections to the historical integrity of the Marcan narrative are not substantial and should be set aside. There was no disciple of John present to report the details of what had taken place, but it was inevitable that what happened would first be whispered about, and then take shape in a popular report. Mark narrates what was being said at that time.

---

65 *Ant.* XVIII. v. 2. The fortress, which was also a splendid palace, had been built by Herod the Great near the village of Machaerus. It possessed commodious quarters suitable for an extended stay and festive occasions (cf. Josephus, *War* VII. v. 2).

66 See below on Ch. 9:11-13. Justin, *Dial.* 49, 4-5 early interpreted the death of John in terms of the reference Jesus made in Ch. 9:11-13.

THE HERODIAN FAMILY

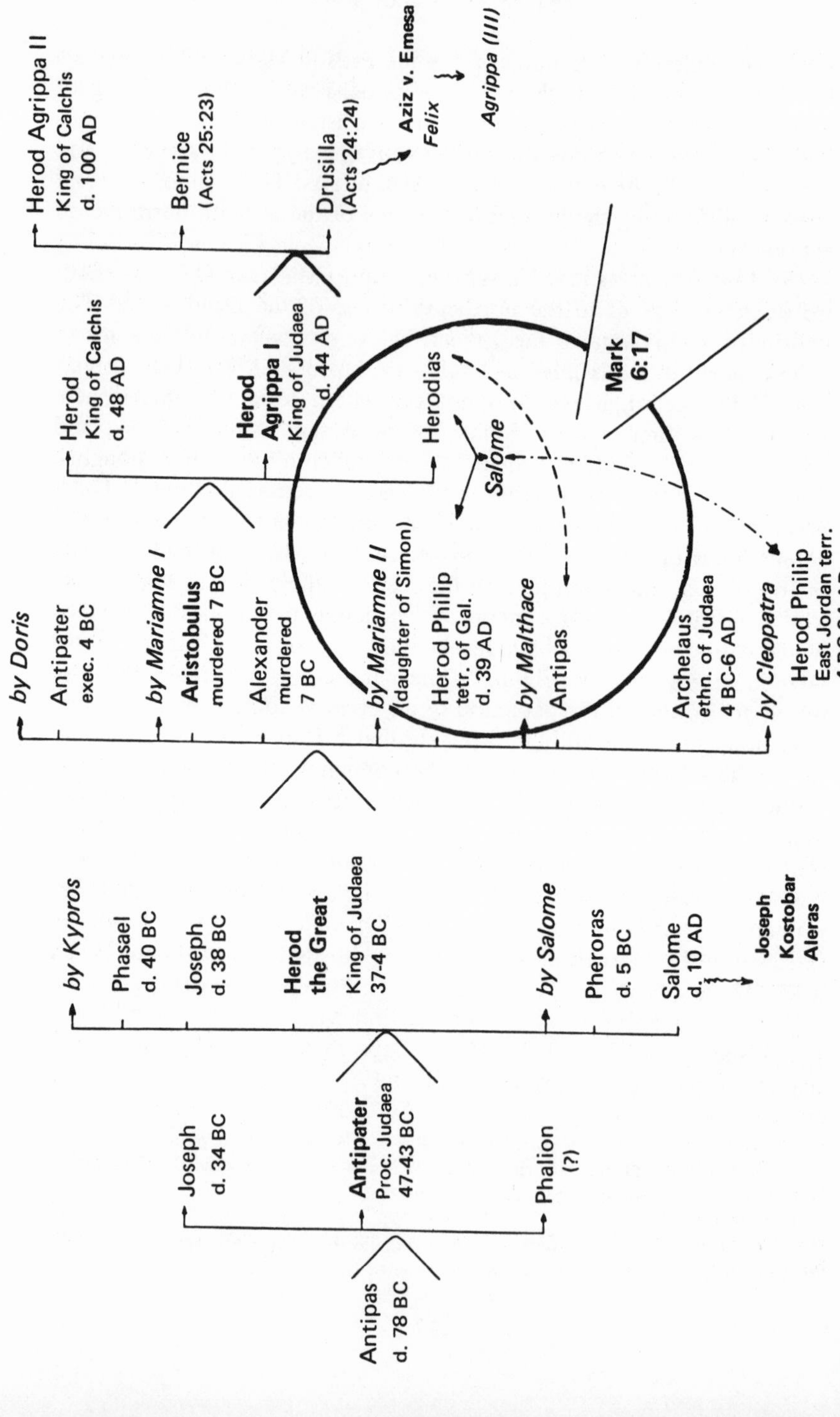

17-18 In supplement to the incidental report of John's imprisonment in Ch. 1:14, Mark now provides the details clarifying the situation. With a boldness appropriate to his office, John had denounced the unlawful marriage of Antipas to Herodias. Not even the royal house was exempt from the call to radical repentance. When John had ministered on the eastern bank of the Jordan River near Bethany he was in Perea, and it is probable that Antipas had taken him prisoner during a sojourn in this area.[67] The fortress-palace of Machaerus, which served as the military headquarters for the region, was not far from this place. Herod's motives for arresting the Baptist appear to have been mixed. John's preaching was politically explosive. The powerful Nabatean forces across Herod's border posed a definite threat to his security, and the tetrarch could not afford to have the provincials also inflamed against him. Nevertheless, he recognized that John was a man of God and sought to keep him in protective custody against the vindictive intentions of his wife. Herodias was the daughter of Aristobulus (the son of Herod and Mariamne), and the niece of Antipas.[68] She was near her fortieth year at the time of her second marriage.[69] Her union with Antipas was adulterous and shocking because the Mosaic Law clearly prohibited marriage to a brother's wife while the brother was yet alive (Lev. 18:16; 20:21).[70] This flouting of the Law in high places could not but call forth the stern denunciation of the wilderness prophet.

19-20 It is impossible to know whether John had addressed the royal court directly or not. It seems clear, however, that just as the weak Ahab had blurted out his troubles to Jezebel, Antipas had not concealed from Herodias what John was saying. The prophet's charge infuriated her. She nurtured a sustained grudge against John and desired to silence his disturbing accusation in a manner that had ample precedent in the Herodian annals–arranged "accident" or execution. Antipas would not

---

[67] C. H. Kraeling, *op. cit.*, pp. 8-10, 93.

[68] Lev. 18:13 explicitly forbids the marriage of a nephew to his aunt, but says nothing of the marriage of an uncle to his niece. While such marriages were allowed by some rabbis they were contested by others, by the Sadducees and the provisions of the Damascus Covenant (cf. TB *Yebamoth* 55a, b; *Baba Bathra* 115b; CD v. 7-11). There is no reflection on this aspect of the Law in Mark or Josephus.

[69] Aristobulus was strangled *ca.* 7 B.C., and Josephus mentions a younger sister to Herodias, Mariamne, in *War* I. xxviii. 1.

[70] Josephus, *Ant.* XVIII. v. 4 notes the public sense of shock at Herodias' repudiation of her first husband, especially because a daughter, Salome, had been born from this marriage.

permit this, for he had a superstitious fear of John whom he recognized as a righteous and holy man. The imprisonment of John was thus a compromise measure; it silenced his proclamation to the people, but could be rationalized as a protective measure against the whims of his wife. More weak than cruel, Herod listened to John with an undeniable fascination. John's word left him perplexed, and in anguish. Yet he found a strange pleasure in the authoritative preaching of this holy man, whose stringent life gave added power to his probing word. Too weak to follow John's counsel, he nevertheless had to listen.

21-23 While Herodias had been restrained from executing her wrath upon John for a period of time, an appropriate occasion presented itself when Herod celebrated his birthday with a banquet for the leading courtiers and men of his province.[71] The narrative seems to imply that she was biding her time, but that she deliberately sent her daughter into the feast to dance, in order to induce Herod to grant her desire. This understanding offers the most plausible explanation for Salome's dance.

The terms describing the guests at the banquet are of special interest: "his great men, his commanders of battalions, and the first persons of Galilee." The first term, which occurs only here in the Gospels, is appropriate to an oriental environment; Tacitus uses it of the barons of Armenia who resisted the Roman incursions, while in the context of Belshazzar's feast it designates the petty lords of the monarch.[72] In Mark the "great men" are the inner circle of the tetrarch's government. The second term has distinctly Roman overtones, *chiliarch* being the usual equivalent to the Latin *tribunus militum,* designating "commanders of a thousand."[73] The term is appropriate to Herod's tetrarchy, where his hosts would be only at battalion strength. A second Roman term occurs in verse 27, which in conjunction with the present reference indicates the court and administration of a petty Jewish prince who patterned his establishment after the imperial model. The leading men of Galilee are presumably Herod's courtiers, men of substance who pos-

[71] Verse 21 follows logically after verse 19; verse 20 provides a parenthetical explanation of why Herodias was unable to kill John. The Herodians apparently celebrated their birthdays in this fashion regularly, for Josephus mentions a similar feast on a birthday of Agrippa (*Ant.* XIX. vii. 1).

[72] Gr. μεγιστᾶνες, Tacitus, *Annals* XV. 27; Dan. 5:23 LXX, cited by A. N. Sherwin-White, *Roman Society and Roman Law in the New Testament* (Oxford, 1963), p. 137.

[73] *Ibid.,* pp. 124, 137.

sessed both the leisure and inclination to accompany him to Machaerus whenever Antipas was resident there.

Josephus identifies the name of Herodias' daughter as Salome. She was later married to the tetrarch Herod Philip, who was considerably older than she was, and after his death in 34 A.D. to another Herodian named Aristobulus.[74] She was, apparently, in her middle teens at the time of her infamous performance.[75] That she was not yet married seems clear from the fact that she was still under the influence of her mother; certainly no prince would have permitted his wife to perform artistically before the company of assembled men. The dance was unquestionably lascivious, designed to captivate and further the ends of the dancer. It appears to have had its origins not in a Semitic context but in a distinctly Hellenistic one.[76] The performance pleased both Herod and his guests, perhaps precisely because it was the princess who danced. They had undoubtedly seen professional dancers in the past, but Mark seems to stress that it was actually the daughter of Herodias who performed. In a boisterous manner appropriate to the feast and the presence of his chief men, Herod invited the girl to specify what her reward should be, sealing his words with an oath. The invitation, together with the formulation, "unto the half of my kingdom," recalls especially the words of Ahasuerus to Esther (Esth. 5:3, 6). It is clear, however, from parallel references that Herod is employing a proverbial reference for generosity[77] which Salome understood was not to be taken prosaically. Generosity suited the occasion, and would undoubtedly win the assent of his guests.

---

74 Josephus, *Ant.* XVIII. v. 4.

75 Mark's term κοράσιον occurs eight times in Esther (e.g. 2:2, 9) to designate a young girl of marriageable age.

76 H. Lesêtre, "Danse," *DB* II (1909), col. 1289. It is clear that in Roman circles dancing was generally considered indecent at this time; cf. Cicero, *Pro Murena* 14, "to dance a man must be intoxicated or insane"; Suetonius, *Domit.* 8; Horace, *Odes* xxi. 11, 12; xxxii. 1, 2. It is probable that Ecclus. 9:4 is a caution against a woman professional dancer. For this type of dancing within the Herodian household see Josephus, *War* II. ii. 5, where Antipater, the son of Salome, accuses Archelaus of giving himself to intoxication and sensuous dancing during the night. For the dance itself and parallels to a princess dancing see H. Windisch, "Kleine Beiträge zur evangelischen Überlieferung," *ZNW* 18 (1917), pp. 73-81; G. Dalman, "Der Tanz der Tochter des Herodias," *Palästinajahrbuch* 14 (1918), pp. 44-46.

77 I Kings 13:8; Lk. 19:8. On the invitation, "Ask me . . . and I will give you . . ." and its background in adoption formulae see K. H. Rengstorf, "Old and New Testament Traces of a Formula of the Judean Royal Ritual," *Nov Test* 5 (1962), pp. 229-244. Legal questions stemming from Herod's oath are discussed by J. D. M.

24-25 If the supposition that Salome danced at the instigation of her mother is correct, Herodias had not fully revealed her intention. She had merely instructed her daughter to perform in such a manner as to win Herod's approval. When Salome asked what she should claim for herself, Herodias responded with a bluntness and promptness which betrays calculation–the head of John the Baptist. She had waited for this moment. Now that it had come she found it satisfying. Her request in no way shocked Salome, who hastened back at once to Herod to demand the head of John. The grim detail "on a platter" seems to be her own, an expression of black humor inspired by the banquet yet in progress.

26-28 The request of Salome, expressed with arrogance and malice, immediately sobered Antipas. Only moments before he had revelled in boisterous conviviality; now he experienced the deepest grief. [78] Herod was filled with conflicting feelings. He was reluctant to grant the request but finally decided that he had no other choice since he had sealed his invitation with an oath in the presence of his great men. As had to happen, [79] Herod gave the order that the girl's demand was to be honored.

The designation for the guardsman charged with the execution transliterates the Latin form *speculator*. The *speculatores* were a well-known division of the imperial guard at Rome. These soldiers served as a police force, and in the pages of Tacitus tend to figure in moments of military intrigue. [80] The use of the Latin term for the guardsman ordered to execute John is appropriate to the context, and offers further illustration of Herod's attempt to pattern his court after the imperial administration. John was beheaded in the dungeon of the fortress, and in due course the head was presented on a platter, first to Salome, and then to her mother.

Derrett, "Herod's Oath and the Baptist's Head," *Bib Zeit* 9 (1965), pp. 49-59, 233-246.

[78] Gr. περίλυπος, used in Mark only here and in Ch. 14:34 where it describes the piercing agony of Jesus in Gethsemane.

[79] For this interpretation of εὐθύς see D. Daube, *The Sudden in Scripture* (Leiden, 1964), p. 54.

[80] Gr. σπεκουλάτωρ cf. Tacitus, *Hist.* i. 24-25; ii. 73, on which see A. N. Sherwin-White, *op. cit.,* pp. 109 f., 124.

29 It is difficult to know how long after John had been slain that word of his death reached his disciples. It is probable that they were not far from the fortress in order to serve him in any way they could. Their final act of ministry was to take up his corpse and place it in a tomb, presumably in the vicinity of Machaerus. The death of John, however, did not bring the Baptist movement to an end,[81] nor was this the final time Herod would be forced to remember John. The ministry of Jesus stirred his sober reflection on John whom he had beheaded. Then in A.D. 36 the Nabatean hordes swept down upon him to avenge the humiliation suffered by the daughter of Aretas. They administered a stinging defeat to Antipas which the people interpreted as an act of God avenging the murder of John the Baptist.[82]

The focus of Ch. 6:17-29 is on the suffering of John. Yet the remarkable fact is that the Baptist only provides the occasion for the record; John himself is always in the background. The single emphasis of the account is what *they* do to him. What Mark understands by this enigmatic suffering scene is clarified in Ch. 9:9-13.[83]

3. The Provision of Rest in the Wilderness. Ch. 6:30-34

30 And the apostles gathered themselves together unto Jesus; and they told him all things, whatsoever they had done, and whatsoever they had taught.
31 And he saith unto them, Come ye yourselves apart into a desert place, and rest a while. For there were many coming and going, and they had no leisure so much as to eat.
32 And they went away in the boat to a desert place apart.
33 And *the people* saw them going, and many knew *them,* and they ran together there on foot from all the cities and outwent them.
34 And he came forth and saw a great multitude, and he had compassion on them, because they were as sheep not having a shepherd: and he began to teach them many things.

---

[81] For an account of the later Baptist movement, and especially of the Mandeans, see C. H. Kraeling, *op. cit.,* pp. 158-187; O. Cullmann, *op. cit.,* pp. 25-30.

[82] Josephus, *Ant.* XVIII. v. 1-3, on which see C. H. Kraeling, *op. cit.,* pp. 88-90.

[83] Rightly stressed by W. Wink, *op. cit.,* pp. 13-17.

The decision to divide Ch. 6:30-44 at verse 34 is one of convenience, which permits a consideration of the return of the disciples and the withdrawal to a wilderness-place before attention is concentrated upon the feeding of the multitude. The degree of variation displayed in modern treatments of this question indicates the relative difficulty of discerning the evangelist's intention.[84] The division adopted presupposes that Mark has prefaced the feeding miracle by two small introductory passages which are thematically united.[85] The first describes the return of the disciples and their rest in a wilderness-place (Ch. 6:30-32), while the second tells of the gathering of the multitudes to the wilderness and Jesus' compassion upon them (Ch. 6:33-34).

30 At the conclusion of their mission to the Galilean villages the disciples returned to Jesus. He had commissioned them to be his emissaries (Ch. 6:7-13), and it is appropriate to this circumstance that they should report to him how they had fulfilled their commission. The designation of the Twelve as "the apostles," which occurs only here in Mark's Gospel, has specific reference to the mission they have just undertaken. In this context the term is descriptive of the disciples' function rather than an official title, and could be rendered "missionaries." It was in consequence of their mission of preaching and exorcism in Galilee that the Twelve were designated "apostles," i.e. those who had been sent forth and empowered by Jesus.[86]

31-32 The mission activity of the Twelve had caught the attention of large numbers of people, who pursued after the disciples even as earlier they had sought the benefactions of Jesus. Mark conveys the impression of one group following another as he reports that "many were coming

---

[84] M. J. Lagrange, *op. cit.*, p. 165; E. Lohmeyer, *op. cit.*, p. 122 and J. Bowman, *op. cit.*, p. 155 prefer to view Ch. 6:30-44 as a unit. K. Aland, *op. cit.*, p. 205 divides the unit into Ch. 6:30-31 and 32-44; C. E. B. Cranfield, *op. cit.*, p. 213 finds the break between verses 33 and 34; V. Taylor, *op. cit.*, pp. 317 f., 322 and K. Tagawa, *Miracles et Évangile* (Paris, 1966), pp. 140-148 support the division into two units, with the break after verse 34. It is difficult to say with confidence that one solution is more satisfactory than the others which have been proposed.

[85] Cf. U. Mauser, *op. cit.*, pp. 134-136.

[86] See above on Ch. 6:7-9. K. H. Rengstorf, *TWNT* I (Eng. Tr. 1964), pp. 424-437 provides a full discussion of the relevant texts. Cf. J. Dupont, "Le nom d'apôtres a-t-il été donné aux douze par Jésus," *Or Syr* 1 (1956), pp. 267-290; R. P. Meye, *op. cit.*, pp. 173-191.

and going," with the result that the Twelve had no leisure to eat.[87] Jesus' directive to withdraw to a wilderness-place signifies more than a deserved rest after strenuous labor. What is in view is the concept of rest within the wilderness. Mark indicates this by repeating the expressions "a wilderness-place apart" in verses 31 and 32.[88] The site toward which the disciples set sail cannot be identified with any degree of certainty; but this was not important to the evangelist. What was significant was the character of the place to which Jesus and his disciples withdrew, and this is sufficiently indicated by the descriptive phrase "wilderness-place." That God provides rest for his people within the wilderness is a recurring theme in the Scripture.[89] It was the literal rest of the wilderness generation led by Moses and Joshua which became the type of the final rest promised to the people of God in a second exodus in the preaching of Isaiah and Jeremiah.[90] The ancient hope of rest within the wilderness is to be fulfilled as Jesus gathers his disciples to a wilderness-place that they may be by themselves. The disciples and the multitudes who pursue them prove to be the people of the new exodus. The presence of Jesus and the provision of God will give to this time of withdrawal the character of rest within the wilderness.

33-34 The second introductory unit is thematically united to the first by wilderness motifs. Its purpose is to indicate that the withdrawal of the multitude from the several Galilean villages to the wilderness where they experienced Jesus' compassion was the direct result of the mission activity of the Twelve. By accenting the relationship of the multitude to the disciples ("they saw *them,* and they recognized *them* and they ran on foot from all the towns and got there ahead of *them*") Mark shows that the provision of rest in the wilderness was the ultimate intention behind the disciples' commission by Jesus.

---

87 Like Jesus in a similar circumstance. See above on Ch. 3:20.

88 On the significance of Mark's phrase κατ' ἰδίαν, "alone" or "apart," see U. Mauser, *op. cit.,* pp. 119-124. He concludes that the passages in Mark containing the phrase "alone" concern either instruction about the necessity of suffering or about the life-giving power of Jesus. Invariably the facet of special revelation is in view.

89 E.g. Deut. 3:20; 12:9 f.; 25:19; Josh. 1:13, 15; 21:44; Ps. 95:7-11; Isa. 63:14; Jer. 31:2; Heb. 3:7-4:13, on which see U. Mauser, *op. cit.,* pp. 33, 41, 73 f.

90 Isa. 63:14 (in the context of Ch. 63:10-14); Jer. 31:2 (in the context of Chs. 30:23-31:6).

The comparison of the people to "sheep not having a shepherd" is an allusion to Num. 27:17 and Ezek. 34:5.[91] In the context of both of these passages, Mark's statement belongs to the wilderness theme. In Num. 27:17 Moses prays that the Lord will appoint a leader to take his place prior to his death in the wilderness lest the people "be as sheep which have no shepherd." It is significant that God appointed as shepherd Joshua, whose name in the Septuagint is "Jesus." In Ezek. 34 the shepherd image is also associated with the wilderness. There is no shepherd for the sheep, but God promises the coming of a faithful shepherd, "my servant David" (Ch. 34:23), who will establish a covenant of peace, causing the people to "dwell securely in the wilderness" (Ch. 34:25). In verse 34 Mark proclaims Jesus on the background provided by these passages: he is the one appointed by God to be the leader of the people in their exodus into the wilderness; he is God's servant David who provides rest for the people in the wilderness.[92] These theological notes are not extraneous to Mark's presentation. They provide the indispensable background for understanding the feeding narrative which follows. The multitude who pursue Jesus and the disciples are representative of Israel once more in the wilderness. There they experience the compassion of the Messiah, who teaches them "at length" concerning the Kingdom of God.[93] In the carefully constructed twofold introduction to the feeding narrative it is the wilderness motif which exhibits the deeper significance that Mark found in the events he records. The time of rest in the wilderness has come when the Son of God establishes meal-fellowship with his people.

4. The Provision of Bread in the Wilderness. Ch. 6:35-44

35 And when the day was now far spent, his disciples came unto him, and said, The place is desert, and the day is now far spent;

---

[91] On the metaphor see W. Tooley, "The Shepherd and Sheep Image in the Teaching of Jesus," *Nov Test* 7 (1964), pp. 15-25; G. Ziener, "Die Brotwunder im Markusevangelium," *BZ*, n.f. 4 (1960), pp. 282-285.

[92] Cf. U. Mauser, *op. cit.*, p. 135.

[93] The note that Jesus had compassion upon the multitude (Chs. 6:34; 8:2) is confined to Mark and Matthew among the Synoptic Gospels. For Mark's distinctive attitude toward the multitude see B. Citron, "The Multitude in the Synoptic Gospels," *ScJTh* 7 (1954), pp. 408-418, and especially pp. 416 f. (on Mk. 6:34).

36 send them away, that they may go into the country and villages round about, and buy themselves somewhat to eat.
37 But he answered and said unto them, Give ye them to eat. And they say unto him, Shall we go and buy two hundred shillings' worth of bread, and give them to eat?
38 And he saith unto them, How many loaves have ye? go *and* see. And when they knew, they say, Five, and two fishes.
39 And he commanded them that all should sit down by companies upon the green grass.
40 And they sat down in ranks, by hundreds, and by fifties.
41 And he took the five loaves and the two fishes, and looking up to heaven, he blessed, and brake the loaves; and he gave to the disciples[94] to set before them; and the two fishes divided he among them all.
42 And they all ate, and were filled.
43 And they took up broken pieces, twelve basketfuls, and also of the fishes.
44 And they that ate the loaves[95] were five thousand men.

The account of the feeding of the multitude on the shores of Lake Gennesaret possesses a particular significance in the framework of Mark's Gospel. Its elaborate introduction (Ch. 6:30-34), the extended dialogue with the disciples (Ch. 6:35-38), as well as subsequent references to this occasion (Chs. 6:52; 8:17-21) and its sequel in the feeding of the four thousand (Ch. 8:1-10), show that the evangelist regarded this event as crucial for understanding the dignity of Jesus. Its position in the Marcan framework after the account of Herod's feast juxtaposes the sumptuous oriental aura of the Herodian court with the austere circumstances in which Jesus satisfied the multitude with the staples of a peasant's diet. In spite of the tetrarch's pretensions to royalty, the people are as leaderless as sheep who possess no shepherd.[96] In contrast to the drunken debauchery of the Herodian feast, Mark exhibits the glory of God unveiled through the abundant provision of bread in the wilderness where Jesus is Israel's faithful shepherd.

---

94 P^{45} 𝔎 A D W Θ λ φ *pl* latt $sy^{s\,p\,h}$ aeth read "his disciples," probably rightly. Mark normally speaks of "his disciples" and rarely of "the disciples" (Chs. 8:1; 9:14; 10:10, 13, 24; 14:16).

95 The words "the loaves" are omitted by P^{45} ℵ D W Θ λ 565 700 *al* latt sy^s sa, perhaps under the influence of Mt. 14:21.

96 In I Kings 22:17; II Chron. 18:16 and Judith 11:19 the metaphor occurs in the context of battle where Israel has no king to give leadership to the people.

35-38 The disciples felt compelled to call Jesus' attention to the lateness of the hour and the scarcity of provision for the evening meal which was close at hand. They may have sensed a particular responsibility for the people who had followed them from the several villages in which they had ministered. From the perspective of their need it was imperative that the people be dismissed to find food in the surrounding countryside and villages. The norms of practical judgment appeared to support their proposal, although the impracticality of so large a company flocking to the neighboring towns seems not to have been considered. They were utterly unprepared for Jesus' instruction to provide for the needs of the multitude. This is evident from the astonishment expressed in their question about purchasing bread, which is disrespectful in tone, but points unmistakably to the impossibility of complying with Jesus' order. Two hundred denarii was roughly equivalent to the entire year's wage of a day laborer,[97] and it is clear that the Twelve did not have such a sum at their disposal. Jesus' refusal to let the issue rest by insisting that they count their reserves of bread forces the recognition that the situation was beyond human resourcefulness. Five small barley loaves and two salted or roasted fish were insignificant in the presence of such need, and the disciples might have echoed Moses' cry of anguish in the wilderness: "Where shall I find meat to give to all these people? . . . Shall all the fish of the sea be gathered together for them, to satisfy them?" (Num. 11:13, 22).

The extended conversation of Jesus with his disciples concerning bread is the distinctive element in the Marcan account of the feeding of the multitude. Jesus, in contrast to the circumstances depicted in all of the other miracles, appears deliberately to create the situation in which the people must be fed. His instructions to the disciples to feed the people and to count their reserves of bread signify unambiguously that the food had to be provided through the disciples, not from the multitude. Jesus knows from the beginning what he will do and the exchange with the Twelve moves toward a well-defined end. His instructions to the disciples, which perplex and baffle them, are intended to lead them to understanding. The Twelve, however, display an increasing lack of understanding; their attitude of disrespect and incredulity declares that

[97] According to Mt. 20:2 ff. the denarius was the standard day-wage; Jn. 6:7 indicates that 200 denarii was not sufficient to provide a morsel for each person. On the Roman silver denarius see E. Rogers, *Handy Guide to Jewish Coins* (London, 1914), pp. 67 ff.

the conduct of Jesus is beyond their comprehension. This dialogical structure of the Marcan account gives to it a particular tone and provides the basis for the criticism that the disciples did not understand because their hearts were hardened (Ch. 6:52).[98]

39-40 At the command of Jesus the vast gathering was constituted into table-companies in preparation for the meal.[99] Two details of the Marcan account are narrowly related to the wilderness motif noted in verses 30-34. (1) The reference to "the green grass" is not in contradiction to the description of the locale as "wilderness." The concept of the wilderness is broad enough to include pastures sufficient for the grazing of flocks, particularly after the winter rains. Yet the vivid description is most intelligible when read in the larger context provided by the introduction to the feeding narrative. The transformation of the desert into a place of refreshment and life through the power of God is an aspect of the wilderness tradition which is prominent in the prophets. By divine intervention the land of curse will become fat pastures where the sheep will be gathered and fed by the true shepherd (Ezek. 34:26 f., 29). The Lord who causes his people to recline in green pastures (Ps. 23:1) evokes the shepherd imagery of verse 34 and implies that the wilderness is already being changed into the land of fertility and rest.[100] (2) The arrangement of the crowd into field-groups of hundreds and fifties recalls the order of the Mosaic camp in the wilderness (e.g. Ex. 18:21). This detail is particularly striking because the documents of Qumran use these subdivisions to describe true Israel assembled in the desert in the period of the last days.[101] If this concept is presupposed in verse 40, the multitude who have been instructed concerning the Kingdom is characterized as the people of the new exodus who have been

---

98 E. Lohmeyer, *op. cit.*, pp. 125 f.; K. Tagawa, *op. cit.*, pp. 151-153 find this triple exchange of demands and responses between Jesus and the disciples, the total lack of comprehension on the part of the disciples, and the ambiguity of Jesus' words and attitude highly characteristic of the Johannine style.

99 Gr. συμπόσια συμπόσια = חֲבוּרוֹת חֲבוּרוֹת: the text denotes a group of people eating a fellowship meal together. E. Stauffer, *Jesus and His Story* (New York, 1960), pp. 82 f. sees in the reference an allusion to the celebration of the Passover in Galilee in A.D. 31, but this appears to over-interpret Mark's expression, in spite of Jn. 6:4.

100 U. Mauser, *op. cit.*, pp. 136 f.; G. Friedrich, "Die beiden Erzählungen von der Speisung in Mark. 6, 31-44; 8, 1-9," *ThZ* 20 (1964), pp. 10-22.

101 CD xiii. 1; 1QS ii. 21; 1QSa i. 14 f.; 1QM iv. 1-5.

summoned to the wilderness to experience messianic grace. Through these elements of the wilderness complex Mark portrays Jesus as the eschatological Savior, the second Moses who transforms a leaderless flock into the people of God.

41 In Judaism it was a stringent rule that nothing should be eaten without thanking God before and after the meal.[102] On this occasion Jesus performed the duty of the host in pronouncing the blessing over the loaves and the fish. Mark's sequence of words describes the characteristic procedure at ordinary Jewish meals[103] and indicates that Jesus faithfully followed the accepted form: he took the bread in his hands, pronounced the blessing, broke the bread into pieces and distributed it. The only deviation from normal practice was that while praying Jesus looked toward heaven rather than downward, as prescribed.[104] This is not an ordinary meal, and it is proper to see in Jesus' prayer not only the customary praise and thanksgiving but a reliance upon the Father for the extraordinary power necessary to meet the people's need. The object of the blessing pronounced was not the loaves and the fish, but "the Lord," since every prayer before a meal began with the blessing of the name of God: "Praise unto thee, O Lord our God, King of the world." The continuation of the prayer depended on the nature of the food involved; in the case of bread, blessing was invoked on God, "who makes bread to come forth from the earth."[105] This recognition that the bread was God's provision was confirmed by those who were present with their "Amen." In the act of blessing God

---

[102] Tos. *Berachoth* IV. 1; TJ *Berachoth* 10a; TB *Berachoth* 35a. The biblical foundation for this practice was found in Lev. 19:24; Deut. 8:10. See H. W. Beyer, *TWNT* II (Eng. Tr. 1964), pp. 760-762.

[103] There is a persistent desire on the part of commentators to find in the formula "he blessed, and broke the loaves, and gave . . . " overtones of the eucharist (cf. Ch. 14:22), in spite of the fact that identical language occurs in the non-eucharistic context of Acts 27:35, and is inevitable when describing an ordinary Jewish meal. For a careful consideration and rejection of the eucharistic interpretation see G. H. Boobyer, "The Eucharistic Interpretation of the Miracle of the Loaves in St. Mark's Gospel," *JThS* n.s. 3 (1952), pp. 161-171, and for a dissenting opinion K. Tagawa, *op. cit.*, pp. 134-138, 153.

[104] S-B*K* II (1924), p. 246.

[105] G. Dalman, *Jesus-Jeschua* (Leipzig, 1922), p. 124 suggests that on this occasion Jesus used a freer form of the benediction congruent with the Lord's Prayer: "Blessed be Thou, our Father in heaven, who gives us today our necessary bread."

the few loaves and fish were consecrated to the service of the Kingdom. The actual fact of the miracle is not recounted and cannot be described. Whether the bread increased in the hands of Jesus or in the hands of the disciples who distributed it was not considered important in the tradition. Here the Kingdom of God was functioning. The God who gave manna in the wilderness and who made startling provision for his servants Elijah and Elisha [106] now gives to the people their daily bread, visibly and yet in a hidden manner. [107]

42-44 The text is emphatic that the loaves and fish were miraculously increased. In sharp contrast to the deficiency of funds and the scarcity of food at hand Mark poses "all" who "eat and are filled" with much left over, in spite of the vast size of the gathering. In contrast to a sacramental meal in which the people receive only a morsel, Mark emphasizes that their hunger was fully satisfied. When they returned to the wilderness in response to the mission of the Twelve the Galileans met the Lord who "opens his hand and satisfies the desire of every living thing" (Ps. 145:16). Reflecting the traditional respect for bread as the gift of God, it was a regulation that scraps which had fallen upon the ground during a meal were to be gathered. [108] The fragments were collected in the small wicker baskets [109] that every Jew carried with him as a part of his daily attire. Each of the disciples returned with his basket full. The quantity of the remaining fragments witnesses to the fulness of the meal and confirms the satisfaction noted in verse 42. The arrangement

---

[106] Ex. 16 (the manna); I Kings 17:7-16 (the multiplication of the oil and meal for the widow of Zarephath); II Kings 4:1-7 (the increase of the pot of oil), 42-44 (the feeding of 100 men with twenty loaves of barley). For rabbinic accounts see TB *Ta'anith* 24b, 25a; *Yoma* 39a and the discussion of H. van der Loos, *op. cit.*, pp. 624-632.

[107] S. F. H. J. Berkelbach van der Sprenkel, *Het evangelie van Markus* (Amsterdam, 1937), *ad loc.* comments: "In the midst of the wilderness, among the sheep without a shepherd, there stands one who breaks bread; the Messianic feast transcends realism and its confusions. God's kingdom opens, they eat and are filled, without knowing how." See further, H. Clavier, "La Multiplication des pains dans le Ministère de Jésus," in *Studia Evangelica* I, ed. F. L. Cross (Berlin, 1959), pp. 441-457; A. G. Hebert, "History in the Feeding of the Five Thousand," in *Studia Evangelica* II, ed. F. L. Cross (Berlin, 1964), pp. 65-72.

[108] S-B*K* I (1922), p. 687; IV. 2 (1928), pp. 625 ff.

[109] Gr. κόφινος. They were used to hold such items as a light lunch and general odds and ends. They were so much a symbol of the Jew that Juvenal twice described him with reference to the *cophinus: Satires* iii. 14; vi. 542.

of the multitude in table companies and field groups would permit a quick estimation of the number present. Five thousand men was an immense gathering since large neighboring towns like Capernaum and Bethsaida had only 2000-3000 inhabitants each.

The miracle took place before the multitude, but there is no indication in the Marcan text that they had any realization of what was taking place. The simplicity of the meal Jesus provided is congruous with his general reluctance to perform miracles and give signs; there was nothing extraordinary in the peasants' fare which would call attention to itself. The messianic meal remained hidden from the thousands. The event is intended to be revelatory to the disciples alone. They are the ones who prompt the action, who bring the loaves and fish, who distribute the meal and who gather the fragments. In contrast to their usually passive stance Jesus actively involved them in the total proceeding. His extended discussion with them prior to the event baffled them, while his wordless disclosure of his divine power through the event exceeded all understanding. In the eyes of the people Jesus remained an enigmatic prophetic teacher (cf. Ch. 6:14 f.), but he should have been recognized by the disciples as the Son of God at whose disposal are all of the riches of his Father. The people fail to perceive who Jesus is and they do not understand him. The disciples do not understand him although they were given an abundant opportunity to see his glory. That is why they alone are reproved for their hardness of heart and their failure to grasp the meaning of the miracle of the loaves in the subsequent narrative (Chs. 6:52; 8:17-21).

It is appropriate to see in the feeding of the multitude a fresh affirmation of the promise that the Messiah will feast with men in the wilderness (Isa. 25:6-9).[110] The austerity of the meal, however, is more reminiscent of the manna in the wilderness than of the rich fare promised for the eschatological banquet. Moreover, the absence of an enduring relationship between Jesus and the people indicates that the fellowship which they shared was essentially that which exists between a host and his guests. The meal was eschatological to the degree that the people experienced rest in the wilderness and were nurtured by the faithful Shepherd of Israel, but it pointed beyond itself to an uninterrupted

110 Cf. E. Stauffer, "Zum apokalyptischen Festmahl in Mk 6, 34 ff.," *ZNW* 46 (1955), pp. 264-266; A. Richardson, "The Feeding of the Five Thousand," *Interpretation* 9 (1955), pp. 147-149; J. F. Priest, "The Messiah and the Meal in 1QSa," *JBL* 82 (1963), pp. 95-100.

fellowship in the Kingdom of God. In the center of the event stands Jesus, who creates the situation and arranges everything that pertains to the meal. He orders the camp in their groups, takes and breaks the bread and divides the fish, and through his hands the miracle unfolds for those who have eyes to see. If the crowd has been described as sheep without a shepherd, Jesus is presented as the Shepherd who provides for all of their needs so that they lack nothing.

5. The Lord of the Sea. Ch. 6:45-52

45 And straightway he constrained his disciples to enter the boat and to go before *him* unto the other side to Bethsaida,[111] while he himself sendeth the multitude away.
46 And after he had taken leave of them, he departed into the mountain to pray.
47 And when even was come,[112] the boat was in the midst of the sea, and he alone on the land.
48 And seeing them distressed in rowing, for the wind was contrary unto them, about the fourth watch of the night he cometh unto them, walking on the sea, and he would have passed by them:
49 but they, when they saw him walking on the sea, supposed that it was a ghost,[113] and cried out;

---

111 The text is attested by the great majority of witnesses, but it creates the difficulty that Bethsaida was on the northeast shore of the lake, in the region where the feeding took place according to Lk. 9:10, not on "the other side." It is better to accept the Caesarean text, which omits εἰς τὸ πέραν and gives only πρὸς (εἰς) Βηθσαϊδάν: P^{45} W λ *q* sy^s. For a defense of the primitiveness of this reading see L. Vaganay, "Mk 6:45," *RB* 49 (1940), pp. 5-32. The longer reading of Mark appears to be a conflated variant reuniting the shorter reading supported by the Caesarean text with the different reading of Mt. 14:22. Mark evidently uses εἰς τὸ πέραν to indicate a change of location by boat where the destination of the voyage is unspecified (cf. Chs. 4:35; 5:21; 8:13 with 6:32, 53; 8:10) or quite general (Ch. 5:1). See further C. C. McCown, "The Problem of the Site of Bethsaida," *JPOS* 10 (1930), pp. 32-58; J. O'Hara, "Two Bethsaidas or One?" *Scripture* 15 (1963), pp. 24-27.

112 P^{45} D λ 22 28 251 697 *a b d ff* g^2 i adds πάλαι, "already," which may be primitive. Cf. ἤδη, "already" in Mt. 14:24.

113 Gr. φάντασμα, sy^s reads δαιμόνιον, while I Enoch 60:16 speaks of the "spirit" of the sea which is "masculine and strong." The sea, like the wilderness, was regarded as the dwelling place for demons.

50 for they all saw him, and were troubled. But he straightway spake with them, and saith unto them, Be of good cheer: it is I; be not afraid.
51 And he went up unto them into the boat; and the wind ceased; and they were sore amazed in themselves;
52 for they understood not concerning the loaves, but their heart was hardened.

The second occasion when Jesus demonstrated his sovereignty over the sea, like the stilling of the storm (Ch. 4:35-41), is connected with the Sea of Galilee. The earlier event focused attention on the authority of Jesus' word; here his whole person is involved as he walks across the rough water. On both occasions the disciples fail to understand who Jesus is and experience stark fear and amazement.[114] The incident is more firmly welded into the context than most of the paragraphs belonging to the Galilean ministry. The dismissal of the crowd, the hurried departure of the disciples under constraint, and the reference to the loaves in verse 52 inseparably link the narrative with the feeding of the multitude.[115] When the third person plural of the narration is transposed to the first person plural of direct discourse the section reads like the excited report of one of the Twelve who had experienced terror upon seeing the Lord of the Sea.

45-46 The abruptness with which Jesus constrained the disciples to return to their boat and directed them to Bethsaida Julias in the territory of Herod Philip suggests a crisis which is unexplained in the Marcan narrative. The wilderness plays a prominent role, however, in the several messianic uprisings of the first century, and Jn. 6:14 f. states that the people recognized Jesus as the promised eschatological Prophet (cf. Mk. 6:14 f.) and determined to proclaim him king. The tension of messianic excitement was dangerously in the air after the meal in the desert. The hurried dismissal of the disciples prevented them from adding fuel to the fire by revealing to the people the miraculous character of the evening meal. Jesus remained to pacify and dismiss the unruly crowd. His retreat to the hillside for prayer and the subsequent withdrawal from

---

114 For a development of the parallel see H. J. Ebeling, *Das Messiasgeheimnis und die Botschaft des Marcusevangelisten* (Berlin, 1939), pp. 152-154.

115 A dissenting opinion has been registered by T. Snoy, "La rédaction marcienne de la marche sur les eaux (Mc., VI, 45-52)," *Eph Th Lov* 44 (1968), pp. 205-241, who fails to appreciate the internal connection between the two episodes.

Galilee are the direct result of the outburst of enthusiasm which followed the feeding of the multitude. Jesus refused to be the warrior-Messiah of popular expectations.[116]

This analysis is confirmed when the reference to Jesus in prayer is seen in the context of Mark's structure. The evangelist speaks of Jesus' withdrawal to a solitary place for prayer after the excitement of the sabbath activity in Capernaum (Ch. 1:35-39), after the miracle of the loaves (Ch. 6:45 f.), and following the Last Supper (Ch. 14:26-42). In each case it is night and Jesus finds himself in a moment of crisis prompted by the enthusiasm of the crowds or the impending passion.[117] On this occasion it was the threat inherent in irresponsible excitement which prompted Jesus to retreat from the people. As at the beginning of his ministry (Ch. 1:12 f.), Jesus' presence in the wilderness provoked the renewal of temptation: refusing the acclaim of the multitude he gave himself to a long period of solitude in order to affirm his obedience to the Father.

47 By the time Jesus had finished praying it was the dark hours before dawn and the disciples were well out to sea. The observation that the boat was on the sea and Jesus was alone on the land seems labored until it is seen as an element in a recurring pattern in Mark. Whenever the master is absent from the disciples (or appears to be so, as in Ch. 4:35-41), they find themselves in distress. And each time they experience anguish it is because they lack faith (Chs. 4:35 ff.; 6:45 ff.; 9:14 ff.).[118] This is clearly the case in this episode where the physical exhaustion of the disciples was aggravated by stark terror when they encountered what they believed to be a night spectre. Mark's notice indicates that the crowd has dispersed and brings into focus the principals in the drama which unfolded on the sea.

48-50 The reason that Jesus came to the disciples across the rough sea about 3:00 A.M. was that he had seen his disciples exerting themselves against a strong wind which blew presumably from the north or north-

---

116 For the suggestion that Jesus prevented a messianic uprising see H. G. Wood, "Interpreting This Time," *NTS* 2 (1955-56), pp. 265 f.; H. Montefiore, "Revolt in the Desert? (Mark vi. 30 ff.)," *NTS* 8 (1962), pp. 135-141.

117 R. H. Lightfoot, "A Consideration of Three Passages in St. Mark's Gospel," *In Memoriam E. Lohmeyer* (Stuttgart, 1951), pp. 110-115. See on Ch. 1:35-39 above.

118 G. Minette de Tillesse, *Le secret messianique dans l'Évangile de Marc* (Paris, 1968), pp. 411-418.

east and drove them off their course. Because the text stresses that Jesus' coming to the disciples was the direct result of his perceiving their distress, the explanation that "he meant to pass by them" seems enigmatic, if not alien to the context. Among the several proposals that have been offered three are worthy of serious consideration. (1) The words record the impression that the disciples had at that time that the spectral figure intended to pass by them. The complex of verses 48-50 becomes intelligible when transposed into the first person: "He meant to pass by us, but when we saw him walking upon the sea we thought it was a ghost, and cried out; for we all saw him and were terrified."[119] (2) The several modern translations, which create the impression of an independent and more or less isolated statement, fail to represent Mark's intention. The text should be rendered, "for he intended to pass their way." The initial particle is to be understood in an explicative sense rather than as a coordinating conjunction; it introduces a subordinate clause clarifying why Jesus came walking on the water. Verse 48 thus forms a composite whole: when Jesus saw that the disciples were wearing themselves out, he already felt the desire to reveal his presence to them by passing their way. This proposal is grammatically feasible and introduces cohesion and balance into the account.[120] (3) For Mark the event is a theophany, a manifestation of the transcendent Lord who will "pass by" as God did at Sinai before Moses (Ex. 33:19, 22) or on Horeb before Elijah (I Kings 19:11). The text simply uses the language of theophany familiar from the Septuagint.[121] It is possible that the evangelist intends his readers to recognize an allusion to Job 9:8, 11: "he walks upon the waves of the sea . . . If he goes by me, I will not see him, and if he passes by me, I will not recognize him." In this instance the divine appearance occurred for the very purpose of being seen. In wonderful fashion Jesus put his authority at the disposal of the disciples and passed by to assure them of his presence with them.

The disciples reacted to Jesus' appearance with terror, convinced that they had encountered a water spirit. The popular belief that spirits of the night brought disaster is illustrated by a tradition preserved in the

119 C. E. B. Cranfield, *op. cit.*, p. 226.

120 H. van der Loos, *op. cit.*, pp. 652 f. For this use of καί see Bl-D-F § 442, 9 (pp. 228 f.).

121 J. Schneider, *TWNT* II (Eng. Tr. 1964), pp. 681 f.; A. M. Denis, "Jesus' Walking on the Waters. A Contribution to the History of the Pericope in the Gospel Tradition," *Louvain Studies* 1 (1967), pp. 284-297. Denis calls attention to Job 9:8, but seems not to have seen the relevance of the continuation in verse 11.

Talmud: "Rabbah said, Seafarers told me that the wave that sinks a ship appears with a white fringe of fire at its crest, and when stricken with clubs on which is engraven, 'I am that I am, Yah, the Lord of Hosts, Amen, Amen, Selah,' it subsides."[122] When Jesus perceived the terror of the disciples he allayed their fears and corrected their delusion with a summons to courage. The emphatic "I" in verse 50 is ambiguous. It can be understood as a normal statement of identity ("it is I, Jesus"), but it can also possess deeper significance as the recognized formula of self-revelation which rests ultimately on the "I am that I am" of Ex. 3:14. Not only the immediate context of the walking upon the water but the words with which the emphatic "I" is framed favor the theophanic interpretation. The admonitions to "take heart" and to "have no fear" which introduce and conclude the "I am he" are an integral part of the divine formula of self-revelation (e.g. Ps. 115:9 ff.; 118:5 f.; Isa. 41:4 ff., 13 ff.; 43:1 ff.; 44:2 ff.; 51:9 ff.). In the darkness, when the disciples are deceived by their eyes, Jesus affirms his identity with the words "I am he; fear not." But the emphatic overtone should not be missed and is confirmed by the evangelist's continuation in verse 51 f.[123]

51-52 Jesus assured the disciples with his word and his presence. When he joined them in the boat the wind suddenly died down. Since the abatement of the wind may be ascribed to natural causes it is unnecessary to find here an additional demonstration of Jesus' sovereignty. The disciples, however, were utterly astonished. They were undoubtedly physically drained from their rowing against a strong head-wind and emotionally drained from their experience of terror. They had no categories for understanding Jesus' presence with them in the boat. Mark alone explains that they had failed to understand about the loaves and that their hearts were hardened (verse 52; cf. Ch. 8:17). The disciples certainly realized that the multitude had been fed with five loaves and two fish, but they had failed to grasp that this event pointed beyond

---

[122] TB *Baba Bathra* 73a; cf. TB *Megillah* 3a; I Enoch 60:16; Wisd. 17:3 f., 15, on which see S-B*K* I (1922), p. 691.

[123] This understanding is reflected in the Palestinian Syriac as well as in the new Hebrew text of R. L. Lindsey, *A Hebrew Translation of the Gospel of Mark* (Jerusalem, 1969), p. 111, חִזְקוּ, אֲנִי הוּא, אַל תִּירָאוּ. For a full discussion of the relevant texts see E. Stauffer, *TWNT* II (Eng. Tr. 1964), pp. 345-354 (p. 352 for Mk. 6:50); *idem, Jesus and His Story* (New York, 1960), pp. 174-195; H. Zimmermann, "Das absolute ἐγώ εἰμι als die neutestamentliche Offenbarungsformel," *BZ* 4 (1960), pp. 54-69, 266-276.

itself to the secret of Jesus' person. Because they were not truly open to the action of God in Jesus they had missed the significance of the miracle of the loaves for them, and saw only "a marvel." That is why they displayed not confidence and joy in Jesus' unexpected presence but faithless panic.[124] Mark's concluding explanation is important in three respects: (1) it indicates that some events in Jesus' ministry are "parabolic" in that they provide the key to other events.[125] If the disciples had understood the miracle of the loaves they would have recognized Jesus' identity as the sovereign Lord who walks upon the waves of the sea. (2) The problem of understanding is not intellectual, but existential; it is a matter of faith. The disciples did understand Jesus' incidental instructions and they understood that the multitude had been fed. But their confused reaction to Jesus indicates that they failed to recognize that God was acting in history through him. Their misunderstanding reflects unbelief. (3) The disciples' reaction to Jesus' *actions* (as well as his teachings) throughout Mark's Gospel is characterized by non-understanding. In tracing this lack of understanding to "hardness of heart" Mark indicates that at this stage in Jesus' ministry the disciples are not essentially different from his opponents, who also fail to recognize his unique character and exhibit hardness of heart (cf. Chs. 3:5; 10:5).

The proper framework for understanding this unusual episode is provided by the OT. There the power of the Lord over seas and rivers, storms and wind, is repeatedly proclaimed. As the creator of the sea God subdues it and treads upon the waves in demonstration of his majesty. Because he is the Lord men do not need to be afraid no matter how the sea may rage or the wind blow. Jesus' appearance on the Sea of Galilee must be appreciated as a reality and a sign that the living God has come nearer to men in the revelation of the Son. Jesus had no intention of simply passing by his disciples in a display of enigmatic glory. His walking upon the water proclaimed that the hostility of nature against man must cease with the coming of the Lord, whose concealed majesty is unveiled in the proclamation "I am he." At an early date this

---

124 E. Stauffer, *New Testament Theology* (New York, 1955), p. 182 comments: "The heart that does not want to be fortified through grace, fortifies itself against God, becomes hardened and stubborn, and refuses to hear or see anything divine, but all the same in the last resort fumes against itself."

125 Cf. M. E. Glasswell, "The Use of Miracles in the Marcan Gospel," in *Miracles*, ed. C. F. D. Moule (London, 1965), pp. 154-162.

episode was interpreted as a pledge of Christ's aid; it provided the martyrs with the assurance of Jesus' saving nearness to all who believe and obey him.[126]

6. Healing in the Region of Gennesaret. Ch. 6:53-56

53 And when they had crossed over, they came to the land unto Gennesaret,[127] and moored to the shore.[128]
54 And when they were come out of the boat, straightway *the people* knew him,
55 and ran about that whole region, and began to carry about on their beds those that were sick, where they heard he was.
56 And wheresoever he entered, into villages, or into cities, or into the country, they laid the sick in the marketplaces,[129] and besought him that they might touch if it were but the border of his garment:[130] and as many as touched him were made whole.

53 The account of healing in the region of Gennesaret is the evangelist's summary of Jesus' activity just prior to his departure for the coastal cities of Tyre and Sidon (Ch. 7:24). It is tied to its context as the natural sequel to the account of the storm at sea which subsided when Jesus

---

126 See Acts of Thomas 66; Acts of Peter 7; (Christian) Sibylline Oracles VI. 13; VIII. 273 f.

127 Gr. Γεννησαρέτ, but more correctly Γεννησάρ as in I Macc. 11:67; Josephus, *Ant.* XIII. v. 7; XVIII. ii. 1; *War* III. x. 7; Targ. Num. 34:11. This reading is preserved in D *it* vg^{2} mss. sy$^{s c p}$ bo. TJ *Megilla* I. 70a mentions a village by this name, although Mark's reference is evidently to the plain; note the reference to "the whole region" in verse 55.

128 Gr. καὶ προσωρμίσθησαν which is absent from D W Θ 1 28 209 565 700 *it* sy$^{s p}$ geo arm. F. C. Burkitt, "W and Θ: Studies in the Western Text of St. Mark," *JThS* 17 (1916), pp. 19 f. proposed that the words are original, but that they were dropped by almost all texts at a very early time. The textual critic Origen restored them in the third century.

129 Gr. ἐν ταῖς ἀγοραῖς. Strictly speaking, only the larger towns had marketplaces, but the term appears to include here open spaces. This opinion is reflected in the reading of D 565 700 latt ἐν ταῖς πλατείαις, "in the wide roads (or streets)."

130 Gr. κράσπεδον can denote the hem of a garment, but it may also refer to the tassel (צִיצִת) which the Israelite was commanded to wear on the four corners of his outer garment (according to Num. 15:38 f., Deut. 22:12), if Jesus observed the Mosaic law on this point. See S-B*K* IV (1928), pp. 276-292.

joined his disciples in the boat (Ch. 6:51). Although the disciples had rowed toward Bethsaida, a short distance from the northeast corner of the lake, the strong head-wind appears to have driven them severely southward. The fertile plain of Gennesaret extended for about three miles between Capernaum and Tiberias along the western shore of the Sea of Galilee, and in the first century was thickly populated.[131]

54-55 Though the people were not expecting Jesus, he was immediately recognized. He was well known from his ministry at Capernaum and reports of his healing power had penetrated the entire region (cf. Ch. 1:28). The presence of Jesus created an immense excitement. Mark's picture of the people hastening from place to place as reports of his presence were received, carrying their sick on mattresses, graphically conveys the impression of a determined effort to seize an unexpected opportunity for healing. The healing of a paralyzed man who had been carried to Jesus on a mattress (Ch. 2:1-12), as well as of others who had been brought to him (Ch. 1:32-34), undoubtedly had been the subject of bazaar conversation in many towns and cities and created the climate of expectation which greeted Jesus in Gennesaret.

56 Whenever Jesus entered villages, cities or hamlets the report that he was coming had preceded him. He found the sick assembled in the marketplace or any open space where they could be carried in anticipation of his arrival, convinced that if they could only touch the fringe of his garment they would be restored to health. The statement that as many as touched him were healed is to be understood in the light of Mark's treatment of this mutual relationship between Jesus and the afflicted in Ch. 5:25-34. What was involved was not simply material contact with Jesus' clothing, but the touch of faith. At the same time, this vignette is reminiscent of other crowds which had clamored to touch Jesus in a feverish mood of excitement bordering on hysteria (see on Ch. 3:7-10) and recalls an earlier situation when Jesus found it necessary to avoid towns and cities altogether (Ch. 1:45). The works of Jesus appear to be an epiphany of divine power and the people treat him as a miracle worker or divine man whose power is released through

---

[131] G. Dalman, *Orte und Wege Jesu*[3] (Leipzig, 1924), pp. 184 ff. On the relationship of this summary to its context see H. Hegermann, "Bethsaida und Gennesar, eine traditions- und redaktionsgeschichtliche Studie zu Mc. 4-8," in *Judentum, Urchristentum, Kirche,* ed. W. Eltester (Berlin, 1960), pp. 130-140.

touch.[132] In this connection the absence of any reference to preaching or teaching activity is significant. The people are not prepared for Jesus' proclamation of the word, and the public ministry interrupted in Ch. 6:31 has not been resumed. They understand only that power is channeled through his person. Jesus patiently bears with their limited insight and graciously heals those who reach out to him from the bed of affliction.

132 For the role played by physical contact in the miracles reported by Mark see G. Minette de Tillesse, *op. cit.*, pp. 53-55.

CHAPTER 7

7. Defilement According to the Tradition. Ch.7:1-8

1 And there are gathered together unto him the Pharisees, and certain of the scribes, who had come from Jerusalem, [1]
2 and had seen that some of his disciples ate their bread with defiled, [2] that is, unwashen hands.
3 (For the Pharisees, and all the Jews, except they wash their hands diligently, [3] eat not, holding the tradition of the elders; [4]

---

[1] This punctuation implies that it was the scribes from Jerusalem who saw the disciples eating with unwashed hands, and obscures the fact that verses 2 and 5 form a single sentence. The words ἰδόντες... ἄρτους in verse 2 are dependent upon the main verb ἐπερωτῶσιν ("they questioned") which Mark cannot introduce until verse 5 because of the explanatory parenthesis in verses 3-4. It is preferable to place a period after verse 1, as in the Nestle text, and to understand "the Pharisees and the scribes" as the subject of verses 2 and 5. This interpretation finds support in Caesarean, Western and Antiochian manuscripts which show that a full stop was read after verse 1 and that the absence of a main verb in verse 2 appeared awkward: W Θ λ φ *al* latt sa 𝔎 insert ἐμέμψαντο ("they blamed") after ἄρτους; D adds κατέγνωσαν ("they condemned"); sy^p h inserts "they complained."

[2] Gr. κοινός. This word, together with the related verb, provides the unifying motif for this unit; the adjective recurs in verse 5 while the verb occurs in verses 15, 18, 20 and 23. It means "ritually unclean," as in I Macc. 1:47, 62, yet possesses a technical nuance which is unusual in Mark. M. Smith, *Tannaitic Parallels to the Gospels* (Philadelphia, 1951), pp. 31 f. points out that κοιναῖς χερσίν is equivalent to סתם ידים, an expression which appears frequently in the Jerusalem and Babylonian Talmuds. Expressions with סתם, which may be translated "as is," refer to objects which are neither certainly pure nor impure. This meaning of κοινός occurs also in Acts 10:14, 28; 11:18 and probably in Rom. 14:14; Heb. 10:29; Rev. 21:27. Mark here preserves one of the fine distinctions in Pharisaic rules about the cleanness of foods and displays an accuracy on a question of ritual purity which is distinctive to this pericope. The question of Jesus' impurity following contact with the leper (Ch. 1:41) or the woman with the flow of blood (Ch. 5:27-30) is simply ignored. Jesus was relatively unconcerned about ritual defilement, as is demonstrated by his association with "sinners." God did not demand the kind of purity which necessitated withdrawal from ordinary humanity.

[3] The ASV apparently reads πυκνά (supported by ℵ W *f g* vg sy^p h bo goth), which means "often," "frequently," but can be interpreted in the sense of "vigorously." It is necessary, however, to read the more difficult πυγμῇ with A B (D) L Θ and the great majority of manuscripts. The expression πυγμῇ νίπτεσθαι is so difficult that it was omitted in Δ sy^s sa and is left untranslated in the RSV. For a discussion of various proposals which have been put forth, see P. R. Weis, "A Note on πυγμῇ," *NTS* 3 (1956-57), pp. 233-236; K. L. Schmidt, *TWNT* VI (1959), pp. 915-917; S. M. Reynolds, "ΠΥΓΜΗΙ (Mark 7, 3) as 'Cupped Hand'," *JBL* 85

4 and *when they come* from the marketplace,[5] except they bathe
themselves,[6] they eat not; and many other things there are,
which they have received to hold, washings of cups and pots,
and brasen vessels.)[7]
5 And the Pharisees and the scribes ask him, Why walk[8] not
thy disciples according to the tradition of the elders, but eat
their bread with defiled hands?
6 And he said unto them, Well[9] did Isaiah prophesy of you
hypocrites, as it is written,

This people honoreth me with their lips,
But their heart is far from me.
7 But in vain do they worship me,
Teaching *as their* doctrines the precepts of men.

8 Ye leave the commandment of God, and hold fast the tradition of men.

(1966), pp. 87 f.; and especially M. Hengel, "Mc 7, 3 πυγμῇ: Die Geschichte einer exegetischen Aporie und der Versuch ihrer Lösung," *ZNW* 60 (1969), pp. 182-198.

[4] Gr. τὴν παράδοσιν τῶν πρεσβυτέρων, the equivalent of the Hebrew phrase מסרת הזקנם; cf. Josephus, *Ant.* XIII. x. 6, who speaks of "the traditions of the fathers." Here "elders" designates honored Jewish teachers of the Law whose legal decisions were handed down as authoritative by the scribes. Elsewhere in Mark (e.g. 8:31; 11:27) the term denotes the contemporary religious leaders of the Jews.

[5] This understanding of the ASV, RSV finds support in D W and a number of Itala and Vulgate MSS, which insert ὅταν ἔλθωσιν ("when they come") before ἀπ' ἀγορᾶς. It is possible, however, that the text correctly transmits a Semitic idiom which should be recognized: ἀπ' ἀγορᾶς means "(anything) from the market-place." This is the understanding of the Arabic Diatessaron 20:20 ("They were accustomed not to eat what is sold from the market-place except they washed it") and finds support in the Sahidic and Ethiopic versions. See M. Black, *An Aramaic Approach to the Gospels and Acts*[2] (Oxford, 1954), p. 37.

[6] Gr. βαπτίσωνται, supported by A D W Θ 𝔎 λ φ latt sys p bo Or and preferred by the Nestle text. The word denotes the more thorough form of ritual washing necessitated by the defiling contacts of the market-place, but was considered difficult to those unfamiliar with Jewish customs. This accounts for the variant ῥαντίσωνται supported by א B *pc* sa. On the technical distinction between washing, sprinkling and bathing see R. Meyer, *TWNT* III (Eng. Tr. 1965), p. 421.

[7] Gr. ξεστῶν, which may be a corruption of the Latin *sextarius* which appears in rabbinic Hebrew as a loan-word and denotes a capacity measure, roughly one pint or half a liter. It came to mean a pitcher or jug without reference to the amount contained. See A-G, p. 550. A D W Θ *al,* most minuscules and versions, Origen add καὶ κλινῶν, "and couches," which is accepted by E. Lohmeyer, *Das Evangelium des Markus*[16] (Göttingen, 1963), p. 140, n. 5, but is rejected by all modern translations and critical editions of the text.

[8] The use of "walk" in the sense of living or conducting one's life is thoroughly Semitic; cf. II Kings 20:3; Prov. 8:20; Eccl. 11:9; Jn. 8:12; Rom. 6:4; 8:4.

[9] Gr. καλῶς means here "truly" or "yes, indeed," as in Ch. 12:32.

The material of these verses has no definite connection with the preceding narratives and it is impossible to determine when or where the incident took place. In form the material resembles the accounts of controversy grouped in Chs. 2:1-3:6, and this unit could easily have been positioned there. For that reason Mark's placement of the discussion concerning defilement is instructive. It stands in the center of the section that extends from Chs. 6:7 to 8:26, and functions as the formal prelude to three miracle narratives in which Jesus extends his grace to Gentiles. Its central position is similar to that occupied by the discourse on parables (to which it has important structural parallels), which stands in the middle of Chs. 3:7-6:6 and is also followed by three accounts of Jesus' power. This is one more indication that prior to the redaction of the tradition Mark had a clear conception of the structure and arrangement he has followed in the building of the Gospel.

A sustained concern with defilement, traditional and real, indicates that Mark intends Ch. 7:1-23 to be taken as a single unit. The subdivision of the unit at verses 8 and 13 allows a consideration of the material in its logical divisions: the charge of the scribes and Pharisees and Jesus' initial response (verses 1-8), the counter-charge that the scribal tradition is in conflict with the Law (verses 9-13), and finally the exposition of true defilement (verses 14-23). These are, however, three phases of a unified argument which focuses upon essential differences between Jesus and recognized interpreters of the Law. The distinctive feature of Mark's treatment of this episode is his clarification of terms and issues unfamiliar to his readers (verses 2b-4, 11) and his careful delineation of the relevance of this discussion to the Church (verses 19b-23).

1-2a Jesus' teaching differed fundamentally from that of the Pharisees on essential points of common piety. This has already been illustrated with respect to sharing table-fellowship with outcasts (Ch. 2:15-17), fasting (Ch. 2:18-22) and Sabbath observance (Ch. 2:23-28), and is now exhibited in regard to ritual defilement. This significant category extended beyond various washings to the distinctions between ritually clean and unclean foods and the vast complex of dietary laws. The reference to the Jerusalem scribes recalls the sharp conflict that was instigated by their charge that Jesus exercised the power of Beelzebul and was himself a possessed man (Ch. 3:22-30). It serves notice that far more is involved in the exchange between the scribes and Jesus than a rabbinic debate in which alternative decisions will be preserved and made the subject of further consideration. The eating of bread without proper concern for the removal of ritual defilement was merely the immediate occasion for this confrontation. Its ultimate occasion was Jesus' evident disregard for the whole structure of oral tradition which examined virtually every aspect of personal and corporate life and sought to regulate it in a manner consistent with the Law under conditions often vastly different from those in which the Law was first handed down. In areas where the Law was silent the tradition was vocal, drawing the conclusions felt to be implicit in the mandates of the written code. The result was a vast legal complex, oral in form but definite in formulation, which was entrusted to the scribes, the recognized interpreters of the Law, and was regarded as binding upon all Israel.

2b-4 Aware that most of his readers will not understand the technical nature of the scribal charge nor its background in Jewish practice, Mark provides a simple definition of defilement and a thumbnail sketch of Pharisaic practice. The evangelist has been criticized for ascribing Pharisaic practice to "all the Jews," since the common people, the so-called "sinners" (see on Ch. 2:15), certainly were not careful about ritual washings. In generalizing his explanation Mark was following accepted Jewish practice in describing Jewish customs to a Gentile audience. A close parallel is provided by the Letter of Aristeas § 305: "And as the custom of *all the Jews,* they washed their hands and prayed to God." The same distinctions in practice which were current in first-century Judaism could be observed in the second century B.C. when this document was composed, but were not considered relevant to the issue under discussion.

The biblical mandate that the priests had to wash their hands and feet prior to entering the Tabernacle (Ex. 30:19; 40:13) provided the foundation for the wide-spread practice of ritual washings in Palestinian and diaspora Judaism. At least as early as the second century B.C. many Jews voluntarily assumed the purity laws of the priests and regularly washed their hands before morning prayer.[10] The accompanying benediction was designed not for the priests, but for laymen: "Blessed be Thou O Lord, King of the universe, who sanctified us by thy laws and commanded us to wash the hands."[11] The custom of washing the hands

---

[10] E.g. Judith 12:7; Letter of Aristeas § 305; Sibylline Oracles III. 591-593.
[11] TB *Berachoth* 60b.

before eating bread was also grounded in priestly practice, in the conviction that daily food should be eaten as if it were priestly food. By the third century A.D. the eating of bread without washing was strongly condemned,[12] and this seems to have been a tendency already evident in Jesus' day. The Pharisees surpassed the priests in their zeal to safeguard themselves from ritual defilement and were strong proponents of "the priesthood of all believers" in the sense that they considered the priestly regulations to be obligatory for all men. It is important to appreciate the concern to sanctify ordinary acts of life which lay behind this extension of priestly regulations to the laity. Its finest intention was the demonstration that all Israel was devoted to God and the Law, and the fulfilment of the injunction: "You shall be holy to me" (Lev. 20:26). The Pharisees were convinced that the strict discipline of human conduct was the necessary prelude to the true acknowledgment of God as sovereign.[13]

To restore Levitical purity after defilement it was necessary to cleanse by water, and Mark refers to the most common act of cultic cleansing, the washing of the hands,[14] which was formally required only before the consumption of bread. The washing was accomplished by pouring water on the hands,[15] and this fact excludes all suggestions of immersing the hands from Mark's reference in verse 3. The evangelist correctly specifies that a *handful of water* was required.[16] The position of the hand was cupped, with the fingers flexed to allow the water to pass between them so as to reach all parts of the hand. By cupping the hand the entire hand could be washed with a very small quantity of water.[17]

---

12 TB *Soṭah* 4b; *Shabbath* 62b.

13 E.g. TB *Nazir* 23b: "Let a man study the Law and fulfill precepts even with impure motives, for in time he will learn to do so from good motives."

14 נטילת ידים. See important discussions of cultic uncleanness and cultic cleansing by R. Meyer, *TWNT* III (Eng. Tr. 1965), pp. 418-423; H. Danby, "The Rules of Uncleanness," in *The Mishnah* (Oxford, 1933), pp. 800-804.

15 E.g. M. *Yadaim* II. 1, "If a person poured water over one of his hands with a single rinsing, his hand is clean."

16 So M. Hengel, *op. cit.*, p. 197: "The πυγμῇ of Mk 7:3 is apparently a Latinism on the analogue of the Latin *pugnus, pugillus,* meaning 'a handful'." This corresponds to the requirement of M. *Yadaim* I. 1, 2 and finds support in related statements in the Talmud, e.g. TB *Shabbath* 62b, "I wash my hands with both hands full of water."

17 S. Reynolds, *op. cit.*, p. 88 cites a letter received from Professor Saul Lieberman: "The custom of shaping the hands like cups when they were washed for ritual purposes from a vessel was most probably very old. The opening of the χειρονιπτήρ was usually not a large one; water in Palestine was valuable. When

A distinction was maintained between this type of washing, sprinkling, and bathing or the immersion of the hands up to the joint of the fingers, and apparently it is this third category of ablutions to which reference is made in verse 4 in connection with food purchased in the market-place.[18] Up to this point Mark's statements are factual and accurate. It is probable that a tone of irony is intended, however, when he makes a sweeping reference to the oral tradition ("and many other things there are, which they have received to hold") and concludes his catalogue with reference to the "washing of cups and pots and copper vessels." There may be here a certain justifiable impatience with the mass of detail which was later codified in the Mishnah tractate *Kelim* (Vessels), but it has the effect of exposing the oral law to ridicule. Mark's final remark serves to broaden the issue from the washing of hands to cultic cleansing *per se*.

5 The sentence begun in verse 2a is completed in verse 5. Ostensibly the issue raised by the Pharisees and their scribes was the failure of certain of the disciples to observe the purity laws. The crucial element in the question as formulated, however, concerns walking according to the tradition of the elders. The binding character of the decisions handed down by honored Jewish teachers of the Law was an essential component in Pharisaic thinking. It was Jesus' failure to support the validity of the oral law which made him an object of concerted attack by the scribes. The question posed is clearly a challenge to Jesus himself, and in his response, no reference is made to the disciples. The deeper intention behind the question of eating with defiled hands is suggested by a passage in the Mishnah: "But whom did they place under a ban? Eleazar ben Enoch, because he cast doubt on (the tradition of the Elders concerning) the cleansing of hands."[19]

---

one forms the hand like a loose fist the narrow stream of water covers at once the entire outer and inner surface of the hand. Water is saved in this way. For purposes of cleanliness it was sufficient to pour some water on part of the hand, which could subsequently be spread all over the hand by rubbing both hands. Pouring water on 'cupped hands' immediately indicated ritual washing in preparation for a meal."

18 E.g. TB *Ḥullin* 106a, "the ablution of the hands before (eating) profane things is practiced up to the joint," and this is supported by a gloss to Mk. 7:4 in the Harklean Syriac VS. The description "profane" qualifies things (vessels, food) that have not been consecrated, but which are not impure of necessity.

19 M. *Eduyoth* V. 6. See further, W. G. Kümmel, "Jesus und der jüdische Traditionsgedanke," *ZNW* 33 (1934), pp. 105-131; H. Merkel, "Jesus und die Pharisäer," *NTS* 14 (1968), pp. 194-208.

6-8 The question of the scribes receives a twofold answer. An immediate reply is provided by the pointed citation of Isa. 29:13, introduced with the ironic comment "Well did Isaiah prophesy of you hypocrites!" This quotation is directly applied to the scribes and Pharisees in verse 8. A second answer is provided by the pregnant saying addressed to the crowd in verses 14 f., which exposes the deeper issue of the source of defilement which remains unaffected by cultic cleansing.

The quotation differs slightly in form from the Septuagint text and may have been drawn from a florilegium of prophetic passages used in Rome. It is probable that Jesus himself cited the Hebrew text or the Targum currently used in the synagogue. It has often been held that the charge of abandoning the commandment of God for the tradition of men (in verse 8) depends for its validity upon the Greek text where it differs from the Hebrew. This is clearly not the case. The Massoretic text contrasts formal lip-service to God with devotion from the heart and concludes, "this fear of me is a commandment of men which has been taught (to them)." This is certainly relevant to the larger issue of the oral tradition which was diligently handed down to each generation of the Pharisees. It implies that even the concern to sanctify all of life, which is presupposed in the assumption of the priestly purity laws, rests less upon *the commandment* above all others, the love of God with the whole heart (Deut. 6:4; cf. Mk. 12:28-34), than upon a tradition which has been received and passed on as an expression of formal piety. This gives pointedness to the charge of hypocrisy which emphasizes the contradiction between what a man seems to be in the opinion of his peers and what he is before God. In the outward appearance of their piety the Pharisees were impeccable since they scrupulously observed numerous prescriptions and commandments. It was, nevertheless, a lie because they had not surrendered themselves to God.[20]

Jesus' sharp rebuttal sets in radical opposition the commandment of God and the halakhic formulations of the scribal tradition. Theoretically, the oral law was a fence which safeguarded the people from

---

[20] Cf. G. Bornkamm, *Jesus of Nazareth* (New York, 1960), p. 104: "What does this conception of the law reveal? Evidently this: the law has become separated from God and has become man's real authority. It no longer leads to a meeting with God, but rather frustrates it. Correspondingly man has retreated behind his deeds and achievements–as well as behind his guilt. God is concealed behind the law and man behind his achievements and works. Law and performance are the two sides of the protecting wall, behind which man takes up his own position and asserts himself before God."

infringing the Law. In actuality it represented a tampering with the Law which resulted inevitably in distortion and ossification of the living word of God. The exaggerated reverence with which the scribes and Pharisees regarded the oral law was an expression of false piety supported by human precepts devoid of authority. Jesus categorically rejects the authority of the oral law.

8. THE CONFLICT BETWEEN COMMANDMENT AND TRADITION. Ch. 7:9-13

9 And he said unto them, Full well [21] do ye reject the commandment of God, that ye may keep [22] your tradition.
10 For Moses said, Honor thy father and thy mother; and, He that speaketh evil of father or mother, let him die the death: [23]
11 but ye say, If a man shall say to his father or his mother, That wherewith thou mightest have been profited by me is Corban, [24] that is to say, Given *to God;*
12 ye no longer suffer him to do aught for his father or his mother;
13 making void the word of God by your tradition, which ye have delivered: and many such like things ye do.

9 Jesus' counter-charge that the scribes and Pharisees have abandoned the commandment of God in their zeal to observe the oral tradition

[21] Gr. καλῶς. RSV "You have a fine way . . . ! "

[22] For τηρήσητε there is a variant reading στήσητε ("that you may *establish* your tradition") which is strongly supported by Western, Caesarean and Antiochian texts: D W Θ 1 28 209 565 *it* sys p arm goth Cyp Aug. As the more difficult reading it should perhaps be read.

[23] Gr. θανάτῳ τελευτάτω. In the LXX the dative of a cognate noun is used with a verb to translate the infinitive absolute used with a finite verb in Hebrew. Here it should be translated "let him surely die." See C. F. D. Moule, *An Idiom Book of New Testament Greek*2 (Cambridge, 1960), pp. 177 f.

[24] Gr. κορβᾶν, a transliteration of קָרְבָּן, "an offering," "a gift devoted to God." The word is used by Josephus who defines it as δῶρον θεοῦ (i.e. a gift devoted to God) in *Contra Apionem* I. 22. For a careful discussion of the OT roots of this expression and its development as a dedicatory formula in the first century see J. T. Milik, "Trois tombeaux juifs récemment découverts au Sud-Est de Jérusalem," *Studii Biblici Franciscani Liber Annus* 7 (1956-57), pp. 232-239; H. Hommel, "Das Wort Korban und seine Verwandten," *Philologus* 98 (1954); J. A. Fitzmyer, "The Aramaic Qorbān Inscription from Jebel Ḫallet eṭ-Ṭuri and Mark 7:11 / Matt. 15:5," *JBL* 78 (1959), pp. 60-65; K. H. Rengstorf, *TWNT* III (Eng. Tr. 1965), pp. 860-866.

does not stand unsupported. The charge is reaffirmed in verse 9 with biting irony and is then illustrated concretely with reference to the conflict between the fifth commandment and the position of the elders on the sanctity of an oath. The scribes had referred deferentially to the oral law as "the tradition of the elders" (verse 5); Jesus cited Isaiah in support of his claim that it deserved to be designated "the tradition of men" (verses 7-8), an example of human cleverness. He now baldly labels it "your tradition" and affirms that in order to establish it God's commandment is nullified. Jesus refused to permit his adversaries to invoke against him a tradition which was capable of violating the Law of God.

10-12 The theoretical foundations of oral law were traced backward through a chain of tradition extending from the elders and the men of the Great Synagogue to the prophets and Joshua to Moses himself.[25] Jesus, therefore, cites Moses against the developments in legal casuistry which were an essential component of the scribal tradition. The fifth commandment is cited in both its positive and negative formulations in almost literal agreement with the Septuagint text of Ex. 20:12a (= Deut. 5:16a) and 21:16.[26] The second text indicates the seriousness of an offense against parents: the death penalty was decreed for those who cursed their parents or treated them with contempt.[27] In spite of Moses' unequivocal affirmation of filial responsibility, the effect of the scribal tradition on the binding character of an oath, even when uttered rashly, was to prohibit compliance with the commandment.

Qorban is a technical term within the priestly tradition of the OT (its use is limited to Lev., Num. and Ezek.) where it always denotes an offering made to God. In Mark's explanatory note the term "gift" is a technical designation for an oblation precisely as in the Greek text of Lev. 2:1, 4, 12 f. A fine contemporary parallel to the use of *qorban* in Mark has been provided by a recently recovered Jewish ossuary inscription: "All that a man may find-to-his-profit in this ossuary (is)

---

25 M. *Aboth* I. 1-3.

26 Cf. Lev. 20:9; Deut. 27:16; Prov. 20:9a; Ezek. 22:7.

27 In the LXX κακολόγος translates קלל, which in the pi'el and hiphil means to curse, rather than simply to abuse or speak ill of. C. Schneider, *TWNT* III (Eng. Tr. 1965), p. 468 translates Mk. 7:10b, "Whoso curseth father or mother shall die the death." According to scribal interpretation, the death penalty was decreed only for those who cursed their parents in the name of God, M. *Sanh.* VII. 4, 8.

an offering to God from him who is within it."[28] The importance of this inscription is that it preserves the formula in its completeness and furnishes a concrete example of how the formula was used. It indicates that Jesus was referring to a dedicatory-formula which was commonly used by Jews in the last centuries B.C. and well into the Christian era. The basic purpose of the formula was to place a ban on something, reserving it for sacred use and withdrawing it from profane use by another person. The vow creates a prohibition with regard to an object and fixes upon it the character of an offering dedicated to God. This did not necessarily mean that the object declared *qorban* had actually to be offered to God; it signified rather that it was withdrawn from its intended use and was no longer available for a particular individual "as if it were an offering." In the hypothetical situation proposed by Jesus, if the son declared his property *qorban* to his parents, he neither promised it to the Temple nor prohibited its use to himself, but he legally excluded his parents from the right of benefit.[29] Should the son regret his action and seek to alleviate the harsh vow which would deprive his parents of all of the help they might normally expect from him, he would be told by the scribes to whose arbitration the case was submitted that his vow was valid and must be honored.[30] Jesus' statement that the scribes do not allow him to do "anything" for his parents is not extreme. The renunciation of all profitability extended beyond financial support to such practical kindness as assistance in the performance of religious duties or the provision of care in sickness.[31]

---

28 Translated by J. A. Fitzmyer, *op. cit.*, p. 62. Fitzmyer points out that a variety of formulae existed side by side, some of which were more expanded and formal like that of the ossuary inscription and others of which were more abbreviated like the one to which Jesus referred. The developments represented in the Mishnaic tractate *Nedarim* ("Vows") are discussed on pp. 64 f.

29 Z. W. Falk, "On Talmudic Vows," *HTR* 59 (1966), pp. 309-312. G. W. Buchanan, "Some Vow and Oath Formulas in the New Testament," *HTR* 58 (1965), pp. 319-324 prefers to find in the reference to *qorban* a minced imprecatory oath on the analogy of rabbinic formulations of the second century: "'*Korban!* [may these evils fall upon me] if from me you receive benefit'."

30 M. *Nedarim* V. 6 is particularly instructive because it shows that there were cases in which a son's vow which created a breach between father and son could not be set aside even with the best will on the part of the son. S-B*K* I (1922), p. 716 provides an account of such a case in Beth-Horon. The practice of alleviating vows pronounced without prior deliberation is of uncertain date. See the discussion of K. Rengstorf, *TWNT* III (Eng. Tr. 1965), pp. 863 f.

31 S-B*K* I (1922), p. 714; K. Rengstorf, *op. cit.*, p. 865.

13 The scribes sought to satisfy God's legal claim; the recognition of the validity of a vow fulfills the letter of the commandment in Num. 30:1 f.[32] If, on the basis of a vow, the claims of God must be upheld even in opposition to those of a man's parents, that is because God's claims are fundamentally higher than man's and must be given precedence. This argument acquires special force if *qorban* in this case signifies a genuine transference of parental claims to God and the transfer of property to the Temple. But Jesus categorically rejects the practice of using one biblical commandment to negate another. This interpretation of Num. 30:1 f. seized upon the letter of the passage in such a way as to miss the meaning of the Law as a whole. It is in this context that the citation of Isa. 29:13 is particularly intelligible. For Jesus this is God's own judgment on the scribal attempts to satisfy his legal claim. The quotation indicates that Jesus is not so much attacking a particular scribal practice as he is showing that the scribes cannot properly honor God. In their concern for the fulfilment of the letter of Scripture they forget that the Law was provided not for its own sake but to benefit men. It is an expression of God's covenant faithfulness as well as of his righteousness and in no circumstance was obedience to one commandment intended to nullify another. The fault lay not in the commandments but in an interpretive tradition which failed to see Scripture in its wholeness. Jesus implicated the scribes who stood before him in this indictment when he referred pointedly to "your tradition, which you have delivered." They are not merely passive guardians of an inherited tradition but have had an active and responsible role in shaping and transmitting the oral law. The case of the *qorban* vow, Jesus adds, is not an isolated example, but one of many which could be cited where the intention of Scripture had been obscured by the scribal tradition.

9. TRUE DEFILEMENT. Ch. 7:14-23

14 And he called unto him the multitude again,[33] and said unto them, Hear me all of you, and understand:

---

[32] Cf. Sifre Num. § 153 on Ch. 30:3.

[33] There is no clear antecedent to πάλιν and 𝔎 A W Θ λ φ 33 700 p*m* sy$^{s\ p}$ sa bo read πάντα: "And he called the *whole* crowd." If πάλιν ("again") is correct, it may be a conscious reference to Ch. 4:1-20, to which there are other parallels in this passage. Cf. Ch. 10:1 "and again, as his custom was, he taught them."

15 there is nothing from without the man, that going into him
can defile him; but the things which proceed out of the man
are those that defile the man.[34]
17 And when he was entered into the house from the multitude,
his disciples asked of him the parable.[35]
18 And he saith unto them, Are ye so without understanding
also? Perceive ye not, that whatsoever from without goeth
into the man, *it* cannot defile him;
19 because it goeth not into his heart, but into his belly, and
goeth out into the draught?[36] *This he said,* making all meats
clean.[37]
20 And he said, That which proceedeth out of the man, that
defileth the man.
21 For from within, out of the heart of men, evil thoughts proceed, fornications, thefts, murders, adulteries,
22 covetings, wickedness, deceit, lasciviousness, an evil eye, railing, pride, foolishness:
23 all these evil things proceed from within, and defile the man.

14-15 Jesus' demonstration of the contradiction between the halakhic tradition and the scriptural commandment was designed to shame and silence his adversaries. The question asked by the scribes and Pharisees in verse 5 receives a more direct reply in the teaching of verses 14b-15. Essential to a biblical consideration of defilement and cleansing is the question of the source of defilement and it is this deeper issue which Jesus now exposes through a single pregnant statement addressed to

---

[34] Verse 16, "If anyone has ears to hear, let him hear," is omitted by ℵ B L Δ* 28 102 bo (most MSS) geo[1] and by the several critical editions of the Greek text. It is read by 𝔎 A D W Θ λ φ *pl* latt sys p sa (most MSS) bo (some MSS), apparently to bring Ch. 7:15 f. in harmony with Ch. 4:3-9 where a parable is introduced and concluded with a call to hearing. The balance of probability is against its authenticity here.

[35] Gr. παραβολή, which here has the meaning "a pregnant saying," as in Ch. 3:23-27.

[36] Gr. ἀφεδρών, "a latrine." Codex D reads ὀχετόν, which probably means a sewer (as in Herodian V. viii. 9; VII. vii. 7).

[37] The completion of the ellipsis by making καθαρίζων πάντα τὰ βρώματα grammatically dependent upon καὶ λέγει αὐτοῖς in verse 18 is almost certainly correct. This interpretation was first proposed by the Greek Fathers (Origen, Chrysostom, Gregory Thaumaturgus) and has won almost universal support. For a dissenting opinion see H. N. Ridderbos, *The Coming of the Kingdom* (Philadelphia, 1962), p. 332 n. 35.

the crowd. The solemn call to attentive hearing recalls the summons of Ch. 4:3 and has its ultimate background in the prophetic call to hearing which provides the setting for the revelation of the word of God.[38] It indicates that what follows is of revelatory significance and that it demands careful reflection.

With a mode of expression calculated to provoke thought, Jesus sets in radical opposition material purity and moral purity.[39] The meaning of the first half of the riddle was intelligible in the light of the controversy with the scribes: a man is not defiled by what he eats, even when his hands are not properly washed. The second half, however, remained enigmatic, for it stands without an immediate context. The principle that uncleanness comes from within and not from without is grounded in the biblical teaching concerning the heart as the source of all spiritual and moral conduct,[40] but this was not apparent to the crowd or to the disciples. The implications of Jesus' teaching that nothing external to men defiles were to have far-reaching consequences for the Church, which Mark spells out in the light of further revelation in verse 19b. Here, however, Jesus' expression is general and enigmatic. It did not abrogate the Mosaic laws on purification or erase the distinctions between clean and unclean and declare them invalid. It rather attacked the delusion that sinful men can attain to true purity before God through the scrupulous observance of cultic purity which is powerless to cleanse the defilement of the heart. It is this latter emphasis which is stressed in the exposition to the disciples in verses 17-19a.

---

[38] E.g. Micah 1:2 "Hear, you peoples, all of you!" Cf. Wisd. 6:1 "Listen therefore, O kings, and understand," where the cry of Divine Wisdom reflects the prophetic stance.

[39] The antithetic parallelism is typically Semitic. V. Taylor, *The Gospel According to St. Mark* (London, 1952), p. 343 suggests that the phrases εἰσπορευόμενον εἰς αὐτόν and ἐκπορευόμενα are "explanatory additions, for they are detachable and are characteristic of Mark's vocabulary." In this case the original saying is more provocative: "Nothing outside a man can defile him: the things which are from a man are what defile him."

[40] In addition to the passages collected by F. Baumgärtel, *TWNT*. III (Eng. Tr. 1965), pp. 606 f. note Jer. 17:9 f.: "The heart is deceitful above all things and desperately corrupt: who can understand it? I the Lord search the mind and try the heart." The concept of moral purity is also integral to the scribal tradition, and the passages gathered by R. Meyer, *TWNT* III (Eng. Tr. 1965), p. 423 should be consulted. See further A. W. Argyle, "'Outward' and 'Inward' in Biblical Thought," *ExT* 68 (1957), pp. 196-199; C. E. Carlston, "The Things that Defile (Mark vii. 14) and the Law in Matthew and Mark," *NTS* 15 (1968-69), pp. 75-96.

17-19a It is in the nature of a pregnant saying that its tenor is not immediately apparent. The pattern of public teaching in parabolic speech and private interpretation to the disciples was characteristic of Jesus' ministry according to Ch. 4:33 f., and Mark frequently designates "the house" as the place of revelation (Chs. 9:28, 33; 10:10).[41] In view of the character of the riddle in verse 15 an inquiry by the disciples was quite natural. Their lack of understanding, however, indicates that in spite of their privileged relationship to Jesus they are not fundamentally different from the crowd. The failure of the disciples to understand Jesus' mighty acts and teaching is particularly emphasized in this section of the Gospel (Chs. 6:52; 7:18; 8:14-21) and is traced to hardness of heart.

The new element in Jesus' interpretation is the specific reference to "the heart." In Semitic expression the heart is the center of human personality which determines man's entire action and inaction. This key to the statement in verse 15 was already available in the citation of Isa. 29:13: "This people honors me with their lips, but *their heart* is far from me." Jesus now makes this explicit when he traces the source of defilement to the heart, and shows that in an ultimate sense "food" and "the heart" have nothing to do with each other. The relevance of this explanation to the question posed in verse 5 is apparent: fulfilling the dictates of the oral law on cultic purity does not alter the heart of man with its warring impulses: the minutiae of the tradition are powerless to remove the pollution from the heart, the source of defilement in the actions of men. Jesus has no intention of denying that the purity laws occupy a significant place in the Mosaic code (Lev. 11:1-47; Deut. 14:1-20) or of detracting from the dignity of men who suffered death rather than violate the Law of God governing unclean foods (I Macc. 1:62 f.). Rather he presses home the recognition that the ultimate seat of purity or defilement before God is the heart.

19b-23 The form of the concluding verses deserves careful attention. The elliptical expression in verse 19b ("cleansing all meats") is almost certainly an interpretative comment of the evangelist which drew out the implications of Jesus' statement. Verse 20 introduces an indirect, rather than a direct quotation and represents Mark's paraphrase of what

[41] For a treatment of this motif see G. Minette de Tillesse, *Le Secret Messianique dans l'Évangile de Marc* (Paris, 1968), pp. 228-237, 242-248.

Jesus said.[42] The possibility of catechetical influence on the arrangement of verses 21-22 is clear and is suggested by the symmetrical arrangement of the list in its present form: the general category "evil thoughts" is followed by six nouns in the plural denoting evil acts and six nouns in the singular denoting moral defects or vices.[43] These combined features support the hypothesis that in verses 19b-23 there is another example of a word addressed to the Christian reader of the Gospel. It represents Mark's interpretation of the word and explanation of Jesus.

The Church vacillated in its attitude toward the Jewish food laws and did not resolve this issue without anguish and controversy (Gal. 2:11-17; Rom. 14:14; Col. 2:20-22). The question of table-fellowship with Hellenistic Christians and even of the admission of Gentiles to the Church hinged upon the decisions which were taken with regard to cultic purity. The thrice-repeated vision which Peter received in Joppa, with its sharp admonition, "What God has cleansed you must not call common," had a decisive influence on the Church's recognition that the purity laws had fulfilled their function and were abolished (Acts 10:9-16; 11:2-18; 15:7-29). The ancient ritual prescriptions were only a sign of a more profound interior purification: that which God has purified (Acts 10:15). In the light of this further revelation to Peter (which offers the closest parallels in vocabulary to the language of defilement in Mk. 7)[44] it could be seen that Jesus' statement in verse 15 called into question not only the voluntary assumption of the priestly purity laws but the whole ritual system. "This he said, cleansing all meats" is Mark's comment to his readers in Rome, some of whom may have continued to find this conclusion difficult (cf. Rom. 14:14). It expresses the implication of Jesus' teaching, but not what he actually said at the time.[45]

Mark does not linger on this insight but develops Jesus' explanation at the point where he had placed the emphasis–upon the heart as the center of the whole inner life and source of human action. The structure of the exposition follows the pattern of verses 18-19 where the substance of verse 15a was repeated (verse 18b) and then explained (verse 19a). Similarly, the substance of verse 15b is repeated in verse 20, followed

---

42 In verse 20 ἔλεγεν δὲ ὅτι introduces an indirect quotation in contrast to καὶ λέγει αὐτοῖς in verse 18, which introduces a direct quotation.

43 The list in Mt. 15:19 consists of only seven vices; after the general category "evil thoughts" the order of the decalogue is followed: murder, adultery and fornication, theft, false-witness and slander.

44 Rightly stressed by M. Smith, *op. cit.*, pp. 31 f.

45 Cf. G. Minette de Tillesse, *op. cit.*, p. 147.

by the explanation (verses 21-23). The source of true defilement in men is the human heart, and the tragedy of man's having to sin reaches its demonic fulfilment in man's wanting to sin. There is no heart in which this radical evil has failed to take root. The catalogue of sinful acts and dispositions which flow from the heart is thoroughly Jewish in character.[46] At the head of the list is "evil thoughts" which stand behind the evil actions of men. Fornication is a broad term covering all acts of sexual immorality; it is wider than adultery, which presupposes the breach of the marriage bond, and "licentiousness," which carries the nuance of open immorality.[47] Theft, murder and adultery occur side by side in the decalogue and in Hos. 4:2. "Acts of coveting" may include deeds committed in lust since this word is frequently associated with other terms denoting sexual sins.[48] "Wickedness" appears to be a general term denoting acts of deliberate malice. "Deceit" implies the components of cunning and treachery. "An evil eye" is a Semitic expression for stinginess (Deut. 15:9; Ecclus. 14:10; 31:13) or for that grudging jealousy with which a man looks upon the possessions of another.[49] "Railing" can refer to "slander" (as in the RSV) directed toward a man, but in the OT it always describes an affront to the majesty of God, and a more accurate translation would be "blasphemy." "Pride" carries the nuance of arrogance which expresses itself in self-approbation. "Foolishness" describes the dominant disposition of the man who is morally and spiritually insensitive; he does not know God and he does not wish to know him. These acts and dispositions, Jesus affirms, are what defile a man and they have their source in a heart which is in open rebellion against God.

This explanation places the question of defilement and purity on a fundamentally different plane than that presupposed by the scribes and

---

46 C. E. B. Cranfield, *The Gospel According to St. Mark*² (Cambridge, 1963), p. 242 has shown the distinctly biblical flavor in the catalogue: of the twelve items, ten occur in the LXX, while another is used in two other translations of Hosea. More significant is the recovery of a pre-Christian Jewish parallel in 1QS iv. 9-11. It has frequently been held that the Marcan list reflects Hellenistic or Pauline influence, but there is no valid reason for holding that the list cannot go back to Jesus, at least in its essential form. Cf. Mk. 10:19.

47 Cf. B. W. Bacon, "The Apostolic Decree against πορνεία," *Exp* 8th series 7 (1914), pp. 40-61; G. Harder, *TWNT* VI (1959), pp. 562-566.

48 G. Delling, *TWNT* VI (1959), pp. 266-274.

49 In Ecclus. 35:8, 10 ἀγαθὸς ὀφθαλμός (literally, "a good eye") denotes generosity. Cf. W. Michaelis, *TWNT* V (Eng. Tr. 1967), p. 377.

Pharisees. By this interpretation Jesus does not alleviate the demand for purity but sharpens it. The requirement of cultic purity possessed an inner value and justification as a symbol pointing beyond itself to God's demand for spiritual and moral purity. The capacity for fellowship with God is not destroyed by material uncleanness of food or hands; it is destroyed by personal sin. With this fundamentally biblical insight the older ritual concept of purity is transcended. At the same time every human attempt to manipulate the law and to make it manageable and complimentary to human self-complacency is shown to be useless and impious. It reduces men to the category of those who seem to honor God at the very moment their heart is removed from his judging and saving action. The focus upon the desperate need for the renewal and cleansing of the human heart lends to the entire discussion the character of a messianic sign.

10. The Faith of a Gentile. Ch. 7:24-30

24 And from thence he arose, and went away into the borders[50] of Tyre and Sidon.[51] And he entered into a house, and would have no man know it; and he could not be hid.

25 But straightway a woman, whose little daughter had an unclean spirit, having heard of him, came and fell down at his feet.

26 Now the woman was a Greek,[52] a Syrophoenician by race. And she besought him that he would cast forth the demon out of her daughter.

27 And he said unto her, Let the children first be filled: for it is not meet to take the children's bread and cast it to the dogs.

---

[50] Gr. τὰ ὅρια Τύρου. Ὅριον in the singular means "border" or "boundary," but in the plural "territory or district." Cf. RSV "the region of Tyre"; Ch. 7:24, 31 should be corrected accordingly.

[51] The words καὶ Σιδῶνος are omitted by D L W Δ Θ 28 565 latt. sys pal Or. Their presence in other texts may reflect assimilation to Mt. 15:21 and Mk. 7:31. The joint reference to Tyre and Sidon is commonly used in the OT to designate the pagan world. Cf. Mk. 3:8.

[52] The woman is not Greek by nationality, as the following words indicate. The designation indicates that she was Greek-speaking or Hellenistic in culture. It is better to translate "Now the woman was a Gentile"; cf. W. Bauer in A-G, p. 251, "a Gentile woman."

28 But she answered and saith unto him, Yea,[53] Lord;[54] even the dogs under the table eat of the children's crumbs.
29 And he said unto her, For this saying go thy way; the demon is gone out of thy daughter.
30 And she went away unto her house, and found the child laid upon the bed, and the demon gone out.

Mark's placement of the incident in the district of Tyre immediately following the discussion of clean and unclean provides a concrete example of Jesus' disregard for the scribal concept of defilement. It invites comparison with Acts 10:9 ff. where Peter, after being instructed in a trance not to regard as defiled what God has cleansed, ministered to the household of Cornelius in Caesarea. His free association with members of the household in repudiation of the old regulation prohibiting a Jew from visiting a Gentile (Acts 10:28 f.; 11:3) translates the revelation he has received into action. Jesus' response to a Gentile woman of faith and humility in the pagan environment of Tyre is the appropriate consequence of his teaching in Ch. 7:15. When Ch. 7:24-30 is seen as the intended sequel to Ch. 7:1-23, the faith of the Syrophoenician woman contrasts dramatically with the determined unbelief of the Pharisees and the scribes from Jerusalem, while her witty reply to Jesus indicates a degree of understanding which puts the disciples to shame (cf. 7:17 f.). It is possible that Mark regards this episode as a symbol and prophecy of the gospel which will be proclaimed with power in the Gentile world. There can be no doubt that Gentile readers would be vitally interested in the account.[55]

24 The territorial district of Phoenicia was tangent to Galilee some twenty miles northwest of Capernaum. In his search for privacy Jesus

---

53 The "yes" is omitted in P45 D W Θ φ 565 *b c ff*1 *i* arm and may have been added to the Marcan text from the parallel in Mt. 15:27. If it is original, ναί, ... καί has the meaning "yes ... but ... "

54 κύριε, which probably should be translated "sir," recognizing a formula of deep respect. This is the sole instance of this vocative of address in Mark (unless κύριε is read in Chs. 1:40; 10:51). T. A. Burkill, "The Syrophoenician Woman: The Congruence of Mark 7:24-31," *ZNW* 57 (1966), pp. 33-35 champions the translation "Lord," and finds here an anticipation of the confession of Jesus as Son of God in Ch. 15:39. This is unlikely since Mark never uses ὁ κύριος of Jesus in narrative sections.

55 Cf. T. A. Burkill, *op. cit.*, pp. 23-37; J. Jeremias, "The Gentile World in the Thought of Jesus," *Bulletin of the Studiorum Novi Testamenti Societas* 3 (1952), pp. 18-28; *idem, Jesus' Promise to the Nations* (Chicago, 1958).

seems to have left the plains of Gennesaret (Ch. 6:53-56) and proceeded northward. It is impossible to know how far he penetrated into this Hellenistic environment since "the region of Tyre" simply designates the district of which Tyre was the metropolitan center.[56] This was apparently Jesus' only excursion beyond the ancient borders of Israel and throughout his ministry he avoided having much contact with Gentiles. He does not seem to have entered any town of the district; the text is explicit that he wished to escape notice (cf. Ch. 9:30). This proved impossible, for he had already had contact with a delegation from Tyre and Sidon (Ch. 3:8) and the fame of his power over sickness and demonic possession had preceded him.

The purpose of Jesus' withdrawal to Tyre was to secure the rest which had been interrupted both in the wilderness (Ch. 6:30-34) and in the district of Gennesaret (Ch. 6:53-56). The house provided a place of retreat for Jesus with his disciples. Mark's reference to the house serves two purposes. It indicates to men engaged in missionary activity the necessity for rest (cf. Ch. 6:31). At the same time, persons who come seeking Jesus in a house are presented sympathetically in the Gospel as having full confidence in the Lord (Ch. 2:1-5; 3:20; 7:24-30).[57]

25-26 In the course of events Jesus was approached by a woman whose non-Jewish character is stressed. She was a member of the Hellenized citizen class in the Phoenician republic of Tyre, a Gentile by birth and culture. She is designated a Syrophoenician because Phoenicia belonged administratively to the province of Syria and was distinguished from Libophoenicia with its center at Carthage in North Africa.[58] The woman had had no previous contact with Jesus but had heard of his ability to cast out demons, and her own daughter was demon-possessed.[59] What this entailed for a child is sufficiently suggested by a later account where acute convulsions and uncontrollable falling into fire or water are the

---

[56] On the geographical questions raised by this pericope see G. Dalman, *Orte und Wege Jesu*[3] (Leipzig, 1924), pp. 211 f.; C. Kopp, *Die heiligen Stätten der Evangelien* (Regensburg, 1959), p. 288.

[57] K. Tagawa, *Miracles et Évangile* (Paris, 1966), pp. 119 f.

[58] Diodorus Siculus xix. 93; Polybius iii. 33; Strabo xvii. 3, 9.

[59] Greek authors admitted the existence of possession by unclean spirits, e.g. Sophocles, *Ajax* 244; Eusebius, *Praeparatio Evangelica* IV. xxiii. 4. On the demonic in Hellenistic thinking see W. Foerster, *TWNT* II (Eng. Tr. 1964), pp. 6-9; F. Hauck, *TWNT* III (Eng. Tr. 1965), pp. 415 f.; K. Kleinknecht, *TWNT* VI (1959), pp. 336 f., 343-350.

symptoms of possession in a young boy (Ch. 9:17 f., 20-22, 26). The mother's anguish over her daughter's condition is thoroughly understandable and does much to explain her bold persistence in begging Jesus to expel the demon from her child. Her prostration at Jesus' feet was a mark of deep respect as well as of profound grief.[60]

27-28 The brief exchange between Jesus and the woman brings the account to its climax. Jesus promises her nothing, but develops a comparison between the children and the small dogs of the household which amounts to a refusal. The comparison can be understood on two quite distinct levels. It seems appropriate to interpret Jesus' statement on the background provided by the OT and later Judaism where the people of Israel are designated as the children of God.[61] Understood in this light, Jesus acknowledges the privileges of Israel and affirms that the time has not yet come for blessing to be extended to the Gentiles. "Let the children first be fed" has reference to God's election of Israel and his appointment that the gospel be proclaimed "to the Jew first and (then) to the Greek" (Rom. 1:16; 2:9 f.; Acts 3:26; 13:46). By reference to the distinction between the claims of the children of the household and the pet dogs Jesus sharply differentiates between the claims of Israel and those of the Gentiles upon his ministry, which is restricted to Israel.[62] This is certainly the deeper meaning behind Jesus' words, but it may legitimately be asked if the woman possessed the background necessary to appreciate the distinction drawn between Jews and Gentiles and the prerogative of Israel in the divine intention. The text stresses her Hellenistic background, whereas this common interpretation of the comparison presumes a high degree of theological sophistication. Moreover, while Gentiles are sometimes described as dogs by the Jewish tradition, par-

---

60 For the desire to find in προσέπεσεν πρὸς τοὺς πόδας αὐτοῦ the thought of "stumbling" or "falling against" see A-G, p. 723 προσκόπτω 1b, p. 725 προσπαίω, προσπίπτω 2.

61 E.g. Ex. 4:22; Deut. 14:1; 32:6; Isa. 1:2; Jer. 31:9; Hos. 11:1; Jubilees 1:24 f., 28; Rom. 9:5. In M. *Aboth* III. 15 it is affirmed: "Blessed are Israel, for they were called children of God; still greater was the love [of God] because it was made known to them that they were called children of God, as it is written, 'You are the children of the Lord your God' [Deut. 14:1]."

62 This is clearly affirmed in the tradition preserved by Mt. 15:24, "I was sent only to the lost sheep of the house of Israel." It is the absence of this interpretive key in Mark which prompts the question whether this is the only level on which Jesus' statement is intelligible.

ticularly with reference to their vices,[63] there is no parallel to the use of the pet dogs of the household in this pejorative sense. Yet Jesus' statement and the woman's reply depend upon the nuance in the diminutive "little dogs" (which are admitted to the house and can be found under the table at meal time in contrast to the yard dogs or the stray scavengers of the street). It is therefore doubtful that Jesus intended a reference to the Gentiles or that the woman understood his statement in this sense. On the contrary, he alludes to a current domestic scene, particularly in a Hellenistic household. The table is set and the family has gathered. It is inappropriate to interrupt the meal and allow the household dogs to carry off the children's bread. On this level of understanding the metaphor is intelligible in the life-situation depicted in Ch. 7:24 ff. It has specific reference to the necessity for rest, which accounts for Jesus' presence in the district and to the woman's intrusion upon that rest.[64] It seems probable that the woman, at least, understood Jesus' statement on this practical (non-theological) level.

Jesus' apparent refusal to help in a situation of clear need conveys an impression of harshness and insensitivity. His reluctance to act immediately on the woman's behalf may be due to the fact that in the Hellenistic world in the first century there were many "miracle-workers" who attracted popular followings. In Galilee Jesus had been regarded as one of these "divine men" and the crowds had thronged him for his benefactions (see on Chs. 3:7-10; 6:53-56). The power of God, however, is properly released not in a context of superstition and magic but in response to faith. Jesus therefore put before the woman an enigmatic statement to test her faith. The irony of comparison is intended to invite a renewed appeal.[65]

---

[63] E.g. TB *Ḥagigah* 13a, "As the sacred food was intended for men, but not for the dogs, the Torah was intended to be given to the Chosen People, but not to the Gentiles"; Pirqe Rabbi Eliezer 29, "Whoever eats with an idolater is like a man who eats with a dog"; Exodus Rabba IX. 2 on 7:9, "The ungodly are like dogs." See for a discussion of the background to this usage O. Michel, *TWNT* III (Eng. Tr. 1965), pp. 1101-1104. On the diminutives in Mark see D. C. Swanson, "Diminutives in the Greek New Testament," *JBL* 77 (1958), pp. 134-151; Bl-D-F § 111. 1, 3 (pp. 60 f.).

[64] K. Tagawa, *op. cit.*, pp. 118-120 understands "the children" to be the disciples who need rest; Jesus insists by this parabolic word on the necessity of rest. "If Jesus agrees to the demand of the woman, he cannot rest nor allow his disciples to breathe: thus this is 'to carry off the children's bread'" (p. 120).

[65] H. Clavier, "L'ironie dans l'enseignement de Jésus," *Nov Test* 1 (1956), pp. 3-20; J. Jónsson, *Humour and Irony in the New Testament* (Reykjavík, 1965), pp. 142 f., 179, 192 f. speaks of the "irony of refusal" in discussing this passage.

The woman clearly understood this and did not hesitate before the apparent obstacle before her. She felt no insult in the comparison between children of the household and the pet dogs. Instead she neatly turned it to her advantage: the crumbs dropped by the children, after all, are intended for the dogs! Jesus' comparison is not rejected but carried one step further, which modifies the entire scene: if the dogs eat the crumbs under the table, they are fed *at the same time* as the children (and do not have to wait, as implied by the affirmation in verse 27a). Indeed, let the children be fed, but allow the dogs to enjoy the crumbs. There does not have to be an interruption of the meal, for what she requests is not the whole loaf but a single crumb. The acceptance of the comparison, the clever reply, and the profound respect for Jesus in her address show that her confidence in his power and good will has not been shaken.

29-30 The irresistible confidence of the woman in Jesus delighted him. Her interpretation of his statement bore eloquent witness both to her humility and her simple trust in his power to confront the demonic when all human help fails. This is the faith which is alone capable of receiving miracle. She placed herself unconditionally under Jesus' lordship and received his acknowledgment and promise: "on the ground of this saying, go." The command to return home is important, for in Mark Jesus speaks in this manner each time he perceives the profound confidence of those who request healing (Chs. 2:11; 5:34; 7:29; 10:52).[66] No word of healing was spoken, but the woman was given the strong assurance that the demon had been expelled from her daughter. She returned home where she found her child lying on her bed where the demon had cast her with a final convulsion before leaving (cf. Ch. 9:26). Presumably she was exhausted, but her state of calmness indicated that the paroxysms of possession were past and her person healed.[67]

In later tradition this account was retold and embellished. The mother

---

66 K. Tagawa, *op. cit.*, pp. 117-121. In Ch. 2:5 Jesus perceives "their faith"; in Chs. 5:34 and 10:52 ὕπαγε is united to the statement "Your faith has made you well." The absence of an explicit reference to faith in Ch. 7:24-30, therefore, should not obscure the fact that Mark here provides a concrete illustration of radical faith.

67 On healings at a distance see H. van der Loos, *The Miracles of Jesus* (Leiden, 1965), pp. 328-333. The authority invested in Jesus knows no regional frontiers.

was given the name Justa and her daughter received the name Berenice.[68] Mark, however, reduces the story to its bare minimum and presents this episode as an example of true faith toward the person of Jesus. While the scribes and Pharisees forget the reality of life in their attachment to casuistry and the disciples remain dull and hard-hearted (Ch. 7:1-23), a Hellenistic woman shows a profound confidence in Jesus and is not disappointed in her expectations.

11. Healing in the Decapolis. Ch. 7:31-37

31 And again he went out from the borders of Tyre, and came through Sidon[69] unto the sea of Galilee, through the midst of the borders of Decapolis.
32 And they bring unto him one that was deaf, and had an impediment in his speech;[70] and they beseech him to lay his hand upon him.
33 And he took him aside from the multitude privately, and put his fingers into his ears, and he spat, and touched his tongue;[71]
34 and looking up to heaven, he sighed, and saith unto him, Ephphatha,[72] that is, Be opened.

---

68 E.g. Pseudo-Clementine *Homilies* II, 19: "There is among us a certain Justa, a Syrophoenician . . . whose little daughter was tormented by a serious disease, and who came to our Lord, calling upon him and begging him to heal her daughter"; III. 73; IV. 1, 4, 6; XIII. 7. On these passages see W. Bauer, *Das Leben Jesu im Zeitalter der neutestamentlichen Apokryphen* (Tübingen, 1909), p. 517; J. Smit, *De Daemoniacis in Historia Evangelica* (Rome, 1912), pp. 412 f.

69 P45 𝔎 A N W λ φ 22 28 *pl q* sy sa geo arm read καὶ Σιδῶνος, which may represent an early attempt to deal with the geographical difficulty of the verse as it stands.

70 Gr. μογιλάλον which occurs in the NT only here and in the LXX only in Isa. 35:6 (Ex. 4:11 in the versions of Aquila, Symmachus and Theodotion; Isa. 56:10, Aquila). It denotes speaking with severe difficulty, rather than mute. This is supported by the variant reading μογγιλάλον ("hoarse of speech") in B3 L W Δ *et al* φ 28 33 118 579 892 *pl* and by ἐλάλει ὀρθῶς in verse 35.

71 P45 W 0131 sys Ephraem and the Arabic Diatessaron 21:3 speak of spitting upon the fingers before thrusting them into the man's ears and this order is defended as original by P. L. Couchoud, "Notes de critique verbale sur St. Marc et St. Matthieu," *JThS* 35 (1934), p. 12.

72 Gr. ἐφφαθά. I. Rabinowitz, "'Be Opened' = Ephphatha (Mark 7:34): Did Jesus Speak Hebrew?" *ZNW* 53 (1962), pp. 229-238 opposes the common assumption that this word is Aramaic on the ground that no such form existed in any of the varieties of Western Aramaic. His proposal that the word is Hebrew and trans-

35 And his ears were opened, and the bond of his tongue was loosed, and he spoke plain.
36 And he charged them that they should tell no man: but the more he charged them, so much the more a great deal they published it.
37 And they were beyond measure astonished, saying,
He hath done all things well;
he makes even the deaf to hear,
and the dumb to speak.

The episode of the healing of a man with defective hearing and speech is recorded only by Mark. The significance the evangelist finds in this incident is apparent when the account is seen in its larger context. In Ch. 6:31-7:37 Mark has presented a cycle of tradition which includes the feeding of the multitude, the encounter with Pharisaic unbelief and acts of healing. With Ch. 8:1 a new cycle is introduced, which follows a similar pattern,[73] climaxed by the confession of Ch. 8:27-30. The recognition of this parallel in structural arrangement sheds light on the function of Ch. 7:31-37 in the Marcan outline. It serves to bring the first cycle of tradition to a close on a doxological note. The focus of the entire account is on the confession that Jesus does all things well.

31 The Phoenician republic of Sidon was located on the coast some twenty miles north of Tyre. Jesus apparently journeyed northward to the district of Sidon and then turned southeastward through Philip's territory toward a point on the eastern shore of the Lake of Galilee within the region of the Decapolis. The route followed is only vaguely indicated and cannot be retraced now,[74] but it may have been designed to preclude the necessity of entering Galilee. Jesus remained in territory with strong

---

literates the masculine singular imperative of the niphal stem of פתח is accepted by J. A. Emerton, "MARANATHA and EPHPHATHA," *JThS* 18 (1967), pp. 427-431. Cf. R. L. Lindsey, *A Hebrew Translation of the Gospel of Mark* (Jerusalem, 1969), p. 115: אֶפָּתַח וּפֵרוּשׁוֹ הִפָּתַח:. For the bearing this evidence has on the question of the language of Jesus see R. H. Gundry, "The Language Milieu of First-Century Palestine. Its Bearing on the Authenticity of the Gospel Tradition," *JBL* 83 (1964), pp. 404-408; H. P. Rüger, "Zum Problem der Sprache Jesu," *ZNW* 59 (1968), pp. 113-122.

[73] Cf. L. Cerfaux, "La section des pains" in *Recueil Lucien Cerfaux* I (Gembloux, 1954), pp. 471-485, and see below on Ch. 8:1-10.

[74] For two quite different estimates of the situation see G. Dalman, *op. cit.*, p. 214; and K. Tagawa, *op. cit.*, pp. 29 f.

Gentile associations. The location of the episode in the Decapolis, however, proves nothing as to the participants since there were sizeable colonies of Jews in nearly all of the cities.[75] It is difficult from the text to determine whether the crowd which approached Jesus was Jewish or Gentile in complexion.

32 A crowd brought to Jesus a man with defective hearing and speech. He was deaf and had a speech impediment so severe he could not articulate his words. He apparently suffered from a spasmodic condition of the tongue which can extend to the facial muscles as well. If the man had been born deaf and mute he would not have learned to speak and would possess no concept of language. This was not the situation. He had become deaf later in life apparently as a result of disease or injury and could speak only with great effort.[76] Mark's use of an extremely rare word to describe the man's speech defect is almost certainly an allusion to Isa. 35:5f. which celebrates God as the one who comes in order to unstop the ears of the deaf and to provide song for the man of inarticulate speech. The fulfilment of the prophecy was expected in the Days of the Messiah in the exegetical tradition of the rabbis.[77] By means of the biblical allusion Mark provides his readers with a sign that the promised intervention of God took place in the ministry of Jesus. The reference points forward to the confession of faith in verse 37.

The request for the laying on of hands (cf. Chs. 5:23; 6:5) indicates the presence of Jews or of Gentiles who were familiar with this Jewish practice in connection with blessing and healing. The great surprise exhibited by the people when the afflicted man spoke clearly suggests that they had not expected healing, but had brought the man to Jesus for his blessing.

33-35 Jesus took the man aside from the crowd in order to establish contact with him. He regarded the personal relationship between himself and the sick to be of supreme importance, and in this instance all of his actions are intelligible in the light of the necessity of communicating with a person who had learned to be passive in life. Through touch and the use of spittle Jesus entered into the mental world of the

---

[75] See E. Schürer, *Die Geschichte des jüdischen Volkes im Zeitalter Jesu Christi*³ II (1898), pp. 115-148 and the references cited there.

[76] H. van der Loos, *op. cit.*, pp. 523-529.

[77] Genesis Rabba 95; Midrash Tehillin 146:8.

man and gained his confidence.[78] He stretched open his ears and made it clear to him that he wished to make his tongue alive with his own life. Jesus prayed with him and for him and openly expressed the strong emotion he seems to have always felt in the presence of the ravages of demonic possession and disease. This sequence of actions indicated to the man that he was to expect healing from the one who stood before him. The act of healing itself was accomplished with the word of liberation addressed not to the defective auditory organs but to the man as a whole person: "Be opened."

The results of Jesus' actions are simply described: the ears were opened, the tongue was loosened, and the man began to speak clearly. The loosening of the tongue followed immediately upon the opening of the ears. There are parallels in Hellenistic texts to the statement that "the tongue was loosened" which have prompted the suggestion that this affliction was due to demonic possession; Jesus liberated the man from the fetters of the demon responsible for his severe condition.[79] There is nothing in the Marcan text, however, to support this proposal and it is better to regard the phrase as a figurative description of the cure. Mark has stressed Jesus' encounter with the demonic throughout the first half of the Gospel and it can be presumed that he would have stated that the man was possessed by a deaf and dumb spirit if this were the case.

The healing did not consist in the fact that the man spoke, but that he spoke without defect. His command of language confirms that he had not been born deaf and dumb. His normal speech formed the surprising contrast to his former stammering.

36-37 Jesus' repeated injunctions to be silent concerning what had taken place were immediately disregarded; those who had witnessed the healing were exuberant and engaged in kerygmatic activity (cf. Chs.

---

78 Spittle was regarded as an important curative force in Judaism and Hellenism. Cf. J. Preuss, *Biblisch-talmudische Medizin* (Berlin, 1911), pp. 96 ff., 321 f.; H. van der Loos, *op. cit.*, pp. 306-309; and pp. 313-321 on the significance of touch in healing.

79 A. Deissmann, *Light from the Ancient East*[4] (New York, 1927), pp. 304-307; accepted by J. Behm, *TWNT* I (Eng. Tr. 1964), p. 750; C. E. B. Cranfield, *op. cit.*, p. 252; *et alia*. On the other hand, J. M. Robinson, *The Problem of History in Mark* (London, 1957), pp. 40 f., while finding "exorcism language" in the account, notes that "the hostile opposition which characterized the exorcism narratives" is missing from this account, which is not specifically an exorcism.

1:45; 5:20). The parallel with Ch. 1:44 f. is particularly close since the violation of the injunction is described in both places as "proclamation," the technical designation for preaching the gospel. The identical language in Ch. 1:44 f. and Ch. 7:36 suggests that the purpose of the injunction was to avoid a recurrence of the situation which developed subsequent to the healing of the leper when the presence of crowds in each town clamoring for Jesus' healing touch hindered his movement and interrupted his preaching mission. It was apparently Jesus' intention to remain in the region of the Decapolis for a period of time and he did not wish to be regarded as a Hellenistic wonder-worker.

The narrative concludes with a confession of faith which focuses on the messianic significance of the incident. In their excitement the crowd generalized the healing,[80] perhaps with reference to what they had previously heard (cf. Chs. 3:8; 5:20) and was now confirmed by what they had seen. But Mark intends an allusion to Isa. 35:5 f.[81] The choral exclamation of the crowd is the response of faith which recognizes in all the works of Jesus the promised intervention of God.

---

80 The presence of the plurals τοὺς κωφούς . . . καὶ ἀλάλους is obscured in English translation. M. Dibelius, *Die Formgeschichte des Evangeliums*[4] (Tübingen, 1961), p. 73 finds here "the conclusion of a number of stories rather than the acclamation of the people to Jesus who is just passing by."

81 There appear to be echoes of Gen. 1:31 (cf. Ecclus. 39:16: "All the works of the Lord are exceedingly good") and Isa. 29:18-23, but the primary reference is to Isa. 35:5-6, anticipated by μογιλάλον in verse 32. J. Héring, "καλῶς πάντα πεποίηκεν. Remarques sur Marc 7, 37," *Coniectanea Neotestamentica* 11 (1947), pp. 91 ff., on the basis of a comparative study of Mk. 7:37 and Mt. 15:31, proposed that the text should read:

κυλλοὺς παντελεῖς πεποίηκεν	"He has made the lame whole
καὶ τοὺς κωφοὺς ποιεῖ ἀκούειν	And he makes the deaf to hear
καὶ ἀλάλους λαλεῖν	and the dumb to speak."

The chief value of this proposal is that it eliminates all other echoes and more pointedly directs attention to Isa. 35:5-6. It remains, however, only an interesting conjecture which lacks sufficient cogency to set aside the vast weight of the textual tradition.

CHAPTER 8

In Ch. 8:1-30 Mark presents a sequence of events which is parallel in structural arrangement and motif to Chs. 6:31-7:37. He intends for this parallel to be recognized, for the tradition he records in Ch. 8:17-21 points back to the crucial importance of the two feeding narratives. The extent of the structural parallel is evident from the following table:

Ch. 6:31-44	Feeding of the Multitude	Ch. 8:1-9
Ch. 6:45-56	Crossing of the Sea and Landing	Ch. 8:10
Ch. 7:1-23	Conflict with the Pharisees	Ch. 8:11-13
Ch. 7:24-30	Conversation about Bread	Ch. 8:13-21
Ch. 7:31-36	Healing	Ch. 8:22-26
Ch. 7:37	Confession of Faith	Ch. 8:27-30

The table has been deliberately simplified to set forth the pattern that can be recognized from the material. A more careful arrangement might exhibit the degree of dissimilarity in these two cycles of tradition. The individual units in each section exhibit marked differences in vocabulary and formulation; they have been drawn from independent cycles of tradition consisting of different episodes. The evangelist, however, is responsible for the arrangement and redaction of the material in terms of the motif of understanding. After both feedings the failure of the disciples to understand the significance of the sign of the broken bread is stressed (Ch. 6:52; Ch. 8:14-21). Between these points Jesus solemnly calls the multitude and the disciples to understand (Ch. 7:14-18). By skillful arrangement of the material Mark indicates that it was necessary for the Lord to repeat the sequence of acts and teaching a second time before their significance dawned upon the disciples. Their ears remained deaf to Jesus' teaching and their eyes blind to his glory (Ch. 8:18). In this respect the incidents which conclude the two cycles are significant. The opening of the ears of one who was deaf (Ch. 7:31-36) and of the eyes of one who was blind (Ch. 8:22-26) prefigure the unstopping of the deaf ears of the disciples and the opening of their eyes. This was the necessary prelude to the confession of the messianic dignity of Jesus (Ch. 8:27-30).

12. The Provision of Bread in the Decapolis. Ch. 8:1-10

1 And in those days, when there was again a great multitude,
and they had nothing to eat, he called unto him his disciples,
and saith unto them,
2 I have compassion on the multitude, because they continue
with me now three days, and have nothing to eat:
3 and if I send them away fasting to their home, they will faint [1]
on the way; and some of them are come [2] from far.
4 And his disciples answered him, Whence shall one be able to
fill these men with bread here in a desert place?
5 And he asked them, How many loaves have ye? And they
said, Seven.
6 And he commanded the multitude to sit down on the ground:
and he took the seven loaves, and having given thanks, [3] he
brake, and gave to his disciples, to set before them; and they
set them before the multitude.
7 And they had a few small fishes: and having blessed them, [4]
he commanded to set these also before them.
8 And they ate, and were filled: and they took up, of broken
pieces that remained over, seven baskets. [5]

---

[1] Gr. ἐκλύεσθαι, used of weakness caused by hunger in Judg. 8:15; 1 Kings 14:28; Isa. 46:1; Lam. 2:19; I Macc. 3:17 LXX.

[2] Gr. ἥκασιν supported by ℵ A D N W Θ 𝔎 λ 28 33 69 565 700 *pm* latt sy$^{s\ p}$ arm goth aeth sa. The more familiar form εἰσίν is read by B L Δ 892 bo, but ἥκασιν is clearly to be preferred. Mark apparently intends the phrase ἀπὸ μακρόθεν ἥκασιν to echo Josh. 9:6, 9 or Isa. 60:4 or both. See the suggestive development of this phrase by F. W. Danker, "Mark 8:3," *JBL* 82 (1963), pp. 215 f.

[3] Gr. εὐχαριστήσας, in contrast to εὐλογῶ in Ch. 6:41. Both words represent the Semitic בֵּרֵךְ, but the preference for εὐχαριστῶ here is seen as a Hellenistic element supporting the Gentile orientation of the passage. Cf. W. L. Knox, *Some Hellenistic Elements in Primitive Christianity* (London, 1944), pp. 3-5; J. Jeremias, *The Eucharistic Words of Jesus*[2] (Oxford, 1955), p. 119.

[4] It is preferable to omit αὐτά ("them") with D E G H S U V Ω 22 33 118 472 579 700 *pm q* and to explain its presence in so many good MSS as due to the ignorance of Gentile scribes concerning Jewish practice. The object of the blessing was not the loaves or the fish, but the Lord (see on Ch. 6:41). If Mark did write εὐλογήσας αὐτά the passage should be translated "having blessed [God's Name] over them."

[5] English translation obscures the presence of σπυρίς here (in contrast to κόφινος in Ch. 6:43). The σπυρίς was a rope or mat basket sufficiently large to carry a man (Acts 9:25). The remains of the seven σπυρίδες were thus more extensive than the twelve κόφινοι mentioned in Ch. 6:43.

9 And they were about four thousand: and he sent them away.
10 And straightway he entered into the boat with his disciples,
and came into the parts of Dalmanutha.[6]

The degree of similarity in situation and language between Ch. 6:34-44 and Ch. 8:1-9 has prompted the question whether there were indeed two occasions in Jesus' ministry when the multitudes were fed. The dominant critical opinion is that there was one event which was reported in various forms in the tradition and a highly divergent version provided the basis for the second feeding reported in Ch. 8:1-9.[7] The improbability that the disciples would have forgotten the first feeding so soon is particularly important in this critical evaluation, since in Ch. 8:4 they make no reference to an earlier feeding. This argument deserves careful examination. The most striking similarities in language are inherent in the situation depicted–the feeding of a multitude with peasants' fare in an isolated area when Jesus began the meal with the customary blessing of God's name.[8] Allowances should be made in this regard for the tendency to assimilate the language of the two narratives through

[6] Gr. Δαλμανουθά poses a difficult puzzle complicated by textual variants and conjectures. Dalmanutha is completely unknown apart from this reference; in the parallel passage Mt. 15:39 stands Magadan, which was located near ancient Gerasa on the eastern side of the lake. This finds support in several of the variant readings for Mk. 8:10 (P^{45} D^{corr} it sy^s Origen Eusebius *Onomasticon* 134, 18), but these may simply reflect assimilation to the text of Matthew. The chief difficulty with this variant is that it places Jesus on the wrong side of the lake. C. Kopp, *Die heiligen Stätten der Evangelien* (Regensburg, 1959), pp. 232, 246 ff., considers Dalmanutha to be almost certainly identical with Magdala, a town near Tiberias on the western side of the lake. This proposal finds support in the Caesarean text of Mk. 8:10 where Μαγδαλα is read by Θ λ φ 209 271 317 sy^{pal}. For a review of proposed conjectural emendations based on a presumed Aramaic text see E. Lohmeyer, *Das Evangelium des Markus*[16] (Göttingen, 1963), pp. 154 f. and for the geographical questions involved J. Sickenberger, "Dalmanutha," *ZDPV* 57 (1934), pp. 281-285; P. Tielscher, "Dalmanutha," *ZDPV* 59 (1936), pp. 128-132; B. Hjal-Hansen, "Dalmanutha," *RB* 53 (1956), pp. 372-384.

[7] H. van der Loos, *The Miracles of Jesus* (Leiden, 1965), p. 620; K. Tagawa, *Miracles et Évangile* (Paris, 1966), p. 129; G. Ziener, "Das Brotwunder im Markusevangelium," *BZ* 4 (1960), pp. 282-285, among many others.

[8] Both incidents are situated in the wilderness (Ch. 6:35; Ch. 8:4); the question "How many loaves have you?" recurs (Ch. 6:38; Ch. 8:5); the command to recline is expressed by the same vocable (Ch. 6:39; Ch. 8:6); the meal is initiated in the same way (Ch. 6:41; Ch. 8:6); on both occasions "they ate and were filled" (Ch. 6:42; Ch. 8:8); the fragments were gathered after each meal (Ch. 6:43 f.; Ch. 8:8 f.); the dismissal of the crowd was followed by a journey in the boat (Ch. 6:45; Ch. 8:9 f.).

repeated use in teaching and worship. There can be no doubt about striking divergences in vocabulary, detail and situation between the two accounts, most of which were already noted by Jerome in his commentary on Mt. 15:32 ff. [9] More significant is the fact that Jesus reminds his disciples of two feedings in Ch. 8:19 f. The rejection of the historicity of Ch. 8:1-9 requires the assignment of Ch. 8:14-21 to the limbo of creative redaction or false tradition. The perplexity of the disciples in Ch. 8:4 is intelligible in context. Jesus declared his concern for the crowd but he had not said how he planned to meet their need. In this setting Ch. 8:4 is equivalent to the question: What do *you* intend to do? Jesus had taken the initiative to provide for the crowd and he must clarify how he will satisfy their hunger. It would have been presumptuous for the disciples to have assumed that Jesus would, as a matter of course, multiply a few loaves as he had done on an earlier occasion. There is no intrinsic improbability about Jesus feeding a vast gathering in the Decapolis with loaves and fish and the historical integrity of the account should be accepted. [10] Mark clearly understood that there were two occasions when Jesus miraculously fed a multitude.

1-3 The second feeding of a multitude occurred in the vicinity of Lake Gennesaret. It may be deduced from the reference to the Decapolis in Ch. 7:31 and the general reference to time in Ch. 8:1 that Jesus remained on the eastern shore of the lake where a mixed population of Jews and pagans lived. Mark does not specify the purpose for this sojourn, but the presence of a multitude which has spent three days in Jesus' company implies an intensive teaching ministry. [11] The text emphasizes the need of the people: they have been for three days in an isolated location

[9] *Comm. in Matth.* P. L. XXVI, 112. Even among the so-called parallel expressions there are striking differences, e.g. the distinction between κοφίνων and σπυρίδες in describing the gathered fragments not only in Ch. 6:43 and Ch. 8:8 but in Ch. 8:19 f. Among differences may be noted the duration of the crowd's stay in the wilderness (Ch. 6:35, one day; Ch. 8:2, three days); the numbers of the loaves and fish, the fragments, and those present (Ch. 6:38, 42-44; Ch. 8:5, 8 f.); the absence of the exchange between Jesus and the disciples (Ch. 6:36-38), and of the references to the distinctive wilderness motifs (Ch. 6:34, 39 f.) in the second account. Moreover, in the first feeding the disciples raise the question of what is to be done about the crowd, but the initiative is taken by Jesus in the second.

[10] See further G. Friedrich, "Die beiden Erzählungen von der Speisung in Mk. 6, 31-44; 8, 1-9," *ThZ* 20 (1964), pp. 10-22; J. Knackstedt, "Die beiden Brotvermehrungen im Evangelium," *NTS* 10 (1964), pp. 309-335.

[11] It is tempting to see in the three-day ministry the sanctification of the people in preparation for an epiphany of the Lord's glory, on the analogy of Ex. 19:10 f.

and their provisions have been exhausted. They have already engaged in fasting and have been weakened through hunger. While some of the people are from villages and towns nearby, others must travel a distance to reach home. This is the practical situation that calls forth Jesus' compassion, which is an expression of the gracious disposition of God toward men. The sole purpose of the feeding is to meet the physical needs of the multitude, who chose to be nourished by Jesus' word rather than bread.

Two details are particularly striking in the Marcan setting to the second multiplication of the loaves. (1) In Ch. 6:34 the ground of Jesus' compassion is that the people are like sheep who possess no shepherd. Jesus provides the leadership they lack *by teaching them.* The relationship established in the text is between compassion and teaching, while the feeding of the multitude is a subsequent act. In Ch. 8:2 f. the ground of Jesus' compassion is that the people have been so long without food. Jesus meets their need *by feeding them.* The relationship emphasized by the text is between compassion and feeding. (2) In Ch. 6:35-37 the disciples ask Jesus to dismiss the crowd, which has spent the greater part of a day with him in order that they may seek provisions in neighboring towns and villages. Mark implies that they interrupted Jesus' teaching in order to call his attention to this practical consideration. On this second occasion Jesus is thoroughly aware of the practical issues involved in dismissing the crowd without nourishment and he takes the initiative in calling the attention of the disciples to this urgent situation. These differences amount to striking divergence in situation, motivation and detail between the two accounts.

4-5 On both occasions that Jesus fed a multitude he involved his disciples in his action. It is clear from Ch. 8:17-21 that Jesus considered their understanding of his feeding of the people as the necessary prerequisite to their understanding of his person. The disciples' question in verse 4 stresses their inadequacy to the situation and indicates that Jesus alone can act on behalf of the people. In Ch. 6:37 they had not envisioned that a multitude could be fed and they emphasized the impossibility of the situation with disrespectful irony. There is an indirectness in the response of Ch. 8:4 which is different in tone and function. It serves to refer the question of procuring bread back to Jesus and is tantamount to asking, What do you intend to do? [12] Jesus' counter-

[12] M. J. Lagrange, *Évangile selon Saint Marc* (Paris, 1947), pp. 202 f. finds a further nuance in the question: Everyone knows that God gave bread to his people

question concerning the number of loaves available to them, on the other hand, is equivalent to the affirmation, I know what I am going to do.

6-7 The feeding of the multitude with bread and small fish recalls in outline the action of Jesus with the five thousand on the (presumably) western shore of the lake. There is, however, no reference to the lush pastures or to the grouping of the people into table and field companies, and the evangelist makes no attempt to develop any of the wilderness motifs inherent in the situation as in the earlier account. Assuming that the multitude was representative of the mixed population of the region, the blessing of God's name before the distribution of the bread would have been a new action to many of them. This may explain the unusual pronouncement of thanksgiving over fish in verse 7. The pronouncement of blessing over bread is the normal Jewish practice for beginning a meal, but the blessing of God's Name prior to the distribution of the fish seems to have been intended to teach the people to thank God for their daily food. The offering of praise and thanksgiving acknowledges that the multiplied food is the gracious provision of God.

8-10 The highly compressed narrative stresses the satisfaction of the people's need, the abundance of the provision as witnessed by the seven large rope baskets of fragments that remained over, and the vastness of the crowd that had gathered. It is common to find a symbolic significance in the numbers recorded here (and in Ch. 6:43 f.): the four thousand represent the Gentiles from the four corners of the world, while the seven baskets prefigure the seven leaders of the Hellenistic Church in Jerusalem. All such symbolic interpretation finds little support in the Marcan text. The numbers are carefully noted because they were important in the tradition preserved in Ch. 8:17-21. As for the composition of the multitude, it has been common since the time of Augustine to assign the first feeding to the nourishment of Israel and the second to the Gentiles.[13] There can be no doubt of the Gentile associations of the Decapolis and of Mark's interest in the apostolic mission to the Gentiles.

---

in the desert (cf. Ex. 16:32). Only a miraculous provision of bread can satisfy the need.

[13] See e.g. A. Richardson, "The Feeding of the Five Thousand," *Interpretation* 9 (1955), pp. 144-149; G. Friedrich, *op. cit.,* pp. 10-22; A. Shaw, "The Marcan Feeding Narratives," *The Church Quarterly Review* 162 (1961), pp. 268-278.

The units of tradition brought together in Ch. 7:1-30 (and perhaps Chs. 7:1-8:9) have important implications for the Gentile mission. Moreover, there are nuances in the language and phraseology of Ch. 8:1-9 which suggest a Gentile orientation. [14] In view of the mixed population of the area, however, it is probable that both Jews and Gentiles sat down together in meal fellowship on this occasion, and this prefigured Jesus' intention for the Church. This seems to be a more realistic approach to the historical situation than the desire to find an exclusively Gentile audience in Ch. 8:1-9. [15]

After dismissing the crowd Jesus left the Decapolis and returned to the western side of the lake and Galilee. Within the limits of our knowledge of Palestinian geography in the first century it is impossible to identify Dalmanutha. The argument that this site was identical with Magdala is worthy of serious consideration, [16] but must await confirmation from new evidence before it is accepted as definitive.

13. The Request for a Sign. Ch. 8:11-13

11 And the Pharisees came forth, and began to question [17] with him, seeking of him a sign from heaven, [18] trying [19] him.
12 And he sighed deeply in his spirit, and saith, Why doth this

---

14 The situation of the incident in the Decapolis, the allusive use of ἀπὸ μακρόθεν ἥκασιν in Ch. 8:3b, the substitution of εὐχαριστῶ for εὐλογῶ in Ch. 8:6 and of σπυρίδες for κοφίνων in Ch. 8:8. See F. W. Danker, *op. cit.*, pp. 215 f.; W. L. Knox, *op. cit.*, pp. 3-5; R. C. Horn, "The Use of the Greek New Testament," *Lutheran Quarterly* 1 (1949), p. 301.

15 G. H. Boobyer, "The Miracles of the Loaves and the Gentiles," *ScJTh* 6 (1953), pp. 77-87 argues that both feedings took place on the eastern side of the lake and involved Gentiles. His argument is unconvincing because he fails to discuss the distinctly Jewish wilderness motifs in Ch. 6:30-44.

16 C. Kopp, *op. cit.*, pp. 232, 246 ff.

17 Gr. συζητεῖν, which conveys more the nuance of disputing or arguing with someone (cf. Chs. 9:14, 16; 12:28); RSV "they began to argue with him." The expression implies that there was a prior discussion, the content of which is not indicated, which was then terminated with the demand for a sign.

18 Gr. ἀπὸ τοῦ οὐρανοῦ, which is probably a Semitic idiom for "from God." So K. H. Rengstorf, *TWNT* VII (1964), p. 233: This expression simply acknowledges that God is the ultimate author of the sign. It does not specify the sphere in which the sign is to be exhibited.

19 RSV "to test him" is better in the light of the background to the Pharisaic demand in Deut. 18:18-22.

generation seek a sign? verily I say unto you,[20] There shall no sign be given unto this generation.[21]
13 And he left them, and again entering into *the boat*[22] departed to the other side.

11 This brief passage is abruptly introduced without reference to time, place, or the circumstances which led to the demand for a sign. The connection with the immediate context is not explicit. The presence of the Pharisees implies the western shore of the lake, and this is confirmed by the reference to the crossing and subsequent arrival at Bethsaida in Ch. 8:13, 22. The text further implies a prior discussion, the content of which is unspecified, which was climaxed by the demand for "a sign from heaven." It appears to be Mark's intention that this fragment of conversation be regarded as an extension of the controversy reported in Ch. 3:22-30. This is suggested by the position of these verses, in parallel with Ch. 7:1-5 which specifically mentions the scribes from Jerusalem (cf. Ch. 3:22), and by the use of the solemn 'Amen' formula which points back to Ch. 3:28. Subsequent to the encounter with the Jerusalem authorities who accused Jesus of being in league with Satan, the Pharisees resumed the debate which led to the request for a sign. This reconstruction provides a definite context for Ch. 8:11-13 and indicates the direction which must be pursued for a proper understanding of the passage.

The concept of a sign is intelligible from the OT and later Jewish

---

[20] Gr. λέγω ὑμῖν is omitted by P[45] W and this is defended as original by G. W. Buchanan, "Some Vow and Oath Formulas in the New Testament," *HTR* 58 (1965), p. 325 because it brings the passage into conformity with oath formulae in the OT and rabbinic literature (e.g. Num. 5:19-22; Deut. 27:15 f.).

[21] Gr. εἰ δοθήσεται contains a Semitic idiom for strong negation (cf. οὐ δοθήσεται in the parallel passage, Mt. 16:4), in which εἰ = אִם, implying an imprecation. N. D. Coleman, "Some Noteworthy Uses of εἰ or εἶ in Hellenistic Greek, with a Note on St. Mark viii. 12," *JThS* 28 (1926-27), pp. 159-167 denied that εἰ was a particle of negation and treated it as an emphatic particle in accordance with Hellenistic usage. He translated the text: "I tell you truly, there shall indeed be given to this generation a sign!" In response F. C. Burkitt, "Mark viii. 12 and εἰ in Hellenistic Greek," *JThS* 28 (1926-27), pp. 274-276 showed that the Semitic idiom was recognized and translated as a negative by the Syriac and Coptic versions (and by W Δ 5 φ and Origen who comments εἰ . . . τοῦτ' ἔστιν οὐ δοθήσεται). For the Semitic formulae underlying the Greek text see G. W. Buchanan, *op. cit.*, pp. 324-326.

[22] The interpretation of the ASV, RSV "into the boat" is made explicit in a number of manuscripts: P[45] 𝔎 A D W Θ 0131 λ φ 33 565 579 700 *al* it sy sa bo.

literature.[23] It signifies a token which guarantees the truthfulness of an utterance or the legitimacy of an action. Prophetic statements which could not be verified were frequently accompanied by a sign which authenticated the prophecy. In that context a sign is a further prophecy to be fulfilled within a short period of time.[24] The special characteristic of a sign is that there is a coincidence between a prior prophecy and a subsequent event. In other instances a sign is a token performed at once to verify a certain proposition.[25]

The recognition that a sign is primarily an evidence of trustworthiness, not of power, sheds light on this verse. It indicates that the demand for a sign is not a request for a miracle. Jesus' miracles are never designated as signs in Mark's Gospel, nor were they considered to be signs by the Pharisees. They regard Jesus' miracles as ambiguous actions whose meaning must be confirmed by a sign.[26] They had witnessed his mighty works but had concluded they were of demonic agency (Ch. 3:22-30). That is why the Pharisees demand a sign in spite of Jesus' deeds. The request for a sign is a demand that he demonstrate the legitimacy of his actions. In this context "a sign from heaven" signifies a public, definitive proof that God is with him. In this light, the qualifying phrase "testing him" is important; it refers to the biblical provision for testing if a prophet has been sent by God (Deut. 13:2-6; 18:18-22). The demand for a sign is the equivalent to the question of the Jerusalem authorities in Ch. 11:30: what is the source of your authority?

12 Behind the demand for a sign was the prior, firm conviction that Jesus' authority was demonic in origin, his works an expression of black magic (see on Ch. 3:22). Jesus was thoroughly aware of the hostility and unbelief of the Pharisees. The emotion displayed in his deep sigh was an expression of indignation and grief (cf. Ch. 3:5). There is a note of exasperation in the question, Why does this generation seek a sign? which reflects on the perverseness and unbelief of a people who oppose

---

[23] See the comprehensive treatment of K. H. Rengstorf, *TWNT* VII (1964), pp. 199-261, and especially pp. 207-220, 223-227. Of particular importance is the concept of אוֹת as "token," pp. 209-212.

[24] For a discussion of I Sam. 2:30-33; I Kings 20:1 ff.; Isa. 7:10 ff.; TB *Sanhedrin* 98a see O. Linton, "The Demand for a Sign from Heaven (Mk. 8, 11-12 and Parallels)," *Stud Theol* 19 (1965), pp. 123-126.

[25] *Ibid.*, p. 127 provides an instructive analysis of TB *Baba Mezia* 59b.

[26] K. H. Rengstorf, *TWNT* VII (1964), p. 233.

themselves to the revelation of God's grace (cf. Chs. 8:38; 9:19).[27] What Moses experienced from the wilderness generation (Deut. 32:5-20; Ps. 95:10), Jesus experienced in his day. His absolute rejection of the demand for a sign[28] is expressed in a solemn formula of adjuration implying self-imprecation. The formula is abbreviated, as in Ps. 95:11,[29] but may be filled out on the analogy of II Kings 6:31: "May God do so and more to me if ever a sign is given to this generation!" This form of speech is a direct reflection of Scripture rather than popular usage. It would be understood immediately to signify that no sign will be given to authenticate Jesus' authority.

Jesus' refusal of a sign has important historical and theological significance. Historically, the demand for a sign expressed the desire to judge Jesus according to norms defined by scribal interpretation. If Jesus had granted a sign, his adversaries would have invoked the sanctions of Deut. 13:2-5 against him. Jesus was conscious of acting under the direction and authority of the Spirit of God (Ch. 1:11 f.; 3:28). He had already pronounced the scribal norms decayed and sterile (Ch. 7:1-23) and he now rejects their pretentiousness categorically. Theologically, the demand for unmistakable proof that God is at work in Jesus' ministry is an expression of unbelief. It represents the attempt to understand the person of Jesus within categories which were wholly inadequate to contain his reality. The call for a sign is a denial of the summons to radical faith which is integral to the gospel. Jesus rejects the way of signs as fundamentally wrong because it precludes personal decision in response to the word of revelation.[30]

---

[27] F. Büchsel, *TWNT* I (Eng. Tr. 1964), p. 663; M. Meinertz, "'Dieses Geschlecht' im Neuen Testament," *BZ* 1 (1957), pp. 283 ff.

[28] On the Matthean parallel with its reference to the sign of Jonah (Mt. 12:38 f.; 16:4) see A. Vögtle, "Der Spruch vom Jonaszeichen," in *Synoptische Studien Festschrift Alfred Wikenhauser* (München, 1953), pp. 230-275; K. H. Rengstorf, *TWNT* VII (1964), pp. 231 f.

[29] Mk. 8:12 is the sole example of the apocopated curse formula in the NT, apart from the citations of Ps. 95:11 in Heb. 3:11; 4:3, 5. Since Ps. 95:10 speaks derisively of "this generation," it is possible that Jesus intends an allusion to Ps. 95:10 f. in his double affirmation. G. Minette de Tillesse, *Le secret messianique dans l'Évangile de Marc* (Paris, 1968), p. 379 calls attention to Ezek. 14:1-3; 20:1-3 where the Lord refuses to listen to the elders of the people. In Ezek. 20:3 his refusal is sealed with an oath, as in Mk. 8:12.

[30] See further G. Delling, "Botschaft und Wunder im Wirken Jesu," in *Der historische Jesus und der kerygmatische Christus,* ed. H. Rostow and K. Matthiae (Berlin, 1960), pp. 389-402; K. Tagawa, *op. cit.,* pp. 75-80.

13 Jesus' abrupt departure from the Pharisees gave visible expression to his indignation. Nothing good could be expected to result from further discussion with them, and he crossed over the lake to the eastern shore once more. The Pharisees had demonstrated that they lacked the discernment to see that the tokens of the Kingdom were visible in his words and actions. The sharp cleavage between Jesus and the Pharisees indicates that the gospel remains hidden from unbelief.

14. The Failure to Understand. Ch. 8:14-21

14 And they forgot to take bread; and they had not in the boat with them more than one loaf.
15 And he charged them, saying, Take heed, beware of the leaven of the Pharisees and the leaven of Herod.[31]
16 And they reasoned one with another, saying, We have no bread.[32]
17 And Jesus perceiving it saith unto them, Why reason ye,[33] because ye have no bread? do ye not yet perceive, neither understand? have ye your heart hardened?[34]
18 Having eyes, see ye not? and having ears, hear ye not?[35] and do ye not remember?

---

31 Predominantly Caesarean texts refer to the leaven of the "Herodians," a correction influenced by Chs. 3:6; 12:13: P^{45} G W Δ Θ λ φ 22 28 60 251 565 679 *i k* sa geo arm.

32 There are many textual variants to this clause. The great majority of Greek MSS have ἔχομεν, supported by some MSS of the Itala, vg $sy^{p\ h}$, and this reading is followed by the ASV, RSV. It is preferable to read ἔχουσιν with P^{45} B (D) W λ it sa bo, as in the critical editions of the Greek text. It is then better to understand ὅτι as an indirect interrogative: "they discussed with one another *why* they had no loaves." For a defense of this translation see C. H. Turner, "Marcan Usage," *JThS* 27 (1925-26), p. 59.

33 After τί διαλογίζεσθε the Caesarean texts refer to the disciples as ὀλιγόπιστοι: P^{45} W Θ Φ φ 28 124 565 700 sy^{hmg} geo^2 arm. This adjective was probably introduced through Mt. 16:8, but it is thoroughly in harmony with Mk. 8:17-21 and deserves consideration.

34 Gr. πεπωρωμένην is interpreted as blindness of heart in D sy^s vg, and this understanding finds support in the following words of verse 18. See especially L. Cerfaux, "'L'aveuglement d'esprit' dans l'Évangile de Saint Marc," *Le Muséon* 49 (1946), pp. 267-279; J. B. Tyson, "The Blindness of the Disciples in Mark," *JBL* 80 (1961), pp. 261-268.

35 The text is near to the LXX formulation of Jer. 5:21; Ezek. 12:2, but with overtones of Isa. 6:9 f. clearly audible. Particularly the link between hardness/blindness of heart and understanding points to Isa. 6:10. See Tillesse, *op. cit.*,

19 When I brake the five loaves among the five thousand, how many baskets full of broken pieces took ye up? They say unto him, Twelve.
20 And when the seven among the four thousand, how many basketfuls of broken pieces took ye up? And they say unto him, Seven.
21 And he said unto them, Do ye not yet understand?

14-15 The reference to the one loaf within the boat ties these verses to the preceding account where Jesus returned to the lake, leaving the Pharisees standing on the shore. The sequence of developments seems to be clear. In the abrupt departure the disciples had forgotten to take bread with them. Jesus chose this opportunity to caution his disciples about "the leaven of the Pharisees" because he wanted them to hear his warning while the impact of the encounter reported in Ch. 8:11f. was fresh. When the disciples interpreted Jesus' words as an indirect reproach for their failure to bring provisions and began quarreling concerning whose responsibility it was to procure bread, he reproached them for their failure to understand. The intimate connection between Ch. 8:14-21 and the preceding verses determines the context for the interpretation of verse 15.[36]

The metaphor of leaven turns on the ability of a minute amount of yeast to impregnate the material with which it is mixed with its own fermentation. In both Jewish and Hellenistic circles leaven was a common metaphor for corruption.[37] In this context the reference draws upon the Jewish understanding of leaven as the evil will and its expression. The disciples are warned against the evil disposition of the Pharisees who ask for a sign when their judgment has already been

---

p. 272; J. Gnilka, *Die Verstockung Israels. Isaias VI, 9-10 in der Theologie der Synoptiker* (München, 1961), p. 33. Cf. Oxyrhynchus Logia iii. 8, "My soul grieves over the sons of men because they are blind in their hearts and cannot see."

[36] Verse 15 is commonly regarded as an isolated saying of Jesus which has been inserted into this context artificially due to the association of leaven and bread, e.g. C. H. Turner, "Marcan Usage," *JThS* 26 (1924-25), p. 150; E. Lohmeyer, *op. cit.*, p. 127 among others. Not only is this contrary to Mark's customary practice in dealing with the sayings of Jesus but the removal of verse 15 would disrupt the continuity of thought in verses 14-21. See G. Ziener, "Das Bildwort vom Sauerteig Mk 8, 15," *TrierThZ* 67 (1958), pp. 247 f.; R. P. Meye, *Jesus and the Twelve* (Grand Rapids, 1968), pp. 68-72.

[37] E.g. TB *Berachoth* 17a; Plutarch, *Moralia* II, 659 B; I Cor. 5:6-8; Gal. 5:9. Cf. H. Windisch, *TWNT* II (Eng. Tr. 1964), pp. 902-906.

passed. The reference to Herod is intelligible if Dalmanutha (Magdala?) was in the neighborhood of Tiberias where Antipas had his capital. In Ch. 6:14-16 Herod had betrayed a hostile interest in Jesus, and a tradition not recorded by Mark indicates his own desire to see a sign (Lk. 23:8). The figure of leaven thus describes the disposition to believe only if signs which compel faith are produced.[38] In contrast, Jesus' warning constitutes a fresh call to faith and understanding apart from signs.

16 The disciples heard only a reference to bread.[39] They discovered their lack of provisions and began quarreling about whose irresponsibility accounted for this situation. The overt reference to the Pharisees and to Herod was simply ignored. The dispute among the disciples, which indicated how completely they were absorbed in their temporal preoccupations, was the immediate occasion for Jesus' sharp condemnation of the lack of understanding in men whose privileged position should have led them to perceive the truth of his person and the importance of hearing his word.

17-18 Jesus' rebuke is expressed in a series of sober questions which focus on the persistent blindness displayed by the Twelve (cf. Chs. 4:13, 40; 6:52; 7:18). Repeated exposure to Jesus' teaching and mighty works had not led to reflection on their significance but to a basic insensitivity and dullness. Mark does not attribute the severity of the rebuke to the failure of the disciples to grasp the allusion to a sign-oriented disposition

---

38 K. Tagawa, *op. cit.,* pp. 77 f. R. P. Meye, *op. cit.,* pp. 68 f. sees the connection between leaven and the request for a sign, but then interprets Jesus' miracles as signs already given. Jesus' rejection of the way of signs in Ch. 8:12 stands opposed to this interpretation. There is a persistent desire to find in the reference to the Pharisees and Herod an allusion to a possessive, self-seeking nationalism bound up with a false, political-messianic hope. E.g., E. Lohmeyer, *op. cit.,* p. 157; G. H. Boobyer, "The Eucharistic Interpretation of the Miracle of the Loaves in St. Mark's Gospel," *JThS* n.s. 3 (1952), pp. 170 f. Lohmeyer goes so far as to find reference to Herod Agrippa I (41-44 A.D.). There is nothing in the context which lends support to such an interpretation.

39 The rabbinic references listed by S-B*K* I (1922), p. 729 show that "leaven" can be understood as meaning "leavened bread." A. Negoiță and C. Daniel, "L'énigme du levain. Ad Mk. viii. 15; Mt. xvi. 6; et Lc. xii. 1," *Nov Test* 9 (1967), pp. 306-314 feel that the disciples should have recognized the play on words intended, since in first-century Aramaic חֲמִירָא (leaven) and אֲמִירָא (word, teaching) were homonyms.

in verse 15, but to their failure to perceive the meaning of Jesus' presence with them. The indignant questions concerning hardness of heart and blindness of disposition echo the description of Israel in prophetic literature (Jer. 5:21; Ezek. 12:2; Isa. 6:9 f.) and are related to the distinction between the crowd and the Twelve in Ch. 4:11 f. There those who are "outside" were contrasted with the disciples who listen to Jesus' word. Here the Twelve appear to be no better than the crowds who profit from Jesus' miracles without reflection and who seek his teaching without applying it to themselves.

19-20 By question and answer Jesus leads the disciples back to the two feedings of a multitude. The numbers are precisely given and the types of baskets used on each occasion to collect the fragments are carefully distinguished. The disciples remembered the facts perfectly and responded to Jesus' questions without hesitation. Nevertheless, they failed to understand the significance of what had taken place before their eyes. They were no different from the unseeing crowd! It is this harsh reality of their existence that Jesus calls to their attention with his reference to the feeding of the five thousand and of the four thousand.

The two multiplications of the loaves were recalled by the quarrel concerning bread. At the same time they indicate that Jesus' mighty works (as well as his teaching) were parabolic in the sense that they pointed beyond themselves to the secret of his own person. The feedings are thus not mentioned in compensation for the refusal to provide a sign, as if they were a kind of sign themselves. The concept of signs presupposes the existence of categories according to which a judgment may be passed, but there are no traditional categories which can grasp the feedings. The reference to the loaves thus calls into question the desire to think in terms of signs and reinforces the teaching of verse 15. The broken fragments of bread force attention upon the presence of Jesus as that which has meaning for men. It is this fact which the contrast between the demand for a sign and the miracles of the loaves seeks to make precise.[40]

21 The pointed climax indicates that the disciples have not yet understood the secret to which Jesus' works pointed. The introductory words, "and he was saying to them" are an indication of paraphrase or sharp reduction of what Jesus said in order to focus on the most salient

---

[40] Rightly stressed by K. Tagawa, *op. cit.*, pp. 77 f.

point.[41] The word which follows is addressed to the Christian audience of the Gospel as well as to the disciples. What they should understand from the miracles of the loaves is the secret that Jesus is none other than the Messiah and Lord. It is tempting to find a veiled reference to this in the language of verse 14b: Jesus is the one true loaf that is with the disciples in the boat. The repeated question concerning understanding (verses 18, 21) indicates that the didactic goal of Jesus' ministry to the disciples has not been attained and points forward to the miracle of understanding which leads to the confession of Ch. 8:27-30.

15. The Opening of Blind Eyes. Ch. 8:22-26

22 And they came unto Bethsaida.[42] And they bring to him a blind man, and beseech him to touch him.

23 And he took hold of the blind man by the hand, and brought him out of the village; and when he had spit on his eyes, and laid his hands upon him, he asked him, Seest thou aught?[43]

24 And he looked up,[44] and said, I see men; for I behold *them* as trees, walking.[45]

---

41 Cf. above on Chs. 2:27 f.; 7:20.

42 The reference is to Bethsaida Julias, which the tetrarch Philip advanced from a village to the dignity of a city, both in terms of its population and grandeur. But despite its reorganization and new name it remained a mere toparchic capital (of Gaulanitis), and not a true city (Josephus, *Antiquities* XVIII. ii. 1). This point is important because the reference to κώμη in verses 23 and 26 is usually taken to indicate that this unit of tradition was not originally connected with Bethsaida, e.g. R. Bultmann, *The History of the Synoptic Tradition* (Oxford, 1963), pp. 64 f.; K. Tagawa, *op. cit.*, p. 132 n. 2. It is necessary to interpret κώμη in the light of Josephus, *War* III. iii. 2, who remarks on the large agricultural villages located in Galilee: "the very many villages that are here are everywhere so full of people, because of the richness of their soil, that the very least of them contained more than 15,000 inhabitants." Mark's reference to κώμη is correct. See A. N. Sherwin-White, *Roman Society and Roman Law in the New Testament* (Oxford, 1963), pp. 127-131. On Bethsaida Julias see G. Dalman, *Orte und Wege Jesu*[3] (Leipzig, 1924), pp. 178 f., 189; C. Kopp, *op. cit.*, pp. 230 ff. The variant reading supported by some western texts, "Bethany" (D 262 it goth), has no claim to originality.

43 Gr. εἴ τι βλέπεις. On the use of εἰ to introduce a direct question see C. F. D. Moule, *An Idiom-Book of New Testament Greek*[2] (Cambridge, 1960), pp. 151, 158.

44 Gr. ἀναβλέψας, which here means "to look up," but in Ch. 10:51 "to recover one's sight."

45 There are many textual variants to this statement which smooth out its roughness, but the text of ℵ B *al* sy[s] followed in the ASV, RSV is to be preferred.

25 Then again he laid his hands upon his eyes; and he looked steadfastly, and was restored, and saw all things clearly.[46]
26 And he sent him away to his home, saying, Do not even enter into the village.[47]

22 The crossing reported in Ch. 8:13 brought Jesus and the Twelve to the capital of the district of Gaulanitis, Bethsaida Julias, situated on the northeastern shore of the Sea of Galilee in the territory of Herod Philip (cf. Ch. 6:45). This was one of the large sites on the lake which had the size of a city but the organization of a village, and Mark's designation of it as such in verse 23 is precise. There a number of persons brought a blind man[48] to Jesus and begged him to touch the man in healing.

23-25 It is difficult to be certain why Jesus led the blind man out of the town. It was not his usual procedure to isolate himself from a congregation of people when healing or exorcising unclean spirits (Chs. 1:23-28; 3:1-5; 9:14-27), and he does not do so on a later occasion when he restored the sight of Bar-Timaeus (Ch. 10:46-52). Moreover, in all of the redactional summaries where Mark speaks of healing and exorcism he indicates the presence of crowds around Jesus (Chs. 1:32-34; 3:7-12; 6:53-56). If it is proper to speak of a tendency in Mark, the sphere of miracle is public rather than secret.[49] The three exceptions to this general observation derive, apparently, from a set of circumstances inherent in the situation itself. This is certainly true in Ch. 5:35-43 where Jesus excludes the scornful, unbelieving group of professional

---

[46] Gr. τηλαυγῶς, literally "clearly from afar." This rare word indicates that the man could see everything clearly at a distance.

[47] Gr. μηδὲ εἰς τὴν κώμην εἰσέλθῃς is supported by ℵ B L W λ (except 118) 209 sys p sa bo. The North African text (*c k q*) with the support of D presupposes the reading μηδενὶ εἴπῃς εἰς τὴν κώμην ("do not speak to anyone in the village") and this text is defended as original by C. H. Turner, "Marcan Usage," *JThS* 26 (1924-25), p. 18; 29 (1927-28), p. 2; P. L. Couchoud, "Notes de critique verbale sur St. Marc et St. Matthieu," *JThS* 34 (1933), p. 122. The Caesarean and Byzantine families of texts conflate the two readings. For the commentary the text of the major uncials is accepted as primitive.

[48] For a wealth of background material on the blind and prescribed remedies for diseases of the eye in antiquity see J. Preuss, *Biblisch-talmudische Medizin* (Berlin, 1911), pp. 313 ff.

[49] K. Tagawa, *op. cit.*, pp. 161-163. Tagawa denies that Ch. 8:23 has anything to do with Mark's so-called "secrecy phenomena." It is rather inherent in the tradition which the evangelist received.

mourners from the revelation of his life-giving power. In Ch. 7:33 the removal of the man from the crowd was an important action in establishing communication with an individual who had learned to be passive in society. This may provide the key to Ch. 8:23 as well. When Jesus took the blind man's hand and led him outside the city he established a personal relationship to him that was an important element in the man's confidence that his cure could be expected from Jesus. Beyond this, the restoring of sight to a blind person among the mixed population of Bethsaida would have led to the type of false veneration that Jesus constantly avoided (Ch. 1:35-39, 45; 3:7-9; 6:45).

The application of spittle to the eyes and the laying on of hands in healing have significant parallels in Jewish practice and in the Gospel (see on Chs. 6:5; 7:33). By these actions Jesus entered into the thought-world of the man and established significant contact with him. The report of the healing, however, contains three elements which are without parallel in the evangelical tradition: (1) Jesus' question if his action has been effective ("Do you see anything?"); (2) the explicit reference to only partial healing ("I can actually see people, but they look to me like trees–only they're walking!"); (3) the laying on of hands a second time, resulting in complete restoration of sight ("I see everything clearly–even at a distance"). These features distinguish this incident of healing from all of the others and suggest that the man's sight was restored only gradually and with difficulty. It is impossible to recover the larger context of the situation which would shed light on many questions prompted by these unique features.

The reference to men like trees walking indicates that the man had not been born blind. Persons blind from birth do not have an exact idea of objects and cannot properly visualize a tree. On the other hand, optical images become modified as blindness continues, and the visualization of men under the form of trees indicates that the man had been blind for a long period of time.[50] The vivid progression from verse 24 to verse 25 expresses something of the man's excitement and intense involvement in the dynamics of his recovery of sight,[51] and stresses the completeness of the restoration.

---

50 H. van der Loos, *op. cit.*, p. 420.

51 This is more apparent in the Greek text where ἀναβλέπειν, διαβλέπειν and ἐμβλέπειν indicate a climax in seeing: he looked up, opened his eyes wide and had a clear view of everything. Cf. A-G, pp. 180 (διαβλέπω), 254 (ἐμβλέπω).

26 The instruction to go home (cf. Chs. 2:11; 5:19) was reinforced with the admonition, "Do not (first) go into the town." It is common to find here a further instance of an injunction to silence (cf. Chs. 1:44; 5:43; 7:36), and this is made explicit in certain strands of the textual tradition which report the instruction, "Say nothing to anyone in the town." If this represents a valid interpretation of the intention behind the instruction, it is appropriate to find here a precaution Jesus found necessary because on other occasions spectacular healings had actually led to an interruption of his planned ministry (Ch. 1:44f.). The statement occurs, however, without qualification in a narrative which displays unique traits and it is perilous to insist that the purpose behind Jesus' final instruction must conform to his apparent intention on other occasions.[52]

Like making the deaf to hear and the dumb to speak, the restoring of sight to the blind was the promised action of God (Ps. 146:8; Isa. 29:18; 35:5). In this regard Ch. 8:22-26 invites comparison with Ch. 7:31-37 where the theological point that the promised intervention of God has taken place in the ministry of Jesus is established by an allusion to Isa. 35:5f. and a confession of faith (Ch. 7:32, 37). Both of these accounts are preserved only by Mark and it is almost certain that he regarded them as forming a pair. He has placed them in parallel positions in relation to the two feeding miracles and both concern healings promised in Isa. 35:5-6. The relationship between these distinct episodes is underlined by striking linguistic agreements in the opening two verses of each account where the situation is described.[53] After that the accounts diverge and display equally striking differences which arise not only out of the situation but from the language and structure of the units themselves. To cite only two examples, there are no biblical allusions in Ch. 8:22-26, and there is no counterpart to the confession of faith in Ch. 7:37. These "omissions" are apparently deliberate to force the recognition that the healing of Ch. 8:22-26 comes under the rubric of Isa. 35:5 provided in Ch. 7:31-37, and finds its appropriate conclusion only in the confession of faith recorded in Ch. 8:27-30.[54] This sup-

---

[52] For the interpretation that the final instruction was given to ensure the full recovery of the man see S. Eitrem, *Some Notes on the Demonology of the New Testament* (Oslo, 1950), p. 47.

[53] See the tables set out by V. Taylor, *The Gospel according to St. Mark* (London, 1952), pp. 368f. and G. Minette de Tillesse, *op. cit.*, pp. 57-62.

[54] For the close parallelism in structure between Ch. 8:22-26 and Ch. 8:27-30 see R. H. Lightfoot, *History and Interpretation in the Gospels* (London, 1935),

position finds confirmation from the conversation with the disciples which immediately precedes the healing of the blind man. In Ch. 8:18 Jesus speaks of the blindness and deafness of the Twelve who continue to show themselves insensitive to his person and word. An action as radical as the literal unstopping of deaf ears and loosening of a bound tongue and the opening of blind eyes was required to lead them to understanding and confession. That action was precipitated by Jesus' extension of grace to a deaf man with defective speech in the Decapolis and to a blind man outside of Bethsaida, and Mark has underscored this fact by linguistic and structural arrangement. In this context the confessions of Ch. 7:37 and Ch. 8:29 acquire a deeper significance for the Christian community for which Mark prepared the Gospel: in both passages they recognize their Lord. In Ch. 7:37 they sing a hymn to Christ who has done all things well, making the deaf to hear and the dumb to speak; in Ch. 8:29 they recognize the Messiah who has just opened the eyes of the blind. [55]

16. The Recognition of the Messiah. Ch. 8:27-30

27 And Jesus went forth, and his disciples, into the villages of Caesarea Philippi: [56] and on the way he asked his disciples, saying unto them, Who do men say that I am?

28 And they told him, saying, John the Baptist; and others, Elijah; but others, One of the prophets.

---

pp. 90 f.; A. Richardson, *Miracle-Stories of the Gospels* (New York, 1942), pp. 84-90, among others. The structural pattern follows the outline:

Ch. 8:22	Situation	Ch. 8:27
Ch. 8:23-24	Partial Sight	Ch. 8:27-28
Ch. 8:25	Sight	Ch. 8:30
Ch. 8:26	Injunction to Silence	Ch. 8:30

It is obvious from Ch. 8:32 that even the confession that Jesus is the Messiah represents only partial sight, but the analogy drawn between the two units is suggestive.

55 G. Minette de Tillesse, *op. cit.*, p. 61; U. Luz, "Das Geheimnismotiv und die markinische Christologie," *ZNW* 56 (1965), pp. 14 f., among others.

56 In contrast to Bethsaida, Caesarea Philippi was a genuine city in the technical Hellenistic sense; it controlled an extensive territory and possessed the privilege of minting its own money. Mark's phrase designates a toparchic capital and its subordinate villages. See A. H. M. Jones, *Cities of the Eastern Roman Provinces* (Oxford, 1937), pp. 277 n. 67, 283 f. n. 76; A. N. Sherwin-White, *op. cit.*, pp. 127-131.

29 And he asked them, But who say ye[57] that I am? Peter answereth and saith unto him, Thou art the Christ.[58]
30 And he charged them that they should tell no man of him.

Mark has placed at the center of his narrative the recognition that Jesus is the Messiah. The pivotal importance of this moment is indicated by the fact that already in the first line of the Gospel the evangelist designates Jesus as the Messiah. Yet between Ch. 1:1 and Ch. 8:29 there is no recognition of this fact in spite of a remarkable sequence of events which demanded a decision concerning Jesus' identity. By arrangement and emphasis Mark indicates the crucial significance which he finds in the events which clustered around the sojourn in the territory of Herod Philip.[59] Jesus' display of extraordinary power astonished his countrymen and provoked the question of the source of his authority and wisdom, but his true dignity remained unrecognized (Chs. 1:27; 2:7; 6:2). His association with sinners and disregard for accepted conventions of piety so scandalized the guardians of an inherited tradition that they could think only in terms of the demonic (Chs. 2:15-20; 3:22-30; 7:1-5). The recognition of the demons communicated nothing to the bystanders but frenzied opposition to Jesus (Chs. 1:24 f.; 3:10 f.; 5:7 f.). The disciples raised the question of Jesus' identity but found no categories by which they could understand him (Ch. 4:41; 6:51 f.), and failed to penetrate the veiledness which characterized his words and works (Ch. 8:17-21). By weaving these several strands of the tradition together in the first half of the Gospel, Mark creates a climate of tension which can be resolved only by the recognition of Jesus' dignity. The pointed question of Ch. 8:21, "Do you not understand?" cries for the answer provided in Ch. 8:29, "You are the Messiah."

The central importance of Peter's confession in the Marcan structure is confirmed by the sharp change of tone and orientation which it in-

---

[57] The position of ὑμεῖς in the Greek text (separated from the verb and placed at the beginning of the sentence) is emphatic: i.e. "you whom I have chosen and trained, in contrast with other men."

[58] Gr. ὁ χριστός, which represents the Hebrew מָשִׁיחַ and the Aramaic מְשִׁיחָא, should be rendered "the Messiah" or "the Anointed (of the Lord)." By assimilation to Mt. 16:17 א L 157 sy^pal add ὁ υἱὸς τοῦ θεοῦ and W φ 543 sy^p ὁ υἱὸς τοῦ θεοῦ τοῦ ζῶντος.

[59] Cf. Polybius xvi. 18; xxviii. 1; Josephus, *Antiquities* XV. x. 3; XVIII. ii. 1; *War* I. xi. 3; II. ix. 1. See further E. Schürer, *Geschichte des jüdischen Volkes im Zeitalter Jesu Christi*[4] II (Leipzig, 1907), pp. 204-208; G. Dalman, *op. cit.*, Ch. XI.

troduces. If there had been earlier indication that Jesus would be taken away from the disciples (Ch. 2:20) or that his adversaries determined to destroy him (Ch. 3:6), they remained veiled allusions to what appeared to be a distant event. In direct response to Peter's declaration, however, Jesus spoke of the necessity of his passion with a directness which scandalized the disciples (Ch. 8:31-33). The distinctive theology of the cross and resurrection implied by this announcement dominates the remainder of the Gospel. The recognition that Jesus is the Messiah is thus the point of intersection toward which all of the theological currents of the first half of the Gospel converge and from which the dynamic of the second half of the Gospel derives. In no other way could Mark more sharply indicate the historical and theological significance of the conversation in the neighborhood of Caesarea Philippi.[60]

27 Jesus led his disciples some 25 miles north from Bethsaida (Ch. 8:22) to the district of Iturea dominated by Caesarea Philippi, the residence of Herod Philip. The capital was located at the source of the Jordan River on the slopes of Mount Hermon in a region famed for its beauty and fertility. When the area was first given to Herod the Great by Augustus he built a temple in honor of the emperor near a grotto consecrated to the Greek god Pan. In 3 B.C. Philip rebuilt the neighboring village of Paneas as his residence and named the new city in honor of Caesar. The area was thus dominated by strong Roman associations, and it may be theologically significant that Jesus' dignity was first recognized in a region devoted to the affirmation that Caesar is lord. Here Jesus questioned his disciples concerning what was popularly being said concerning him. In Mark the questions of Jesus frequently lead to a new teaching (cf. Chs. 9:33; 12:24, 35). The purpose of this question was to prepare for the more personal question of verse 29 and the radically new teaching of verses 31 ff. Moreover, in the Gospel the term "men" is usually shaded to mean those from whom revelation remains veiled (Chs. 1:17; 7:7 f.; 9:31; 10:27; 11:30) as opposed to the disciples who have been extended special grace.[61] The double question of verses 27 and 29 thus permits a sharp differentiation between the inadequate opinions of "men" and the affirmation of faith uttered by Peter.

---

60 For a helpful survey of modern treatments of Ch. 8:27-30 see G. Minette de Tillesse, *op. cit.*, pp. 293-302.

61 E. Lohmeyer, *op. cit.*, p. 162.

28 The response to Jesus' question indicates that the truth concerning his dignity and function remains veiled from the people. In Ch. 6:14 f. the same popular opinions were presented in the same order.[62] While it is important to distinguish between these points of view, they are equally inadequate. The conviction that Jesus is John or Elijah indicates that he is nothing in himself but only the eschatological realization of a more recent or more distant past event. The affirmation that he is an ordinary prophet fails to distinguish between Jesus and the messengers of God who had appeared so many times throughout Israel's history. All three opinions assign to Jesus only a preparatory role and deny to him the definitive role associated with consummation and the achievement of salvation.

29 By question and response the contrast between those who perceive and acknowledge Jesus' messianic dignity and those who know him only in an inadequate way is clearly presented. The fact that Jesus led the disciples to this affirmation of faith is significant. He elicited the open avowal of his messiahship at this time because it was imperative to define the dimensions of his messianic ministry and to set forth what this would require of his followers.

The declaration that Jesus is the Messiah was made by Peter, whom Jesus had set apart for a decisive future role in building up the people of God when he bestowed upon him his new name (Ch. 3:16).[63] Here, as later, he functioned as the spokesman for the Twelve (cf. Chs. 9:5; 10:28; 11:21; 14:29). In Mark Peter's confession is given in its simplest, most direct and moving form.[64] The basic meaning of "Messiah" is

---

[62] The reference to John the Baptist is only intelligible in the light of Ch. 6:14-29, and it is evident that Mark intends his readers to recognize this earlier mention of popular opinion. For the distinction between the three convictions see above on Ch. 6:14 f., and for the relationship between Ch. 6:14-16 and Ch. 8:28 see G. Minette de Tillesse, *op. cit.,* pp. 310-312.

[63] E. Stauffer, *New Testament Theology* (New York, 1955), p. 31 comments: "As the Twelve took a central place inside the people of God, so Peter took a central place within the twelve.... He is no prize specimen, either as a thinker or a character. He speaks only the 'things that be of men.' Satan himself can talk through him. Our sources speak of these matters with relentless candor. Does that mean they were attacking Peter and his privileged position? On the contrary, the Gospels intend to make clear the unimpeachable basis of Peter's privilege, try to show what kind of man Peter is and what God has wrought in him–so that no man should glory in his presence."

[64] On the relationship between the Marcan and Matthean accounts of the con-

passive, "the one anointed by God." It implies divine election and appointment to a particular task and a special endowment of power for its performance. In the OT the royal, priestly and prophetic offices are associated with an anointing with oil which symbolized consecration to God's service and enjoyment of the divine protection (e.g. Ex. 29:7, 21; I Sam. 10:1, 6; 16:13; I Kings 19:16; Ps. 105:15; Isa. 61:1 ff.). The expectation of a future anointed leader was grounded in the promise of a faithful ruler from David's line (cf. II Sam. 7:14-16; Isa. 55:3-5; Jer. 23:5; 4 Q Patriarchal Blessings i. 3-4, "the righteous Messiah, the Branch of David"). In later Judaism the term "Messiah" became increasingly fluid in the emergence of a variety of messianic projections; the concept of a Davidic Messiah was only one strand of expectation among many.[65] The thought of a special relationship to God and to the people of God, however, remained dominant. In the first century the crucial question concerned the function of messiahship, and it was precisely at this point that Jesus' teaching concerning his own function stood in radical opposition to contemporary expectations.[66] Peter's confession recognized that Jesus was the appointed agent of God whose coming marks the fulfilment of the divine promise and the realization of Israel's hopes. Of the deeper and more costly dimensions of messiahship, however, he had no intimation.

30 False and narrow hopes clustered about the designation "Messiah" in the first century, and Jesus showed a marked reluctance to use this title himself (cf. Ch. 12:35-37; 14:61 f.). He clearly knew himself to be "the anointed of the Lord" but his destiny was to be fulfilled along lines other than those projected for the royal figure of popular expectations. Peter's affirmation was an exultant expression of faith. The subsequent narrative, however, indicates that it was also a reflection of a profound

---

fession see A. Vögtle, "Messiasbekenntnis und Petrusverheissung. Zur Komposition Mt. 16:13-23 Par," *BZ* 1 (1957), pp. 252-272; 2 (1958), pp. 85-103; O. Cullmann, *TWNT* VI (1964), pp. 103-109.

65 For useful surveys of texts see M. de Jonge, "The Use of the Word 'Anointed' in the Time of Jesus," *Nov Test* 8 (1966), pp. 132-148; E. Lohse, *TWNT* VIII (1969), pp. 483-488. Particularly important for Pharisaic convictions is Psalms of Solomon 17:23 ff.; 18:1-10; see below on Ch. 12:35-37.

66 Cf. J. B. Frey, "Le conflict entre le Messianisme de Jésus et le Messianisme des Juifs de son temps," *Biblica* 14 (1933), pp. 133-149; 269-293. For a recent positive evaluation of Jesus' own messianic consciousness see O. Betz, "Die Frage nach dem messianischen Bewusstsein Jesu," *Nov Test* 6 (1963), pp. 20-48.

misunderstanding (Ch. 8:31-33; 10:35 ff.). The disciples as yet had no way of knowing what conception Jesus had of his messianic vocation and it was imperative that they should not be allowed to fill the content of the term with their own dreams. Peter's words were correct in themselves, but his conception was wrong, and Jesus sternly charged them to tell no one about him, precisely as he had done earlier when the demons identified him (Ch. 1:25; 3:12).[67] The explanation for this injunction is provided immediately in verse 31, where Jesus begins to define what it means for him to be the Messiah.

V. The Journey to Jerusalem. Chs. 8:31-10:52

With verse 31 an entirely new orientation is given to the Gospel.[68] This change is defined by the explicit and new teaching concerning the necessity of Jesus' passion and by a sharp change in tone. In the Marcan structure, Jesus' prophecy of his rejection and suffering is his response to Peter's confession of faith. The following section is entirely dominated and structured by this solemn pronouncement, which is repeated twice more (Chs. 9:31; 10:33 f.). In no other Gospel do the three cardinal announcements of forthcoming humiliation have as structured a function as they do in Mark. They furnish the framework, the tone and the subject of Chs. 8:31-10:52.[69] The primary purpose of this

---

67 On the use of ἐπιτιμᾶν in Ch. 8:30 see K. Tagawa, *op. cit.,* p. 174 n. 1. For the Christians of Rome who read Mark, the confession "You are the Messiah" was precisely their profession of faith, but now illumined by the humiliation of the cross and the vindication of the resurrection.

68 The general consensus that the second half of the Gospel begins with Ch. 8:27 recognizes the intimate relationship between Peter's confession and the first prophecy of the passion in Ch. 8:31. This prophecy introduces the distinctively new elements of the second half, and characteristically commentators speak of Ch. 8:31 ff. when discussing the new section (e.g. R. P. Meye, *op. cit.,* pp. 73-80; T. A. Burkill, *Mysterious Revelation* [Ithaca, N.Y., 1963], pp. 168-171). It is better, therefore, to recognize Ch. 8:31 as the beginning of the second half of the Gospel. K. Tagawa, *op. cit.,* pp. 49-55 properly cautions against exaggerating the differences between the two halves of the Gospel.

69 Typical of many treatments of this material is G. Strecker, "The Passion- and Resurrection Predictions in Mark's Gospel (*Mark* 8:31; 9:31; 10:32-34)," *Interpretation* 22 (1968), pp. 421-442. Strecker recognizes an original pre-Marcan form of the passion/resurrection prophecy, but regards Ch. 9:31 and Ch. 10:33 f. as derived from Ch. 8:31 which reflects a sharpening of the prophecy after the event. For a defense of the essential authenticity of the three prophetic announcements

section is to explain what it means for Jesus to be the Messiah and what it requires to be identified with him. In the movement of the Gospel it serves to bring Jesus near Jerusalem where his suffering will be accomplished. Throughout this section there is sustained emphasis upon the journey to Jerusalem. Already in Ch. 8:27 Jesus and the Twelve were "on the way" among the villages of Caesarea Philippi; in Ch. 9:30 they make their way through Galilee, stopping briefly in Capernaum (Ch. 9:33); by Ch. 10:1 they have entered Judea near the lower Jordan; when interrupted by a wealthy man they are again "on the way" (Ch. 10:17), but not until Ch. 10:32 f. is the destination of the journey announced: "we are going to Jerusalem." The meaning of the journey to Jerusalem is defined by the repeated announcements of Jesus' passion: he goes to Jerusalem to fulfill his messianic destiny. He leads his disciples in the way of the cross by instructing them concerning the necessity of his sufferings and of the requirement this imposes upon them. [70]

The fact that Jesus' solemn declaration is repeated three times within a section entirely devoted to the mystery of the sufferings of the Messiah and his people indicates its crucial importance for the theology of Mark. The three cardinal pronouncements constitute the first of three movements in a programmatic pattern. The confession of Ch. 8:29 was a moment of revelation and insight. Nevertheless, the disciples failed to understand the significance of Jesus' messiahship, and Mark underscores this failure after each of Jesus' affirmations of his rejection and humiliation: Peter rebuked him (Ch. 8:32); the disciples did not understand, and were afraid to ask, and reasoned who was greater (Ch. 9:32 ff.); they were amazed and afraid, James and John asked for the places of honor in his glory, and the others were indignant (Ch. 10:35-37, 41). On each of these occasions Jesus called the Twelve to authentic discipleship involving humility, service and suffering (Chs. 8:34-38; 9:33-37; 10:38-45). The parallel themes of Jesus' suffering in fulfilment of the will of God, misunderstanding, and the call to true discipleship exhibit emphases which Mark regarded as so essential for his community to understand that he made them the heart of his Gospel.

The change of tone is stressed by the evangelist as well as by the

---

see A. Feuillet, "Les trois grandes prophéties de la Passion et de la Resurrection des évangiles synoptiques," *Rev Thom* 67 (1967), pp. 533-560; 68 (1968), pp. 41-74.

[70] Cf. U. Luz, *op. cit.,* pp. 24 f.; E. Schweizer, *Lordship and Discipleship* (London, 1960), pp. 11-21.

tradition he incorporates. In Ch. 4:33 f. Mark stressed that parabolic, veiled speech characterized Jesus' ministry before the people ("And with many such parables he was speaking the word to them, to the degree that they were able to hear it"). The veiled reference to Jesus' death in Ch. 2:20 offers an example of his parabolic speech. In Ch. 8:32, however, Mark states "and he was speaking the word openly (and with frankness)," in reference to the unmistakable note of rejection and violent death in Ch. 8:31. Moreover, in Ch. 8:34 Jesus calls the crowd and speaks to them in the same forceful, open terms he addresses to the disciples (in contrast to Ch. 7:14-15, 17-23). This openness is theologically significant within the larger context of Jesus' messianic self-revelation in the Gospel of Mark. It points beyond Jesus' hiddenness, which reaches its climax on the cross, to his revealed glory. In the cross and resurrection of Jesus the secret of the Kingdom is thoroughly veiled as well as gloriously revealed. Mark exposes this tension, which is inherent in the gospel, through the reaction of the disciples to Jesus' sober teaching throughout Chs. 8:31-10:52.

1. The Sufferings of the Messiah: the First Major Prophecy of the Passion. Ch. 8:31-33

31 And he began[71] to teach them, that the Son of man must[72] suffer many things,[73] and be rejected by the elders, and the

[71] Gr. ἄρχεσθαι is frequently paraphrastic, reflecting a Semitic idiom, but here carries its full weight; it introduces the beginning of a new section and a new teaching. Cf. U. Luz, *op. cit.*, pp. 20-23.

[72] Gr. δεῖ has its proper background in Dan. 2:28 f., 45 LXX, Theodotion; Mk. 13:7, 10; Rev. 1:1; 4:1. In these contexts there is the suggestion of cosmic catastrophe and God's judicial intervention. In Ch. 8:31 it refers to a compulsion, behind which is the expressed will of God, and corresponds to γέγραπται ("it is written") in Chs. 9:12; 14:21, 49. Behind historical occurrence there stands an unrecognized divine plan.

[73] For the Semitic-Palestinian idiom behind πολλὰ παθεῖν see D. Meyer, "ΠΟΛΛΑ ΠΑΘΕΙΝ," *ZNW* 55 (1964), p. 132, who points to the Assumption of Moses 3:11. W. Michaelis, *TWNT* V (Eng. Tr. 1967), p. 915 suggests that behind παθεῖν stands the root סבל, which can mean "to bear, to endure," influenced by Isa. 53:4, 11. The reference in πολλά is then to the fullness or totality of the human guilt the Son of Man had to bear. Both parts of this formula might thus stand under the influence of Isa. 53. R. L. Lindsey, *A Hebrew Translation of the Gospel of Mark* (Jerusalem, 1969), p. 119 translates לִסְבֹּל הַרְבֵּה.

chief priests,[74] and the scribes, and be killed, and after three days rise again.
32 And he spake the saying openly.[75] And Peter took him, and began to rebuke him.[76]
33 But he turning about, and seeing his disciples, rebuked Peter, and saith, Get thee behind me,[77] Satan; for thou mindest not the things of God, but the things of men.

It was imperative for Jesus to teach the disciples what it means to acknowledge that he is the Messiah. That teaching is provided in verse 31. Jesus' statement regarding his impending death and resurrection is a

---

[74] Gr. καὶ τῶν ἀρχιερέων, found also in Chs. 11:18, 27; 15:10, 11. The plural is rare, because ἀρχιερεύς designates the high priest, and only one man held this office at a time. In Josephus, however, the plural designates in addition to the acting high priest, former high priests and members of the privileged families from which the high priests were selected (e.g. *War* II. xvii. 3). On this use, which is apparent in Ch. 8:31, see E. Schürer, *op. cit.*, II, pp. 238-267; J. Jeremias, *Jerusalem zur Zeit Jesu*³ (Göttingen, 1962), II B, pp. 33-40.

[75] The Old Latin manuscript *k* (North Africa), sy^s and the Arabic Diatessaron attest an early variant which connects the open proclamation of the word with the period following Jesus' resurrection: "... and after three days rise again. And (then) he will speak the Word openly." Some support for this may be found in the reference to "the gospel" in verse 35, and in Ch. 9:9 (silence until after the Son of Man is risen); 9:30 (secrecy in connection with the second major prophecy); and the so-called "shorter ending" to Mark (see on Ch. 16); cf. also Jn. 16:25. This reading is defended as authentic by F. C. Burkitt, "St. Mark viii. 32: A Neglected Various Reading," *JThS* 2 (1900-1901), pp. 111-113; P. L. Couchoud, *op. cit.*, p. 123; E. Lohmeyer, *op. cit.*, p. 167. In favor of the text adopted by the critical editions and all modern English versions is not only the overwhelming support of the textual tradition but the appropriateness of these words within the Marcan context. Cf. Jn. 7:26; 18:20, where the opposition between open proclamation and secret teaching corresponds to the difference between authoritative, truthful speech and false, heretical doctrine; see M. Smith, *Tannaitic Parallels to the Gospels* (Philadelphia, 1951), pp. 155 f., who finds a polemic note in the contrast between Mk. 4:11 and 8:32.

[76] This statement proved embarrassing in sectors of the early Church and various attempts to soften it or to remove the reference to Peter's rebuke of Jesus are reflected in the textual tradition. Thus sy^s *c k* present Peter in an entirely different light: "But Simon Peter, in order to spare him, spoke to him."

[77] It is difficult to decide what nuance should be heard in the command, ὕπαγε ὀπίσω μου. If this means "away," "get out of my sight," this is the only passage in Mark where ὀπίσω with the genitive is used in the sense of "away from"; in Chs. 1:17, 20; 8:34 it signifies "follow after" as a disciple. The thought may be "return to your rank," i.e., be a true follower of mine and not one who speaks for Satan rather than God.

prophetic utterance. Its intention, like that of most of the OT prophecies, was not to record history in advance but to provide certainty that when these events took place they represented what God had planned and fulfilled. The full import of prophecy cannot be grasped until after the event. That solemn pronouncement, however, has a function beyond the information it conveys concerning Jesus' passion. It follows immediately on verse 30 as the explanation of the stern command not to speak to anyone concerning Jesus' identity. It was not necessary that the people recognize that he is the Messiah until after he had fulfilled his messianic vocation through death and resurrection (Ch. 9:9; 13:9 f.; 14:9; cf. Ch. 4:21-23). This is the only time in Mark that an injunction to silence is explained and it provides the key to all of the previous injunctions to silence. The necessity of the passion in obedience to the will of God accounts for the so-called secrecy phenomena in the Gospel. The "messianic secret" is God's intention to provide salvation through a suffering Savior who is identified with the people by his free decision to bear the burden of judgment upon human rebellion.[78] The repeated injunctions to silence throughout the Gospel of Mark are an expression of Jesus' fidelity to the divine plan of salvation. That plan, though announced in Scripture, was unrecognized in Israel. The function of Jesus' prophetic declaration in verse 31 is to make clear what the disciples could have known had they possessed the thought of God as expressed in Scripture (verse 33). The close association of Ch. 8:31-33 with the declaration of Ch. 8:29 indicates that confession in itself is insufficient to establish Christian faith. Jesus had to lead the disciples beyond messianic confession to an awareness of the dimensions of messiahship as defined by the revealed will of God.

31 In his response to Peter's confession Jesus neither accepted nor refused the designation "Messiah." He spoke of "the Son of Man" who

---

[78] G. Minette de Tillesse, *op. cit.,* p. 321: "The messianic secret expresses in Mark the irrevocable and free decision of Jesus to embrace his passion, because this is the divine will. It is this fact which is expressed by δεῖ, 'must.' If Jesus had allowed his glory as Son of God to shine everywhere, if he had permitted to the crowds their delirious enthusiasm, if he had allowed the demons to howl their servile confession, if he had permitted the apostles to divulge everywhere their sensational discovery, the passion would have been rendered impossible and the destiny of Jesus would have issued in triumph, but a triumph which would have been wholly human (Ch. 8:33) and which would not have accomplished the divine plan of salvation." Cf. pp. 415-417.

could anticipate suffering and rejection issuing in violent death and resurrection, and this disclosure, which is described as new teaching, dominates the remainder of the Gospel. It is generally recognized that "the son of man" is not a genuine Greek idiom, but a literal translation of the Aramaic *bar-nash/bar nasha'*. This expression was in common use, both as a noun (= man) and as a substitute for the indefinite pronoun (= someone, anyone, a certain one) in early as well as in later stages of the development of the Galilean dialect. In a recent fresh examination of the total corpus of early Palestinian Aramaic, G. Vermès has offered conclusive evidence that the idiom sometimes functioned as a circumlocution for "I."[79] It occurs with this meaning primarily in sentences containing an allusion to humiliation, danger or death, although use of the idiom in reference to one's self was sometimes dictated by humility or modesty.[80] Geographically, the idiom is Palestinian-Galilean, and it is well attested in the earliest strata of Galilean Aramaic (represented by the Palestinian Pentateuch Targum, the Jerusalem Talmud and Genesis Rabba). This has important bearing on Ch. 8:31. It indicates that it was not necessary that the disciples should have recognized in Jesus' usage of "the son of man" any more than the circumlocution for "I." The explicit reference to humiliation would account for the indirect idiom. Only in the light of Jesus' subsequent teaching concerning the enthronement and judging function of the Son of Man (Chs. 8:38; 13:26; 14:62) was it possible to recognize an allusion to the mysterious figure of Dan. 7:13 f. to whom God appointed celestial glory, dominion over all nations and an everlasting kingdom. Peter's strong protest was not because he recognized a reference to Dan. 7 or realized the unspeakable incongruity between the transcendent majesty of the Son of Man and Jesus' prophecy of suffering. It was rather the in-

---

[79] "The Use of בר נשא בר נש in Jewish Aramaic," Appendix E in M. Black, *An Aramaic Approach to the Gospels and Acts*[3] (Oxford, 1967), pp. 310-328. Vermès stresses the importance of distinguishing between various types of Aramaic writings and the variety of speech forms. Particularly important are the instances of בר נש in monologues and dialogues, since these provide the true parallel to the Gospels.

[80] *Ibid.*, pp. 320-326. One example may illustrate this idiomatic usage: Jacob of Kefar Nibburaya gave a rabbinic ruling. When his adversary, Rabbi Haggai, heard the ruling he sent Rabbi Jacob the order "Come and be scourged!" to which Rabbi Jacob replied "Should בר נש be scourged who proclaims the word of Scripture?" (Gen. Rabba VII. 2). The use of בר נש as an indirect idiom for "I" is confirmed by the parallel passage, Num. Rabba XIX. 3, which contains the reply of Rabbi Haggai: "Yes, because *you* did not give the right ruling."

congruity between "Messiah" (Ch. 8:29) and Jesus' affirmation which accounts for his reaction. This illustrates the ambiguity of the idiom which made it singularly appropriate to express the tension between concealment and revelation in Jesus' ministry.

Mark clearly understands and intends the old biblical context of Son of Man as defined in the vision of Daniel 7.[81] Even in this first prophetic announcement of his coming suffering Jesus made a veiled allusion to his own identity as the transcendent Son of Man. But in this context Son of Man receives a deep paradoxical meaning; the man of transcendent glory goes the way of suffering and his hidden majesty will be revealed only after his rejection by the leaders of Israel and his violent death. The designation is thus appropriate to a comprehensive theology of history extending from glory (Dan. 7:13 f.) through humiliation (Mk. 8:31) to glory (Mk. 8:38). "Son of Man" occurs fourteen times in the Gospel of Mark. Its significance to the evangelist, as Jesus' own self-designation, deserves special attention. It is useful to distinguish four categories of text:

Son of Man in Mark[82]

A	Ch. 2:10	The authority to forgive sins
	Ch. 2:28	The Lord of the Sabbath
B	Ch. 8:31	Prophecy of the Passion
	Ch. 9:31	Prophecy of the Passion
	Ch. 10:33 f.	Prophecy of the Passion

[81] Many interpreters believe that "Son of Man" in the Gospels reflects an awareness of the apocalyptic tradition found in the so-called "Similitudes of Enoch" (I Enoch 37-71), where "the Son of Man" receives the title "Messiah" (Ch. 48:10; 52:4) and performs vital messianic functions associated with features of the Jewish national hope (Chs. 48:4-10; 53-54; 62-63). The classic study of this material is by E. Sjöberg, *Der Menschensohn im Äthiopischen Henochbuch* (Lund, 1946). The Son of Man in I Enoch is a transcendent heavenly figure who functions as the eschatological judge and is intimately identified with God's elect. Yet he is himself nowhere subjected to humiliation and suffering. Moreover, while the conception in Enoch is dependent on Dan. 7:13 f., the Son of Man is not described as "coming with the clouds" as in Daniel and in Mk. 13:26; 14:62. See now C. Colpe, *TWNT* VIII (1969), pp. 422-429; J. C. Hindley, "Towards a Date for the Similitudes of Enoch. An Historical Approach," *NTS* 14 (1968), pp. 551-565.

[82] For this chart and its discussion I am endebted to G. Minette de Tillesse, *op. cit.*, pp. 364-394.

C	Ch. 9:9	Resurrection
	Ch. 9:12	Sufferings
	Ch. 10:45	His life is a ransom for the many
	Ch. 14:21	Goes (to death)
	Ch. 14:21	Betrayed
	Ch. 14:41	Betrayed
D	Ch. 8:38	Will come in glory
	Ch. 13:26	Will come on the clouds
	Ch. 14:62	Will come on the clouds

The two texts of Group A represent the sole use of Son of Man in the first half of the Gospel and have been shown to represent Mark's use of this designation to indicate the theological significance of an incident for his Christian reader. [83] The six texts of Group C are allusions to the three prophetic announcements of the passion in Group B. The remaining passages (Groups B and D) consist of three cardinal texts announcing Jesus' suffering balanced by three texts promising his parousia in glory. The close formulation between the three texts in each series indicates the importance of this teaching, both historically, at the level of Jesus' ministry to the disciples, and existentially, at the level of the evangelist and his community. There can be no understanding of the gospel (or of the Gospel of Mark) apart from an appropriation of these separate, but related, phases of Jesus' ministry on behalf of the people of God. In the Gospel of Mark there exists a reciprocal relationship between these two series of texts. The open announcement of coming suffering which is made possible by the recognition that Jesus is the Messiah liberates the messianic glory which had remained veiled even in the presence of Jesus' extraordinary works (Ch. 9:1-9). The tension between concealment and openness in the self-revelation of God's Son is thus exhibited in the texts of Groups B and D. Only the eye of faith can perceive the identity between the broken figure upon the cross and the transcendent majesty of the enthroned Son of Man whose coming consummates history and initiates universal judgment.

This paradox indicates how intimately these six cardinal texts are related to "the messianic secret." The nerve-center of the secret is the necessity of the passion in the plan of God. But the manifestation of the glory of the Son of Man is also an integral part of the design for redemp-

---

[83] For "Son of Man" in the Christian community see Acts 7:56; cf. Jn. 9:35 f.; Rev. 1:13; and later texts discussed by C. Colpe, *TWNT* VIII (1969), pp. 466-481.

tion. The incisive promise, "you will see," repeated three times (Chs. 8:38-9:1; 13:26; 14:62), can only refer to an open and definitive unveiling of what God has kept concealed. Only then will it be recognized by all men that the glorious Son of Man entered into his triumph only through rejection and abject humiliation. This is central to Mark's theology, and to the structure of his Gospel. The texts of Groups B and D are complementary: on three occasions Jesus solemnly announces the necessity of his passion, and on three occasions he affirms in awesome fashion the glorious manifestation of the Son of Man.

Reflection upon Ps. 110:1 and Dan. 7:13 f. exercised profound influence upon the formulation of the texts referring to Jesus' enthronement and coming in majesty. It is more difficult to detect the influence of Dan. 7 on the prophecies referring to the sufferings of the Son of Man. In connection with these texts, however, there is an insistence that the key is provided by Scripture (Chs. 9:12; 14:21 "as it is written"; Ch. 8:31 "must," because it is God's announced will). There can be no proper grasp of Mark's theology apart from a recovery of the texts of Scripture to which reference is made. The extent of the biblical nuances can be shown only in a careful examination of the individual passages themselves. It is clear, however, that the prophecies of the passion reflect an identification of the Son of Man with the suffering Servant of the Lord as set forth in Isa. 52:13-53:12.[84] A rich range of texts informed Jesus' understanding of his messianic vocation, but the suffering and atoning work of the Servant appears to have provided the matrix for his reflection upon his mission. Mark does not have to develop this tradition; it already existed in the churches[85] and he presupposes it when he builds the traditional sayings about the destiny of the Son of Man into the heart of his Gospel.

Jesus' interpretation of "Messiah" in terms of a theology of suffering is an index to his realism as well as his awareness of the Father's will.

---

84 Allusions to Isa. 53 were present in the tradition which Mark received (see on Chs. 8:31; 9:12, 31; 10:45; 14:24). This needs to be reaffirmed in the face of a growing tendency to see little, if any, Isaianic influence on the formulation (e.g. M. D. Hooker, *Jesus and the Servant* [London, 1959]; *idem, The Son of Man in Mark* [London, 1967]). For a positive assessment of this influence see J. Jeremias, *The Servant of God in the New Testament* (Chicago, 1957), pp. 96 f.; J. Coppens, "Le fils d'homme daniélique et les relectures de Dan., VII, 13, dans les apocryphes et les écrits du Nouveau Testament," *Eph Th Lov* 37 (1961), pp. 5-51.

85 E.g. Rom. 4:25 ("he was put to death for our trespasses") reproduces exactly the Targum to Isa. 53:5; cf. Rom. 8:32.

The scribes regarded him as blasphemous (Ch. 2:7) and demonic (Ch. 3:22-30); the legal provisions against men deemed "heretics" or "seducing prophets" were explicit; the murder of John the Baptist indicated the destiny of God's appointed messengers (Ch. 6:17-29; cf. Ch. 12:2-8). The Scriptures were explicit that the Servant of the Lord experiences rejection, stark humiliation and death on behalf of the people of God. These several strands of prophecy and experience are drawn together in the solemn declaration that the Son of Man must suffer many things. [86]

The necessity, under which Jesus' suffering, death and resurrection stand, belongs to the mysterious divine work of judgment and salvation in the last time. The statement that the Son of Man *must* suffer many things points to the overruling purpose of God and reflects Jesus' conviction that the intention revealed in Scripture attains its fulfilment in the shame of the crucifixion as well as in the triumph of the resurrection. The disciples may behold in Jesus' submission to the divine will the perfect human response to the regal claims of God. If the formula "suffer many things" stands under the influence of Isa. 53:4, 11 it is equivalent to "bear (the sins of) many" (cf. Ch. 10:45). In the light of Isa. 53, Jesus' humiliation is an obedient suffering in execution of a divine commission. [87] The extent of this humiliation is defined in terms of rejection and violent death. Jesus asserts that he will be made the object of the testing wisdom and insight of the Jewish authorities, and will be rejected. An allusion to Ps. 118:22 is confirmed by Ch. 12:10, where Jesus quotes the passage about the rejected stone precisely before

---

[86] An introduction to the extensive literature on Son of Man and the complexity of the issues is offered by J. Coppens and L. Dequeker, *Le Fils de l'Homme et les Saints du Très Haut en Danièl VII, dans les Apocryphes et dans le Nouveau Testament* (Louvain, 1961); O. Cullmann, *The Christology of the New Testament*² (Philadelphia, 1963), pp. 137-192; A. J. B. Higgins, *Jesus and the Son of Man* (London, 1964); H. E. Tödt, *The Son of Man in the Synoptic Tradition* (Philadelphia, 1965); J. Jeremias, *Abba* (Göttingen, 1966), pp. 15-67, 139-152, 191-229; F. H. Borsch, *The Son of Man in Myth and History* (London, 1967); C. Colpe, *TWNT* VIII (1969), pp. 403-481; I. H. Marshall, "The Synoptic Son of Man Sayings in Recent Discussion," *NTS* 12 (1965-66), pp. 327-351; R. Maddox, "The Function of the Son of Man according to the Synoptic Gospels," *NTS* 15 (1968-69), pp. 45-74; M. Black, "The 'Son of Man' Passion Sayings in the Gospel Tradition," *ZNW* 60 (1969), pp. 1-8; A. J. B. Higgins, "Is the Son of Man Problem Insoluble?" in *Neotestamentica et Semitica*, ed. E. E. Ellis and M. Wilcox (Edinburgh, 1969), pp. 70-87.

[87] See W. Michaelis, *TWNT* V (Eng. Tr. 1968), pp. 914-916; C. Maurer, "Knecht Gottes und Sohn Gottes im Passionsbericht des Markusevangeliums," *ZThK* 50 (1953), pp. 1-38.

the high priests, scribes and elders (cf. Ch. 11:27; Acts 4:11).[88] The reference to these three prominent classes of men who together constituted the Sanhedrin indicates the totality of the failure to recognize Jesus and stresses that all of the leaders of Israel must equally assume responsibility for the rejection of the Son (cf. Ch. 14:64). The general term "and be killed" implies a violent death (cf. I Thess. 2:14) but provides no hint of crucifixion. The form that Jesus' death would assume was not apparent until the crisis of the conflict with authority in Ch. 15.[89] The precise nature of the humiliation and its inscrutable paradox were only very gradually revealed to the disciples.

Jesus' prophecy announced not only suffering and death, but victory and vindication expressed through resurrection (cf. Ch. 9:9, 31; 10:34; 14:28). In Isaiah the final triumph of the Servant is presented as a triumph over death itself (Isa. 52:13; 53:10-12), and this assurance is reflected in Jesus' reference to his own resurrection after three days. The fundamental OT passage on resurrection in the first century, however, was Hos. 6:1 f. Hosea spoke about the national revival by God of a contrite and repentant Israel: "Come, let us return to the Lord; for he has torn, that he may heal us; he has stricken, and he will bind us up–after two days he will revive us; on the third day he will raise us up, that we may live before him." By the first century the passage had come to be interpreted eschatologically of the consolation of Israel in the last days, sealed by resurrection. This interpretation is reflected in the Targum read in the synagogue in connection with the call to repentance in preparation for the Day of Atonement:

> "They will say: Come, and let us return to the service of the Lord; for he who has smitten us will heal us; and he who has brought ruin upon us will give us rest.
> He will revive us on the days of consolation which are about to come;
> On the day of the resurrection of the dead he will raise us up and we shall be revived before him."

---

[88] In rabbinic literature Ps. 118:22 is applied to Abraham (Pirqe Rabbi Eliezer 24) and to David (TB *Pesaḥim* 149a; Targum to Ps. 118:22 f.), types of the righteous man who is shamefully treated by men in authority. Only in medieval Jewish writings was it applied to a rejected Messiah. See S-B*K* I (1922), pp. 875 f.

[89] Apart from a single metaphorical use of "cross" in Ch. 8:34, neither the substantive nor the verb "to crucify" occurs in Mark until Ch. 15, which is concerned with the actual crucifixion. There the words occur 10 times.

Reflection upon this interpretation of Hos. 6:2 also may have informed Jesus' conviction concerning his resurrection "after three days." [90] While there is some evidence that "after three days" can be regarded in a Semitic context as equivalent to "on the third day" (Gen. 42:17 f.; II Chron. 10:5, 12), it is probable that Jesus' reference to three days was an indefinite expression for a short period of time. A conviction, grounded upon Scripture, was that "the Holy One, blessed be he, does not leave his own in distress for more than three days." [91] The reference to resurrection already points forward to Ch. 8:38 where Jesus warns the people of the Son of Man's enthronement as eschatological judge. The opposition and rejection experienced at the hands of Israel's leaders will be overturned in startling fashion.

32-33 When the disciples looked back upon Jesus' statement they were amazed at the openness with which he had spoken to them. Even in private discourse he had never spoken as clearly concerning his mission and destiny as he did on this occasion. Mark's term for open speech denotes an outspokenness that conceals nothing. The comment that Jesus was speaking the word openly indicates the decisive character of this incident in the context of Jesus' persistent use of veiled, parabolic speech (Ch. 4:33 f.). Peter's reaction shows that it was impossible to miss what Jesus intended to say, even though the divine necessity for his suffering appeared inconceivable.

Mark describes Peter's impetuous action in sharp terms, employing the same strong vocable used throughout the Gospel in connection with the silencing of the demons: he *rebuked* Jesus (cf. 1:25; 3:12). How difficult it was to reconcile the designation "Messiah" and suffering is well illustrated by the Targum to Isa. 53, where the positive statements are interpreted to refer to King Messiah but the sufferings to the people. [92]

---

[90] So J. Dupont, "Ressuscité 'le troisième jour'," *Biblica* 40 (1959), pp. 742-761; M. Black, "The 'Son of Man' Passion Sayings in the Gospel Tradition," *ZNW* 60 (1969), pp. 5-8.

[91] Midrash Tehillim on Ps. 22, § 5, with allusions to Gen. 22:4; 42:17; Ex. 15:22; II Kings 20:5; Isa. 2:16; Jonah 2:1; Hos. 6:1 f. Cf. J. B. Bauer, "Drei Tage," *Biblica* 39 (1958), pp. 354-358 for other examples of "three days" indicating an indefinite short period.

[92] It is a matter of debate whether the Targum to Isa. 53 represents the form of the Targum actually used in the first decades of the first century or whether it reflects a deliberate redaction influenced by later Jewish-Christian polemics centered in the prophecy of the suffering Servant. See G. Minette de Tillesse, *op. cit.*, p. 387 and n. 5 for the pertinent bibliography.

The rebuke indicates that Jesus' declaration was radically new and that the disciples were totally unprepared to receive it: a rejected Messiah was incompatible with Jewish convictions and hopes. Peter's reaction was therefore understandable but presumptuous, and it is not allowed to stand.

The presence of the other disciples, who undoubtedly shared Peter's conviction that Jesus was wrong, necessitated a sharp and open rebuke. Jesus called them to witness that he resolutely refused the temptation represented in Peter's words. It had been appointed by God that the Messiah was to achieve victory over the forces of evil in the world through the shame of the cross. The suggestion that he should refuse the passion may be construed as a temptation coming from Satan himself who desires to thwart the divine plan of salvation (cf. Chs. 1:12 f.; 3:23 ff.).[93] The sharpness of the rebuke stems from the suggestion of disobedience to God's will and the frustration of a course of events which will lead to the enthronement of the Son of Man, the achievement of the salvation of his elect, and the judgment of the world (Ch. 8:38). Jesus, therefore, unmasks the source of Peter's thought and commands him to return to his rank as a true disciple. His response to Jesus' solemn prophecy betrayed no higher level than that characteristic of unregenerate human nature. An inability to accept a suffering Savior involves the refusal of the will of God, whose sovereign disposition of the problem of sin and human rebellion fails to conform to the niceties of human expectations (cf. Isa. 55:8 f.). Jesus shows no inclination to justify the ways of God to men. He simply affirms that the way of the cross is the will of God.

2. The Requirements for Following Jesus. Chs. 8:34-9:1

34 And he called unto him the multitude with his disciples, and said unto them, If any man would come[94] after me, let him deny himself, and take up his cross, and follow me.

---

[93] See B. Noack, *Satanás und Sotería* (Lund, 1948); W. Foerster, *TWNT* VII (1964), pp. 158 f.

[94] The variant text "to follow," supported by P[45] C* 𝔎 D W Θ λ 22 28 157 565 700 *pl* latt sa aeth Origen apparently reflects assimilation to the form of the saying in Mt. 10:38.

35 For whosoever would save his life[95] shall lose it;[96] and whosoever shall lose his life for my sake and[97] the gospel's shall save it.
36 For what doth it profit a man, to gain the whole world, and forfeit his life?
37 For what should a man give in exchange for his life?
38 For whosoever shall be ashamed of me and of my words[98] in this adulterous and sinful generation, the Son of Man also shall be ashamed of him, when he cometh in the glory of his Father with the holy angels.
9:1 And he said unto them, Verily I say unto you, There are some here of them that stand *by,* who shall in no wise taste of death,[99] till they see the kingdom of God come with power.

This section consists of a group of short, pungent sayings which concern personal commitment to Jesus in circumstances which require courage

---

95 Gr. ψυχή, which presupposes a continuity with OT usage where נֶפֶשׁ designates man in his totality, his vitality, his profound dynamism which includes his appetite for the good things of life but also his frailty threatened by death. See now G. Dautzenberg, *Sein Leben bewahren. Ψυχή in den Herrenworten der Evangelien* (München, 1966).

96 This expression presupposes the Semitic idiom אִבֵּד נַפְשׁוֹ, "to trifle away one's life." This idiom always presupposes an active element which may not be apparent in "lose"; it implies that the loss is attributable to the will or the fault of the one who suffers it. See A. Oepke, *TWNT* I (Eng. Tr. 1964), pp. 394 f., who refers to Sifre Numbers § 131 which refers to individuals who spoiled their lives through their own acts, which brought them to destruction.

97 P45 D 28 700 it (some MSS) sys aeth arm Origen omit ἐμοῦ καί, which results in the reading "whosoever shall lose his life for the sake of the gospel." The omission may be accidental.

98 Gr. με καὶ τοὺς ἐμοὺς λόγους. W *k** sa Tertullian omit λόγους, which yields "whoever shall be ashamed of me and mine" (i.e. Jesus' followers). This reading is accepted as primitive by C. H. Turner, "Marcan Usage," *JThS* 29 (1927-28), p. 2; T. A. Burkill, *op. cit.,* p. 170 n. 3, among others. The only other example of ἐμός in the Gospel occurs in Ch. 10:40 where ἐμόν = "mine." Moreover, D it (some MSS) syc Origen omit λόγους in the parallel passage, Lk. 9:26. The formulation "me and my words," however, is analogous to "for my sake and the gospel's" in verse 35 and should be retained with the vast number of MSS.

99 To "taste death" is a Semitism unknown to the OT (cf. "the bitterness of death," I Sam. 15:32), although there are several examples of this formula in rabbinic literature: e.g. Genesis Rabba to 1:31; 3:22; TB *Yoma* 78b; cf. Heb. 2:9. R. Le Déaut, "Goûter le calice de la mort," *Biblica* 43 (1962), pp. 82-86 has called attention to two clear examples of the expression "to taste the cup of death" in Codex Neofiti I, the complete recension of the Palestinian Pentateuch Targum (to Deut. 32:1). The expression is otherwise extremely rare.

and sacrifice. They appear to have been brought together in the tradition or by the evangelist through catchword association. They reflect similar formulation and vocabulary.[100] Mark includes this unit, which concerns essential requirements for being a follower of Jesus, because of a strong pastoral concern for his own people. Here he speaks beyond the historical situation in Jesus' ministry to a church harassed by persecution, their ranks decimated by the subtle as well as more overt pressures exerted against Christians in imperial Rome. Mark shows that this situation is quite normal. Jesus had called his own disciples to the realization that suffering is not only his destiny but theirs. The humiliation of the Messiah, announced in Ch. 8:31, is the mysterious prototype of that of the Christian. But even as Jesus spoke of death followed by resurrection, his followers may look beyond a pagan tribunal to the tribunal of the Son of Man where loyalty to Jesus will be honored with vindication. This unit amounts to a call for complete and confident identification with Christ.

34 The reference to the crowd is sudden and unexpected (cf. Ch. 7:15; 8:1), but serves a vital function in the narrative. By calling the crowd Jesus indicates that the conditions for following him are relevant for all believers, and not for the disciples alone. This had important implications for the Christians in Rome and elsewhere. It indicated that the stringent demand for self-renunciation and cross-bearing extends not only to Church leaders but to all who confess that Jesus is the Messiah. It was the Lord's intention that those who follow him should not be detached observers of his passion, but men who grow in faith and understanding through participation in his sufferings. Only in following on the way to the cross is it possible to understand either the necessity of Jesus' humiliation or Jesus himself. The common address of these sober words to the crowd and the disciples recognizes that there is no essential difference between them when confronted with the sufferings of Christ: both alike have very human thoughts uninformed by the will of God

---

100 The first five statements are connected by γάρ, and the sixth by Mark's usual formula for concluding a discourse or introducing a paraphrase of a much longer conversation, καὶ ἔλεγεν αὐτοῖς. Εἴ τις θέλει (34) corresponds to ὃς γὰρ ἐὰν θέλῃ (35); τί γὰρ ὠφελεῖ (36) corresponds to τί γὰρ δοῖ (37); verses 35-37 are joined together by the catchword ψυχή; verse 38 and Ch. 9:1 reflect the same sentence structure and word order, ὅταν ἔλθῃ . . . corresponding to ἕως ἂν ἴδωσιν . . . See J. Sundwall, *Die Zusammensetzung des Markus-Evangeliums* (Åbo, 1934), pp. 56 f.

(Ch. 8:33), and it was imperative for them to know what it means to follow Jesus. Precisely in following on the way to the cross the distinction between a privileged group and those outside (Ch. 4:11) disappears.[101] "Following" in this context does not possess the technical meaning of "discipleship," but refers to that common commitment to Jesus which distinguishes all Christians from those who fail to recognize him as God's appointed Savior.[102]

Jesus stipulated that those who wish to follow him must be prepared to shift the center of gravity in their lives from a concern for self to reckless abandon to the will of God. The central thought in self-denial is a disowning of any claim that may be urged by the self, a sustained willingness to say 'No' to oneself in order to be able to say 'Yes' to God. This involves a radical denunciation of all self-idolatry and of every attempt to establish one's own life in accordance with the dictates of the self.[103] This demand is reinforced and intensified by the horrifying image of a death march. Bearing the cross was not a Jewish metaphor, and Jesus' statement must have sounded repugnant to the crowd and the disciples alike. The saying evokes the picture of a condemned man going out to die who is forced to carry on his back the cross-beam upon which he is to be nailed at the place of execution.[104] By the time Mark prepared his Gospel this had become cruel reality, both for Jesus

---

101 E. Schweizer, "Zur Frage des Messiasgeheimnis bei Markus," *ZNW* 56 (1965), pp. 1-8. On "the crowd" in Mark see K. Tagawa, *op. cit.*, p. 59; G. Minette de Tillesse, *op. cit.*, pp. 415 f.

102 On this distinction see R. P. Meye, *op. cit.*, pp. 122-125; H. Kahlefeld, "Jünger des Herrn," *Geist und Leben* 30 (1957), pp. 1-6. Both of these studies stress that discipleship implies the will of Jesus that specific men should follow him and their response. Ch. 8:34 is not a call to discipleship but a statement regarding the conditions for *following* Jesus.

103 H. Schlier, *TWNT* I (Eng. Tr. 1964), pp. 469-471.

104 D. R. Fletcher, "Condemned to Die. The Logion on Cross-Bearing: What does it Mean?" *Interpretation* 18 (1964), pp. 156-164: "Every hour is the last hour. Every successive hour and day, self is to be found by being lost. Let the disciple refuse himself: let him think constantly as one who feels the weight of the hateful beam across his back and knows himself condemned to die. This is his existential calling while the reign of God is being brought in" (p. 164). While the metaphor is not found in older rabbinic literature, death under the Romans was a sufficiently familiar sight in Palestine to provide the basis of the saying. The Roman governor of Syria, Varus, was credited with having crucified 2,000 Jews (Josephus, *Ant.* XVII. x. 4-10; cf. *War* II. xii. 6, xiv. 9; V. xi. 1). On this saying see further A. Fridrichsen, "Sich selbst verleugnen," *Coniectanea Neotestamentica* 2 (1936), pp. 1-3; J. Schneider, *TWNT* VII (1964), pp. 577-579.

and the Church. Jesus' words were a sober caution that the commitment for which he asked permitted no turning back, and if necessary, a willingness to submit to the cross in pursuance of the will of God. His followers must be prepared to die, for they share in the same veiledness that permits his own humiliation. The call to follow Jesus, which recapitulates the action in which self-denial and cross-bearing are to be manifested, provides a vivid reminder that suffering with the Messiah is the condition of glorification with him (Rom. 8:17).

35 This statement, which exposes the ambivalent concept of life, follows meaningfully the call to disown self and to be prepared to sacrifice life itself in verse 34. The irreplaceability of life, which is considered elemental for earthly existence, is shown to be the crucial issue in reference to eternal existence. Jesus' words envision men before a court where denial of association with him will bring release while affirmation of "Jesus and the gospel" issues in martyrdom. He thoroughly appreciates the frailty of human life threatened by death, but warns that the man who seeks to secure his own existence by denial of his Lord brings about his own destruction. Paradoxically, the man who yields his life in loyalty to Jesus safeguards it in a deeper sense. The contrast between ordinary human life and life as the expression of the eschatological salvation which Jesus provides in verse 35b indicates the irony in the alternation between "save" and "suffer loss" in verse 35a. It defines an opposition corresponding in sharpness to the distinction between eternal loss and salvation. Jesus' pregnant statement deals realistically with the concrete, existential character of the dynamism of life. The theology of life affirmed is grounded in the paradox that a man can guarantee that dynamism only by sacrificing it.[105]

The context in which denial or confession is determinative of life is "Jesus and the gospel." The absoluteness of Jesus' claim upon the allegiance of man to his own person was affirmed unequivocally here for the first time. Prior to this it was possible to hear a call for commitment to his message, but now the locus of commitment is Jesus himself. The identity between Jesus and the message is underlined by the reference to suffering for the gospel, which is found only in Mark, and may have been added by the evangelist as an explanatory comment with

---

[105] G. Dautzenberg, *op. cit.*, pp. 51-64. Rabbinic "parallels" are exceedingly rare; cf. Aboth de Rabbi Nathan II. 35 "Whoever preserves one word of the Law preserves his life, and whoever blots out one word of the Law will lose his life."

particular relevance to the Christians in Rome.[106] In the second half of Mark "the gospel" always denotes the message announced by the Church, of which Jesus is the content (Chs. 8:35; 10:29; 13:10; 14:9), precisely as in Ch. 1:1. Mark knew experientially that for the gospel men abandoned their goods (Ch. 10:29) and gave their lives (Ch. 8:35). It is possible that he has preserved an early Christian slogan, "for Christ and the gospel," for which believers suffered and overcame.[107]

36-37 In developing the thought of the supreme value of life in its deepest sense, Jesus employed language drawn from commercial life: profit, gain, loss, give in exchange. A comparison of values is the proper setting for a consideration of profit and loss. Corresponding to the advantage gained–the whole world–is the payment which must be forfeited–authentic life.[108] But the ledger involves values which cannot really be compared. The loss even of ordinary human life is in no way compensated by winning the world; how much more is this true of eternal life! The pointed rhetorical questions of verses 36-37 suggest reflection on Ps. 49:7-9, where the Psalmist is speaking of men "who trust in their wealth and boast of the abundance of their riches": "Truly no man can ransom himself, or give to God the price of his life, for the ransom of his life is costly and can never suffice that he should continue to live on forever, and never see the Pit." The absurdity of the man who secures his own life (verse 35a) in preference to participation in the salvation provided by God (verse 35b) emphasizes the fateful consequences of denying Jesus, even when human life is at stake. When a man has forfeited eternal life, he experiences absolute loss, even though he may have won the approval of the whole world with his denial of Jesus and the gospel.

38 Each of Jesus' successive statements reinforced the irony of verse 35a, that the man who gains his life through denial of Jesus and the gospel suffers infinite loss. The character of the loss is now defined with

[106] F. J. McCool, *Formatio Traditionis Evangelicae* (Rome, 1955), pp. 72-74.

[107] E. Lohmeyer, *op. cit.*, p. 171; G. Minette de Tillesse, *op. cit.*, pp. 404-409; W. Marxsen, *Der Evangelist Markus*² (Göttingen, 1963), pp. 77-101.

[108] A. Stumpff, *TWNT* II (Eng. Tr. 1964), pp. 888 f.: If the reference is to winning the world in terms of missionary outreach, "the loss is one which can be incurred in and with this activity." The continuation in verse 38 suggests rather that what is involved is winning *the approval of the world* through denial of Jesus and the gospel.

reference to the final judgment which has been committed to the Son of Man. Verse 38 is parallel in structure to verse 35 and complementary in intention. It returns to the situation envisioned in verse 35 and carries it to its final consequences. The motive for denial of Jesus and his words is shame born out of an anxiety for one's life and a basic unwillingness to be made an object of contempt in the world.[109] Ashamed of past association with the Lord, the decision to seek approval from the world rather than from him exposes the Lord himself to contempt. This defines the seriousness of denial in terms of its immediate consequences for the world before whom Jesus and the gospel must be confessed. The world is defined qualitatively as "an adulterous and sinful generation," an expression colored by the strictures of the prophets against idolatry (cf. Isa. 1:4, 21; Ezek. 16:32; Hos. 2:4). Denial confirms the world in its idolatrous character and approves the unfaithfulness to God expressed in its rejection of Jesus and of those who display uncompromising loyalty to him.

Denial, however, entails ultimate consequences for the man who is ashamed of Jesus, for the Son of Man will expose him to contempt when he comes to execute the final judgment. Jesus' veiled reference to his future role is appropriate because of the presence of the crowd. This is the only occasion when Jesus used the designation "Son of Man" publicly prior to his arraignment before the High Priest, where he spoke in circumstances of the utmost veiledness (Ch. 14:62), and his reserve is consistent with the messianic veiledness throughout his ministry. The critical opinion that Jesus spoke of the Son of Man as a person distinct from himself reflects a failure to perceive the eschatological and literary parallelism in this statement, in which an element of the first clause is introduced in a different manner in the second clause. In verse 38a Jesus refers to himself in the first person; in verse 38b he refers to himself by the designation most appropriate to the glory of the parousia when he will come for judgment. The statement receives its pregnant significance precisely because Jesus and the Son of Man are the *same*

---

[109] The Shepherd of Hermas exposes the situation of Christians in Rome in the early second century in terms reminiscent of Mk. 8:38; e.g. *Similitudes* IX. xiv. 6: "Do you see then whom he [the Son of God] supports? Those who bear his name with their whole heart. He then was their foundation and he supports them joyfully, because they are not ashamed to bear his name"; IX. xxi. 3: "the double-minded, when they hear of affliction, become idolaters through their cowardice, and they are ashamed of the name of their Lord."

person, and the denial of Jesus entails the denial of the final Judge himself.[110] For this startling reason the criterion for a man's acceptance or rejection before the Son of Man is his loyalty or disloyalty to Jesus now. The judgment of those who range themselves against Jesus is the corollary of the vindication and salvation of those who have faithfully followed him. The underlying irony in the situation depicted derives from the veiledness which characterized Jesus' earthly ministry: he is one of whom men may be ashamed, but he will be openly revealed as the one who possesses the glory of his Father.

The reference to the Father's glory and to the accompanying train of angels (cf. Ch. 13:26 f.) serves to set Jesus' entire ministry in a doxological perspective. Jesus was sent to reveal the glory of God in a world whose intoxication with its own glory is well expressed in the thought of gaining the world (Ch. 8:36). He can accomplish his mission only if his own glory means nothing to him and the Father's glory means everything. For Jesus this required submission to the contempt and shame of the cross. But God does not fail to recognize his self-renunciation and cross-bearing, and the hour comes when the Son of Man is exhibited glorified by the Father for whose sole glory he lived and died.[111] This had immediate relevance for the persecuted and justly frightened Christians in Mark's congregation. In Jesus' own commitment to the Father they possessed a paradigm for their commitment to him and to the gospel. The sober words of Ch. 8:34-38 represented not theoretical reflections but the law of life by which Jesus gauged his own conduct in a world hostile to God. His vindication and coming triumph provided assurance that they would share in his glory if they held fast their commitment to him (cf. Ch. 13:9-13).

---

110 M. Black, *op. cit.*, pp. 3-5; R. Maddox, *op. cit.*, pp. 49 f.
111 E. Stauffer, *op. cit.*, pp. 28 f.

CHAPTER 9

1 The introductory formula, "and he was saying to them," indicates that Jesus' solemn affirmation is the conclusion to a larger discourse of which only the most salient point has been preserved (see on Ch. 2:27). Ch. 9:1 serves an important function in the structure of Chs. 8:34-9:1. The call to responsible commitment (Ch. 8:34) is followed by the contrast between a man who secures his own existence through denial and one who is killed because of his unwavering confession of Jesus and the gospel (Ch. 8:35). The statements which follow explore the consequences of denial (Ch. 8:36-38), but refer only by implication to those whose commitment will lead to their death. Absolute allegiance to Jesus demands response, and this is provided in Ch. 9:1. In context, Jesus' prophecy is a word of comfort addressed to those who heed his call to follow him in spite of the cost involved. The Semitism "taste death" alludes to the harsh reality of violent death contemplated in Ch. 8:35b; men who are faithful to Jesus and the gospel will lose their lives. But they are given the assurance that this anomalous situation is for a determined period of time and they shall see an open manifestation of God's sovereignty "with power." The solemn introduction with which Jesus prefaces his words, "Amen, I say to you," guarantees their truthfulness. His promise is grounded upon absolute certainty.[1]

It has been shown that in the Gospel of Mark the Kingdom of God and the person of Jesus are so integrally bound together as to be inseparable.[2] This has important bearing on Ch. 9:1. The concept of "the Kingdom of God come with power," like the concept of the Son of Man

---

[1] See on Ch. 3:28; 8:12. The presence of the "Amen" formula has important bearing on the authenticity of this saying. "No evidence [exists] that the early Church felt free to create sayings prefaced with the solemn asseveration ἀμὴν λέγω ὑμῖν." See A. Moore, *The Parousia in the New Testament* (Leiden, 1966), pp. 175-177. Moore surveys the wide range of interpretation provoked by Ch. 9:1 on pp. 92-107, 125-131; cf. C. E. B. Cranfield, *The Gospel according to Saint Mark*[2] (Cambridge, 1963), pp. 286-288, 484 f.

[2] See on Ch. 1:14 f.; 4:11. The Kingdom has been brought near with Jesus' coming; his authority and power in confronting powers hostile to God signal its real, though proleptic, presence. Nevertheless, the presence of the Kingdom in Jesus' person and work remains a secret far removed from the obvious, irrefutable, unambiguous display of sovereignty men would have welcomed. This inherent tension is basic to Chs. 8:34-9:1.

coming with glory (Ch. 8:38), has a strictly Christocentric orientation. It refers to an event which provides an open manifestation of Jesus' dignity. Jesus' solemn affirmation expresses from a different perspective the fundamental surprise enunciated in Ch. 8:38: the ambiguity of the situation in which God's sovereignty may be questioned, his anointed emissary treated with contempt, and his people exposed to shame will be resolved in a revelation of definitive power. Essential to both Ch. 8:38 and Ch. 9:1 is the contrast between concealment and revelation which expresses the tension between the hidden character of Jesus' earthly ministry and his manifestation in glory and power at the consummation. The function and the perspective of these two passages, however, is not the same. Ch. 8:38 served to warn those who choose to stand with the world in its contempt for Jesus that his apparent weakness and openness to humiliation will be reversed in an awesome manifestation of his glory as the eschatological Judge. The function of Ch. 9:1, with its reference to "the Kingdom come with power," is to provide certainty that the Son of Man will indeed come with glory, and that those who now share his sufferings will also share in his exaltation.[3] Its reference is to an event sufficiently near that certain individuals present will be privileged to see a manifestation of the sovereignty of God in a triumphal unveiling of Jesus' dignity.[4] Nothing short of this can satisfy the expectation prompted by Jesus' promise, which is intended to strengthen the people of God for their coming ordeal. The tension of their own "hiddenness" in a world which seeks to lead them to denial and which heaps abuse upon them when they are steadfast is acute, and requires an open manifestation of God's sovereignty.

The immediate sequel to Jesus' solemn promise is the account of the transfiguration (Ch. 9:2-8). This indicates that Mark understood Jesus' statement to refer to this moment of transcendent glory conceived as

---

[3] The relationship between Ch. 8:38 and Ch. 9:1 reflects an old biblical pattern. In the OT the assurance that God will intervene decisively in history is based on his past and present activity in redemptive history. Corresponding to this, Ch. 9:1 announces an event soon to be accomplished which will provide fresh evidence of God's sovereign direction of history toward the consummation when the Son of Man will be revealed in glory (Ch. 8:38).

[4] A. Moore, *op. cit.*, p. 127 n. 4 rightly stresses that in Ch. 9:1 it is not said that death will exclude some of those present from seeing the announced event. All that is required by Jesus' statement is that "some" will see a further irruption of the power and sovereignty of God before they experience the suffering foreseen in Ch. 8:34-35. The basis of selection is left entirely unspecified.

an enthronement and an anticipation of the glory which is to come.[5] It is instructive to compare II Peter 1:16-18, which speaks of "the power and the parousia of our Lord Jesus Christ." Peter made known to his churches the power *that was to be revealed* at Jesus' coming in terms of the glory *which had been revealed* in the transfiguration. This expresses precisely the relationship between Ch. 8:38 (parousia) and Ch. 9:1 (transfiguration). The transfiguration was a momentary, but real (and witnessed) manifestation of Jesus' sovereign power which pointed beyond itself to the parousia, when he will come "with power and glory" (Ch. 13:26).[6] The fulfilment of Jesus' promise a short time later (Ch. 9:2) provided encouragement to the harassed Christians in Rome and elsewhere that their commitment to Jesus and the gospel was valid. The parousia is an absolute certainty. The transfiguration constituted a warning to all others that the ambiguity which permits the humiliation of Jesus and of those faithful to him will be resolved in the decisive intervention of God promised in Ch. 8:38.[7]

3. The Transfiguration: the Glory of the Son. Ch. 9:2-8

2 After six days Jesus taketh with him Peter, and James, and John, and bringeth them up into a high mountain apart by themselves: and he was transfigured[8] before them;

---

[5] Cf. S. S. Smalley, "The Delay of the Parousia," *JBL* 83 (1964), pp. 41-46; J. Schierse, "Historische Kritik und theologische Exegese der synoptischen Evangelien erläutert an Mk. 9, 1," *Scholastik* 29 (1959), pp. 520-536. The transfiguration is full of overtones suggesting the parousia: the emphasis on the visible manifestation of Jesus' dignity (Ch. 9:2, 4, 8-9), the cloud reminiscent of God's self-revelation and self-veiling, the voice in confirmation of Jesus' sonship. The command to listen to him reinforces the challenge of Ch. 8:34-38.

[6] It also points proleptically to the resurrection, although Mark does not stress this until Ch. 9:9. The Roman Church was familiar with the (pre-Pauline) Palestinian confession that Jesus had been declared the Son of God *with power* through the resurrection (Rom. 1:3-5; cf. II Tim. 2:8). Cf. H. N. Ridderbos, *The Coming of the Kingdom* (Philadelphia, 1962), pp. 503-507.

[7] Cf. E. Trocmé, "Marc 9, 1: Prédiction ou Réprimande?" in *Studia Evangelica*, ed. F. L. Cross (Berlin, 1964), pp. 259-265.

[8] Gr. μετεμορφώθη describes a transformation that is outwardly visible. Cf. J. Behm, *TWNT* IV (Eng. Tr. 1967), pp. 755-759: "The miracle of transformation from an earthly form into a supraterrestrial, which is denoted by the radiance of the garments, has nothing whatever to do with metamorphosis in the Hellenistic sense but suggests the context of apocalyptic ideas" (p. 758). See Dan. 12:3; II Baruch 51:3, 5, 10, 12; I Enoch 38:4; 104:2; IV Ezra 7:97.

3 and his garments became glistening, exceeding white, so as no
fuller[9] on earth can whiten them.
4 And there appeared unto them Elijah with Moses: and they
were talking with Jesus.
5 And Peter answereth and saith to Jesus, Rabbi, it is good for
us to be here: and let us make[10] three tabernacles,[11] one for
thee, and one for Moses, and one for Elijah.
6 For he knew not what to answer; for they became sore afraid.
7 And there came a cloud overshadowing[12] them: and there
came a voice out of the cloud, This is my beloved Son:[13] hear
ye him.
8 And suddenly looking round about, they saw no one any more,
save Jesus only with themselves.

In Mark, the transfiguration is a dramatic indication of the resplendent glory which belongs to Jesus as God's unique Son. As a revelation of the concealed splendor of the Son of Man, the event points forward to the advent promised in Ch. 8:38, when Jesus' status as the eschatological Judge will be manifested to the world. The episode provides a personal

---

9 A fuller is one who cleans and prepares woollen cloth by the use of nitrium ("fuller's earth").

10 A characteristic Marcan construction (cf. Chs. 10:36, 51; 14:12; 15:9) is found in Caesarean and Western texts which insert θέλεις before ποιήσωμεν: "Do you wish us to make . . . ?" For a defense of this reading, supported by D W Θ φ 543 565 *b ff*² *i*, see C. H. Turner, "Marcan Usage," *JThS* 29 (1927), p. 3.

11 Gr. σκηνάς. It is difficult to know which nuance is appropriate to "tabernacles," since σκηνή is used to translate סֻכָּה, "booth" (Lev. 23:42 f.), in which case Peter is thinking of the shelters made of intertwined branches which were used in connection with the Feast of Tabernacles, or אֹהֶל, "tent," in which case the reference is to the Tent of Meeting where God met with Moses (Ex. 27:1). See the discussion of H. Bornhäuser, *Sukka* (Giessen, 1935), pp. 126-128; H. Riesenfeld, *Jésus transfiguré* (Lund, 1947), pp. 146-205; W. Michaelis, "Zelt und Hütte im biblischen Denken," *Ev Th* 14 (1954), pp. 24-49; *idem, TWNT* VII (1964), pp. 369-382; W. R. Roehrs, "God's Tabernacles among Men – A Study of the Transfiguration," *ConThMon* 35 (1964), pp. 18-25.

12 Gr. ἐπισκιάζειν, which here has the nuance of enveloping or concealing, rather than "overshadowing." See A. Oepke, *TWNT* IV (Eng. Tr. 1967), pp. 908 f.

13 This expression contains an allusion to Gen. 22:2, 12, 16, where ὁ υἱός ὁ ἀγαπητός means "only son"; cf. Mk. 12:6. God proclaims, This is my Isaac. For this understanding see C. H. Turner, "Ο ΥΙΟΣ ΜΟΥ Ο ἈΓΑΠΗΤΟΣ," *JThS* 27 (1926), pp. 113-129; and for the Isaac typology, E. Best, *The Temptation and the Passion* (Cambridge, 1965), pp. 169-173. On the targumic association of the sacrifice of Isaac with Passover see R. Le Déault, *La nuit pascale* (Rome, 1963), pp. 170-178.

and preliminary revelation that he whom the disciples follow on a way marked by suffering and humiliation is the Son of Man whose total ministry has cosmic implications. Ch. 9:2-8 serves as a prelude to Chs. 14:1-16:8 and corresponds in function to Isa. 52:13-15 in relationship to Ch. 53:1-12: it offers assurance that despite apparent abandonment by God, Jesus is the Lord's Servant who prospers in the task he has been sent to accomplish. The revelation of Jesus' mysterious, transcendent dignity serves to confirm Peter's acknowledgment that Jesus is the Messiah (Ch. 8:29), and Jesus' own prophecy of his impending passion and vindication (Ch. 8:31). The event is oriented toward the disciples (Ch. 9:2 "before *them*," 4 "appeared to *them*," 7 "This is my beloved Son: listen to him") to strengthen them in their commitment and to prepare them for the sufferings which they must share.

The theory that the transfiguration is a misplaced account of a resurrection appearance of the Lord continues to find support[14] in spite of the solid objections which have been marshalled against such an interpretation.[15] It is necessary to recognize in the narrative the presence of details which ground the event in history: the precise time reference (Ch. 9:2), the designation "Rabbi" and the proposal of verse 5. Mark clearly believed that he was reporting a factual event which had primary significance for the disciples as a disclosure of Jesus' transcendent sonship. While the language used to describe the event was supplied from the vocabulary of theophany in the OT and in Jewish apocalyptic, the actual content of the revelation finds its closest parallel in the witness

---

[14] E.g. C. E. Carlston, "Transfiguration and Resurrection," *JBL* 80 (1961), pp. 233-240.

[15] Cf. G. H. Boobyer, *St. Mark and the Transfiguration Story* (Edinburgh, 1942), pp. 11-16; C. H. Dodd, "The Appearance of the Risen Christ: An Essay in Form-Criticism of the Gospels," in *Studies in the Gospels,* ed. D. E. Nineham (Oxford, 1955), pp. 9-35. Note that all of the canonical accounts of resurrection appearances begin with Jesus' absence, while he is present from the beginning in Ch. 9:2-8. Moreover, in resurrection narratives the spoken word of the Risen Lord has a prominent place, but in Ch. 9:2-8 Jesus is silent. The theory of a misplaced resurrection account leaves unexplained the appearance of Moses and Elijah, Peter's designation of Jesus as "Rabbi" and his impetuous statement (Ch. 9:5). After listing five points of contrast between Ch. 9:2-8 and accounts of post-resurrection appearances, Dodd adds: "To set over against these points of difference I cannot find a single point of resemblance. If the theory of a displaced post-resurrection appearance is to be evoked for the understanding of this difficult *pericope,* it must be without any support from form-criticism, and indeed in the teeth of the presumption which formal analysis establishes" (p. 25).

of the heavenly voice at Jesus' baptism with its attendant cosmic overtones (Ch. 1:9-11). There is room for discussion concerning the form of the event (i.e. it is possible that the disciples saw a vision of Elijah and Moses and heard the heavenly voice within the scope of that vision) but the transfiguration as an entity must be regarded as an act of revelation for which God was responsible.

The desire to find the Feast of Tabernacles implicitly in the background of the transfiguration account is based on details within the text, especially the reference to the "booths" in verse 5.[16] The Feast of Tabernacles, like the Passover, had come to have significant reference to the final deliverance promised by God. The several elements in the account, however, can be traced back to the reports of Moses' ascent to Sinai and his vision of the glory of God (Ex. 24:12-18); a more decisive influence seems to have been exerted upon the narrative from this tradition rather than from any other.[17] The transfiguration scene develops as a new "Sinai" theophany with Jesus as the central figure.

2-3 The precise temporal reference ("after six days") is unusual in Mark and indicates that the evangelist attached special importance to this episode.[18] The six days appear to refer back to the whole complex of teaching which followed Peter's affirmation of Jesus' messianic dignity, and more particularly to the solemn promise of Ch. 9:1. The unveiling of Jesus' glory in the presence of the three disciples corresponds to the assurance that *some will see*. The transfiguration is presented in the terminology of a theophany which reveals the powerful coming of the Kingdom of God. Understood in this light, the precise time reference in verse 2 recalls Ex. 24:16 f. where six days designates a time of preparation for the reception of revelation. Mark evidently regarded Jesus' announcement of his approaching suffering as the preparation required for witnessing the disclosure of Christ's true character. In this way the suffering and glorification of Jesus are as intimately associated at the

---

[16] H. Riesenfeld, *op. cit.*, pp. 146-205, 265 ff.; C. W. F. Smith, "Tabernacles in the Fourth Gospel and Mark," *NTS* 9 (1963), pp. 130-146. Cf. Ezek. 37:27; 43:7, 9; Joel 3:21; Zech. 2:10 f.; 8:3, 8; 14:16-19 for the expectation that God would pitch his tent among his people in the last days.

[17] See U. Mauser, *Christ in the Wilderness* (Naperville, Ill., 1963), pp. 111-118.

[18] Elsewhere precise notes of time are found only in the passion narrative (Chs. 14:1, 12, 17; 15:1, 25, 33, 34, 42; 16:2) and it is necessary to go to Ch. 14:1 to find a close parallel to Ch. 9:2.

beginning of the narrative as at its close when Jesus speaks of the Son of Man as an object of contempt (Ch. 9:12).[19] The choice of Peter, James and John to see the transfiguration corresponds to the privileged relationship these three disciples shared with Jesus on other occasions (Chs. 5:37; 13:3; 14:33) and served to qualify them as witnesses to the event after Jesus' resurrection (Ch. 9:9). The "high mountain" recalls the theophanies on the mountain of God (Sinai, Ex. 24; Horeb, I Kings 19) where Moses and Elijah received a vision of the glory of God. In the choice of location Jesus was not merely seeking solitude. In order to bring the feeling and thoughts of the disciples closer to the significance of the hour he used the evocative significance of the mountain in the wilderness tradition of the OT.[20]

Before the eyes of his most intimate disciples the human appearance of Jesus was perceptibly altered in accordance with the splendor of the transfigured world. For a brief moment the veil of his humanity was lifted and Jesus' body presented itself in the form of tenuously material light. In the OT the glory of God is always conceived as shining brilliance or bright light. The reference to the glistening character of Jesus' clothing reflects this concept and the language of apocalyptic where the image of radiance and resplendent light is borrowed to describe the glory of the Messiah.[21] As a revelation of the hidden quality of Jesus' life the transfiguration was an anticipation and guarantee of an eschatological reality: the glory of the Consummator. The disciples thus saw a disclosure of the mystery of the parousia (Ch. 8:38), when there will be a vindication of the glory of God superseding all previous revelations of that glory, at Sinai or elsewhere.

---

[19] If H. Riesenfeld (*op. cit.*, pp. 267 f.) is correct in referring the six days to the period between the Day of Atonement and the Feast of Tabernacles, the timing of Jesus' announcement concerning his sufferings (Ch. 8:31) is particularly appropriate.

[20] W. Foerster, *TWNT* IV (Eng. Tr. 1967), pp. 486 f. For a suggestive treatment of "the mountain of revelation" see J. Bowman, *The Gospel of Mark* (Leiden, 1965), pp. 157 f. On the actual site of the transfiguration, which was probably Mount Hermon (9,000 feet), see G. Dalman, *Orte und Wege Jesu*[3] (Leipzig, 1924), pp. 202 ff.; C. Kopp, *Die heiligen Stätten der Evangelien* (Regensburg, 1959), pp. 300 ff.

[21] G. von Rad and G. Kittel, *TWNT* II (Eng. Tr. 1965), pp. 238-242, 248 f.; J. Behm, *TWNT* IV (Eng. Tr. 1967), pp. 758 f.; W. Gerber, "Die Metamorphose Jesu, Mark. 9, 2 f., par," *ThZ* 23 (1967), pp. 385-395. On the related concept of the robe of glory see H. Riesenfeld, *op. cit.*, pp. 115-129. Cf. Rev. 1:13-16.

4 It was appropriate that Jesus, whose work was inaugurated in the wilderness at his baptism and whose way through the desert was directed by the Spirit (Ch. 1:9-13), should be accompanied in this moment of high revelation by the eminent prophets of the wilderness who stand by his side to testify to his character and mission. Jesus is the one in whom the promise of the second exodus becomes a reality. Moses appears as the representative of the old covenant and the promise, now shortly to be fulfilled in the death of Jesus, and Elijah as the appointed restorer of all things (Chs. 1:2 f.; 9:11). The stress on Elijah's presence at the transfiguration[22] indicates that the fulfilment of "all things" has arrived (Ch. 9:12). The transfiguration is the prelude to the passion, and Elijah is there to testify to the ultimate importance of the impending events in an historical sequence which culminates in consummation. The presence of Elijah with Moses thus has eschatological significance in the specific sense that they proclaim the coming of the end.

5-6 Peter's impulsive response is in keeping with his character and the numinous nature of the incident. He recognizes two of the most eminent figures in the history of revelation and feels that it is good that he and the sons of Zebedee are present so they can serve Jesus and his heavenly attendants. His proposal to build three tabernacles evidently rests upon a misunderstanding of the significance of the situation. The desire to erect new tents of meeting where God can again communicate with men implies that Peter regards the time of the second exodus as fulfilled and the goal of the sabbath rest achieved.[23] He is anxious to find the fulfilment of the promised glory now, prior to the sufferings Jesus had announced as necessary. His comment reflects a failure to appreciate that the transfiguration was only a momentary anticipation of the glory of the consummated kingdom. The blessings of the new age, which will be shared by *all* the people of God (Ch. 13:26 f.), cannot be secured until Jesus has accomplished the sufferings which are integral to his appointed task, culminating in his death. Mark's explanatory comment indicates that the three disciples were quite unable to grasp the messianic significance of what they had witnessed. The direct involve-

---

22 The mention of Elijah before Moses is unusual, but Elijah is much in Mark's thoughts at this time (Chs. 8:28; 9:11) and this may account for the order. Cf. J. Jeremias, *TWNT* II (Eng. Tr. 1964), pp. 938 f.; IV (Eng. Tr. 1967), pp. 857-863, 867.

23 U. Mauser, *op. cit.,* pp. 113 f.

ment of God in sending Moses and Elijah and the character of the glory of Christ were tokens of the eschatological judgment announced in Ch. 8:38. The fear that the disciples manifested is understandable in this context. At the same time, the occurrence of the transfiguration between Jesus' announcement of his approaching passion (Ch. 8:31) and the conversation with the disciples on the way down the mountain (Ch. 9:11-13) indicates that Peter's words in verse 5 reflect the same erroneous concept of God's intention as his response in Ch. 8:32.[24] The way through the wilderness has not been terminated by the disclosure of Jesus' unique glory.

7 The response of God to Peter's proposal discloses the real significance of this event. The appearance of a cloud enveloping Jesus, Moses and Elijah served to distinguish the witnesses from the participants in the unveiling of Jesus' parousia glory. This prepared the disciples to hear the solemn admonition addressed to them. The theophany is depicted in the language of the OT where the cloud is frequently the symbol of God's presence and protection (e.g. Ex. 16:10; 19:9; 24:15f.; 33:1). It is particularly significant that the correlation of the cloud and the voice is limited to the exodus accounts of the Pentateuch, as in the instance of the theophany on Sinai (Ex. 24:16). The cloud is God's tabernacle, the pavilion which both reveals and conceals his glory. The one whom God hides within his pavilion bears a special relationship to him (Ps. 29:5). In the case of both Moses and Elijah the epiphany of the glory of God served to vindicate their mission during their respective ministries in the wilderness. This is also the function of the cloud and the heavenly voice on this occasion. When Jesus began his mission in the wilderness of Judea the voice of God declared him to be the beloved Son, the object of his elective pleasure (Ch. 1:11). Now on the wilderness mountain the voice is heard again, reaffirming the Father's approval and confirming Jesus' dignity as the transcendent Son, although he has assumed the role of the rejected, suffering Servant of Isa. 53. Jesus' obedience to his messianic vocation is vindicated by God, precisely at

---

[24] Peter's use of the title "Rabbi" (Chs. 9:5; 11:21; 14:45; cf. "teacher" [Chs. 4:38; 10:35; 13:1]) is surprising, almost as if no discovery of Jesus' messianic dignity had been made among the villages of Caesarea Philippi. It provides one more indication that the disciples do not really understand what messiahship means. On the honorific title see E. Lohse, *TWNT* VI (1959), pp. 962-966; A. Schulz, *Nachfolgen und Nachahmen* (München, 1962), pp. 19-45.

the point where Jesus has announced what obedience entails (Ch. 8:31). The presence of the cloud and the solemn declaration of the voice affirm the same truth: Jesus is the unique Son of God who enjoys the unbroken presence and approval of the Father.

The spoken content of the revelation deserves careful attention. The first clause affirming Jesus' unique filial relationship to God provides the immutable ground for the solemn admonition in the second clause. Because Jesus is God's only Son the disciples are exhorted to hear and obey him. The stress upon Jesus' present status as the Son of God indicates that the transfiguration is more than an enacted promise of future glory. The unchanging fact of his transcendent sonship is the constant presupposition of his words, which reveal the will of God. The command "listen to him," which reinforces this insight, contains an allusion to Deut. 18:15 and serves to identify Jesus as the eschatological Prophet like Moses to whom Israel must listen because he is the final bearer of the word of God. The exhortation has bearing upon all of Jesus' words, but has particular relevance to the new instruction Jesus had been giving to his followers concerning the necessity of his sufferings and of their participation in his humiliation. There can be no doubt that Mark intended his congregation in Rome to take this word to heart.

8 When the cloud lifted, Moses and Elijah had vanished. Jesus alone remained as the sole bearer of God's new revelation to be disclosed in the cross and resurrection. Moses and Elijah had also followed the path of obedience, but having borne witness to Jesus' character and mission, they can help him no more. The way to the cross demanded the submission of the Son and Jesus must set out upon it alone. The transfiguration, however, has disclosed a new aspect of God's truth: Jesus is himself the new Tabernacle of divine glory. His word and deed transcend all past revelation. This was the truth with which the disciples were confronted when they realized they were once again alone in the presence of Jesus.

4. The Coming of Elijah. Ch. 9:9-13

9 And as they were coming down from the mountain, he charged them that they should tell no man what things they had seen, save when the Son of man should have risen again from the dead.

10 And they kept the saying,[25] questioning among themselves what the rising again from the dead should mean.[26]
11 And they asked him, saying, *How is it* that the scribes say that Elijah must first come?
12 And he said unto them, Elijah indeed cometh first, and restoreth all things:[27] and how is it written of the Son of man,[28] that he should suffer many things and be set at nought?[29]
13 But I say unto you, that Elijah is come, and they have also done unto him whatsoever they would,[30] even as it is written of him.

9 The terse conversation during the descent from the mountain was provoked by Jesus' instruction to tell no one what had taken place until

---

25 While the construction could mean that they kept in mind the statement concerning the resurrection it is more likely that Mark means that they obeyed the injunction to silence. For the evangelist's interest in this matter cf. Chs. 1:43, 45; 7:36.

26 The widely supported reading τὸ ἐκ νεκρῶν ἀναστῆναι (א A B C L Θ *pl q* sa bo goth) may represent a correction of the concrete but awkward text supported by the Western and Caesarean families (D W λ φ latt sys p geo Tatian), ὅταν ἐκ νεκρῶν ἀναστῇ: "They discussed among themselves what 'When he shall rise again from the dead' means." On this understanding, the disciples were not perplexed concerning the reference to the resurrection, but to the resurrection *of the Son of Man from the dead.*

27 Gr. ἀποκαθιστάνει πάντα, an allusion to Mal. 3:23 LXX (= M.T. 4:5), καὶ ἀποκαταστήσει, "and he will restore ..." Cf. A. Oepke, *TWNT* I (Eng. Tr. 1964), pp. 387-389.

28 The undeniably abrupt shift from Elijah to Jesus has prompted the conjecture that the reference to the Son of Man stems from a misunderstanding. If the primitive tradition spoke of *that* Son of Man, i.e. that man or prophet (as in Ezekiel), then Ch. 9:11-13 referred originally only to Elijah (see W. Wink, *John the Baptist in the Gospel Tradition* [Cambridge, 1968], p. 14). This ingenious proposal attains smoothness at the expense of the Marcan intention to link the sufferings of Elijah with those of the Son of Man.

29 Gr. ἐξουδενηθῇ, literally "considered as nothing," is an allusion to Isa. 53:3 where Aquila and Symmachus have ἐξουδενωμένος. The expression "suffer many things" is an appropriate summary of all that is written in Isa. 53 concerning the Servant of the Lord. Cf. also Ps. 21 (M.T. 22): 6 LXX and Ps. 118:22 in the textual tradition preserved in Acts 4:11. See C. Maurer, "Knecht Gottes und Sohn Gottes im Passionsbericht des Markusevangeliums," *ZThK* 50 (1953), p. 28.

30 For a defense of the interesting reading presupposed by the North African MS *k* (καὶ ἐποίησεν ὅσα ἔδει αὐτὸν ποιῆσαι, "and he did whatsoever it was necessary for him to do") see P. L. Couchoud, "Notes de critique verbale sur St. Marc et St. Matthieu," *JThS* 34 (1933), pp. 123 f.

after his resurrection. The clear implication of this statement is that the period of concealment is to be followed by a time of open proclamation when his status as the transfigured Son and eschatological Judge is to be announced to all (cf. Chs. 13:10; 14:9). This exhortation is of special interest, however, because it is the only instance in the Gospel where Jesus sets a limit to the silence enjoined. William Wrede seized upon this injunction and found in it the keystone to Mark's theological attempt to explain why Jesus had remained unrecognized as the Messiah during his earthly career. [31] What Wrede failed to perceive was the intention behind the injunction, which must be viewed within the larger context of Chs. 8:29-9:13. The fundamental misunderstanding of Jesus' messianic vocation reflected in Ch. 8:29-33 is still evident in Ch. 9:6-10. Peter is deeply impressed with Jesus' stature as the Messiah and the transfigured Son of God, but he and the other disciples find the necessity of the passion completely incomprehensible (Chs. 8:32 f.; 9:5 f., 30, 32). Jesus prohibits the telling of what they had seen and perceived because their enthusiasm was based on a superficial preconception of what messiahship and sonship signifies. Jesus' injunction in verse 9 is actually a challenge to perceive and proclaim the exalted Son of Man within the context of his historical ministry marked by suffering and rejection, culminated by death on the cross. The unaltered presupposition of Jesus' reference to his resurrection from the dead is the theological necessity to accept the passion in all of its dimensions. Within the will of God Jesus can be the exalted, resurrected Son of Man only as he is the suffering, rejected Son of Man (Ch. 9:12b). The reference to his resurrection is appropriate because this event is already a first realization of the majesty of the Son of Man at his parousia. The reality of his exaltation as the transfigured Son, however, can be appreciated only when the significance of his sufferings has been grasped. The response of the disciples in verse 10 implies that Jesus' resurrection will itself be the precondition for the disciples to understand this fact.

---

[31] *Das Messiasgeheimnis in den Evangelien* (Göttingen, 1901), pp. 66-71. In discussing Wrede's interpretation, R. G. Newman (*Tradition and Interpretation in Mark* [Ann Arbor, 1965], p. 215 n. 1) stresses a failure "to perceive the dimension of Mark's intentionality with reference to his contemporaries' misunderstanding as the stimulus which guides Mark's redaction." The emphasis upon the passion in Mark serves to correct an overemphasis upon Jesus as the exalted Son of God at the expense of his humanity and humiliation.

10 The disciples obeyed Jesus' injunction, but were puzzled concerning its meaning. It can be assumed that they were thoroughly familiar with the concept of the resurrection of the dead as the climactic event of the last day (cf. Chs. 6:14, 16; 12:18-27). What perplexed them was what this rising from the dead of the Son of Man could mean. This is explicit in the textual tradition supported by Caesarean and Western manuscripts, where the precise form of Jesus' reference in verse 9 is repeated in verse 10, and it is the necessary implication in the text followed by the ASV or RSV as well. The disciples' real question is, What have death and resurrection to do with the Son of Man? They possessed no categories by which they could distinguish between Jesus' statements concerning his resurrection and those concerning his parousia, and the relationship between these two distinct events remained obscure. Jesus' reference to his death and resurrection after three days may have led them to expect a duplicate of Elijah's experience of translation (cf. Ch. 8:31 with II Kings 2:17), or some similar experience of exaltation following humiliation. The place of Jesus' passion and death, together with his resurrection, was the unexpected and incomprehensible middle term between the present and the magnificent future assured by the transfiguration. What bothered the disciples specifically, then, was the phrase "from among the dead," together with the implication that time would yet remain before the consummation for the proclamation of what they had seen.

11 The disciples' question concerning Elijah is relevant at this point in the discussion. The presence of Elijah at the transfiguration (Ch. 9:4 f.), as well as Jesus' reference to the resurrection,[32] suggested that the consummation was imminent. But if this is true, where is Elijah who must prepare the people for the searching judgment of God (cf. Mal. 3:1 f.; 4:5 f.; Ecclus. 48:10)? It is probable that this question actually masks an objection to Jesus' announcement of his suffering and death, for the restoration Elijah is to effect just prior to the end makes messianic suffering unnecessary.

The reference to scribal teaching sheds light on a polemic use of the biblical teaching concerning the return of Elijah before the day of the Lord to discredit the impression created by Jesus' authoritative word

[32] The only passage in early scribal sources that associates Elijah's return and ministry with the resurrection is M. *Soṭah* IX. 15, which gives evidence of being a later appendix to the original tractate.

and deed. In the earliest sources the primary task of Elijah is to prepare the people of God for the reception of salvation through repentance.[33] An early tradition, however, links the prophet's return with the restoration of the flask of anointing oil (*Mekilta* to Ex. 16:33), and this conception is presupposed in the later scribal objections to Jesus' messiahship as expressed by Trypho in Justin's famous *Dialogue:* "The Messiah–if he has indeed been born and exists anywhere–is unknown and does not even know himself, and has no power, until Elijah comes to anoint him and make him known to all" (*Dial.* 8,4; cf. 49,1; Jn. 7:27). If this is the general scribal concept to which the disciples refer, it serves to reinforce their objection to Jesus' tacit allusion to his death in verse 9. The appearance of Elijah with Jesus upon the mountain of transfiguration could only be the anticipated return. What room for sufferings remains?

12 Jesus acknowledged that the affirmation that Elijah must come first and restore all things was certainly correct (cf. Mal. 3:23 LXX=4:5 f. M.T.). The fact that the Scripture also affirms that the Son of Man must experience suffering and rejection, however, indicates that Elijah's task as the restorer cannot signify what the disciples apparently believe it to mean. The reference to the sufferings of the Son of Man is undeniably abrupt, but serves to qualify the facile assumptions of the disciples as well as the scribes[34] and responds to the more fundamental, unexpressed question concerning the necessity for suffering which lies hidden in the question of verse 11. In verse 9 Jesus had spoken of his resurrection from the dead; his suffering and rejection is introduced in verse 12b by way of explanation. The allusion to Isa. 53:3, where the Servant experiences rejection and is treated as an object of contempt, reinforces

---

[33] In addition to Mal. 4:5 f.; Sir. 48:10, cf. Pirqe Rabbi Eliezer 43 (25a): "Without repentance Israel will not be redeemed... They will fulfill the great repentance only when Elijah of blessed memory comes, as it is said... (Mal. 4:5)"; Sifré Deut. § 41 "If you (plural) keep the Law, expect Elijah, as it is said... (Mal. 4:5)"; IV Ezra 6:26, "And the men will appear who were translated, who have not tasted death from the day of their birth, and the hearts of those who dwell on the earth will be changed and they will be turned to a new mind." See further J. Jeremias, *TWNT* II (Eng. Tr. 1964), pp. 931-934.

[34] The relationship between the two clauses is clarified by the recognition of the underlying μέν... δέ construction (with καὶ πῶς in 12b substituting for the δέ): on the one hand Elijah comes first to restore all things, but on the other hand the Scripture affirms that the Son of Man must suffer many things and be rejected. It is necessary that all the Scripture be fulfilled, not only those passages concerning Elijah.

Jesus' insistence that his sonship is misunderstood unless it is perceived that his exaltation is inseparably bound up with his humiliation. The response to the disciples' question concerning Elijah by a further question concerning the rejection of the Son of Man has a deeper intention, however. Basic to Jesus' understanding of Elijah's function is the restoration through repentance promised in Mal. 4:6, and fulfilled in the prophetic ministry of John the Baptist. Verse 12b serves as a warning that the sufferings of John and his shameful rejection do not disqualify him from fulfilling the role of Elijah nor do Jesus' sufferings discredit him as the transcendent Son of Man.

13 Jesus' veiled affirmation implicitly identifies John the Baptist as the eschatological messenger promised in Mal. 4:5 f. John is the Elijah sent by God because he fulfilled the function expected of Elijah, leading the people to renewal through repentance and forgiveness. His sufferings at the hands of Herod and Herodias (Ch. 6:14-29), which are indicated by an idiomatic expression denoting absolute and arbitrary power (cf. II Macc. 7:16), strengthen the identity of John with Elijah, who in his own ministry was harassed by a wicked woman and a weak king (I Kings 19:2, 10).[35] The startling character of this identification needs to be appreciated. The secret of Jesus' messianic vocation, conditioned by suffering as well as exaltation, leads to the disclosure of John's vocation as Elijah.[36] That the identification is not made explicit is consistent with the restraint Mark has exercised elsewhere when dealing with Jesus'

---

[35] It is necessary to assume that the phrase "even as it is written of him" has reference to the prophet Elijah in the framework of his historical ministry. No passage of Scripture associates suffering with Elijah's eschatological ministry, and there is no evidence that pre-Christian Jewish apocalyptic circles expected Elijah to face suffering upon his return. In fact, the concept of Elijah's sufferings is alien to the Jewish expectations of his role as the Restorer.

[36] For an incisive analysis of this "Elijanic secret" see W. Wink, *op. cit.*, pp. 15-18. Wink comments: "Thus the identification of John with Elijah was both an act of typological-prophetic confidence and at the same time a bold, utterly amazing affirmation which turns the tables on the Jewish expectations as radically as does the reinterpretation of messiahship involving Jesus. What is expressed is the quite offensive paradox that the heavenly Elijah should be this captive, murdered prophet: a *dead* Elijah. This identification cannot be said to be a simple apologetical retort to the Jewish protest that Elijah must first come, for this 'answer' is just as offensive as the statement that the crucified Jesus is the Messiah, and it operates on the same assumptions. In Mark's hands the Elijah expectation is radicalized and transformed even while the old framework is preserved" (p. 15).

identity. Thus in Ch. 1:2-8 the Baptist's resemblance to Elijah is simply suggested without comment and his ministry is placed under the rubric of Mal. 3:1 rather than Mal. 4:5 f. The failure of the disciples to understand Jesus' teaching about his own sufferings (Chs. 8:32 f.; 9:6, 10, 11, 32) undoubtedly extended to their comprehension of the sufferings of Elijah as well. John's identity, like that of Jesus himself, remains hidden until after the resurrection. Paradoxically, the vindication of John's ministry comes through his death and the violation of every human right. He participates in God's sovereign purpose which triumphs in apparent defeat. John's obscurity and ignominious death express all the ambiguity and suffering of Christian existence in the interval before the parousia. In this sense, John provides an example for the persecuted Christians in Rome. What *they* (Antipas and Herodias) did to him, *they* (men hostile to God) will do to men whose allegiance to Jesus and the gospel is unwavering (Ch. 13:9-13).[37] The significant point, however, is that he suffered as Elijah and his ministry demonstrated that the fulfilment of "all things" was at hand. The ambiguity between his true dignity and his hiddenness in the world will be resolved only at the parousia when the people of God will be vindicated by the Son of Man who shared their sufferings and rejection. The reference to Elijah's sufferings thus underscores the point made in verse 9: glory comes only after humiliation.

5. The Healing of a Possessed Boy. Ch. 9:14-29

14 And when they came to the disciples, they saw[38] a great multitude about them, and scribes questioning them.
15 And straightway all the multitude, when they saw him, were greatly amazed, and running to him saluted him.
16 And he asked them,[39] What question ye with them?

---

[37] *Ibid.*, pp. 17, 40 f., 110.

[38] One branch of the textual tradition introduces the story from Jesus' perspective: ἐλθὼν ... εἶδεν, "and when he had come ... he saw ..." (𝔎 A C D Θ *al*, most minuscules, latt sy bo geo^2 aeth). The plural forms (ἐλθόντες ... εἶδον), however, are strongly supported (ℵ B L W Δ Ψ 892 1324 *k* sa arm) and conform more to Mark's style elsewhere in the Gospel. They may represent an echo of eyewitness report: "having come ... we saw ..."

[39] The ambiguity of the pronoun is the occasion for the variant reading τοὺς γραμματεῖς ("the scribes") in 𝔎 A C sy^p. This may be a correct interpretation in the light of verse 14, but the reading is clearly secondary.

17 And one of the multitude answered him, Teacher, I brought unto thee my son, who hath a dumb spirit;
18 and wheresoever it taketh him, it dasheth him down: and he foameth, and grindeth his teeth, and pineth away[40]: and I spake to thy disciples that they should cast it out; and they were not able.
19 And he answereth them and saith, O faithless generation,[41] how long shall I be with you? how long shall I bear with you? bring him unto me.
20 And they brought him unto him: and when he saw him, straightway the spirit tore him grievously; and he fell on the ground, and wallowed foaming.
21 And he asked his father, How long time is it since this hath come unto him? And he said, From a child.
22 And oft-times it hath cast him both into the fire and into the waters, to destroy him: but if thou canst do anything, have compassion on us, and help us.
23 And Jesus said unto him, If thou canst![42] All things are possible to him that believeth.
24 Straightway the father of the child cried out, and said,[43] I believe; help thou mine unbelief.
25 And when Jesus saw that a multitude came running together,[44] he rebuked the unclean spirit, saying unto him, Thou dumb and deaf spirit, I command thee, come out of him, and enter no more into him.

---

[40] Gr. ξηραίνεται may connote "becomes stiff" (cf. RSV "becomes rigid") or "becomes exhausted," "wastes away" in the sense of exhibiting the pallor of complete exhaustion. Perhaps the first nuance is to be preferred.

[41] After ἄπιστος P^{45} W φ 543 *pc* add καὶ διεστραμμένη, bringing the text of Mark into harmony with Mt. 17:17; Lk. 9:41 (and Deut. 32:5): "faithless and perverse generation."

[42] Gr. τὸ εἰ δύνῃ in which the article τό is used to introduce a citation, in this instance of the father's words in verse 22: "so far as the 'if you can' is concerned [I tell you] all is possible to him who believes." See Bl-D-F § 267:1 (p. 140). The phrase appeared obscure and was altered at both ends: τό is suppressed in P^{45} D Θ φ *al*, while 𝔎 A D Θ φ *pm* latt sy$^{p\,h}$ add πιστεῦσαι after δύνῃ, missing the idiom altogether.

[43] Under influence of "cried out," 𝔎 D nearly all minuscules latt sy$^{p\,h\,pal}$ add μετὰ δακρύων ("with tears"). The words are absent from P^{45} א A* B C* L W Δ Ψ 28 700 1216 *k* sy^{s} sa bo arm aeth geo and clearly should be omitted.

[44] Gr. ἐπισυντρέχειν has not been found elsewhere. For the suggestion that it represents the Aramaic idiom רְהַט עַל = "to rush against," see M. Black, *An Aramaic Approach to the Gospels and Acts*[3] (Oxford, 1967), p. 85 n. 3.

26 And having cried out, and torn him much, he came out: and *the boy* became as one dead; insomuch that the more part said, He is dead.
27 But Jesus took him by the hand, and raised him up; and he arose.
28 And when he was come into the house, his disciples asked him privately, *How is it* that we could not cast it out?
29 And he said unto them, This kind can come out by nothing save prayer.[45]

Mark's account of this incident is vivid and detailed: verses 14b-16, 21-24 and 26-27 have no parallel in Matthew or Luke. The impression conveyed is that the episode has been reported from the point of view of one of the disciples who returned with Jesus from the mountain. The return from the glory of the transfiguration to the reality of demonic possession serves to reinforce the theme that Jesus enters into his glory only through confrontation with the demonic and the suffering this entails (cf. Ch. 9:19). The relationship between Ch. 9:2-13 and Ch. 9:14-29 corresponds to that between Jesus' baptism, with its theophanic note, and the trial in the desert where he confronted Satan (Ch. 1:9-13). The stress upon the powerlessness of the disciples is an element not found elsewhere in the evangelical tradition, but this is closely related to their failure to understand Jesus or the power released through him.[46] The episode exhibits the disaster which occurs when men from whom the power of faith may be expected are proven to be void of power when it is needed. The healing of the possessed boy demonstrates what faith expressed through prayer could have accomplished, even though Jesus was absent from the disciples. There are pastoral overtones throughout the account, which has pointed relevance for the community

---

[45] Most MSS add καὶ νηστείᾳ, "and fasting." The authorities supporting the omission are few, but important (א B *k* geo[1] Clement-Alex), and should be followed. The textual tradition of Mt. 17:21; Acts 10:30; I Cor. 7:5 indicates a strong tendency to add references to fasting where none originally existed. Moreover, Jesus had expressly sanctioned the disciples' discontinuance of fasting so long as he was with them (Ch. 2:18-22). For a discussion of the text see B. M. Metzger, *The Text of the New Testament* (Oxford, 1964), p. 203; and for a defense of the addition, on the ground that prayer and fasting are a symbolic reference to Jesus' death on the cross, see G. Minette de Tillesse, *Le Secret messianique dans l'Évangile de Marc* (Paris, 1968), pp. 98 f.

[46] On this relationship see H. J. Ebeling, *Das Messiasgeheimnis und die Botschaft des Marcus-Evangelisten* (Berlin, 1939), pp. 172-178.

of Rome, which felt itself to be powerless and defeated in the absence of the Lord at a critical moment in its own experience.

14-15 The scene at the base of the mountain is vividly sketched. The dispute, in which the disciples, the scribes and certain of the by-standers were taking part, had so engrossed the crowd that they had not seen Jesus and the other three men approaching. The presence of the scribes may indicate witnesses sent out by the Sanhedrin in Jerusalem to gather evidence against Jesus, who was suspected of misleading the people.[47] The prescribed procedure, which demanded a thorough investigation by official envoys, offers an explanation for the presence of scribes from Jerusalem at other points in Jesus' ministry (Chs. 3:22-30; 7:1-5). If this supposition is correct, the dispute undoubtedly concerned not only the failure of the disciples but the more basic question concerning their authorization to attempt an exorcism.

Verse 15 has the character of a marginal note, presenting Mark's comment on the fact reported: in seeing Jesus, the people were astonished. The astonishment of the crowd was occasioned by the presence of Jesus, rather than by any particular aspect of the event (such as his unexpected arrival at a critical moment).[48] In the Gospel expressions of fear and astonishment serve to emphasize the revelatory content and christological significance of many incidents. The evangelist wishes to stress that the person of Jesus himself provokes astonishment (cf. Ch. 10:32). This is the only instance where the respectful salutation of Jesus, presumably with the word of greeting "peace to you," by the multitude is reported. It is appropriate to the notice that the people were astonished when they saw him.

---

[47] For the relevant texts see E. Stauffer, *Jesus and His Story* (New York, 1960), pp. 206 f., Appendix II "The Provisions against Heretics," Nos. 33, 34, 43.

[48] So G. Bertram, *TWNT* III (Eng. Tr. 1965), p. 6; K. Tagawa, *Miracles et Évangile* (Paris, 1966), pp. 105-110. Mark makes no attempt to explain the amazement of the crowd, but places Jesus in the center of the narrative as its sole occasion, as in Ch. 10:32a. K. Tagawa attempts to bring out the evangelist's intention through paraphrase: "One day, Jesus came toward his disciples at the moment when they were discussing–it is Jesus of whom I am speaking! He is astonishing. –As the crowd assembled around him . . . " (p. 107). On the other hand, there is no basis for the opinion that every coming of Jesus is in the manner of a theophany (e.g. G. Minette de Tillesse, *op. cit.*, p. 92) or for the supposition that Jesus' face was radiant like Moses' face when he descended from the mountain (Ex. 34:29 f.). The charge of Ch. 9:9 would be senseless if Jesus' appearance called attention to what had taken place upon the mountain.

16-18 Jesus' question was probably addressed to the scribes, who had taken advantage of his absence to embarrass the disciples still further. He was answered, however, by a man from the crowd–the one who was most deeply concerned–the father of a possessed boy who had brought his son to Jesus for healing. His respectful address "Teacher," which carries the same nuance as "Rabbi" in Ch. 9:5, together with the emphatic declaration "I brought my son to you," indicates an expectation of deliverance based upon conviction. Without answering the question of verse 16 directly, he explained the situation which had erupted in the intense dispute between the disciples and the scribes.

The description of the destructive energy released at unexpected intervals by the demonic spirit indicates the seriousness of the boy's condition. Violent convulsions, foaming at the mouth, involuntary gnashing of the teeth, rigidness followed by utter exhaustion, resemble the symptoms of the major form of epilepsy.[49] The reference to a dumb and deaf spirit (Ch. 9:17, 25) implies that the child's situation was aggravated by an inability to speak or hear. What was involved, however, was not simply a chronic nervous disorder but demonic possession. The violence of the seizures, and the reference to repeated attempts to destroy the youth by hurling him into a fire or water (Ch. 9:20, 22, 26), indicate that the purpose of demonic possession is to distort and destroy the image of God in man. That this destruction should be heaped upon a child only serves to indicate how radical the issue is between demonic power and Jesus, the bestower of life (Ch. 9:27).

The father had appealed to the disciples to exercise the power known to belong to Jesus because the principle basic to discipleship was that "the messenger of a man is as the man himself."[50] In Jesus' absence the disciples stood in his place and were regarded as he is. It was therefore legitimate to expect that they possessed the power of their master. For their part, the disciples had good reason to believe that they could cast out the demon because they had been commissioned to expel demons in the context of their mission, and they had been successful

---

[49] There is surprising unanimity in diagnosing the boy's condition as epilepsy. The relevant source material on epilepsy in antiquity is presented by J. Preuss, *Biblisch-talmudische Medizin* (Berlin, 1911), pp. 341-345; H. van der Loos, *The Miracles of Jesus* (Leiden, 1965), pp. 404 f. For a recent examination of the narrative by a medical doctor see J. Wilkinson, "The Case of the Epileptic Boy," *ExT* 79 (1967), pp. 39-42. J. Smit, *De Daemoniacis* (Rome, 1913), p. 473 finds resemblances to epilepsy, but cautions that there are also differences.

[50] Cf. K. H. Rengstorf, *TWNT* I (Eng. Tr. 1964), pp. 415, 425.

(Ch. 6:7, 13). They undoubtedly tried in various ways to heal the boy, but they were inadequate to the resistance they encountered. They possessed the power of God only in personal faith, but during Jesus' absence an attitude of unbelief and self-confidence, based on past success, had exposed them to failure. Their inability appears to have shaken the father's confidence in Jesus' ability to do anything (cf. Ch. 9:22 "if you can"). He appealed for Jesus' help directly only after another violent convulsion, and then with doubt and hesitation.

19 Jesus' poignant cry of exasperation is an expression of weariness which is close to heart-break (cf. Chs. 3:5; 8:12). This is brought into sharp relief when his exclamation is seen to be a personal word addressed to the disciples, who alone had failed at the crucial moment. Although they had been privileged to be with Jesus and possessed the charism of healing, they had been defeated through unbelief when they stood in his place and sought to exercise his power. The lack of faith and hardness of heart reproved on other occasions (Chs. 4:40; 6:50, 52; 8:17-21) continued to characterize the disciples and betrayed a costly failure to understand the nature of their task and of the relationship that they must sustain to Jesus. The qualitative overtones in "unbelieving generation" suggest that the disciples remain indistinguishable from the unregenerate men who demand signs but are fundamentally untrue to God (Ch. 8:12, 38). The rhetorical questions, "how long shall I be with you? how long shall I bear with you?" express the loneliness and the anguish of the one authentic believer in a world which expresses only unbelief. The opposition expressed between "I" and "you" in these statements is seen in its true character only when it is recognized that what God says of his relationship to faithless Israel (cf. Isa. 63:8-10), Jesus now says of his relationship to the future community of faith. It is a measure of Jesus' infinite patience that he continues to instruct the Twelve and prepare them for the day in which they will stand in his place and continue his work (Chs. 3:14 f.; 9:28 f.; 14:28; 16:7).

20-22 The antipathy between Jesus and the demonic realm is evident in the violence of the seizure the boy experienced when he was brought before the Lord. By reducing the son to complete helplessness the unclean spirit betrayed his malicious intent to destroy the child and his utter contempt for Jesus. It is evident that the Lord was deeply moved. His question concerning the length of time the boy had been subject to such attacks shows his deep humanity and concern, for the source of the question is compassion. The father was deeply alarmed and saw in this new convulsion one more incident in a series of near-fatal seizures which could only end in disaster if help was not forthcoming. His distress is well expressed in the desperate cry, "If you can do anything, have compassion on us, and help us." At the same time, his words contain a concealed accusation against the powerlessness of the disciples, which has led him to doubt Jesus' ability to offer real assistance to his son.

23-24 Jesus seized upon the father's words at the point where they were most tempered with doubt: "if you can." Verse 23 can be paraphrased, "As regards your remark about my ability to help your son, I tell you everything depends upon your ability to believe, not on mine to act." By this reversal of intent, Jesus indicates that the release of the man's son from possession is not to be a response to the conditional "if you can," as if his power were something to be elicited through challenge. What is to be tested in the arena of experience is not Jesus' ability, but the father's refusal to set limits to what can be accomplished through the power of God. In its struggle with temptation, faith must always free itself from the disastrous presumption of doubt, in the certainty that with God nothing is impossible (Ch. 10:27), and that his majesty becomes most visible when human resources have become exhausted. Jesus thus calls for that faith which bows its head before the concealed glory of God (cf. Chs. 5:36; 11:23 f.). The parallel in expression between Ch. 9:23 and Ch. 10:27 indicates that through faith the believer shares in the sovereign rule of God and therefore, either actively or passively, experiences miraculous power.[51] In this instance, healing is to be the response to radical faith in Jesus, through whom the power of God is released.

---

[51] W. Grundmann, *TWNT* II (Eng. Tr. 1964), pp. 302 f. E. Stauffer, *New Testament Theology* (New York, 1955), pp. 168 f. comments: "faith is the assertion of a possibility against all probabilities, in spite of any contrary indication provided by our experience of life or the realities of the world, and in constant battle against temptation (Mk. 9:23). What is it that differentiates this faith from mere illusion, which breaks down upon the hard rock of reality? It is not a faith which reaches vaguely into the void, but one that firmly trusts Jesus Christ. Such a faith has nothing else than Jesus Christ in the middle of a world which scoffs at all our hopes and fears. It fastens on to Jesus Christ with all the strength at its command, and if the demonic power of the storm becomes overpowering, then the last resources of man's nature give vent to the cry, 'Lord, I believe; help thou mine unbelief' (Mk. 9:24)."

The father's response indicates that he understands Jesus' words in this light, for he immediately relates the solemn declaration concerning faith to himself. His cry expresses humanity and distress at being asked to manifest radical faith when unbelief is the form of human existence. At the same time that he affirms his faith, he associates himself with the rebuke addressed to the disciples: this generation is always unbelieving. The ambivalence in his confession is a natural expression of anxiety in the earnest desire to see his son released, but it is also a candid plea for help at that point where his faith is ready to fail. The exchange between Jesus and the father established the personal relationship necessary for the accomplishment of the release.

25-27 The statement that Jesus acted because he saw that a multitude was rapidly gathering is consistent with the reserve he exercised on other occasions when exorcising malignant spirits. The reference to the crowd, however, is puzzling. It is natural to think of the crowd mentioned in verse 14, although there has been no mention of withdrawal from the people, as in Chs. 7:33; 8:23. It is possible that others began to converge upon the spot as word of Jesus' presence spread. The reference, however, must remain obscure. The release was effected through Jesus' authoritative word. The expression of the command both positively and negatively served to make it clear that the attacks were now to be a thing of the past.[52] The double rebuke of the unclean spirit may have been prompted by the display of contempt for Jesus exhibited in the severe convulsion reported in verse 20. That malicious action was repeated at the moment of exorcism with such violence that the boy took on the appearance of a corpse–so much so that most of the people said he was dead. The expression "became as one dead" implies that he was not dead, although there was clearly room for discussion concerning this (cf. Ch. 5:39-42). But the accumulation of the vocabulary of death and resurrection in verses 26-27, and the parallelism with the narrative of the raising of Jairus' daughter, suggest that Mark wished to allude to a death and resurrection. The dethroning of Satan is always a reversal of death and an affirmation of life. There is a nuance in this instance, however, which must be appreciated. There appears to be a definite

[52] On the twofold command, which occurs elsewhere in both Jewish and Hellenistic sources (e.g. Josephus, *Antiquities* VIII. ii. 5; Philostratus, *Vita Apollonii* IV. 20), see S. Eitrem, *Some Notes on the Demonology of the New Testament* (Oslo, 1950), p. 26.

heightening of demonic resistance to Jesus which can be traced in the sequence Ch. 1:23-27–Ch. 5:1-20–Ch. 9:14-29. In this instance the disciples are powerless before the demon's tenacious grip upon the child and Jesus is successful only by the costly means of death and resuscitation. [53] The healing of the possessed boy thus points beyond itself to the necessity of Jesus' own death and resurrection before Satan's power can be definitively broken.

28-29 These verses have the character of an epilogue to the account, which ends with verse 27. Without the epilogue, the theme of the powerlessness of the disciples would remain incomplete and unexplained. A withdrawal to a house where Jesus may be questioned in private by the disciples is recorded in Chs. 4:10; 7:17; 9:28 and 10:10, and on each occasion these conversations provide supplementary teaching reserved for the disciples alone. In the house Jesus emphasizes the theological point of an incident. In this instance the final conversation relates to the central theme of the unit, for the epilogue qualifies the faith of verse 23 as the faith that prays.

In response to the inevitable question of why they had failed, Jesus explained to the disciples that such malign evil spirits can be expelled only by a full reliance upon the unlimited power of God expressed through prayer. This response contains at least the implicit criticism that the disciples had failed because they had not acted in prayer and sincere faith. The stress that prayer alone is efficacious, however, is striking because in Judaism the recitation of the *Shema* (Deut. 6:4-6), and of Psalms 3 and 91 was considered a powerful agent against evil spirits. [54] In the early Church the efficacy of fasting was championed and this emphasis has left its mark upon almost the entire manuscript tradition of verse 29. Jesus, however, spoke only of prayer as the source of faith's power and the means of its strength. The disciples had been tempted to believe that the gift they had received from Jesus (Ch. 6:7) was in their control and could be exercised at their disposal. This was a subtle form of unbelief, for it encouraged them to trust in themselves rather than in God. They had to learn that their previous success in expelling demons provided no guarantee of continued power. Rather the power of God must be asked for on each occasion in radical reliance

---

[53] G. Minette de Tillesse, *op. cit.*, pp. 96-99; H. Riesenfeld, "Die fientlige andarna (Mk. 9:14-29)," *Svensk Exegetisk Årsbok* 22-23 (1957-58), pp. 64-74.

[54] Cf. S-B*K* I (1922), p. 760.

upon his ability alone. When faith confronts the demonic, God's omnipotence is its sole assurance, and God's sovereignty is its only restriction. This is the faith which experiences the miracle of deliverance.

6. The Second Major Prophecy of the Passion. Ch. 9:30-32

30 And they went forth from thence, and passed through Galilee; and he would not that any man should know it.
31 For he taught his disciples, and said unto them, The Son of Man is delivered up into the hands of men, and they shall kill him; and when he is killed, after three days he shall rise again.
32 But they understood not the saying, and were afraid to ask him.

30 The re-entrance into Galilee marks a return to familiar territory, but the public ministry which had stirred the province was not to be resumed. This was simply the first leg of the journey from the territory of Herod Philip through Galilee and Perea to Jerusalem. The subject of the brief section covering the return to Galilee (Ch. 9:30-50) is Jesus' instruction of the Twelve, first concerning his destiny, and then their responsibility toward one another and toward men of faith beyond their immediate circle. Jesus' intention that his presence in Galilee should be unrecognized reflects not only the desire to instruct the disciples without interruption but a sense of compulsion to press toward Jerusalem where his messianic mission is to be fulfilled.

31 The three prophecies of the passion are distinct in narrative setting and formulation, and should be regarded as separate utterances.[55] The second major prophecy differs from the first (Ch. 8:31) in not speaking of a divinely imposed necessity, but of a fact so certain it can be described as accomplished ("is delivered"). It is also briefer in formulation, referring to abandonment to the will of men, violent death and resurrection. The stress on suffering and rejection is absent, perhaps because these aspects of Jesus' humiliation were re-emphasized in Ch. 9:12b.

---

[55] For relevant bibliography see the notes to Ch. 8:31, and for a treatment of Son of Man, and the phrase "be killed and after three days rise again," the discussion at that point.

The element which is new is the notice that the Son of Man will be delivered up (or handed over) into the hands of men (cf. Ch. 14:41). "To deliver up" or "hand over" is an important concept in the context of lawsuits and in the Jewish theology of martyrdom. More than simply the coming of an individual into another's power, the term connotes the actual fulfilment of God's will as expressed in Scripture. Particularly in martyrdom, God is the one who permits (or hinders) the handing over in fulfilment of his deeper purposes. "Into the hands of men" reinforces the concept of abandonment, as is evident in Jer. 33 (M.T. 26):24 where the full phrase occurs: "given over into the hands of the people to be put to death." After the betrayal by Judas and Jesus' arrest, it was natural to associate the terminology of "handing over" with that act of treachery (cf. Chs. 3:19; 14:41). The background of the term in Scripture, however, indicates that the thought is more profound: Jesus will be delivered into the hands of men by God, and what takes place on the level of historical occurrence has ultimate significance because it centers in the eschatological action of God. The precise wording of verse 31 may have been influenced by Isa. 53:6, 12 (LXX), where the expiatory death of the Servant is prominently in view. Jesus' statement indicates that God's redemptive will provides the key to understanding his passion.

32 The failure of the disciples to understand Jesus' meaning (cf. Ch. 9:10) and their fear of discussing it with him combine to suggest their apprehension and Jesus' essential loneliness on the way to Jerusalem. They cannot penetrate his meaning, and they are afraid to do so because they suspect that to know more would be painful. The text of verse 31 is not obscure, but Jesus may have used an ambiguous Aramaic expression which can mean exaltation or crucifixion.[56] This may explain both the fear of the disciples to inquire more precisely concerning his meaning and their readiness to be preoccupied with questions of precedence in Jesus' Kingdom (Ch. 9:33 f.; 10:35-37).

---

[56] The proposal of G. Kittel, "אִזְדְּקִיף = ὑψωθῆναι = gekreuzigt werden," *ZNW* 35 (1936), pp. 282-285 has recently been taken up by M. Black, "The 'Son of Man' Passion Sayings in the Gospel Tradition," *ZNW* 60 (1969), p. 7: "It is tempting moreover to attribute this ambivalent Aramaic expression to Jesus himself: if uttered in the context of Mk. 9:31 par, the failure of the disciples to understand (ἠγνόουν) is intelligible; Mark's present text is not obscure, but an ambiguous אזדקיף would certainly leave the hearers puzzled. Was it exaltation or was it crucifixion?"

7. True Greatness. Ch. 9:33-37

33 And they came[57] to Capernaum: and when he was in the house he asked them, What were ye reasoning on the way?
34 But they held their peace: for they had disputed one with another on the way, who *was* the greatest.
35 And he sat down, and called the twelve; and he saith unto them, If any man would be first, he shall be last of all, and servant of all.[58]
36 And he took a little child, and set him in the midst of them: and taking him in his arms, he said unto them,
37 Whosoever shall receive one of such little children in my name, receiveth me, and whosoever receiveth me, receiveth not me, but him that sent me.

The instruction given to the disciples "in the house" in Capernaum extends through verse 50. It consists of a group of sayings which appear to have been built up primarily through catchword-association, in which one saying is linked to another through a related expression.[59] Ch. 9:38-42 seems to have been joined to Ch. 9:33-37 through the recurring phrase "in my name" (verses 37, 38, 39, 41). The warning against offending "one of these little ones" in verse 42 was prompted by association with "one of these little children" in verse 37, while the formulation "whoever shall offend ... it were better for him" in verse 42 attracted the sayings concerning the offending hand, foot and eye where the symmetry in phrasing is particularly evident (verses 43, 45, 47). The reference to the unquenchable fire of hell in verse 48 served to recall the proverb that everyone shall be salted with fire (verse 49), which is itself linked to the final thoughts by the key word "salt." The series of catchwords

[57] The tendency to present a new unit from Jesus' perspective, observed in verse 14 above (note 38), is evident in the reading ἦλθεν ("he came"), supported by C 𝔎 A L N Θ *pc f q* sy^s bo.

[58] Verse 35b is omitted by D *d k,* perhaps unintentionally, while the clause "last of all" is omitted by λ.

[59] The composition of Ch. 9:33-50 has been studied often, and in detail: L. Vaganay, "Le schématisme du discours communautaire à la lumière de la critique des sources," *RB* 60 (1953), pp. 203-44; *idem, Le Problème synoptique, Une hypothèse de travail* (Tournai, 1954), pp. 361-404; R. Schnackenburg, "Mk 9, 33-50" in *Synoptische Studien A. Wikenhauser* (München, 1954), pp. 184-206; A. Deschamps, "Du discours de Marc IX, 33-50 aux paroles de Jésus," in *La Formulation des Évangiles* (Bruges, 1957), pp. 152-177; F. Neirynck, "La Tradition des paroles de Jésus et Marc 9, 33-50," *Concilium* 20 (1966), pp. 57-66.

and recurring phrases were aids to memorization and it is probable that teaching given historically on several occasions was brought together for catechetical purposes. At the same time, there is an appropriateness to the material in this context which must be recognized. The unity of Ch. 9:33-50 is imposed through the Semitic device of *inclusio,* in which there is a return to the beginning of a section at its conclusion. The final word in verse 50 ("Be at peace with one another") has pointed relevance to the strife reported in verses 33 f., while the material introduced within the section has direct bearing on the missionary character of the Twelve–and of the Church.

33-34 When Jesus asks a question of the disciples, his intention is to provide new teaching (cf. Ch. 8:27, 29, 31). The direct question concerning the heated discussion on the way to Capernaum proved embarrassing to the disciples. It was difficult to be honest that the point of the dispute had been who was the greatest among them. Their silence recalls the silence of Jesus' adversaries before his pointed question in the synagogue at Capernaum (Ch. 3:4). The question of greatness could be posed from the vantage point of understanding, as in Logion 12 of the Gospel of Thomas: "The disciples said to Jesus, We know that you will go away from us. Who is it that will then be great over us?" In Mark, however, the dispute over greatness indicates the degree to which the disciples had failed to understand Jesus' solemn affirmation concerning his abandonment to the will of men (Ch. 9:31 f.). It also shows how impregnated they were with the temper of their own culture where questions of precedence and rank were constantly arising.[60]

35 The question of precedence was resolved on the authority of Jesus: he who wishes to be first must determine to be the servant of all. This surprising reversal of all human ideas of greatness and rank is a practical application of the great commandment of love for one's neighbor (Ch. 12:31; Lev. 19:18) and a reaffirmation of the call to self-denial which is the precondition for following Jesus (Ch. 8:34, where the formulation

---

[60] Cf. A. Schlatter, *Der Evangelist Matthäus* (Stuttgart, 1935), p. 543: "At all points, in worship, in the administration of justice, at meals, in all dealings, there constantly arose the question who was the greater, and estimating the honor due to each was a task which had constantly to be fulfilled and was felt to be very important." To the material which was available to Schlatter may be added the texts from Qumran: e.g. 1QS ii. 20-23; v. 20-24; vi. 3-5, 8-10; 1QSa ii. 11-22.

"whoever wishes to come after me" is parallel to "whoever wishes to be first" in Ch. 9:35). The order of life for the disciples in their relationship to each other is to be the service of love. By transforming the question of greatness into the task-orientation of service, Jesus established a new pattern for human relationships which leaves no occasion for strife or opposition toward one another.[61] The disciples' thoughts were upon the period of glory, when questions of rank seemed appropriate (cf. Ch. 10:35-37); Jesus redirected them to his insistence that the way to glory leads through suffering and death. The point of suffering is here located in the service to be accomplished, where service means specifically sacrifice for others. The disciples cannot order their relationships as they please but are to recognize in one another men under whom they place themselves as servants. Jesus thus decided their question in a way which is in keeping with his proclamation of his own messianic vocation (cf. Ch. 10:43-45). This was clearly recognized in Polycarp's exhortation to the men whose task was to discharge the office of servants in the church at Philippi: "Likewise must the deacons be blameless . . . walking according to the truth of the Lord, who was 'the servant of all'" (*ad Phil.* 5:2).

36-37 Taking an illustration from life, Jesus set a young child from the home among the ambitious disciples. The taking of the child into his arms recalls Ch. 10:13-16, where Jesus' love for children is evident. His action on this occasion, however, introduces an enacted parable. The child is set before the Twelve as an example of *discipleship,* and the fact that the same Aramaic word means "child" and "servant" lends to his presence the character of a dramatized play on the affirmation in verse 35.[62] The disciples are to identify themselves with children and become "the little ones" who have no basis for pretensions to greatness. The statement that to receive a little child is equivalent to receiving Jesus (verse 37a) must, therefore, be interpreted of the disciples.[63] This is confirmed by the vocabulary of the formulation and by the immediate context. "Receive" must be understood in the same sense this word has

---

[61] W. Grundmann, *TWNT* IV (Eng. Tr. 1967), p. 533.

[62] M. Black, "The Markan Parable of the Child in the Midst," *ExT* 59 (1947-48), pp. 14-16.

[63] See O. Michel, "'Diese Kleinen'–eine Jüngerbezeichnung Jesu," *ThStKr* 108 (1937-38), pp. 401-415; J. R. Michaels, "Apostolic Hardships and Righteous Gentiles. A Study of Matthew 25:31-46," *JBL* 84 (1965), p. 37.

in Ch. 6:11, where it refers to the welcome extended to the disciples because they come as Jesus' representatives. The mission context of Ch. 6:7-13 provides the key to verse 37 where "the child" comes in Jesus' name, as his representative. "The child" only represents Jesus if he has been sent by him, in accordance with the legal principle that the emissary of a man is as the man himself. Because he comes in Jesus' name, invested with his authority, he is to be received. The vocabulary of hospitality appears in verse 41 as well, where Jesus speaks of the cup of water extended to the disciples because they come "in the name of the Messiah." In verse 42, a follower of Jesus is in view when he speaks of "one of these little ones who believe in me," and the image of the child is once more invoked. There is thus a clear progression in thought in verses 35-37: the admonition to become "the servant of all" in verse 35 is reinforced by the parabolic action of verse 36. But with the admonition to fulfill the disciple's vocation by becoming "one of these children" is linked the assurance of identification with Jesus. The Lord says, in effect, whoever receives you, receives me and the Father who sent me (verse 37). This provision lends to the servant's task the greatest dignity. At the same time Jesus associates himself with the posture of the servant, in anticipation of the startling declaration of Ch. 10:45.

8. Exorcism through Jesus' Name. Ch. 9:38-42

38 John said unto him, Teacher, we saw one casting out demons in thy name, and we forbade [64] him, because he followed not us. [65]

39 But Jesus said, Forbid him not: for there is no man who shall do a mighty work in my name, and be able quickly to speak evil of me.

---

[64] Gr. ἐκωλύομεν, a conative imperfect which should be translated "we tried to prevent him." J. H. Moulton and W. F. Howard, *A Grammar of New Testament Greek*³ I (Edinburgh, 1908), p. 129 point out that the form implies that the man refused to be stopped in his good work.

[65] The final clause is omitted by Western and Caesarean MSS (D W X λ φ 28 565 *al* it arm), which insert ὃς οὐκ ἀκολουθεῖ ἡμῖν after δαιμόνια (i.e. "we saw a certain man in your name casting out demons, who does not follow us, and we tried to prevent him"). The text of the ASV, RSV is supported by ℵ B C L Δ Θ sy^s sa bo, but may represent assimilation to the textual form of Lk. 9:49. If the Western and Caesarean texts are followed, the point is the man's apparent lack of authorization rather than merely a narrow sectarianism on the disciples' part.

40 For he that is not against us is for us.
41 For whosoever shall give you a cup of water to drink, because ye are Christ's, [66] verily I say unto you, he shall in no wise lose his reward.
42 And whosoever shall cause one of these little ones that believe on me [67] to stumble, it were better for him if a great millstone [68] were hanged about his neck, and he were cast into the sea.

38 The assurance that a special and intimate relationship exists between Jesus and the Twelve (verse 37) prompted John to call Jesus' attention to an unsuccessful attempt to prevent an unauthorized use of his power and name by an anonymous exorcist. This is the only time when Mark calls attention to John alone. It is striking, however, that after each of the three major prophecies of the passion the evangelist inserts the response of one of the three disciples who were closest to Jesus: Peter (Ch. 8:32 f.), John (Ch. 9:38), and James, with John (Ch. 10:35-37). Mark shows in this way that even the most privileged of the disciples failed to understand what the passion signified for their life and mission. The use of the first person plural ("we saw... we forbade him... not following us") indicates that John was speaking for all of the disciples.

What had disturbed the Twelve was the exercise of Jesus' power and name by a stranger who had not been authorized to do so. He was not

---

66 Gr. ἐν ὀνόματι, ὅτι Χριστοῦ ἐστε is rather unusual and has called forth variants, the most important being the addition of μου after ὀνόματι (א* C³ D W Δ Θ φ 28 118 124 565 700 latt sy^hmg sa bo aeth Origen) and the substitution of ἐμόν instead of Χριστοῦ in א*. If the text is accepted as given, translate "on the ground that you belong to the Messiah" or "because you bear the Messiah's name." It is unlikely, however, that Jesus used the designation "Messiah" in this way, for it is contrary to his usage elsewhere in the Synoptic Gospels and leaves unexplained the reading in Sinaiticus, which suggests that what Mark wrote was ἐν ὀνόματι ὅτι ἐμοί ἐστε (i.e. "on the ground that you are mine"). This agrees perfectly with the reading "ashamed of me and mine" (i.e. my disciples) in Ch. 8:38, supported by W *k** sa Tertullian (and preferred by many commentators). Cf. G. Minette de Tillesse, *op. cit.*, pp. 330 f.

67 The words "on me" (εἰς ἐμέ) are omitted by א C* Δ *b ff² i k*, sa bo, while D *a d* read "one of these little ones who *has faith.*" The support for the text adopted for the ASV, RSV, however, is strong and should be accepted.

68 Gr. μύλος ὀνικός, i.e. a large millstone turned by an ass in contrast to a smaller one turned by hand and frequently attended by a woman. Cf. TB *Mo'ed Qatan* 10b; *Kiddushin* 29b for references to large millstones turned by animals.

even a member of Jesus' company; yet he had refused to listen to the disciples when they sought to restrain his activity. John's complaint is significant, for it reveals an awareness that only the Twelve had been commissioned by Jesus and were authorized to act in his name, i.e. as his representatives and with his power. The irony of John's disclosure, at this point in the narrative, is that in Ch. 9:14-18 the disciples themselves had been powerless in a situation involving demonic resistance to exorcism. The action of the Twelve toward a stranger who was effective in exercising Jesus' power only points to their own ineptness and lack of understanding (cf. Num. 11:27-29, where Joshua wishes to forbid the unauthorized exercise of the gift of prophecy). The Twelve had an unduly narrow perspective toward the work of God. The man had grasped that an essential dimension of Jesus' mission was the confrontation and defeat of Satan. The use of Jesus' name (i.e. "I command you to come out in Jesus' name!") shows an awareness that it was Jesus who ordered the action, which was accomplished by his sovereign will. In the light of the experience of Jewish exorcists who misused Jesus' name, without understanding (Acts 19:13-16; cf. Mt. 7:21-23), it is necessary to affirm that the name of Jesus discloses its authentic power only when a man joins Jesus in faith and obedience to the will of God.[69] The fact that Jesus' power was active in the man, bringing release to men who had been enslaved to demonic possession, marks him as a believer. His action was an effective witness to the imminent Kingdom of God.

39-40 Jesus opposed the narrow exclusivism of the Twelve with an open and generous spirit. The disciples' action was an abuse of their authority, for they had presumed to speak for Jesus where they had no competence. Qualifying the prohibition "Do not forbid him" is the recognition that a mighty work was being done and that Jesus' name was being proclaimed. The proverbial statement "he will not lightly

---

[69] H. Bietenhard, *TWNT* V (Eng. Tr. 1967), pp. 227 f. There is a rather persistent line of interpretation which sees in the action of the strange exorcist an example of magic, e.g. A. Oepke, *TWNT* III (Eng. Tr. 1965), p. 213: "Although the conduct of the strange exorcist of Mk. 9:38 ff. par is rooted in a superstitious use of the name so far as he himself and those around him are concerned, Jesus endorses him. His answer implies neither approval nor condemnation of the superstition." This is to over-interpret the text, and misses the essential point of the passage, namely the unauthorized use of the name, not its superstitious misuse (as in Acts 19:13-16). See further E. Wilhelms, "Der fremde Exorzist," *Stud Theol* 3 (1950-51), pp. 162-171.

speak evil of me" entails subtle humor, to which there are formal parallels in Jewish sources.[70] With this remark Jesus gently contrasts the effectiveness of the unknown exorcist with the ineffectiveness of the Twelve. Concurrently, it expresses the important point that the use of Jesus' name involves a recognition of his authority. It was not necessary to be a direct follower of Jesus to share in a conflict which has cosmic dimensions; opposition to Satan unites the man to Jesus in his distinctive mission (cf. Ch. 3:27). The real ground of the prohibition is provided in the epigrammatic statement in verse 40.[71] The sharp recognition of only two sides ("against us" and "for us") radicalizes the demand to welcome participation in the mission, even from unexpected quarters. If anyone is working for the cause to which Jesus and the Twelve are committed, he cannot work against it at the same time.

41 The reference to the person who gives a drink of water to a disciple on the ground that he belongs to Jesus concretely illustrates the principle of verse 40 and indicates how wide is the range of participation in the mission which Jesus envisions. The offering of a cup of water to quench the biting thirst induced by the burning heat of the eastern sun is an act of hospitality (cf. verse 37) as well as an example of the humble service commended to the disciples in verse 35. It becomes a significant act when the drink is offered to a man *because he is a disciple and belongs to Jesus.* This statement presupposes the same frame of reference integral to verse 37, that the emissary of a man is as the man himself, and what is done to the emissary is done to the one who sent him. Jesus thus recognizes that the cup of water is extended to himself, and that this act of kindness is actually a token of faith and obedience. That is why he solemnly promises that the one who declares himself "for us" by this tangible action will not lose his reward. He will have a place in the Kingdom of God with the disciples and with Jesus, with whom he has identified himself in this small way. The reference to "his reward" carries no thought of deserving or of merit, for there is

---

[70] S-B*K* II (1924), p. 19; C. Schneider, *TWNT* III (Eng. Tr. 1965), p. 468.

[71] E. Wilhelms, *op. cit.,* p. 165 cites Cicero's defense of the Pompeiani before Caesar: "Let that maxim of yours, which won you your victory, hold good. For we have often heard you say that, while we considered all who were not with us as our enemies, you considered all who were not against you your friends." Cf. Mt. 12:30=Lk. 11:23 with the first principle, and with the second the variant to Mk. 9:40 in Oxyrhynchus Papyri 1224 (fol. 2r col. 1): "He who is not against you is for you. He who today is far from you may tomorrow be near to you."

no way in which a cup of water may be conceived as *meriting* participation in the Kingdom. It serves rather to stress God's awareness of all who share in the extension of Jesus' work, and to emphasize that there are no distinctions between "trivial" and "important" tasks. There is only faith and obedience, shown in devotion to Jesus, and wherever these qualities exist they call forth the approval of God.

42 The relationship of verse 42 to the larger discussion introduced by John's reference to an unknown exorcist in verse 38 is not generally recognized.[72] It receives no support from the parallel in Mt. 18:15, the paragraphing in the critical editions of the text or in any modern translation of the Scripture. There is, nevertheless, good reason to believe that in Mark's intention verse 42 provides the final comment on the disclosure that the disciples had tried to prevent a man from exorcising demons in Jesus' name. The warning against causing "one of these least ones" to stumble in their faith follows naturally upon verse 41, with which it shares an introductory "whoever" clause ("Whoever gives to you a cup of water ... And whoever causes one of these little ones who believe on me to stumble ..."). The explicit reference to those who believe in Jesus looks back upon the concrete action described in verse 41, and presumably in verses 38 f. as well. The stern warning has immediate relevance for those who had sought to prevent the exercise of faith in Jesus' name, and corresponds in severity to the word addressed to Peter when he sought to turn Jesus from the path of obedience (Ch. 8:33). Verse 42 performs the same function as Ch. 8:33: it serves to expose a grievous misconception and by graphic language to impress the seriousness of the matter indelibly upon the disciples' hearts.

In verse 37 Jesus had designated the disciples as "the children" who were to be received in his name. Here the designation "the little ones" is extended to other followers whose allegiance to Jesus is no less exemplified in their own spheres of labor (exorcism, hospitality) than is true of the Twelve. The description points to the secret that they bear a concealed or future dignity because they believe in Jesus and act in his name. The parallel designation underscores the irony that those

---

72 While commentators generally find the humble members of the Christian community (e.g. C. E. B. Cranfield, *op. cit.*, p. 313) or less often the disciples (e.g. O. Michel, *TWNT* IV, Eng. Tr. 1967, pp. 651 f.) in verse 42, only three studies known to me associate verse 42 with verse 38: A. Loisy, *Les évangiles synoptiques* II (Ceffonds, 1907), p. 77; W. Grundmann, *Das Evangelium nach Markus* (Berlin, 1962), *ad loc.* and K. Tagawa, *op. cit.*, p. 178.

who are to be received because they belong to Jesus (verse 37) should be the occasion of causing to fail in their faith others who equally belong to him. In such an eventuality, Jesus implies, the punishment incurred will be so severe it would have been better for a man if he had been drowned before he could have committed so grievous an offense. The graphic reference to the millstone around the neck and being cast into the sea would not have been lost upon the disciples, who undoubtedly had heard of the punishment inflicted by the Romans in Galilee on some of the leaders of the insurrection under the early Zealot leader, Judas the Galilean (cf. Acts 5:37).[73]

9. The Demanding Requirements of Discipleship. Ch. 9:43-50

43 And if thy hand cause thee to stumble, cut it off: it is good for thee to enter into life maimed, rather than having thy two hands to go into hell,[74] into the unquenchable fire.[75]
45 And if thy foot cause thee to stumble, cut it off: it is good for thee to enter into life halt, rather than having thy two feet to be cast into hell.
47 And if thine eye cause thee to stumble, cast it out: it is good for thee to enter into the kingdom of God with one eye, rather than having two eyes to be cast into hell,
48 where their worm dieth not, and the fire is not quenched.
49 For everyone shall be salted with fire.[76]

---

[73] Cf. Suetonius, *De Vita Caesarum* i. 67; Josephus, *Antiquities* XIV. xv. 10, reports the drowning of Herod's supporters by Galileans who rebelled.

[74] Gr. γέενναν, a transliteration of the Hebrew expression for the valley of Hinnom to the south of old Jerusalem, where infants were formerly sacrificed to Moloch (Jer. 7:31; 19:5 f.; 32:35). This site was desecrated by Josiah (II Kings 16:3; 21:6; 23:10) and consigned to the burning of offal. Here, literally, the fire was not quenched and the worm never died, and it is not surprising that Gehenna came to denote the place of divine punishment during the Intertestamental period (e.g. I Enoch 27:2, "This accursed valley is for those who are accursed for ever"; 90:26 f.; IV Ezra 7:36; M. *Aboth* I. 5; V. 19 f.). See J. Jeremias, *TWNT* I (Eng. Tr. 1964), pp. 657 f.

[75] Verses 44 and 46, which are identical in form with verse 48, are omitted by ℵ B C L W Δ Ψ λ 22 28 565 892 *al k* sy^{s} sa bo geo arm and should not be read. They were apparently added in later MSS to round out the poetical parallelism evident in verses 47 f.

[76] Verse 49 is found in three major textual forms. The reading adopted in the critical editions of the text and followed by the ASV, RSV and most modern

50 Salt is good: but if the salt have lost its saltness, wherewith will ye season it? Have salt in yourselves, and be at peace one with another. [77]

43-48 These verses constitute a call to concrete obedience which renews the radical demands of discipleship enunciated in Ch. 8:34-38. In contrast to verse 42, where Jesus spoke of causing someone else to fall away from him, these stern warnings relate to the ensnaring of oneself in sin. The issue remains the same, however. In the specific context, the offense is in the question of decision for the Kingdom of God, which cannot be divorced from the person of Jesus himself and the exercise of faith. It is particularly important to appreciate the eschatological framework of Jesus' words concerning radical self-punishment of an offending member of the body. The sharp contrast between departure (or, being cast) into hell and entrance into life (or the Kingdom) presupposes the situation of the final judgment in which the decision of God (or the Son of Man, cf. Ch. 8:38) concerning each man is irreversible and entails eternal consequences.

It was not a Palestinian custom to refer to an abstract activity but to the specific member of the body which is responsible for it. [78] For this

---

translations is strongly attested (ℵ B L W Δ λ 565 700 *et al* sy^s sa bo geo arm). A longer text adds to these words καὶ πᾶσα θυσία ἁλὶ ἁλισθήσεται ("and every sacrifice must be salted with salt," supported by A C N X Θ *al pl* φ 28 892 1071 *al pl f l q r* vg sy^p h aeth and followed by the AV). This reading has been supported by H. Zimmermann, "'Mit Feuer gesalzen werden.' Eine Studie zu Mk 9:49," *Theol Quart* 139 (1959), pp. 28-39, but the addition appears to represent a marginal gloss influenced by Lev. 2:13. In D *a b c d ff i k* the gloss (in the form, "For every sacrifice will be salted with salt") supplanted the main reading. P. L. Couchoud, *op. cit.*, p. 124 (followed by E. Lohmeyer, *op. cit.*, p. 197 n. 2) has proposed that the original reading is preserved in the North African MS *k*. The Latin text presupposes the reading πᾶσα δὲ οὐσία ἀναλωθήσεται, which must be understood in connection with verse 48: "where their worm shall not die, nor their fire be quenched, and all (their) substance shall be destroyed." This proposal finds some support in Ψ, which reads ἀναλωθήσεται in place of the second ἁλισθήσεται in the longer reading, while οὐσία could have given rise to the introduction of θυσία. The chief problem with Couchoud's conjecture is that some allusion to salt is necessary to account for the association of verse 50 with verse 49. This provision is satisfied by the shorter text adopted in the critical editions. See further Tj. Baarda, "Mark ix. 49," *NTS* 5 (1958-59), pp. 318-321.

[77] Verse 50c is an instance in Greek of two imperatives in conditional parataxis joined by the consecutive καί; translate "have salt in yourselves, *then* you will be able to maintain peace with one another." See Bl-D-F § 442:2 (p. 227).

[78] F. Horst, *TWNT* IV (Eng. Tr. 1967), pp. 560 f.

reason, Jesus speaks of the offending hand, foot and eye, all members which have highly important functions to fulfill. They characterize a man concretely as one who acts and who is responsible for his actions. The representation of the members as the acting subject ("if your hand leads you to offend") belongs to the realism of Jewish thought. The radical demand that the hand or foot should be hacked off or the eye plucked out if they expose a man to the danger of final rejection juxtaposes the relative value of physical life with the absolute value of that authentic, imperishable life which is bestowed by God alone. Jesus did not hesitate to call for the renunciation of possessions (Ch. 10:21), family (Ch. 10:28 f.) and of life itself (Ch. 8:34 f.) if these things stood in the way of following him; here he demands the complete sacrifice of the sinful activity of the member. This was not a demand for physical self-mutilation, but in the strongest manner possible Jesus speaks of the costliest sacrifices. For the sake of the unconditional rule of God the members of the body must not be placed at the disposal of sinful desire. The sinful member must be renounced in order that the whole body be not cast into hell. Conversely, concern for the preservation of a hand, a leg or a foot must not lead a man to denial of the sovereignty of God or his allegiance to Jesus. This thought found heroic exemplification in the history of Jewish martyrdom (e.g. II Macc. 7:2-41, where the sacrifice of limbs and life is accepted in order to be true to God and to receive life from his hand) and was to play a crucial role in the martyr Church as well. Whatever in one's life tempts one to be untrue to God must be discarded, promptly and decisively, even as a surgeon amputates a hand or a leg in order to save a life.[79]

What is designated "life" in verses 43 and 45 means specifically "life with God," as the parallel with "the kingdom of God" in verse 47 indicates. In the related context of Ch. 10:17-31, this reality is qualified as "eternal life" (Ch. 10:17, 30). In contrast with entrance into life Jesus speaks of "departure into hell, to the unquenchable fire" (verse 43). The final phrase does not appear in verses 45 and 47; it may represent Mark's explanation of the word "Gehenna," which would be unfamiliar to Gentile readers, on the basis of Isa. 66:24 (cited in verse 48). In Jewish

---

[79] H. Hommel, "Herrenworte im Lichte sokratischer Überlieferung," *ZNW* 57 (1966), pp. 1-23 calls attention to classical and Hellenistic parallels which speak of a willingness to sacrifice a hand, foot or some other part of the body in order to pursue philosophy or the truth.

sources Gehenna was associated with the eschatological fires of hell [80] and conveyed an image of extreme horror. Entrance into hell indicates spiritual ruin in the starkest terms. This thought is reinforced with the citation of Isa. 66:24 in verse 48, which speaks of the punishment of the sin of rebellion against God. As the final word of the prophecy of Isaiah the passage was thoroughly familiar to the disciples as a vivid picture of a destruction which continues endlessly. [81] The contrast drawn between spiritual life and spiritual death in Ch. 8:35-37 is here redrawn in concrete, tangible terms to sharpen the issue of radical obedience in the context of costly sacrifice.

49 This brief logion, which is preserved by Mark alone, speaks of a different kind of fire–the fire of purification. While verse 48 applies to the rejected, verse 49 has reference to those who are true to God in a hostile world. The thought of the sacrifice of an offending member of the body (verses 43-47) is here carried a step further: every disciple is to be a sacrifice for God (cf. Rom. 12:1). In the OT the Temple sacrifices had to be accompanied by salt (Lev. 2:13; Ezek. 43:24; cf. Ex. 30:35). The salt-sacrifice metaphor is appropriate to a situation of suffering and trial in which the principle of sacrifice cultivated with respect to the individual members of the body is now severely tested. The disciples must be seasoned with salt, like the sacrifice. This will take place through fiery trials (cf. I Peter 1:7; 4:12), through which God will purge away everything contrary to his will. [82] Understood in this way, Jesus' word is a challenging pronouncement on suffering which shed light on the experience of the Church in Nero's Rome. Its preservation in "the teaching manual" of a community facing persecution is fully intelligible.

---

[80] E.g. TB *Rosh Ha-Shanah* 16b; IV Ezra 7:36; II Baruch 59:10; 85:13; Sibylline Oracles I, 103; II, 291; IV, 186.

[81] When Isa. 66:22-24 was read in the synagogue, verse 23 was repeated in order to bring the reading to a conclusion with a word of comfort. Verse 24 has left its mark on Jewish documents of the Intertestamental period, e.g. Ecclus. 7:17, "Humble yourself greatly; for the punishment of the ungodly is fire and worms"; Judith 16:17, "Woe to the nations that rise up against my people! The Lord almighty will take vengeance upon them in the day of judgment; he will give their flesh to fire and worms; they shall weep in pain for ever." This is the conception presupposed in verses 43-48.

[82] F. Hauck, *TWNT* I (Eng. Tr. 1964), p. 229. J. Jeremias, *TWNT* I (Eng. Tr. 1964), p. 658 finds here a reference to the purificatory character of the final fire of judgment.

50 The reference to salt in verse 49 supplies the dominant note for verse 50. Here, however, the associations of salt are no longer cultic, but domestic. Two observations on Palestinian life furnish the background to Jesus' pithy comments. The maxim that "the world cannot survive without salt" (Tractate *Sopherim* XV. 8) is a vivid reminder that salt was a necessity of life in the ancient world because it preserved food from putrefaction. On the other hand, Pliny the Elder had already observed that the salt from the Dead Sea can lose its savory quality and becomes insipid (*Hist. Nat.* 3, 31, 34).[83] Jesus' words presuppose these two truths. The logion concerning salt, however, must be interpreted by the context, which sets forth the demanding requirements of discipleship. The disciples have an eschatological responsibility toward men in a world which is subject to the judgment of God. Jesus warns them that they can lose that salt-like quality which can mean life for the world. Here salt typifies that quality which is the distinctive mark of the disciple, the loss of which will make him worthless. This can only be his allegiance to Jesus and the gospel (cf. Ch. 8:35, 38). The exhortation to guard their salt-like quality in order to be at peace with one another has direct bearing on the situation of strife which provoked the conversation in verses 33 ff. What is to set one man apart from another is not distinctions of rank or worth, but the quality of "saltness." Strife is resolved and peace restored when men recognize in one another a common commitment to Jesus and the gospel, and to the servant's vocation.

[83] Salt from the Dead Sea which is mixed with gypsum and other impurities acquires a stale and alkaline taste. For the Jewish parallel "If the salt becomes insipid, how shall it be salted?" (TB *Bekhoroth* 8b), which in context seems to be a scoffing reference to Jesus' statement, see F. Hauck, *TWNT* I (Eng. Tr. 1964), p. 229.

CHAPTER 10

10. The Question of Divorce. Ch. 10:1-12

1 And he arose from thence, and cometh into the borders of Judaea and beyond the Jordan:[1] and the multitudes[2] come together unto him again; and as he was wont, he taught them again.

2 And there came unto him Pharisees,[3] and asked him, Is it lawful for a man to put away *his* wife? trying him.

3 And he answered and said unto them, What did Moses command you?

4 And they said, Moses suffered to write a bill of divorcement, and to put her away.

5 But Jesus said unto them, For your hardness of heart he wrote you this commandment.

6 But from the beginning of the creation, male and female made he them.

---

1 The text of verse 1a is found in three variant traditions. The ASV, RSV follow the critical editions of the Greek text supported almost exclusively by Alexandrian witnesses (א B C* L Ψ 892 1009 sa bo): "he came into the territories of Judea and Transjordan." A variant text, supported by Caesarean and Western authorities (C^2 D G W Δ Θ λ φ 28 565 579 *al* latt $sy^{s\,p}$ arm geo Augustine), reflects the geographical situation in the days of Ptolemy the astronomer (*ca.* A.D. 130-160): "he came into the territories of Judea beyond Jordan." Still another variant belongs to a later stage of the tradition when it has come to be thought that Perea was no more than a bridge between Galilee and Jerusalem (A 𝔎 157 569 575 700 *pl* sy^h aeth): "he came into the territories of Judea by the farther side of Jordan." For a full geographical and textual commentary see T. W. Manson, "The Cleansing of the Temple," *BJRL* 33 (1951), pp. 272 f.

2 Mark nowhere else uses the plural, and the singular ὁ ὄχλος is read by Western and Caesarean authorities (D W Θ φ 28 565 700 *al* it sy^s geo^2). This reading is defended as original by C. H. Turner, "Marcan Usage," *JThS* 29 (1927), pp. 4 f. If the plural is correct, it may be intended to suggest the different crowds which gathered on different occasions, a viewpoint championed by Manson, *op. cit.*, pp. 273 f.

3 The words προσελθόντες Φαρισαῖοι are absent in the Western MSS (D it sy^s Origen) and they may well have come into the other witnesses through the influence of the parallel in Mt. 19:3. If the Western text is read ἐπηρώτων will be an indefinite plural, i.e. "people asked him." C. H. Turner, *op. cit.*, p. 5 has shown that this is consistent with Mark's style elsewhere (e.g. Ch. 10:13).

7 For this cause shall a man leave his father and mother, and shall cleave to his wife;[4]
8 and the two shall become one flesh: so that they are no more two, but one flesh.
9 What therefore God hath joined together, let not man put asunder.
10 And in the house the disciples asked him again of this matter.
11 And he saith unto them, Whosoever shall put away his wife, and marry another, committeth adultery against her:
12 and if she herself shall put away her husband, and marry another, she committeth adultery.[5]

1 Mark's account of the Galilean ministry is terminated with Ch. 9. From this point forward the narrative moves swiftly and relentlessly toward its inevitable climax in Jerusalem. Verse 1 is a summary passage, reporting a further stage in the journey toward the Judean capital and the resumption of a public ministry. From Capernaum (Ch. 9:33) Jesus came into southern Palestine. The order in which the provinces are listed

---

[4] The final clause is omitted by ℵ B Ψ 892* l^{48} sy^{s} goth and probably reflects assimilation to Mt. 19:5 (and Gen. 2:24).

[5] Verse 12, which is peculiar to Mark, is found in three main forms, each of which has attracted its defenders. The ASV, RSV follow the critical editions in accepting the almost exclusively Alexandrian reading (ℵ B C L Δ Ψ 517 579 892, 1342 sa bo aeth). This form of the text is adopted by most modern commentators and is defended on both textual and intrinsic grounds by G. Minette de Tillesse, *Le Secret messianique dans l'Évangile de Marc* (Paris, 1969), pp. 231-234 (among others), who considers the formulation to be shaped for the Graeco-Roman legal situation. The variant reading, "If a woman should divorce her husband and should marry another," supported by Byzantine and certain other MSS (A W 𝔎 λ 22 118 1071 *pl f* g^{2} r^{2} vg sy$^{p\ h}$ geo^{1} Augustine), is accepted by M. J. Lagrange, *Évangile selon Saint Marc* (Paris, 1947), pp. 260 f. on the ground that it accounts best for the textual variants. A third text, which differs substantially from the first two in speaking of a woman separating from her husband (without divorce) and marrying another, has strong Western and Caesarean support (D Θ φ 28 543 565 700 *a b ff* (*k*) *q* sy^{s} arm). This text has strong claim to priority since it represents a textual tradition current at Antioch, Caesarea, Carthage, Italy and Gaul at least as early as A.D. 150. Moreover, the situation envisioned (desertion and remarriage) is precisely that of Herodias and is appropriate to the importance this issue assumed in connection with the death of John the Baptist (see Ch. 6:17-29). This third text is assumed to be the original one in the commentary. See further, D. Daube, *The New Testament and Rabbinic Judaism* (London, 1956), pp. 366-368; J. Dupont, *Mariage et divorce dans l'Évangile de Matthieu 19, 13-12 et parallèles* (Bruges, 1959), pp. 61-63; N. B. Stonehouse, *Origins of the Synoptic Gospels* (Grand Rapids, 1963), pp. 27-28.

(Judea and Perea) suggests that he went south across the mountains of Samaria into Judea, following the ordinary route for pilgrims on their way to the Holy City (cf. Lk. 9:51-53).[6] At some point he crossed over the Jordan into Perea, which was part of the territory of Herod Antipas. The itinerary marks a return to the Jordan region where John the Baptist had conducted his ministry and had suffered imprisonment and martyrdom. If Jesus had been associated with John for any length of time it is possible that in coming to southern Judea and Perea he was returning to an area and people he knew well. His reputation in these areas is attested by Ch. 3:8, although it is not clear whether it was established by direct knowledge or report. In both Judea and Perea Jesus began teaching crowds of people once more, resuming a public ministry which had been discontinued some time before he left Galilee (Ch. 9:30). This aspect of his ministry was concluded when Jesus went up to Jerusalem, by way of Jericho, for the Passover, or perhaps the Feast of Tabernacles (see Ch. 10:46-11:10).

2 On the question of the lawfulness of divorce the Pharisees and their scribes (and perhaps the majority of the Jewish people) were agreed: divorce was permitted in accordance with the provisions of Deut. 24:1. The only point of real dispute concerned the interpretation of the phrase "something shameful" in Deut. 24:1, which constituted the grounds upon which divorce was to be permitted. From the beginning of the first century variant opinions had polarized into two camps. The followers of Shammai argued that something morally shameful was in view, particularly adultery, but also a failure to observe the Jewish law which prescribed great reserve for a wife. The followers of Hillel argued that in addition to any moral fault, anything which caused annoyance or embarrassment to a husband was a legitimate ground for a divorce suit.[7] It seems likely, however, that far more than this rabbinic dispute was in the background of the question posed in verse 2. The question was hostile in its intention, as Mark indicates by the qualifying phrase

---

[6] K. Tagawa, *Miracles et Évangile* (Paris, 1966), pp. 34 f.; T. W. Manson, *op. cit.*, pp. 273 f.

[7] M. *Gittin* IX. 10; TB *Gittin* 90a; TJ *Soṭah* I. 1. 16b; Num. R. IX. 30. For treatments of the Jewish legislation on divorce see S-B*K* I (1922), pp. 312-320; J. Bonsirven, *Le divorce dans le Nouveau Testament* (Tournai, 1948), pp. 7-24; M. R. Lehmann, "Gen. 2:24 as the Basis for Divorce in Halakhah and New Testament," *ZAW* 72 (1960), pp. 263-267; T. V. Fleming, "Christ and Divorce," *JThS* 24 (1963), pp. 541-554.

"tempting him," and this larger context of temptation is very important to the passage as a whole. The question of the lawfulness of divorce and remarriage had been the immediate occasion for John the Baptist's denunciation of the conduct of Herod Antipas and Herodias (Ch. 6:17f.) and had led to his violent death. In Perea Jesus was within the tetrarch's jurisdiction. The intention behind the question, apparently, was to compromise Jesus in Herod's eyes, perhaps in the expectation that the tetrarch would seize him even as he had John. The cooperation between the Herodians and the Pharisees, first mentioned in ominous terms in Ch. 3:6 and reiterated in Ch. 12:13, may be a part of the historical situation presupposed in the narrative.

3-4 Jesus cut across the casuistry of the Jewish legal tradition with a direct appeal to the Law (cf. Ch. 7:1-23; 10:17-20). In asking what Moses *commanded* it is evident that Jesus was calling for positive instruction (perhaps specifically the instruction of Gen. 2:24). His questioners answered with an exception and a permission, summarizing Deut. 24:1: Moses permitted divorce providing a certificate of divorce was given to the wife. This provision assumes the practice of divorce and describes a right to which a wife is entitled: she is to be given a bill of divorce which authenticates her release from the marriage contract and affirms her right to remarry.[8] The Mosaic provision was made for the contingency of divorce, but did not in itself determine whether that contingency was right or wrong. Its primary function was to provide a degree of protection for the woman who had been repudiated by her husband.[9]

---

[8] On the so-called Mosaic permission in Deut. 24:1 see J. Murray, *Divorce* (Philadelphia, 1961), pp. 3-16; R. C. Campbell, "Teaching of the Old Testament concerning Divorce," *Foundations* 6 (1963), pp. 174-178. On the certificate of divorce see P. C. Hammond, "A Divorce Document from the Cairo Geniza," *JQR* 52 (1961), pp. 131-153 (dated A.D. 1054, which at the time was thought to be the only one which had been preserved from antiquity, but see now the divorce documents of Murabba'at No. 19 [in Aramaic] and No. 115 [in Greek] published in *Discoveries in the Judaean Desert* II, ed. P. Benoit, J. T. Milik and R. de Vaux [Jerusalem, 1961] and discussed by E. Lövestam, "ΑΠΟΛΥΕΙΝ– en gammalpalestinensisk skilsmässoterm," *Sv Ex Års* 27 [1962], pp. 132-135).

[9] D. Daube, "Repudium in Deuteronomy," in *Neotestamentica et Semitica* (Edinburgh, 1969), pp. 236-39 argues that the main reason for introducing the certificate was to enable a woman to prove that she was divorced. Prior to the Mosaic provision there might be dire consequences if she or her family wrongly believed that a divorce had taken place.

5 Jesus' forceful retort is a denunciation of human sinfulness which serves to clarify the intention of the Mosaic provision. In Deut. 24:1 divorce is tolerated, but not authorized or sanctioned. When Jesus affirmed that Moses framed the provision concerning the letter of dismissal out of regard to the people's hardness of heart, he was using an established legal category of actions allowed out of consideration for wickedness or weakness. What is involved is the lesser of two evils, and, in this instance, a merciful concession for the sake of the woman.[10] Jesus' purpose is to make clear that the intention of Deut. 24:1 was not to make divorce acceptable but to limit sinfulness and to control its consequences. This had direct bearing on the question of the lawfulness of divorce posed in verse 2. The Mosaic provision in Deut. 24:1-4 was in reality a witness to the gross evil which arose from, or even consisted in, a disregard of the creation ordinance of marriage as set forth in Gen. 1:27; 2:24. The situation that provided the occasion for the permission of divorce was one of moral perversity which consisted in a deliberate determination not to abide by the will of God. Such stubborn rebellion against the divine ordinance is the essence of hard-heartedness. The calloused attitude which could be taken in regard to divorce is well illustrated by the counsel of a respected teacher, Joshua ben Sira (*ca.* 200 B.C.): "If she go not as you would have her go, cut her off and give her a bill of divorce" (literally "cut her off from your flesh," a reflection on the phrase "they shall be one flesh" in Gen. 2:24) (Ecclus. 25:26). Jesus' judgment regarding hard-heartedness presupposes the abiding validity and obligation of the original divine institution of marriage, and the force of his pronouncement here, and in the following verses, is to obliterate the Mosaic tolerance. In this abrogation of the divorce tolerated under Moses there is applied a stringency which raises jurisprudence to the level of the intrinsic requirement of the Law of God.[11]

6-8 The appeal to the creation narrative lifts the discussion to a higher plane by relating it to the purpose of God with regard to marriage. The citation of Gen. 1:27 and 2:24 does not reflect an arbitrary decision as to God's will but entails an appeal over against legislation based upon fallen history to the true nature of human existence as it was revealed

---

10 See D. Daube, "Concessions to Sinfulness in Jewish Law," *JJS* 10 (1959), pp. 1-13.

11 J. Murray, *op. cit.*, pp. 27 f.

from the beginning of the creation.[12] The Mosaic permission was a departure from the creation ordinance and from the practice to which it obligated men. The original constitution of the race as male and female is the basis of marriage.[13] The creation of the two sexes is resolved in unity through marriage, as instituted by God. It was recognized in certain strands of the scribal tradition that Gen. 2:24 commits both husband and wife to mutual fidelity and forbids adultery.[14] The deduction drawn by Jesus in verse 8b ("so then they are no longer two, but one flesh") affirms the indissolubility of marriage against a husband's repudiation of his wife. The significant aspect of Jesus' teaching at this point is that the interdiction of divorce is subservient to the proclamation of the unity of marriage, expressing a reaction against the frequently low esteem of women, even in Judaism.

9 Jesus' final pronouncement grounds the sanctity of marriage in the authority of God himself. This is consistent with the biblical perspective, which never considers husband and wife alone but always in the presence of God, subject to his commands and aided by his grace. God intended that the purpose of marriage should be unity and that the obligations of marriage should be taken seriously. The decisive "No" to divorce provides the required safeguard against human selfishness which always threatens to destroy marriage.[15] It also warns that the man who dissolves a union sanctioned by God inevitably stands under the divine judgment. This warning has in view the husband, rather than a judicial authority,

---

[12] E. Lohmeyer, *Das Evangelium des Markus*[16] (Göttingen, 1963), pp. 198 f.; J. C. Margot, "L'indissolubilité du mariage selon le Nouveau Testament," *Rev Theol Phil* 17 (1967), pp. 391-403.

[13] Cf. J. Murray, *op. cit.*, p. 29: "Marriage is grounded in this male and female constitution: as to its nature it implies that the man and the woman are united in one flesh; as to its sanction it is divine; and as to its continuance it is permanent. The import of all this is that marriage from its very nature and from the divine nature by which it is constituted is ideally indissoluble. It is not a contract of temporary convenience and not a union that may be dissolved at will."

[14] TB *Sanhedrin* 57b; TJ *Kiddushin* I. 1. cited by M. Lehmann, *op. cit.*, p. 265. An appeal to the creation ordinance was not common in Jewish discussions of marriage and divorce, but at Qumran Gen. 1:27 is cited in favor of monogamous and indissoluble marriage (see CD iv. 13-v. 5).

[15] J. Murray, *op. cit.*, p. 33: "Divorce is contrary to the divine institution, contrary to the nature of marriage, and contrary to the divine action by which the union is effected. It is precisely here that its wickedness becomes singularly apparent–it is the sundering by man of a union God has constituted. Divorce is the breaking of a seal which has been engraven by the hand of God."

since in Jewish practice divorce was effected by the husband himself. Behind this solemn prohibition there is a deep concern for personal relationships. Jesus does not envisage marriage as it is at times but as it can and should be–a call to fidelity, peace and love.[16] The conclusion to the public discussion shows that this has not been a rabbinic discussion concerning the interpretation of the Law, but an authoritative teaching, astonishingly different from that of the scribes (cf. Ch. 1:22). The prophetic character of the teaching implies a veiled, messianic proclamation of the Kingdom drawn near in the person of Jesus himself. The disciples are shown that even the ordinances of the Law are not to be followed blindly but are to be carefully considered in the light of the highest standards which Scripture exemplifies. In this historical and geographical context, Jesus' pronouncement confirms the bold testimony of John and condemns equally Antipas and Herodias.

10-11 In the subsequent discussion with the disciples Jesus declared without qualification that a man who divorces his wife and marries another commits adultery against her.[17] The use of the word "adultery" directs the disciples back to the absolute command of God (Ex. 20:14) and clarifies the seriousness of the issue. The new element in this teaching, which was totally unrecognized in the rabbinic courts, was the concept of a husband committing adultery against his former wife. According to rabbinic law a man could commit adultery against another married man by seducing his wife (Deut. 22:13-29) and a wife could commit adultery against her husband by infidelity, but a husband could not be said to commit adultery against his wife.[18] The unconditional form of Jesus' statement served to reinforce the abrogation of the Mosaic permission in Deut. 24:1. This sharp intensifying of the concept of adultery had the effect of elevating the status of the wife to the same dignity as her husband and placed the husband under an obligation of fidelity.

---

16 R. Pesch, "Die neutestamentliche Weisung für die Ehe," *Bib Leb* 9 (1968), pp. 208-221.

17 There is here no reflection on the situation created in the event of adultery, but rather a concentration upon the abrogation of the Mosaic provision concerning divorce and upon the practice of divorce both in Jewish and Gentile circles. On the relationship of Ch. 10:11 to Mt. 19:9; Lk. 16:18 see J. Murray, *op. cit.*, pp. 50-54; and for a different evaluation G. Delling, "Das Logion Mark x. 11 (und seine Abwandlungen) im Neuen Testament," *Nov Test* 1 (1956), pp. 263-274; G. Minette de Tillesse, *op. cit.*, pp. 231 f.

18 F. Hauck, *TWNT* IV (Eng. Tr. 1967), pp. 730-732.

12 The right of a wife to divorce her husband was not recognized by Jewish law[19] and even in Roman law was a relatively recent development near the end of the Republic (*ca.* 50-40 B.C.). If the reading supported by the Western and Caesarean families of texts is correct,[20] Jesus did not speak of divorce in verse 12, but of desertion and remarriage. The woman who deserts her husband to marry another man is as guilty of the sin of adultery as the man who divorces his wife and remarries. This was a pointed judgment upon the conduct of Herodias, who had deserted her husband Philip to marry Antipas. The fact that she had sent her former husband a letter of separation[21] did not alter the sinful, adulterous character of her action. The historical context of Jesus' statement and its vindication of the Baptist's denunciation of this adulterous union (Ch. 6:17f.) was apparently lost to view in later strands of the textual tradition. The form of the text found in the ASV, RSV, which presupposes that a wife possesses the ability to divorce her husband, may represent an adaptation of Jesus' statement to the legal situation which prevailed in Rome and elsewhere in the Empire. This was a logical extension of the principle set forth in Ch. 10:11-12. The change brought verse 12 into parallel structurally with verse 11 and had immediate relevance for the Gentile churches.

11. The Blessing of the Children. Ch. 10:13-16

13 And they were bringing unto him little children, that he should touch them: and the disciples rebuked them.[22]

---

[19] In cases of impotence, denial of conjugal rights, and unreasonable restriction of movement, a wife could sue for divorce, but even in such instances the divorce remained the husband's act. See S-B*K* II (1924), p. 23.

[20] See above, n. 5. It is interesting to compare with this form of the text Ecclus. 23:22-23. After a long passage on the adulterer (Ch. 23:16-21), ben Sira continues: "So it is with a woman who leaves her husband and provides an heir by a stranger. For first of all, she has disobeyed the law of the Most High; second, she has committed an offense against her husband; and third, she has committed adultery through harlotry and brought forth children by another man." Cf. Rom. 7:2f. which speaks of a woman living with another man while her husband is alive, but makes no mention of divorce.

[21] Josephus, *Antiquities* XVIII. v. 4.

[22] Gr. αὐτοῖς read by ℵ B C L Δ Ψ 579 892 1342 *c k* bo. The variant found in the vast majority of MSS, τοῖς προσφέρουσιν, is an attempt to resolve the ambiguity of αὐτοῖς, which grammatically may refer to the children themselves. The masculine gender of the pronoun will exclude the common conception that

14 But when Jesus saw it, he was moved with indignation, and said unto them, Suffer little children to come unto me; forbid them not: for to such belongeth the kingdom of God.
15 Verily I say unto you, Whosoever shall not receive the kingdom of God as a little child, he shall in no wise enter therein.
16 And he took them in his arms, and blessed them, laying his hands upon them.

13 The account of Jesus blessing the children furnishes an appropriate sequel to the pronouncements on the sanctity of marriage in Ch. 10:2-12. Although the circumstances are sketched in the barest possible manner and all references to time and place are absent, the situation is clear: children were brought to the Master in order to request his blessing for their future life.[23] Jesus' subsequent action in taking the children into his arms suggests that quite young children were involved. The terms employed by Mark in describing the initial action, however, are ambiguous: the verb may mean "bring" without implying the idea of carrying (cf. Ch. 7:32; 11:2, 7), while in Ch. 5:39-42 the same descriptive term, a young child, is used of a girl of twelve years. Although it is natural to think that the children were brought by their mothers, the masculine gender of the pronoun in the statement that the disciples rebuked *them* points rather in the direction of their fathers, or even to children themselves, the older ones bringing the younger ones to Jesus. This latter idea tends to be confirmed by verse 14, where the prohibition "Do not forbid *them*" has clear reference to the children. It is not said why the disciples sought to interfere and considered children unimportant to him. Their action was actually an abuse of their authority and stems from that same lack of perception which had led them to interfere with an unknown exorcist who was exercising the power of Jesus' name effectively (see on Ch. 9:38). And, significantly, it called forth the same solemn prohibition: "Do not forbid" (Ch. 9:39).

14 The reference to Jesus' indignation at the disciples' rebuff of the children is confined to Mark's account alone.[24] The suggestion of im-

---

it was (primarily) mothers who were bringing their children to Jesus. It is necessary rather to think of fathers or of children who were responsible for this action.

[23] For parallels among the rabbis see S-B*K* I (1922), pp. 807 f.

[24] Only here in the Gospels is Jesus described as indignant, but cf. the strong emotion expressed in Ch. 1:41, 43; 3:5; 7:34; 9:19.

patience and irritation is strengthened by the sharp staccato effect of the positive and negative commands regarding the children, achieved by asyndeton: "Let the children approach me; do not prevent them" (without an intervening connective).[25] The disciples' attempt to turn the children aside because they were unimportant is one more instance of a persistent tendency to think in wholly human, fallen categories which Jesus had rebuked on earlier occasions (Chs. 8:33; 9:33-37). The Kingdom of God belongs to children, and to others like them who are of no apparent importance, because God has willed to give it to them. That is why these children are to be given access to Jesus, in whom the Kingdom has drawn near (see on Ch. 1:15). Unlike adults, who do not want anything to be given to them, children are comparatively modest and unspoiled. The Kingdom belongs to such as these because they receive it as a gift. The ground of Jesus' surprising statement is not to be found in any subjective quality possessed by children but rather in their objective humbleness and in the startling character of the grace of God who wills to give the Kingdom to those who have no claim upon it.

15 This solemn pronouncement is directed to the disciples, but has pertinence for all men confronted by the gospel because it speaks of the condition for entrance into the Kingdom of God.[26] The demand that a man become as a little child calls for a fresh realization that he is utterly helpless in his relationship to the Kingdom. The Kingdom is that which God gives and that which a man receives. Essential to the comparison developed in verse 15 is the objective littleness and helplessness of the child, which is presupposed in verse 14 as well. The Kingdom may

---

[25] The proper parallel to Ch. 10:13 f. is Ch. 9:38 f. There is no justification in the Marcan context for finding in Ch. 10:13-16 an encouragement to infant baptism (on the ground that κωλύειν is a word associated with baptism in the early Church), as urged by A. Oepke, *TWNT* V (Eng. Tr. 1967), p. 650; O. Cullmann, *Baptism in the New Testament* (London, 1950), pp. 71-80, among others.

[26] It is commonly charged that verse 15 interrupts the natural sequence of verses 14 and 16, which speak of children in the plural while verse 15 speaks of the child. Moreover, Matthew has placed it in a different context (Ch. 18:3). It is possible that verse 15 was an independent logion which Mark has introduced into this context; it is nevertheless wholly appropriate to this context and depends on the same essential comparison presupposed in verse 14, the objective helplessness of the child. See J. Blinzler, "Kind und Königsreich Gottes nach Markus 10, 14. 15," *Klerusblatt* 38 (1934), pp. 90-96; A. Goettmann, "L'attitude fondamental du disciple d'après les Synoptiques: l'enfance spirituelle," *Bible et Vie Chrétienne* 77 (1967), pp. 32-45.

be entered only by one who knows he is helpless and small, without claim or merit. The comparison "receive . . . as a little child" draws its force from the nature of the child to take openly and confidently what is given.[27] The unchildlike piety of achievement must be abandoned in the recognition that to receive the Kingdom is to allow oneself to be given it.[28] Jesus is emphatic that the man who does not receive the Kingdom now, simply and naturally as the children received him, will not enter into it when it is finally established in the consummation. What is specifically in view is the reception of the gospel and of Jesus himself as the one in whom the Kingdom has come near (see on Chs. 8:35, 38; 9:1).

16 Jesus' final action was as significant as his words. His genuine love of children, and the tenderness expressed in taking them into his arms and blessing them through prayer and laying on of hands, can only be properly appreciated within the context of the calloused attitudes toward children that still prevailed within Hellenistic society in the first century. A papyrus dated Alexandria, June 17, 1 B.C., contains a letter of instruction from a husband to his expectant wife, who he supposes may have had her child: "if it was a male child, let it live; if it was a female, cast it out."[29] Jesus' action in honoring the children offered concrete illustration that the blessings of the Kingdom are freely given. In context, the bestowing of the blessing constituted a fresh reiteration of the call to true discipleship and obedience to the intention of God.

---

[27] Cf. A. Oepke, *TWNT* V (Eng. Tr. 1967), p. 649: "The child's littleness, immaturity, and need of assistance, though commonly disparaged, keep the way open for the fatherly love of God, whereas grown-ups so often block it."

[28] An alternative interpretation has been proposed by W. K. L. Clarke, *New Testament Problems* (London, 1929), pp. 36-38, and F. A. Schilling, "What Means the Saying about Receiving the Kingdom of God as a Little Child (τὴν βασιλείαν τοῦ θεοῦ ὡς παιδίον)? Mk x. 15; Lk xviii. 17," *ExT* 77 (1965), pp. 56-58. They read παιδίον as an accusative and insist that the comparative phrase must be taken with "Kingdom" and not with the one who receives it. The meaning is that one receives the Kingdom as one receives a little child, which recalls the formulation of Ch. 9:37 and places the rebuke of the children in verse 13 in a sharper light. For a critique of this proposal see E. Lohmeyer, *op. cit.*, pp. 204 f.

[29] Oxyrhynchus Papyrus IV, No. 744, lines 9 f., cited by A. Deissmann, *Light from the Ancient East*[4] (New York, 1929), pp. 167-170. Cf. Apuleius, *Metamorphoses* x. 23; Ovid, *Metamorphoses* ix. 675-679 for similar instructions; Justin, *Apology* I, 27 ff. for a severe condemnation of the custom of exposing infants, and the Epistle of Diognetus 5:6 for the boast that Christians do not expose their children.

12. Riches and the Kingdom of God. Ch. 10:17-27

17 And as he was going forth into the way, there ran one to him, and kneeled to him, and asked him, Good Teacher, what shall I do that I may inherit eternal life?

18 And Jesus said unto him, Why callest thou me good? none is good save one, *even* God.

19 Thou knowest the commandments, Do not kill, Do not commit adultery,[30] Do not steal, Do not bear false witness, Do not defraud,[31] Honor thy father and mother.

20 And he said unto him, Teacher, all these things have I observed from my youth.

21 And Jesus looking upon him loved him,[32] and said unto him, One thing thou lackest: go, sell whatsoever thou hast, and give to the poor, and thou shalt have treasure in heaven: and come, follow me.

22 But his countenance fell at the saying, and he went away sorrowful: for he was one that had great possessions.[33]

---

[30] The normal order of the commandments (following the M.T. and LXX[A F]) is supported by ℵ[corr] B C *pc* sy[s] sa bo. The reverse order (the seventh commandment before the sixth) is supported by A W 𝔎 Θ λ 28 latt goth Clement of Alexandria, in agreement with Lk. 18:20, Ex. 20:12-16, LXX[B] and the Nash Papyrus. D *k* Irenaeus support the reading "Do not commit adultery, do not commit fornication," and this quite different text was adopted by C. H. Turner, "Marcan Usage," *JThS* 29 (1927), p. 5, who called attention to Ch. 7:21 where both adultery and fornication are listed, and urged that murder was the sin least likely to be in question. It seems more likely, however, that πορνεύσῃς is a scribal error for φονεύσῃς and that the normative order should be followed.

[31] Gr. Μὴ ἀποστερήσῃς is omitted by B* K W Δ Π Ψ λ φ 28 69 579 700 *al* sy[s] geo arm Irenaeus Clement of Alexandria and by the parallel passages Mt. 19:18; Lk. 18:20. The phrase would tend to be eliminated from a list of commandments drawn from the Decalogue, and should be retained. In Classical Greek ἀποστερεῖν is used of the refusal to return property or money deposited with another for safe-keeping; in the LXX it denotes the withholding of wages earned (cf. Ex. 21:10; Deut. 24:14[A]; Ecclus. 4:1). Commentators usually regard it as representing the tenth commandment, but it seems more likely that it is a variant form of the eighth or ninth commandments. Cf. Ezek. 33:15.

[32] It is difficult to be certain what nuance should be read in the statement that Jesus loved him. W. Bauer (A-G, p. 4) translates "became fond of him," but allows for the possibility that the text speaks of a loving gesture, i.e., "he embraced him," and he is followed in this interpretation by E. Lohmeyer, *op. cit.*, p. 211.

[33] Gr. κτῆμα, which in later usage came to be restricted to the meaning "landed property." Perhaps the text should be translated, "because he possessed great estates."

23 And Jesus looked round about, and saith unto his disciples, How hardly [34] shall they that have riches enter into the kingdom of God!
24 And the disciples were amazed at his words. But Jesus answereth again, and saith unto them, Children, how hard is it for them that trust in riches [35] to enter into the kingdom of God! [36]
25 It is easier for a camel to go through a needle's eye, than for a rich man to enter into the kingdom of God.
26 And they were astonished exceedingly, saying unto him, [37] Then who can be saved?
27 Jesus looking upon them, saith, With men it is impossible, but not with God: for all things are possible with God.

Mark appears to regard Ch. 10:17-31 as a single unit expressing the essence of Jesus' teaching concerning entrance into the Kingdom of God. This unit occupies a crucial position in the Marcan outline. It follows Ch. 10:13-16, where entrance into the Kingdom is defined as the gift of God bestowed upon those who acknowledge their helplessness in relationship to the Kingdom. It precedes the third major prophecy of the passion, which sharpens the demand to follow Jesus on the way to the cross. Within this context the major emphases of Ch. 10:17-31 are brought into focus. The call to self-denial in order to follow Jesus, sounded earlier in Ch. 8:34-38 and Ch. 9:33-37, is repeated in verse 21. The demand imposed upon the man who wishes to enter the Kingdom (cf. Ch. 9:42-50) is heightened, and the utter impossibility of attaining

---

[34] The RSV is clearer: "How hard it will be for those who have riches to enter the kingdom of God."

[35] While the text followed by the ASV is supported by the vast majority of MSS and versions, the words τοὺς πεποιθότας ἐπὶ (τοῖς) χρήμασιν should be omitted with B W Δ Ψ *k* sa bo aeth, translating with the RSV "How hard it is to enter the kingdom of God!" The addition appears to be an attempt to link Jesus' statement more closely to the incident and to soften the radical character of his affirmation.

[36] Verse 25 occurs before verse 24 in D 235 *a b ff*2 and this order is favored by V. Taylor, *The Gospel according to St. Mark* (London, 1952), pp. 430-432. The inversion is suspect, however, as a scribal attempt to improve the sense.

[37] The text followed by the ASV has good support (ℵ B C Δ Ψ 892 sa bo), but the variant reading ἑαυτούς (i.e. "saying among themselves") may well be correct. It is strongly attested (A D K [M*] W X Θ Π λ φ *pl* it syp h Augustine) and agrees with Marcan usage (e.g. Chs. 1:27; 11:31; 12:7; 16:3; cf. 4:31; 8:16; 9:34).

the Kingdom through human achievement is underscored in verse 27. The incident of the wealthy man who sought out Jesus in order to learn the requirements for securing eternal life provides the setting for a startling proclamation of the demands and the nature of the Kingdom.

It is customary to subdivide the unit between verses 22 and 23, and this paragraphing is reflected in most editions and translations of the text. It is clear, however, that Jesus' statement regarding the danger of riches is a direct comment on the rejection of the call given in verse 21 and furnishes the necessary sequel to the encounter of verses 17-22. An attractive proposal is that the incident should be regarded as extending through verse 24a, the comment of Jesus in verse 23 together with the note of astonishment in verse 24a terminating the report. The subsequent section, verses 24b-27, would be in the nature of an appendix joined to the incident because of its appropriateness to the situation.[38] This would explain the essential repetition of verse 23 in verse 24b and the repeated statement that the disciples were amazed (verse 24a, verse 26a). While the question regarding the rewards of discipleship is appropriate to this context and may have been prompted historically by the refusal of Jesus' call, verses 28-31 are easily detachable from verses 22-27 and may be considered independently.[39]

17 Behind this recorded incident, with its vivid details, there stands the remembrance of a concrete encounter with Jesus which has left its mark on the tradition. The eager approach of a man while Jesus was setting out on his way, his kneeling posture, the formal address together with the weighty character of his question–all suggest deep respect for Jesus and genuine earnestness on the part of the man himself. He came to consult Jesus as a distinguished rabbi and showed him the deference reserved for revered teachers of the Law.[40] In the OT and subsequent Judaism only God is characteristically called "good," although it was possible to speak in a derived sense of "the good man" (e.g. Prov. 12:2; 14:14; Eccl. 9:2; Mt. 12:35). The designation of Jesus as "good teacher,"

---

[38] This is the analysis of N. Walter, "Zur Analyse von Mk 10:17-31," *ZNW* 53 (1962), pp. 206-218, who argues that a break occurs between verse 24a and 24b rather than between verses 22 and 23.

[39] See C. E. B. Cranfield, "Riches and the Kingdom of God: St. Mark 10:17-31," *ScJTh* 4 (1951), pp. 302-314; W. Zimmerli, "Die Frage des Reichen nach dem ewigen Leben," *EvTh* 19 (1959), pp. 90-97; S. Légasse, *L'Appel du riche (Mc 10, 17-31 et paralleles)* (Paris, 1966).

[40] K. H. Rengstorf, *TWNT* II (Eng. Tr. 1964), pp. 152-157.

however, is virtually without parallel in Jewish sources [41] and should be regarded as a sincere tribute to the impression he had made upon the man, whether "good" be understood to signify "kind," "generous," or some other quality of goodness. The question concerning the inheritance of eternal life, which has formal parallels in early Jewish material, [42] places the discussion which follows in an eschatological perspective. The form of the question (*"What must I do* to inherit eternal life?") implies a piety of achievement which stands in contrast to Jesus' teaching that a man must *receive* the Kingdom (or life) as a gift from God in his helplessness (Ch. 10:15). In the light of verse 20, the man evidently thought that there were conditions to be fulfilled beyond those set forth in the Law.

18-19 Jesus responded by directing attention away from himself to God, who alone is the source and norm of essential goodness. The apparent repudiation of the epithet "good" only serves to radicalize the issue posed by the question of verse 17. The inquirer's idea of goodness was defined by human achievement. He undoubtedly regarded himself as "good" in the sense that he was confident that he had fulfilled the commandments from the time he first assumed their yoke as a very young man; now he hopes to discover from another "good" man what he can do to assure eternal life. Jesus' answer forces him to recognize that his only hope is an utter reliance upon God, who alone can bestow eternal life. The referral of the question to God, bowing before the Father and giving him the glory, places Jesus' response within the context of the lordship of God. In calling in question the man's use of

---

[41] In contrast to Hellenism, where ὦ ἀγαθέ or ὦ βέλτιστε tended to become a conventional form of address, the Jews did not speak to one another in this way. S-B*K* II (1924), p. 24 cites only one (fourth century) Jewish parallel to the expression, TB *Ta'anith* 24b, and there the expression "good teacher" is uttered by a heavenly voice in a dream. In the Testaments of the Twelve Patriarchs the expression "a good man" (Simeon 4:4, 7; Dan. 1:4; Asher 4:1) or "a good heart" (Simeon 4:7; Zebulun 7:2) occurs, but this does not go beyond the biblical examples cited. See W. Grundmann, *TWNT* I (Eng. Tr. 1964), pp. 14-16.

[42] "To inherit eternal life" becomes a fixed expression in Judaism, as in Psalms of Solomon 14:6, which speaks of inheriting life, the life assigned by God to the righteous (cf. Ps. Sol. 3:16; 14:10; I Enoch 38:4; 40:9; 48:3; II Macc. 7:9; IV Macc. 15:3). W. Zimmerli, *op. cit.*, p. 95 has called attention to TB *Berachoth* 28b (Baraitha) where the question is asked, "What must I do to enter life and participate in it?" and the answer is given in terms of Ezek. 33:15 with its demand to walk in the statutes of life and to commit no iniquity.

"good," Jesus' intention is not to pose the question of his own sinlessness or oneness with the Father, but to set in correct perspective the honor of God.[43] He took seriously the concept of the envoy which stands behind the formulation of Ch. 9:37, and desires to be known only in terms of his mission and the one who sent him.

The appeal to the commandments serves to reinforce this emphasis and responds more directly to the question, What must I do? Jesus' response echoes the OT teaching that the man who obeys the Law will live (e.g. Deut. 30:15 f.; Ezek. 33:15 and often). With the exception of the prohibition of fraud, which appears to be an application of the eighth and ninth commandments, the requirements cited are drawn from the Decalogue (Ex. 20:12-16; Deut. 5:16-20). They clearly and incisively focus upon relationships with others as the discernible measure of a man's reverence for God and obedience to his mandates.[44] Jesus does not accept as good any other will than the will of God revealed in the Law. His affirmation of the commandments is a demand for obedient action which recognizes both the sovereignty of God and the existence of the neighbor.

20-21 The impulsive reply of the man indicates that he had made the Law the norm of his life and that he was confident that he had fulfilled its demands perfectly.[45] "From a youth" has reference to a boy's twelfth year when he assumed the yoke of the commandments and was held responsible for their performance (cf. M. *Berachoth* II. 2; Lk. 2:42). From that time forth he had observed "all these." Yet his question to Jesus suggests that behind a façade of security there was a heart which had lost much of its security. Concerned with the dimensions of his own piety, he had lost his delight in God with the result that he lacked

---

[43] See B. B. Warfield's classic treatment of this text, "Jesus' Alleged Confession of Sin," *Princeton Theological Review* 12 (1914), pp. 177-228 and W. Grundmann, *TWNT* I (Eng. Tr. 1964), pp. 15 f.

[44] Cf. J. Calvin, *Institutes of the Christian Religion* II. viii. 52 f. The focus upon the commandments dealing with a man's neighbor is found equally in Rom. 13:9. No discussion of Jesus' regard for the Law, however, is complete without a careful consideration of Ch. 12:28-34. See the insightful treatment of W. Gutbrod, *TWNT* IV (Eng. Tr. 1967), pp. 1059-1065.

[45] Cf. S-B*K* I (1922), p. 814: "That man possesses the ability to fulfill the commandments of God perfectly was so firmly believed by the rabbis that they spoke in all seriousness of people who had kept the whole Law from A to Z." It is necessary only to refer to Paul's affirmation in Phil. 3:6, "as to righteousness under the Law, blameless."

the approval of God. Nevertheless, there was an earnestness in the man which Jesus recognized. The response of verse 21 is not intended to shame him by exposing the real depth of the commandments but is an expression of genuine love for him. The one thing he lacks is the self-sacrificing devotion which characterizes every true follower of Jesus. For this reason Jesus invites him to follow him now and to experience the demands of life and the Kingdom with the Twelve. Keeping the individual commandments is no substitute for the readiness for self-surrender to the absolute claim of God imposed through the call of the gospel. Jesus' summons in this context means that true obedience to the Law is rendered ultimately in discipleship. This man will achieve the perfect observance of the Law when he surrenders himself and follows Jesus. Self-surrender implies a renunciation of his own achievement and the reception of messianic forgiveness through which a man is released to stand under the Law and to offer the obedience of love.

The specific form of the sacrifice Jesus demanded of this man is not to be regarded as a general prescription to be applied to all men, nor yet as a demand for an expression of piety that goes beyond the requirements of the Law. The command to sell his property and to distribute the proceeds to the poor was appropriate to this particular situation. The subsequent reduction to poverty and helplessness would dramatize the fact that man is helpless in his quest for eternal life, which must be bestowed as the gift of God. Scribal legislation prohibited the giving away of all one's possessions precisely because it would reduce a man to poverty.[46] Nevertheless, Jesus' call for resolute sacrifice in order to do the will of God does not exceed that which the Law requires nor that which he himself had voluntarily assumed. The assurance of "treasure in heaven" reflects an idiom that was current in Judaism,[47] which allowed Jesus to enter the thought-world of his contemporaries. Here, however, it is stripped of its customary associations of merit (as if selling one's property and giving the money received to the poor will *earn* a significant reward), since the promised treasure signifies the gift of eternal life or salvation at the revelation of the Kingdom of God.

---

46 M. *Arakhin* VIII. 4; TB *Kethubim* 50a limits the amount to be distributed in almsgiving to one-fifth of one's property. Cf. TB *Baba Bathra* 116a: "poverty is worse than all the plagues of Egypt."

47 S-B*K* I (1922), pp. 429-431; F. Hauck, *TWNT* III (Eng. Tr. 1965), pp. 136-138. When the Jewish proselyte, King Monobazus of Adiabene, was chided for bestowing so much of his wealth upon the poor and afflicted, he replied, "I need to accumulate an imperishable treasure for the age to come" (Tos. *Peah* IV. 18).

The deepest answer to the question of verse 17, however, lies not in the command to sell all but in the call to follow Jesus.[48] Jesus separated persons from their normal historical existence (cf. Chs. 1:16-20; 2:14; 3:13 f.) in order to introduce them to a new quality of existence based upon fellowship with himself. This means that the command to follow Jesus is an invitation to lay hold of authentic life offered as a gift in his own person.[49] Jesus' demand is radical in character. He claims the man utterly and completely, and orders the removal of every other support which could interfere with an unconditional obedience. The terms defined by Jesus clarify what following signifies (cf. Ch. 10:28),[50] and indicate that Jesus himself is the one answer to the man's quest for life.

22 The response to Jesus' call is vividly described: the man's face fell, etched with disappointment and sorrow because he possessed great estates.[51] For the first time Mark indicates that the man was rich. His tragic decision to turn away reflects a greater love for his possessions than for life (cf. Ch. 4:19). What accounts for the rich man's failure is the call of the Kingdom of God with its demand for resolute self-denial (cf. Ch. 8:34). The refusal of the call only serves to accentuate the greatness of the renunciation demanded and the uniqueness of the Twelve as those who had abandoned everything in order to follow Jesus. The conclusion to the interview with Jesus indicates that in the case of this man the Law had not yet fulfilled its function, for its historical task is

---

48 Rightly stressed by W. Zimmerli, *op. cit.*, p. 97.

49 N. Walter, *op. cit.*, pp. 212-215 argues that this incident was first remembered in the tradition as attesting that the only way to life is the following of Jesus. Later the interest shifted to the man's refusal of Jesus' call because he had many possessions.

50 G. Minette de Tillesse, *op. cit.*, p. 261 suggests that it is at this point that Mark sees the element that distinguishes the gospel from the OT: the demand to abandon all and follow Jesus.

51 Later tradition seized on this refusal and elaborated the account in terms influenced by Lk. 16:19-25. In the Gospel according to the Hebrews, which speaks of two rich men, the second "began to scratch his head, being displeased, and then the Lord said to him, How can you say: I have kept the law and the prophets? For it is written in the Law, You shall love your neighbor as yourself, and look, many of your brothers, sons of Abraham, are clad in filth, dying from hunger, and your house is full of many good things but none at all go out from it to them" (Ps - Origen, *Comm. in* Mt. XV. 14, text in K. Aland, *Synopsis Quattuor Evangeliorum* [Stuttgart, 1964], p. 340).

to bring man's satisfaction with this world to an end and to quicken within him a thirst for righteousness and life.

23-25 Jesus' comment on the difficulty encountered by the rich in entering the Kingdom of God draws its force from the refusal of this particular rich man to abandon everything and to follow him. This action demonstrated how easy it was to become so attached to wealth that even an earnest man forgets what is infinitely more important. Jesus' warning implies that only in meeting the demand for radical sacrifice and following is entrance into the Kingdom secured, reinforcing the specific instruction of verse 21. In Judaism it was inconceivable that riches should be a barrier to the Kingdom, since a significant strand of OT teaching regarded wealth and substance as marks of God's favor (e.g. Job 1:10; 42:10; Ps. 128:1-2; Isa. 3:10 and often). If a related strand of the tradition recognized the poor as the special objects of God's protection (e.g. Deut. 15:7-11; Prov. 22:22 f.), the possession of wealth permitted generous gifts to those in need. This aspect of personal and public concern was one of the three major pillars of Jewish piety (almsgiving, fasting and prayer). The affirmation of verse 23 was shocking precisely because it entails the rejection of the concept of merit accumulated through the good works accomplished by the rich, which was presupposed in contemporary Judaism. There is no mark of God's special favor in possessions, nor in the lack of them. The peculiar danger confronting the rich, however, lies in the false sense of security which wealth creates and in the temptation to trust in material resources and personal power when what is demanded by the Law and the gospel is a whole-hearted reliance upon God.

When the disciples expressed their surprise, Jesus repeated his solemn warning in an absolute form: how hard it is to enter the Kingdom of God. The repetition of this sober affirmation is calculated to provoke careful reflection on the part of every man confronted with the call of the gospel. In verse 25, however, Jesus states that it is impossible for a rich man to enter the Kingdom of God. The reference to the camel and the needle are to be taken literally, for the disciples' reaction in verse 26 stems from a statement of real impossibility. The camel was the largest animal found on Palestinian soil. The violent contrast between the largest animal and the smallest opening expresses what, humanly speaking, is impossible or absurd.[52]

---

[52] Rabbinic sources reflect a variant form of the image: "Perhaps you are

26-27 The disciples were more bewildered than before. They understood that the manner in which Jesus spoke of the rich in fact blocks the way for *any* man to achieve entrance into the Kingdom, and they were frightened by this implication. Their anxious question is eschatological in nature: Who will be found in the Kingdom?[53] Jesus' response in verse 27 provides the key to the sober declarations in the immediate context and to the gospel he proclaimed. Salvation is completely beyond the sphere of human possibilities; every attempt to enter the Kingdom on the basis of achievement or merit is futile. Yet even the rule of the impossibility of entrance into the Kingdom for the rich is limited by the sovereign action of God himself. The ability and the power to effect deliverance reside in God alone (cf. Rom. 8:7). "Eternal life," "salvation," or "entrance into the Kingdom" describe a single reality which must be bestowed as his gift to men. The conclusion to the account rejoins the beginning in directing attention to the ability and goodness of God, and constitutes the basis for the renewal of a theology of hope.

13. The Rewards of Discipleship. Ch. 10:28-31

28 Peter began to say unto him, Lo, we have left all, and have followed thee.

---

from Pumbeditha, where they draw an elephant through the eye of a needle" (TB *Baba Metzia* 38b, refined in TB *'Erubin* 53a "... through the eye of a fine needle"); "This is proved by the fact that a man is never shown in a dream a date palm of gold or an elephant going through the eye of a needle," i.e. something absurd or impossible (TB *Berachoth* 55b). On this image see P. Minear, "The Needle's Eye. A Study in Form-Criticism," *JBL* 61 (1942), pp. 157-169; J. Jónsson, *Humour and Irony in the New Testament* (Reykjavík, 1965), pp. 110 f.; O. Michel, *TWNT* III (Eng. Tr. 1965), pp. 593 f. (with further bibliography).

[53] S. Légasse, "Jesus a-t-il annoncé le Conversion Finale d'Israël? (A propos de Marc x. 23-27)," *NTS* 10 (1964), pp. 480-487 finds in verse 26 the question of the messianic salvation promised to Israel. Jesus cites Gen. 18:14, recalling the omnipotence of God in a context of promise to Abraham. Like Paul in Rom. 11, Jesus announced the final conversion of Israel. This conclusion, however, is not obvious from the context, and in addition to Gen. 18:14 Jesus' statement that all things are possible to God recalls Job 10:13 LXX ("Having these qualities in yourself, I know that all things are possible, for nothing is impossible to you"); 42:2; Zech. 8:6 LXX ("Thus says the Lord, the Almighty, Because it will be impossible for the remainder of this people in these days, shall it be impossible for me?"). Cf. W. Grundmann, *TWNT* II (Eng. Tr. 1964), p. 308.

29 Jesus said, Verily I say unto you,[54] There is no man that
hath left house, or brethren, or sisters, or mother, or father,[55]
or children, or lands, for my sake, and for the gospel's sake,
30 but he shall receive a hundredfold now in this time, houses,
and brethren, and sisters, and mothers, and children, and
lands, with persecutions; and in the world to come eternal
life.[56]
31 But many *that are* first shall be last; and the last first.

28 Peter often acted as the spokesman for the Twelve and he did so on this occasion (cf. Chs. 8:29, 32; 9:5; 11:21). His affirmation recalls the invitation extended in verse 21 and was perhaps prompted by it. In contrast to the refusal of Jesus' call by a man who valued his wealth above eternal life, they had abandoned everything in order to follow Jesus (Ch. 1:16-20; 2:14). There appears to be a note of self-congratulation in this announcement. It reflects the same tendency to think of the honors that will be received in the Kingdom before the nature of the mission has been understood that was encountered in Ch. 9:33 (cf. Ch. 10:35-37). Nevertheless, Peter's declaration shows that he has understood Jesus' words in the absolute sense they bear in verse 21.

29-30 Jesus' response defines Christian existence in terms of promise and persecution, and history as the interplay of blessedness and suffering. The contrast between the present age and the age to come is thoroughly Palestinian in character[57] and expresses the tension between promise and fulfilment in the life of faith. The frank recognition of the loss that allegiance to Jesus and the gospel may entail (cf. Ch.

54 On this important expression see Ch. 3:28.

55 The clause ἢ γυναῖκα (or wife) is added in C 𝔎 A Φ Ψ φ 157 *pl f q* and in many MSS and VSS in the parallel text Mt. 19:29, perhaps under the influence of Lk. 18:29 or simply because the reference to children presupposes the presence of wives.

56 The Western text (D it) reduces verses 29-30 to a single statement: "whoever has left house and sisters and brothers and mother and children and fields with persecution, shall receive eternal life in the age to come." In the text of the critical editions the items in verse 29 are joined by the disjunctive ἢ ("or"), while those in verse 30 by the conjunctive καί ("and"); the effect is to emphasize that what is gained far outweighs what has been lost.

57 See H. Sasse, *TWNT* I (Eng. Tr. 1964), pp. 202-207. The thought of receiving compensation both in this age and in the age to come recalls M. *Aboth* V. 19, which speaks of the disciples of Abraham.

13:12 f.)[58] is conditioned by the promise that all that is lost in one society (verse 29) will be regained a hundredfold in the new society created by the dynamic of the gospel (verse 30). This reassurance is addressed to any man who suffers loss for Jesus and the gospel. God takes nothing away from a man without restoring it to him in a new and glorious form. Jesus' reference to the new family which will compensate for the loss sustained in one's own family finds its preparation in Ch. 3:31-35. The omission of a reference to the father in verse 30 is undoubtedly intentional since God himself is the head of the new spiritual family (cf. Ch. 11:25, "Your Father in heaven"). Over against the blessings of the new society stands the sharp realism in the reference to persecution, which clarifies what identification with Jesus and the gospel entails (Ch. 8:34 f.; cf. Ch. 4:17).[59] This has pointed relevance to the church in Rome where suffering for the name of Christ became the reality and norm of Christian experience (cf. I Peter 4:14, 16). Paradoxically, the first part of Jesus' promise (fellowship with other believers) found its deepest realization within the context of the persecution through which the Church became identified as the suffering people of God. The promise of eternal life in the age to come looks beyond the conflicts of history to the triumph assured through radical obedience to the will of God.

31 The final statement, with its antithetic parallelism obtained through the inversion of its clauses, is a piece of "floating tradition" which occurs in other contexts as well (Mt. 20:16; Lk. 13:30). In the Marcan context it is clearly eschatological and speaks of the reversal of every earthly gradation of rank in the age to come. It is difficult, however, to determine whether it is intended to confirm the promise which Jesus has just given to the Twelve (verse 30), or as a warning against the presumption voiced in the outburst of verse 28. It is perhaps better to regard it as a powerful summation of Jesus' teaching concerning the nature of discipleship as service, on the analogy of Ch. 9:35. If the dis-

---

[58] Cf. the related logion in the Coptic Gospel of Thomas, Logion 55: "Jesus said: He who does not hate his father and his mother will not be able to be my disciple; and he who does not hate his brothers and his sisters and does not bear his cross, as I have, will not be worthy of me."

[59] J. Jónsson, *op. cit.*, p. 193 finds in the reference to persecution an instance of "educational irony." For an interesting study of this passage see Bo Reicke, "The New Testament Conception of Reward," in *Aux Sources de la Tradition Chrétienne,* ed. O. Cullmann and P. Menoud (Paris, 1950), pp. 195-206.

ciples thought that they would enter the Kingdom because they had left everything behind, or considered discipleship a matter of giving up possessions now in order to receive a reward later, Jesus shattered these false conceptions. What he demanded was a total, radical commitment to himself, sustained in the act of following him faithfully. In return he gave the Twelve the responsibility to accept the consequences of commitment, supported by his presence and the promise of God.

14. The Third Major Prophecy of the Passion. Ch. 10:32-34

32 And they were on the way, going up to Jerusalem; and Jesus
was going before them: and they were amazed; and they that
followed were afraid.[60] And he took again the twelve, and
began to tell them the things that were to happen unto him,
33 *saying,* Behold, we go up to Jerusalem; and the Son of man
shall be delivered unto the chief priests and the scribes; and
they shall condemn him to death, and shall deliver him unto
the Gentiles:

---

[60] The form of verse 32a is difficult and has prompted textual variation, conjectural emendation and extended discussion. The text adopted in the critical editions has Alexandrian and Caesarean support (א B C* L Δ Θ Ψ 1 565 *pc* bo sa). The final clause ("and those who followed were afraid") is omitted by D K 28 157 700 *pc a b,* while οἱ δέ is replaced by conjunctive καί in A 𝔎 *et al* 118 892 1071 *pl l q r* vg sy geo, but both of these variants appear to be attempts to simplify and smooth out the text. A commonly held point of view is that the passage speaks of two distinct groups who were following Jesus: (1) the Twelve, who were amazed, and (2) other followers, including the women mentioned in Ch. 15:40 f., who were afraid. Nothing in the larger context of the passage lends support to this interpretation. Moreover, an examination of Mark's use of the vocabulary of amazement and fear indicates that it is futile to attempt any real discrimination between these expressions which will explain why the evangelist speaks of the amazement of one group and the fear of another (cf. Chs. 1:27; 9:32; 10:24; 12:12; 16:5 f., 8). Considerations of context and Marcan usage tend to indicate that only *one* group of followers is indicated, the Twelve, who show amazement and fear in Jesus' presence (as in Ch. 9:32; cf. Chs. 4:38-41; 6:49-51). When Mark wishes to indicate the presence of a group in addition to the Twelve, he does so clearly (cf. Ch. 10:46). The final clause in verse 32a is an instance of a Marcan after-thought (as in Ch. 2:15), providing an additional commentary on the impression created by Jesus' presence. On this complex question see R. P. Meye, *Jesus and the Twelve* (Grand Rapids, 1968), pp. 159-164; K. Tagawa, *op. cit.,* pp. 108-110; and for a dissenting point of view V. Taylor, *op. cit.,* pp. 437 f.; C. E. B. Cranfield, *The Gospel according to St. Mark*[2] (Cambridge, 1963), p. 335.

34 and they shall mock him, and shall spit upon him, and shall scourge him, and shall kill him; and after three days he shall rise again.

32 Each of the three major prophecies of the passion is set within the context of the journey, but now for the first time Jerusalem is named as the destination where Jesus will accomplish his mission. Jerusalem was the holy city set upon a hill, and it was normal to speak of "going up" to Jerusalem and the Temple.[61] There is a note of solemnity in the vivid picture of Jesus walking before his frightened disciples, inflexible in his determination to do the will of God (cf. Isa. 50:7 f.). The action of Jesus walking ahead of the Twelve corresponds to rabbinic custom,[62] but far more than this is involved. The description anticipates the action of the Risen Lord promised in Chs. 14:28; 16:7, and evokes the image of the powerful Savior who leads his people with purpose and direction. The person of Jesus is central in the scene sketched in verse 32a. What awakens amazement and terror in the disciples who follow is not the recognition that the road leads to Jerusalem nor an awareness of what will be accomplished there, but Jesus himself. The power of the Lord, who holds in his hands his own destiny as well as that of the people of God, is manifested for Mark and his readers in the awe and dread which characterize those around him (cf. Ch. 9:32).[63]

The solemn announcement concerning Jerusalem, and the suffering and vindication to be experienced there, is elaborately introduced. The notice that Jesus "took again the Twelve" simply means that he gathered the disciples around him to make precise the purpose of the journey, which had been disclosed earlier in less specific terms (Chs. 8:31; 9:12, 31). On each occasion the Twelve alone were the recipients of this prophetic instruction.

33-34 Of Jesus' three prophecies of his suffering and death, the third is the most precise.[64] Its relationship to the earlier utterances and to the

---

[61] Cf. J. Schneider, *TWNT* I (Eng. Tr. 1964), p. 519.

[62] Cf. G. Kittel, *TWNT* I (Eng. Tr. 1964), p. 213.

[63] G. Bertram, *TWNT* III (Eng. Tr. 1965), p. 7; K. Tagawa, *op. cit.*, pp. 108-110; E. Lohmeyer, *op. cit.*, p. 220.

[64] For the form of the prophecy and a treatment of several of its more significant details see the discussion of Ch. 8:31 and Ch. 9:31.

course of events reported in the Passion Narrative may be seen in the following table: [65]

	Ch. 8:31	*Ch. 9:31*	*Ch. 10:33-34*	*Passion Narrative*
(1) Delivered to the chief priests and scribes	—	(X)	X	Ch. 14:53
(2) Sentenced to death	(X)	—	X	Ch. 14:64
(3) Delivered to the Romans	—	—	X	Ch. 15:1, 10
(4) Mocked, spit upon, scourged	—	—	X	(Ch. 14:65); Ch. 15:15-20
(5) Executed	X	X	X	Ch. 15:20-39, 44
(6) Resurrected	X	X	X	Ch. 16:1-8

The greater detail in the third prophecy and its close correspondence with Jesus' subsequent experience have led many commentators to affirm that the formulation has been shaped by the Passion Narrative itself. [66] This judgment is by no means necessary. Jesus was aware of the balance of power among the various authorities in Palestine and could calculate precisely the procedure which would be followed in carrying out a sentence of death. The more precise details in verse 34 are actually enumerated in the inverse order in which they occur in Ch. 15:15-20; moreover, there has been no attempt to conform the vocabulary of the prophecy to the fulfilment (see Ch. 15:15). It is far more likely that the form of the prophecy indicates Jesus' reflection on such OT texts as Ps. 22:6-8, where the righteous Sufferer is cruelly mocked, and Isa. 50:6, which speaks of scourging and spitting as the tokens of contempt to which the righteous Servant is exposed. It is appropriate to see in verses 33-34 a further revelation of sufferings which Jesus will assume in fulfilment of his messianic vocation.

---

[65] This table has been adapted from V. Taylor, *op. cit.,* p. 346 and G. Minette de Tillesse, *op. cit.,* p. 376.

[66] V. Taylor, *op. cit.,* p. 437: "In its precision the third [prediction] is a *vaticinium ex eventu,*" and this judgment is repeated often. On the failure of the disciples to be prepared for Jesus' betrayal and death when he had spoken so plainly see G. W. Barker, W. L. Lane, and J. R. Michaels, *The New Testament Speaks* (New York, 1969), pp. 105-110.

The new element in the prophecy is the sharp distinction between Jesus' condemnation by the Jewish authorities and the execution of the sentence of death by the Gentiles, who are mentioned for the first time in the context of the passion (cf. Acts 3:13). Delivery to the Gentiles reveals that Jesus will be held in contempt by his own countrymen, for the Gentiles are the last people to whom the Messiah of the people of God should be handed over. The actions defining his humiliation are carried out by the Gentiles. Mockery (cf. Ch. 15:20) and spitting (cf. Ch. 15:19) are forms of derision to which Jesus will be exposed, while the scourging (cf. Ch. 15:15; cf. Jn. 19:1) is more closely related to his violent death, in accordance with the Roman law that scourging always accompanied a capital sentence.[67] Nothing is said of crucifixion, but this could be presupposed under the circumstances of Roman jurisdiction.[68] In Jerusalem, as nowhere else, Jesus will fulfill his mission. Beyond the abject humiliation disclosed in the sober terms of verse 34 lies the assurance of vindication through resurrection.

15. Rank, Precedence and Service. Ch. 10:35-45

35 And there came near unto him James and John, the sons of Zebedee,[69] saying unto him, Teacher, we would that thou shouldest do for us whatsoever we shall ask of thee.

36 And he said unto them, What would ye that I should do for you?[70]

---

[67] See the references cited by C. Schneider, *TWNT* IV (Eng. Tr. 1967), p. 517 n. 17.

[68] Cf. Plato, *Republic* II, 5, 361e: "The just man will be scourged, tortured, bound, blinded with fire, and when he has endured every kind of suffering will at last be impaled on the cross." This passage is cited by E. Stauffer, *Jesus and His Story* (New York, 1960), p. 170, who comments: "There can be no doubt that Jesus never read the works of Plato. But he knew human beings at least as well as Socrates or Plato. And he knew that his era was the setting for a conflict of quite another sort from the conflict between the righteous and the unrighteous–namely the struggle between God and the world. In view of this, if for no other reason, Jesus must have foreseen his violent death from the very beginning."

[69] The identification of James and John as the sons of Zebedee is a precision unnecessary in the light of Chs. 1:19; 3:17 and may stem from a primitive stage when this incident had an independent existence.

[70] Verse 36 is omitted by the North African MS *k*, while in D the words τί θέλετέ με are omitted, resulting in the reading "I will do it." Other minor variants attempt to smooth out the construction of the text.

37 And they said unto him, Grant unto us that we may sit, one
on thy right hand, and one on *thy* left hand, in thy glory.
38 But Jesus said unto them, Ye know not what ye ask. Are ye
able to drink the cup that I drink? [71] or to be baptized with
the baptism that I am baptized with?
39 And they said unto him, We are able. And Jesus said unto
them, The cup that I drink ye shall drink; and with the baptism
that I am baptized withal shall ye be baptized:
40 but to sit on my right hand or on *my* left hand is not mine to
give; but *it is for them* for whom [72] it hath been prepared. [73]
41 And when the ten heard it, they began to be moved with indignation concerning James and John.
42 And Jesus called them to him, and saith unto them, Ye know
that they who are accounted to rule over the Gentiles lord it
over them; and their great ones exercise authority over them.
43 But it is not so among you: but whosoever would become
great among you, shall be your minister;
44 and whosoever would be first among you, shall be servant
of all.
45 For the Son of man also came not to be ministered unto, but
to minister, and to give his life a ransom [74] for many. [75]

---

71 Normally the usage of the present indicates an action already begun. The question posed could thus be translated: Can you drink the cup that I am in the process of drinking? More probably the underlying Aramaic would be interpreted as a future, in which case it points forward to the passion. Cf. Mt. 20:22 τὸ ποτήριον ὃ ἐγὼ μέλλω πίνειν.

72 In minuscule 225 it (sys c) sa aeth the text is read ἄλλοις ἡτοίμασται, i.e. "it is prepared for others." This reading, which reflects an alternate division of the uncials ΑΛΛΟΙΣ (which could be read either as ἀλλ' οἷς or ἄλλοις), is preferred by P. L. Couchoud, "Notes de critique verbale sur St. Marc et St. Matthieu," *JThS* 34 (1903), p. 125, but is probably of Marcionite origin. See B. M. Metzger, *The Text of the New Testament* (Oxford, 1964), p. 13.

73 The addition of the phrase "by my Father" in ℵ* Θ Φ λ 22 91 251 299 697 1071 1342 syhmg represents assimilation to Mt. 20:23, but expresses what is implied.

74 Gr. λύτρον, which occurs in the NT only here and in the parallel text, Mt. 20:28. The position of the words which follow, ἀντὶ πολλῶν ("in place of many") shows that they depend on the noun λύτρον and not on the verb δοῦναι. On this important concept, which expresses the essence of Mark's understanding of Jesus' death, see J. Jeremias, "Das Lösegeld für Viele (Mk. 10:45)," *Judaica* 3 (1947/48), pp. 249-264; S. Lyonnet, "De notione redemptionis," *Verb Dom* 36 (1958), pp. 129-146; N. Levinson, "Lutron," *ScJTh* 12 (1959), pp. 277-285; F. Büchsel, *TWNT* IV (Eng. Tr. 1967), pp. 341-349; A. Feuillet, "Le logion sur la rançon," *RevSciPhTh* 51 (1967), pp. 365-402; H. J. B. Combrink, *Die diens van Jesus. 'n Eksegetiese beskouing oor Markus 10:45* (Groningen, 1968).

75 The authenticity of verse 45 has been denied on various grounds. The saying,

Ch. 10:32-45 is structurally parallel with Ch. 9:30-37. The second and third major prophecies of the passion (Ch. 9:30-32; Ch. 10:32-34) are both followed by an exposure of the presumption of the disciples (Ch. 9:33 f.; Ch. 10:35-37) and by Jesus' instruction concerning humility and service (Ch. 9:35-37; Ch. 10:42-45). This incident reveals that in spite of Jesus' repeated efforts since Peter's confession at Caesarea Philippi to inculcate in his disciples the spirit of self-renunciation demanded by the cross, the sons of Zebedee have understood his intention very superficially. Their ambitious request brings discredit upon them, while the indignation of the other ten disciples reflects a similar preoccupation with their own dignity. The pronouncement of Jesus concerning the servant vocation of the Son of Man, who seals his service with the sacrifice of his life for the many, goes beyond the instruction given to the disciples in Ch. 9:35-37, and brings the question of rank, precedence and service into profound pastoral and theological perspective.

35-37 In the request of James and John the misunderstanding which attended each of the previous prophecies of Jesus' suffering asserted itself in a blatant form. The disciples had failed completely to grasp the significance of Jesus' teaching that he would be treated with contempt and be put to death. The request of the sons of Zebedee for places of honor in the glory of the Son of Man immediately follows Jesus' announcement that they were going to Jerusalem and after three days the Son of Man will rise. The enthusiasm reflected in the sweeping terms of verse 35, and the form of the petition in verse 37, in the context of approaching the royal city, show that the brothers regard Jesus as the eschatological Lord who goes to Jerusalem to restore the glory of the fallen throne of David. The question of rank, involving an inflated understanding of their own position, is best explained in the context of

---

however, is thoroughly Palestinian in vocabulary (Son of Man, give one's life, καί as an explanatory conjunction, the many) and character (the synonymous parallelism, the form of verse 45a in which the idea is expressed first negatively and then positively, and the association of the phrase "to give his life" with "a ransom for many"). The Semitic character of verse 45 appears clearly when its expression is compared with I Tim. 2:6. Those who deny the genuineness of Jesus' saying too easily assume that its ideas are exclusively Pauline and do not sufficiently recognize that Pauline thought is rooted in Palestinian tradition. For a defense of the authenticity of Ch. 10:45 see F. Büchsel, *TWNT* IV (Eng. Tr. 1967), pp. 341 f.; A. Feuillet, *op. cit.*, pp. 367-385; L. Morris, *The Apostolic Preaching of the Cross*[2] (Grand Rapids, 1955), pp. 26-35.

royal messiahship.[76] The request may be for the places of honor at the messianic banquet[77] or for the positions of eminence and authority at the parousia, when Jesus is enthroned as the eschatological judge (see Chs. 8:38; 13:26). The place of honor is the seat on the right, and next to it, the seat on the left (cf. I Kings 2:19; Ps. 110:1; I Esdras 4:29; Ecclus. 12:12; Josephus, *Antiquities* VI. xi. 9). The announcement of Jerusalem as the goal of the journey suggested that Jesus' glory was imminent (cf. Ch. 9:1).

38-39 Jesus' response is as sharp as the probing questions in Ch. 7:17 or Ch. 8:20. Taking account of what immediately follows, the sense appears to be as follows; you do not know that in requesting to participate in my glory you ask at the same time to share my painful destiny, an indispensable condition of my glorification.[78] It must be stressed that the question of verse 38 calls for a negative reply. The sufferings and death which await Jesus, expressed by the two images of the cup and baptism, belong to the unique messianic mission of the Son of Man. Verse 38 expresses an impossibility, and not the requisite condition for association with Jesus' glory. Jesus' pointed question contains at least an implied condemnation of the proud pretensions of James and John. Their desire to share the messianic glory of Jesus, without taking account of the distance which separates them from their Master, is insensitive that this would entail participation in his sufferings and in his messianic death for the salvation of men.

In interpreting the enigmatic language of the cup and baptism it is crucial to recognize that these images do not bear the same significance when applied to Jesus and when applied to the disciples. The cup and baptism signify that Jesus in his passion will be the voluntary sacrifice for the sins of men; when applied to the disciples in verse 39 these images suggest their moral participation in Jesus' passion.[79]

To share someone's cup was a recognized expression for sharing his

---

76 J. B. Tyson, "The Blindness of the Disciples in Mark," *JBL* 80 (1961), pp. 261-268.

77 Were James and John asking for a confirmation that the places they occupied in the fellowship meals which the Twelve shared with Jesus would be their seats when his glory was openly unveiled? Cf. Jn. 13:23-25 (where John appears to be reclining on Jesus' right hand).

78 A. Feuillet, "La coupe et le baptême de la passion (Mc, x, 35-40; cf. Mt, xx, 20-23; Lc, xii, 50)," *RB* 74 (1967), pp. 363 f.

79 *Ibid.*, pp. 370-388.

fate.[80] In the OT the cup of wine is a common metaphor for the wrath of God's judgment upon human sin and rebellion,[81] and this understanding was kept alive into the first century.[82] The total ruin which the cup represents is willed by God and constitutes a divine judgment. In interpreting verse 38 it is necessary to see the cup as a designation of judgment. Jesus boldly applied to himself the image of the cup used by the prophets to threaten the enemies of God with his divine vengeance. The cup which Jesus must drink has reference to divine punishment of sins which he bears in place of the guilty (cf. Chs. 10:45; 14:24). The reality which the image represents is expressed in Isa. 53:5: "he was wounded because of our sins, bruised because of our iniquities; *the chastisement which gives us peace has been upon him,* and it is by his sufferings that we are healed."[83]

The image of baptism is parallel to that of the cup.[84] In popular Greek usage the vocabulary of baptism was used to speak of being overwhelmed by disaster or danger, and a similar metaphorical use of submersion is present in Scripture.[85] The texts of the OT, however, do not demonstrate that to be submerged signified submission to a fearful death, and it is this which is required in the context. Apparently Jesus called his passion a baptism (cf. Lk. 12:50) because he and the disciples were

---

80 For an extensive survey of OT and rabbinic references see S-B*K* I (1922), pp. 836-38. This thought is rare beyond biblical and Jewish literature, but cf. Plautus, *Casina* 933 where "that he should drink the same cup I drink" *(ut eodem poculo quo ego bibi biberet)* signifies to have him experience the same fate as I do. Cf. Martyrdom of Polycarp 14:2, "I bless thee, because thou hast counted me worthy to share . . . in the cup of thy Christ," where martyrdom is in view.

81 Cf. Ps. 75:8; Isa. 51:17-23; Jer. 25:15-28; 49:12; 51:7; Lam. 4:21 f.; Ezek. 23:31-34; Hab. 2:16; Zech. 12:2. See L. Goppelt, *TWNT* VI (1959), pp. 149-153; W. Lotz, "Das Sinnbild des Bechers," *Neue Kirchliche Zeitschrift* 28 (1917), pp. 396-407.

82 E.g. Psalms of Solomon 8:14 f.: "They left no sin undone in which they did not surpass the heathen. Therefore, God mingled for them a spirit of wandering, and gave them to drink a cup of undiluted wine, that they might become drunken"; 1QpHab xi. 10-15; Martyrdom of Isaiah 5:13; Palestine Pentateuch Targum to Deut. 32:1. See R. Le Déaut, "Goûter le calice de la mort," *Biblica* 43 (1962), pp. 82-86.

83 A. Feuillet, *op. cit.*, pp. 370-377.

84 *Ibid.*, pp. 377-382; G. Delling, "ΒΑΠΤΙΣΜΑ, ΒΑΠΤΙΣΘΗΝΑΙ," *Nov Test* 2 (1957), pp. 92-115.

85 E.g. Ps. 42:7; 49:3 (Symmachus used βαπτίζειν), 15; 69:2 (Aquila used βαπτίζειν), 15; Job 9:31 (Aquila used βαπτίζειν); 22:11; Isa. 43:2; Jonah 2:3-6. For the metaphor in the context of divine judgment see Isa. 30:27 f.

familiar with John's rite of repentance, which he called "baptism" and set in an explicit context of God's judgment upon human sin. Jesus understood that his baptism expressed his solidarity with sinful men and signified his willingness to assume the burden of the judgment of God (see on Ch. 1:2-11). The baptism which he anticipates is his death upon the cross in fulfilment of his messianic vocation. [86] Applied to Jesus, the images of the cup and baptism signify that he bears the judgment merited by the sins of men (cf. Ch. 14:36; 15:34). While informed by the OT motifs, the primary key for interpreting the parabolic language of verse 38 is Jesus' messianic task.

In verse 39 the two images are paradoxically applied to James and John. They indicate that the brothers will participate in the sufferings of Jesus (cf. I Peter 4:13). There must be a solidarity between the Son of Man and his disciples, and this is expressed not only by their grateful acceptance of his protection and favor, but also by their following his example of humility and service, if necessary to the extent of death. The description of discipleship implied conforms to Ch. 8:34-38. The reference, however, is neither exclusively nor necessarily to martyrdom, for the image of baptism is not found in this sense in Christian literature until the turn of the second century. [87] Rather Jesus prophesies that the sons of Zebedee, like himself, will endure great tribulation and suffering for the gospel (cf. Acts 12:2; Rev. 1:9).

The two brothers are confident that they are prepared to share Jesus' destiny, even in reference to suffering if this is the necessary prelude to glory. Their naïve reply only serves to indicate that they were as incapable of understanding the full import of Jesus' reference to his cup and baptism as they were of grasping the real significance of his prophecy of the passion.

40 Jesus' denial of the right to set men on his right or left hand is consistent with his refusal to accept even the appearance of an arbitrary authority. His prerogatives are limited by his submission to the Father,

---

[86] A. Feuillet, *op. cit.*, pp. 380-382; G. Delling, *op. cit.*, pp. 95-97.

[87] The tradition that John, as well as his brother James, was martyred is based on late and unreliable reports that "Papias says in his second book that John the Theologian and James his brother were killed by the Jews" (cited by Philip of Side [*ca.* 450] and George Harmartolos [9th century]). Neither Irenaeus nor Eusebius, both of whom knew Papias' work well, mentions such a tradition and Irenaeus' testimony that John lived to a peaceful old age in the province of Asia is against it (*Adv. haer.* ii. 22). On this question see A. Feuillet, *op. cit.*, pp. 358-363.

and Jesus frankly admitted this (cf. Ch. 13:32; Acts 1:7). The appointment of the places of honor is the Father's prerogative, and James and John are only given the assurance that these will be assigned to those who have been prepared by him.

41-44 The other ten disciples were indignant because they were jealous of their own dignity and fearful lest the two brothers should secure some advantage over them. Their insensitivity to the seriousness of the moment links them with James and John, and suggests the cruel loneliness with which Jesus faced the journey to Jerusalem. It also indicates the degree to which selfish ambition and rivalry were the raw material from which Jesus had to fashion the leadership for the incipient Church.

In seeking to impress the truth of Ch. 9:35 on the Twelve, Jesus contrasted the conduct of Gentile rulers with the submission to service and sacrifice which is appropriate to discipleship. It is probable that his most direct contact with the expression of power and authority by the petty rulers of Palestine and Syria and the great lords of Rome was through the coins which circulated in the land. To cite only two examples, the denarius that was used for paying taxes (cf. Ch. 12:16) portrayed Tiberius as the semi-divine son of the god Augustus and the goddess Livia; the copper coins struck by Herod Philip at Caesarea Philippi showed the head of the reigning emperor (Augustus, then Tiberius) with the emperor's name and the inscription: "He who deserves adoration." [88] There is biting irony in the reference to those who give the illusion of ruling (cf. Jn. 19:11) but simply exploit the people over whom they exercise dominion. In their struggle for rank and precedence, and the desire to exercise authority for their own advantage, the disciples were actually imitating those whom they undoubtedly despised.

Jesus consciously opposes to the order of earthly rule the vocation of the servant. The synonymous parallelism between verses 43 and 44 identifies the household servant and the slave as men whose activities are not directed toward their own interests but to those of another. The order of life for the common dealings of the disciples is to be love expressed in the form of service. This transforms the question of rank and greatness into the task of service: only by service does one become great. On the other hand, high rank ("first," "greatest") deserves recog-

---

88 For these and other examples see E. Stauffer, *op. cit.*, pp. 54-58.

nition in the community when it is rooted in the service which Jesus commands (cf. Ch. 9:35). The Twelve are summoned to become the compassionate community and to recognize that the performance of an act of compassion as an expression of pure devotion to Jesus is at one and the same time worship and service (cf. I Cor. 9:19; II Cor. 4:5; Gal. 5:13; I Peter 5:3).[89]

45 The reversal of all human ideas of greatness and rank was achieved when Jesus came, not to be served, but to serve. He voluntarily veiled his glory as the Son of Man (cf. Chs. 8:38; 13:26; 14:62) and assumed the form of a slave who performed his service unto death because this was the will of God (cf. Phil. 2:6-8). In verse 45, which subsumes verses 43-44, the death of Jesus is presented as his service to God and as a vicarious death for many in virtue of which they find release from sin. Each of the components of this highly compressed saying is significant. The formulation "The Son of man came . . . " places the entire statement in the context of Jesus' messianic mission (cf. Ch. 2:17). The service in which the royal will of the Son of Man is displayed is fulfilled in his giving of himself. In a Jewish frame of reference this expression was characteristically used of the death of the martyrs (e.g. I Macc. 2:50; 6:44; Mekilta to Ex. 12:1). In this context it expresses the element of voluntariness or self-sacrifice in the death of Jesus who offers himself in obedience to the will of God. His death has infinite value because he dies not as a mere martyr but as the transcendent Son of Man.

The ransom metaphor sums up the purpose for which Jesus gave his life and defines the complete expression of his service. The prevailing notion behind the metaphor is that of deliverance by purchase, whether a prisoner of war, a slave, or a forfeited life is the object to be delivered. Because the idea of equivalence, or substitution, was proper to the concept of a ransom, it became an integral element in the vocabulary of redemption in the OT.[90] It speaks of a liberation which connotes a servitude or an imprisonment from which man cannot free himself. In the context of verse 45a, with its reference to the service of the Son of Man, it is appropriate to find an allusion to the Servant of the Lord in Isa. 53, who vicariously and voluntarily suffered and gave his life for

---

89 See further P.H. Boulton, "Διακονέω and its Cognates in the Four Gospels," in *Studia Evangelica,* ed. K. Aland *et al.,* I (Berlin, 1959), pp. 415-422.

90 For a treatment of the relevant material see O. Procksch, *TWNT* IV (Eng. Tr. 1967), pp. 328-335.

the sins of others. The specific thought underlying the reference to the ransom is expressed in Isa. 53:10 which speaks of "making his life an *offering for sin.*"[91] Jesus, as the messianic Servant, offers himself as a guilt-offering (Lev. 5:14-6:7; 7:1-7; Num. 5:5-8) in compensation for the sins of the people. The release effected by this offering overcomes man's alienation from God, his subjection to death, and his bondage to sin. Jesus' service is offered to God to release men from their indebtedness to God.[92]

The thought of substitution is reinforced by the qualifying phrase "a ransom *for the many.*" The Son of Man takes *the place* of the many and there happens to him what would have happened to them (cf. Ch. 8:37: what no man can do, Jesus, as the unique Son of Man, achieves). The many had forfeited their lives, and what Jesus gives in their place is his life. In his death, Jesus pays the price that sets men free. The sacrifice of the one is contrasted with those for whom it is made, in allusion to Isa. 53:11 f. In rabbinic literature, and even more strikingly at Qumran, "the many" is a technical term for the elect community, the eschatological people of God.[93] The majestic figure of the Son of Man is linked here with the community which will be vindicated and saved in the eschatological judgment because Jesus goes to his death innocently, voluntarily and in accordance with the will of God. This corresponds perfectly with the main thought of Isa. 53. The ultimate meaning of Jesus' vicarious suffering and his giving himself as a ransom, however, can be understood only from the reality of his life, death and resurrec-

---

[91] Or possibly Isa. 53:12, where 1 Q Isa.[a] reads "and for their sins they were stricken," in contrast to the M.T. "and made intercession for the transgressors." The reading attested at Qumran is presupposed in Testament of Benjamin 4:8 (ὑπὲρ ἀνόμων παραδοθήσεται καὶ ὑπὲρ ἀσεβῶν ἀποθανεῖται), Isa. 53:12 LXX (καὶ διὰ τὰς ἁμαρτίας αὐτῶν παρεδόθη), and Paul understands the text in the same way (Rom. 4:25; I Cor. 15:3). On this question see J. Jeremias, *op. cit.*, pp. 262-264; H. W. Wolff, *Jesaja 53 im Urchristentum*[2] (Berlin, 1950), pp. 64-70; C. Maurer, "Knecht Gottes und Sohn Gottes im Passionsbericht des Markusevangeliums," *ZThK* 50 (1953), pp. 1-38; E. Lohse, *Märtyrer und Gottesknecht* (Göttingen, 1955), pp. 97-102. For the dissenting opinion that Isa. 53 does not have any bearing on Ch. 10:45, see C. K. Barrett, "The Background of Mark 10:45," in *New Testament Essays*, ed. A. J. B. Higgins (Manchester, 1959), pp. 1-18.

[92] F. Büchsel, *TWNT* IV (Eng. Tr. 1967), p. 344. The larger discussion (pp. 344-349), putting Ch. 10:45 in biblical-theological perspective, is well worth consulting.

[93] Cf. R. Marcus, "*Mebaqqer* and *Rabbim* in the Manual of Discipline vi, 11-13," *JBL* 75 (1956), pp. 298-302; H. Huppenbauer, "רב, רוב, רבים in der Sektenregel (1 QS)," *ThZ* 13 (1957), pp. 136 f.; J. Jeremias, *TWNT* VI (1959), pp. 543-545.

tion as narrated in the Gospel. In Mark there is complete correspondence between the ransom saying and the death of Jesus. Because Jesus' will is synchronous with the will of God he must die in the place of guilty men (Ch. 8:31, 33). This is what it means for him to offer his life as a ransom for the many.

This painful and glorious destiny of the Son of Man is something unique to his mission and in a definite sense is incommunicable: only he can accomplish this service. Nevertheless, his submission to the servant's vocation is here proposed as an example to the Twelve, who are summoned to pattern their lives after the humility of the Son of Man. Jesus' sacrifice of his own glory is the ground of a renewal of life to self-sacrificial obedience. The disciples were to experience this power of his death in themselves. That John, the son of Zebedee, ultimately understood Jesus' intention is clear from I John 3:16: "He laid down his life for us; and we ought to lay down our lives for the brethren."

16. The Faith of Blind Bartimaeus. Ch. 10:46-52

46 And they came [94] to Jericho: and as he went out from Jericho, with his disciples and a great multitude, the son of Timaeus, Bartimaeus,[95] a blind beggar, was sitting by the way side.
47 And when he heard that it was Jesus the Nazarene,[96] he began to cry out, and say, Jesus, thou son of David, have mercy on me.
48 And many rebuked him, that he should hold his peace: but he cried out the more a great deal, Thou son of David, have mercy on me.
49 And Jesus stood still, and said, Call ye him. And they call the blind man, saying unto him, Be of good cheer:[97] rise, he calleth thee.

---

94 The tendency to focus attention solely upon Jesus when introducing an incident accounts for the singular ἔρχεται in D it sy^{s}. For a similar alteration of the plural to a singular see Ch. 9:14, 33.

95 Mark customarily introduces the Aramaic formation first, followed by the Greek (e.g. Chs. 3:17; 7:11, 34; 14:36), and it is possible that the inverse order in Ch. 10:46 points to a primitive scribal gloss. The Old Syriac Gospels (sy$^{s\ c}$) have "Timaeus, the son of Timaeus," but this may reflect an attempt to simplify the text. Bartimaeus is apparently a patronymic of Aramaic origin, i.e. בַּר טִמְאַי, "the son of Timai." Cf. S-B*K* II (1924), p. 25, who mentions a Rabbi Joshua bar Timai.

96 See on Ch. 1:24.

97 See on Ch. 6:50. Θάρσει occurs seven times in the NT, and apart from this

50 And he, casting away his garment,[98] sprang up, and came
to Jesus.
51 And Jesus answered him, and said, What wilt thou that I
should do unto thee? And the blind man said unto him, Rabboni,[99] that I may receive my sight.
52 And Jesus said unto him, Go thy way; thy faith hath made
thee whole. And straightway he received his sight, and followed him in the way.

46 The incident involving the blind beggar, Bartimaeus, is the last of the healing miracles recorded by Mark. The vividness with which the story is told as well as the precision with which it is located at Jericho on the final stage of Jesus' journey to Jerusalem is apparently due to eyewitness report. Jericho was located about five miles west of the Jordan and eighteen miles northeast of Jerusalem. The old city had badly deteriorated by the first century, but extending southward the new city built by Herod as the site for his magnificent winter palace was renowned for its singular beauty and fertility.[100] The crowd which came out of the city with Jesus and his disciples plays almost no role in the ensuing drama; it most likely consisted of pilgrims on their way

instance, it is always the word of Jesus. Mark may have been thinking of Isa. 35:4-5: "Say to them that are of a fearful heart, Be strong, fear not: behold your God . . . will come and save you. Then the eyes of the blind shall be opened."

[98] Gr. ἀποβαλών, "to throw off, to let go." In minuscule 565, supported by sy[s] aeth, the text reads ἐπιβαλών, "to put on," and this reading is preferred by E. Lohmeyer *(op. cit.*, p. 226) on the ground that it conforms to the oriental custom that the first thing that a man does when called before a superior is to clothe himself (cf. Jer. 1:17; Jn. 21:7; Acts 12:8). This does not, however, appear to be a sufficient ground for setting aside an almost uniform textual tradition.

[99] Gr. Ραββουνί is a strengthened form of "Rabbi," and means "my lord," "my master." Found only here and in Jn. 20:16 (where "Teacher" is added in translation) in the NT, the Aramaic form רַבּוֹנִי is relatively frequent in the Palestine Pentateuch Targum (e.g. Gen. 32:19; 44:5, 18; Ex. 21:4, 5, 8) where it designates a human lord. In Mt. 20:33; Lk. 18:41 Rabboni is replaced by κύριε (i.e. Sir), and this reading is found in Mark in 409 geo[1] (while D *a b ff i* sy[s] read κύριε ῥαββεί). See E. Lohse, *TWNT* VI (1959), pp. 962-966.

[100] On Roman Jericho see G. Dalman, *Orte und Wege Jesu*[3] (Leipzig, 1924), pp. 257-259; C. Kopp, *Die heiligen Stätten der Evangelien* (Regensburg, 1959), pp. 312-315; J. L. Kelso, "New Testament Jericho," *BA* 14 (1951), pp. 34-43. P. Ketter, "Zur Lokalisierung der Blindenheilung bei Jericho," *Biblica* 15 (1934), pp. 411-418 argues that the miracle took place between Old and New Jericho; while Matthew and Mark are thinking of Israelite Jericho, Luke has in mind Herodian Jericho (cf. Mt. 20:29; Mk. 10:46 with Lk. 18:35).

to Jerusalem for the feast (cf. Ps. 42:4). Though the road which led from Jericho to the capital passed through desolate mountainous country and was notoriously unsafe, it was much travelled. The presence of a blind beggar just outside the city gates, on the pilgrimage way, was a common sight in the Near East. The preservation of his name is unusual, and is limited to the Marcan account. Mark so rarely records names in connection with incidents of healing (only Ch. 5:22) that it is probable that the Son of Timai was known in the later Church.

47-48 It is evident that Bartimaeus has heard about Jesus of Nazareth and that his relentless crying of "Son of David, have mercy upon me" reflects a conviction, formed on the basis of what he had heard, that Jesus could restore his sight. Nevertheless, it is difficult to be certain of the significance of the component parts in his appeal for help. "Have mercy upon me" is a cry directed to God by the afflicted in the Psalter (e.g. Ps. 4:1; 6:2; 41:4, 10; 51:1; 109:26; 123:3). In this context it may be a general plea for God's goodness and mercy which is channeled through his servant, Jesus. The nuance in "Son of David" is more difficult to determine. Unlike Matthew and Luke, Mark had made little of this theme. Jesus is addressed as Son of David only here (cf. Chs. 11:9-10; 12:35-37). There is no indication in the text that he rejected the title. The command that the blind man be called (verse 49) rather implies that he paid it particular attention. If it is proper to understand the designation in its messianic context (cf. Isa. 11:1 ff.; Jer. 23:5 f.; Ezek. 34:23 f.; 4QPatriarchal Blessings i. 3-4, "the righteous Messiah, the branch of David"), the epithet is closely related to the confession of Ch. 8:29 (cf. Ch. 15:32). Presumably, Jesus did not silence the beggar (in contrast to Ch. 8:30) because he is at the threshold of Jerusalem where his messianic vocation must be fulfilled. The "messianic secret" is relaxed because it must be made clear to all the people that Jesus goes to Jerusalem as the Messiah, and that he dies as the Messiah.[101] This may be the natural way to interpret the designation, and it is probable that Mark's readers understood the epithet in this messianic context (cf. Rom. 1:3). The problem is that Bartimaeus' use of "Son of David" is confined to his period of blindness before he has gained Jesus' attention. When he stands in the presence of Jesus he addresses him respectfully as "my master," but there is no suggestion of messianism in this

101 Cf. G. Minette de Tillesse, *op. cit.*, pp. 283-293; E. Lohmeyer, *op. cit.*, pp. 223-227.

title of honor. If the request to see reflects a messianic conviction that Jesus is the one through whom the promises of Isa. 35:4-5; 61:1 are fulfilled, this is not made explicit in the text (in contrast to Ch. 7:37). For these reasons it is, perhaps, better to find in "Son of David" a respectful form of address colored by the vivid Davidic associations of Jerusalem but informed by the conviction that Jesus was the instrument of God for bringing healing and blessing to the land. It is not necessary to conclude that Bartimaeus knew of Jesus' Davidic lineage or recognized that he was the Messiah. It is evident from Ch. 11:10 (cf. Acts 4:25) that those who had no direct Davidic descent could speak of "our father David" (with the implication that they were the sons of David). All that is required by the ensuing narrative is that the blind man recognized Jesus as the one from whom he could expect the gracious mercy of God. The ambiguity in "Son of David" permitted Mark's readers to hear his cry as an acknowledgment of Jesus' messianic dignity.[102]

Those in the crowd who rebuked the beggar undoubtedly regarded his shouting as a nuisance and resented the thought of any possible delay. They had probably become quite hardened to seeing beggars along the roadside, and especially at the city gates, crying for alms. Undeterred, the man resolutely continued his chant until he succeeded in drawing Jesus' attention to himself.

49-50 Jesus took the initiative in directing that the blind man should be called. The rebuke of those who had attempted to silence the beggar was not allowed to stand (cf. Ch. 10:13 f.), for even on the way to Jerusalem Jesus had time for a man who appealed for his help in faith. The encouragement offered to Bartimaeus assured him that Jesus was concerned with his plight and relieved the anxiety and distress expressed in his cry. His response was dramatic and decisive. He cast aside his outer garment, which he had spread on the ground in front of him to receive alms, sprang up, and came, apparently unaided, to Jesus.

51-52 Jesus did not exercise his power arbitrarily or impersonally but in the context of a genuine involvement which established the existence of faith sufficient to receive the gift of healing from God. For this purpose questions or brief conversations are frequently an element in the healing narratives of the Gospel (e.g. Chs. 2:5-11; 5:30-34; 7:27-29;

---

[102] See further E. Lohse, *TWNT* VIII (1969), pp. 482-492.

9:21-24). The cause of Bartimaeus' distress was clear, but Jesus' question is designed to strengthen his faith by encouraging him to express it forthrightly. The response, "Master, let me receive my sight," acknowledged Jesus as the one who can make the blind to see (Ch. 8:22-26; Isa. 35:5). It was recognized by the Lord as an affirmation of confident trust in the gracious mercy of God and his power to heal (cf. Ch. 5:34). The healing was immediate: "he received his sight and followed him in the way." That Bartimaeus followed Jesus does not mean that he became a disciple, like one of the Twelve, but that he joined the crowd of pilgrims who were accompanying the Master.[103] It would undoubtedly be his intention to go up to the Temple in order to offer the sacrifice of thanksgiving for his sight. The following "on the way" contrasts dramatically with his former sitting "along the way" and anticipates Ch. 11:1-11 when the pilgrims enter Jerusalem with the ancient songs of praise. Mark may have had in mind the contrast between the Son of David, who has in his company the former blind man, and the warrior king, who had recognized in the blind and the lame only an obstacle to be destroyed in the taking of Jerusalem (II Sam. 5:6-8). Jesus had fulfilled the condition for entrance into Jerusalem (taking away the blind, II Sam. 6:5) by restoring sight to the blind beggar in the way. The healing of Bartimaeus displays, without any concealment, the messianic dignity of Jesus and his compassion on those who believe in him, and throws in bold relief the blindness of the leaders of Israel, whose eyes remained closed to his glory.

---

[103] R. P. Meye, *Jesus and the Twelve* (Grand Rapids, 1968), pp. 164-166, who rightly stresses that in contrast to the call addressed to the Twelve, Jesus tells Bartimaeus, "Go your way." The fact that Bartimaeus' way is also the way of Jesus is certainly significant, but it does not warrant the identification of this following with discipleship.

CHAPTER 11

VI. MINISTRY IN JERUSALEM. Ch. 11:1-13:37

The arrival at the outskirts of Jerusalem marks the beginning of a new section. From this point forth all of the subsequent events occur in and around Jerusalem. The concern of this new unit is Jesus' prophetic ministry in Jerusalem, consisting of the symbolic actions accomplished during the first three days in the city (Ch. 11:1-25) and the conflict with priestly and scribal authorities which his presence provoked (Ch. 11:27-12:37). Jesus continued to prepare the disciples for their future ministry, instructing them concerning believing prayer (Ch. 11:20-25) and exhorting them to watchfulness in the specific context of mission and suffering (Ch. 13:1-37). The limits of the section are determined by the Passion Narrative, which opens with a new note of time and explicit reference to the Passover (Ch. 14:1).

At the outset the narrative is set within a framework of three successive days and the recurring pattern of entrance into the city during the day but withdrawal to Bethany on the eastern slopes of the Mount of Olives in the evening (Ch. 11:11f., 19f.). The third day begins with Ch. 11:20, but it is not said when it ended, unless the instruction on the Mount of Olives (Ch. 13:3-37) is intended to mark the close of the third day. The precise temporal links between the units of tradition in Ch. 11:1-25 are simply lacking in Ch. 11:27-12:44, and it is conceivable that the five conflict situations in Jerusalem, like the corresponding sequence of conflict in Galilee (Ch. 2:1-3:6), actually took place over an extended period of time. This raises one of the most difficult questions of the Marcan outline. It is traditional to compress the sequence of events in Ch. 10:46-16:8 into a single week, extending from Palm Sunday to Easter. This understanding is at least as old as the fourth century, when it was customary to celebrate liturgically Jesus' entry into Jerusalem on the Sunday before Easter, and it has solid support in Jn. 12:1, 12-15. Yet it is very difficult to determine whether Mark understood the tradition in Ch. 11:1-16:8 to cover a single week. There is no reference to the Passover until Ch. 14:1, which does not possess any chronological link with the preceding section, and Mark does not say that Jesus came to Jerusalem for the Passover. It has been plausibly argued that the cries of Hosanna, the branches of green in the hand, the allusions to Ps. 118 and Zech. 9-13, and the reference to the Mount of Olives, as well as the interest in the Temple and its relation to the

Gentiles, in Ch. 11:1-19 are more appropriate to the Feast of Tabernacles in the Fall than to the Passover in the Spring.[1] Moreover, Jesus' reference to teaching daily in the Temple in Ch. 14:49 appears to imply a longer ministry than that presupposed in the traditional chronology. The Marcan narrative, considered in itself, could conceivably permit a Jerusalem ministry extending from Tabernacles to Passover, a period of approximately six months, as opposed to the thought of a single, final week. The question may be left open, for it has important bearing on the interpretation of the subsequent narrative.

1. The Entry into Jerusalem. Ch. 11:1-11

1 And when they drew nigh unto Jerusalem, unto Bethphage and Bethany, at the Mount of Olives, he sendeth two of his disciples,
2 and saith unto them, Go your way into the village that is over against you: and straightway as you enter into it, ye shall find a colt[2] tied, whereon no man ever yet sat; loose him and bring him.
3 And if anyone say unto you, Why do ye this? say ye, The Lord[3]

---

[1] Cf. C. W. F. Smith, "No Time for Figs," *JBL* 79 (1960), pp. 315-327; *idem,* "Tabernacles in the Fourth Gospel and Mark," *NTS* 9 (1963), pp. 130-146; T. W. Manson, "The Cleansing of the Temple," *BJRL* 33 (1951), pp. 271-282.

[2] Gr. πῶλος designates simply a young animal, and with this meaning stands in connection with a number of zoological designations (elephant, camel, ass, gazelle); when it stands alone in Greek sources it connotes a (young) horse, and this meaning is preferred here by W. Bauer, "The 'Colt' of Palm Sunday (Der Palmesel)," *JBL* 72 (1953), pp. 220-229. Yet in the LXX, as in the papyri, πῶλος is used of the colt of an ass (cf. Gen. 32:15; 49:11; Judges 10:4; 12:14; Zech. 9:9), and on the basis of Zech. 9:9 the ass was understood to be *the* beast of the Messiah (see *Berachoth* 56b Baraitha; Bereshith Rabba 75, 98; Tanchuma Genesis 2a; Pirqe Rabbi Eliezer 32). Since the πῶλος in Ch. 11:2, 5, 7 is a sacred, messianic animal, it is inconceivable that πῶλος should be understood as "horse." So H. W. Kuhn, "Das Reittier Jesu in der Einzugsgeschichte des Markusevangeliums," *ZNW* 50 (1959), pp. 82-91; O. Michel, "Eine philologische Frage zur Einzugsgeschichte," *NTS* 6 (1959), pp. 81 f.; *idem, TWNT* VI (1959), p. 960.

[3] The capitalization indicates that the translators of the ASV, RSV assumed that Jesus meant himself in this reference to ὁ κύριος, and this understanding has the support of K. Tagawa, *Évangile et Miracle* (Paris, 1966), p. 169 n. 3, and G. Minette de Tillesse, *Le Secret messianique dans l'Évangile de Marc* (Paris, 1968), p. 396, among others. Nevertheless, this is contrary to Marcan usage and it is unlikely that Jesus would have referred to himself in this way (cf. Ch. 14:13 f. in

hath need of him; and straightway he will send him back hither.[4]
4 And they went away, and found a colt tied at the door without in the open street;[5] and they loose him.
5 And certain of them that stood there said unto them, What do ye, loosing the colt?
6 And they said unto them even as Jesus had said: and they let them go.
7 And they bring the colt unto Jesus, and cast on him their garments; and he sat upon him.
8 And many spread their garments upon the way, and others branches,[6] which they had cut from the fields.
9 And they that went before, and they that followed, cried, Hosanna;[7] Blessed *is* he that cometh in the name of the Lord:
10 Blessed is the kingdom that cometh, *the kingdom* of our father David: Hosanna in the highest.
11 And he entered into Jerusalem, into the temple; and when he had looked round about upon all things, it being now eventide, he went out unto Bethany with the twelve.

The association of Ch. 10:46-52 with Ch. 11:1-11 undoubtedly reflects historical sequence and marks a fulfilment of Isa. 29:18-19: "In that

---

a parallel circumstance: "The Teacher says, Where is my guest room . . . "). While ὁ κύριος may be deliberately ambiguous, it is preferable to translate "The owner has need of him," and to assume that the owner was with Jesus at this time. A message to the effect that the owner wanted his colt and would return it shortly would account for the response described in verses 5-6.

[4] It is preferable to understand the final clause of verse 3 as part of the message, as in the RSV; it is an assurance that the owner will send the colt back without delay.

[5] Gr. ἐπὶ τοῦ ἀμφόδου. On the basis of Justin, *Apology* I, 32 ("the foal of the ass was bound to a vine at the entrance of the village") P. L. Couchoud, "Notes de critique verbale sur St. Marc et St. Matthieu," *JThS* 34 (1933), p. 126 suggested emending the text of verse 4 to πρὸς ἄμπελον δεδεμένος. He suggested that the error crept in through the similarity between ΑΜΦΟΔΟϹ/ΑΜΠΕΛΟϹ, when the allusion to Gen. 49:11 was no longer recognized. This proposal is accepted by E. Lohmeyer, *Das Evangelium des Marcus*[16] (Göttingen, 1963), p. 230 n. 4, but must remain merely an interesting conjecture.

[6] Gr. στιβάς denotes leaves, leafy branches, or perhaps rushes gathered from the fields. Palm branches are mentioned only in Jn. 12:13. If palms were involved, they would have been brought from Jericho by the pilgrims, since they were not native to Jerusalem.

[7] Gr. Ωσαννα is a transliteration of אושענא, the Aramaic form of הוֹשִׁיעָה־נָּא and means "save, we pray" or "save now." Cf. E. Lohse, "Hosianna," *Nov Test* 6 (1963), pp. 113-119.

day the deaf shall hear the words of a book, and out of their gloom and darkness the eyes of the blind shall see. The meek shall obtain fresh joy in the Lord, and the poor among men shall exult in the Holy One of Israel." The Marcan account of the entry into Jerusalem is characterized by vivid detail and yet is remarkably restrained in its messianic assertion. It carries forward the unveiling of Jesus' majesty and office in an enigmatic way which becomes plain only in the light of subsequent events. For the readers of the Gospel, the entire scene has evident messianic significance. The entry itself, however, was ambiguous and its meaning was concealed even from the disciples, according to Jn. 12:16. In interpreting the account it is important to appreciate the tension between messianic assertion and restraint.

Jesus himself took the initiative in preparing for his entry into the city. The precise instructions concerning the colt of an ass never before ridden possess a profound symbolic significance which could only be messianic. It was not customary for pilgrims to enter Jerusalem riding upon an ass; the final stage of the pilgrimage was generally completed on foot. The great messianic oracle, Zech. 9:9, already contained the three essential elements of the Marcan account: the entry ("See, your king comes"), the messianic animal ("riding upon an ass, even upon a colt, the foal of an ass"), and the jubilation of the people ("Rejoice greatly, O daughter of Zion").[8] Yet Mark does not cite this oracle, and Jesus' fulfilment of the prophecy occurred in circumstances that paradoxically concealed the meaning of his action. The presence of the crowds, the greens, the antiphonal chanting of the Hallel Psalms, the feeling of exultation when the city comes into view, mark the final stage of the pilgrimage even if Jesus was not present. It is probable that the strewing of the pilgrim's way with greens cut from the fields and with outer clothing marks a moment of high enthusiasm intended to honor a pilgrim engaged in a prophetic mission. Yet the demonstration was apparently not so significant as to attract the attention of the Roman authorities, and the exultation in Ch. 11:9-10 stops short of messianic assertion. When Jesus entered the city the group of pilgrims who had accompanied him quickly dispersed, and he appears to have come to the Temple accompanied only by the Twelve.

While Mark knew that he was narrating the entry of the Messiah into Jerusalem and the coming of the Lord to his Temple, he has not allowed this later understanding to color his account. At the time only

---

[8] H. W. Kuhn, *op. cit.*, p. 90; G. Minette de Tillesse, *op. cit.*, pp. 284-287.

Jesus knew the messianic significance of his action. He intended to conform his entry to the prophecy of Zech. 9:9. His action was a veiled assertion of both the fact and the character of his messiahship; it affirmed that the royal way involved humility and suffering.[9] Only later did the disciples recognize that the Scripture had been fulfilled, and that Jesus had come to Jerusalem as the Messiah. The messianic hiddenness which characterized Jesus' entire ministry was preserved in the ambiguity of the entry, and it is important not to exaggerate its character.

1-3 Jesus came from Jericho to the Mount of Olives, rising over 2600 ft. high and stretching from north to south on the east side of Jerusalem. The pilgrimage road led through Bethany on the eastern slopes of the mountain, across the Kidron Valley to the northern gate of the city. Bethphage was a village or district close to Jerusalem. It is described in rabbinic literature as falling within the precincts of Jerusalem, marking the limits within which items for the Temple could be prepared or used.[10] Bethany, located at the second milestone from the city (Jn. 11:18), was the final station on the road from Jericho to Jerusalem.[11] Although Bethany would be reached before Bethphage, the order of mention in verse 1 is apparently dictated by the reference to Jerusalem, followed by the village which was nearer to the city. In the OT the Mount of Olives is designated as the place of the future eschatological revelation of God's glory (Zech. 14:1-9; cf. Ezek. 43:2-9),[12] although its association with the resurrection of the dead and with the coming of the Messiah belongs to the post-Christian period.[13]

---

9 The rabbis were embarrassed to explain how the Messiah could be content with so humble an entry as prescribed in Zech. 9:9. The explanation was found in Israel's preparedness for his coming: "Behold, the Son of Man comes 'on the clouds of heaven' and 'lowly and riding an ass.' If they (Israel) are worthy, 'with the clouds of heaven'; if they are not worthy, 'lowly, and riding upon an ass'" (TB *Sanhedrin* 98a). Was Jesus' entry a declaration of Israel's unworthiness?

10 Cf. Tosephta *Meilah* I. 5; M. *Menachoth* XI. 2; TB *Menachoth* 78b; *Sanhedrin* 14b, 86b; *Soṭa* 45a. See I. Löw, "Bethphage," *Revue des Études Juives* 62 (1911), pp. 232-235; G. Dalman, *Orte und Wege Jesu*³ (Leipzig, 1924), pp. 244-246.

11 G. Dalman, *op. cit.*, pp. 265-267; C. Kopp, *Die heiligen Stätten der Evangelien* (Regensburg, 1959), pp. 328 f.

12 Cf. W. Schmauch, "Der Ölberg," *TLZ* 7 (1957), pp. 391-396.

13 On the basis of Zech. 14:1 ff.; Josephus, *Antiquities* XX. viii. 6 = *War* II. xiii. 5; Targum to Cant. 8:5; Sepher Elijahu (in A. Jellinek, *Beth ha-Midrash* III, 65-68), E. Lohmeyer, *op. cit.*, p. 229, G. Minette de Tillesse, *op. cit.*, pp. 284 f., among others, argue that already in the first century it was expected that the Messiah would appear on the Mount of Olives, but the texts adduced do not

Jesus took the initiative in sending two of his disciples (cf. Ch. 6:7; 14:13) into the nearby village (presumably Bethphage) to untie a young, untrained ass and to bring it to him. His precise knowledge concerning the animal and its availability suggests prearrangement with the owner (cf. Ch. 14:12-16), who may have been with Jesus at the time. While this point is not made explicit in the text, it tends to be confirmed by the fact that the message concerning the colt is not directed to the owner but to anyone who might question the disciples' action. The character of the message is also consistent with this interpretation: the owner wants his colt and will return it without delay. The description of the colt as one which had never been ridden is significant in the light of the ancient provision that an animal devoted to a sacred purpose must be one that had not been put to ordinary use (cf. Num. 19:2; Deut. 21:3; I Sam. 6:7). This detail emphasizes the appropriateness of the colt for the sacred task it will perform and characterizes Jesus' entry as a symbolic action possessing profound messianic significance.

The apparently disproportionate length at which the incident of the untying of the colt is related (verses 1-6) suggests that far more is involved than merely the preparation for the entry. The attention given to this phase of the action and the explicit reference to "a colt tied," with its allusion to Gen. 49:11, points to a deeper significance supplied by the Oracle of Judah, Gen. 49:8-12.[14] The allusion to Gen. 49:11 confirms the messianic character which the animal bears in Ch. 11:1-10. It also indicates that the untying of the colt was itself a messianic sign, although it was not recognized as such at that time. In addition to the "colt of an ass," the oracle speaks of the enigmatic "Shiloh who is to come" (Gen. 49:10), and this reference was interpreted messianically in pre-Christian Jewish texts.[15] This interpretation is reflected in the designation "the Coming One" or "He who comes," and the suggestion lies close at hand that the context for understanding the jubilant chant of verse 9, "Blessed is *he who comes* in the name of the Lord," is

---

warrant this assertion. See W. Foerster, *TWNT* V (Eng. Tr. 1967), p. 484 and n. 102.

[14] Cf. H. W. Kuhn, *op. cit.*, pp. 86 f.; J. Blenkinsopp, "The Oracle of Judah and the Messianic Entry," *JBL* 80 (1961), pp. 55-64.

[15] E.g. Gen. 49:10 LXX, Onkelos, Pseudo-Jonathan and Palestine Pentateuch Targums, Num. 23:24; 24:9, 17 LXX; Isa. 11:10 LXX; TB *Sanhedrin* 98a; 4Q Patriarchal Blessings i. 1-6. Cf. P. Prigent, "Quelques testimonia messianiques, leur histoire littéraire de Qumrân aux Pères de l'église," *ThZ* 15 (1959), pp. 419-430.

supplied not only by Ps. 118:25 f. but by Gen. 49:10. The oracle speaks of one whose coming brings messianic fulfilment to Israel and connects his coming with an ass tied to a vine. Mark appears to have presupposed this understanding in the formulation of verses 1-6.[16]

4-6 The execution of the command is recorded in terms identical with Jesus' instruction:

command	*execution*
(a) "Go into the village . . . "	(a') "They went away . . . "
(b) "Untie it and bring it"	(b') "They untied it"
(c) "If anyone says to you . . . say . . . "	(c') "Those who were there said to them . . . And they told them . . . "

This correspondence is intelligible if Mark found in the untying of the colt a symbolic action with reference to Gen. 49:10 f. In the absence of any mention of the owner the presumption is that he was not present in the village when the disciples came. If the message specified his desire for the colt this would account for the lack of interference reported in verse 6.

7-8 The disciples placed their outer garments on the colt in place of a saddle, and Jesus began his ride to the gates of Jerusalem. What is described in verse 8 appears to have been a spontaneous expression of homage to Jesus. The pilgrims may have believed that he had come to Jerusalem in fulfilment of a prophetic mission. The spreading of the garment upon the way is similar to the royal salute given to Jehu (II Kings 9:12 f.), or the gesture of profound respect shown to Cato of Utica when he was about to leave his soldiers (Plutarch, *Cato Minor* 7). The reference to the branches of green and the antiphonal singing recalls the entry into Jerusalem of Simon, the last of the five Hasmonean brothers, on a triumphal occasion (I Macc. 13:51). A note of jubilation and excitement is evident in the text. Yet the action described does not appear to possess a messianic significance, for there is no explicit

[16] The relationship between Gen. 49:10 f. and Zech. 9:9 is stressed in Bereshith Rabba XCVIII. 8 to Gen. 49:11, and is a commonplace in the interpretation of the entry into Jerusalem among the Fathers (e.g. Justin, *Apology* I, 32, *Dialogue with Trypho* 53; Pseudo-Clementine *Homilies* 49, *Recognitions* i. 49-50; Irenaeus, *Adv. haer*. IV. x. 2).

acknowledgment of Jesus' majesty in the acclamation of verses 9-10. It was a brief moment of enthusiasm outside the city walls which would have been appropriate to a royal enthronement, but was scarcely distinguishable from the exultation which characterized other groups of pilgrims when the City of David, with its magnificent Temple, came into view.

9-10 Those who went before Jesus and those who followed behind began the chanting of one of the great psalms of ascent to the Holy City. The Hallel Psalms (Ps. 113-118) were used liturgically in connection with Passover and Tabernacles,[17] serving as a focus for prayer, praise and thanksgiving for every pious Jew. The substance of Ps. 118:25 f. is cited in verse 9, while the response in verse 10 provides a commentary upon the quotation. The chiastic structure of verses 9-10 suggests the antiphonal character of the singing:

(a) Hosanna!
(b) Blessed is he who comes in the name of the Lord!
(b') Blessed is the coming kingdom of our father David!
(a') Hosanna in the highest!

"Hosanna" is properly a prayer invoking God's saving action ("save us"), but through liturgical use it came to be dissociated from its original meaning and could be used as a shout of acclamation (like "Hallelujah") or as a greeting in addressing pilgrims or a famous rabbi. In Ps. 118:26 a blessing is pronounced upon the pilgrims who have come up to the festival, and this is perhaps the normal way to understand verse 9b. "Blessed in the name of the Lord be he who comes" formed part of a customary form of religious greeting. Yet the formulation is ambiguous and Mark may well have intended his readers to detect a deeper, messianic significance in the phrase "he who comes in the name of the Lord" (cf. Gen. 49:10).[18] The rabbis interpreted Ps. 118:25 f. with

---

[17] The strongest argument for a Tabernacles setting for the entry into Jerusalem is found in the reference to the branches of greenery in connection with the use of "Hosanna." At Tabernacles the pilgrims carried bundles of palm, myrtle and willow, which were shaken whenever the word "Hosanna" occurred in the liturgy (M. *Sukkah* III. 3-9). Cf. G. W. MacRae, "The Meaning and Evolution of the Feast of Tabernacles," *CBQ* 22 (1960), pp. 251-276, and the articles cited in n. 1.

[18] J. Schneider, *TWNT* II (Eng. Tr. 1964), pp. 669 f. argues that the praise of the people is for the coming Messiah and the coming Kingdom.

reference to David or to the final redemption,[19] and this understanding appears to explain the reference to "the kingdom of our father David" in verse 10. The substance of the antiphonal response is provided in the fourteenth of the Eighteen Benedictions (Palestinian recension) when prayer was offered daily for the restoration of the kingdom of David. The final Hosanna (Save us, thou who dwellest in the highest) is an appeal for God to inaugurate the era of salvation. The verse expresses a popular type of messianic hope without identifying Jesus as the Messiah. Despite the enthusiasm of their homage, there is no awareness on the part of the people that the time of fulfilment has actually arrived and that the Kingdom has actually drawn near in the person of Jesus himself (cf. Ch. 1:14 f.).

11 Once within the city, the crowd of pilgrims seems to have quickly dispersed. The lateness of the hour is natural enough since they had come from Jericho, nearly eighteen miles away. Jesus seems to have gone to the Temple alone, or accompanied by the Twelve. In recording this visit to the Temple Mark has no intention of depicting Jesus as a pilgrim who has come to Jerusalem for the first time and has a natural desire to see "all things." The point is rather that Jesus is the Lord of the Temple, who must inspect its premises to determine whether the purpose intended by God is being fulfilled (cf. Mal. 3:1). The whole of the Temple precincts are denoted in the comprehensive term used by the evangelist,[20] but it is probable that Jesus proceeded no further than the Court of the Men. His survey, which took in all that could be seen, provided the ground of his action the following day. In the company of the Twelve Jesus withdrew to Bethany, as he was to do each of the successive evenings. Commentators have spoken of a *dénouement* in verse 11 and of the quiet ending of the entire section. The ending is quiet, but it is the quiet before the storm!

2. The Unproductive Fig Tree. Ch. 11:12-14

12 And on the morrow, when they were come out from Bethany, he hungered.

---

[19] TB *Pesachim* 119a; Midrash Tehillim to Ps. 118, § 22, 244a.

[20] Cf. G. Schrenk, *TWNT* III (Eng. Tr. 1965), pp. 232-237; J. Simons, *Jerusalem in the Old Testament* (Leiden, 1952), pp. 381-435 (on the Herodian Temple).

13 And seeing a fig tree afar off having leaves, he came, if haply[21] he might find anything thereon: and when he came to it, he found nothing but leaves; for it was not the season for figs.
14 And he answered and said unto it, No man eat from thee henceforth for ever.[22] And his disciples heard it.

The difficulties presented by this incident involving a fig tree covered with leaves but without fruit are well known. It is usually treated as a miracle of destruction, and the question naturally arises if the cursing of the fig tree–for so Peter understands verse 14 (Ch. 11:21)–is really consistent with what is otherwise known of Jesus' character. The juxtaposition of the two seemingly contradictory assertions in verse 13 heightens the difficulty, for the explicit statement that it was not the season for figs appears to make Jesus' action arbitrary and meaningless. These problems have often been regarded as an insuperable obstacle to accepting the account in its present form.[23] It is said that the narrative had its origin in a local legend concerning a withered fig tree in the vicinity of Bethany,[24] or that Jesus' parable of the unproductive fig tree (Lk. 13:6-9) has been transformed in the course of tradition into a factual account.[25] More commonly, the final clause of verse 13 is regarded as a gloss, inserted at a time when it was believed that the incident occurred near the time of Passover; when the gloss is removed, the account gains credibility because it has reference to the time of the fig harvest, in close proximity to the Feast of Tabernacles.[26]

It is not necessary to resort to such expedients. Jesus evidently used

---

21 Gr. εἰ ἄρα, where the inferential ἄρα means "in these circumstances."

22 Gr. μή (here μηκέτι . . . μηδείς) with the optative expresses a negative wish or a formal prohibition.

23 Cf. T. W. Manson, *op. cit.*, p. 279: "It is a tale of miraculous power wasted in the service of ill-temper . . . and as it stands it is simply incredible."

24 First proposed by E. Schwartz, "Der verfluchte Feigenbaum," *ZNW* 5 (1904), pp. 80-84 and now supported by K. Tagawa, *op. cit.*, p. 35, in spite of the cogency of M. J. Lagrange's comment that "a withered fig tree is too ordinary a thing to give birth to a legend" (*L'Évangile selon saint Marc*[8] [Paris, 1947], p. 299).

25 H. van der Loos, *The Miracles of Jesus* (Leiden, 1965), pp. 692-696; L. Goppelt, *TWNT* VI (1959), p. 20; C.-H. Hunzinger, *TWNT* VII (1964), pp. 756 f., among others. It should be noted, however, that there is not the slightest allusion to the parable in Ch. 11:12-14, 20 f.

26 In addition to the works cited in n. 1, J. van Goudoever, *Biblical Calendars* (Leiden, 1959), pp. 261-265.

his hunger as an occasion for instructing the Twelve. If the incident occurred in the period approaching Passover, the parenthetical statement in verse 13c is incontrovertible and suggests that Jesus had no expectation of finding edible figs. Events have meaning beyond their face value; they become significant as they are interpreted. The unexpected and incongruous character of Jesus' action in looking for figs at a season when no fruit could be found would stimulate curiosity and point beyond the incident to its deeper significance. His act was an example of prophetic realism similar to the symbolic actions of the OT prophets (e.g. Isa. 20:1-6; Jer. 13:1-11; 19:1-13; Ezek. 4:1-15). The prophets frequently spoke of the fig tree in referring to Israel's status before God (e.g. Jer. 8:13; 29:17; Hos. 9:10, 16; Joel 1:7; Micah 7:1-6), while the destruction of the fig tree is associated with judgment (Hos. 2:12; Isa. 34:4; cf. Lk. 13:6-9). In this context the fig tree symbolizes Israel in Jesus' day, and what happens to the tree the terrible fate that inevitably awaited Jerusalem. The explanation was already put forth by Victor of Antioch, in the oldest existing commentary on Mark, that Jesus had "used the fig tree to set forth the judgment that was about to fall on Jerusalem." This is certainly the evangelist's understanding of the episode, for in the Gospel of Mark Jesus' action in the Temple is firmly embedded within the fig tree incident. The a-b-a structure of Ch. 11:12-21 (fig tree–cleansing of the Temple–fig tree) serves to provide a mutual commentary on these two events. Just as the leaves of the tree concealed the fact that there was no fruit to enjoy, so the magnificence of the Temple and its ceremony conceals the fact that Israel has not brought forth the fruit of righteousness demanded by God. Both incidents have the character of a prophetic sign which warns of judgment to fall upon Israel for honoring God with their lips when their heart was far from him (cf. Ch. 7:6).[27]

12-13 The incident involving the fig tree occurred on the next day when Jesus and his disciples were returning from Bethany to Jerusalem. Jesus' hunger accounts principally for the fact that he came to the tree to see if there was fruit upon it. It is important to stress, however, that neither his hunger nor his disappointment in the failure to find fruit is

---

[27] So also M. J. Lagrange, *op. cit.,* pp. 292-294, 298 f.; C. E. B. Cranfield, *The Gospel according to Saint Mark*[2] (Cambridge, 1963), pp. 356 f.; G. Friedrich, *TWNT* VI (1959), p. 844. Cf. J. W. Doeve, "Purification du Temple et dessèchement du figuier," *NTS* 1 (1954-55), pp. 297-308.

cited as the ground of the pronouncement in verse 14. While Jesus was initially prompted by physical hunger in this situation, he used the occasion for a prophetic symbolic action of far-reaching significance. On the protected eastern side of the Mount of Olives fig trees can be seen in leaf at the end of March or the beginning of April. Only early green figs, which actually appear before the leaves, could be expected at this time, and they are disagreeable in taste and are not ordinarily eaten. They are not ripe before June, and quite commonly they all fall off, so that after some days the fig tree has only leaves.[28] This corresponds to the situation depicted in verse 13, where the point lies in the difference between the tree's appearance from a distance and its true condition, which a closer inspection reveals.

The explicit statement that it was not the season for figs presupposes that the season involved is the spring month of Nisan in which the Passover falls. It has often been urged that this clause is a gloss that was imposed upon the text at a time when its Tabernacles orientation had been forgotten. There is no textual support for this proposal, and it must be rejected as an expedient designed to alleviate the problematic character of verse 13. Such parenthetical comments are typically Marcan and occur throughout the Gospel (e.g. Chs. 1:16; 5:42; 7:3-4, 19; 13:14). C. H. Bird has called attention to the function of those parenthetical clauses in Mark which begin with the conjunction "for"; when Jesus alludes to the Scriptures without explicitly quoting them, frequently a clause introduced by "for" indicates that a biblical passage, word, or idea is to be recalled by the immediate situation. Mark uses such clauses to create striking sentences which are always the mark of a deeper symbolic meaning (e.g. Ch. 1:16, rooted in the OT metaphor of fishing set forth in Jer. 16:16).[29] In Ch. 11:13 the final clause should be translated, "and the significant thing about this is that it was not even the season for figs." It has been suggested that the passage to which allusion is made is Micah 7:1-6. Bewailing the absence of righteousness in Israel the prophet compared the land to a gleaned vineyard and exclaimed, "I desire the first ripe fig" (Mic. 7:1). These words were in

[28] On these questions see F. Goldman, *La Figue en Palestine à l'époque de la Mišna* (Paris, 1911); I. Löw, *Die Flora der Juden* (Berlin, 1928), pp. 224-254; G. Dalman, *Arbeit und Sitte in Palästina* I. 2 (Leipzig, 1928), pp. 378-381; 556-564. A convenient summary appears in T. W. Manson, *op. cit.*, pp. 277 f.

[29] C. H. Bird, "Some γάρ clauses in St. Mark's Gospel," *JThS* n.s. 4 (1953), pp. 171-187. Bird refers to this construction as "allusive γάρ," and suggests an allusion to Isa. 28:4.

Jesus' mind as he approached the fig tree, and Mark has used the parenthetical clause in verse 13c to point to the Scriptural text which elucidates the event.[30] A more comprehensive commentary is offered by Jer. 8:13, which occurs in the context of God's judgment upon the land because of the false scribe and priest: "When I would gather them, says the Lord, there are no grapes on the vine, nor figs on the fig tree; even the leaves are withered, and what I gave them has passed away from them." The parenthetical clause in verse 13 is thus a deliberate Marcan device, and rather than being a dissonant note to be removed from the score, it is the key to its primary theme.

14 Jesus addressed a formal prohibition to the tree, which said nothing of its destruction but only that no one will eat of its fruit. Nevertheless, Peter interprets Jesus' action in the categories of a curse on the following day when the tree was found withered (Ch. 11:21).[31] What was involved was a prophetic sign warning of God's judicial action against the nation. In context, verse 14 is equivalent in function to Ch. 12:9, where the figure of the vineyard is parallel to the symbolism of the fig tree. Jesus' words are an expression of judgment which anticipates his judging action in the Court of the Gentiles (Ch. 11:15-17). The statement that his disciples were listening to him points forward to the sequel to the account in Ch. 11:20f.

3. The Expulsion of the Merchants from the Temple Precincts. Ch. 11:15-19

15 And they come to Jerusalem: and he entered into the temple, and began to cast out them that sold and them that bought in the temple, and overthrew the tables of the money-changers, and the seats of them that sold the doves;

---

[30] J. N. Birdsall, "The Withering of the Fig Tree (Mark xi. 12-14, 20-22)," *ExT* 73 (1962), p. 191; A. de Q. Robin, "The Cursing of the Fig Tree in Mark xi. A Hypothesis," *NTS* 8 (1962), pp. 276-281.

[31] For attempts to eliminate the offense of the cursing by replacing the curse by sadness and disappointment on the part of Jesus see B. Violet, "Die Verfluchung des Feigenbaumes" in *Eucharisterion* (Festschrift H. Gunkel) II (Göttingen, 1923), pp. 135-140; T. W. Manson, *op. cit.*, p. 280. G. Stählin, *TWNT* V (Eng. Tr. 1967), p. 429 speaks of "the wrath of the eschatological judge who has full power to destroy . . . and who has already used this power." The "offensive" aspect here and elsewhere in the Gospel stresses the seriousness of the situation.

16 and he would not suffer that any man should carry a vessel
through the temple.
17 And he taught, and said unto them, Is it not written, My
house shall be called a house of prayer for all the nations?
but ye have made it a den of robbers.
18 And the chief priests and the scribes heard it, and sought [32]
how [33] they might destroy him: for they feared him, for all
the multitude was astonished at his teaching.
19 And every evening [34] he went forth out of the city.

This incident within the Temple precincts only comes into perspective when the great importance that Judaism at that time accorded to everything which concerned the Temple of Jerusalem is remembered. The splendor of Herod's Temple, the immense crowds of pilgrims which assembled there on the occasion of the principal feasts, and the fanaticism with which the Jews defended the sacred precincts until the disaster of A.D. 70 provide an index to the veneration which attended the Temple. On the Mount of Olives, which was considered a part of the Temple precincts for ritual purposes, there were four markets where pilgrims could buy doves and other ritually pure objects of sacrifice for Temple offerings (TJ *Ta'anith* IV. 8). These markets were not under the jurisdiction of the High Priest, but of the Sanhedrin. Although it is commonly assumed that the commercial use of the Court of the Gentiles was a practice of long standing, there is actually no evidence that traffic in ritually pure items took place in the Temple prior to A.D. 30. V. Eppstein has argued that the sale of animals in the Temple forecourt was an innovation of recent date, introduced by Caiaphas, who wished to set up a market which would be in punitive competition with the traditional markets on the Mount of Olives. The rabbinic evidence marshalled in support of this thesis indicates that the markets of the Temple and of the Mount of Olives had been the subject of impassioned quarrels

---

32 The meaning of the parataxis (καὶ ἤκουσαν . . . καὶ ἐζήτουν . . .) is "When they heard, they began to seek . . ."

33 Gr. πῶς is used in an indirect sense and the clause implies a deliberate question: How are we to destroy him? Cf. 14:1, 11.

34 Gr. ὅταν ὀψὲ ἐγένετο, which should probably be translated "And when evening came" as in the RSV and the Jerusalem Bible, or "when it got late," with C. E. B. Cranfield, *op. cit.*, p. 359. The particle ὅταν in Mark usually means "when" and not "whenever."

during this period, while the existence of the four markets on the Mount of Olives is presumptive evidence that the transaction of business in sacrificial objects inside the Temple was not an established institution, but an exceptional and shocking license introduced by Caiaphas forty years before the destruction of the Temple, i.e. *ca.* A.D. 30.[35] The presence of certified markets on the Mount of Olives nullified any argument in support of the use of the Court of the Gentiles for similar purposes. Jesus' action expressed his deep indignation at the flagrant violation of the divinely announced purpose for the Temple. The use to which the forecourt was devoted entrenched the entire people in disobedience to God. In order to halt this deplorable situation he inflicted blows upon the guilty and drove them from the court.[36] This is the only act of violence recorded of the Lord, and it is understandable as a public demonstration of zeal for God's honor.

The absence of any immediate counter-action on the part of the Temple authorities[37] is surprising but intelligible. While the incident disturbed the activity in the Court of the Gentiles, it did not interrupt the functioning of the Sanctuary. Moreover, Jesus' action was too ambiguous in character to be directly revolutionary.[38] His violent expulsion of the merchants could be explained within a current of active pietism which openly appealed to Phinehas and his zeal for God (Num. 25:6-12; Ps. 106:28-31; Ecclus. 45:23 f.; I Macc. 2:54),[39] or as an exercise of prophetic authority within the tradition of Jeremiah (Jer.

---

[35] V. Eppstein, "The Historicity of the Gospel Account of the Cleansing of the Temple," *ZNW* 55 (1964), pp. 42-58.

[36] E. Trocmé, "L'expulsion des marchands du Temple," *NTS* 15 (1968-69), pp. 17-19 speaks of "an abuse which was commensurate with their crimes," and stresses the point that there was no threat to life in the Lord's action.

[37] On the number and placement of the Temple police see V. Eppstein, *op. cit.*, pp. 46 f.

[38] E. Trocmé, *op. cit.*, pp. 2, 5, 17-22. N. Q. Hamilton, "Temple Cleansing and Temple Bank," *JBL* 83 (1964), p. 371 makes the point that Jesus "did not take anything. He did not burn or destroy records of indebtedness. He did not lead any force which could be interpreted as a revolutionary army. He simply suspended the economic function of the temple without taking any advantage of the act. Soon he left the temple, and presumably operations returned to normal." For a balanced appraisal and rejection of the proposal that the expulsion of the merchants entailed a carefully prepared and executed military operation by a troop of men disciplined and knowledgeable in the arts of war see E. Trocmé, "Jesus Christ et le Temple: éloge d'un naïf," *Rev Hist Phil Rel* 44 (1964), pp. 245-251.

[39] Cf. W. R. Farmer, "The Patriarch Phineas," *ATR* 34 (1952), pp. 26-30.

7:1-15; 26:1-15), or as the coming of the Lord to his Temple, whose purging action is the immediate prelude to judgment (Mal. 3:1-5).[40]

15-16 The Court of the Gentiles was a wide enclosure which provided access to the interior parts of the Temple precincts, from which it was separated by a high partition-wall. While it was protected by certain regulations prohibiting the use of the forecourt as a thoroughfare, it was generally considered to have little sacred significance. In a country where the circulating currency consisted primarily of Roman money, provision had to be made for the Jews to pay the annual Temple tax "after the shekel of the Sanctuary" as commanded in Ex. 30:13-16. In the first century all Temple dues had to be paid in Tyrian coinage, since the Tyrian shekel was the closest available equivalent to the old Hebrew shekel. To make the necessary exchange the tables of the money changers were set up in the provinces on Adar 15, and in the Temple forecourt on Adar 25 (M. *Shekalim* I. 3), five days before the first of Nisan, when the tax was due. The slight surcharge permitted in the exchange (1/24 of a shekel) was intended to cover loss resulting from the wear of coins in circulation (M. *Shekalim* I. 7). No information is available concerning the date when the tables were taken down, but presumably this was done in the provinces on Adar 25 and in the Temple on Nisan 1.[41] The specific reference to the tables of the money changers in the Temple forecourt tends to date Jesus' action between Adar 25 and Nisan 1, i.e. more than two weeks before Passover.

Doves were the recognized offering of the poor, required for the purification of women (Lev. 12:6; Lk. 2:22-24), the cleansing of lepers (Lev. 14:22), and other purposes (Lev. 15:14, 29). The installation of stalls for the sale of animals and of other requirements for the sacrifice such as wine, oil and salt, had the effect of transforming the Court of

---

[40] On the more specialized question of the relationship of the Synoptic account of the cleansing of the Temple to the Johannine report, and more particularly of the possibility of two cleansings, see F. M. Braun, "L'expulsion des vendeurs du temple (Mt. xxi. 12-17, 23-27; Mc. xi. 15-19, 27-33; Lc. xix. 45-xx. 8; Jo. ii. 13-22)," *RB* 38 (1929), pp. 178-200; R. H. Lightfoot, *The Gospel Message of St. Mark* (Oxford, 1950), pp. 70-79; I. Buse, "The Cleansing of the Temple in the Synoptics and John," *ExT* 70 (1958-59), pp. 22-24.

[41] Cf. V. Eppstein, *op. cit.*, pp. 43-46, 56; J. Liver, "The Half-Shekel Offering in Biblical and Post-Biblical Literature," *HTR* 56 (1963), pp. 173-198. The provisions governing late payment of the tax (M. *Shekalim* III. 1f.; VI. 5) imply the possibility of exchange at other times as well, although on a greatly reduced scale.

the Gentiles into an oriental bazaar and a cattle mart.[42] Jesus was appalled at this disregard for the sanctity of an area consecrated for the use of Gentiles who had not yet become full proselytes to Judaism. His action in driving out the merchants and their patrons, overturning the tables of the money changers and the seats of those who sold doves, and standing guard over the court to prohibit its use as a thoroughfare, was an astonishing display of zeal for God's honor and respect for the sacredness of the Temple precincts. Ironically, Jesus' spirited protest entailed a rigorous application of existing provisions, which prohibited anyone from entering the Temple Mount with a staff, sandals or his wallet, and which specifically denied the right to make of the forecourt "a short by-path" (M. *Berachoth* IX. 5; TB *Berachoth* 54a). The reference to the vessels of the Temple in verse 16, in conjunction with the expulsion of the merchants in verse 15, indicates that Jesus was acting in fulfilment of the obligation laid upon him by Zech. 14:21: "and every vessel in Jerusalem and Judah shall be sacred to the Lord of hosts . . . and there shall no longer be a trader in the house of the Lord of hosts on that day."[43] By purging the Temple forecourt Jesus bore witness to the conditions of "that day" when God would gather the righteous Gentiles to his Temple to worship him (cf. Zech. 14:16).

17 The scriptural warrant for Jesus' violent action is solemnly introduced. The quotation is drawn from Isa. 56:7 and agrees exactly with the LXX text. The prophecy speaks of a destiny and a function which God has designed for his house, and occurs in the midst of promises which describe his generous purposes both for his people Israel and for all the nations. While the designation of the Temple as a house of prayer is ancient (cf. I Kings 8:28-30; Isa. 56:7 twice; 60:7 LXX), the clause "for all the nations" is found only in Isa. 56:7 and in Mark's summary of Jesus' teaching. This notice indicates that Jesus expelled the merchants from the Court of the Gentiles in order to safeguard rights and privileges sanctioned by God. The use of the forecourt as an open market effectually prevented the one area of the Temple which was available to the Gentiles from being a place of prayer.

---

[42] Cf. M. *Shekalim* IV. 7 f.; V. 3-5. At the Passover in A.D. 66 the worshippers required an estimated 255,600 lambs (Josephus, *War* VI. ix. 3; cf. *War* II. xiv. 3). See N. Q. Hamilton, *op. cit.*, pp. 366-369.

[43] *Ibid.*, p. 372; C. Roth, "The Cleansing of the Temple and Zech. 14:21," *Nov Test* 4 (1960), pp. 174-181. Cf. Hos. 9:15, "Because of the wickedness of their deeds, I will drive them out of my house."

The second part of Jesus' protest recalls the language of Jer. 7:11 and sets in sharp opposition what the Temple has become with what it must be in God's intention. The perfect tense in the statement "You *have made* it a cave of marauders" stresses the irremediable character of the action of the priestly authorities and points forward to the stern warning in Ch. 13:2. It is possible that the strong term "robbers" or "marauders" should be understood in the more technical sense it bore in the works of Strabo and Josephus, where it describes those engaged in anti-government guerrilla warfare. Jesus would then be saying that the Temple authorities had prepared the way for the Temple to be turned into a Zealot stronghold.[44] On the other hand, the distinctive vocabulary is already a part of Jeremiah's denunciation of the false sense of security bred by the presence of the Temple of the Lord in his own day and may be intended to evoke the larger context of Jer. 7:11 where the destruction of the land is prophesied. In that case the merchants are described as marauders, not so much because they were involved in fraudulent practices but because they were insensitive to the holiness of the area where they practiced their trade. By expelling them from the forecourt Jesus freed the place where the Gentiles were allowed for worship. In view of the explicit citation of Isa. 56:7 and the allusion to Jer. 7:11, speculation that Jesus' action was aimed at reform or abolition of the Temple worship is irrelevant.[45] He is depicted as making possible the worship of the Gentiles at the feast of the Passover which commemorated God's redemption of his people. The importance of this would not be lost upon Mark's readers in the predominantly Gentile Church of Rome.

18-19 Jesus' legitimate censure of the priestly authorities for their misuse of the Temple is presented as the immediate occasion for the fateful decision which leads directly to his arrest and crucifixion.[46] The expulsion of the merchants may have seemed to them to signal the emergence of a new Zealot leader who could only be considered as

---

[44] Cf. G. W. Buchanan, "Mark 11, 15-19: Brigands in the Temple," *HUCA* 30 (1959), pp. 169-177, who points to Ch. 15:7 and Lk. 13:1f. for the possibility of zealotic activity in the Temple, but prefers to see in Ch. 11:17 a reference to the events of A.D. 68-70 when the Temple was unquestionably a Zealot stronghold.

[45] Rightly stressed by C. W. F. Smith, *op. cit.*, pp. 321f.

[46] J. Blinzler, *Der Prozess Jesu*[3] (Ratisbonne, 1960), pp. 55, 57 considers the expulsion the principal reason for the hostility of the Jewish authorities against Jesus. See also the suggestive essay of N. Q. Hamilton, *op. cit.*, pp. 365-372.

a center of grave disorders. Nevertheless, the coalition between the chief priests and the scribes (cf. Chs. 11:27; 14:1, 43, 53) is ironical in the light of the congruence of Jesus' action with a rigorous reading of scribal law (see on verse 16). In contrast to the hostile response of the chief priests and the scribes, the people were spellbound at this impressive display of authority. The statement that they were astonished at Jesus' teaching tends to indicate that the introduction to verse 17 should be taken literally: Jesus was teaching them, and only the most salient point of that teaching has been preserved (cf. Ch. 14:49). Yet in Ch. 1:27 an authoritative act is called "a new teaching," and this extended meaning of the term may be intended here. The people are astonished, but there is no indication that they have penetrated the veil of Jesus' messianic dignity. Jesus' popularity with the people explains why the authorities did not order his immediate arrest but discussed how they could destroy him without creating a popular disturbance of major proportions. Verse 18 has the effect of showing that it was not the Jewish people that are rejected but the Temple authorities and their scribal supporters (cf. Ch. 3:6). It also serves to bring Jesus' work on behalf of the Gentiles in close connection with his death.[47]

The account is abruptly terminated by Jesus' withdrawal from the city at the close of the day (Ch. 11:11). This brief notice prepares for the sequel to the incident of the fig tree in Ch. 11:20f. and for the important discussion reported in Ch. 11:27-12:12, with its ominous foreshadowing of the destiny of the Son and his adversaries.

4. The Withered Fig Tree, Faith and Prayer. Ch. 11:20-25

20 And as they passed by in the morning, they saw the fig tree withered away from the roots.[48]
21 And Peter calling to remembrance saith unto him, Rabbi, behold, the fig tree which thou cursedst is withered away.
22 And Jesus answering saith unto them, Have faith in God.[49]

---

[47] R. H. Lightfoot, *op. cit.*, pp. 62-69.

[48] A comparison of the Marcan text (ἐξηραμμένην ἐκ ῥιζῶν) with Hos. 9:16 LXX (τὰς ῥίζας αὐτοῦ ἐξηράνθη) suggests that the evangelist had in mind the text from Hosea.

[49] A number of MSS (א D Θ φ 28 33 61 543 565 700 1071 it sy[s] geo[1] arm) insert Εἰ before ἔχετε, so that the last words of verse 22 serve as the introduction to the strong assertion in verse 23. This variant is probably due to assimilation to Mt. 21:21 or Lk. 17:6.

23 Verily I say unto you, [50] Whosoever shall say unto this mountain, Be thou taken up and cast into the sea; and shall not doubt in his heart, but shall believe that what he saith cometh to pass; he shall have it.
24 Therefore I say unto you, All things whatsoever ye pray and ask for, believe that ye receive them, and ye shall have them.
25 And whensoever ye stand praying, forgive, if ye have aught against anyone, that your Father also who is in heaven may forgive you your trespasses. [51]

20-21 The initial verses of this new section form the sequel to verses 12-14, and complete the incident within which the expulsion of the merchants from the Court of the Gentiles gains perspective. The detail that the tree was withered from the roots indicates the totality of its destruction (cf. Job 18:16; 31:12; Ezek. 17:9; Hos. 9:16) and demonstrates that no one will in the future eat fruit from the tree (verse 14). The remark that Peter remembered (cf. Ch. 14:72) suggests that the entire incident was associated with the Petrine memoirs in the tradition. Jesus made no attempt to interpret the event, but it is clear that the withering of the tree served as a vivid warning of impending judgment (Ch. 13:2; cf. Ps. 90:6; Joel 1:12; Hos. 9:16). [52]

22-24 If the connection between verses 20 f. and verse 22 is historical, it implies that the source of Jesus' authority is his unbroken relationship with the Father. These sayings on faith and prayer, however, occur in quite scattered contexts in the Synoptic Gospels [53] and may have been uttered on different occasions. In Mark they constitute a summons to faith and to action consistent with that faith. The brief saying in verse 22 is commonly interpreted as an exhortation to have faith in God. It is possible that it should be understood as an encouragement rather than an exhortation: you have the faithfulness of God (cf. Hab. 2:4). On this understanding the solemnly introduced assurances of verses 23-24 are grounded explicitly on God's faithfulness and not on the ability of

---

[50] See above on Ch. 3:28.

[51] Verse 26 is rightly omitted in the ASV, RSV and all modern translations of the text. It is absent from ℵ B L W Δ Ψ 565 700 892 *pc* g^2 *k l* r^2 sy^s sa bo geo arm, and represents an addition from Mt. 6:15; cf. Mt. 18:35.

[52] See further the larger discussion introducing Ch. 11:12-14.

[53] Ch. 11:23 = Mt. 17:20; Lk. 17:6; with Ch. 11:24 cf. Mt. 7:7; 18:19; Lk. 11:9; with Ch. 11:25 cf. Mt. 6:14 f.

a man to banish from his heart the presumption of doubt. Basic to both of these alternative ways of reading the text is the concept of faith as a quiet confidence in the power and goodness of God who accomplishes *everything*. The corollary to faith is miracle, and in this immediate context faith is unwavering trust in miraculous divine help.[54]

The Dead Sea is visible from the Mount of Olives and it is appropriate to take the reference to "this mountain" quite literally. An allusion may be intended to Zech. 14:4. In the eschatological day described there the Mount of Olives is to be split in two, and when the Lord assumes his kingship "the whole land shall be turned into a plain" (Zech. 14:10). The prayer in question is then specifically a Passover prayer for God to establish his reign.[55] What is affirmed is God's absolute readiness to respond to the resolute faith that prays (cf. Isa. 65:24). What distinguishes the faith for which Jesus calls from that self-intoxication which reduces a man and his work to a fiasco is the discipline of prayer through faith. When prayer is the source of faith's power and the means of its strength, God's sovereignty is its only restriction. The assertion in verse 24 reiterates this assurance in more comprehensive and general terms. The man who bows his head before the hidden glory of God in the fulness of faith does so in the certainty that God can deal with every situation and any difficulty and that with him nothing is impossible (Ch. 10:27).

25 While there is no textual evidence for the omission of verse 25, this saying stands under strong suspicion of being a gloss, influenced by Mt. 6:14 f. While the distinctive vocabulary and phraseology ("if you have anything against someone... your Father who is in heaven... forgive you your trespasses") is unparalleled in Mark, it is decidedly Matthean in character (cf. Mt. 5:23; 6:9, 14 f.). Matthew appears to follow Mark in this pericope, but only through Ch. 11:24, which may suggest that his copy of Mark actually concluded this section with verse

---

[54] R. Bultmann, *TWNT* VI (1959), p. 206; K. Tagawa, *op. cit.*, p. 116. For a powerful statement on the relationship between faith and prayer in these verses see E. Stauffer, *New Testament Theology* (New York, 1955), pp. 168 f., 171.

[55] C. H. Bird, *op. cit.*, p. 177 believes the reference is to "the mountain of the house of the Lord" (cf. Isa. 2:2-4; Micah 4:1-3) and understands the final clause of verse 23 to refer to Jesus himself and the destruction of the Temple. It seems better to understand the text in this specific way than to find a general assertion of the ability of the disciples to do the impossible. Cf., however, I Cor. 13:2, where Paul appears to allude to this saying in quite general terms.

24. Moreover, the transition between verses 24 and 25 is abrupt, since Jesus has been talking about faith, while the new saying speaks of forgiveness. Ch. 11:26 is a clear case of a transfer from Mt. 6:15 which did not take place in the best MSS but shows how easily a passage from one Gospel could become attached to the context through catchword association.[56] Yet none of these arguments is decisive in itself,[57] and verse 25 actually differs in formulation from Mt. 6:14 to a greater degree than is usual in cases of Synoptic transfer. Verse 25 must be considered as a logion in its own right. Its formulation has been influenced by the liturgical language of the Lord's Prayer. K. Stendahl has shown through paraphrase that it is thoroughly appropriate to this context, which is concerned with omnipotent prayer: "When you stand and pray–especially if you expect your prayer to share in the power of the messianic age–forgive if you have something against somebody..."[58] The effect of the juxtaposition of verses 23-24 and 25 is to suggest that not only faith but also the willingness of the Christian to forgive conditions the efficacy of prayer. The conjunction of these two thoughts in Mark affirms that the right to pray the prayer envisioned in verses 23-24 belongs only to brothers who are mutually reconciled and united in a community of faith.[59]

5. The Authority of Jesus. Ch. 11:27-33

27 And they come again to Jerusalem; and as he was walking in the temple, there come to him the chief priests, and the scribes, and the elders;

---

[56] So H. F. D. Sparks, "The Doctrine of the Divine Fatherhood in the Gospels," in *Studies in the Gospels,* ed. D. E. Nineham (Oxford, 1955), pp. 243-245, who concludes that the verse is a gloss.

[57] K. Stendahl, "Prayer and Forgiveness," *Sv Ex Års* 22-23 (1957-58), pp. 76 f. n. 8 properly cautions that παράπτωμα is a hapax legomenon in Matthew as well as in Mark; the fact that verse 26 follows Matthew more closely than verse 25 makes it possible to see verse 25 as original in Mark; Matthew already deviates considerably from Mk. 11:24 and may well have preferred to have the saying on prayer and forgiveness in the context of his teaching about prayer; the unique occurrence of the designation "Father in heaven" in Mark suggests liturgical language known to Mark but not quite natural for his own style.

[58] *Ibid.,* p. 86.

[59] J. Murphy-O'Connor, "Péché et Communauté dans le Nouveau Testament," *RB* 74 (1967), pp. 177 f.

28 and they said unto him, By what authority [60] doest thou these things? or who gave thee this authority to do these things?
29 And Jesus said unto them, I will ask of you one question, [61] and answer me, and [62] I will tell you by what authority I do these things.
30 The baptism of John, was it from heaven, [63] or from men? answer me.
31 And they reasoned with themselves, saying, If we shall say, From heaven, he will say, Why then did ye not believe him?
32 But should we say, From men [64]–they feared the people: for all verily held John to be a prophet. [65]
33 And they answered Jesus and say, We know not. And Jesus saith unto them, Neither tell I you by what authority I do these things.

Chs. 11:27-12:25 is important for its indication that hostility to Jesus came from all the influential groups within Judaism. [66] The implied judgment upon the chief priests and elders in Ch. 11:27-33 is sustained in the parable of the vineyard which immediately follows (Ch. 12:1-11). The climax of that section serves both as the application of the parable and as the reproach of the authorities, who have rejected both John and Jesus. The leading idea of the whole section is that the leaders of the Jewish people have rejected the will of God. The vineyard parable

---

[60] Gr. ἐξουσία. See above on Ch. 1:22, 27.

[61] Gr. λόγον, which here means "matter," "point," i.e. "I will ask you about a single point."

[62] The imperative followed by "and" may be used in place of a conditional clause. The thought is, "and if you answer me, then I will tell you . . ."

[63] "Heaven" is a circumlocution for God, in keeping with a common Jewish idiom; cf. Dan. 4:26; Mk. 14:61 f. and the discussion of H. Traub, *TWNT* V (Eng. Tr. 1967), pp. 512, 521 f.

[64] It is better to adopt the punctuation of the ASVmg, RSV: "But shall we say, 'From men'?"

[65] Gr. ὄντως qualifies ἦν, not εἶχον; it has been put in the main clause for emphasis. Therefore translate with the ASVmg, RSV: "for all held that John was a *real* prophet."

[66] This is rightly stressed by B. R. Halson, "A Note on the Pharisees," *Theology* 67 (1964), pp. 248-251, and forgotten, e.g. by G. Baumbach, "Jesus und die Pharisäer. Ein Beitrag zur Frage nach dem historischen Jesus," *Bibel und Liturgie* 41 (1968), pp. 112-131, who argues that the portrayal of Jesus' adversaries has been influenced by the existing situation at the time when the Gospels were written. For a more balanced presentation see H. Merkel, "Jesus und die Pharisäer," *NTS* 14 (1968), pp. 194-208.

develops this judgment into a panorama of redemptive history. The representatives of the Sanhedrin who question Jesus are like the leaders of Israel throughout its history who have continually rejected God's messengers, from the prophets to the Son.

27-28 Jesus apparently made the Temple the focal-point of his ministry throughout the duration of his final period in Jerusalem (cf. Chs. 11:11, 15-18, 27; 12:35, 41; 13:1-2; 14:49). He was probably walking in one of the several porches of the Temple precincts when he was approached by representatives of the Sanhedrin (see on Ch. 8:31; cf. Chs. 14:43, 53; 15:1). While it is improbable that the high court would conduct a formal inquiry in public, the fact that each of the three constituent groups was represented indicates the alarm that Jesus had occasioned. The specific point of concern ("these things") was the expulsion of the merchants from the Temple forecourt, together with the popular response to Jesus' ministry (Ch. 11:18; cf. Ch. 12:12, 37). They ask by what right does Jesus act with power within the Temple, by a right deriving from his own authority (i.e. as a prophet), or by one grounded in the commission given to him by another? The Sanhedrin was concerned to learn why Jesus performed what appears to be an official act if he possesses no official status. The question posed is important from the point of view of the "secrecy" phenomena of the Gospel, for it proves that Jesus had never said openly that he was the Messiah, the institutor of an entirely new economy, [67] or even a prophet.

29-30 Answering a question by another question was a common rabbinic custom, especially in the context of debate (cf. Ch. 10:2-3). What is distinctive here is that Jesus makes his answer depend entirely on theirs. Their decision about John will determine their decision about him. [68] Jesus stakes his own authority entirely on that of the Baptist, and his declaration of solidarity with John is, in essence, a statement about the eschatological crisis which both knew to be at hand. John and Jesus stand in common opposition to those who disregard the will of God. The reference to John is appropriate because already in his ministry the Baptist had effected that split between the people and their leaders which characterized Jesus' ministry in the Temple (Chs. 11:18; 12:38).

---

67 Cf. G. Minette de Tillesse, *op. cit.*, pp. 152 f.

68 See J. Kremer, "Jesu Antwort auf die Frage nach seiner Vollmacht. Eine Auslegung von Mk 11, 23-33," *Bib Leb* 9 (1968), pp. 128-136.

The alternative posed by Jesus delimits the question and allows only two possible conclusions: from God, or from men. The counter-question clearly implies that Jesus' authority, like that of the baptism of John, is grounded in a commission from God (cf. Ch. 9:37).[69]

31-32 Jesus' counter-question had the immediate effect of putting his adversaries in a state of embarrassment. They recognized their dilemma: if they acknowledged John's prophetic authority they would expose themselves to the charge of unbelief. They also realized that they would be compelled to acknowledge that Jesus' authority comes from God. The second conditional sentence is broken off in the middle, but the apodosis is clear from the context: if they affirm that John's authority was from men (i.e. not from God), they will discredit themselves in the eyes of the people, who could turn against them in wrath. Both John and Jesus were regarded by the people as genuine prophets, and for this reason in both instances the authorities "feared" the people (Chs. 11:18, 32; 12:12).

33 The spokesmen for the group sought to evade the issue with a confession of ignorance, implying that they had suspended their judgment. Jesus, therefore, refused to answer their probing question beyond the veiled, indirect answer implied in his counter-question. The fact of his authority remained. Jesus' authority presupposes a divine commission and authorization with power; the specific feature of this authority is that it is inseparable from the proclamation that the Kingdom of God has drawn near (see on Ch. 1:15).[70]

---

[69] Is the reference to the Baptist an allusion to an earlier expulsion of the merchants from the Temple forecourt, carried out under the Baptist's authority (Jn. 2:13-22)? If so, it is no accident that when Jesus cleanses the Temple on his own messianic authority he answers the challenge of the authorities with a reminder of John's baptism.

[70] W. Foerster, *TWNT* II (Eng. Tr. 1964), p. 569.

CHAPTER 12

6. THE PARABLE OF THE DEFIANT TENANTS. Ch. 12:1-12

1 And he began to speak unto them in parables.[1] A man planted a vineyard, and set a hedge about it, and digged a pit for the winepress, and built a tower, and let it out to husbandmen, and went into another country.
2 And at the season he sent to the husbandmen a servant, that he might receive from the husbandmen of the fruits of the vineyard.
3 And they took him, and beat him, and sent him away empty.[2]
4 And again he sent unto them another servant; and him they wounded in the head, and handled shamefully.
5 And he sent another; and him they killed: and many others; beating some, and killing some.
6 He had yet one, a beloved son[3]: he sent him last unto them, saying, They will reverence my son.
7 But those husbandmen said among themselves, This is the heir; come, let us kill him, and the inheritance shall be ours.
8 And they took him, and killed him, and cast him forth out of the vineyard.
9 What therefore will the Lord[4] of the vineyard do? He will come and destroy the husbandmen, and will give the vineyard unto others.
10 Have you not read even this scripture:
The stone which the builders rejected,
The same was made the head of the corner;
11 This was from the Lord,
And it is marvellous in our eyes?
12 And they sought to lay hold on him; and they feared the multitude; for they perceived that he spake the parable against them[5]: and they left him, and went away.

---

1 Gr. ἐν παραβολαῖς is used adverbially and means simply "parabolically," as in Ch. 3:23. For an introduction to Jesus' use of parables see the opening remarks to Ch. 4.

2 Gr. κενόν here means "empty-handed," as in the LXX expression τινὰ κενὸν ἐξαποστέλλειν (Gen. 31:42; Deut. 15:13; Job 22:9).

3 Gr. ἀγαπητόν means here "only" son, as in Gen. 22:2, 12, 16; Jer. 6:26 LXX. See above on Ch. 1:11.

4 It is better to translate κύριος as "owner," in keeping with the parable Jesus has been telling (cf. verse 1, "a man planted a vineyard").

5 Gr. πρὸς αὐτούς is better translated "with reference to them."

The Parable of the Defiant Tenants reflects the social background of Jewish Galilee in the first century, with its great landed estates and the inevitable tension between the absentee-owners and the dispossessed, land-hungry peasantry who cultivated the land as tenant-farmers. Recent study of the Zenon papyri and of the rabbinic parables has shown that situations very closely analogous to that of the parable actually existed in Palestine both around 280 years prior to Jesus' ministry and for some time afterward. [6] Detailed analysis of the imagery of the parable has further shown that from this point of view Ch. 12:1-9 is a genuine parable, and not an allegory. It belongs to the general category of judgment parables; it is a dramatic presentation of a life situation which invites a judgment from the hearers. Jesus' parable served to expose the planned attempt against his own life, and God's judgment against the planners. Recent criticism has tended to view the account in the Gospel of Thomas (Logion 65) as preserving the parable in its most primitive form; [7] but there are serious objections to this judgment. [8]

---

[6] See the valuable discussions of C. H. Dodd, *The Parables of the Kingdom*, revised edition (London, 1963), pp. 93-98; J. Jeremias, *The Parables of Jesus*[6] (New York, 1962), pp. 70-77; and most recently, M. Hengel, "Das Gleichnis von den Weingärtnern Mc 12, 1-12 im Lichte der Zenonpapyri und der rabbinischen Gleichnisse," *ZNW* 59 (1968), pp. 9-31. On the Zenon papyri see especially V. Tcherikover, "Palestine under the Ptolemies," *Mizraim* 4/5 (1937), pp. 7-90.

[7] In the Gospel of Thomas the parable is free from allegorical features, the number of servants is reduced to two, the reference to Isa. 5:2 at the beginning is lacking, the servants are not murdered but only violently beaten, and in place of the rhetorical questions of Ch. 12:9 is the typical admonition "He who has ears to hear, let him hear!" This form is championed as primitive by C. H. Dodd, *op. cit.*, p. 96 n. 22; J. Jeremias, *op. cit.*, pp. 70-77; B. M. F. van Iersel, *Der "Sohn" in den synoptischen Jesusworten*[2] (Leiden, 1964), pp. 124-145; G. Minette de Tillesse, *Le Secret messianique dans l'Évangile de Marc* (Paris, 1968), pp. 288-290, among others.

[8] W. Schrage, *Das Verhältnis des Thomas-Evangeliums zur synoptischen Tradition und zu den koptischen Evangelienübersetzungen* (*BZNW* 29, Berlin, 1963), pp. 137-141 has demonstrated by his comparison of the Coptic Gospel of Thomas and the Sahidic translation of the Synoptic Gospels that Thomas is dependent upon the Sahidic VS, and that in a late form. On p. 139 he shows that Logion 65 shows especially the influence of the Lucan version of the parable (Lk. 20:9-19), and is convinced that in Thomas there has been a conscious de-allegorizing reduction produced from the Synoptic Gospels, without access to independent tradition (pp. 7 f.). M. Hengel, *op. cit.*, p. 5 remarks: "We are thrust back upon Mark as preserving presumably the oldest form." See also W. G. Kümmel, "Das Gleichnis von den bösen Weingärtnern (Mark 12. 1-9)," in *Aux Sources de la Tradition Chrétienne* (Mélanges M. Goguel, ed. O. Cullmann and Ph. Menoud. Paris, 1950), pp. 120-131.

The Marcan account is solidly grounded in Semitic tradition[9] and may be regarded as a faithful representation of the parable Jesus told on this occasion.

1 Jesus addressed his parables to the representatives of the Sanhedrin who came to question him concerning the nature and source of his authority, for they are the most natural subject of the verbs found in verse 12 (cf. Ch. 11:18). The initial details of the parable, in which the careful construction of the vineyard is described, are derived from Isa. 5:1 f. The allusion to the Song of the Vineyard (Isa. 5:1-7) has been regarded as a later, allegorical addition to Jesus' parable, since it has no parallel in Lk. 20:9 or the Gospel of Thomas, but this is to misunderstand the Lord's intention. He deliberately appealed to Isa. 5:1 f. in order to force his hearers to draw the conclusion that the parable concerns their abuse of the position they have assumed. This parable was told for the purpose of being understood, and Mark underlines this fact in verse 12. The construction of the vineyard, however, is only preliminary to the situation depicted. The story concerns a landowner who leased a vineyard to tenant farmers who agreed to work the land in his absence. Since the whole of the upper Jordan valley and a large part of the Galilean uplands were in the hands of foreign landlords at this time, such a practice was common. A contract stipulated for the payment of rent in the form of a portion of the produce.[10] The crucial detail is that the owner is living abroad, for the subsequent conduct of the tenants is intelligible only under the existing conditions of absentee ownership.

2-5 At the proper time the owner sent his agent to collect the rent. A previously unpublished papyrus clarifies the reference to "the fruits of the vineyard" in verse 2 since it refers to different kinds of wine, including a cheap wine designated for the slaves of the state. The same papyrus reports a dispute between the agent of the finance minister who owned a vast estate in Beth Anath in Galilee and hostile farmers who were withholding certain quantities of grapes, wine and corn. While

---

9 On the Semitisms in the parable see the list of twelve items in M. Hengel, *op. cit.*, pp. 7 f. n. 31.

10 C. H. Dodd, *op. cit.*, p. 93 n. 17 refers to Oxyrhynchus Papyri 1631, 1689, 1968 for examples of contracts stipulating for payment of rent in kind. During the Ptolemaic period covered by the Zenon Papyri, wine stood high on the export list from Palestine and Phoenicia.

the agent refers to the contract made with the employment-agent of the toparchy, the farmers speak of a "petition" which they themselves have drawn up in their own interest.[11] This was the type of situation which could erupt into the kind of violence Jesus described when he spoke of the indignities heaped upon the first two agents, climaxed by the murder of the third. Having met the owner's appeal for his rental with a defiance that stopped at nothing, the sequel of the story in the murder of the son and presumed heir is inherent in the logic of the situation. The detail in verse 5b, however, that the owner sent many others, was intended by Jesus to force his listeners beyond the framework of the parable to the history of Israel. In the OT the prophets are frequently designated "the servants" of God (cf. Jer. 7:25 f.; 25:4; Amos 3:7; Zech. 1:6) and it is natural to find a reference to their rejection in the words "beating some, and killing others."

6-8 The owner, realizing the seriousness of the situation, sent his son to deal with it. The words "they will respect my son" are not didactic reflection on God the Father's expectation in sending Jesus to Israel, since the parable teaches that Jesus did not expect that. They are an integral part of the parable, and are intelligible on the assumption that the owner was living in a distant foreign land. It could be expected that the son of the owner would command the respect which had been denied to the slaves who had represented him previously.[12] The murder of the son and the final indignity of casting his body over the wall of the vineyard without burial provide the climax of iniquity demanded by the plot of the story. The seizure of the property is illumined by the contemporary legal situation.[13] The arrival of the son allowed the tenant

---

[11] M. Hengel, *op. cit.*, pp. 12-14.

[12] J. Jeremias, *op. cit.*, pp. 72 f. correctly points out that in the sending of the son, Jesus had his own sending in mind, but that the messianic significance of the son would remain veiled from his hearers since there is no evidence that the title "Son of God" was applied to the Messiah in pre-Christian Palestinian Judaism. In the rabbinic parable of the defiant tenants (Sifré Deut. 32:9 § 312) the son is interpreted as the patriarch Jacob, i.e. as representing the people of Israel. So also W. G. Kümmel, *op. cit.*, p. 130.

[13] See especially E. Bammel, "Das Gleichnis von der bösen Winzern (Mc 12, 1-9) und des jüdische Erbrecht," *RIDA* 3rd ser. 6 (1959), pp. 11-17; J. D. M. Derrett, "Fresh Light on the Parable of the Wicked Vinedressers," *RIDA* 3rd ser. 10 (1963), pp. 11-41; M. Hengel, *op. cit.*, pp. 18-39. A piece of land could be lawfully possessed, if it fell within the category of ownerless property, if even a small portion of it had been "marked out, fenced, or provided with an entrance" (M. *Baba Bathra*

farmers to assume that the owner had died and that his sole heir had come to claim his inheritance. Under specified circumstances an inheritance could be regarded as "ownerless property," which could be lawfully claimed by anyone, the prior right of ownership belonging to the claimant who comes first. This was the case when an inheritance was not claimed within a specified period of time. This provision of law explains why the tenants assume that if they murder the son (and presumed heir), they may take unhindered possession of the vineyard. It would become "ownerless property" which they can claim as the actual occupants of the land.

9 The integrity of verse 9 has been questioned because it refers back to Isa. 5:5 LXX, and Jesus did not ordinarily answer his questions. The details of his answer, however, are inherent within the logic of the situation. The murder of the son exhibited the outrageous defiance of the tenants in a most emphatic way. Their foolish assumption that the owner was dead and his property available for seizure would be shattered on the hard rock of reality. The owner would have recourse to governmental intervention to forcibly subdue the mutinous tenants,[14] after which he would naturally lease the vineyard to others. The allusion to Isa. 5:1-7 both at the beginning and conclusion of the parable is a deliberate appeal to those who were plotting Jesus' death to understand the ultimate seriousness of what they were doing. The fact that in Isa. 5 the vineyard itself is at fault, while in Jesus' parable it is only the defiant tenant-farmers, indicates that he directed his words specifically to the leaders of the people, and not to the people themselves. Within the scope of the parable the inevitable consequence of the rejection of the son was decisive, catastrophic judgment. This points to the critical significance of the rejection of John and of Jesus which is so prominently in view in Ch. 11:27-12:12, for what is involved is the rejection of God. Without declaring his own transcendent sonship, Jesus clearly implies that the Sanhedrin has rejected God's final messenger and that disaster will ensue. The sacred trust of the chosen people will be transferred to the new Israel of God.

III. 3). A garden which had belonged to a proselyte who died intestate was successfully claimed by marking it with a sign (TB *Baba Bathra* 54a).

[14] C. H. Dodd, *op. cit.*, p. 95 appeals to the example of Brutus, who collected a debt from the corporation of Salamis by arranging for the dispatch of a force of cavalry obtained from the governor of Cilicia (see Cicero, *Ad Atticum* V. 21; VI. 1).

10-12 The quotation of Ps. 118:22 f. agrees exactly with the LXX form of the text.[15] The passage refers to one of the building blocks gathered at the site of Solomon's Temple which was rejected in the construction of the Sanctuary but which proved to be the keystone to the porch.[16] Introduced with the language of debate, the citation is intended to sharpen the application of the parable to Jesus and his immediate listeners. It confirms the identification of Jesus as the son in the parable and contrasts his despised and rejected status with the glorious exaltation to which God has appointed him. The note of rejection followed by vindication sounded in the first prophecy of the passion (see on Ch. 8:31) is here expressed with the covert, but clear terms of the biblical text. In rabbinic literature the rejected stone of Ps. 118:22 was understood with reference to Abraham, David or the Messiah, while the expression "the builders" was sometimes used of the doctors of the Law.[17] Here the text serves as a warning that God will reverse the judgment of men with regard to his final messenger in a startling display of his power, turning apparent defeat into triumph (cf. Acts 4:11; I Peter 2:7).

The representatives of the Sanhedrin who heard Jesus speak would naturally find the clue to his meaning in the explicit allusion to Isa. 5:1-7 and in their own experience of hostility toward him. The parable, with its reflection on the history of Israel as marked by rebellion and unfaithfulness in spite of divine grace, amounted to a biting condemnation of their failure as leaders of the people. They understood its tenor only too well. The emphasis on understanding in verse 12 is new (contrast Ch. 4:11 f., 33 f.) and suggests that the secret of the Kingdom is on the point of being publicly revealed.[18] What is significant is that Jesus himself took the initiative to disclose increasingly the secret of his own person, although the men to whom he directed his words were blinded by rage to the truth. Only the presence of crowds of people prevented them from laying violent hands on Jesus there in the Temple. The con-

---

[15] In the Gospel of Thomas an allusion to Ps. 118:22 follows the parable as a separate logion (66): "Jesus said: Show me the stone which the builders rejected. It is the keystone."

[16] Cf. J. Jeremias, *TWNT* I (Eng. Tr. 1964), pp. 792 f.; IV (Eng. Tr. 1967), p. 278; L. W. Barnard, "The Testimonium Concerning the Stone in the New Testament and the Epistle of Barnabas," in *Studia Evangelica* III, ed. F. L. Cross (Oxford, 1964), pp. 306-313.

[17] Cf. S-B*K* I (1922), pp. 875 f.

[18] G. Minette de Tillesse, *op. cit.*, pp. 218 f., 287-293 speaks of Jesus' progressive and regular withdrawal of the veil from his own identity until the secret is openly disclosed in Ch. 14:62.

clusion of the account echoes Ch. 11:18 f. and suggests that verse 12 may mark the close of the third day in Jerusalem.

The question of Jesus' authority introduces a sequence of five conflict situations in Jerusalem (Ch. 11:27-12:37) corresponding to the similar sequence of conflict in Galilee in Ch. 2:1-3:6. D. Daube, however, has suggested that the four accounts which follow show an awareness of the traditional structure of the early Passover liturgy. [19] The sequence of questions proposed corresponds to four types of questions recognized by the rabbis: questions of wisdom, which concern a point of law (cf. Ch. 12:13-17); of mockery, which frequently bear on the resurrection (cf. Ch. 12:18-27); of conduct, which center in relationship to God and men (cf. Ch. 12:28-34); and of biblical exegesis, which often concern the resolving of an apparent contradiction between two passages of Scripture (cf. Ch. 12:35-37). It is only in the Passover eve liturgy that the four types of questions appear in this particular order, and there the first three questions are posed by a wise son, a wicked son and a son of simple piety. The fourth is posed by the head of the family himself. This arrangement sheds light on the sequence of questions in Ch. 12:13-37. Daube's suggestion is attractive that in this section of the Gospel we are in touch with elements of the tradition which were already associated with the Passover eve celebrations among the Christians in the first decades after the resurrection and may account for the grouping and order of the sequence in Mark's Gospel.

7. The Question Concerning Tribute. Ch. 12:13-17

13 And they send unto him certain of the Pharisees and of the Herodians, [20] that they might catch him in talk. [21]
14 And when they were come they say unto him, Teacher, we know that thou art true, and carest not for anyone; for thou

[19] D. Daube, "Evangelisten und Rabbinen," *ZNW* 48 (1957), pp. 119-126; *idem*, "The Earliest Structure of the Gospels," *NTS* 5 (1959), pp. 174-187. The schema to which Daube makes reference is found with variation in the order of the questions in Mekilta Ex. 13:8, § 4; TJ *Pesachim* X 37d; TB *Niddah* 69b-71a.

[20] On the Pharisees see above on Ch. 2:16; 7:1; 8:11; and on the Herodians Ch. 3:6. A coalition between these two groups is mentioned as early as Ch. 3:6.

[21] Gr. ἵνα αὐτὸν ἀγρεύσωσιν λόγῳ, "that they might catch him in (an unguarded) statement." 'Αγρεύειν ("to catch") occurs only here in the NT, and is used figuratively as in Prov. 5:22; 6:25 f. LXX.

regardest not the person of man, but of a truth teachest the way of God: Is it lawful to give tribute [22] unto Caesar, or not?
15 Shall we give, or shall we not give? But he, knowing their hypocrisy, said unto them, Why make ye trial of me? [23] bring me a denarius, that I may see it.
16 And they brought it. And he saith unto them, Whose is this image and superscription? And they said unto him, Caesar's.
17 And Jesus said unto them, Render unto Caesar the things that are Caesar's, and unto God the things that are God's. And they marvelled greatly at him.

13 The account is abruptly introduced without any statement of time or place, but it is appropriate to situate this encounter with certain Pharisees and Herodians in one of the porches of the Temple (cf. Chs. 11:27; 12:35). Presumably they had been sent by certain members of the Sanhedrin or by leaders in their respective groups. They may well have been Galileans with previous contact with Jesus who had come to Jerusalem to celebrate the feast (cf. Lk. 23:7), and it is possible that their question, so carefully devised to discredit or imperil Jesus, was the result of the joint deliberations mentioned in Ch. 3:6. These men were anxious to entangle Jesus "in his word" because in his word they sensed his claim to absolute authority and consequently his threatening character. If they could snare him into making an unguarded statement they might be able to succeed in destroying him.

14-15a The opening remarks addressed to Jesus were designed to close the way to any possible evasion of a painful and difficult question. By reminding Jesus that he was a man of integrity who paid no attention to the opinions of men but taught absolute commitment to the way of life commanded by God, his adversaries intended to force him to face squarely the issue they had decided upon. It is important to appreciate

[22] Gr. κῆνσον transliterates the Latin term *census* and reflects the impact made by the introduction of the Roman taxation into the Judean province in A.D. 6. In place of this term D Θ 124 565 1071 *k* sy$^{s\ p}$ read ἐπικεφάλαιον ("poll-tax"), and this variant is preferred by C. H. Turner, "Marcan Usage," *JThS* 29 (1928), pp. 7 f.

[23] After τί με πειράζετε P^{45} F G N W Θ Σ λ φ 13 28 33 543 565 579 *q* sy^{h} sa geo arm have ὑποκριταί, which may be correct. Cf. P. L. Couchoud, "Notes de critique verbale sur St. Marc et St. Matthieu," *JThS* 35 (1934), pp. 19 f. On the charge of hypocrisy see above on Ch. 7:6.

the emotional trauma which pervaded the issue of the tribute money ever since it had first been imposed on the Roman province of Judea in A.D. 6.[24] At that time Judas the Galilean had seen in the census which was the prelude to the taxation an introduction to slavery and an affront to the sovereignty of God (cf. Josephus, *Antiquities* XVIII. i. 1; Acts 5:37). The Zealots resolutely refused to pay the tax because it acknowledged Caesar's domination over them.[25] The Pharisees resented the humiliation implied in the tax but justified its payment, while the Herodians supported it on principle. In asking if it was allowed by the Law of God to pay the tribute money it could be assumed that the Pharisees were concerned chiefly in the moral and religious implications of the question, and the Herodians with its political or nationalistic ramifications. In point of fact the question was insincere. Its object was to force Jesus into a compromising position either theologically or politically. The form of the question ("shall we give, or shall we not give it?") was skillfully designed to thrust Jesus on the horns of a dilemma. An affirmative answer would discredit him in the eyes of the people, for whom the tax was an odious token of subjection to Rome.[26] A negative reply would invite reprisals from the Roman authorities.

15b-16 Jesus recognized that the question was not sincere but represented one more attempt to discover something which could be used against him (see on Ch. 8:11; 10:2). There is an understandable note of exasperation in the pointed question, Why are you putting me to the test? While the command to bring a denarius implies that neither Jesus nor his adversaries had one, there is little evidence that in the first century there was a general, deep-rooted objection to handling and

---

[24] Cf. Josephus, *Antiquities* V. i. 21 and the interesting material brought together by E. Stauffer, *Jesus and His Story* (New York, 1960), pp. 21-32. There is a wealth of technical material in S. L. Wallace, *Taxation in Egypt from Augustus to Diocletian* (Princeton, 1938) and H. Loewe, *"Render Unto Caesar": Religious and Political Loyalty in Palestine* (Cambridge, 1940).

[25] Cf. S-B*K* I (1922), p. 884. According to Hippolytus, *Omnium haeresium confutatio* ix. 26, the Zealots would not handle or look upon any coin which bore an image.

[26] G. Minette de Tillesse, *op. cit.,* pp. 153 f. sees the dilemma differently: if Jesus says "Yes," he must renounce his messianic pretensions. There is no indication, however, either in the title of address used by the questioners in verse 14 or in the general probabilities of the situation, that Jesus' messianic dignity is the real issue at stake.

gazing upon coins bearing a human effigy.[27] The only coin that was accepted for payment of taxes in Judea, as throughout imperial territory, was the Roman denarius. This was a small silver coin that was worth normally about eighteen cents. The denarius of Tiberius portrayed the emperor as the semi-divine son of the god Augustus and the goddess Livia and bore the (abbreviated) inscription "Tiberius Caesar Augustus, Son of the Divine Augustus" on the obverse and "Pontifex Maximus" on the reverse. Both the representations and the inscriptions were rooted in the imperial cult and constituted a claim to divine honors.[28] The unhesitating reply to Jesus' question in verse 16, that the image and inscription were Caesar's, indicates that the coin was well known to the delegation through common circulation and use.

17 In his reply Jesus seized on the admission that the image and inscription were Caesar's.[29] The acceptance and usage of Caesar's coinage implicitly acknowledged his authority and therefore the obligation to pay the tax. The portrait and legend demonstrated the right of the sovereign who coined the money to demand tribute from the provincials, in keeping with the common understanding that the emperor owned the coins which bore his image. There are obligations to the state which do not infringe the rights of God but are grounded in his appointment (cf. Rom. 13:1-7; I Tim. 2:1-6; Tit. 3:1 f.; I Peter 2:13-17). By recognizing the relative autonomy of the civil authority in the first part of his response, Jesus showed himself opposed to any belief in an essentially theocratic state and to any expectation of an imminent eschatological consummation of his own mission. But by distinguishing so sharply between Caesar and God he tacitly protested against the idolatrous claims advanced on the coins. There is always inherent in civil authority a tendency to reach

---

27 In contrast to the third-century Rabbi Nahum ben Simai, who gained the title of "holy" among his contemporaries because he would not so much as look at a coin which bore any sort of effigy (TJ *'Abodah Zarah* 42c; TB *Megillah* 72b). See H. Loewe, *op. cit.*, pp. 87 f.

28 See E. Stauffer, *Christ and the Caesars* (Philadelphia, 1955), pp. 112-137, together with the material assembled by A. Deissmann, *Light from the Ancient East*[4] (New York, 1927), pp. 252, 338-384.

29 The logion in verse 17 occurs in Egerton Papyrus No. 2 (Fragment 2 recto) and in the Coptic Gospel of Thomas, Logion 100. Both versions, however, differ substantially from each other and from the Synoptic wording. These divergent sayings are studied by J. N. Sevenster, "Geeft den keizer wat des keizers is, en Gode wat Gods is," *Nederlands Theologisch Tijdschrift* 17 (1962), pp. 21-31, who concludes that they should not be used for interpreting Jesus' statement in verse 17.

beyond its appointed function,[30] a tendency which leads to self-transcendence. The temptation to self-glorification which always accompanies power was particularly clear in the extravagances of the imperial cult, with its deification of the state and its civil head. Jesus emphatically rejected this insolent confusion between man and God; divine honors belong to God alone. The second part of his response, seen in the total context of Jesus' life and teaching, shows that the duties toward God and Caesar, though distinct, are not completely separate, but are united and ruled by the higher principle of accomplishing in all things the will of God.[31] Because men bear the image of God they owe their total allegiance to him.

There is gentle irony in Mark's closing comment that his adversaries marvelled greatly at Jesus. It is appropriate that men who had come to ensnare Jesus through unguarded statement should sense the devastating effect of the authority displayed in his word.[32]

8. The Question Concerning the Resurrection. Ch. 12:18-27

18 And there come unto him Sadducees, who say that there is no resurrection; and they asked him, saying,
19 Teacher, Moses wrote unto us, If a man's brother die, and leave a wife behind him, and leave no child, that his brother should take his wife, and raise up seed unto his brother.
20 There were seven brethren: and the first took a wife, and dying left no seed;
21 and the second took her, and died, leaving no seed behind him; and the third likewise:
22 and the seven left no seed. Last of all the woman also died.

---

[30] This was already realized by Aristotle (*Politica* III. vii. 7; VI. i. 1-3), and found ample illustration in men like Antiochus Epiphanes or Pompey whose arrogance in assuming divine prerogatives was duly noted in Jewish literature (cf. Mekilta to Ex. 15:11; Psalms of Solomon 2:29; II Macc. 9:8). Cf. Ch. 13:14.

[31] Cf. L. Goppelt, "The Freedom to Pay the Imperial Tax," in *Studia Evangelica* II (ed. F. L. Cross, Berlin, 1963), pp. 183-194. On the larger issues posed by the question of Christian political responsibility see K. Barth, *Against the Stream* (London, 1954), pp. 13-54; O. Cullmann, *The State in the New Testament* (London, 1957); C. E. B. Cranfield, "The Christian's Political Responsibility according to the New Testament," *ScJTh* 15 (1962), pp. 176-192.

[32] Cf. G. Kittel, *TWNT* IV (Eng. Tr. 1967), pp. 106-108.

23 In the resurrection[33] whose wife shall she be of them? for the seven had her to wife.
24 Jesus said unto them, Is it not for this cause that ye err, that ye know not the scriptures, nor the power of God?
25 For when they shall rise from the dead, they neither marry, nor are given in marriage; but are as angels in heaven.
26 But as touching the dead, that they are raised; have ye not read in the book of Moses, in *the place concerning* the Bush,[34] how God spake unto him, saying, I *am* the God of Abraham, and the God of Isaac, and the God of Jacob?
27 He is not the God of the dead, but of the living: ye do greatly err.

18 It is commonly assumed that the Sadducees were an aristocratic party consisting of the high priestly and other leading families of Jerusalem. Actually questions of their origin and development as well as their political and theological orientation are problematic because no certain Sadducean documents have been preserved. The sources describing the Sadducees are frequently conflicting in their reports and antagonistic in intention. The theory of a fundamental relationship between the Sadducees and the Temple is itself based on late source material and conjecture. Of the 28 high priests who held office in the 107-year period between Herod's appointment of Ananel and the destruction of the Temple, only Ḥanan ben Ḥanan, who held office for three months, is identified as a Sadducee by Josephus (*Antiquities* XX. ix. 1). The disputes between Sadducean and Pharisaic scribes show a pronounced interest in the Temple but do not warrant the assertion that the Temple hierarchy was by conviction Sadducean or was inclined to follow the traditions of the Sadducees. It is probable that the Sadducees began as a political faction which supported the legitimacy of the Hasmonean throne over the protest of the purists who insisted on a separation of the priestly and royal prerogatives or who looked for a revival of the Davidic kingdom. They also championed the sovereign's

---

[33] At this point 𝔎 A Γ Θ Φ λ (φ) *pl* latt sys bopt add ὅταν ἀναστῶσιν, i.e. "in the resurrection, when they are raised . . . " Though these additional words are missing from some of the more significant MSS, the tautology reflects Semitic idiom and is probably original.

[34] Gr. ἐπὶ τοῦ βάτου is a customary Jewish manner of referring to the narrative concerning the burning bush in Ex. 3:1-6. See above on Ch. 2:26, and cf. Rom. 11:2, where ἐν Ἠλείᾳ refers to I Kings 19:1-10. Other Jewish examples are collected in S-B*K* II (1924), p. 28.

authority over the judiciary, in opposition to the concept of a separation of powers which would assign to a self-perpetuating establishment of ordained scribes absolute authority in questions of Jewish law. After the death of the last of the Hasmonean contenders, Mattathias Antigonus II, the Sadducees tended to assume a merely negative role, repudiating the authority of the Pharisaic scribes and rejecting their innovations both in the definition of the Law and in the details of halakhic regulation.[35]

A firm belief in the resurrection was an integral element in popular Jewish piety as expressed in the second benediction of the Shemoneh 'Esreh ("Blessed be thou, O Lord, who raises the dead") or in the doxology to be pronounced in a cemetery, "He will cause you to arise. Blessed be he who keeps his word and raises the dead!" (Tos. *Berachoth* VII. 5).[36] The Sadducees, who took their doctrinal stance from the Pentateuch, were notorious for their rejection of this belief as a later innovation, and the provision of M. *Sanhedrin* X. 1 was directed against them: "Whoever says that the resurrection of the dead cannot be deduced from the Torah has no part in the Age to Come."[37]

19-23 The use of Scripture and an illustrative story to pose a challenge to an accepted interpretation is typical of scribal discussion. This suggests that the delegation which posed their problem to Jesus consisted of Sadducean scribes who, like their counterpart among the Pharisees (cf. Ch. 2:16), were specialists in biblical interpretation. They referred to the Mosaic provision for levirate marriage, freely citing Deut. 25:5 f., and tailored the story of the woman and her seven husbands, all of whom died childless, to show that the ordinance had been literally fulfilled. The story may have been adapted from a popular version of the book of Tobit (for a woman married to seven husbands, all of whom died childless, cf. Tobit 3:8, 15; 6:13; 7:11; for levirate marriage, cf. Tobit 4:12; 6:9-12; 7:12 f.). Their intention is to expose a belief in the

---

35 For the details in support of this reconstruction see V. Eppstein, "The Gospel Account of the Cleansing of the Temple," *ZNW* 55 (1964), pp. 50-54; *idem*, "When and How the Sadducees were Excommunicated," *JBL* 85 (1960), pp. 213-224; R. Meyer, *TWNT* VII (1964), pp. 35-46. Cf. E. E. Ellis, "Jesus, the Sadducees and Qumran," *NTS* 10 (1964), pp. 274-279.

36 See the texts cited by A. Oepke, *TWNT* I (Eng. Tr. 1964), pp. 369 f.

37 Cf. TJ *Ḥagigah* IV 77b: "Elisha ben Abuya said, 'There is no resurrection of the dead'." See further Acts 23:6-8; Josephus, *Antiquities* XVIII. i. 4; *War* II. viii. 14; *Aboth de Rabbi Nathan* (recension B) 5 and the discussion of R. Meyer, *TWNT* VII (1964), pp. 46 f.

resurrection to ridicule with their confident question, "In the resurrection, whose wife will she be?"

24-25 Jesus responded with two counter-questions, each of which is balanced with a positive statement. The root of the Sadducean error was a failure to understand the tenor of the Scriptures or the power of God. When properly understood, the passage cited in verse 26 bears eloquent witness to the truth of the resurrection, while God's power is revealed in his ability to vanquish death and bestow the gift of life.[38] The Sadducees were mistaken about the character of the resurrection life. The text deals only with the concrete point of marriage, which is germane to the specific problem posed, but points beyond this immediate issue. In opposition to the current Jewish conception that earthly relationships will be resumed after the resurrection,[39] Jesus affirmed that the resurrection life is comparable to the life enjoyed by the angels. Its great purpose and center is communion with God.

26-27 Jesus maintained the fact of the resurrection life by an appeal to Scripture and to God's covenant faithfulness. It is significant that the passage cited, Ex. 3:6, is drawn from the Pentateuch, that part of Scripture acknowledged by the Sadducees to be authoritative. The greater part of commentary opinion denies to Ex. 3:6 even an implicit affirmation of the resurrection of the dead, and finds here a rabbinic type of argumentation that is without relevance for contemporary thought.[40] Precisely here, however, Jesus is concerned to rectify the error of the Sadducees, which has its source in an inability to understand

---

[38] C. K. Barrett, *The Holy Spirit and the Gospel Tradition*² (London, 1958), pp. 74 f. suggests that Jesus was thinking of a passage in the *Amidah* prayer which includes the words "You quicken the dead with great mercy . . . and keep your faith with those who sleep in the dust," and was known as גְּבוּרוֹת (i.e. "the powers [of God]").

[39] Cf. S-B*K* I (1922), pp. 888-890, and for the truth affirmed by Jesus I Enoch 104:4, "You shall have great joy as the angels in heaven"; II Baruch 51:10, the righteous "shall be made like the angels." For the Sadducean rejection of the belief in angels, see Acts 23:8.

[40] It is common to refer to TB *Sanhedrin* 90b, where Rabbi Gamaliel II deduces the resurrection from Num. 11:9 ("in order that you may prolong your days on the land which God has promised to your fathers to give *to them*") on the ground that they must themselves be the beneficiaries of the promise. In a similar manner Rabbi Johanan deduces from Num. 18:28 that Aaron must be alive all the time the law is in effect. Jesus' argument is far more profound than this.

the Scriptures. It is therefore necessary that Jesus should rectify that error and remove that ignorance by teaching which is objectively true, on the truthfulness of which he rests his authority and which possesses permanent value.

F. Dreyfus has shown that the text cited by Jesus has, in a strictly literal sense, a much more profound significance than has been generally appreciated and that it can set forth in all its fulness the biblical doctrine of the resurrection.[41] In the official Jewish prayers used in the first century the phrase "the God of Abraham, of Isaac, and of Jacob" was used in reference to God as the protector and Savior of the three patriarchs. Twice daily in the second benediction of the Shemoneh 'Esreh the pious Jew thanked God for the protection he had been for the fathers, which assured him of God's continual faithfulness to Israel in his own generation: "Blessed be thou, O Lord, God of Abraham, God of Isaac and God of Jacob, God most high ... our shield and the shield of our fathers, our confidence in all generations. Blessed be thou, O Lord, the shield of Abraham." In the seventeenth benediction the formula "our God and the God of our fathers" is clarified by the phrase "for your blessing upon them, for the love and mercy which you have granted to us and that you have shown to our fathers before us." In these and related benedictions[42] what is repeatedly in view is the initiative taken by God on behalf of the patriarchs because of his covenant fidelity, and not the response of fidelity on the part of men. The phrase "the God of ..." is synonymous with helper, savior, and is rooted in the concept of God's provision of redemption.

This first century (and earlier) interpretation of the formula is completely in harmony with the literal sense of Ex. 3:6. By designating himself the God of Abraham, Isaac and Jacob in the context of his self-revelation to Moses, the Lord presented himself as the God of the covenant concluded with the patriarchs; but here the accent is placed primarily on the action of God who protected the fathers and provided

---

[41] F. Dreyfus, "L'argument scripturaire de Jésus en faveur de la résurrection des morts (Marc, XII, 26-27)," *RB* 66 (1959), pp. 213-224. I have sought to summarize this important article in the paragraphs which follow.

[42] Among the passages cited by Dreyfus are Prayer of Manasseh 5:1; Assumption of Moses 3:9 ("God of Abraham, God of Isaac, God of Jacob, remember the covenant which you made with them ... as you have promised to them"); Jubilees 45:3; Testament of Reuben 4:10; Testament of Simeon 2:8; Testament of Joseph 2:2; 6:7; Testament of Gad 2:5; III Macc. 7:16; Wisdom of Solomon 9:1; 1QM x. 8; xiii. 1-2, 7, 13; xiv. 4; Judith 9:11.

for their deliverance. The sense of the self-designation of God in Ex. 3:6 is "As I have been the God of your fathers," i.e., their guide, helper and sustainer, "so I will be your savior in your present affliction." The formula recurs in Ex. 3:6, 15, 16; 4:5 precisely in passages in which God promises salvation and deliverance to his people, and serves as a guarantee of that deliverance.

This understanding sheds light on Jesus' triumphant affirmation in verse 27, which could be rendered, "He is not the protector, the savior of the dead, but of the living." The concept "God of the dead" implies a blatant contradiction, especially in the context of the Sadducean understanding of death as extinction, without the hope of resurrection. If God has assumed the task of protecting the patriarchs from misfortune during the course of their life, but fails to deliver them from that supreme misfortune which marks the definitive and absolute check upon their hopes, his protection is of little value. But it is inconceivable that God would provide for the patriarchs some partial tokens of deliverance and leave the final word to death, of which all the misfortunes and sufferings of human existence are only a foretaste. If the death of the patriarchs is the last word of their history, there has been a breach of the promises of God guaranteed by the covenant, and of which the formula "the God of Abraham, of Isaac and of Jacob" is the symbol. It is in fidelity to his covenant that God will resurrect the dead. In citing Ex. 3:6 Jesus showed how resurrection faith is attached in a profound way to the central concept of biblical revelation, the covenant, and how the salvation promised by God to the patriarchs and their descendants in virtue of the covenant contains implicitly the assurance of the resurrection. It was the failure to appreciate the essential link between God's covenant faithfulness and the resurrection which had led the Sadducees into their grievous error.

9. The Question Concerning the Great Commandment. Ch. 12:28-34

28 And one of the scribes came, and heard them questioning together, and knowing that he had answered them well, asked him, What commandment is the first of all?
29 Jesus answered, The first is, Hear, O Israel; The Lord our God, the Lord is one;
30 And thou shalt love the Lord thy God with all thy heart, and

with all thy soul, and with all thy mind,[43] and with all thy strength.
31 The second is this, Thou shalt love thy neighbor as thyself. There is none other commandment greater than these.
32 And the scribe said unto him, Of a truth, Teacher, thou hast well said that he is one; and there is none other but he.
33 And to love him with all the heart, and with all the understanding, and with all the strength, and to love his neighbor as himself, is much more than all whole burnt offerings and sacrifices.[44]
34 And when Jesus saw that he answered discreetly, he said unto him, Thou art not far from the kingdom of God. And no man after that durst ask him any question.

28 The question concerning the great commandment was asked by a scribe who was well impressed with the appropriateness of Jesus' words in the preceding discussion.[45] He was not necessarily a Pharisee, since the Sadducees also had their interpreters of the Law.[46] A distinction between lighter and weightier, smaller and greater commandments was an inevitable feature of Palestinian piety, since it was traditional to speak of the 613 individual statutes of the Law.[47] The basis of distinguishing between small and great commandments was generally the nature of the demand (in the case of commandments) or of the propitiation demanded (in the case of prohibitions which had been infringed). Both the question and its presuppositions stem from a piety of human achievement, supported by scribal interpretation of the biblical mandates.

---

[43] The phrase "and with all thy mind" is omitted by D *pc* it, perhaps rightly. The omission brings the citation of Deut. 6:5 into harmony with the threefold reference in the MT and LXX, and with the reference to the commandment in verse 33. "Soul" and "mind" represent a double translation of the Semitic term נֶפֶשׁ.

[44] Gr. ὁλοκαύτωμα καὶ θυσία often appear together in the LXX and differentiate sacrifices which were wholly consumed from those in which the flesh was eaten by the worshippers.

[45] For a defense of the originality and antiquity of the Marcan account (answering objections which have been raised), see S. Légasse, "Scribes et disciples de Jésus," *RB* 68 (1961), pp. 483-489.

[46] Cf. S-B*K* IV (1928), pp. 339-352; S. Légasse, *op. cit.*, pp. 497-502; J. Jeremias, *Jerusalem zur Zeit Jesu* II B (Göttingen, 1958), pp. 101-114.

[47] S-B*K* I (1922), p. 900; W. Grundmann, *TWNT* IV (Eng. Tr. 1967), p. 535 n. 31.

29-31 Jesus' response goes much deeper than the distinction between small and great commandments and shows that he understood the question to concern the principle of Law. The attempt to summarize the whole Law in a single utterance was remembered in anecdotes concerning some of the early scribal teachers. When challenged by a Gentile, Hillel the Elder (*ca.* 40 B.C.-A.D. 10) replied: "What you yourself hate, do not do to your neighbor: this is the whole Law, the rest is commentary. Go and learn it."[48] For Jesus the whole Law is summarized in the will of God which calls for the love which is a whole-hearted response to God and to the neighbor.[49]

Mark alone reports that Jesus introduced his answer with the opening words of the *Shema*ʿ (Deut. 6:4). Their use by the pious Jew as a prayer and a confession of faith every morning and evening dates very probably to the second century B.C.[50] The first words of the formula were of such importance that their omission in the Jewish milieu presupposed in the Marcan narrative would be scarcely intelligible. They indicate that the command to love God is an obligation which stems from his uniqueness as God and his gracious favor in extending his covenant love to Israel. It is *the Lord our God* who is to be loved with a completeness of devotion which is defined by the repeated "all." Because the whole man is the object of God's covenant love, the whole man is claimed by God for himself. To love God in the way defined by the great commandment is to seek God for his own sake, to have pleasure in him and to strive impulsively after him. Jesus demands a decision and readiness for God, and for God alone, in an unconditional manner. Clearly this cannot be the subject of legal enactment. It is a matter of the will and

---

[48] TB *Shabbath* 31a (cf. Tobit 4:15). Other examples may be found in S-B*K* I (1922), p. 907.

[49] This combination of Deut. 6:5 and Lev. 19:18 has a number of antecedent parallels in Jewish material: e.g. Testament of Issachar 5:2 "Love the Lord and the neighbor"; 7:6 "I loved the Lord and every man with all my heart"; Testament of Dan. 5:3 "Love the Lord with all your life and one another with a true heart"; Testament of Reuben 6:9; Testament of Judah 18:3; Testament of Zebulun 5:3; Testament of Gad 6:1; Sifré Deut. 3:29; Sifra Lev. 19:18. Cf. J. B. Stern, "Jesus' Citation of Dt 6, 5 and Lv 19, 18 in the Light of Jewish Tradition," *CBQ* 28 (1966), pp. 312-316.

[50] Cf. Letter of Aristeas § 160; Jubilees 6:14; Josephus, *Antiquities* IV. viii. 13; 1QS x. 1-3, 9-11, 13 f.; 1QH xii. 4-7. There is a wealth of material on the *Shema*ʿ in S-B*K* IV (1928), pp. 189-207, and J. Jeremias, *The Prayers of Jesus* (London, 1967), pp. 66-81.

action.[51] The love which determines the whole disposition of one's life and places one's whole personality in the service of God reflects a commitment to God which springs from divine sonship.[52]

This commitment finds expression in a similar commitment to men. Jesus responds to the question about the *first* commandment with reference to the first and second because they are inseparable. A whole-hearted love for God necessarily finds its expression in a selfless concern for another man which decides and acts in a manner consistent with itself. In the second commandment God addresses men as they are, sinners who love themselves, and claims them as such for love to the neighbor. In Lev. 19:18 the neighbor is defined by the prior reference to "the sons of your own people" in the first part of the verse, and this understanding was presupposed in the first century.[53] Jesus freed the commandment from this restriction in reference, with his startling teaching concerning the neighbor in Lk. 10:25-37. This definition of the will of God and its fulfilment as the combined and inseparable love for God and love for men left an indelible impression on subsequent apostolic teaching (cf. Rom. 13:8-9; Gal. 5:14; Jas. 2:8).[54]

32-34a These verses, which record the approving response of the scribe and Jesus' recognition of his favorable disposition in the perspective of the Kingdom of God, are confined to the Marcan account. The omission of the divine name in the reaffirmation of the *Shema*ʿ ("he is one") is typically Jewish, and stems from a respect for the name of God grounded in the third commandment (Ex. 20:7). The qualifying phrase "and there is no other beside him" is drawn from Deut. 4:35 (cf. Ex. 8:10; Isa. 45:21). The surprising feature in the scribe's response is the declaration that the double law of love is superior to sacrifice. The common scribal

---

51 G. Quell and E. Stauffer, *TWNT* I (Eng. Tr. 1964), pp. 29, 44 f.

52 W. Grundmann, *TWNT* IV (Eng. Tr. 1967), pp. 535 f.

53 Whenever רע ("neighbor") occurs in the legal sections of the Law it is always understood by the early legal commentaries to mean "fellow-Jew." Cf. Sifré Deut. 23:26: "By the general rule, since the word רע is used (this law) does not refer to (the property of) others" (i.e. Gentiles). See M. Smith, "Comments on Taylor's Commentary on Mark," *HTR* 48 (1955), pp. 50 f. and nn. 38, 40.

54 For an extended exposition of Ch. 12:29-31 see K. Barth, *Church Dogmatics* I/2 (Edinburgh, 1936), pp. 381-454. See further G. Bornkamm, "Das Doppelgebot der Liebe," *Neutestamentlichen Studien für R. Bultmann* (*BZNW* 21, Berlin, 1954), pp. 85-93; H. Montefiore, "'Thou Shalt Love Thy Neighbor as Thyself'," *Nov Test* 4 (1962), pp. 157-170.

position is well summarized in the maxim of Simon the Just (*ca.* 200 B.C.): "The world rests on three things: the Law, the sacrificial worship, and expressions of love" (M. *Aboth* I. 2). But there are also statements in rabbinic literature which are attached explicitly or implicitly to OT texts like I Sam. 15:22; Hos. 6:6; Prov. 21:3 which affirm the superiority of the moral life, and especially of love, to cult and sacrifice.[55] A careful reading of the texts indicates that "love" is understood as benevolence expressed in works of love which are set above sacrifice because of their atoning significance (cf. *Aboth de Rabbi Nathan* IV. 2). This concept falls short of expressing that inner commitment to God for his own sake which Jesus had affirmed. The explicit statement that the scribe answered discreetly implies an unreserved acknowledgment of the demand expressed in the double commandment of love for God and men.

Jesus' statement, "you are not far from the Kingdom" is deliberately ambiguous and was undoubtedly intended to provoke reflection. The scribe's openness and humility before God exhibited a favorable disposition, while his enthusiastic approval of Jesus' teaching revealed an attraction toward the one through whom God had brought the Kingdom near to men in an eschatological and messianic perspective. The account does not concern a rabbinic discussion about the heart of the Mosaic Law, but a proclamation of the demands of the messianic Kingdom.[56]

34b The silence of Jesus' adversaries is significant in the context of debate (cf. Ch. 3:4). It is difficult to know whether this brief comment refers to the discussions which precede or is intended to introduce the following account concerning the Davidic descent of the Messiah.[57] The latter alternative has much to commend it, since the silence of those who had questioned Jesus will then explain the initiative he took in posing the question which is the core of Ch. 12:35-37. The issue, however, must be left open.

---

55 S. Légasse, *op. cit.,* p. 484, citing TB *Sukkah* 49b; *Berachoth* 55a; Deut. Rabba V, 201d.

56 G. Minette de Tillesse, *op. cit.,* p. 151.

57 In Mt. 22:46 the comment is placed at the end of the next section; in Lk. 20:40 at the end of the previous section. S. Légasse, *op. cit.,* p. 485 prefers to take it as the introduction to Ch. 12:35-37.

10. The Question Concerning David's Son. Ch. 12:35-37

35 And Jesus answered and said, as he taught in the temple, How say the scribes that the Christ is the son of David?
36 David himself said in the Holy Spirit,
The Lord said unto my Lord,
Sit thou on my right hand,
Till I make thine enemies the footstool of thy feet.
37 David himself calleth him Lord; and whence is he his son? And the common people heard him gladly.

35 The question concerning the Davidic lineage of the Messiah finds its larger context in the general expectation of a restored kingdom. Popular hopes, heightened by the celebration of redemption in the festival season, found expression in the pilgrim chant, "Blessed be the kingdom of our father David which is coming" (Ch. 11:10). The conviction that national deliverance would be achieved under Davidic leadership was an integral element of both scribal and sectarian piety, and the matter of the fulfilment of the divine promise to David (II Sam. 7:11-16) was in the air.[58] The Davidic sonship of the Messiah was a scribal tenet firmly grounded in the old prophetic literature (Isa. 9:2-7; 11:1-9; Jer. 23:5 f.; 30:9; 33:15, 17, 22; Ezek. 34:23 f.; 37:24; Hos. 3:5; Amos 9:11). Although the precise terminology "son of David" is not attested until the middle of the first century B.C. (Ps. Sol. 17:23), the designation soon became common for the messianic deliverer among early Palestinian teachers.[59]

Jesus' challenge was not designed to deny the word and prophecy of Scripture but to raise the crucial issue of its proper meaning.[60] Verse 35 should be understood in the sense, "What do the scribes mean when

---

58 In 4QFlorilegium i. 11-13 the promise to David (II Sam. 7:11c, 12bc, 13, 14a) is interpreted by reference to a messianic interpretation of Amos 9:11. This latter passage is similarly interpreted in CD vii. 16; TB *Sanhedrin* 96b, 97a; cf. Acts 15:16 f., representing sectarian, scribal and early Christian preoccupation with the fulfilment of the promise.

59 E.g. R. José ben Qisma (*ca.* A.D. 110), TB *Sanhedrin* 98a; R. Johanan ben Torta (*ca.* A.D. 130), TJ *Ta'anith* IV. 8, 68d; R. Jehuda ben Il'ai and R. Nehemia (*ca.* A.D. 150), TB *Sanhedrin* 97a. See E. Lohse, *TWNT* VIII (1969), pp. 484-486.

60 R. P. Gagg, "Jesus und die Davidssohnfrage. Zur Exegese von Markus 12. 35-37," *ThZ* 7 (1951), pp. 18-30 argues that Mark has preserved only the ending of an original conflict story. The opening question was lost in the course of tradition, but some opponent seems to have asked if Jesus taught that the Messiah would be David's son. So in similar accounts Jesus replied with a counter-question designed

they say that the Messiah is the son of David?" and verse 37, "In what sense then is he his son?" Those questions are calculated to provoke thoughtful reflection upon the character of the Messiah in the perspective of the OT witness to his lordship. What is in view is *the relationship* of the Davidic sonship to the Messiah's transcendent majesty. Among the scribes this would be recognized as a Haggada-question, a question of exegesis concerned with the reconciliation of two seemingly contradictory points of view expressed in Scripture.[61] The unity of different biblical passages was stressed by demonstrating their harmony, which depends upon bringing them into a correct relationship to each other. In a Haggada-question it is shown that two affirmations are true, but each is concerned with a different situation or a different epoch. Jesus, then, posed the question how the Davidic descent of the Messiah (which is attested by the Scriptures) is to be harmonized with the equally supported affirmation that the Messiah is David's Lord.[62]

36-37 The initial question is immediately followed by a reference to what David said under the inspiration of the Holy Spirit. The elaborate introduction to the citation shows that David is regarded as a prophetic witness to the supreme dignity of the Messiah.[63] In the psalm David clearly affirmed that the divine promise concerned not himself, but the Messiah. Here only among the sayings of Jesus is the authority of an OT passage traced to its inspiration.[64] The question closely follows the

to escape a trap by breaking off a dangerous conversation. It seems better, however, to hold that Jesus seized the initiative to point to the disparity between the narrow political hopes associated with popular messianism and the intention of Scripture. The formulation of verse 35 invites comparison with Ch. 9:11 f.: in both contexts Jesus does not question the accuracy of the scribal teaching but he probes the intention of the biblical texts undergirding that teaching.

[61] See D. Daube, *The New Testament and Rabbinic Judaism* (London, 1956), pp. 158-163, and the articles cited in n. 19 above; E. Lohse, *op. cit.*, p. 488.

[62] E. Lövestam, "Die Davidssohnfrage," *Sv Ex Års* 27 (1962), pp. 74-80. It is the failure to recognize that Jesus was posing a Haggada-question which has led a number of commentators to affirm that Jesus denied the Davidic descent of the Messiah, e.g. R. Bultmann, *The History of the Synoptic Tradition* (New York, 1963), pp. 136 f.; E. Lohmeyer, *Das Evangelium des Markus* (Göttingen, 1963), p. 262; B. van Iersel, "Fils de David et fils de Dieu" in *La venue du Messie* (Bruges, 1962), pp. 121-123, 130.

[63] For related references see E. Lohse, *TWNT* VIII (1969), p. 486.

[64] Cf. C. K. Barrett, *op. cit.*, pp. 107-112. The contention that Ps. 110 is Maccabean in date is now disproved by the recovery of a complete Psalter from Qumran which has been dated in the third century B.C.

LXX text of Ps. 110:1, with minor variations.[65] In the Hebrew text the initial reference to "the Lord" translates the tetragrammaton *Yahweh*, the covenant name of God, while the second ("to my Lord") renders *Adonai*. Jesus' citation of the passage would have point only if the scribes of his day recognized with him the messianic reference in the text.[66] The purpose of the provocative question in verse 37 is to invite thought and decision. If David referred to the Messiah as his "Lord," he understood that the one who would receive the promise was far greater than himself.

The brief Marcan account capsulizes a larger discussion in terms of its most salient point. Light is shed upon this discussion by other NT passages (Acts 2:29-34; 13:23-39; Heb. 1:5-13) in which the relationship of the Davidic sonship of Jesus the Messiah is linked to his exaltation in terms of Ps. 110:1. In these texts the prophetic promise to David serves as the starting point for the proclamation of Jesus as the Savior whose resurrection and exaltation marked the fulfilment of the promise. Jesus is the fulfiller of Scripture, in this case, the promise to David.[67]

This primitive Christian understanding provides the context for properly interpreting the Marcan text. Jesus' questions do not imply that there will be an exaltation of the Messiah through which he is affirmed as David's Lord, in opposition to his Davidic sonship; nor is the contrast between the Messiah's humiliation and subsequent exaltation when he is unveiled as David's Lord. Rather the question posed by Jesus concerns the messianic fulfilment of the promise announced in Ps. 110:1 and anticipates his own resurrection and exaltation to God's right hand. The point made is that David himself distinguished between his earthly, political sovereignty and the higher level of sovereignty assigned to the Messiah. The Messiah is not only "son of David"; he is also, and especially, his Lord. His role is not to restore on earth the Davidic

---

65 Following the text supported by B D W Ψ 28 l^{1353} sy^s sa bo geo Diatessaron, ὑποκάτω is substituted for ὑποπόδιον and the article is omitted before κύριος.

66 The earliest rabbinic evidence for the messianic interpretation of Ps. 110:1 is Bereshith Rabba LXXXV, 153a (second half of the 3rd century A.D.). The absence of earlier evidence appears to reflect the Jewish-Christian debate. Thus in Justin, *Dialogue with Trypho* 32 f., 56, 83 it is said that the Jews interpreted the psalm of Hezekiah. Cf. S-B*K* IV (1933), pp. 452-465. Jesus' use of Ps. 110:1 led to its free citation in the early church. Within the NT there are more references or allusions to this verse than to any other OT passage.

67 E. Lövestam, *op. cit.*, pp. 75-77.

kingdom or the sovereignty of Israel. He does not simply extend the work of David, but comes to establish a wholly different Kingdom, the throne of which is situated at God's right hand. It is thus the question of another kind of fulfilment to the promise than that which contemporary Judaism expected. The political-nationalistic concept of the messianic mission supported by the scribes is simplistic. [68]

When Jesus posed his question within the Temple precincts he stood before his suffering and death (cf. Chs. 10:32-34; 11:18; 12:12). He knew himself to be in a situation of conflict for the salvation of the people of God. The battle would not be fought against Rome or any other earthly power, and it had no national-political goals. It was rather against the demonic powers of the spiritual world that he set himself. Victory demanded configuration with the suffering Servant in obedience to God, fully trusting in the vindication promised in Ps. 110:1. God's promise to David is fulfilled by the cross which, for Jesus, is the prelude to resurrection.

This interpretation strikes at the heart of the national-political understanding of the Davidic promise. To the question, "In what sense, then, is the Messiah David's son?" no satisfactory answer could be given from a scribal viewpoint. Only from the perspective of the New Covenant is the answer provided: already in the exaltation of the Messiah to God's right hand is the promise of everlasting dominion fulfilled (II Sam. 7:13, 16; Ps. 110:1). [69] In this way the Scriptures affirming Davidic sonship and the Messiah as David's Lord were united.

Jesus' rhetorical statements imply a veiled self-affirmation. They suggest, but do not explicitly affirm, that his sonship is more than a matter of human descent and that his dignity is transcendent. Behind Ch. 12:35-37 stands the same Christology affirmed in the confessional formulations of Rom. 1:3 f.; II Tim. 2:8: the son of David is the exalted Lord who now reigns at God's right hand, having fulfilled the expectation of Israel according to a modality startlingly different from scribal interpretation. [70]

---

[68] So J. Gnilka, "Die Erwartung des messianischen Hohenpriesters von Qumran und des Neue Testament," *Rev Qum* 2 (1959/60), pp. 416-418; G. Minette de Tillesse, *op. cit.*, pp. 331-333.

[69] E. Lövestam, *op. cit.*, pp. 79-81.

[70] See W. Michaelis, "Die Davidssohnschaft Jesu als historisches und kerygmatisches Problem" in *Der historische Jesus und der kerygmatische Christus*, ed. H. Rostow and K. Matthiae (Berlin, 1961), pp. 317-330.

If it is proper to view verse 37b as a concluding comment to the preceding discussion, it serves to identify the common people with Jesus. They sensed the discomfort of the scribes and responded enthusiastically to his teaching, without necessarily penetrating its significance. It is possible, however, that Mark intended a reference to Jesus' Temple ministry as a whole (cf. Ch. 14:49). In that case, these words provide a general comment upon the popular response to an extended ministry, which is summarized in the five conflict-stories of Ch. 12:13-37.

11. The Warning Concerning the Scribes. Ch. 12:38-40

38 And in his teaching he said, Beware of the scribes, who desire to walk in long robes, [71] and to have salutations in the marketplaces,
39 and chief seats in the synagogues, and chief places at feasts:
40 they that devour widow's houses, and for a pretence make long prayers; these shall receive greater condemnation.

38-39 Jesus' warning against scribal abuses is introduced in a most general way. No attention is given to details of time and place or to the specific circumstances which called forth this denunciation. It appears to have found its place in the Marcan outline through topical association with the preceding paragraph: in Ch. 12:35-37 the teaching of the scribes is exposed as simplistic and misleading; here their self-intoxication is placed under the judgment of God. While Ch. 12:28-34 indicates that Jesus' relationship with the scribes was not always strained, throughout the Gospel Mark has noted a sustained conflict with the scribes from Jerusalem [72] (see Chs. 3:22-30; 7:1-5; 11:18, 27f.; 12:12). The new note sounded in this pericope is the bold attack upon the love of deference in men whose preoccupation with the Law should have made them singularly zealous that God alone should receive the praise of men.

The scribe was distinguished by his linen robe, a long white mantle

[71] For ἐν στολαῖς E. Lohmeyer, *op. cit.*, p. 263 n. 2 prefers ἐν στοαῖς, "in cloisters," corresponding to ἐν ταῖς ἀγοραῖς, "in the marketplaces." While support for this conjecture may be found in the Old Syriac Gospels ($sy^{s\ pal.}$ to Ch. 12:38; sy^{c} to Lk. 20:46), the absence of Greek MS support suggests that the translation variant arose through a scribal error.

[72] For wealth of information concerning the Jerusalem scribes see J. Jeremias, *Jerusalem in the Time of Jesus* (Philadelphia, 1969), pp. 233-245.

reaching to the feet and provided with a long fringe. White linen clothes were regarded as a mark of distinction, so that men of eminence (priests, Levites, scribes), or those who wished to parade their position, wore white and left bright colors to the common people.[73] By the majority of the people the scribes were venerated with unbounded respect and awe. Their words were considered to possess sovereign authority. When a scribe passed by on the street or in the bazaar people rose respectfully. Only tradesmen at their work were exempted from this display of deference.[74] The scribe was greeted with titles of deepest respect: "Rabbi," "Father," "Master,"[75] and there is evidence that in the first century A.D. the designation "Rabbi" was undergoing a transition from its former status as a general title of honor to one reserved exclusively for ordained scribes.[76] When the important men of Jerusalem gave a feast they considered it an ornament to the feast to have a distinguished scribe and his pupils there. The highest places were assigned to them, and the scribe was given precedence in honor over the aged, and even over parents.[77] In the synagogues as well the seat of honor was reserved for him; he sat at the front with his back to the chest containing the Torah, in full view of the congregation. Jesus condemned the scribes for their desire for these tokens of status and for the self-satisfaction they perpetuated.

40 The shift in emphasis from the desire for deference to the abuse of privilege suggests that it is better to read a full stop at verse 39 and to regard verse 40 as a separate, and independent, charge. In the first century A.D. the scribes lived primarily on subsidies, since it was forbidden that they should be paid for exercising their profession.[78] While few scribes were reduced to begging, an abundance of evidence shows

---

[73] Cf. S. Krauss, *Talmudische Archäologie* I (Leipzig, 1910), pp. 144 f., 547 ff.; W. Michaelis, *TWNT* IV (Eng. Tr. 1967), pp. 244, 246; K. H. Rengstorf, "Die στολαί der Schriftgelehrten. Eine Erläuterung zu Mark 12, 38" in *Abraham unser Vater, Festschrift O. Michel* (Leiden, 1963), pp. 383-404.

[74] TB *Kiddushin* 33a.

[75] E.g. TJ *Berachoth* II. 1, 4b. 24 (Rabbi), TB *Makkoth* 24a (*'abi,* "my Father" and *mari,* "my master"). Cf. Matt. 23:7; Lk. 20:46.

[76] J. Jeremias, *op. cit.,* p. 236.

[77] *Ibid.*, p. 244, citing TJ *Ḥagigah* II. 1, 77b.

[78] M. *Aboth* I. 13; M. *Bekhoroth* IV. 6; TB *Nedarim* 37a, 62a: "Do not make of the Torah a spade with which to dig," i.e. you must not accept payment for teaching the Law.

that the Jerusalem scribes belonged to the poorer classes.[79] The extension of hospitality to them was strongly encouraged as an act of piety; it was considered particularly meritorious to relieve a scribe of concern for his livelihood. Many well-to-do persons placed their financial resources at the disposal of scribes, and it was inevitable that there should be abuses.[80] The charge that the scribes "devoured widows' houses" refers to the fact that they sponged on the hospitality of people of limited means. The accusation that on the pretext of deep piety they made of public prayers an opportunity to win the esteem of men indicates the peril in the loss of perspective in the service of God.[81] This displacement of the honor of God from the center of concern is what distinguished the scribes from Jesus and exposed them to the searching judgment of God.

This stern denunciation of scribal practices concludes the Marcan account of Jesus' public ministry. The incident which follows, like the Olivet discourse, centers in teaching directed to the disciples. By terminating the public ministry with this account the evangelist points to the sharp opposition between Jesus and the Jewish authorities which led inevitably to events recalled in the passion narrative.

12. The Widow Who Gave Everything. Ch. 12:41-44

41 And he sat down over against the treasury, and beheld how the multitude cast money into the treasury: and many that were rich cast in much.

42 And there came a poor widow, and she cast in two mites, which make a farthing.[82]

43 And he called unto him his disciples, and said unto them,

---

79 See J. Jeremias, *op. cit.*, pp. 111-116.

80 TB *Soṭah* 22b (Baraitha) speaks of scribes whose zeal was directed toward the things of this world and not to those of the age to come; Assumption of Moses 7:6 describes the scribes as "gluttons"; and Josephus, *Ant.* XVII. ii. 4 says that the Pharisees (and most scribes were Pharisees) made men believe they were highly favored by God and that women were deceived by them. Cf. J. Jeremias, *op. cit.*, pp. 113 f.

81 For a powerful statement of the temptation to which the Church is exposed in history to become more concerned with its own piety than with the Lord see E. Stauffer, *New Testament Theology* (New York, 1956), pp. 203 f.

82 Jerusalem Bible: "two small coins, the equivalent of a penny." See below, n. 84.

Verily I say unto you, This poor widow cast in more than all they that are casting into the treasury:
44 for they all did cast in of their superfluity; but she of her want did cast in all that she had, even all her living.

41-42 This brief account has the character of a postscript to the preceding paragraph. It serves to sharpen the contrast between the sham righteousness of the scribes and that wholehearted devotion to God which characterized an unnamed widow whose poverty was absolute. It is equally a transitional passage to the prophetic discourse which follows, for its setting is the Court of the Women. It was as Jesus left the sacred precincts with his disciples that he prophesied the complete destruction of the Temple complex (Ch. 13:1-2). The sequence of movement envisioned in Ch. 12:41-13:2 is natural and undoubtedly reflects what happened upon a single occasion.

Jesus was seated upon a bench watching the people bring their contributions to the Temple treasury. According to the Mishnah, *Shekalim* VI. 5, there were thirteen trumpet-shaped receptacles for this purpose which were placed against the wall of the Court of the Women. [83] In contrast to many wealthy persons who brought "much" Jesus noticed a woman whose poverty could be estimated from the size of her gift. She cast into the receptacle two of the smallest copper coins which circulated in Palestine. [84] For the benefit of his Roman readers Mark

---

[83] Cf. G. Schrenk, *TWNT* III (Eng. Tr. 1966), p. 236. Mark's use of the singular to describe the receptacle indicates one of the thirteen boxes. For the plural see Neh. 12:44 (LXX II Esdras 22:44, ἐπὶ τῶν γαζοφυλακίων τοῖς θησαυροῖς), "over the receptacles for contributions." Paul Billerbeck (S-B*K* II [1924], pp. 37-45) suggests that the reference is to the treasury itself, and that the amount of a gift and the purpose for which it was intended were declared audibly by the donor to the priest in charge. While this would explain how Jesus knew the precise amount of the widow's gift, it does not find support in the Marcan passage, which speaks only of Jesus *seeing* the donors make their contribution.

[84] The tiny *lepton* was first minted during the Maccabean period. While its small size made legible stamping difficult, it has been possible to determine particular patterns and to assign coins recovered from excavations to the reigns of Herod the Great, Archelaus, the praefect Valerius and the praefect Pilate. The *lepton* was worth about one four-hundredth part of a shekel, or roughly 1/8 of a cent. For help in identifying Palestinian coinage see F. Prat, "Le cours des Monnaies en Palestine au temps de Jésus-Christ," *RSR* 15 (1925), pp. 441-448; C. Seltmann, *Greek Coins* (London, 1933); and for the lepta D. Sperber, "Mark xii. 42 and its Metrological Background. A Study in Ancient Syriac Versions," *Nov Test* 9 (1967), pp. 178-190.

computes their value in terms of Roman coinage.[85] The fact that the woman gave two coins was significant, for she could easily have kept one for herself.

43-44 Jesus saw in the widow an example which the disciples needed to appreciate. They undoubtedly felt that those who were wealthy had made the significant contribution, since so much more could be accomplished with the sizable gifts they brought (see on Ch. 10:25-26). What was the value of two almost-worthless coins in comparison to such munificence? Prefacing his statement with his solemn Amen,[86] Jesus overturned this facile assumption of conventional piety. What the Twelve had failed to appreciate was the total commitment to God that the widow's gift represented. In contrast with those who brought a gift from their abundance, she gave all that she had, even her whole living.

The rabbinic literature contains a similar account: a priest rejected the offering of a handful of meal from a poor woman. That night in a dream he was commanded: "Do not despise her. It is as if she had offered her life."[87] This account, like the evangelical narrative, serves to stress the qualitative difference between God's perspective and man's: "man looks on the outward appearance, but the Lord looks upon the heart" (I Sam. 16:7). There is, however, an added dimension to the evangelical narrative which is provided by its context in the gospel. The woman sacrifices *what is necessary,* all she had.[88] It was this that the disciples needed to understand, for the call to the gospel is a call for absolute surrender to God and total trust in him.

---

85 Mark's κοδράντης, a transliteration of the Latin *quadrans,* supports the view that he was writing in the West, since the *quadrans* was not in circulation in the east. See W. M. Ramsay, "On Mark xii. 42," *ExT* 10 (1898/99), pp. 232, 336.

86 See above on Ch. 3:28.

87 Leviticus Rabba III, 107a.

88 So L. Simon, "Le sou de la veuve. Marc 12/41-44," *Études Théologiques et Religieuses* 44 (1969), pp. 115-126.

CHAPTER 13

13. The Olivet Discourse. Ch. 13:1-37

In the Gospel of Mark there is no passage more problematic than the prophetic discourse of Jesus on the destruction of the Temple. The questions posed by the form and content of the chapter and by its relationship to the Gospel as a whole are complex and difficult and have been the occasion of an extensive literature.[1] The Olivet discourse is unique as the longest uninterrupted course of private instruction recorded by Mark. Moreover, it is the only extended speech attributed to Jesus by the evangelist. The interpretation of Mark 13 is inevitably colored by critical decisions concerning the character and function of the material, its structured arrangement and essential authenticity.

The Olivet discourse occupies a special position in the Marcan outline. It provides the bridge between Jesus' public ministry, culminating in the conflict with the Temple authorities (Chs. 11:11-12:12), and the Passion Narrative, where the conflict with authority is the occasion of Jesus' condemnation and death (Ch. 14:1f., 9f., 42-65). By locating the eschatological discourse in this crucial position, and by recurring reference to the destruction of the Temple in the context of Jesus' trial and execution (Chs. 14:58; 15:29, 39), the evangelist points to the relationship which exists between the judgment upon Jerusalem implied by the discourse and the death of Jesus. This theological understanding is reflected by the literary form of verses 5-37. In form Jesus' words are a farewell address providing instruction and consolation for his disciples just prior to his death. Ch. 13 unites prophecy concerning the

---

[1] A comprehensive survey of the literature on Mark 13 was presented by G. R. Beasley-Murray, *Jesus and the Future. An Examination of the Criticism of the Eschatological Discourse, Mark 13 with special reference to the Little Apocalypse Theory* (London, 1954), which was followed by *A Commentary on Mark Thirteen* (London, 1957). Since that time at least six major monographs have been published: G. Neville, *The Advent Hope. A Study of the Context of Mark 13* (London, 1961); L. Hartman, *Prophecy Interpreted. The Formulation of Some Jewish Apocalyptic Texts and of the Eschatological Discourse Mark 13 Par* (Lund, 1966); A. L. Moore, *The Parousia in the New Testament* (Leiden, 1966); J. Lambrecht, *Die Redaktion der Markus-Apokalypse: Literarische Analyse und Strukturuntersuchung* (Rome, 1967); R. Pesch, *Naherwartungen. Tradition und Redaktion in Mark 13* (Düsseldorf, 1968); L. Gaston, *No Stone on Another. Studies in the Significance of the Fall of Jerusalem in the Synoptic Gospels* (Leiden, 1970), all with full bibliographies of the relevant journal articles.

future with exhortation regulating the conduct of the disciples in the period when the Master will no longer be with them, and this is characteristic of a farewell discourse.[2]

The character of the discourse is further defined by its parenetic framework.[3] It consists of admonition supported by reference to apocalyptic events which must take place within the plan of God. The emphasis upon parenesis, and even the detail of the constant form of address in the second person plural, are features which serve to distinguish Mark 13 from Jewish apocalyptic documents contemporary with it. At transitional points in the discourse Mark's arrangement of Jesus' words is punctuated by the characteristic word, "take care" (verses 5, 9, 23, 33). In verse 5 this exhortation introduces Jesus' answer to the disciples' question concerning the destruction of the Temple. They are to "take care" that they are not deceived by the course of events into thinking that the end has come. This warning is repeated in verse 9 with reference to the disciples themselves and the prospect of their suffering. Persecution does not mean that the end has come, nor is it an occasion for the loss of hope. It is rather an occasion for witness to the nations, for this must take place before the end comes. What is required for vindication is patient endurance (verse 13). Verses 14-23 speak of an appalling sacrilege, the great tribulation, and a final wave of false messianic pretenders and prophets. The people of God, however, have been forewarned and must "take care" to avoid being deceived (verse 23). Following the description of the parousia (verses 24-27) and instruction regarding the time (verses 28-32), the final parable is introduced by the admonition, "Take care, watch" (verse 33).

The speech-pattern evident throughout the discourse may be analyzed as paraclesis supported by a statement introduced by the conjunction

---

[2] The fully developed form in the Testament of the Twelve Patriarchs has its origins in such OT passages as Gen. 49, Deut. 33, Josh. 23 and I Sam. 12. In the NT cf. Acts 20:17-35, II Timothy and II Peter. See J. Munck, "Discours d'adieu dans le Nouveau Testament et dans la littérature biblique" in *Aux Sources de la Tradition Chrétienne* (Neuchâtel, 1950), pp. 155-170; E. Stauffer, *New Testament Theology*[5] (New York, 1963), pp. 344-347. The Olivet discourse was recognized as a farewell address in form by F. Busch, *Zum Verständnis der synoptischen Eschatologie, Markus 13 neu untersucht* (Gütersloh, 1938), p. 44.

[3] The parenesis is carried forward by such terms as βλέπετε (verses 5, 9, 23, 33), μὴ θροεῖσθε (verse 7), μὴ προμεριμνᾶτε (verse 11), ὁ ὑπομείνας (verse 13), μὴ πιστεύετε (with regard to false prophets, verse 21), μάθετε (verse 28), γινώσκετε (verse 29), ἀγρυπνεῖτε (verse 33) and γρηγορεῖτε (verses 35, 37).

"for."[4] Paraclesis denotes both exhortation expressed in the imperative and consolation expressed in the indicative, as in verses 5-8.

Take care that no one leads you astray.	paraclesis (imperative, verse 5b)
For many will come in my name saying that 'I am he' and they will lead many astray.	*for* – reason (verse 6)
And when you hear of wars do not be disturbed.	paraclesis (imperative, verse 7a)
For this must take place, but it is not yet the end.	*for* – reason (verse 7b)
For nation will rise against nation and kingdom against kingdom. There will be earthquakes in various places, there will be famines.	*for* – reason (verse 8a)
These are the beginning of the pangs.	paraclesis (indicative, verse 8b)

The recognition of this pattern indicates that the apocalyptic instruction is not an independent element in the discourse. It has been introduced to provide the supporting reason for the exhortation. Far from being the main point stressed by Jesus, these developments are presupposed as something known from the Scriptures, from which Jesus draws out the consequences for his disciples. The discourse is actually structured and sustained by the nineteen imperatives found in verses 5-37.

This observation indicates that the primary function of Ch. 13 is not to disclose esoteric information but to promote faith and obedience in a time of distress and upheaval. With profound pastoral concern, Jesus prepared his disciples and the Church for a future period which would

---

4 L. Gaston, *op. cit.,* pp. 14, 50-53 has called attention to the importance of γάρ in Ch. 13. He remarks: "The importance of this word would have been noticed long ago were it not for the unfortunate fact that it is missing in several places from the Nestle text, even though it is required by a synoptic comparison and is well attested. γάρ appears at the beginning of v. 6, 7b, 8, 9b, 11b, 19, 22, 33 and 35. With the exception, therefore, of the longer sections 14-18 and 24-27, every apocalyptic element is attached to its context by a γάρ" (p. 52). Cf. Ch. 8:34-38, which moves progressively from exhortation to eschatology, where every sentence is connected to the preceding one by γάρ (verses 35, 36, 37, 38).

entail both persecution and mission. The discourse clearly presupposes a period of historical development between the resurrection and the parousia. The relationship of the necessity of suffering to the experience of vindication and glory established in Ch. 8:34-38 is stressed once again by the announcement of the manifestation in glory of the Son of Man in the context of eschatological suffering for the people of God.

This message was of profound significance for the Christians of Rome, harassed by persecution and disturbed by the rumors of the developments in Palestine in the sixties. The inclusion of the eschatological discourse in the Gospel was motivated by the same pastoral concern that had prompted Jesus' teaching. Mark cautions his readers that the community is to find its authentic eschatological dimension not in apocalyptic fervor but in obedience to Jesus' call to cross-bearing and evangelism in the confidence that this is the will of God which must be fulfilled before the parousia. Jesus' words provided a bed-rock for Christian hope. The witness of the eschatological community not only focuses on the suffering Son of Man whose crucifixion and resurrection comprise the core of the gospel but also looks forward to the triumphant Son of Man whose appearance represents the one event in light of which the present is illumined. This fact enabled Mark to face the crisis of the sixties with realism and hope. [5]

An analysis of the structure of Ch. 13 must take account of the key phrase "these things." The disciples ask when *these things* will take place, and what is the sign that *all these things* are about to be accomplished (verse 4). [6] The italicized words are reference-points throughout the discourse. Jesus announces the sufferings which can be expected (verses 5-23) as well as the final victory which terminates the period of trial (verses 24-27). In verse 23, at the conclusion of the sketch of the historical events which must precede the in-breaking of salvation, Jesus cautions, "Take care, I have told you beforehand *all things*." The announcement of the salvation which follows these events is then expressed in the classic formulation of the parousia. There is a correspondence between the question of verse 4, "Tell us when *these things*... will be accomplished" and the response of Jesus in verse 23, "I have told you... *all things*." Verses 29-30 return to these reference points: "When-

---

[5] See C. B. Cousar, "Eschatology and Mark's *Theologia Crucis*. A Critical Analysis of Mark 13," *Interpretation* 24 (1970), pp. 326-328, 331.

[6] Gr. ταῦτα..., ταῦτα... πάντα.

ever you see *these things* happening... and this generation shall not pass away until *all these things* take place." The vocabulary demands that these statements be considered in relationship to verses 4 and 23. They cannot have reference to the cosmic dissolution described in verses 24-25 since these are phenomena which accompany the parousia, not preliminary events which point to it. *These things* in verse 29 refers to the entire discourse from verses 5-23, with special reference to verses 14-23. [7] They provide the evidence for which the disciples asked. The point of Jesus' warning is that these preliminary events must not be mistaken as evidence that the end has come. The events to be fulfilled within the generation of Jesus' contemporaries (verse 30) should be regarded for what they are, preliminary events only. The parousia cannot take place until after they have occurred. They are the necessary precursors of the parousia, yet in themselves they do not determine the time of that event, which is known only to God (verse 32). [8] The thrust of Jesus' discourse, as Mark has recorded it, is to warn the disciples not to be disturbed by the preliminary signs nor to confuse them with the end itself.

Understood in this light, these words of Jesus do not stand in any tension with the saying which follows about not knowing the time of the master's return. Since the preliminary events do not rigidly fix the date of the parousia, vigilance rather than calculation is required of the disciples and of the Church. These considerations, based on Marcan vocabulary and structure, demonstrate that verses 32-37, with their demand for confident faith and vigilance, should not be regarded as an afterthought, inserted by the evangelist. They constitute Jesus' true answer to the disciples' question. [9]

---

[7] So W. Michaelis, *Der Herr verzieht nicht die Verheissung* (Bern, 1942), pp. 30 ff.; J. R. Michaels, *The Church Vigilant. An Examination of* ΓΡΗΓΟΡΕΙΝ and ΑΓΡΥΠΝΕΙΝ *in the New Testament* (Diss. Harvard, Cambridge, Mass., 1962), pp. 94-96; G. Minette de Tillesse, *Le Secret messianique dans l'Évangile de Marc* (Paris, 1968), pp. 422-424; A. L. Moore, *op. cit.,* pp. 131-135; C. B. Cousar, *op. cit.,* p. 325.

[8] Cf. G. Minette de Tillesse, *op. cit.,* p. 423 who comments: "This manner of relating verse 30 and verse 32 to two distinct events is not imposed upon us by apologetic concerns, but by the simple redactional analysis of the chapter: πάντα ταῦτα, we argue, can only relate to the question of verse 4, while the day and the hour, unknown even to the angels, can only designate the parousia. The almost insoluble contradiction faced by those authors who wish to relate verse 30 and verse 32 to the same event is a powerful confirmation of our analysis."

[9] J. R. Michaels, *op. cit.,* p. 99.

The OT plays an essential part in the structure and imagery of the prophetic discourse. L. Hartman has argued convincingly that the eschatological discourse has at its foundation an exposition or meditation based on texts in Daniel about "the last things," to which other OT passages were joined by common themes and key words.[10] The resultant prophetic discourse employed a reinterpretation of the OT prophecies of the Day of the Lord as the basis for pastoral exhortation. A form of this teaching circulated in the churches as an authoritative tradition at least two decades before Mark prepared his Gospel. It was known to Paul and cited by him as "a discourse of the Lord" (I Thess. 4:15) in the teaching he transmitted to his churches. In this tradition a parenetic exposition of the OT was combined with words of Jesus on watchfulness and on the unexpected occurrence of the end. The discourse existed in this form at the latest a few years prior to A.D. 50, since Paul must have come in contact with it before his arrival in Thessalonica.[11] If Hartman is correct, Jesus' words have had a significant prehistory before they were finally recorded in the pages of the Synoptic Gospels. This Christian life situation, in which the tradition was used to provide guidance in actual church situations as well as to supply teaching on eschatology, may help to resolve some of the complex questions raised by a comparison of the Olivet discourse in the Synoptic Gospels.[12] The fact that Paul, some fifteen years after Jesus' death, clearly attributed the first link in the chain of transmission to the Lord himself has important bearing on the substantial authenticity of the tradition incorporated in Mark 13. While it is possible that the form of the discourse has experienced modification in the course of its transmission, the attempt to deny the factual content of this speech to Jesus is unwarranted.

A common critical assumption is that Ch. 13 is a Marcan construction, the integral parts of which are unlike in origin. Elements of Jewish apocalyptic, authentic sayings of Jesus and pronouncements of Christian prophets, it is argued, have been forged into a unified discourse by

---

[10] L. Hartman, *op. cit.,* pp. 145-177; cf. F. Busch, *op. cit.,* pp. 63-120. Hartman points especially to Dan. 7:8-27; 8:9-26; 9:24-27; 11:21-12:13, and to some extent Ch. 2:31-45.

[11] For the details see L. Hartman, *op. cit.,* pp. 178-205, 211-213.

[12] Cf. L. Gaston, *op. cit.,* pp. 8-64, 244-369 for an attempt to unravel the relationship between the Synoptics.

Marcan redaction.[13] This assumption, however, is in conflict with the practice of the evangelist. In Ch. 4, for example, the several parables are preserved as distinct units of tradition and have not been considered as the basis for composing a discourse concerning the Kingdom of God.[14] The evidence provided by a comparative study of the structure and content of Ch. 13 with earlier and later eschatological sections in the NT[15] supports the contention that Mark received this discourse pre-formed, as the teaching of Jesus, and that he incorporated it into his Gospel without substantial alteration.[16]

(a) Jesus' Prophecy of Impending Destruction. Ch. 13:1-4

1 And as he went forth out of the temple,[17] one of his disciples saith unto him,
Teacher, behold, what manner of stones and what manner of buildings!
2 And Jesus said unto him, Seest thou these great buildings? There shall not be left here one stone upon another, which shall not be cast down.[18]

---

[13] E.g. W. G. Kümmel, *Promise and Fulfillment* (Naperville, 1957), pp. 60 f.; W. Marxsen, *Mark the Evangelist* (Nashville, 1969), pp. 151-206; cf. C. B. Cousar, *op. cit.*, p. 322, "The chapter . . . is unquestionably a composition of the Evangelist containing Jewish or Jewish-Christian apocalyptic material, traditional sayings, and redactional comments tightly woven together."

[14] Rightly stressed by F. Flückiger, "Die Redaktion der Zukunftsrede in Markus 13," *ThZ* 26 (1970), pp. 396 f. Flückiger pushes the redaction of the discourse back to a pre-Marcan stage, as does L. Gaston, *op. cit.*, pp. 41 f.

[15] E.g. I Thess. 4-5, II Thess. 2, II Peter 3, Rev. 6. See especially L. Hartman, *op. cit.*, pp. 178-205, 211-213 and A. L. Moore, *op. cit.*, pp. 152 f.

[16] So G. R. Beasley-Murray, *A Commentary on Mark Thirteen* (London, 1957), pp. 4-18; A. L. Moore, *op. cit.*, pp. 152-180; L. Hartman, *op. cit.*, p. 172; F. Flückiger, *op. cit.*, pp. 397, 408; cf. L. Gaston, *op. cit.*, pp. 13, 41 f.

[17] Gr. ἱερόν denotes the entire Temple complex, not simply the sanctuary, as the exclamation of the disciple makes clear. By NT times the term for the sanctuary was ναός.

[18] A longer form of the text, which refers not only to the destruction of the Temple but states that a new Temple will be raised up, is found in D W it Cyprian: "there will not be left stone upon stone that will not be thrown down, and in three days another will be erected without hands." The expansion is an interpretation of Mark in accordance with John 2:19 since it employs the verb ἀνίστημι rather than οἰκοδομεῖν (as in Mk. 14:58). Such expansions are not uncommon in Codex D. See C. H. Turner, "Western Readings in the Second Half of St. Mark's Gospel," *JThS* 29 (1928), pp. 8 f.

3 And as he sat on the mount of Olives over against the temple,
Peter and James and John and Andrew asked him privately,
4 Tell us, when shall these things be?
And what shall be the sign when these things are all about to
be accomplished?

1 The occasion of Jesus' prophecy of the impending destruction of the Temple was the awe and reverence with which the disciples regarded the spectacle of the Temple area. They were astonished at the magnificence of the construction and adornment of the sanctuary and its complex of courts, porches, balconies and buildings. They particularly marvelled at the massive size of the stones which were used in the structure and substructure of the Temple. Remarking on Herodian masonry, Josephus states that "the Temple was built of hard, white stones, each of which was about 25 cubits in length, 8 in height and 12 in width" (*Antiquities* XV. xi. 3). On another occasion he remarks that these huge stones were also ornate (*War* V. v). The buildings of the area which prompted the disciple's comment would include not only the sanctuary itself with its magnificent façade but its series of enclosures and the related structures of smaller buildings joined to it by colonnaded courts, covering approximately 1/6 of the old city of Jerusalem. This complex of stone was one of the most impressive sights in the ancient world, and was regarded as an architectural wonder. The rabbis had little respect for Herod and his successors, but they said, "he who has not seen Jerusalem in her splendor has never seen a desirable city in his life. He who has not seen the Temple in its full construction has never seen a glorious building in his life."[19] As a mountain of white marble decorated with gold[20] it dominated the Kidron gorge as an object of dazzling beauty.

2 Jesus' response was the startling prediction that "not one stone will be left upon another which shall not be thrown down."[21] The most striking feature of this prophecy is its emphatic definiteness. The double

19 TB *Sukkah* 41b (Baraitha); *Baba Bathra* 4a (Baraitha). For a full bibliography on the Temple see G. Schrenk, *TWNT* III (Eng. Tr. 1965), pp. 230 f. and for a reliable account of the Herodian Temple as reconstructed by archeological research see J. Simons, *Jerusalem in the Old Testament* (Leiden, 1952), pp. 381-435. Cf. A. Parrot, *The Temple of Jerusalem* (London, 1957); R. K. Harrison, *Archaeology of the New Testament* (New York, 1964), pp. 18 f.

20 The Roman historian Tacitus was sufficiently pleased by the building to describe it as "a temple of immense wealth" (*History* V. 8).

21 F. Flückiger, *op. cit.*, pp. 404 f. has argued that the original form of Jesus'

negatives, which occur twice in verse 2,[22] already suggest the total nature of the devastation, while the description "stone upon stone" removes all possible misconception about the extent of the destruction envisaged.[23] A variant of the saying is found in Luke 19:44, where Jesus addresses the city with the solemn warning that the days are coming when "they will not leave one stone upon another in you."[24] Paradoxically, the prophet Haggai had used the phrase "stone upon stone" in his appeal to the people to resume the work of rebuilding the Temple (Hag. 2:15). Now Jesus announces the approach of a day when utter devastation will overtake the city and the Temple will be systematically dismantled.

This disturbing prophecy must be understood in the context of Jesus' teaching concerning the Temple on an earlier occasion. It actually forms the expected sequel to Ch. 11:17. There, in a pronouncement of judgment upon the misuse of the Temple, Jesus cited Jer. 7:11. In the context of that passage the destruction of the Temple by Nebuchadnezzar is seen as God's punishment of the rebelliousness of Judah in the time of Jeremiah (Jer. 7:12-14). The failure of the Temple authorities in Jesus' day to respect God's intention with reference to the Temple created the climate in which its ruin was certain. Jesus' prediction was fulfilled with awful finality in the destruction of Jerusalem by the legions of Rome in A.D. 70. After fire had raged through the Temple precincts Titus ordered the demolition of the Temple in the course of which buildings were leveled to the ground.[25] Isolated fragments of the substructures and of

words contained the double prophecy of the destruction of the Temple and the building of a new sanctuary. He bases his argument on the longer formulation in Ch. 14:58 (cf. Ch. 15:29; John 2:19). On this understanding, the announcement of the destruction of the Temple is not simply a judgment oracle but is at the same time a prophecy of messianic redemption. Against this proposal, however, see L. Gaston, *op. cit.*, pp. 12, 67-243. L. Hartman, *op. cit.*, p. 220 rightly observes that the shorter and longer forms of Jesus' words have existed side by side in the tradition from the beginning.

22 Gr. οὐ μὴ ἀφεθῇ . . . οὐ μὴ καταλυθῇ.

23 In the use of ἀφεθῇ and καταλυθῇ an aorist subjunctive replaces the future, a change that often suggests emphasis. See E. D. Burton, *Syntax of the Moods and Tenses in New Testament Greek*³ (Edinburgh, 1955), p. 78. The verb καταλυθῇ ("thrown down") is itself an emphatic compound.

24 For a discussion of this logion in context, see L. Gaston, *op. cit.*, pp. 355-360.

25 Cf. Josephus, *War* VII. i. 1: "Caesar [Titus] ordered the whole city and the Temple to be razed to the ground." For a wealth of information see F. M. Abel, "Topographie du Siège de Jérusalem en 70," *RB* 56 (1949), pp. 238-258. The conquest and destruction of the Temple are reviewed on pp. 252-255.

the old city wall which have been recognized by archeological research only confirm the degree to which Jesus' prophecy was fulfilled.[26]

This prophecy bears no trace of having come into existence after the event. There is no allusion to the destruction of the Temple by fire (cf. Josephus, *War* VI. iv. 17). Moreover, it is eminently suited to its context, since in the preceding narratives the Temple precincts have been the principal scene of Jesus' activity (Chs. 11:11, 15, 25; 12:35) and his teaching has stressed the judgment under which Israel stands (Chs. 11:14, 20; 12:9, 40). The terminology reflects a knowledge of OT formulation, but the detail "no stone left upon another" only describes what usually took place during the conquest of cities in antiquity.[27] Jesus' word of judgment marks a continuation of ancient prophecy, along the lines of Micah 3:12 and Jer. 26:18.[28] As the Lord of the Temple, Jesus announces its destruction in close connection with the establishment of his sovereign dignity (see on Ch. 11:11-21). The prophecy is distinctly eschatological in its significance.[29] Mal. 3:1-6 had described the coming of the Lord to his Temple in the context of judgment for the refining and purifying of his people. In this context the destruction of the Temple in A.D. 70 is to be understood as the judgment of God upon the rebelliousness of his people, and not simply the response of Imperial Rome to insurrection. Significant strands of Jewish literature also attributed the fall of Jerusalem to the sin of her people.[30]

---

26 Cf. J. Simons, *op. cit.*, p. 435: "If Christ's prophecy about the destruction of the Herodian Temple, not a stone of which was to remain in place ... referred to the temple proper or to the entire block of buildings within the outer enclosure, no prophecy has been fulfilled more literally, since the very site of the sacred edifice and the disposition of all the accessory buildings have become matters of discussion."

27 Cf. C. H. Dodd, "The Fall of Jerusalem and the 'Abomination of Desolation,'" *Journal of Roman Studies* 37 (1947), pp. 49-51; L. Hartman, *op. cit.*, p. 240.

28 For later prophecies of destruction prior to A.D. 70 see TJ *Yoma* 43c, 61 (Baraitha) and TB *Yoma* 39b; Josephus, *War* VI. v. 3. For details see J. Neusner, *A Life of Rabban Yohanan Ben Zakkai ca. 1-80 C.E.* (Leiden, 1962), pp. 105-110; L. Gaston, *op. cit.*, pp. 442-444. Cf. C. H. Dodd, "The Prophecy of Caiaphas. John XI, 47-53" in *Neotestamentica et Patristica* (Leiden, 1962), pp. 134-143.

29 Cf. G. Schrenk, *op. cit.*, pp. 238 ff.

30 E.g. TB *Shabbath* 119b, where there are a series of formulations, "Jerusalem was destroyed only because ... ," and a variety of transgressions are recounted. Cf. Testament of Levi 14:1; 15:1, "Therefore, my children, I have learned that at the end of the ages you will transgress against the Lord, stretching out hands to wickedness ... Therefore the Temple, which the Lord shall choose, shall be laid waste through your uncleanness, and you shall be captives throughout all nations.

3-4 These verses introduce the actual discourse. The short journey from the city to the Mount of Olives furnished a most imposing view of the sanctuary area.[31] The route followed by Jesus and the Twelve probably led through a gate in the north wall of the city and then eastward across the Kidron Valley, defined on the west by the high ridge on which the city of Jerusalem stood and on the east by the gentle slopes of Olivet. Because the Temple was set at the crest of the western ridge it loomed over the valley and would have been fully visible throughout the journey. When they reached the western slope of the Mount of Olives the four disciples whom Jesus first called (Ch. 1:16-20) privately asked him to clarify his pronouncement. In a vision Ezekiel had seen the Shekinah glory depart from the Sanctuary to the Mount of Olives, leaving the Temple defenseless against attack (Ezek. 9:3; 10:18 f.; 11:23), while Zechariah spoke of the Mount of Olives as the locus of redemption in the last days (Zech. 14). These rich biblical associations between the Temple and the Mount of Olives appear to inform the disciples' question.[32]

In the Gospel of Mark a question from the disciples often furnishes the introduction to a section of teaching (cf. Chs. 4:10 ff.; 7:17 ff.; 9:22 f.; 10:10 ff.). In this instance the disciples asked a single question expressed in two parallel clauses.[33] Both clauses relate to the prophecy of verse 2. In Semitic parallelism the second clause may expand or explain the first. In the Marcan formulation of the question, the second clause resembles Dan. 12:7. When Daniel asked how long it would be to the end the divine messenger replied, "when the shattering of the power of the holy people comes to an end, *all these things will be ac-*

And you shall be an abomination unto them, and you shall receive reproach and everlasting shame from the righteous judgment of God."

[31] Cf. J. Simons, *op. cit.*, p. 435: "To reconstitute the dazzling panorama enjoyed by Christ's contemporaries from the top of the Mount of Olives will ever remain an unrealizable wish."

[32] For the significance of the Mount of Olives as a locus of revelation see W. Schmauch, *Orte der Offenbarung und der Offenbarungsort im Neuen Testament* (Berlin, 1956), pp. 58-66.

[33] The parallelism has been widely recognized by interpreters. Cf. C. F. Burney, *The Poetry of Our Lord* (Oxford, 1925), pp. 16, 20 f.; M. Black, *An Aramaic Approach to the Gospels and Acts*[3] (Oxford, 1967), pp. 105, 117; L. Hartman, *op. cit.*, pp. 221 f.; G. Minette de Tillesse, *op. cit.*, p. 425; L. Gaston, *op. cit.*, p. 12 *et alia.*

complished." [34] In this context historic events are seen as the immediate prelude to the intervention of God. If an allusion to Dan. 12:7 is intended in verse 4b, the second clause indicates that the disciples understood Jesus' prophecy of the destruction of the Temple in its eschatological perspective. The question of verse 4 envisions one event, the devastation of the Temple, but it is clearly recognized that this cannot be an isolated incident. The phrase "these things" in verse 4a, which clearly refers to the prophecy of verse 2 and the judgment implied, already envisions a complex of events associated with the destruction. The phrase "all these things" in verse 4b is parallel in its intention and reference. [35] What is envisioned is a judgment that will be of ultimate significance to Israel. It is assumed by the disciples that the fall of Jerusalem and the destruction of its sanctuary is the prelude to consummation. The question provides evidence of implicit faith in Jesus' word and deep concern.

(b) Warning Against Deception. Ch. 13:5-8

5 And Jesus began to say unto them, Take heed that no one lead you astray.
6 Many shall come in my name, saying, I am he; and shall lead many astray. [36]
7 And when ye shall hear of wars and rumors of wars, be not troubled:
these things must needs come to pass; [37] but the end is not yet.

---

[34] LXX: συντελεσθήσεται ταῦτα πάντα; cf. Mk. 13:4b, μέλλῃ ταῦτα συντελεῖσθαι πάντα. On this parallel see L. Hartman, *op. cit.*, pp. 145, 220-222.

[35] So G. Minette de Tillesse, *op. cit.*, p. 425; L. Hartman, *op. cit.*, p. 221; L. Gaston, *op. cit.*, p. 12.

[36] L. Gaston, *op. cit.*, p. 14 has argued that verse 6 and verse 7b should be introduced by the preposition γάρ (for). Both Matt. and Luke appear to have read a γάρ in Mark in verse 6 and it is probable that it should be read along with A D it sy *al.* The case for γάρ in verse 7b is even stronger: ℵ 𝔎 A D L Θ it sy *pl.* Logically, the γάρ is necessary in these verses, for it indicates the reason for the warnings expressed in verse 5 and verse 7a. See above, pp. 445 f.

[37] Gr. δεῖ γενέσθαι may reflect Dan. 2:28 LXX, where this expression is used with reference to the last days (cf. Dan. 2:29, 45; 8:19; Rev. 1:1; 4:1; 22:6). The use of δεῖ elsewhere in Mark refers to a necessity imposed by the sovereign will of God. See above on Ch. 8:31.

8 For nation shall rise[38] against nation, and kingdom against kingdom;
there shall be earthquakes in divers places;
there shall be famines:
these things are the beginning of travail.[39]

5-6 Jesus' response forms an extended prophecy designed to prepare his followers for the period of distress which must precede the coming of the Son of Man. The reply provides an answer to the question of verse 4 concerning the destruction of the Temple. At the same time it serves to bring this incident within the perspective of the events which are preliminary to the end of time. The purpose of this first section of the discourse is to discourage a false sense of imminence and to urge vigilance in the turmoil and stress which precedes the catastrophe overtaking Jerusalem. The primary element in Jesus' counsel is exhortation motivated by deep pastoral concern for his people. In solemnly warning the disciples about the danger of deception by false prophets or by a misreading of the significance of contemporary events, Jesus stood in the main line of the prophetic tradition. The formulation of his prophecy has been strongly influenced by the language of the OT, which furnishes parallels to nearly every phrase in this section.[40]

The admonition "take heed" introduces a call to vigilance which is sounded throughout the chapter, appearing again in verses 9, 23 and 33. In verse 5 it is prompted by the ever present danger that the people of God may be led astray by false leaders who appear in a situation of crisis. In the OT it is the false prophets who lead Israel astray (e.g. Jer. 23:13, 32; 29:8 f.), and this understanding of verse 6 is reflected in the Old Latin MS *k,* which reads "for many false prophets (*pseudoprophetae*) shall come in my name and say I am he." The Greek text, however, is not as clear as this. The interpretation of the peril that is seen depends upon the nuance expressed in the related phrases "in my name" and

[38] W. Bauer[4] (A-G, p. 214) proposes that the proper translation here is "rise in arms." The use of the passive form of the verb, ἐγερθήσεται, suggests that the fulfilment of God's purpose is directly in view, i.e. "shall be raised [by God]."

[39] Gr. ὠδῖνες appears to be a technical phrase corresponding to the rabbinic expression חבלו של משיח, "the birthpangs of the Messiah," referring to the period of distress which precedes the messianic age. On this expression see S-B*K* I (1922), p. 905; IV (1928), pp. 977-986. Cf. II Baruch 27-30; TB *Shabbath* 118a; *Sanhedrin* 98b.

[40] See especially L. Hartman, *op. cit.,* pp. 147-150.

"I am he." The first phrase was a technical expression designating an appointed emissary or representative (see on Ch. 9:37, 39) and would ordinarily mean "claiming to be sent by me." Its close association with the ambiguous "I am he," however, points in another direction. In the Semitic world the "name" of a person denotes his dignity and power.[41] Understood in this manner, "in my name" signifies "arrogating to themselves the title and authority which properly belong to me."[42] The enigmatic phrase "I am he" is intelligible in this light. As used by Jesus, these words have been generally understood to constitute a claim of dignity which finds its significance in God's own self-designation.[43] The deceivers will claim this dignity for themselves. Thus Jesus cautions his disciples that men will emerge in the crisis who will falsely claim to have the theophanic name and power of the Messiah and they will lead many astray.[44] Their intention will be to lead men to believe that the time of vigilance is past.

The reference in verse 6 is to be understood primarily in terms of the messianic pretenders who throughout the first century won momentary support from segments of the Jewish population by the promise to provide the tokens of redemption that would validate their claims.[45] A succession of false messiahs appeared and gathered followers, but the movements which took their impetus from them were dissipated with their capture and death. They represented a misplacement of hope that could only yield deception and disaster.

---

[41] Cf. H. Bietenhard, *TWNT* V (Eng. Tr. 1967), pp. 272, 276.

[42] So E. Stauffer, *TWNT* II (Eng. Tr. 1965), p. 353; A. Feuillet, "Le discours eschatologique sur la ruine du Temple," *RB* 55 (1948), p. 490; C. E. B. Cranfield, *The Gospel According to St. Mark*² (Cambridge, 1963), p. 395.

[43] Cf. Ex. 3:14; Deut. 32:39; Isa. 41:4; 47:8, 10 LXX and see above on Ch. 6:50. See further, D. Daube, "The 'I Am' of the Messianic Presence" in *The New Testament and Rabbinic Judaism* (London, 1956), pp. 325-329; H. Zimmermann, "Das absolute 'Ich bin' in der Redeweise Jesu," *TrierThZ* 69 (1960), pp. 13 ff.; *idem*, "Das absolute 'Εγώ εἰμι als die neutestamentliche Offenbarungsformel," *BZ* 4 (1960), pp. 54-69, 226-276; A. Haiduk, "'*Ego eimi*' bei Jesu und seine Messianität," *Communio Viatorum* 6 (1963), pp. 55-60.

[44] On the possible background for this statement in Dan. 8:25 see L. Hartman, *op. cit.*, pp. 160 f.

[45] Cf. Josephus, *Antiquities* XX. v. 1; viii. 5-6, 10; *War* II. xiii. 3; xvii. 8-9; VI. v. 2; VII. viii. 1; xi. 1 and the suggestive essay by W. K. L. Clarke, "A Prophet Like Unto Me" in *New Testament Problems* (London, 1929), pp. 39-47. The material in Josephus is conveniently summarized by U. Mauser, *Christ in the Wilderness* (Naperville, 1963), pp. 56-58.

7-8 Jesus warned that it was also possible to misinterpret the significance of contemporary events such as war or natural disasters. When the disciples hear of armed conflict or the threat of war, they are not to be disconcerted or diverted from their task. These developments fall within the sovereign purpose of God, who controls the historical destinies of the nations. These things *must* happen, but they do not signify the end, or even that the end is near. Anxiety excited by war is a common theme in the OT (e.g. Isa. 13:6ff.; 17:14; Jer. 4:19ff.; 6:29ff.; Joel 2:1ff.; Nah. 2:11). The Bible frequently depicts war as a time of divine visitation (e.g. Isa. 14:30; 19:2). It would have been natural for the disciples to have seen in the outbreak of conflict in the land or in the disturbances of A.D. 62-66, when rumors of revolt were common, a sign that the end was imminent.[46] Wars, in themselves, however, do not indicate that the consummation is at hand.

This is emphasized in verse 8 when Jesus reiterates what he has said about war and refers to a complex of disorders frequently associated in Scripture with divine intervention in the historical process. The formulation "nation against nation, kingdom against kingdom" echoes the Hebrew text of Isa. 19:2. Earthquakes also have their place in the description of the intervention of God in history,[47] while famine is a frequent aftermath of war.[48] However calamitous and portentous such developments may appear to be they do not signify the breaking in of the end. They constitute only the beginning of a period of suffering which can be expected to become more intense. They point toward the end and provide a pledge that it will come, but in themselves the disorders enumerated in verse 8 are preliminary events only.[49]

To express this fact Jesus used a phrase which became technical in rabbinic literature to describe the period of intense suffering preceding messianic deliverance, "the birthpangs (of the Messiah)." In the OT the pangs of birth are a recurring image of divine judgment, often in the context of God's eschatological action (cf. Isa. 13:8; 26:17; Mic. 4:9f.;

---

[46] To the vocabulary of verses 7-8 there is a profusion of OT parallels which describe the end-time as a period of war and horror. See F. Busch, *op. cit.,* pp. 83 ff.

[47] E.g. Judges 5:4f.; Ps. 18:8ff.; 68:8f.; 77:18; 114:7; Isa. 24:19; 29:6; 64:1, 3. The Roman historian Tacitus refers to earthquakes in Laodicea and Pompeii during the period just before Jerusalem was destroyed (*Annals* XIV. 27; XV. 22).

[48] For prophecies of famine cf. Jer. 15:2; Ezek. 5:17; 14:13; Acts 11:28.

[49] A. Feuillet, *op. cit.,* p. 490 prefers to interpret verse 7c in terms of the end of the judgment of God upon Jerusalem, not the end of the age.

Hos. 13:13; Jer. 4:31; 6:24; 13:21; 22:23; 49:22; 50:43). The insistence that the crises listed in verse 8 are merely "the beginning of travail" suggests that the period before the appearance of the Messiah in triumph may be extended. Events of greater significance and intensity than those described in verses 5-8 may be expected to follow. From this perspective, the parallel statements "the end is not yet" (verse 7c) and "these things are the beginning of travail" (verse 8b) are delay-sayings, designed to prepare the people of God for facing a turbulent world with firm confidence and unwavering faith. For Mark's readers in Rome, harassed by the State and disturbed by the confused reports of turmoil in Galilee and Judea, Jesus' word provided assurance that these events fall within the eschatological purpose of God. Their task is to be vigilant so as not to be led astray and to refuse to be disturbed by contemporary events, which are in God's control.[50]

(c) A Call to Steadfastness Under Persecution. Ch. 13:9-13

9 But take ye heed to yourselves: for they shall deliver you up to councils;[51] and in synagogues shall ye be beaten; and before governors and kings shall ye stand for my sake, for a testimony unto them.[52]
10 And the gospel must[53] first be preached unto all the nations.[54]

---

[50] On the striking correspondence in the order in which the events are described in Ch. 13:5-8 and Rev. 6 (false prophets, war, earthquakes, famine, a pattern of four woes just before the mention of persecution) see M. Rissi, "The Rider on the White Horse," *Interpretation* 18 (1964), pp. 407-418, especially pp. 413 f.

[51] Gr. συνέδρια signifies local Jewish courts, which were to be found not only in Palestine but also in the Diaspora, e.g. Syria and Asia Minor. See E. Lohse, *TWNT* VII (1964), pp. 864 f. According to TB *Sanhedrin* 17b, any city with a Jewish population of 120 persons was qualified to have a Sanhedrin of its own.

[52] Gr. εἰς μαρτύριον αὐτοῖς is better translated "for evidence against them." See above on Chs. 1:44, 6:11 and cf. H. Strathmann, *TWNT* IV (Eng. Tr. 1967), pp. 502 f., who argues that εἰς μαρτύριον followed by the dative refers to objective testimony which incriminates the person involved. Jesus' words envision a situation of suffering and martyrdom which necessitates the view that the apostolic witness is rejected.

[53] Gr. δεῖ denotes a divine constraint and reflects once more on the sovereign purpose of God. See above on verse 7b.

[54] The fact that some MSS (W Θ *b c d ff*[2] *i k r*[2], sy cop) connect καὶ εἰς πάντα τὰ ἔθνη with verse 9 has led G. D. Kilpatrick to propose a punctuation of verses 9-10 according to which the disciples give "evidence against the kings and rulers and all nations" ("Mark XIII 9-10," *JThS* 9 [1958], pp. 81-86). Against this proposal,

11 And when they lead you to judgment, and deliver you up, be not anxious beforehand [55] what ye shall speak: but whatsoever shall be given you [56] in that hour, that speak ye; for it is not ye that speak, but the Holy Spirit.
12 And brother shall deliver up brother to death, and the father his child; and children shall rise up against parents, and cause them to be put to death.
13 And ye shall be hated of all men for my name's sake: but he that endureth to the end, [57] the same shall be saved. [58]

This paragraph consists of three sayings of Jesus which are held together by the catchword "deliver up." The first consists of verses 9 f. and is concerned with being handed over to different authorities for the sake of Jesus. The second (verse 11) promises the support of the Holy Spirit when those arraigned are to defend themselves in courts of law, while the third (verses 12-13) speaks of division in the family. It is probable that this section of the discourse consists of utterances which were spoken on different occasions. The Matthean parallel to these verses is not found in Ch. 24 but in Ch. 10:17-22 in the mission charge to the twelve disciples, while Luke, in another context, transmits a variant of verse 11 as a separate logion (Luke 12:11 f.).

9 The admonition to "take heed to yourselves" introduces a new perspective in the account. While in the preceding verses attention was concentrated on convulsions throughout the Roman world, in verse 9

---

however, is Mark's practice, for in other instances where he uses εἰς μαρτύριον αὐτοῖς (Chs. 1:44; 6:11) these words complete the sentence. Moreover, it would leave the mandate to preach the gospel in verse 10 unqualified and pointless. It is necessary to take καὶ εἰς πάντα τὰ ἔθνη with the words that follow, as in the ASV, RSV, NEB and the Jerusalem Bible. See further A. L. Moore, *op. cit.*, pp. 205 f.

55 Gr. προμεριμνᾶτε for which Codex Ψ substitutes προμελετᾶτε ("do not practice beforehand") while the Byzantine family of MSS adds μηδὲ μελετᾶτε ("nor practice") under the influence of Luke 21:14.

56 Gr. δοθῇ where the passive has been used to avoid the use of the divine name, as in Ch. 6:2.

57 Gr. εἰς τέλος signifies "in an ultimate sense" or "completely" as distinguished from τὸ τέλος, "the end," in verse 7 (for the idiom cf. II Chron. 31:1 LXX; Lk. 18:5; John 13:1; I Thess. 2:16). It is important to observe that structurally all that is said in Ch. 13:9-13 falls under the rubric "the beginning of travail" (verse 8).

58 Gr. σωθήσεται, which in this context should be understood in terms of vindication, as in the related contexts Job 13:16 LXX; Phil. 1:19, 28 (vindication by God).

it is focused upon the prospect of suffering for those who are addressed. The disciples will experience rejection and abuse because of their association with Jesus. His experience will become the cruel prototype of their own.[59] Regarded as apostates by Jewish authorities, they will be arraigned before the local courts and subjected to public scourging in the synagogues as heretical men.[60] After trial before the Jewish courts, they will be turned over to the Gentile authorities, presumably as disloyal provincials who disturb the peace and incite to riot. The double reference, "kings and governors," serves to designate all men of authority. While Jesus' word may be understood within a Palestinian milieu (cf. Chs. 6:14; 15:2; Matt. 27:2), it may also look beyond this local situation to the experience of arrest throughout the Empire. The disciples are instructed to look beyond the tribunal of men to the tribunal of God where the persecutions they have suffered will be reviewed and will provide incriminating evidence against those who have seen in the gospel an offense to God and men.[61]

10 The natural flow of thought between verses 9 and 11 appears to be interrupted by verse 10. Moreover, the vocabulary of the missionary mandate seems to be distinctly Marcan. For these primary reasons the authenticity of verse 10 has often been rejected.[62] The grounds upon which the statement is denied to Jesus, however, are insufficient. The

---

[59] R. H. Lightfoot, *The Gospel Message of St. Mark* (Oxford, 1950), pp. 48-59; E. Larsson, *Christus als Vorbild* (Lund, 1962), pp. 39 ff., have emphasized turns of phrase in verses 9-13 which recur in Chs. 14-15 in reference to Jesus' suffering.

[60] On synagogue beatings see in the Mishnah tractate *Makkoth,* where the rule for punishment set forth in Deut. 25:2-3 is developed and applied in accordance with Jewish legal practice. The synagogue scourge consisted of a strap of calf leather which was divided into four thongs and through which smaller thongs were plaited to make it stronger (TB *Makkoth* 23a). Three, and sometimes twenty-three, judges were required to secure condemnation to scourging in the local synagogues (M. *Sanhedrin* I. 2; TB *Sanhedrin* 10a/b). Deut. 25:3 limited the number of strokes to 40, but according to II Cor. 11:24; M. *Makkoth* III. 10 this was reduced to 39 in actual practice. There were 13 strokes on the breast and 26 on the back, administered by the servant of the synagogue, who usually stood on a stone behind the sentenced person (M. *Makkoth* III. 12). Both men and women were subject to scourging (M. *Makkoth* III. 14). See further C. Schneider, *TWNT* IV (Eng. Tr. 1967), pp. 516, 518 f.

[61] Cf. L. Hartman, *Testimonium Linguae* (Lund, 1963), pp. 64 ff.

[62] E.g. L. Gaston, *op. cit.,* p. 20; W. G. Kümmel, *Promise and Fulfillment* (Naperville, 1957), pp. 83 f.; E. Grässer, *Das Problem der Parusieverzögerung in den synoptischen Evangelien* (Berlin, 1957), pp. 5 f., 159 ff.

thought of a mission to the Gentiles is firmly grounded in the OT (e.g. Isa. 42:6; 49:6, 12; 52:10; 60:6; Ps. 96) and is found in early Pharisaic Judaism as well (e.g. Psalms of Solomon 11:1; 8:17, 43).[63] While Jesus limited his own ministry to Israel he did not hesitate to respond to faith in a Gentile and showed an awareness of the provisional character of the restriction under which he labored[64] (see above on Ch. 7:27). It is appropriate, therefore, to accept the authenticity of verse 10, and to regard it as an independent logion in the gospel tradition.[65] Mark appears to have inserted it here between verses 9 and 11 to make clear that it is the preaching of the gospel which causes offense and public action against the disciples. A concern for evangelism provokes both mission and persecution.

Verse 10 envisages the disciples' active participation in the missionary enterprise. Involvement with mission identifies them with Jesus and exposes them to the rejection he faced. Nevertheless, a divine compulsion stands behind mission activity throughout the world. The proclamation of the gospel to all men is an absolute priority in the divine plan of salvation, and as such is an integral element in God's eschatological purpose.[66] This word of Jesus provided assurance that the Kingdom of God cannot be impeded by any local persecution in Palestine or elsewhere. Despite all opposition, the gospel *must* be preached throughout the world.

The force of the temporal element "first" is that the consummation cannot come until that condition has been satisfied. In itself this detail sheds no light upon the extent of the duration of the period prior to the parousia. If it is proper to understand "nations" in the sense of the Roman world, this imperative was fulfilled at least in a representative

---

[63] D. Bosch, *Die Heidenmission in der Zukunftschau Jesu* (Zürich, 1959), pp. 17 ff.

[64] *Ibid.*, pp. 76 f. G. D. Kilpatrick, "The Gentile Mission in Mark and Mark 13:9-11," in *Studies in the Gospels,* ed. D. E. Nineham (Oxford, 1955), pp. 145-158 has argued that verse 10 envisions a preaching of the gospel among the synagogues of the Diaspora, but makes no provision for a preaching to Gentiles. If this is so, Jesus separates himself from the great prophetic tradition of interest in the Gentiles. Moreover, Mark's evident interest in the Gentile mission indicates that he did not understand verse 10 in this way. Cf. A. Farrer, "An Examination of Mark XIII. 10," *JThS* 7 (1956), pp. 75-79.

[65] Among those recognizing the verse as genuine are D. Bosch, *op. cit.,* pp. 149 ff.; A. L. Moore, *op. cit.,* pp. 86 f.; H. N. Ridderbos, *The Coming of the Kingdom* (Philadelphia, 1962), pp. 376-381, 485 f.

[66] Cf. D. Bosch, *op. cit.,* p. 167; J. Lambrecht, *op. cit.,* pp. 129 f.

sense by A.D. 60 (cf. Rom. 1:5, 8; 10:18; 15:18-24; Col. 1:6, 23). As a necessary preliminary to the end of time, however, the fulfilment of the mandate continually points toward the manifestation of the Son of Man in glory at the consummation.

11 When called to stand before the courts the disciples are not to be filled with anxiety. God will reveal to them what they are to say. In the past he had equipped his servants to speak in the courts of Egypt and Judah (Ex. 4:12; Jer. 1:9), and he graciously promises to do so once again. The speaking in view is not missionary proclamation but is clearly for the purpose of defense. The servant of God would not have to be concerned over Roman judicial procedure or the lack of adequate counsel. He may rely upon the presence of the Holy Spirit, who will inform his word with the power of truth. Jesus' word provides the assurance that God is vitally involved in the confrontation with authority and supplies the ground for Christian boldness.

12-13 Verse 12 serves to make concrete what is said generally in verses 9 and 11 of being handed over to the authorities for trial. It speaks of division within families and betrayal in the context of persecution. The demand for radical commitment which is inherent in the gospel takes precedence over other loyalties and may disrupt the deepest ties between men. This warning may have been prompted by Isa. 19:2, which is echoed in verse 8, for there it is stated "they will fight every man against his brother, and every man against his neighbor." Closely related to this is the targumic interpretation of Mic. 7:2, where the Targum of Jonathan reads: "A man delivers up his brother to destruction," while Mic. 7:4 f. warns, "Put no trust in a neighbor, have no confidence in a friend... for the son treats his father with contempt, the daughter rises up against her mother, the daughter-in-law against her mother-in-law; a man's enemies are the men of his own house." The interpretation of this last verse in the LXX and the Targum correspond to the formulation of verse 13a. The LXX reads, "A man's enemies are *all* the men in his house," while the Targum of Jonathan translates the Hebrew text literally, "those who *hate* a man are the men of his own house." [67] It is prob-

[67] L. Hartman, *Prophecy Interpreted* (Lund, 1966), pp. 168-170. Hartman points out that the text of Micah may also have provided the substratum for verse 13b, since Mic. 7:7 says, "But as for me, I will look to the Lord, I will wait (LXX ὑπομενῶ) for the God of my salvation" (cf. verse 13b ὁ δὲ ὑπομείνας). Does this suggest that verse 13 should be translated "he who waits (for the Lord) completely

able, therefore, that the interpretation of the text of Micah 7 in the synagogue is reflected in the form of verses 12-13a.

The motive for betrayal from within the family may be fanatical hatred of the gospel or the desire to save one's own life by betraying others or the hope to win the approval of the world with the rejection of the claims of Christ (see on Ch. 8:35 f.). In any instance, Jesus left no room for the facile assumption that the assistance of the Holy Spirit promised in verse 11 would result in acquittal. The disciples may expect to be treated with contempt by those closest to them, even as Jesus was regarded by his brothers (see on Ch. 3:20 f.). They can hope to be vindicated before the tribunal of God but they will not escape death at the hands of men.

It is significant that the followers of Jesus will be hated *because of him* (cf. "for my sake" in verse 9). This qualification indicates that the abuse heaped upon the disciples is really intended for Jesus, and that the disciples are persecuted only because they are identified with him. The lash laid upon the back of a Christian was actually intended to strike the Lord (cf. Acts 9:1, 4 f.). It was the sense of a communion of suffering with Jesus that gave to the early Church a sense of privilege that they could assume the hurt which was directed toward Christ (cf. Phil. 1:29 f.; 3:8-11; Col. 1:24). Jesus, however, did not minimize the severity of the testing to which the people of God would be subjected. They are called to be steadfast under persecution and apostasy. At the same time they are encouraged that those who endure their trials with faithfulness will experience vindication before the bar of God, reversing the condemnation of men. This saying amounts to a call for complete reliance upon God in the fulfilment of mission in a hostile world.

That this word should be treasured and recorded in Rome where persecution threatened to divide and decimate the young church should occasion no surprise. The Christians in Rome were regarded as odious despisers of men whose superstitious allegiance to Jesus was worthy of exemplary punishment, and the persecution under Nero had lent a terrible reality to this prophecy. The Gospel of Mark made clear that no suffering had come to them that had not been foreseen by the Lord and experienced by him.[68] Suffering could be borne with patience when

---

will experience vindication"? On the division in families contemplated in Micah 7 and Ch. 13:12 see R. Harrisville, "Jesus and the Family," *Interpretation* 23 (1969), pp. 425-438.

[68] C. B. Cousar, *op. cit.*, pp. 328 f., 332.

it was brought on by the community's determination to bear witness to Jesus in fulfilment of the missionary task.

(d) The Appalling Sacrilege and the Necessity for Flight. Ch. 13:14-23

14 But when ye see the abomination of desolation [69] standing where he [70] ought not (let him that readeth understand), then let them that are in Judea flee into the mountains:
15 and let him that is on the housetop not go down, nor enter in, to take anything out of his house:
16 and let him that is in the field not return back to take his cloak.
17 But woe unto them that are with child and to them that give suck in those days!
18 And pray ye that it be not in the winter.
19 For those days shall be tribulation, such as there hath not been the like from the beginning of the creation which God created [71] until now, and never shall be.
20 And except the Lord had shortened the days, no flesh would have been saved; but for the elect's sake, whom he chose, he shortened the days.
21 And then if any man shall say unto you, Lo, here is the Christ; or, Lo, there; believe it [72] not:

---

69 Gr. τὸ βδέλυγμα τῆς ἐρημώσεως, an expression borrowed from Dan. 9:27; 11:31; 12:11 LXX (cf. I Macc. 1:54), is better translated "the desolating sacrilege" (RSV) or "the appalling sacrilege." Cf. L. Gaston, *op. cit.*, p. 24.

70 Gr. ἑστηκότα is a masculine perfect participle, while the gender of the antecedent would ordinarily demand a neuter. This is an instance of the grammatical structure conforming to the sense intended *(constructio ad sensum)*, on which see Bl-D-F § 134. 3 (p. 74).

71 The phrase "which God created" is redundant and finds no support in the parallel passages and is omitted in Mark by D Θ *al* it. Nevertheless, it is almost certainly to be read as an instance of Marcan expansion to clarify a biblical statement for his Gentile readers, who would not necessarily assume that the creation of the world was the act of God.

72 The command μὴ πιστεύετε is left unqualified and can be completed in one of two ways: "Do not believe it" or "Do not believe him" (where the reference is to "anyone" at the beginning of the sentence).

22 for there shall arise false Christs and[73] false prophets, and shall show signs and wonders, that they may lead astray, if possible, the elect.
23 But take ye heed: behold, I have told you all things beforehand.

Verses 14-23 form a single unit of thought which is controlled by the command to flee when an act of sacrilege, so appalling that it can only invite unparalleled tribulation, is recognized. This extended warning is tied to verse 4 by the reference to "all things" in verse 23 and furnishes the most direct answer to the question of the disciples concerning *when* they could expect the destruction of the Temple.[74] The entire section is to be interpreted in the light of the events which occurred in the turbulent and chaotic period A.D. 66-70.[75]

14 The language of verse 14a is cryptic and difficult. Yet its interpretation is crucial to the understanding of the discourse as a whole. With terminology borrowed from the book of Daniel (Chs. 9:27; 11:31; 12:11) Jesus warned that the appearance of "the appalling sacrilege" signaled that the destruction of the sanctuary was near and that flight from Jerusalem and Judea was imperative.[76] The Semitic expression used in Daniel describes an abomination so detestable it causes the Temple to be abandoned by the people of God and provokes desolation. This mode of expression occurs in passages dealing with persecution and the oppression of the people of God. When the Seleucid ruler Antiochus IV Epiphanes desecrated the Temple in 168 B.C. by erecting a small altar dedicated to Zeus over the altar of burnt offering, upon which he sacrificed a swine, and made the practice of Judaism a capital offense, it was natural to find a fulfilment of Daniel's prophecy in his action (cf. I Macc. 1:54-59; 6:7). Jesus' use of this distinctive expression, how-

---

[73] One line of the Western text (D *pc i k*) omits the reference to false Messiahs, perhaps under the pressure of Deut. 13:2. On this reading, which is to be rejected, verse 22 speaks only of false prophets who attempted to deceive the people through "signs and wonders."

[74] See above, pp. 454 f. Cf. A. Feuillet, *op. cit.*, p. 495.

[75] *Ibid.*, pp. 496-500; cf. H. N. Ridderbos, *op. cit.*, pp. 491-497; L. Gaston, *op. cit.*, pp. 23-26; R. H. Shaw, "A Conjecture on the Signs of the End," *AThR* 47 (1965), pp. 96-102.

[76] Cf. D. Daube, "The Abomination of Desolation," in *The New Testament and Rabbinic Judaism* (London, 1956), pp. 418-437; B. Rigaux, "ΒΔΕΛΥΓΜΑ ΤΗΣ ΕΡΗΜΩΣΕΩΣ (Mc 13, 14; Mt 24, 15)," *Biblica* 40 (1959), pp. 675-683.

ever, indicates that the prophecy was not ultimately fulfilled by the events of the Maccabean period. He warned that there would yet occur an act of profanation so appalling that the Temple would be rejected by God as the locus of his glory (cf. Ezek. 7:14-23). The nature of the profanation is left imprecise, but the use of the masculine participle to modify a neuter noun suggests that Mark found a personification of the abomination in some concrete figure of history. The meaning is well brought out by the NEB: "when you see 'the abomination of desolation' usurping a place which is not *his*." The evangelist appears to have recognized the fulfilment of the prophecy in his own day since he inserts a parenthetical note to the Christian reader to recognize the significance of Jesus' words.[77] The plea that the reader should "understand" is important in the context of an eschatological mystery (cf. Dan. 1:17; 2:21-23; 9:25; 12:13).

Flight is necessary in order to escape the judgment of God that will fall upon the land as the result of sacrilege. The devastation overtaking Jerusalem will affect all Judea and makes flight to the mountains imperative.[78] The tradition of the OT often unites the idea of flight to that of divine judgment (e.g. Gen. 19:17; Jer. 16:16; Ezek. 7:14-16; Zech. 14:5). Ordinarily Jerusalem is regarded as the place of refuge *par excellence* (cf. Isa. 16:3; Jer. 4:6; Zech. 2:11), but in the circumstances described the almost impregnable walls of the city will offer no real defense to its inhabitants. In fact, those who remained in the city during the siege of Jerusalem found themselves helplessly trapped between starvation and violent destruction.

The dominant note in verse 14 is the command to flee. This exhortation is developed or presupposed in each of the subsequent verses as Jesus addresses himself to the urgency for flight (verses 15-16), to circumstances which hinder flight (verses 17-18), to the reason for flight (verses 19-20), and to a final deterrent to flight (verses 21-22). The injunction to flee clearly implies a crisis in history and not the end, when flight will be useless (cf. Rev. 6:15-17).

---

77 It is better to attribute the parenthetical call to understanding to Mark rather than to Jesus since it is consistent with the evangelist's practice elsewhere in the Gospel to address his reader (e.g. Chs. 2:10, 28; 3:30; 7:3-4, 11b, 19b; 9:50b; 16:4b, 8b).

78 L. Hartman, *op. cit.*, pp. 152 f. feels that an allusion to Lot's flight from Sodom (a type of the abomination), as related in Gen. 19, is intended. Cf. Gen. 19:17.

Further light is shed on verse 14 by the fourth-century historian Eusebius. He notes:

> "But before the war, the people of the Church of Jerusalem were bidden in an oracle given by revelation to men worthy of it to depart from the city and to dwell in a city of Perea called Pella. To it those who believed in Christ migrated from Jerusalem. Once the holy men had completely left the Jews and all Judea, the justice of God at last overtook them, since they had committed such transgressions against Christ and his apostles. Divine justice completely blotted out that impious generation from among men" (*Ecclesiastical History* III. v. 3). [79]

The oracle to which Eusebius refers was apparently the saying recorded in verse 14. The circumstances in which it was understood to have been fulfilled are illumined by Josephus in his account of the *Jewish War*. Jewish forces won an impressive victory over the Twelfth Legion commanded by Cestius Gallus in November of 66 (*War* II. xix. 2-9). Many persons in Jerusalem, however, recognized that eventually the Zealot forces would suffer inevitable defeat, and those who were realistic began leaving the city in droves, apparently unimpeded (*War* II. xx. 1). No efforts were marshalled to frustrate desertions from the city until the spring of 68 (*War* IV. vi. 3; vii. 3). Christians in Jerusalem would have had no difficulty leaving the city unless they delayed their departure until a relatively late stage in the conflict.

The prophecy of Daniel concerning the appalling sacrilege had been called to mind in the year A.D. 40 when Caligula laid plans to have an image of himself set up in the Jerusalem Temple (see Philo, *Legatio ad Gaium;* Josephus, *Antiquities* XVIII. viii. 2-9; Tacitus, *History* V. 9). After that catastrophe was averted, Josephus found the fulfilment of Daniel in the events of A.D. 66-70 (*Antiquities* X. xi. 7: "in the same

---

79 Cf. Epiphanius, *De Mensuris et Ponderibus* 15: "For when the city was about to be conquered by the Romans, all the disciples were warned by an angel to leave the city, since it was about to be destroyed completely. Becoming migrants, they dwelt at Pella . . . " Similarly *Adversus Haereses* 29:7; 30:2. These related testimonies were subjected to a critical scrutiny and were rejected by S. G. F. Brandon, *The Fall of Jerusalem and the Christian Church*[2] (London, 1957), pp. 168-178, but see now the response to each of Brandon's objections by S. Sowers, "The Circumstances and Recollection of the Pella Flight," *ThZ* 26 (1970), pp. 305-320. In what follows Sowers' positive contribution is summarized.

manner Daniel also wrote about the empire of the Romans and that Jerusalem would be taken and the Temple laid waste"). He refers to an ancient prophecy concerning the desecration of the Temple *by Jewish hands* and found its fulfilment in a whole series of villainous acts committed by the Zealots in the Temple precincts from the period November 67 to the spring of 68.

> "For there was an ancient saying of inspired men that the city would be taken and the sanctuary burned to the ground by right of war, when it should be visited by sedition and native hands should be the first to defile God's sacred precinct. This saying the Zealots did not disbelieve; yet they lent themselves as instruments of its accomplishment" (*War* IV. vi. 3).

During this period the Zealots moved into and occupied the Temple area (*War* IV. iii. 7), allowed persons who had committed crimes to roam about freely in the Holy of Holies (*War* IV. iii. 10), and perpetrated murder within the Temple itself (*War* IV. v. 4). These acts of sacrilege were climaxed in the winter of 67-68 by the farcical investiture of the clown Phanni as high priest (*War* IV. iii. 6-8). It was in response to this specific action that the retired high priest Ananus, with tears, lamented: "It would have been far better for me to have died before I had seen the house of God laden with such abominations and its unapproachable and hallowed places crowded with the feet of murderers" (*War* IV. iii. 10). Jewish Christians who had met in the porches of the Temple from the earliest days would have found this spectacle no less offensive. It seems probable that they recognized in Phanni "the appalling sacrilege usurping a position which is not his," consigning the Temple to destruction. In response to Jesus' warning they fled to Pella.

The oracle specified that those in Judea were to flee "to the mountains." Since Jerusalem itself is located in the mountains the Christians understood the prophecy to refer to some other range of mountains beyond Judea. The nearest such range was the Transjordanian mountains where Pella is located in the foothills. It can be assumed that by the year 66 there were Gentile Christians in the Decapolis, including Pella, who may have acted as sponsors for the Jerusalem fugitives in that traumatic period.[80]

---

80 A. Feuillet, *op. cit.*, pp. 495 f. and L. Gaston, *op. cit.*, pp. 458-468 similarly interpret the sacrilege in terms of Zealotic excesses committed in the Temple area

15-18 These verses underscore the urgency behind the command to flee to the mountains. Jesus insists upon the necessity of an immediate and rapid flight. A flat roof was commonly used as a place for prayer at midday[81] and was reached by means of an outside staircase. While it is necessary for a man to descend from the roof in order to flee he must not enter his house. At the critical moment a concern for life takes precedence over possessions. Under similar circumstances in the days of Antiochus Epiphanes the aged priest Mattathias and his five sons "fled to the hills and left all that they had in the city" (I Macc. 2:28). The reference to the man working in the fields is appropriate to the rural conditions of much of Judea. The outer garment, designed to shut out the night chill but left upon the ground in another corner of the field, is to be abandoned rather than to risk one's life in returning for it. There is to be no deterrent to flight. The urgency expressed in Jesus' instruction may have been prompted by the description of the utter desolation of Jerusalem in Ezek. 7:14-23. In that context the fate of those who did not flee is vividly described: "the sword is without, pestilence and famine are within; he that is in the field dies by the sword; and him that is in the city famine and pestilence devour. And if any survivors escape, they will be on the mountains . . ." (Ezek. 7:15 f.). Jesus' compassion is evident in his thought of the hardships that will be imposed upon pregnant and nursing mothers forced to flee in difficult circumstances. The peril of flight in winter is that streams swollen by heavy rains would be impossible to cross and could prevent many from reaching a place of refuge. It happened that during the spring of A.D. 68, due to recent rain storms, the Jordan River was too high and swift

---

prior of the siege of the city. For an alternative proposal see F. F. Bruce, "The Book of Daniel and the Qumran Community" in *Neotestamentica et Semitica* (Edinburgh, 1969), p. 231 n. 25.

In the parallel passage (Luke 21:20 f.) the arrival of military forces which surrounded the city, rather than any act of sacrilege in the Temple, is considered the moment for flight. Long before Titus' troops encircled the city, however, the Zealots had taken measures to prevent desertions. It is probable that the reference is to the arrival of Idumean forces who had come in the winter of 68 intending to aid their Zealot allies who were occupying the Temple precincts. They encamped around the city. Thus, when Eusebius says that the Christians left Jerusalem "before the war" he may be saying "before the southern offensive in the spring of A.D. 68." So S. Sowers, *op. cit.*, p. 320. On the Lucan parallel see C. H. Dodd, "The Fall of Jerusalem and the 'Abomination of Desolation'," *Journal of Roman Studies* 37 (1947), pp. 47-54.

81 Cf. Acts 10:9 and the rabbinic references collected in S-B*K* I (1922), p. 952.

for Gadarene fugitives to cross from east to west to seek safety in Jericho (Josephus, *War* IV. vii. 5).

19-20 The reason that flight is so urgent is that a catastrophe without precedent is imminent. The severity of the distress that will accompany the destruction of Jerusalem is vividly suggested through Semitic hyperbole. It is characteristic for oracles of judgment to be couched in language that is universal and radical. The intention is to indicate that through human events God intervenes powerfully to modify the course of history. The entire world feels the vibrations of that intervention. The OT offers numerous examples of this vision of God from the perspective of historical events which are quite localized, e.g. Micah 1:2 ff. depicts the Lord going forth from his sanctuary to punish the crimes of Samaria and Judea: all the earth staggers (cf. Isa. 13:6-10). It is appropriate to the prophetic style of utterance that verses 19-20 be seen in the context of the impending destruction of the Temple. Josephus uses almost identical language in his account of the devastation of Jerusalem (e.g. *War,* proem; I. i. 4; V. x. 5). Emphatic affirmations of this type are not uncommon in the OT and subsequent Jewish literature and must not be interpreted too rigorously (cf. Jer. 30:7; Joel 2:2; Baruch 2:2; I Macc. 9:27; Assumption of Moses 8:1). One example from the Qumran material will be sufficient to illustrate the degree to which Jesus' statement has its parallels. In reference to "the great day of judgment" it is said: "And it shall be a time of distress for all the people redeemed by God, and among all their afflictions there will have been nothing to equal it from its beginning until its end in final redemption" (1QM i. 11-12). Verse 19 conforms in style to the prophetic oracles of judgment which threaten an unprecedented catastrophe which in reality is a judgment of the chosen people to whom God will leave a remnant. In the context of verses 19-20 a distinction is made between the disciples, who escape by flight, and the men of Judea [82] who cannot escape the judgment, except for the remnant which is spared. The destruction of Jerusalem and its sanctuary is in this way situated within the perspective of a universal judgment. [83]

Verse 19 is virtually a citation of Dan. 12:1 ("And there shall be a

---

[82] According to the context, πᾶσα σάρξ in verse 20 must be understood of Judea and Jerusalem. Cf. Jer. 12:12 where a similar expression designates the inhabitants of Judea.

[83] So A. Feuillet, *op. cit.,* pp. 496-500.

time of trouble such as never has been since there was a nation till that time"), although the mode of expression may echo other passages which describe the day when God will visit his people in judgment. The significant addition "and never shall be" clearly indicates that the tribulation is not the distress which accompanies the last days. As great as the oppression will be, it is nevertheless not to be immediately followed by the end, for time will be extended, with the possibility of other, though lesser, tribulations. The fact that this qualification was added to the citation of Dan. 12:1 demonstrates that this section is a prophetic oracle providing instruction for a specific historical situation in which the prophecy of Daniel will be fulfilled.

In this immediate context, the normal sense of the words "no flesh would have been saved" is that no one would have escaped physical death if God had not shortened the period of tribulation. The severity of the judgment reflects upon the abuse of Israel's privileged status provided by the covenant. This lends support to the proposal that it is from within the nation that the appalling act of sacrilege is committed. Yet God's judgment is tempered by his mercy expressed in the curtailment of the period of tribulation. For the idea of the shortening of the days of affliction there is no clear parallel in the OT and only one in later Jewish literature (III Baruch 9).[84] The reference to "the elect" may have been suggested by the continuation of Dan. 12:1 which promises deliverance to the people, "every one whose name shall be written in the book." God's maintenance of the elect is an extension of the OT concept of the remnant which God leaves in Israel as an act of grace and judgment.[85]

21-23 Verses 21-22 have frequently been regarded as a doublet of verses 5-6, and inappropriate to this context. Earlier in the discourse Jesus had warned his disciples not to be deceived by men claiming the dignity which is proper to himself, for the time of the open manifestation of the messianic presence lay yet in the future. The perspective in verses 21-22 is different and is entirely appropriate to a context dominated by the motif of flight. Here the point is rather *not to be deterred from flight* by the claim that the Messiah was here, or there. The internal

---

84 For the text see M. R. James (ed.), *Apocrypha Anecdota* II (Oxford, 1897), p. 91.

85 Cf. R. de Vaux, "Le 'Reste d'Israël' d'après les prophètes," *RB* 40 (1933), pp. 526-539; G. Schrenk, *TWNT* IV (Eng. Tr. 1967), pp. 194-214.

unity of verses 14-23 demands that Jesus' warning at this point be interpreted in this manner. The stress falls on not turning aside when the imperative need is for refuge. Such claims are fallacious and those who make them are not to be believed. The distress described by Jesus does not compel the intervention of the Messiah. While the historical crisis invites a final wave of messianic pretenders and prophets, they will not be able to bring a halt to the tribulation convulsing the land. Flight remains imperative for the people of God. They must not be deceived by a readiness to show signs and wonders which will validate a claim. Already Deut. 13 had warned that men of lies will seek to lead the faithful astray with their signs (cf. Deut. 13:6, 7, 11, 14). The exhortation not to believe those who say, "Look, here is the Messiah" indicates reflection upon the same source. Deut. 13:4 says, "You shall not listen to the words of that prophet," while verse 9 repeats this admonition in connection with the enticing member of the family: "You shall not yield to him or listen to him." In contrast to the extravagant claims of many of those who appeared on the scene during the turbulent years preceding the destruction of Jerusalem [86] stands the refusal of Jesus to provide a sign which will relieve men of the responsibility for faith expressed through commitment (see on Ch. 8:11 f.; cf. Ch. 15:32).

The account of the events preliminary to the destruction of the Temple is rounded off in typical Semitic fashion by returning to the admonition which introduced Jesus' response: "take heed" (verses 5, 23). Here the command is reinforced with the affirmation that the disciples have been adequately forewarned. The "all things" which Jesus has told them corresponds to the request of the disciples to know when "these things are all to be accomplished" (verse 4). From this structural perspective the response to the question of verse 4 is complete with verse 23. All that remains is to announce the final victory of the Son of Man.

(e) The Triumph of the Son of Man. Ch. 13:24-27

24 But [87] in those days, after that tribulation, the sun shall be darkened, and the moon shall not give her light,

---

86 See above, n. 45.

87 Gr. Ἀλλά is a strong adversative implying a contrast to what has just been said. It serves to set verses 24-27 off from the earlier sections of the discourse, and particularly from verses 21-23. The contrast implied may be expressed as follows: "There will be false messianic figures where Jerusalem is judged. Do not be misled

25 and the stars shall be falling from heaven, and the powers that are in the heavens shall be shaken.
26 And then shall they see [88] the Son of Man coming in clouds [89] with great power and glory.
27 And then shall he send forth the angels, and shall gather together his elect from the four winds, from the uttermost part of the earth to the uttermost part of heaven.

24-25 Juxtaposed to the false hopes which will mislead many of the people in the critical moment is the assurance that the period of suffering and distress will be followed by final redemption when the Son of Man will be manifested in power and glory. The correspondence between these two phases of God's eschatological program is indicated only in a general way: "in those days, after that tribulation ..." "In those days" is a stereotyped expression in the OT that came to acquire distinctly eschatological associations from the contexts in which it occurs (e.g. Jer. 3:16, 18; 31:29; 33:15 f.; Joel 2:28 [M.T. 3:1]; Zech. 8:23). In itself, however, it has no determined temporal value. In verse 24 this phrase designates a period subsequent to the days of tribulation described in verses 19-20, but the matter of chronological sequence is left imprecise. It is clear from the structure of the discourse that the parousia cannot take place until after all the preliminary events announced in verses 5-23 have occurred. They are the necessary precursors to the coming of the glorified Son of Man, yet in themselves they do not determine the time of that event. Jesus simply declares the sufferings which can be anticipated (verses 5-23) and the final triumph which will resolve the tensions and paradoxes of historical existence (verses 24-27). The end is contemplated from the standpoint of a concrete event (the destruction of Jerusalem and its sanctuary) which serves as its prelude.

No other section of the eschatological discourse is more indebted to scriptural imagery and language.[90] The entire description is drawn from

---

by them. When the Messiah actually appears his coming will be like this ..." For this reading of the text see D. M. Roark, "The Great Eschatological Discourse," *Nov Test* 7 (1964), pp. 126 f.

88 In Aramaic the indefinite plural is often used for the simple passive. Translate: "And then the Son of Man will be seen ..."

89 The language reflects Dan. 7:13 f., but the detail of the Son of Man's coming upon the clouds is informed by a rich background. When Yahweh comes to administer judgment and to initiate his reign he is carried on the clouds (Isa 19:1; Nah. 1:3; Ps. 18:10; 97:2). See the references collected and discussed by A. Feuillet, *op. cit.*, pp. 69 f.

90 For a convenient table of parallel passages see L. Hartman, *op. cit.*, pp. 156 f.

OT material, which has been brought together through common motifs or keywords which present the coming of the Son of Man in terms of Yahweh's theophany on the Day of the Lord for the gathering of his people. The references to the celestial phenomena which accompany the appearance of the Son of Man are appropriate in this connection. Thus in Joel 2:10 and 3:15 we read of the coming Day of Yahweh: "The sun and the moon are darkened, and the stars withdraw their shining" (cf. Isa. 13:10; 34:4; Ezek. 32:7-8; Amos 8:9).[91] In the prophets and later Jewish apocalyptic writings the dissolution of the cosmic structure frequently orchestrates the intervention of God in history. The imagery employed indicates an important turning point in history, but not necessarily the last act of the historical process. Fundamental to this manner of speaking is the profound concept that the universe is united with man in his destiny, and the prophets, who envisaged a radical reversal in human fortunes, spoke freely of an upheaval in the heavens themselves.[92] In Ch. 13 the judgment upon Jerusalem marks the passing of one era and the establishment of another in which the glory of God is no longer concentrated in the Temple but in the Son of Man. The significance of this fact is expressed in four lines of poetry in verses 24-25, where the first three parallel statements are summed up in the fourth. The language has been profoundly influenced by Isa. 13:10 and 34:4, but there is no actual quotation of either passage. It is possible that Jesus intended a contrast with the signs and wonders of the false prophets (verse 22), in terms of Joel 2:30 f. (M.T. 3:3 f.): "I will give wonders in the heavens and on the earth . . . The sun shall be turned to darkness, and the moon to blood . . . ," which the Targum of Jonathan interprets in the category of signs.[93]

26-27 In these verses all of the actions are attributed to the Son of Man: he not only comes, but he gathers the elect through the ministry of the angels, and the elect are "his." These elements serve to bring the

---

[91] In many of these passages the celestial phenomena occur in conjunction with temporal judgments against Babylon, Egypt, Edom or Assyria. Each of these judgments foreshadows the great day of final judgment and therefore can be described in similar language. For a reading of Joel 2-4 in first-century Jewish perspective see L. Gaston, *op. cit.*, pp. 31-33.

[92] Cf. C. C. McCown, "Symbolic Interpretation," *JBL* 63 (1944), pp. 329-338; A. N. Wilder, "Eschatological Imagery and Earthly Circumstances," *NTS* 5 (1958-59), pp. 229-245.

[93] L. Hartman, *op. cit.*, p. 157 n. 35.

Son of Man into bold relief.[94] His triumph is described in the classic formulation of the enthronement of that mysterious, transcendent figure "like a son of man" in Dan. 7:13f. There are, however, two distinctive features in Jesus' interpretation of that passage. The Son of Man is not, as in Daniel, brought to God's throne. There is, in fact, no allusion to a revelation of God in the context. Instead he comes to gather together the scattered people of God, a function attributed to God in the OT (e.g. Deut. 30:3f.; Ps. 50:3-5; Isa. 43:6; 66:8; Jer. 32:37; Ezek. 34:13; 36:24; Zech. 2:6, 10). This coming as a sovereign in the celestial chariot of the clouds, adorned with power and glory, is properly designated the *parousia* after the analogy with the triumphs celebrated by royal figures and heroes in the Hellenistic-Roman world.[95] Yet it is imperative to recall that Jesus had earlier announced that the Son of Man would be rejected, humiliated and put to death (see on Ch. 8:31) and that the ambiguity in his own historical particularity would be resolved only with his coming in glory as the eschatological judge (see on Ch. 8:38). In this given context the reference to the parousia serves to vindicate Jesus' dignity over against all detractors and the false claims of men (verses 5-6, 21-22). His coming "with the clouds" will mark the end of the veiledness that characterizes both Jesus and the people of God. As such, the parousia provides the kernel of Christian hope, for the triumph of the Son of Man is the one event in the light of which the contradictions of the present are illumined and resolved.

The affirmation that the Son of Man will send forth the angels to gather the elect brings together Deut. 30:4 and Zech. 2:10. In the OT "to scatter to the four winds" (Jer. 9:15; 18:17; Ezek. 5:10, 12; 12:14; 17:21; Zech. 2:10 M.T.) or "to regather from the four winds" / "from every country" / "from the extremities of the earth" (Deut. 30:3-4; Isa. 11:12; 27:13; 56:8; Jer. 23:3; 29:12; 31:8; Ezek. 11:17; 20:34, 41; 28:25; 34:13) are recurring expressions. The first describes the loss of national unity by the elect people as a consequence of their infidelity to God; the second announces the salvation of Israel through a return to spiritual and national unity. The regathering of dispersed Israel is an essential and traditional theme of Jewish eschatological hope (e.g. Tobit 14:7, "all the children of Israel that are delivered in those days, remembering God in truth, shall be gathered together . . . " ; cf. Psalms of Solomon 17:28). When Jesus touched upon this theme in the context

---

94 On the Son of Man see above, pp. 298 ff.

95 Cf. A. Oepke, *TWNT* V (Eng. Tr. 1967), pp. 858-866.

of the eschatological discourse he reinterpreted Israel's hope in a profound way. Until that time the Temple of Jerusalem had been the visible center for the gathering of the scattered chosen people. The destruction of the Temple, however, would not result in their permanent dispersement. On the contrary, it will be followed by the regathering of the new people of God around the Son of Man, that is, around Jesus. The counterpart to the destruction of Jerusalem and the sanctuary is the eschatological salvation of the elect. The remnant of Israel will recover their lost unity through Jesus, the triumphant Son of Man. To be gathered by the Son of Man is to participate in the eschatological community and to experience the messianic blessing. The scope of the activity of the Son of Man through the angels is universal, for Mark's formula "from the ends of the earth to the ends of heaven" synthesizes two OT expressions which mean "everywhere."[96]

(f) The Lesson of the Fig Tree. Ch. 13:28-31

28 Now from the fig tree learn her parable: when her branch has now become tender, and putteth forth its leaves, ye know that the summer[97] is nigh;
29 even so ye also,[98] when ye see these things coming to pass,

---

[96] Deut. 4:32; 30:4; Ps. 19:7 "from one extremity of heaven to the other"; Deut. 13:7 f.; Jer. 12:8: "from one extremity of the earth to the other."

[97] A consideration of the Semitic vocabulary behind the discourse suggests that a play on words may have been intended here. Hebrew קיץ designates not only the warm period of the year, the summer, but also the summer harvest (cf. II Sam. 16:1-2; Isa. 16:9; 28:4; Jer. 8:20; 40:10, 12; 48:32; Micah 7:1). In Amos 8:1-2 it designates summer fruit in a basket, perhaps a basket filled with figs. The basket of קַיִץ signifies that the קֵץ (the critical moment of judgment) has come for the people of Israel who will be punished. The same word play may be intended in verse 28, assuming that Jesus spoke to the disciples in Hebrew (Aramaic קיטא and קיצא does not permit this word play). Cf. I. Löw, "Zum Feigengleichnis," *ZNW* 11 (1910), pp. 167 f. and especially J. Dupont, "La parabole du figuier qui bourgeonne (Mc. xiii. 28-29 et par.)," *RB* 75 (1968), p. 542; M. P. Fernández, "'prope est aestas' (Mc. 13, 28; Mt. 24, 32; Lc. 21, 29)," *Verb Dom* 46 (1968), pp. 361-369.

[98] It has been objected that the words οὕτως καὶ ὑμεῖς with which verse 29 begins do not accord well with verse 28, which was already expressed in the second person plural. See, however, J. Lambrecht, *op. cit.*, pp. 196-198, who points out that the "you" in verse 28 means "you and every man," while in verse 29 it

know ye that he is nigh, [99] even at the doors.
30 Verily I say unto you, This generation shall not pass away, until all these things be accomplished.
31 Heaven and earth shall pass away: but my words shall not pass away.

In this section Jesus responds to the original question of the disciples *when* they may expect to see his prophecy concerning the Temple (verse 2) fulfilled. It is important to review the relationship of these verses to the structure of the discourse. In response to the disciples' question when "these things" will take place and the request for some indication that "all these things" are about to be accomplished, Jesus spoke of the complex of events which find their culmination in the devastation of Judea and the demolition of the Temple. He concluded his remarks with the admonition, "Take care, I have told you beforehand *all things*" (verse 23). The vocabulary of verse 23 underscores the correspondence between the question of verse 4 and the response given in verses 5-23. In verses 29-30 this terminology reappears: "when you see *these things* happening... and this generation shall not pass away until *all these things* occur." The italicized words demand that these statements be considered in relationship to verses 4 and 23. They cannot refer to the celestial upheavals described in verses 24-25 which are inseparable from the parousia (verse 26) and the gathering of the elect (verse 27). These events represent the end and cannot constitute a preliminary sign of something else. The phrase "these things" in verse 29 refers to the entire discourse from verses 5-23, with special reference to the material evidence provided in verses 14-23. The parallel phrase in verse 30 provides the same perspective. Before the passing of a generation, Jerusalem and the Temple will lie in ruins.

---

concerns exclusively the disciples whom Jesus is addressing. A similar transition occurs in Ch. 7:18.

[99] Gr. ἐγγύς ἐστιν is ambiguous. The translation "he is near" presumes that the intended reference is to the parousia described in verses 24-27. A structural analysis of the discourse, however, shows that verse 29 has reference to verses 5-23. It is preferable, therefore, to translate "it is near," finding the antecedent in the appalling sacrilege and tribulation described in verses 14-20. This interpretation finds support from the parallel statement in verse 30, which clearly has reference to verses 14-20. Cf. verse 18 where the same ambiguity exists in the verb γένηται but context demands the translation "Pray that *it* will not happen in winter." See F. Flückiger, *op. cit.*, p. 407; J. Dupont, *op. cit.*, pp. 526-530.

28-29 In contrast to most of the trees of Palestine (the olive, oak, evergreen, terebinth), the fig loses its leaves in the winter, and in contrast to the almond, which blossoms very early in the spring, the fig tree shows signs of life only later. Jesus' parable appeals to this particularity: when the branches of the fig become softened by sap flowing through them and leaves begin to appear one can be certain that winter is past (cf. Song of Sol. 2:11-13) and the warm season is very near. The parable relates the sprouting of the fig tree and the summer in terms of a beginning point and its inevitable sequence. The accent falls not on immediacy but on proximity: when the fig tree becomes green, one is not only certain that summer is coming but that it is near. [100] The Mount of Olives was famous for its fig trees, which sometimes attained a height of 20 or 30 feet. Assuming that Jesus gave this instruction just before the Passover, the fig tree would be in the condition described in the parable, its branches tender, its leaves sprouting. [101] By calling the disciples to observe properly what was immediately at hand Jesus reinforced his exhortation to observe what was happening in Jerusalem and Judea and to recognize its significance.

The application of the parable in verse 29 places the accent on proximity more vigorously: "it is near, at the door." [102] The catastrophe of sacrilege which will profane the Temple (verse 14) will enable the disciples to know that the destruction of the Temple is imminent in the same manner that the coming of summer is imminent to the moment when the fig tree covers itself with leaves. In verse 29 the words "when you see these things happening" appear to be an intentional echo of the beginning of verse 14, "when you see the appalling sacrilege." That catastrophe, which will take place in the Temple, will be the signal for flight from unheard of distress. The parable and its application invite the reader of the Gospel to see in the misfortunes which will overtake Jerusalem the evidence that its devastation and ruin is near.

30-31 Verse 30 is solemnly introduced and emphatically affirmed. [103] It is tied intimately to its immediate context by vocabulary and perspective, "all these things" in verse 30 corresponding to "these things"

---

[100] J. Dupont, *op. cit.*, pp. 531 f.

[101] H. N. and A. L. Moldenke, *Plants of the Bible* (Waltham, Mass., 1952), p. 105.

[102] On the expression ἐπὶ θύραις see J. Jeremias, *TWNT* IV (Eng. Tr. 1965), pp. 173 f.

[103] Gr. ἀμὴν λέγω ὑμῖν. See on Ch. 3:28.

in verse 29. This mode of expression refers to the prophecy of verse 2 and the complex of events preliminary to its fulfilment in verses 5-23. The significance of the temporal reference has been debated,[104] but in Mark "this generation" clearly designates the contemporaries of Jesus (see on Chs. 8:12, 38; 9:19) and there is no consideration from the context which lends support to any other proposal. Jesus solemnly affirms that the generation contemporary with his disciples will witness the fulfilment of his prophetic word, culminating in the destruction of Jerusalem and the dismantling of the Temple.[105] With this word Jesus responds to the initial question of the disciples regarding the time when "these things" will take place.

The declaration of verse 30 is strengthened by the assertion which follows. Verse 31 has its background in the OT where the enduring quality of God and his word is contrasted with the only apparent durability of the created universe (cf. Ps. 102:25-27; Isa. 40:6-8; 51:6). While heaven and earth will be cataclysmically destroyed, Jesus' word is established forever. This claim of high dignity for Jesus' words implies a christological affirmation: what is said of God in the OT may be equally affirmed of Jesus and his word. The prophecy developed on Olivet will surely come to pass.

(g) The Call to Vigilance. Ch. 13:32-37

32 But of that day or that hour knoweth no one, not even the angels in heaven, neither the Son,[106] but the Father.
33 Take ye heed, watch and pray:[107] for ye know not when the time is.

---

[104] The range of interpretation is reviewed by A. L. Moore, *op. cit.*, pp. 131 f. and by E. Lövestam, "En problematisk eskatologisk utsaga: Mark 13:30 par.," *Sv Ex Års* 28-29 (1963-64), pp. 64-80.

[105] So A. Feuillet, *op. cit.*, pp. 82-84; F. Flückiger, *Der Ursprung des christlichen Dogmas* (Zürich, 1955), p. 116.

[106] The phrase οὐδὲ ὁ υἱός proved to be theologically difficult. It is omitted by Codex Montanensis (983) and some Vulgate MSS, and in the parallel passage, Matt. 24:36, by ℵ K L W Δ Π λ 33 565 700 *pm* sy cop. There is no parallel in Luke. On the authenticity of the phrase and verse 32 see B. M. F. van Iersel, *Der Sohn in den synoptischen Jesusworten. Christusbezeichnung der Gemeinde oder Selbstbezeichnung Jesu?* (Leiden, 1961), pp. 117-119; A. L. Moore, *op. cit.*, pp. 99, 191 f.

[107] It is difficult to determine whether the words "and pray" have been added

34 It is as when a man, sojourning in another country, having
left his house, and given authority to his servants, to each one
his work, commanded also the porter to watch.
35 Watch therefore: for ye know not when the lord of the house
cometh, whether at even, or at midnight, or at cockcrowing,
or in the morning;
36 lest coming suddenly he find you sleeping.
37 And what I say unto you I say unto all, [108] Watch.

32 Jesus concluded his response by stressing the responsibility of maintaining vigilance. The duty to watch draws its force from the fact that "no one knows" the critical moment of God's decisive intervention. "That day" evokes a formula consecrated by use in the prophetic Scriptures; it appears with a clearly eschatological resonance in passages which announce the day of Yahweh's appearing (Amos 8:3, 9, 13; 9:11; Mic. 4:6; 5:9; 7:11; Zeph. 1:9 f.; 3:11, 16; Obad. 8; Joel 3:18; Zech. 9:16; 12-14 *passim*). Here it designates an indeterminate date which remains the Father's secret. In the light of its association with the theophany of God on the Day of the Lord it must have primary reference to the parousia, the coming of the Son of Man (verse 26). [109] Jesus thus affirms that no one knows that day or the hour (the smallest unit of time; cf. verse 11) when the Son of Man will appear in glory with power. In order to understand the relationship of this affirmation to the assurance given in verse 30 that the events preliminary to the destruction of the Temple will occur within the experience of that generation, it is necessary to give full force to the adversative particle in verse 32: "I say to you solemnly, this generation shall not pass away away . . . As for that day and that hour, *on the contrary,* no one knows . . . " While the parable of the fig tree illustrates the possibility of observing the proximity of the first event, another comparison is developed in connection with verse 32 which underscores the impossibility of knowing the moment of the

---

here under the influence of Ch. 14:38 or whether their absence in B D it is accidental. They are omitted in the RSV, NEB and Jerusalem Bible. Yet in the critical edition of the Greek text issued by the joint Bible Societies the omission receives only a (D) rating (i.e. very uncertain that the printed text is correct).

108 The extension of the call to vigilance to a wider circle is obscured in D (Θ) it, where verse 37 reads: "But I say to you, Watch."

109 Cf. W. G. Kümmel, *op. cit.,* pp. 36 f.: "Jesus uses this term (ἡ ἡμέρα, ἡ ἡμέρα ἐκείνη) invariably for the end of time in the future." Cf. Ch. 14:25; Matt. 10:15; 25:13; Lk. 10:12; 17:26.

Lord's return. Verses 30 and 32 concern two distinct events (the taking of Jerusalem by the Romans, and the Day of the Lord, respectively).[110]

The accent falls on the words "no one knows," not on the qualification "neither the angels in heaven nor the Son." Very early the clause "nor the Son" attracted the attention of theologians anxious to trace the christological implications in the confession of ignorance,[111] but in this context is it accidental with respect to Jesus' intention. His purpose was not to define the limits of his theological knowledge, but to indicate that vigilance, not calculation, is required. If the Son of Man (interpreting "the Son" by verse 26) and the angels are ignorant of "that day" it is because nothing allows a presentiment of its coming. Its approach is impossible to discern and so to prepare oneself for it. In this respect it stands in sharp contrast to the destruction of Jerusalem, which could be clearly foreseen and its devastation avoided by flight. The day of judgment will arrive so suddenly and unexpectedly that absolutely no one will have the least warning. That is why vigilance and confident faith are required of the disciples and the Church. Correctly understood, the qualification "nor the Son" indicates that even Jesus had to live by faith and to make obedience and watchfulness the hallmark of his ministry.

Jesus recognized one exception to the true ignorance implied: "except the Father." The determination of the critical moment of intervention rests exclusively with him (cf. Acts 1:6-7). On this point the Father has not delegated his authority to anyone, not even to the Son. The one certainty the disciples may have is that the day will come when God will execute his decision to judge the world, and for that purpose he will send forth his Son with the hosts of angels (Ch. 8:38; 13:26 f.). The parousia and the judgment it will inaugurate are matters irrevocably decided. From this perspective the parousia is not conditioned by any other consideration than the sovereign decision of the Father, which remains enveloped with impenetrable mystery.[112]

33-36 The exhortations to vigilance which follow are linked to the fact that the critical moment remains unknowable. The connection with

---

[110] So A. L. Moore, *op. cit.*, pp. 133-135; J. Winandy, "Le Logion de l'Ignorance (Mc, xiii. 32; Mt, xxiv. 36)," *RB* 75 (1968), pp. 71-79.

[111] Cf. B. M. F. van Iersel, *op. cit.*, pp. 117-119.

[112] For an incisive exposition of the tension this introduces in Christian existence in terms of the eschatological motif and the grace motif see A. L. Moore, *op. cit.*, pp. 194-204.

verse 32 and with the brief parable which follows is underlined by reference to an ignorance of God's secret counsel:

verse 32 "No one knows that day or that hour . . . "
verse 33 "For you do not know the critical moment."
verse 35 "For you do not know when the lord of the household comes."

In the parallelism that is developed "that day or that hour," "the critical moment," and the moment of the householder's return are identical expressions for the same reality: the mysterious moment of the divine intervention, which cannot be foreseen. Because the moment of crisis is unknowable, unceasing vigilance is imperative.

This fact is illustrated by the parable of the absent householder, which is peculiar to Mark. A journeying master delegated authority to his servants and assigned each to his work, specifying that the doorkeeper is to watch.[113] These details recall a familiar early Christian pattern of exhortation stressing vigilance and an application of the vigilance concept to the Christian ministry in terms of work and labor.[114] The true servant will want to be actively engaged in his Master's service when he returns. The danger is "lest coming suddenly he find you sleeping" (verse 36). The imagery of a master who first leaves and then returns suddenly, which is integral to the call to watchfulness, is appropriate to the parousia and serves to make the content of "that day" precise. A subordinate feature of the parable is the reference to the four night-watches in verse 35b, which conforms to the Roman reckoning of time (in contrast to the Jewish practice of dividing the night into three watches).[115] As in Ch. 6:48, Mark has transmitted the tradition he received in a form which would be recognized as familiar to his readers.

37 This pregnant statement serves to recall verse 3, where the question which prompted the eschatological discourse was asked privately by

---

113 Cf. P. Joüon, "La parabole du portier qui doit veiller (Mc 13, 33-37) et la parabole des serviteurs qui doivent veiller (Lc 12, 35-40)," *RSR* 30 (1940), pp. 363-368.

114 See J. R. Michaels, *op. cit.*, pp. 63-92, 99-101.

115 See H. Kosmala, "The Time of Cock-Crow," *Annual of the Swedish Theological Institute* 2 (1963), pp. 119 f. For the suggestion that verse 35b programmatically anticipates Mark's chronology of the passion narrative cf. R. H. Lightfoot, *op. cit.*, pp. 48-59.

Peter, James, John and Andrew. The explicit extension of the exhortation to watch to a wider circle, which Mark undoubtedly understood to include the Christians of Rome, suggests that it was Jesus' intention to transcend any distinction between the disciples, to whom he delegated his authority (see on Ch. 6:7), and the Church at large. That which is primarily the duty of the disciple is secondarily the responsibility of the entire community. Each member has "his work" and by completing it he fulfills the obligation to watch.[116] Vigilance is the responsibility of every believer and provides the sole guarantee of preparedness for the Lord's return.

The imperative "take heed, be vigilant" in verse 33 and the related call to "watch" in verses 35, 37 furnish a climax to the exhortations of verses 5, 9, and 23. The stress upon vigilance sustained throughout the discourse suggests that the final call to watchfulness in verse 37 is not focused exclusively upon the last day, but like the previous admonitions, has bearing upon the continuing life of the Church during an age marked by false teachers, persecution and delay in the Lord's return. The phrase "to each his work" in verse 34 tends to strengthen this conclusion. When verses 33-37 are seen in the context of the entire discourse, it is evident that the vigilance of the Church may have as much reference to the perils from within and without delineated in verses 5-23 as to the climactic event of the parousia in verses 24-27.[117] The time of the appearing of the Son of Man in glory is unknown, but the fact that he will come is certain. The Church is called to live vigilantly in the certainty of that coming.

---

[116] J. R. Michaels, *op. cit.*, pp. 101 f., 202-245.

[117] *Ibid.*, pp. 104-107, where the relationship between Ch. 13:33-37 and John 10:1-5 is fruitfully explored.

CHAPTER 14

VII. The Passion Narrative. Ch. 14:1-15:47

In the Gospel of Mark the passion narrative serves to sharpen the perspective from which all of the incidents in Jesus' life and ministry are to be understood. The account of Jesus' betrayal, arrest, condemnation and execution furnishes a climax to the Gospel and brings together motifs and themes developed throughout the account. The conflict with authority, introduced as a matter of record already in Chs. 2:1-3:5, culminated in the decision to seek Jesus' death (Ch. 3:6), and this determination was only reinforced by the developments of the Jerusalem ministry (see on Chs. 11:18; 12:12). The capital offense of blasphemy, which provided the legal basis for Jesus' condemnation by the Sanhedrin (Ch. 14:63 f.), is entered as a charge as early as Ch. 2:7, while Judas is remembered as the one "who betrayed him" (Ch. 3:19) in the traditional list of the Twelve incorporated in Ch. 3:16-19. These notices are taken up and set in historical and theological perspective in the passion narrative.

It is commonly recognized that for Chs. 14-15 Mark had access to a primitive source, whether oral or written, embodying authentic historical remembrance, which he took over virtually intact. [1] He chose only to supplement it with parallel or complementary tradition and to orchestrate it for the development of certain themes. [2] Most of the pericopes found in the account cannot be isolated from their framework without

---

[1] See K. H. Schelkle, *Die Passion Jesu in der Verkündigung des Neuen Testaments. Ein Beitrag zur Formgeschichte und zur Theologie des Neuen Testaments* (Heidelberg, 1949); I. Buse, "St. John and the Marcan Passion Narrative," *NTS* 4 (1957-58), pp. 215-219; X. Léon-Dufour, "Passion (Récits de la)," *DB Suppl* VI (1960), col. 1419-1492. From the Pauline letters and the early sermons in Acts the following elements of the passion narrative may be recognized: Jesus was betrayed, arrested at night, led to the high-priest, condemned by Pilate, crucified. He died on the cross, was buried, was raised from the dead and his tomb was found empty. Cf. Acts 2:23-24; 3:13-15; 4:10; 5:30; 10:39 f.; 13:28-30; 17:3; 26:23; I Cor. 1:23 f.; 11:23-25; 15:3-5; Gal. 6:14; I Tim. 6:13.

[2] Mark's contribution may be seen in the incorporation of Ch. 14:3-9 (the anointing at Bethany); Ch. 14:12-17 (the preparation of the meal); Ch. 14:51 f. (the flight of the young man); Ch. 15:21 f. (Simon of Cyrene, the father of Alexander and Rufus); Ch. 15:43 (the courage of Joseph of Arimathea); Ch. 15:44 f. (the surprise of Pilate that Jesus was already dead).

serious loss. They acquire their significance from the context in which they are located. Indications of time and place, which occur more frequently than in earlier chapters, are usually so securely woven into the fabric of the narrative that they cannot be regarded as editorial links inserted by the evangelist in order to unite originally independent units of tradition. A purely historical preoccupation on the part of the early Church does not seem sufficient to account for the length or the detail of the primitive account. It seems certain that it was in the context of worship that the first elaborations of the essential facts took place.[3] The focus upon the night of the betrayal in the eucharist (cf. I Cor. 11:23) invited extended reflection upon the passion of Jesus, for the episodes which unfold from the prophecy of the betrayal (Ch. 14:18) to the crowing of the cock (Ch. 14:66-72) are unified by their situation in the night and seem to be centered upon liturgical remembrance. Moreover, the Epistle of the Apostles 15:26 (middle of the second century) speaks of a nocturnal vigil which lasts until dawn during which the passion of the Lord was remembered. It is necessary, however, to situate the development of the material in the total framework of early church life, its missionary outreach, its communal instruction, worship and liturgy, and its interaction with the rejection of its message by Judaism at large.

The primordial confession of faith in I Cor. 15:3-5, with its focus upon Jesus' death, burial and resurrection, provided the core of the narrative, which appears to have developed in two successive stages. A brief account of the principal events from the arrest to the resurrection must have existed from the first. In time this was replaced by a longer narrative which recounted the events which led up to the arrest as well. The facts presented were accompanied by a theological interpretation and the terminology itself was impregnated with faith.[4]

The briefer narrative was a kerygmatic presentation of events in the light of prophecy. This development was necessitated by the critical juncture at which the primitive community found itself. Judaism was totally unprepared for a suffering and crucified Messiah. The reaction of Peter when Jesus first announced his passion expresses precisely the

---

[3] Cf. G. Schille, "Das Leiden des Herrn. Die evangelische Passionstradition und ihr 'Sitz im Leben'," *ZThK* 52 (1955), pp. 161-205.

[4] See the treatment of ἀποδοκιμάζειν, παραδιδόναι, πάσχειν, ὥρα, καιρός in K. H. Schelkle, *op. cit.*, pp. 20 f., 70-78.

offense which the proclamation of the cross provoked (see on Ch. 8:31f.). The cross was for the Romans and all provincials an object of infamy. Compelled to justify the course of events, the Christians projected them in the light of the resurrection and the word of prophecy.

The events of the passion narrative owe their interest and their meaning to the resurrection. The evangelists have not reported the history of a death with a cold and detached tone; they invite the auditor to believe in a victory beyond that death. It is this fact of triumph over the grave which accounts for the presence of glory permeating the most humiliating facts. The account of Jesus' rejection and death was passed on by believers with a view to sharing their faith and to bringing faith to birth in others. What is fundamental is the fact of Easter, for the resurrection gave to history a new dimension and permitted the scandalous events which had taken place to be recalled without embarrassment.

Jesus himself had prepared his followers to find in the prophetic Scriptures the key to understanding his sufferings in fulfilment of the sovereign will of God (see on Chs. 8:31; 9:12, 31; 10:33f., 45). The passage that seems to have controlled the Christian interpretation of the events was the prophecy of the Servant of the Lord, and especially Isa. 53:4-12. Here was an account of obedient suffering, expressed by the sustaining of mockery, by silence before accusers, by forgiveness, by intercession for the many, by burial with the condemned, in short, a passion narrative which described the action of God which astounded the people but manifested his triumphant sovereignty.[5] A second group of passages which informed the church's understanding were the psalms of the suffering and victorious righteous one, and especially Psalms 22 and 69.[6] From such sources as these the meaning of the central events of the Christian message were set forth in biblical perspective, thus throwing into bold relief the accomplishment of the will of God.

---

[5] Cf. C. Maurer, "Knecht Gottes im Passionsbericht des Marcus-Evangeliums," *ZThK* 50 (1953), pp. 1-38; J. Jeremias, *TWNT* V (Eng. Tr. 1967), pp. 700-712; A. Vanhoye, "Structure et théologie des récits de la Passion dans les évangiles synoptiques," *Nouvelle Revue Théologique* 89 (1967), pp. 135-163.

[6] For a convenient table of references for the four Gospels see X. Léon-Dufour, *op. cit.*, col. 1430. For Mark he lists the following parallels: Ch. 14:18 (Ps. 41:9); 14:34 (Ps. 42:6); Ch. 15:24 (Ps. 22:18); 15:29 (Ps. 22:7); 15:32 (Ps. 69:9); 15:34 (Ps. 22:1); 15:36 (Ps. 69:21); 15:40 (Ps. 38:11). Cf. H. Gese, "Psalm 22 und das Neue Testament. Der älteste Bericht vom Tode Jesu und die Entstehung des Herrenmahles," *ZThK* 65 (1968), pp. 1-22.

The longer account extended this approach to the preliminary events [7] but also took account of Jesus' prophetic word. He had not only spoken of his coming burial (Ch. 14:8) but had prophesied the betrayal of Judas (Ch. 14:18), the denial of Peter and the desertion of the disciples (Ch. 14:27-31). His word of interpretation of the bread and the cup at the meal especially served to place his death in the context of God's redemptive provision for his people (Ch. 14:22-25).

Mark's arrangement of the narrative falls naturally into two parts. After the introduction of the complementary themes of the plot and the betrayal (Ch. 14:1-11), the evangelist focuses upon the suffering which came to Jesus through betrayal and desertion of those close to him (Ch. 14:12-52). This section consists of a cycle of three progressively ordered accounts centering in the meal (preparation of the meal, the announcement of betrayal, the meal and the interpretation of its elements), augmented by a second cycle describing the progressive realization of abandonment (the prophecy of denial, prayer alone, the arrest and desertion). The second part, emphasizing Jesus' endurance of suffering (Chs. 14:53-15:47), presents successively his judgment by the Jews who condemn him as Messiah (Ch. 14:53-65) and by Pilate who condemns him as King of the Jews (Ch. 15:1-20), followed by his crucifixion, death and burial (Ch. 15:21-47). Within this framework Mark expresses an intensely theological statement concerning Jesus' dignity and achievement. For the first time in this Gospel Jesus, before the Sanhedrin, affirms that he is the Messiah (Ch. 14:62), and it is of utmost significance to the evangelist that he is condemned to death by his contemporaries as the Messiah. In a parallel affirmation Jesus acknowledges before Pilate that he is a king (Ch. 15:1f.), and Mark insists on the fact that it is as King of the Jews that Jesus is sentenced to be crucified. Finally, at the moment of Jesus' death Mark alone among the evangelists brings together the torn veil of the Temple and the confession of the centurion that Jesus is truly Son of God (Ch. 15:38 f.). Here Judaism and the Gentile world, each in its own way, acknowledges Jesus' sovereign dignity. The Marcan passion narrative preserves the kerygmatic character of the primitive account celebrated in the worship and mission outreach of the early Church by exposing the profound redemp-

---

[7] See the suggestive article by F. W. Danker, "The Literary Unity of Mark 14, 1-25," *JBL* 85 (1966), pp. 467-472. Danker finds the literary unity of this section to derive from a creative interaction with Ps. 41 through which Jesus is seen to be the poor man *par excellence* who triumphs over his enemies.

tive efficacy of the death of the Son of God, who freely laid down his life on behalf of the many (see on Ch. 10:45). The reader finds himself confronted with this mystery and is invited to confess by faith that Jesus is the Messiah, the Son of God (Ch. 1:1).

1. The Plot to Seize Jesus. Ch. 14:1-2

1 Now after two days was the feast of the Passover and the unleavened bread: [8] and the chief priests and the scribes sought how they might take him with subtlety, [9] and kill him:
2 for they said, Not during the feast, [10] lest haply there should be a tumult of the people.

1-2 The passion narrative opens with a new note of time, consisting of an explicit reference to the Jewish festival calendar. It is important to observe that this reference has no necessary chronological link with the preceding sections in Mark, and it has been shown that Jesus had been in Jerusalem, apparently, for a period of weeks prior to the Passover (see above on Ch. 11:13, 15). It is proper to find here a new starting point in the narrative and the first of a series of temporal notes which give a degree of precision to the course of events which follow.

In this context "the Passover" designates the festival of redemption celebrated on the 14th of the month Nisan (April/May) and continuing into the early hours of the 15th (between sunset and midnight; cf. Exod. 12:6-20, 48; Num. 9:2-14; Deut. 16:1). This was followed immediately by the Feast of Unleavened Bread on the 15th-21st days of the month

---

[8] The reference to the feast of Unleavened Bread is omitted by D *a ff*[2], perhaps to simplify the text.

[9] Gr. ἐνδόλῳ, "by a stratagem," "by craftiness," is omitted by D *a i r*.

[10] The translation of ἐν τῇ ἑορτῇ is problematic, for ἐν may have a local rather than a temporal nuance. J. Jeremias, *The Eucharistic Words of Jesus*[3] (New York, 1966), pp. 71-73 has proposed the translation "in the presence of the festival crowd" and this suggestion has the support of Luke 22:6 ἄτερ ὄχλου ("in the absence of the multitude"). An alternative proposal urged by N. Turner, *Grammatical Insights in the New Testament* (Edinburgh, 1965), p. 67 is also worthy of consideration. Mark's fondness for parenthesis and the relatively frequent occurrence of the impersonal plural in the Gospel lead Turner to translate: "The chief priests and scribes sought how they might take him by craft and put him to death to avoid an uproar of the people (for the people said [ἔλεγον], 'Not on the feast day!')."

(Exod. 12:15-20; 23:15; 34:18; Deut. 16:1-8). In popular usage the two festivals were merged and treated for practical purposes as the seven-day "feast of the Passover."[11] The distinction between the two phases of the feast found in verse 1 is rarely attested in first-century Jewish sources but reflects OT practice (Lev. 23:3 f.; Num. 28:16 f.; II Chron. 35:1, 17; Ezra 6:19-22). Since the day on which the paschal lambs were sacrificed (the 14th of Nisan) was sometimes loosely designated "the first day of Unleavened Bread,"[12] it is difficult to determine whether the two days should be reckoned from the 15th or the 14th of Nisan. It is probable that the combined phrase indicates the 15th of Nisan, and that the reference here is to some time on the 13th of that month.

The conspiracy of certain of the chief priests and scribes to arrest Jesus and have him quietly put to death expressed an intention that had been nurtured for a long time (Chs. 3:6; 11:18; 12:12). Only the recognition of the popular favor Jesus enjoyed and the fear of an uprising kept them from their purpose. A stratagem was imperative if they were to preserve public order and avoid repressive measures imposed by Rome. During the festival seasons the population of the city swelled from *ca.* 50,000 to 250,000 persons. Demonstrations and riots could always be expected, especially on the part of the excitable Galileans, among whom were many potential supporters of Jesus. The reference in verse 2, then, is to the noise and confusion of an excited crowd, when mob fever, intensified by the hope of redemption associated with the Passover, could seize the people and the situation become uncontrollable.

According to Matt. 26:57 the conspirators gathered at the house of Caiaphas, the high priest, while John 11:47-53 indicates that it was he who pronounced the decisive word. The convergence of these two independent traditions on this detail is sufficient to confirm that it was Caiaphas who was the chief instigator of the plot against Jesus.

---

11 Cf. P. Billerbeck, "Das Passamahl," in S-B*K* IV (1928), pp. 41-76; J. Jeremias, *TWNT* V (Eng. Tr. 1967), pp. 896-900.

12 S-B*K* II (1924), pp. 813-815. Of the references listed J. Jeremias, *The Eucharistic Words of Jesus (op. cit.)*, p. 17 reduces the number to three: TB *Pesachim* 5a; TJ *Pesachim* I. 27a (30) and 27c (43 f.).

2. The Anointing in Bethany. Ch. 14:3-9

3 And while he was in Bethany in the house of Simon the leper, as he sat at meat, there came a woman having an alabaster cruse of ointment of pure[13] nard very costly; and she brake the cruse, and poured it over his head.
4 But there were some[14] that had indignation among themselves, saying, To what purpose hath this waste of the ointment been made?
5 For this ointment might have been sold for above three hundred shillings,[15] and given to the poor. And they murmured against her.
6 But Jesus said, Let her alone; why trouble ye her? she hath wrought a good work on me.[16]
7 For ye have the poor always with you, and whensoever ye will ye can do them good: but me ye have not always.
8 She hath done what she could; she hath anointed my body beforehand for the burying.
9 And verily I say unto you, Whensoever the gospel shall be preached throughout the whole world, that also which this woman hath done shall be spoken of for a memorial of her.

The anointing at Bethany is located in a context of opposition, misunderstanding and impending suffering. The chief priests and scribes are plotting to kill Jesus (Ch. 14:1f.) and Judas is conspiring with them (Ch. 14:10f.). It is probable that in the primitive version of the passion narrative preserved at Rome the report of Judas' faithlessness immediately followed the account of the plot to seize Jesus. The reference to the necessity for a stratagem in verse 1 clearly anticipates verses 10-11,

---

[13] Gr. πιστικῆς has been understood in the ASV as equivalent to πιστῆς (i.e. pure, unadulterated). More probably it should be recognized as a transliteration of the Aramaic פִּיסְתְּקָא, which denotes the pistachio nut, the oil of which was used as a base for costly ointments and perfumes. See M. Black, *An Aramaic Approach to the Gospels and Acts*[3] (Oxford, 1967), pp. 223-225.

[14] In the Western and Caesarean textual tradition it is specified that it was "certain of the disciples" (W φ l^{547} sy^{p}) or simply "the disciples" (D Θ 565 it arm) who disapproved the extravagance. So also Matt. 26:8.

[15] Gr. ἐπάνω δηναρίων τριακοσίων, roughly equivalent to the yearly wage of a day-laborer, since the average daily wage was calculated at a denarius (cf. Matt. 20:2).

[16] RSV "She has done a beautiful thing to me."

while the plot and the betrayal are complementary in intention. By interpolating the account of the anointing in Bethany within this framework[17] Mark achieved a dramatic contrast. The pure devotion of the anonymous woman throws into bold relief the hostility and treachery of the priests and their accomplice. It is further suggested that, at the time men were concerned with securing Jesus' death, Jesus' body was prepared for burial through an act which expressed faith and love.

3 The episode is situated in the village of Bethany on the Mount of Olives, nearly two miles from Jerusalem and the last station on the pilgrim road from Jericho to Jerusalem (see on Ch. 11:1). Throughout his stay in the city Jesus appears to have lodged at Bethany (Ch. 11:11f.). On this occasion he was entertained for a meal in the home of Simon the leper, who is introduced as someone who is well known (cf. Ch. 15:21). While he may have been familiar to some of Mark's readers, the origin of his nickname remains obscure. It is certain that he did not have leprosy at this time. If this incident is identical with the anointing reported in John 12:1-8, the anonymous woman who anointed Jesus may be recognized as Mary, the sister of Martha and Lazarus.[18]

The costly perfume is identified as nard, the aromatic oil extracted from a root native to India.[19] To retain the fragrance of nard, enough ointment for one application was sealed in small alabaster flasks. The long neck of the flask had to be broken to release the aroma.[20] Early in the first century Pliny the Elder (*Natural History* XIII. iii. 19) remarked that "the best ointment is preserved in alabaster." The value of the perfume, and its identification as nard, suggests that it was a family heirloom that was passed on from one generation to another, from mother to daughter. Anointing was a common custom at feasts (cf.

[17] H. Sahlin, "Zwei Fälle von harmonisierendem Einfluss des Matthäus-Evangeliums auf das Markus-Evangelium," *Stud Theol* 13 (1959), pp. 172-179 has argued that Ch. 14:3-9 originally came after Ch. 8:14-21 but was displaced under the influence of the Matthean arrangement of the tradition. There is no evidence to substantiate such a radical rearrangement. Moreover, the practice of intercalating one incident between two phases of a single action is typically Marcan. See above on Chs. 3:20-35; 5:21-43.

[18] The objection that John situates the anointing prior to the entry into Jerusalem is not serious. If Mark has intercalated Ch. 14:3-9 between Ch. 14:1f., 10f., the time reference in Ch. 14:1 cannot govern the occasion of the anointing.

[19] See S. A. Naber, "Νάρδος πιστική," *Mnemosyne* 30 (1902), pp. 1-15; W. H. Schoff, "Nard," *Journal of the American Oriental Society* 43 (1925), pp. 216-218.

[20] A. Veldheuzen, "De alabasten flesch," *ThSt* 24 (1906), pp. 170-172.

Ps. 23:5; 141:5; Luke 7:46), but in this context it is clear that the woman's action expressed pure devotion to Jesus and undoubtedly thanksgiving. In association with the banquet anointing suggested joy and festivity but Jesus found the significance of this act to be far more profound.

4-5 Those present who were indignant at this apparent display of extravagance were undoubtedly the disciples, for the words of Jesus in verses 6-9 are almost certainly addressed to them. The enormous value of the ointment prevented them from appreciating the lavishness of the woman's gift and they censured her. It was natural for them to think in terms of provision for the poor, for it was customary on the evening of Passover to remember the poor with gifts (M. *Pesachim* IX. 11; X. 1; cf. John 13:29).[21] It was also the practice to give as charity one part of the second tithe normally spent in Jerusalem during the feast.[22] The insensitivity of those with Jesus at the banquet table is yet another factor in his isolation from others as the hour of trial approaches, and is an integral part of Jesus' suffering.

6-8 Jesus' defense of the woman sets her act in perspective. He recognized in the generosity of her gift a beautiful expression of love which possessed a deeper significance than she could have possibly understood. The woman's gift was appropriate precisely because of the approaching hour of Jesus' death. F. W. Danker has shown that the meaning of the anointing may be understood in terms of the background provided by Ps. 41, which speaks of the poor but righteous sufferer and his ultimate triumph over his enemies.[23] Like the psalmist, Jesus is the poor but righteous sufferer who, though betrayed by his closest friend

---

[21] J. Jeremias, "Die Salbungsgeschichte Mc 14, 3-9," *ZNW* 35 (1936), pp. 75-82, and J. Bauer, *"Ut Quid Perditio Ista?* – zu Mk 14, 4 f. und Parr," *Nov Test* 3 (1959), pp. 54-56 have suggested that the indignant murmurers were concerned with the duty of almsgiving, while Jesus supported the priority of love above alms. This, however, is to miss the significance of Jesus' response in verses 6-7 and its background in Ps. 41.

[22] See S. Krauss, *Talmudische Archäologie* III (Berlin, 1912), pp. 63-74; M. Katz, "Protection of the Weak in the Talmud," *Columbia University Oriental Studies* 24 (1925), pp. 78-82; A. Cronbach, "The Social Ideas of the Apocrypha and the Pseudepigrapha," *HUCA* 18 (1944), pp. 119-156; E. Bammel, *TWNT* VI (Eng. Tr. 1968), pp. 888-903.

[23] *Art. cit.* in n. 7.

(cf. Ch. 14:18), is confident that God will raise him up and vindicate him. The woman, unlike the dinner guests, perceived that Jesus is the poor man *par excellence* and her deed may be construed as an act of loving kindness toward the poor. The quality for which Jesus commended her was her recognition that the needs of *this* poor sufferer, whom they do not always have, take precedence over the obligation to help the poor who will always be with them. This is emphasized in verse 7, where the contrast developed through an allusion to Deut. 15:11 is not between Jesus and the poor, but between "always" and "not always." The opportunity to benefit the impoverished continues to offer itself but the situation in which a profound expression of love could be extended to Jesus was confined to a fleeting moment. Jesus declared that the woman's act was a valid but proleptic anointing of his body for burial (verse 8). This pronouncement indicates that Jesus anticipated that he would suffer a criminal's death, for only in that circumstance would there be no anointing of the body. [24]

9 In Ps. 41:2 the one who pays heed to the poor has the assurance of blessing from the Lord. Those disciples who had championed the poor by suggesting that the proceeds from the sale of the ointment could be given to them might appear to qualify for such a benediction. It is the woman, however, who receives Jesus' praise for her response to the poor man above all others who is about to suffer for the people of God. By a solemn vow Jesus authoritatively dedicated the anointing to the remembrance of her deed before men. [25] The assurance that the gospel will be preached in the world looks beyond the humiliation of burial, mentioned in verse 8, to the vindication of resurrection which creates the NT concept of "the gospel." Jesus' word clearly reckons with a period between his death and the parousia during which the evangelical tradition would be openly proclaimed. The celebration of the risen Lord

---

24 Cf. D. Daube, "The Anointing at Bethany and Jesus' Burial," *AThR* 32 (1950), pp. 187 f. In the Gospel of Mark this is the only anointing of the body to which reference is made apart from the unfulfilled intention of Ch. 16:1.

25 J. Jeremias, "Mc 14, 9," *ZNW* 44 (1952-53), pp. 103-107, has argued that verse 9 refers not to the church's mission in the world but to the last judgment where the woman will be remembered by God. J. H. Greenlee, "εἰς μνημόσυνον αὐτῆς, 'For her memorial', Mt xxvi. 13; Mk xiv. 9," *ExT* 71 (1960), p. 245 understands the words to signify that the woman's deed served as *her* memorial *to Jesus* in view of his coming death. Against these proposals see the objections marshalled by A. L. Moore, *The Parousia in the New Testament* (Leiden, 1966), pp. 203 f.

would not erase the memory of this unnamed woman whose action anticipated Jesus' death and expressed her profound love for the Master. The incorporation of the tradition of the anointing within the Gospel already marks a fulfilment of Jesus' promise.

3. The Betrayal by Judas. Ch. 14:10-11

10 And Judas Iscariot,[26] he that was one of the Twelve, went away unto the chief priests, that he might deliver him unto them.
11 And they, when they heard it, were glad, and promised to give him money. And he sought how he might conveniently deliver him unto them.

10-11 By introducing the action of Judas at this point Mark sharpens the contrast between the selfless devotion of the woman and the treachery with which the righteous sufferer is greeted by his friend (cf. Ps. 41:9). The brief notice of the willingness of one of the Twelve to betray Jesus is joined to the plot mentioned in verses 1-2 by vocabulary and theme. The chief priests and scribes *were seeking* to arrest Jesus by a stratagem, while Judas *was seeking* an opportunity to hand him over. The primary concern of the Sanhedrin was the avoidance of a riot. The betrayal consisted in the offer to inform the chief priests of an opportunity to arrest Jesus without a public disturbance (cf. Luke 22:6 "in the absence of the crowd"). The offer was welcomed because Judas could lead the Temple guard to Jesus and would prevent any mistake in identity.

That Jesus' betrayer should be one of his own disciples remains enigmatic. No detail in the text permits more than conjecture concerning Judas' motive. With remarkable restraint Mark contents himself with recording the bare facts that Judas collaborated with the Sanhedrin, that he received payment for his services, and that he sought an oppor-

---

[26] For the meaning of Ἰσκαριώθ see above on Ch. 3:19. On Judas see D. Haugg, *Judas Iskarioth in den neutestamentlichen Berichten* (Freiburg, 1930); H. Preisker, "Der Verrat des Judas und das Abendmahl," *ZNW* 41 (1942), pp. 151-155; P. Benoit, "La mort de Judas" in *Synoptischen Studien A. Wikenhauser dargebracht* (Munich, 1953), pp. 1-19; G. Buchheit, *Judas Iskarioth. Legende, Geschichte, Deutung* (Gütersloh, 1954); B. Gärtner, "Judas Iskariot," *Sv Ex Års* 21 (1956), pp. 50-81.

tune moment for the arrest. Judas seems to have responded to an official notice that circulated in Jerusalem: "Now the chief priests had given orders that if anyone knew where he [i.e. Jesus] was, he should let them know, so that they might arrest him" (John 11:57). The need to employ an informer demonstrates how difficult it had become to locate Jesus and seize him in the period just before the Passover.[27]

4. THE PREPARATION OF THE MEAL. Ch. 14:12-16

12 And on the first day of unleavened bread, when they sacrificed[28] the passover,[29] his disciples say unto him, Where wilt thou that we go and make ready that thou mayest eat the passover?

13 And he sendeth two of his disciples, and saith unto them, Go into the city, and there shall meet you a man bearing a pitcher of water: follow him;

14 and wheresoever he shall enter in, say to the master of the house, The Teacher saith, Where is my guest-chamber, where I shall eat the passover with my disciples?

15 And he will himself show you a large upper room furnished[30] and ready: and there make ready for us.

16 And the disciples went forth and came into the city, and found as he had said unto them: and they made ready the passover.

12 A new temporal reference introduces a cycle of tradition centering in the meal commonly designated the Last Supper. The "first day of

---

[27] Cf. E. Stauffer, *Jesus and His Story* (New York, 1960), p. 112: "It may be that Judas, the non-Galilean, had for months been a secret agent of the Jerusalem Sanhedrin assigned to work among the Galilean's disciples. At any rate, he regarded the capture of the man who had been proclaimed a blasphemer and pseudo-prophet (John 11:57) as his bounden duty. For he took an oath pledging himself to commit the betrayal–an oath that may well have included a curse upon himself should he fail to carry out the task he had undertaken."

[28] The indefinite plural and imperfect tense of ἔθυον is better expressed by the rendering "it was customary to sacrifice."

[29] Gr. πάσχα here means "the paschal lamb" in distinction from verse 1 where it denotes the feast day itself. Cf. RSV "when they sacrificed the passover lamb." In verses 12b, 14b and 16b πάσχα designates the passover meal during which the roasted lamb was consumed.

[30] Gr. ἐστρωμένον may have reference to a "paved" or "paneled" room. See W. Bauer[4] (A-G, p. 799).

Unleavened Bread" would ordinarily denote the 15th of Nisan following the celebration of the Passover the previous evening. There is some evidence in the rabbinical literature, however, that the day on which the paschal lambs were sacrificed (the 14th of Nisan) was sometimes loosely designated "the first day of Unleavened Bread." It is necessary, therefore, to interpret the temporal clause in verse 12 in terms of the precision given to it by reference to the slaughter of the passover lambs on the afternoon of Nisan 14.[31]

The chronological note in verse 12 clearly implies that the meal which Jesus celebrated with his disciples was the Passover and that the day of his arrest, condemnation and crucifixion was the 15th of Nisan. The Fourth Gospel, however, appears to situate Jesus' death in the framework of the preparation for the Passover on the 14th of Nisan (John 18:28; 19:14, 31, 42), which would mean that the meal could not have been the Passover. The resolution of this difficulty is one of the most difficult issues in passion chronology.

There are a number of positive elements in the Marcan narrative which substantiate that the Last Supper was a Passover meal. The return to Jerusalem in the evening for the meal (Ch. 14:17) is significant, for the paschal meal had to be eaten within the city walls (M. *Pesachim* VII. 9). An ordinary meal was taken in the late afternoon, but a meal which begins in the evening and continues into the night reflects Passover practice (Exod. 12:8; Jubilees 49:12). The reference to reclining (Ch. 14:18) satisfies a requirement of the Passover feast in the first century when custom demanded that even the poorest man recline for the festive meal (M. *Pesachim* X. 1). While a normal meal began with the breaking of bread, on this occasion Jesus broke the bread during the meal and following the serving of a dish (Ch. 14:18-20, 22). The Passover meal was the one occasion when the serving of a dish preceded the breaking of bread. The use of wine was generally reserved for festive occasions and was characteristic of the Passover (M. *Pesachim* X. 1). Finally, the interpretation of the elements of the meal conforms to Passover custom where the haggadah (or interpretation) is an integral part of the meal.[32] The cumulative evidence supports the claim made in

---

[31] J. Jeremias, *The Eucharistic Words of Jesus*[3] *(op. cit.),* pp. 17 f. The defining of a time reference by a qualifying clause is common in Mark: Chs. 1:32, 35; 4:35; 13:24; 14:30; 15:42; 16:2.

[32] *Ibid.,* pp. 49-61; J. Behm, *TWNT* III (Eng. Tr. 1965), pp. 732-734. G. Ogg, "The Chronology of the Last Supper," in *Historicity and Chronology in the New Testament* (London, 1965), pp. 84-86 concludes that these considerations do not

verses 12, 14 and 16 that the disciples prepared a Passover meal and that the external forms of the Passover were observed at the meal itself.

There are indications that the Fourth Evangelist also regarded the meal which Jesus shared with his disciples as a Passover. The feast takes place within Jerusalem even though the city was thronged with pilgrims (John 12:12, 18, 20; 13:2; 18:1; cf. Mark 14:17). The supper is held in the evening and lasts into the night (John 13:30; cf. Mark 14:17). The meal was ceremonial in character and the participants reclined at table (John 13:12, 23, 25, 28; cf. Mark 14:18). Finally, the walk to Gethsemane followed by the betrayal conforms to the Marcan sequence of events (John 18:1 ff.; Mark 14:26 ff.). In this light it seems that the concern of the priests expressed in John 18:28, that they should not become defiled and so be prohibited from eating "the *pesach*," has reference not to the paschal lamb (which would have been eaten the evening before) but to the *chagigah*, the paschal sacrifices (lambs, kids, bulls) which were offered throughout the festival week. These paschal sacrifices are designated by the term *pesach* in Deut. 16:2 and II Chron. 35:7. If this understanding informed the tradition John has transmitted, the apparent contradiction with the evidence of Mark is removed.[33]

---

demand a Passover understanding. They do, however, demand that Jesus imposed a paschal framework upon the meal.

33 On this understanding the phrase παρασκευὴ τοῦ πάσχα in John 19:14 should not be translated "the Preparation of the Passover" (ASV, RSV) but "the Friday of the Passover week." For παρασκευή, meaning "Friday," cf. Matt. 27:62; Mark 15:42; Luke 23:54; John 19:31; Didache 8. See further J. Jeremias, *op. cit.*, pp. 80 f.

An alternative thesis, involving a three-day passion chronology, has been proposed by Mlle. A. Jaubert: "La date de la dernière Cène," *Revue de l'Histoire des Religions* 146 (1954), pp. 140-173; *idem*, "Jésus et le calendrier de Qumrân," *NTS* 7 (1960-61), pp. 1-30; *idem*, "Les séances du Sanhédrin et les récits de la passion," *Revue de l'Histoire des Religions* 166 (1964), pp. 143-169; 167 (1965), pp. 1-33; *idem*, *The Date of the Last Supper* (Staten Island, 1965); *idem*, "Le mercredi où Jésus fut livré," *NTS* 14 (1968), pp. 145-164. She holds that Jesus was arrested on the Tuesday night preceding the Friday of the crucifixion. The Last Supper, therefore, took place on Tuesday evening in conformity with the prescriptions of the ancient liturgical calendar (based on solar reckoning) attested in the book of Jubilees and at Qumran. This understanding is reflected in the Synoptic Gospels, she contends, while the references in the Fourth Gospel are to the official (lunar) calendar. This proposal has attractive features and has won wide support, but serious objections remain to its acceptance. Chief among these are the following: (i) there is no evidence that Jesus ever followed the ancient sectarian calendar on other festival occasions. (ii) The priests were the masters of the Temple and exercised control over all that had to do with the sacrificing of the paschal victims.

13-16 The episode of the preparation of the paschal meal is parallel in structure with Ch. 11:1-7. The commissioning of two disciples for the performance of a task, the precise knowledge of what they would encounter, and the exact response to be given to the responsible party are features familiar from the earlier account. The two incidents are entirely independent but they have been described according to a common scheme.

While in verse 12 the disciples took the initiative to ask where they should prepare the meal, it is evident that Jesus had made careful advance arrangements. The reference to a man carrying a jar of water who was to be followed to a house suggests a prearranged signal, for ordinarily only women carried water in jars. It would be normal to find a man carrying a wineskin. A sufficient reason for resorting to a means of recognition which would require no exchange of words in the street may be found in the determined search for Jesus and the issuance of a warrant for his arrest implied in John 11:57. Jesus, therefore, commissioned two of the disciples to make the necessary preparations, having engaged an upstairs room where he could celebrate the Passover with his disciples undisturbed. [34] It may be assumed that the owner of the house was a man of courage who had determined to shelter the

---

Even if a company wished to celebrate the feast on a day other than that fixed officially by the Sanhedrin, they would scarcely have had the opportunity to follow their convictions. All were obliged to celebrate the Passover at the official time or to abstain from observing it altogether. (iii) The four evangelists are unanimous that the Last Supper and the arrest took place on the eve of the crucifixion. (iv) The evidence furnished by the *Didascalia* for the Tuesday date of the meal is late and confused, belonging at the earliest to the third century A.D. In fact, of the texts favoring the Tuesday date for the Supper only four expressly speak of Wednesday in connection with the passion, and these originate in a liturgical source intent on justifying a practice of fasting on Wednesday. See further the detailed criticism of G. Ogg in a lengthy review, *Nov Test* 3 (1959), pp. 149-160; J. Blinzler, "Qumran-Kalender und Passionschronologie," *ZNW* 49 (1958), pp. 238-251; E. Kutsch, "Der Kalender des Jubiläenbuches und das Alte und das Neue Testament," *Vetus Testamentum* 11 (1961), pp. 39-47 among others.

[34] E. Stauffer, *op. cit.*, pp. 113-117 argues that there was no lamb on this occasion because Jesus had been condemned as an apostate Jew and as such was forbidden to eat the paschal lamb (although he could share in the bitter herbs and the greens). There is, however, no reason to believe that Jesus would have concurred in the judgment of the Sanhedrin and submitted to its mandate. He presumably sent two of the disciples into the city because they were less well known to the priests than he was and they would have no trouble securing all that was required for the meal.

"heretic" Galilean and his outlawed company of followers. He may have been the one who arranged for the lamb to be sacrificed and who secured the other requirements for the meal. The upstairs rooms would probably be furnished with carpets or couches for the guests to recline on as they ate the meal.

When the disciples entered the city they found that Jesus' instructions were precise, and they prepared the meal. This would include the setting out of the unleavened bread and the wine, the preparation of the bitter herbs and sauce consisting of dried fruit, spices and wine, and presumably the roasting of the passover lamb.

5. The Announcement of the Betrayal. Ch. 14:17-21

17 And when it was evening he cometh with the Twelve.
18 And as they sat [35] and were eating, Jesus said, Verily I say unto you, One of you shall betray me, even he that eateth with me.
19 They began to be sorrowful, and to say unto him one by one, Is it I? [36]
20 And he said unto them, It is one of the twelve, he that dippeth [37] with me in the dish. [38]
21 For the Son of Man goeth, even as it is written of him: but woe unto that man through whom the Son of Man is betrayed! good were it for that man [39] if he had not been born.

17 Since the Jewish day was reckoned from sunset to sunset, the evening marked the beginning of the 15th of Nisan. The Passover meal, which in distinction from ordinary meals began only after sunset and

[35] Gr. ἀνακειμένων should be translated "reclined," so as not to obscure that this requirement of the Passover meal was satisfied.

[36] Gr. μήτι ἐγώ implies a negative answer: "It isn't I, surely?" In the Byzantine and Western textual traditions the response of the disciples is intensified by the addition καὶ ἄλλος· μήτι ἐγώ; perhaps in tacit allusion to Judas.

[37] The reference is to dipping bread and bitter herbs into the bowl of stewed fruit. Cf. RSV, "one who is dipping bread with me." Mark apparently chose to reserve the reference to the unleavened bread to the words of institution in verse 22.

[38] It seems proper to read ἕν (with B C* Θ 565) before τρύβλιον: "in the *same* bowl." To dip one's hand into the bowl together with someone is to share one's meal with him. The expression thus heightens the baseness of the betrayal.

[39] The idiom is more clearly expressed in the RSV: "It would be better for that man if he had not been born."

could last until midnight, had to be eaten within the walls of Jerusalem. Jesus therefore returned to the city after sundown to share the paschal feast commemorating God's deliverance of his people from bondage with the Twelve. The celebration of the Passover was always marked by excitement and the high hope that it would be fulfilled by God's intervention once more. It was observed as "a night of watching unto the Lord" (Exod. 12:42) in the conviction that "in that night they were redeemed and in that night they will be redeemed in the future."[40] Jesus came to the city fully aware that he was to accomplish the Passover in his own person.

The meal was framed within a liturgy whose core was the Passover prayer of the family head and the recitation of the Hallel psalms (Ps. 113-118). When those participating had taken their places, the head of the house began the celebration by pronouncing a blessing, first of the festival and then of the wine (M. *Pesachim* X. 2).[41] Then the paschal company drank the first cup of wine. After this the food was brought in, consisting of unleavened bread, bitter herbs, greens, stewed fruit and roast lamb (M. *Pesachim* X. 3). The son then asked why this night, with its special customs and food, was distinguished from all other nights (M. *Pesachim* X. 4). The family head responded by recalling the biblical account of the redemption from Egypt. This instruction led naturally into the praise of God for the salvation he had provided and the anticipation of future redemption: "So may the Lord, our God, and the God of our fathers, cause us to enjoy the feasts that come in peace, glad of heart at the upbuilding of your city and rejoicing in your service . . . and we shall thank you with a new song for our redemption" (M. *Pesachim* X. 4-6). The new song was the first part of the ancient Hallel (Ps. 113-115), after which a second cup of wine was drunk. Then the head of the house took bread and pronounced over it the blessing of "the Lord our God, Sovereign of the world, who has caused bread to come forth out of the earth" (M. *Berachoth* VI. 1). He then broke the bread in pieces and handed it to those who were at the table, who ate it with the bitter herbs and stewed fruit. Only then did the meal really

---

40 *Mekilta* to Exod. 12:42, XIV. 20a (ed. J. Z. Lauterbach, I [1935], p. 115), where the saying is attributed to R. Jehoshua' b. Ḥananya, *ca.* A.D. 90. Cf. Targum Jerusalem I to Exod. 12:42, "The Messiah who is called 'First' (Isa. 41:27), will come in the first month" (i.e. Nisan); Exod. Rabba XV. 2 to Exod. 12:2.

41 The form of the first blessing is uncertain, but a form for all festivals, based on TB *Berachoth* 49a, may be found in S-B*K* IV (1928), p. 62. The form of the second blessing is preserved in M. *Berachoth* VI. 1; TB *Pesachim* 103a, 106a.

begin with the eating of the roasted lamb, and this was not to extend beyond midnight (M. *Pesachim* X. 9). When the meal had been completed, the head of the family blessed the third cup with a prayer of thanksgiving. There followed the singing of the second part of the Hallel (Ps. 116-118) and the drinking of the fourth cup, which concluded the Passover (M. *Pesachim* X. 7).[42]

In the verses which follow Mark concentrates all of his attention upon two incidents which marked the meal: the moment of the dipping of the bread and the bitter herbs in the bowl of stewed fruit when Jesus spoke of his betrayal (verses 18-21), and the interpretation of the bread and the third cup of wine following the meal itself (verses 22-25).

18-20 The festivity of the meal was shattered when Jesus, with a solemn "Amen," announced that one of those sharing the intimacy of the table-fellowship would betray him. The explanatory words "one who is eating with me" set the pronouncement in the context of Ps. 41:9, where the poor but righteous sufferer laments that his intimate friend whom he trusted and who ate his bread had "lifted his heel" against him.[43] The repeated reference to the inner circle ("one of you," verse 18 and "one of the Twelve," verse 20) and the question "is it I?" expressed by each in turn (verse 19) serve only to intensify the importance of the explanatory clause "one who is eating with me." This is especially apparent in the climactic character of verse 20, which is parallel in form to the pronouncement in verse 18:

Verse 18	*Verse 20*
One of you will betray me, one who is eating with me.	One of the Twelve, one who is dipping with me in the same bowl.

---

[42] See further G. Beer, "Zur Geschichte des Paschafestes," in his edition of *Die Mischna* II *Seder Moëd,* 3. *Traktat Pesachim* (Giessen, 1912), pp. 1-109; T. H. Gaster, *Passover: Its History and Traditions* (New York, 1949); J. B. Segal, *The Jewish Passover from the Earliest Times to A.D. 70* (London, 1963); N. Füglister, *Die Heilsbedeutung des Pascha* (Munich, 1963).

[43] A. Suhl, *Die Funktion der alttestamentlichen Zitate und Anspielungen im Markus-evangelium* (Gütersloh, 1965), pp. 51 f. labels the allusion to Ps. 41:9 "unmistakable," but cautions that the emphasis does not fall on fulfilment as such. Rather the allusion serves to stress the divine will in all that Jesus experiences.

The explicit reference to the dipping of the bread in the bowl of stewed fruit in verse 20 serves to reinforce the allusion to Ps. 41:9.[44] In the timing of Jesus' pronouncement the incongruity of Judas' intention with the intimacy of the paschal fellowship would be apparent to all who were present.[45] Jesus' generosity in sharing this sacred meal with his intimate friends thus stands in contrast to the hypocrisy of the traitor sketched in verses 10-11 and serves to recall the mistreatment of the poor sufferer in Ps. 41.

21 One of the major themes of Ps. 41 is the assurance of ultimate triumph over his enemies' intentions that is given to the righteous sufferer (Ps. 41:10-12). The woe pronounced upon Judas is in line with this expectation, and expresses profound sorrow and pity. In contrast to the blessing of the woman who wins a lasting memorial in accordance with the promise of Ps. 41:2 (Ch. 14:9), Judas is assured of a contrary recompense (cf. Ps. 41:10).[46] There is no vindictiveness in the pronouncement, for the recognition that the approaching death of the Son of Man is in harmony with Scripture serves to set the result of Judas' treachery within the context of God's design.[47] The heinousness of Judas' action, however, is not excused. While the Son of Man goes to his death in accordance with the divine plan, on the other hand it were better for his betrayer had he never been born. The purpose of Jesus' poignant warning is not primarily to affirm the fate of Judas but to underscore his own assurance of vindication. Nevertheless, the betrayer is morally responsible for his action and for the horrible character of its consequences, both for Jesus and for himself.

It is remarkable that Judas is not mentioned by name in the account. He is not introduced as one who asked "is it I?" nor is he identified as the betrayer by Jesus (cf. Matt. 26:25), and there is no reference to the fact that he left the room before the interpretation of the significance of the meal (cf. John 13:26-30). In Mark the stress falls rather upon

---

[44] F. W. Danker, *op. cit.*, pp. 470 f.

[45] Cf. F. C. Fensham, "Judas' Hand in the Bowl and Qumran," *Rev Qum* 5 (1965), pp. 259-261, where it is suggested that the words "with me" indicate that Judas stretched forth his hand at the same moment as Jesus in a gesture declaring that he rejected Jesus' leadership.

[46] F. W. Danker, *op. cit.*, p. 472.

[47] For the suggestion that the Scriptural background is provided by Ezek. 12:1-16 in Targum form see J. Christensen, "Le fils de l'homme s'en va, ainsi qu'il est écrit de lui," *Stud Theol* 10 (1956), pp. 28-39.

the violation of the paschal fellowship by the presence of a traitor who must bear the onus of responsibility for his act, and upon Jesus' knowledge that he will be betrayed by one of the Twelve and that his death is certain. This latter emphasis is set in the perspective of God's redemptive action by the words of institution and the solemn oath which follow in verses 22-25.

6. The Institution of the Lord's Supper. Ch. 14:22-26

22 And as they were eating, he took bread,[48] and when he had blessed, he brake it, and gave to them, and said, Take ye: this is my body.[49]
23 And he took a cup, and when he had given thanks, he gave to them: and they all drank of it.
24 And he said unto them, This is my blood of the covenant,[50] which is poured out for many.

---

[48] It has sometimes been objected that ἄρτος cannot refer to the unleavened bread required by the Passover. See, however, the full treatment of the evidence in the M.T., LXX, Philo and the Mishna in J. Jeremias, *op. cit.*, pp. 63-66, where it is shown that the objection is unfounded. Cf. Exod. 25:30; Lev. 24:7; I Sam. 21:6 LXX and Mk. 2:26).

[49] Codex Bobiensis (*k*), which provides a witness to the earliest Latin VS as used by Cyprian, reads: "... he took bread and pronounced the blessing and broke (it) and gave (it) to them, and they all ate of it; and he said to them 'This is my body.' And he took a cup and pronounced the blessing and gave (it) to them, and they all drank of it; and he said to them, 'This is my blood' ..." The parallelism in the clause that "they all ate" and "they all drank" is a strong argument in favor of the primitiveness of this text. In Mt. 26:26, 28 these statements have been replaced by the liturgical direction "Take, eat" and "Take, drink." It is possible that the formulation of Mk. 14:24, as preserved for us apart from the unique witness of MS *k,* has been brought into harmony with the corresponding passage, Mt. 26:26. If MS *k* preserves the original form of the Marcan text the stress falls on an essential feature of the proceedings, that all ate from one loaf and all drank from one cup. Cf. I Cor. 10:16-17. For a defense of this reading see C. H. Turner, "Western Readings in the Second Half of St. Mark's Gospel," *JThS* 29 (1928), p. 10.

[50] The influence of related liturgical texts (Lk. 22:20; I Cor. 11:25) accounts for the reference to the "new" covenant in the Byzantine textual tradition (cf. AV "the new testament"). In Ch. 14:24 the reading "covenant," without qualification, is well attested (א B C D L W Θ Ψ 565 *d k* cop geo[1]) and should be followed. It has been held that the expression "my blood of the covenant" cannot be primitive because Aramaic does not tolerate a genitive after a noun with a pronominal suffix. This construction, however, is adequately attested in Syriac and examples are found in the Targum to Ps. 68:36; 110:3. See H. Gottlieb, "TO AIMA MOY

25 Verily I say unto you, I shall no more drink of the fruit of the vine,[51] until that day when I drink it new in the kingdom of God.
26 And when they had sung a hymn, they went out unto the mount of Olives.

22 The interpretation of detailed elements in the meal was a fixed part of the Passover liturgy conducted by the head of the household. This occurred after the meal had been served but before it was eaten. When Jesus lifted the platter of unleavened bread he may be presumed to have spoken the Aramaic formula prescribed in the liturgy: "This is the bread of affliction which our fathers ate in the land of Egypt. Let everyone who hungers come and eat; let everyone who is needy come and eat the Passover meal."[52] Each of the other elements was also introduced in the context of Israel's experience in bondage. The bitter herbs served to recall the bitterness of slavery, the stewed fruit, which possessed the consistency and color of clay, evoked the making of bricks as slaves, while the paschal lamb provided a reminder of God's gracious "passing over" of Israel in the plague of death that came to Egypt. While the wording of Jesus' paschal devotions has not been preserved, it is evident that the disciples were prepared for understanding the significance of the words of institution preserved in verses 22-24 by the manner in which Jesus interpreted the components of the meal.

The blessing of God for the gift of bread immediately preceded the meal itself. The head of the family sat up from his reclining position, took a cake of unleavened bread, and recited the blessing over it in the name of all: "Praised be Thou, O Lord, Sovereign of the world, who causes bread to come forth from the earth" (M. *Berachoth* VI. 1). Those present identified themselves with the blessing by saying "Amen." The family-head then broke for each person present a piece and gave it to him, the bread passing from hand to hand until it reached all the guests.

ΤΗΣ ΔΙΑΘΗΚΗΣ," *Stud Theol* 14 (1960), pp. 115-118; J. A. Emerton, "Mark XIV. 24 and the Targum to the Psalter," *JThS* 15 (1964), pp. 58 f.; J. E. David, "τὸ αἷμά μου τῆς διαθήκης, Mt. 26:28: un faux problème," *Biblica* 48 (1967), pp. 291 f.

51 For a discussion and evaluation of the Semitic idiom retained in the variant reading οὐ μὴ προσθῶ πιεῖν found in Western and Caesarean witnesses (D Θ 565 *a f* arm) see B. M. Metzger, *The Text of the New Testament* (New York, 1964), pp. 233 f.

52 N. Glatzer (ed.), *The Passover Haggadah* (New York, 1953), p. 20.

The distribution normally took place in silence, for the explanation of the elements belonged to the Passover devotions, not to the grace before the meal. Contrary to paschal custom, Jesus broke the silence by interpreting the significance of the bread in terms of his own person.

In the course of the Passover, Jesus' word and action with the bread was independent from the word spoken over the cup. The two sayings were originally separated from each other by the sharing of the main body of the meal, and they must be expounded separately. In the figurative saying about the bread, Jesus was not referring to his physical body as such, but to himself. He said: "I am myself this (bread)" or "my person is this (bread)," [53] providing a pledge of his personal presence with them that was to be recalled whenever they broke bread together. The essential action which accompanied this word was not the breaking of the bread, but its distribution. [54] As certainly as the disciples eat the bread which Jesus hands to them, so certainly will he be present with them when they gather for table-fellowship. Jesus' first gift to the disciples was the pledge of his abiding presence with them in spite of his betrayal and death. The first word thus anticipates the resurrection and the real presence of the Lord at the celebration of the eucharist.

23-24 Following the main meal (cf. I Cor. 11:25), the head of the household rose again from his reclining position and exhorted those present to "Speak praises to our God, to whom belongs what we have eaten," to which those present replied, "Praised be our God for the food we have eaten." With his right hand he then took the third cup of red wine mixed with water, and with his eyes on the cup pronounced the prayer of thanksgiving on behalf of all, with the concluding words: "May the All-merciful One make us worthy of the days of the Messiah and of the life of the world to come. He brings the salvation of his king. He shows covenant-faithfulness to his Anointed, to David and to his seed forever. He makes peace in his heavenly places. May he secure peace for us and for all Israel. And say you, Amen." [55] After the company had affirmed

---

[53] So J. Behm, *TWNT* III (Eng. Tr. 1965), p. 736, where the term behind σῶμα is apparently גּוּפִי.

[54] *Ibid.*, p. 735; H. N. Ridderbos, *The Coming of the Kingdom* (Philadelphia, 1962), p. 429. The state of brokenness is not peculiar to this bread, for the ordinary daily meal began with the breaking of bread. A reference in the broken bread to Jesus' violent death is not in harmony with the situation.

[55] N. Glatzer, *op. cit.*, p. 27.

their participation in the blessing with their "Amen," Jesus passed the common cup from which all were to drink, and spoke the second word of institution.

Jesus' saying relates the cup with the red wine to the renewal of the covenant between God and his people. While the word concerning the bread simply promises that Jesus will be with his followers, the primary reference here is to Jesus' blood shed in the context of covenant sacrifice.[56] The allusion to his violent death in the redness of the wine and the reference to the shedding of blood are unmistakable. Yet the cup, whose wine represents Jesus' blood, provides assurance to the disciples that they share in the new divine order which is inaugurated through his death. The cup is thus the pledge that when the people of God meet in table-fellowship, their Master, who goes to his death, is present with the fulness of salvation achieved by this death on behalf of "the many."

The reference to the covenant established in Jesus' blood contains an allusion to Exod. 24:6-8, where the old covenant at Sinai was ratified by the sprinkling of sacrificial blood, and serves to set the whole of Jesus' messianic action in the light of covenant renewal. It also evokes Jer. 31:31-33 where God promises to establish a new covenant with his people in the last days. That promise is now sealed through Jesus' action and the death it anticipates. The saying over the cup directs attention to Jesus as the one who fulfills the divine will to enter into covenant fellowship with his people on a new and enduring basis. The latter part of the saying explains the vicarious character of Jesus' death in terms of Isa. 53:12 and calls to mind the similar formulation of Ch. 10:45.[57] The "many" are the redeemed community who have experienced the remission of their sins in and through Jesus' sacrifice and so are enabled to participate in the salvation provided under the new covenant. Jesus' second gift to his disciples, then, is the assurance that he will be with them as their Savior who establishes the new order through his death. He freely yields his life in order that God's will to save his people may be effected. By his prophetic action in interpreting these familiar parts of the ancient paschal liturgy Jesus instituted something new in which the

---

[56] Cf. E. F. Siegman, "The Blood of the Covenant," *American Ecclesiastical Review* 136 (1957), pp. 167-174; B. Cooke, "Synoptic Presentation of the Eucharist as Covenant Sacrifice," *Theological Studies* 21 (1960), pp. 1-44.

[57] Cf. J. Betz, "Die Eucharistie als sakramentale Gegenwart der Heilsereignisses Jesu nach dem ältesten Abendmahlsberichte," *Geist und Leben* 33 (1960), pp. 166-175.

bread and wine of table-fellowship become the pledge of his saving presence throughout the period of time prior to the parousia and the establishment of the Kingdom of God in its fulness.

25 Jesus' words of promise were confirmed with a solemn oath that he would not share the festal cup until the meal was resumed and completed in the consummation. The sober reference "no more" indicates that this is Jesus' final meal and lends to the situation the character of a farewell. The purpose of his vow of abstinence was to declare that his decision to submit to the will of God in vicarious suffering was irrevocable. [58] Forswearing feasting and wine, Jesus dedicated himself with a resolute will to accept the bitter cup of wrath offered to him by the Father. Yet there is here a clear anticipation of the messianic banquet when the Passover fellowship with his followers will be renewed in the Kingdom of God. [59] Then Jesus will drink the wine "new," where in this context newness is the mark of the redeemed world and the time of ultimate redemption. The reference to "that day" envisions the parousia and the triumph of the Son of Man (see above on Ch. 13:24-27, 32; cf. I Cor. 11:26). Thus in the context of reflecting upon his violent death on behalf of the many, and just prior to the impending events of the passion, Jesus clearly affirmed his vindication and the establishment of an uninterrupted fellowship between the redeemed community and its Redeemer through the experience of messianic salvation.

The cup from which Jesus abstained was the fourth, which ordinarily concluded the Passover fellowship. [60] The significance of this can be appreciated from the fact that the four cups of wine were interpreted in terms of the four-fold promise of redemption set forth in Exod. 6:6-7: "I will bring you out . . . I will rid you of their bondage . . . I will redeem you . . . I will take you for my people and I will be your God" (TJ *Pesachim* X. 37b). Jesus had used the third cup, associated with the promise of redemption, to refer to his atoning death on behalf of the elect community. The cup which he refused was the cup of consummation, associated with the promise that God will take his people to be with him. This is the cup which Jesus will drink with his own in the messianic

---

[58] J. Jeremias, *op. cit.*, pp. 207-218.

[59] Cf. *idem, Jesus' Promise to the Nations* (Naperville, Ill., 1958), pp. 55-73.

[60] Cf. D. Daube, *The New Testament and Rabbinic Judaism* (London, 1956), pp. 330 f.

banquet which inaugurates the saving age to come. The cup of redemption (verse 24), strengthened by the vow of abstinence (verse 25), constitutes the solemn pledge that the fourth cup will be extended and the unfinished meal completed in the consummation, when Messiah eats with redeemed sinners in the Kingdom of God (cf. Lk. 14:15; Rev. 3:20f.; 19:6-9).

26 Among devout Jews it was common to remain together at the table for several hours after the conclusion of the meal, deep in conversation about God's past and future acts of redemption (Tos. *Kethubim* V. 5). The table-fellowship was concluded by the recitation of the second half of the Hallel Psalms. It was customary to sing the Hallel antiphonally, one member of the table company chanting the text, and the others responding to each half verse with the shout of praise, "Hallelujah." Jesus took the words of these psalms as his own prayer of thanksgiving and praise. He pledged to keep his vows in the presence of all the people (Ps. 116:12-19); he called upon the Gentiles to join in the praise of God (Ps. 117); and he concluded with a song of jubilation reflecting his steadfast confidence in his ultimate triumph: "I shall not die, but live, and declare the works of the Lord" (Ps. 118:17). In the assurance that the rejected stone had been made the keystone by God's action Jesus found a prophecy of his own death and exaltation (see above on Ch. 8:31; 12:10f.). When Jesus arose to go to Gethsemane, Ps. 118 was upon his lips. It provided an appropriate description of how God would guide his Messiah through distress and suffering to glory.

Late in the night Jesus and the disciples left the city, perhaps in discrete groups so as not to be conspicuous. They crossed the Kidron valley and began the ascent to the Mount of Olives where the affirmations of the Passover would be tested for their integrity.

7. The Prophecy of Failure and Denial. Ch. 14:27-31

27 And Jesus saith unto them, All ye shall be offended: [61] for it is written, I will smite the shepherd, and the sheep shall be scattered abroad.

---

[61] Gr. σκανδαλίζεσθαι in Mark denotes defection in the face of trial and persecution (e.g. Chs. 4:17; 6:3; 9:42-47). Cf. RSV "fall away."

28 Howbeit, after I am raised up, I will go before[62] you into Galilee.[63]
29 But Peter said unto him, Although all shall be offended, yet will not I.
30 And Jesus saith unto him, Verily I say unto thee, that thou to-day, even this night, before the cock crow twice,[64] shalt deny me thrice.
31 But he spake exceeding vehemently, If I must die with thee, I will not deny thee. And in like manner also said they all.

27-28 The fact that the flow of the narrative would be uninterrupted if a reader jumped from verse 26 to verse 32 suggests that Mark is responsible for the insertion of verses 27-31 at this point. This paragraph indicates that Jesus was thoroughly aware of the course of events which would unfold in the hours ahead and that he would be reunited with his disciples after his resurrection. Within the Marcan outline these verses serve to anticipate important sections of the subsequent account, but especially the flight of the disciples at the time of Jesus' arrest (Ch. 14:43-50) and the denial of Peter (Ch. 14:66-72). Whether the tradition is to be situated in the upper room or on the way to Gethsemane is difficult to determine since there is no evidence in Mark that its position was dictated by sequential considerations (cf. Lk. 22:31-34; Jn. 13:36-38, where the prediction of the denial falls within the meal-sequence).

---

[62] Gr. προάξω can denote a literal walking in front of someone, as in Ch. 10:32, but it is better to understand it in the temporal sense of going somewhere earlier than someone else, as in Ch. 6:45. The saying anticipates a resurrection appearance of Jesus to his disciples in Galilee.

[63] On a third-century papyrus leaf from the Fayum there occurs a fragmentary Greek synopsis of Ch. 14:26-30 and Mt. 26:30-34. The dialogue between Jesus and Peter is briefer and more dramatic than in the canonical texts. Peter's denial is emphasized, but verse 28 is omitted. This text has been designated the Fayum Gospel Fragment, but it may represent only a relatively free citation of a canonical Gospel inserted into a patristic commentary or homily. The fact that the phraseology, when it differs from that of the Synoptic Gospels, tends toward a more classical idiom, lends support to this proposal. The papyrus does not provide a sufficient basis for omitting verse 28. For the text see M. R. James (ed.), *The Apocryphal New Testament*[2] (Oxford, 1955), p. 25.

[64] Gr. δίς is omitted in א C* D W 2148 *l*[76, 150, 950] it arm aeth and in the parallel passage Mt. 26:34; Jn. 13:38. The corresponding ἐκ δευτέρου in Ch. 14:72, however, is strongly attested and provides intrinsic evidence that Mark wrote δίς here.

The prophecy that all the disciples will fall away is supported by the quotation of Zech. 13:7. In the context (Zech. 13:7-9) God commands that the shepherd ("the man who stands next to me") be struck down that the sheep may be scattered as an integral part of a refining process which will result in the creation of a new people of God. This action is associated with the opening of a fountain for the cleansing of sin on behalf of "the house of David and Jerusalem" (Zech. 13:1). The passage to which Jesus referred thus speaks of a necessity which leads to redemption. [65] Even as sheep are scattered in panic when their shepherd falls, so the death of Jesus will cause the disciples to desert him and will mark the loss of the center point for their own communal fellowship. The emphasis in verse 27, however, falls on the offense which Jesus will cause the disciples, for this is the element in the prediction that is seized upon by Peter in his bold affirmation of absolute loyalty (verses 29, 31). "To be offended" at Jesus is the opposite to believing and delighting in him. It implies the desire to be dissociated from him because too close an association with Jesus invites the treatment he receives. [66] Jesus' word emphasizes once again that every time he speaks of his passion, he provokes a crisis for the disciples (see above on Ch. 8:31f.; 9:31f.; 10:32).

The prophecy that the disciples will desert Jesus and be scattered is counter-balanced by the promise of reunion in Galilee following the resurrection. In the context of the announcement of failure and denial on the part of the Twelve, Galilee is designated as the place of restoration to Jesus and renewal. [67] There the scattered sheep will be gathered together and reunited with their Shepherd. The importance of this an-

---

65 For the suggestion that Ch. 14:27-31, 66-72 is an account of the time of testing foreshadowed in Zech. 13:7-14:4 and proclaimed in the sayings of Jesus see M. Wilcox, "The Denial-Sequence in Mark XIV. 26-31, 66-72," *NTS* 17 (1970-71), pp. 426-436.

66 G. Stählin, *TWNT* VII (1964), pp. 348 f.

67 Cf. R. P. Meye, *Jesus and the Twelve* (Grand Rapids, 1968), pp. 82-84. E. Lohmeyer, *Galiläa und Jerusalem* (Göttingen, 1936), pp. 10 ff. found in Ch. 14:28; 16:7 a reflection of Mark's interest in Galilee as the locus of revelation and especially of the parousia. See now, however, the critical evaluation of this thesis in T. A. Burkill, *Mysterious Revelation* (Ithaca, 1963), pp. 252-257: "Supplementary Note E: Galilee and Jerusalem." C. F. Evans, "I will go before you into Galilee," *JThS* n.s. 5 (1964), pp. 3-18 interprets the reference in terms of the Church's mission in the Gentile world. In Ch. 16:7, however, it is the fact that the disciples will *see* the Lord (not that they will proclaim the gospel) which is stressed, and this suggests a resurrection appearance in Galilee.

nouncement is emphasized by its repetition through an angel after Jesus' resurrection (Ch. 16:7). Verse 28 thus points to the resurrection as the point of renewal for a subsequent history. The fact that this promise was given immediately before the events of the passion tended to veil its significance from the disciples. The darkness caused in their thoughts by Jesus' approaching death (cf. verse 31 "if I must die with you . . . ") deprived them of the light of the triumph which was to follow. In this respect verses 27-28 correspond to Ch. 8:31 where Jesus announced he would be killed–and raised up. But Peter fastened only upon the first element in the prophecy (Ch. 8:32), even as he does here.

29-31 The explosive protest of Peter indicates that he found Jesus' comment in verse 27 offensive and that he failed to hear the counter-action proclaimed immediately. In a bold assertion of exception, he separated himself from the others and affirmed his absolute commitment to Jesus. His statement offers a remarkable contrast to the outburst of Ch. 8:32. There Peter denies suffering as Jesus' lot, while here he accepts it not only for Jesus but also for himself (verse 31). The profession of loyalty made by Peter and his companions, however, only serves to heighten the completeness of their failure in the impending hour of crisis.

In a most emphatic manner [68] Jesus solemnly announced that in spite of all good will and the most somber warnings Peter will find him to be a stumbling block and an offense. Before the early morning hours when the second crowing of the cock announces the approaching dawn, [69] Peter will have denied him three times. The reference to a threefold denial indicates the thoroughness with which he will refuse to acknowledge Jesus and the inescapability of the charge that he was offended

---

68 On the solemn "Amen" formula see on Ch. 3:28. The concentrated σὺ σήμερον ταύτῃ τῇ νυκτί, πρὶν ἢ δὶς ἀλέκτορα φωνῆσαι is extremely emphatic.

69 Cock-crow was a proverbial expression for early morning, and there is some evidence among classical writers for a double cock-crowing as a designation of time (cf. Aristophanes, *Ecclesiazusae* 390 f.; Juvenal, *Satires* ix. 107 f.). Since the third of the four Roman night watches was designated "cock-crow" (see on Ch. 13:35), C. H. Mayo, "St. Peter's Token of the Cock Crow," *JThS* 22 (1921), pp. 367-370, suggested that the reference is to a bugle signal for the changing of the guard which would be clearly audible throughout the city. The detail of the two crowings of the cock, however, suggests that the reference is to the rooster. See now H. Kosmala, "The Time of Cock-Crow," *Annual of the Swedish Theological Institute* 2 (1963), pp. 118-120; 6 (1968), pp. 132-134.

because of his master (cf. verse 27a).[70] With vehemence Peter expressed his abhorrence at such a thought and swore he was prepared to accept Jesus' fate as his own. The others present identified themselves with this oath of allegiance. Jesus spoke of scattering and denial; they spoke of a shared destiny. Ironically, a few hours later the disciples had fled (Ch. 14:50) and Peter summoned the same vehemence to support his oath that he did not know the Nazarene (Ch. 14:71). The fulfilment of Jesus' prediction concerning his faithlessness is precisely recorded in Ch. 14:72.

8. Gethsemane. Ch. 14:32-42

32 And they came unto a place which was named Gethsemane:[71] and he saith unto his disciples, Sit ye here, while I pray.
33 And he taketh with him Peter and James and John, and began to be greatly amazed, and sore troubled.
34 And he saith unto them, My soul is exceeding sorrowful even unto death: abide ye here, and watch.
35 And he went forward a little, and fell on the ground, and prayed that, if it were possible, the hour might pass away from him.
36 And he said, Abba,[72] Father, all things are possible unto thee; remove this cup from me: howbeit not what I will, but what thou wilt.
37 And he cometh, and findeth them sleeping, and saith unto Peter, Simon, sleepest thou? couldest thou not watch one hour?
38 Watch and pray, that ye enter not into temptation: the spirit indeed is willing, but the flesh is weak.
39 And again he went away, and prayed, saying the same words.[73]

---

70 Denial means "not to believe" and "not to confess" and so approximates the nuance in "being offended" at Jesus. See H. Riesenfeld, "The Verb ἀρνεῖσθαι" in *In honorem Antonii Fridrichsen, Coniectanea Neotestamentica* 11 (1947), pp. 207-219.

71 Gr. Γεθσημανί transliterates the Hebrew גַּת שְׁמָנֵי, "press of oils."

72 Gr. Ἀββά preserves the Aramaic determinative form אַבָּא, meaning "my Father." On the Aramaic form see J. Jeremias, *The Prayers of Jesus* (London, 1967), pp. 55-57.

73 The final clause (τὸν αὐτὸν λόγον εἰπών) is omitted by Western witnesses (D *a b c d ff*[2] *k*). The singular τὸν . . . λόγον demands the translation "the same request."

40 And again he came, and found them sleeping, for their eyes were very heavy; and they knew not what to answer him.
41 And he cometh the third time, and saith unto them, Sleep on now, and take your rest: [74] it is enough; [75] the hour is come; behold, the Son of Man is betrayed into the hands of sinners.
42 Arise, let us be going: behold, he that betrayeth me is at hand.

That Jesus, shortly before his arrest, prayed to God to be delivered from the suffering which faced him is well established in the tradition, appearing in at least three different early forms (Ch. 14:32-42 and par.; Jn. 17:1-18:1; Heb. 5:7). [76] In the ancient world it was customary to pray aloud almost universally. It may be assumed, therefore, that Jesus' prayer as recorded represents accurately the substance of what he prayed. The Gethsemane tradition was inserted, evidently, where it now stands because it formed an indispensable part of the memories which clustered around the Passion. By locating the episode between the prophecy of the desertion (Ch. 14:27-31) and its fulfilment (Ch. 14:43-50), Mark emphasized that Jesus had to face his hour of crisis utterly alone. What is at the heart of the scene is that mystery in suffering which can

[74] It seems better to take Jesus' words as a reproachful question, as in the RSV: "Are you still sleeping and taking your rest?"

[75] Gr. ἀπέχει is unusually difficult and has called forth a variety of proposals. The translation "enough" (i.e. of sleeping) has some support in certain OL MSS and the Vg but is attested relatively little and late in Greek; "it is a hindrance," or "it is out of place" (cf. H. Hanse, *TWNT* II [Eng. Tr. 1964], p. 828) interprets the expression by the related idiom οὐδὲν ἀπέχει, "nothing hinders" (cf. Plutarch, *Moralia* 433 A, 680 E); "he (i.e. Judas) is paid in full" or "he is taking possession (of me)" appeals to the meaning of ἀπέχειν in the commercial papyri (so J. de Zwaan, "The Text and Exegesis of Mark xiv. 41, and the Papyri," *Exp.* 6th series 12 [1905], pp. 459-472; G. H. Boobyer, "'Απέχει in Mark xiv. 41," *NTS* 2 [1955], pp. 44-48); "the end is pressing" or "is the end far off?" attempts to take into account the Aramaic basis of the word and the Western addition of τὸ τέλος in D W Θ φ 565 1009 1077 1216 1365 it (some MSS) sy arm (so M. Black, *op. cit.*, pp. 225 f.; J. T. Hudson, "Irony in Gethsemane?" *ExT* 46 [1935], p. 382). More recently J. R. Michaels, *The Church Vigilant* (Cambridge, 1962), pp. 205-207, has proposed that ἀπέχει ("it is apart" or "it is separated") indicates a time-lapse between the commands of verse 41a (sleep now and rest) and 41b (awake), much as a dramatist might insert "[Later]" into his script. It seems preferable to translate "it is settled" and to interpret the affirmation by the two statements that immediately follow. See the comm. below.

[76] On the historical value of the Gethsemane tradition see R. S. Barbour, "Gethsemane in the Tradition of the Passion," *NTS* 16 (1970), pp. 234 f.

be penetrated only by those who walk with Jesus in the way of the cross. For Mark's readers, who needed strength for their own hour of trial, the narrative provided an encouragement which they could accept with dignity and gratitude.

This account provides the third instance in the Gospel of Jesus in prayer (see above on Chs. 1:35; 6:46). The similarity of the setting (solitude, night, an awareness of the demonic) and the placement of the three passages at the beginning, at a decisive point in the middle, and at the end of the Gospel, implies that Mark saw in these incidents fundamental events for the understanding of Jesus and his mission.

32 The olive orchard called Gethsemane was part of an estate at the foot of the Mount of Olives. The road up from the Kidron valley would offer a natural boundary on the south, while the dimensions of the estate were most likely marked out by a stone wall. The name is Hebrew, meaning an oil press, and that seems to indicate that the plot of land contained an olive press. This would certainly not have been the only olive orchard with a press on the mountain, but some detail of past association must have distinguished it, so that it had given its name to the estate.[77] This place was familiar to Jesus and the disciples (cf. Lk. 22:39; Jn. 18:2), and in the instruction to wait while he prayed the eleven would have sensed nothing unusual.

33-34 As on other occasions, Jesus separated Peter, James and John from the larger fellowship and took them with him (cf. Chs. 5:37; 9:2). A sufficient reason for his action here may be found in the peculiar responsibility assumed by each of these three to share Jesus' destiny. In the case of Peter, his boisterous avowal in Ch. 14:29, 31 was a matter of immediate past record. Earlier the sons of Zebedee had affirmed their ability to drink Jesus' cup (Ch. 10:38-40), and this confidence is called to mind by the reference to the cup in verse 36. The failure to understand what it means to share Jesus' destiny and to be identified with his sufferings, rather than privileged status, appears to be the occasion for the isolation of the three from the others. Their glib self-confidence exposes them to grave peril of failure in the struggle they

---

[77] C. Kopp, *The Holy Places of the Gospel* (New York, 1963), pp. 335-350. See also H. W. Trusen, "Geschichte von Gethsemane," *ZDPV* 33 (1910), pp. 50-97; B. Meistermann, *Gethsemani* (Paris, 1920); G. Orfali, *Gethsemani* (Paris, 1924).

confront, and for that reason they are commanded to be vigilant. This warning is echoed in verse 37 and repeated in verse 38 where it is sharpened by the allusion to the moment of trial when a man *desires* to be untrue to God. The crisis-character of the hour demands vigilance (see above on Ch. 13:33-37).

The urgency of Jesus' instruction was underscored by his experience of shuddering horror. The suffering which overwhelmed him is forcefully stated: he was "appalled and profoundly troubled,"[78] and spoke of a depth of sorrow which threatened life itself.[79] The unusually strong language indicates that Mark understood Gethsemane to be the critical moment in Jesus' life when the full meaning of his submission to the Father confronted him with its immediacy. In the wilderness he had determined to bear the burden of the judgment of God upon the people (see on Ch. 1:8-13). He had spoken repeatedly and in detail to the disciples about his passion. When he set his face toward Jerusalem he did so with a resolve that "amazed" his disciples and made them afraid (Ch. 10:32). The reference to his baptism and his cup (Ch. 10:38) implies an awareness of the cost of submission to the will of God, and doubtless Jesus had seen other men crucified. His demeanor throughout the approach to the moment of arrest and trial was one of resolute calm. The dreadful sorrow and anxiety, then, out of which the prayer for the passing of the cup springs, is not an expression of fear before a dark destiny, nor a shrinking from the prospect of physical suffering and death. It is rather the horror of the one who lives wholly for the Father at the prospect of the alienation from God which is entailed in the judgment upon sin which Jesus assumes.[80] The horror thus anticipates the cry of dereliction in Ch. 15:34. Jesus came to be with the Father for an interlude before his betrayal, but found hell rather than heaven opened before him, and he staggered. The vivid terminology of verses

---

[78] The vocabulary of the Marcan formulation is found in the variant translations of Ps. 115:2 LXX (M.T. 116:3), while the thought is consistent with the psalmist's depiction of his experience.

[79] On the basis of the formal linguistic parallel in Jonah 4:9 (λυπεῖσθαι ἕως θανάτου), R. Bultmann, *TWNT* IV (Eng. Tr. 1967), p. 323 argues that the meaning is "to be so full of sorrow that I would rather be dead," not "of sorrow which leads to death." This is unsatisfactory in this situation when Jesus knows he is going to die. The meaning is rather "my affliction is so great I am sinking under the weight of it."

[80] L. Goppelt, *TWNT* VI (Eng. Tr. 1968), p. 153.

33-34 prepares for verse 36, where the reference to the cup recalls the description of God's outpoured wrath in the OT as "the cup of staggering" (e.g. Ps. 60:3; Isa. 51:17, 22).

35-36 Separating himself a few yards from the three disciples Jesus prostrated himself and prayed aloud that "the hour" or "this cup" might pass from him. The two expressions are synonymous: both are metaphors for the passion in its deeper redemptive significance. This is evident from the parallel structure of verses 35b and 36a, where the substance of Jesus' prayer is expressed first indirectly and then directly.[81] The reference to "the hour" in verse 35 appears to have been dictated by Jesus' pronouncement that "the hour has come" in verse 41, referring to the moment of his betrayal and arrest with its foreseeable consequences of his execution as a condemned criminal (see above on Ch. 14:18, 21, 24, 27). The meaning of that course of events is informed by the reference to "this cup," which in the light of Ch. 10:38 can only designate the chalice of death and of God's wrath that Jesus takes from the Father's hand in fulfilment of his mission.[82] The thought that the cup could be removed may have come from Isa. 51:17-23 where God, in a proclamation of salvation, summons Jerusalem to arouse from its drunken stupor and to recognize that "the cup of staggering" has been taken away. Yet Scripture also speaks of those who "did not deserve to drink the cup [but] must drink it" (Jer. 49:12). The tension between these alternate expressions of grace and judgment, respectively, seems to be reflected in Jesus' prayer with its confession of God's ability ("all things are possible to you"; cf. Ch. 10:27) and the firm resolve to submit to God's sovereign will. The metaphor of the cup indicates that Jesus saw himself confronted, not by a cruel destiny, but by the judgment of God.

The preservation of *Abba* ("my Father") indicates that Jesus prayed

---

[81] K. G. Kuhn, "Jesus in Gethsemane," *Ev Th* 12 (1952-53), pp. 260-285; T. Lescow, "Jesus in Gethsemane," *Ev Th* 26 (1966), pp. 141-159; and R. S. Barbour, *op. cit.*, pp. 231-234 distinguish two sources for the Gethsemane pericope, one which spoke of "the hour" and the other which spoke of "the cup." When the synthetic parallelism of verses 35-36 is recognized, however, it is unnecessary to follow this critical reconstruction.

[82] See R. Le Déaut, "Goûter le calice de la mort," *Biblica* 43 (1962), pp. 82-86; H. A. Brongers, "Der Zornesbecher," *Oudtestamentische Studiën* 15 (1969), pp. 177-192.

to God in the everyday language of the family. When Jesus addressed God this way he did something new, for in the literature of early Palestinian Judaism there is no evidence of *Abba* being used as a personal address to God. [83] To the Jewish mind the use of this familiar household term would have been considered disrespectful in prayer, and therefore inconceivable. Yet Jesus did not hesitate to speak to God "as a child to its father, simply, inwardly, confidently; Jesus' use of *abba* in addressing God reveals the heart of his relationship with God." [84] In verse 36 *Abba* is an expression of obedient surrender and unconditional faith in the Father.

It is commonly assumed that Jesus went to Gethsemane seeking the sympathy and support of his most intimate disciples and that he returned to them after his periods of prayer to seek some relief from his agonizing isolation. This opinion is almost certainly false. The record of the Gospels is clear that the greater the stress of the approaching passion, the more selfish and confused those around him became. The disciples had continually failed to understand the necessity of the passion (cf. Chs. 8:17-21, 32 f.; 9:32; 10:32, 35 ff.) and were capable of sustaining only the most ordinary kind of affection for Jesus. The Lord had clearly foreseen that at the critical moment they would abandon him (Ch. 14:27-31). True friendship as we experience it–the sharing of inmost thoughts, the exchange of feelings, hopes, sorrows, joys–was a reality that Jesus seems not to have enjoyed, with any continuity, with the Twelve. This was possible with the Father alone, and it is to him, not to the disciples in their frailty, that Jesus turned in this hour of testing.

The complete surrender of the Son in patient obedience to the Father, expressed in *Abba,* is affirmed in the words which qualify the prayer: "if it is possible" (verse 35) and "not what I will, but rather what you will" (verse 36). Jesus' desire was conditioned upon the will of God, and he resolutely refused to set his will in opposition to the will of the Father. Fully conscious that his mission entailed submission to the

---

[83] Cf. J. Jeremias, *The Prayers of Jesus, op. cit.,* p. 67; W. Marchel, "Abba, Pater! Oratio Christi et christianorum," *Verb Dom* 39 (1961), pp. 240-247; R. Baumann, "Abba, lieber Vater. Zum biblischen Gottesbild," *Bibel und Kirche* 22 (1967), pp. 73-78.

[84] J. Jeremias, *op. cit.,* p. 62. The fact that Jesus never allied himself with the disciples in saying "our Father" when he prayed, and that he distinguished between "my Father" and "your Father" in his sayings, indicates that this use of *Abba* expresses a special relationship to God. He is the Son in a unique sense.

horror of the holy wrath of God against human sin and rebellion, the will of Jesus clasped the transcendentally lofty and sacred will of God. [85]

37-38 When Jesus interrupted his praying to return to the disciples he found them "sleeping." It is possible that the description implies a stunned stupor, which permitted them to hear, but not to register, the words of Jesus' prayer until afterwards (cf. Lk. 9:32). From this point forward there is a shift of emphasis in the narrative from the prayer of Jesus to the failure of the three disciples to maintain their vigil.

Jesus came to the disciples primarily because he was concerned for them. This is evident from the reproach directed to Peter because he had failed to watch as well as in the admonition to the three to watch lest *they* experience the most severe testing (verse 38). The opinion that Jesus came seeking the comfort and companionship of the three men is challenged by the structure of the account. Jesus did not ask the main body of the disciples to pray, but to remain while he prayed. He did not instruct the three to watch and pray for him, but for themselves. That the disciples failed to share in Jesus' sufferings was thoroughly predictable (Ch. 14:27). The remarkable element in the scene is that in the midst of an unparalleled agony Jesus twice more came to look after his three vulnerable disciples and to warn them of their danger of failure in the struggle which was about to overwhelm them.

The searching question concerning sleep and the failure to watch is addressed to Peter first because he had affirmed his absolute allegiance to Jesus in a strong statement of exception (Ch. 14:29). The pointed reference to his inability to be vigilant for "one hour" (which perhaps should be taken literally) prepares for the account of his faithlessness in Ch. 14:66-72, while the detail that he was asleep on three occasions when Jesus came to him anticipates his threefold denial. [86] The charge

---

[85] Cf. G. Schrenk, *TWNT* III (Eng. Tr. 1965), p. 49: "The synthesis in Jesus' life of omnipotent and effective will on the one side and patient obedience in lowliness on the other is most clearly and radically expressed in the balanced 'but not what I will, but what you will.' Here the position of the Son is as follows. Humanly he has the possibility of an independent will, but this will exists only to be negated in face of the divine will. Its perfect agreement with the divine will finds agreement in the declaration of this negation."

[86] The distinctive vocabulary of sleep and wakefulness suggests that there is a relationship between the Gethsemane scene and the sayings on eschatological vigilance in Ch. 13:33-37. A purely formal connection is established by the phraseology describing Jesus' "coming" and "finding" in verses 37 and 40 with the

to watch and pray in verse 38, however, is expressed in the plural and is addressed to the three disciples, who stand equally under the obligation to stay awake. The command to watch means to be spiritually awake so as to face the severe sifting of loyalties which was to come in the arrest and death of Jesus. The distinctive component in "temptation," in contrast to other terms for suffering, is that it sets forth the possibility of stumbling and falling into sin. It is an invitation to be untrue to God.[87] The expression is informed by the account of Jesus' trial in the wilderness, where he enters the sphere of Satanic power (see on Ch. 1:12 f.). Verse 38 displays an understanding of temptation as the time and realm in which Satan reigns, and recognizes that what takes place on the level of human encounter has cosmic repercussions in the struggle between God and the demonic.[88] Jesus knows that the disciples will be offended by the course of events and will deny him by their response to the situation. They may be characterized as "flesh" in its weakness, a description of sinful man left to his own inadequate resources who becomes overwhelmed by a situation, his best intentions betrayed by his inability to resist the pressures of the demonic. The "willing spirit" which stands in opposition to the weak flesh is not a better part of man but God's Spirit who strives against human weakness. The expression is borrowed from Ps. 51:12, where it stands in parallel with God's holy Spirit who qualifies a man to speak with boldness before sinners.[89] Spiritual wakefulness and prayer in full dependence upon divine help provide the only adequate preparation for crisis (cf. Ch. 13:11). Jesus prepared for his

---

unexpected return of the householder in the parable of Ch. 13:34-36:

Ch. 14:37	ἔρχεται . . .	εὑρίσκει . . .	καθεύδοντας
Ch. 14:40	ἐλθὼν . . .	εὗρεν . . .	καθεύδοντας
Ch. 13:36	ἐλθὼν . . .	εὕρῃ . . .	καθεύδοντας

J. R. Michaels, *op. cit.*, pp. 249 f., 260-265, has suggested that the fact that the three disciples had been asleep in the crisis hour was an offense with which the Church had to come to terms. It did so by recalling the historical incident as a parenetic illustration to make certain that the Church would not be found sleeping when Jesus came in the parousia. The vigilance pattern, with its characteristic use of γρηγορεῖν, has its origin in the instruction of the three who shared Jesus' vigil in Gethsemane.

87 Cf. K. G. Kuhn, "New Light on Temptation, Sin and Flesh in the New Testament" in K. Stendahl (ed.), *The Scrolls and the New Testament* (New York, 1957), pp. 94-113; H. Seesemann, *TWNT* VI (Eng. Tr. 1968), pp. 31 f.

88 R. S. Barbour, *op. cit.*, pp. 237 f., 242.

89 E. Schweizer, *TWNT* VI (Eng. Tr. 1968), pp. 396 f.; *idem, TWNT* VII (1964), pp. 123 f.

own intense trial through vigilance and prayer, and thus gave to the disciples and to the Church the model for the proper resistance of eschatological temptation.[90]

39-40 Jesus himself observed the prayer vigil commanded in verse 38. He left the disciples and made "the same request" to his Father. The accent in Mark's account, however, falls not on his prayer but on his return to his sleeping followers and the sifting this involved for them. Their eyes were "weighed down"; and as at the transfiguration (Ch. 9:6), "they did not know what to say to him."[91] The evangelist does not even mention the third period of prayer, loosely attaching "the third time" in verse 41 to Jesus' return. This shift of focus to the sleeping disciples who failed to watch recognizes that there was a scandal in the Gethsemane experience which could not be suppressed. It concerned not Jesus, but his immediate disciples who slept when they should have been watching and praying.[92] There is no reason to believe that such an offense was artificially created in the Church; a burden of shame rested upon the three who had come to be regarded as closest to the Lord. Mark faithfully preserved the tradition that only the three were told to watch and that only the three slept. His intention in doing so, however, was to strengthen Christians under persecution in Rome and elsewhere by providing a sober warning that the admonition to watch and pray applies ultimately to all believers, who stand equally exposed to the failure which marked the three disciples (cf. Ch. 13:37).

---

90 The Church is to watch and pray *in order* not to enter temptation. Is the prayer to be offered the Lord's Prayer, which seems to be reflected just beneath the surface of the account? Cf. "Abba, Father" and "your will be done" in verse 36 and the variant to the petition "Lead us not into temptation, but deliver us from the Evil One" in verse 38. Cf. Rom. 8:15; Gal. 4:6.

91 There are unmistakable formal similarities between the transfiguration and Gethsemane in Mark. These include not only the presence of the same three disciples, but the identical use of παραλαμβάνει in Ch. 9:2 and Ch. 14:33, and the statement about not knowing what to answer in Ch. 9:6 and Ch. 14:40. See A. Kenny, "The Transfiguration and the Agony in the Garden," *CBQ* 19 (1957), pp. 444-452.

92 D. Daube, "Evangelisten und Rabbinen," *ZNW* 48 (1957), pp. 119-126 locates the incident in its Passover setting. According to M. *Pesachim* X. 8; TB *Pesachim* 120b, if one member of the group fell asleep the bond was dissolved. Jesus, therefore, requests the disciples to stay awake. When he returned three times and found them sleeping he resolved to go on alone.

41-42 The opening words of verse 41 are to be taken as an ironical demand or a reproachful question.[93] They underscore the utter inability of the disciples to understand the significance of the moment and stress Jesus' isolation in trial. The enigmatic "It is settled" is to be interpreted by the two statements which immediately follow. In verse 35 Jesus had prayed that if it were possible "the hour" might pass from him. He now says "the hour has come," and the possibility contemplated in his prayer has proven invalid. The approach of Judas with a company of men indicates that the matter about which Jesus prayed has been settled: he is going to be handed over to sinners. The two statements "the hour has come" and "the Son of Man is handed over to sinners" are synonymous, the second simply clarifying the tenor of the first declaration. They indicate that the moment is imminent when the power of sin and death will overwhelm Jesus and destroy him. This is Satan's "hour," because "the sinners" are his agents. Jesus has been delivered by God (cf. Ch. 14:21; Rom. 8:32) into the realm of Satanic power from which there is no protection. That the transcendent Son of Man, whose triumph is so emphatically affirmed in Ch. 13:26, should fall into the hands of sinners is conceivable only in terms of the sovereign will of God and the submission of the Son. This concurrence of will is expressed in the command, "Get up. Let us advance to meet them," which accompanies the reference to the approach of the betrayer. As in Ch. 14:18-21 where Jesus first announced his betrayal, there is an alternation between the indirect speech of verse 41, with its reference to the Son of Man (cf. verse 21), and the direct use of the first person in verse 42 (cf. verse 18). While Jesus did not hesitate to speak openly of his betrayal, the reference to the betrayal and death of the Son of Man served to direct attention to the utter seriousness of the offense. Jesus' apparent defenselessness and humiliation in Gethsemane veiled his true dignity. Only after the resurrection did the significance of the transaction concluded there become clear. Just as rebellion in a garden brought Death's reign over man (Gen. 3:1-19), submission in Gethsemane reversed that pattern of rebellion and sets in motion a sequence of events which defeated Death itself (cf. Heb. 5:7-10).

---

93 A. Oepke, *TWNT* III (Eng. Tr. 1965), p. 436.

9. The Betrayal and Arrest of Jesus. Ch. 14:43-52

43 And straightway, while he yet spake, cometh Judas, one of the twelve, and with him a multitude with swords and staves, from the chief priests and the scribes and the elders.
44 Now he that betrayed him had given them a token, saying, Whomsoever I shall kiss, that is he; take him, and lead him away safely.
45 And when he was come, straightway he came to him, and saith, Rabbi; and kissed him.
46 And they laid hands on him, and took him.
47 But a certain one of them that stood by drew his sword, and smote the servant of the high priest, and struck off his ear.
48 And Jesus answered and said unto them, Are ye come out, as against a robber, [94] with swords and staves to seize me?
49 I was daily with you in the temple teaching, and ye took me not: but this is done that the scriptures might be fulfilled.
50 And they left him and fled. [95]
51 And a certain young man followed with him, having a linen cloth cast about him, over his naked body: and they laid hold on him;
52 but he left the linen cloth, and fled naked. [96]

43 Guided by Judas, who possessed knowledge both of the place and the wanted person, the arresting party arrived in Gethsemane to take Jesus into custody. The identification of Judas as "one of the twelve," as if this were not common knowledge, suggests that at this point Mark began incorporating the primitive passion narrative, which in rapid sequence recalled Jesus' arrest, the investigation of the Sanhedrin, the

---

[94] Gr. ληστής more commonly denotes a Zealot leader in the writings of Josephus, and this understanding informs the treatment of this verse by K. H. Rengstorf, *TWNT* IV (Eng. Tr. 1967), p. 261. The translation "robber" is, nevertheless, correct and should be retained. See J. Blinzler, *Der Prozess Jesu*[4] (Regensburg, 1969), pp. 100 f. n. 84.

[95] Gr. ἀφέντες αὐτὸν ἔφυγον πάντες, where the emphatic position of πάντες shows that the accent falls on Jesus' being completely forsaken.

[96] There is widespread agreement among Caesarean, Western and Byzantine witnesses in adding the words ἀπ' αὐτῶν ("from them") to the text. It seems better, however, to follow ℵ B C L Ψ 892 it *aur c k* syp cop aeth in omitting the expression. Not only is the omission strongly attested, but intrinsically it is probable that Mark intended the emphatic ἔφυγεν in verse 52 to reinforce ἔφυγον πάντες in verse 50.

trial before Pilate, his crucifixion and death.[97] Because this was an independent unit of tradition, no prior reference to Judas was assumed. The warrant for Jesus' arrest had been issued by the Sanhedrin, which is indicated by the comprehensive designation "the chief priests, the scribes and the elders" (see on Chs. 8:31; 14:1f.). That the Jewish authorities alone were responsible for the measures taken against Jesus is corroborated by the detail that he was taken directly to the house of the high priest.[98] In addition to the Temple police, who were Levites, the Sanhedrin had at its disposal auxiliary police or servants of the court who were assigned the task of maintaining public order beyond the Temple precincts. They were authorized to make arrests, lead accused persons to the court, guard prisoners and carry out sentences imposed by the court. The arresting party in Gethsemane must have consisted of armed court attendants of this kind.[99] The sword, the wooden staff and the lance are listed as Jewish weapons in M. *Shabbath* VI. 4, while the clubs used by the servants of the high priest are specifically mentioned in an abusive ballad found in the Talmud (TB *Pesachim* 57a Baraitha; Tos. *Menachoth* XIII. 21). The effectiveness of clubs for the quelling of a riot was demonstrated during Pilate's term of office (Josephus, *Antiquities* XVIII. iii. 2; *War* II. ix. 4). While the text speaks of "a multitude," it is important not to overestimate the numerical strength of the force. A large squad was neither necessary nor practical, since it was imperative that an uproar be avoided.

44-45 Judas' betrayal consisted in making known to the Jewish hierarchs the time and place where Jesus could most conveniently be taken into custody without a commotion.[100] The fact that a signal for the arrest had been prearranged confirms that the arresting party were not ac-

---

[97] Cf. J. W. Doeve, "Die Gefangennahme Jesu in Gethsemane. Eine traditionsgeschichtliche Untersuchung," in F. L. Cross (ed.), *Studia Evangelica* (Berlin, 1959), pp. 458-480.

[98] For a careful treatment of Jn. 18:3, 12 see J. Blinzler, *op. cit.,* pp. 87-101. Blinzler rightly points out that if Jesus had been arrested with the help of Roman soldiers, he would certainly have been taken to a Roman prison and not, as all the Gospels testify, brought before the Jewish hierarchs.

[99] *Ibid.,* pp. 126-128.

[100] G. Buchheit, *op. cit.,* pp. 105-107, 141 holds that what Judas betrayed to the chief priests was the messianic secret of Jesus. If this interpretation were correct, it would have been mandatory for Judas to appear before the Sanhedrin as a witness, but there is no evidence that he did so.

quainted with Jesus. The appointed sign was a kiss, the token of homage with which disciples customarily greeted their rabbi.[101] Ironically, both the title "Rabbi" ("my master") and the kiss declared Judas' respect for Jesus, while his act exposed his master to gross contempt. There is little interest in Judas in the account apart from the essential fact that Jesus was handed over to the Sanhedrin through his agency. He is not mentioned in Mark's Gospel after this point.

46 Since Jesus was unarmed and offered no resistance, he was quickly apprehended. The grounds upon which the legality of the arrest was justified are difficult to ascertain. Charges of blasphemy (Ch. 2:7), violation of the Sabbath (Chs. 2:24; 3:2-6), or the practice of magic and sorcery (Ch. 3:22) were at various times urged against Jesus, but no one of these impeachments is specified in the account. In spite of that, the legality of Jesus' arrest cannot be questioned. The body of men who seized him were authorized to do so by the Sanhedrin, the highest Jewish court in the land. If a written warrant for the arrest was required by law (cf. Acts 9:2), it may be assumed that one had been prepared and was in the possession of the leader of the task force. In the Roman provinces, the enforcement of the civil code, and to a large degree criminal law, among the non-citizen classes was normally relegated to the local authorities.[102] A provincial suspected of a crime could be arrested by the Sanhedrin in virtue of the autonomous police powers which this body possessed even under the procurators. There is nothing in the record to indicate that the normal rules of Jewish criminal law were suspended or infringed by the action in Gethsemane.[103]

47 Mark records a single feeble attempt at resistance by an unnamed disciple who struck off the ear of the servant of the high priest with his

---

[101] E.g. TJ *Kiddushin* I. 61c (in connection with Rabbi Joḥanan ben Zakkai, *ca.* A.D. 50). See A. Wünsche, *Der Kuss in Bibel, Talmud und Midrasch* (Berlin, 1911); M. Dibelius, "Judas und das Judaskuss" in *Botschaft und Geschichte* (Tübingen, 1953), pp. 272-297.

[102] E. Bickermann, "*Utilitas crucis.* Observations sur les récits du procès de Jésus dans les Évangiles canoniques," *Revue de l'histoire des religions* 112 (1935), pp. 172-174; L. Wenger, *Die Quellen des römischen Rechts* (Vienna, 1953), pp. 288, 537 n. 16; E. Lohse, *TWNT* VII (1964), pp. 858-868.

[103] The objections that Jesus was arrested at night by armed men and that the Sanhedrin had made use of an informer are satisfactorily answered by J. Blinzler, *op. cit.,* p. 100 n. 81.

sword. According to Jn. 18:10, the assailant was Peter, whose action seems to have been impulsive, and the servant he wounded bore the name Malchus. Since this latter name was in common use among the Nabateans and in Syria,[104] this man may have been a Nabatean Arab or a Syrian who attended Caiaphas as his personal servant. He seems not to have been present in Gethsemane in any official capacity, but doubtless had been charged to bring the high priest a report of the course of the action as soon as possible. In the scuffle Peter managed to get away. He was not pursued because the incident must have seemed of trifling importance once the leader of the whole movement was in their hands.

48-50 Jesus indignantly protested the unusual show of force which had been mustered against him, as if he were an armed robber. He keenly felt the shame and humiliation of being treated as a common criminal. Paradoxically, he had been available for arrest for at least two weeks prior to the Passover (see on Ch. 11:15-16) since he had been teaching publicly in the Temple each day. The contrast between the surprise armed attack by night and Jesus' daily appearance in the Temple indicates that the precautions taken by the auxiliary police were unwarranted and unnecessary, while the affirmation "I was daily *with you* in the Temple" demonstrates that Jesus' captors were Jewish. The comment that this was done that Scripture might be fulfilled immediately calls to mind Isa. 53:12, "he was numbered with the transgressors," but in the light of verse 50, where it is reported that all the disciples fled, it is appropriate to recall Ch. 14:27 where Jesus cited Zech 13:7. The desertion of the eleven marks the fulfilment of that prophecy and of Jesus' word that all of his followers would abandon him that night. No attempt appears to have been made to apprehend the fugitives. The sole concern of the arresting party was Jesus himself.

51-52 These two verses, which are unique to Mark's record, appear to be an appendix to the statement in verse 50 that "all fled." They serve to emphasize the fleeing of the disciples by focusing upon a young man who was present and who also fled. In the search for a clue to the identity of this individual, the linguistic parallel with Gen. 39:12 LXX has been observed (Potiphar's wife "caught him by his garment . . . but

---

[104] *Ibid.*, pp. 98 f. n. 78.

he left his garment in her hands, and fled . . . "),[105] but it is the similarity in situation rather than intended allusion that accounts for the merely formal parallelism. Of greater importance is the fact that in the LXX, the Jewish Apocrypha and Josephus, the term used by Mark designates young men who are exceptionally strong and valiant, or faithful and wise.[106] This observation invites attention to Amos 2:16, where the prophet describes a day of judgment so terrible that "he who is stout of heart among the mighty shall flee away naked in that day." That text seems to offer a more substantial commentary upon this incident. The arrest of Jesus invites the crushing judgment announced by Amos, and not even the valiant shall be able to withstand that day. Yet Christians in Rome and elsewhere who received this tradition would almost certainly understand the reference in terms of an observer who had fled naked into the night when the police sought to seize him. Ordinarily the outer garment was made of wool. The fine linen garment left behind in the hands of a guard indicate that the youth was from a wealthy family, while the absence of an undergarment suggests that he had dressed hastily in order to accompany Jesus. Several Fathers of the Church conjectured that the young man was Mark himself, who is known to have been a resident in Jerusalem (Acts 12:12) and in whose house, it was held by tradition, Jesus celebrated the paschal meal.[107] If this is correct, Mark was an eyewitness to the transactions in Gethsemane. His primary purpose for including this vignette, however, appears to have been to emphasize the fact that *all* fled, leaving Jesus alone in the

---

[105] The formal parallelism is strengthened in the Testament of Joseph 8:3, where the patriarch says he left his garment behind and "fled naked." H. Waetjen, "The Ending of Mark and the Gospel's Shift in Eschatology," *Annual of the Swedish Theological Institute* 4 (1965), pp. 116-120 has argued that a Joseph typology is intended in Ch. 14:51 f. and Ch. 16:5: "The contrast between the fleeing Joseph, who leaves behind his clothes and is unjustly disgraced on the one hand, and the exalted Joseph, who wears splendid garments and is exalted to viceregent on the other, is matched and reproduced by Mark 14, 51 f. and 16, 5" (p. 120). The reference is to Jesus in his humiliation and exaltation. Cf. John Knox, "A Note on Mk. 14:51-52" in S. E. Johnson (ed.), *The Joy of Study* (New York, 1951), pp. 28 f.

[106] *Ibid.,* pp. 115 f. Where νεανίσκος designates an angel, there is some detail in the context which makes this plain. In Ch. 16:5 this detail seems to be the element of revelation.

[107] See J. Weiss, *Das älteste Evangelium* (Göttingen, 1903), pp. 405-407 for a survey of the interpretation of Ch. 14:51 f. in the early Church. Cf. J. H. McIndoe, "The Young Man at the Tomb," *ExT* 80 (1969), p. 125.

custody of the police. No one remained with Jesus, not even a valiant young man who intended to follow him.

10. The Proceedings of the Sanhedrin. Ch. 14:53-65

53 And they led Jesus away to the high priest: and there come together with him all the chief priests and the elders and the scribes.
54 And Peter had followed him afar off, even within, into the court of the high priest; and he was sitting with the officers, and warming himself in the light of the fire.
55 Now the chief priests and the whole council sought witness against Jesus to put him to death; and found it not.
56 For many bare false witness against him, and their witness agreed not together.
57 And there stood up certain, and bare false witness against him, saying,
58 We heard him say, I will destroy this temple that is made with hands, and in three days I will build another made without hands.[108]
59 And not even so did their witness agree together.
60 And the high priest stood up in the midst and asked Jesus, saying, Answerest thou nothing? what is it which these witness against thee?
61 But he held his peace, and answered nothing. Again the high priest asked him, and saith unto him, Art thou the Christ, the Son of the Blessed?
62 And Jesus said, I am:[109] and ye shall see the Son of man sitting at the right hand of Power, and coming with the clouds of heaven.

---

108 It is possible that the qualifying words χειροποίητον and ἀχειροποίητον represent interpretive glosses added by early scribes in order to avoid the mistaken interpretation of Jn. 2:20. They are not found in Ch. 15:29 nor in the Lucan parallel to Ch. 14:58. Cf. E. Lohmeyer, *Das Evangelium des Markus*[16] (Göttingen, 1963), p. 326.

109 The Caesarean text (Θ φ *pc* arm geo Origen), in agreement with Matt. 26:64; Lk. 22:70, reads σὺ εἶπας ὅτι ἐγώ εἰμι, which amounts to a polite admission, but the introductory words convey a nuance ("you say it yourself, not I") which implies that the statement would not have been made had the question not been asked. See Bl-D-F § 441.3 (p. 227). For a defense of the shorter reading, which is followed in the commentary, see J. Blinzler, *op. cit.*, p. 157 n. 64.

63 And the high priest rent his clothes, and saith, What further need have we of witnesses?
64 Ye have heard the blasphemy: what think ye? And they all condemned him to be worthy of death.
65 And some began to spit on him, and to cover his face,[110] and to buffet him, and to say unto him, Prophesy: and the officers received him with blows of their hands.

Serious objections, based on rabbinic legal prescriptions, have been urged against the credibility of Mark's account of the proceedings before the Sanhedrin.[111] These may be considered within the framework of the commentary, but two deserve particular mention. It has been argued that the condemnation of Jesus by the Sanhedrin on the night of the Passover is historically improbable because of the prohibition of capital trials on feast days (cf. M. *Yom Tob* V. 2; Tos. *Yom Tob* IV. 4; Philo, *Migration of Abraham* § 91). Pentateuchal law (Deut. 13:12; 17:13; 21:21), however, required that in the case of particularly serious offenses, the execution should serve as a deterrent so that "all Israel should hear it and fear" (Deut. 17:13). In early Tannaitic exegesis this was taken to mean that the offender should be punished on one of the

---

[110] The phrase καὶ περικαλύπτειν τὸ πρόσωπον is omitted by D *a f* sy[s], and this shorter reading is defended by R. H. Gundry, "LMṬLYM: 1Q Isaiah[a] 50, 6 and Mark 14, 65," *Rev Qum* 2 (1960), pp. 559-567. See however J. Blinzler, *op. cit.*, pp. 164-166, and the interpretation of the apparently misunderstood detail of the covering of the face in the commentary below.

[111] E.g. Paul Winter, *On the Trial of Jesus* (Berlin, 1961), *passim;* T. A. Burkill, *op. cit.*, pp. 304-318. Cf. H. H. Cohn, "Reflections on the Trial and Death of Jesus," *Israel Law Review* 2 (1967), pp. 332-379; *idem, The Trial and Death of Jesus* (New York, 1971), who defends the historicity of the appearance before the Sanhedrin but develops the thesis that the court attempted to rescue Jesus from the Romans. Knowing that Pilate was going to judge Jesus the next morning, the high priest wished to prevent the Romans from executing a Jew who happened to enjoy the love of the people. The plan adopted was to arrest Jesus and bring him before the Sanhedrin, which sought to find witnesses who would testify to his innocence. The council also attempted to induce Jesus to plead not guilty and to promise to make no further disturbance. Their efforts proved fruitless because Jesus continued to assert his messianic claims, and as a result had to be turned over to Pilate. The Marcan account of the proceedings can only be explained by the tendency to shift the burden of responsibility for Jesus' death from the Roman procurator, where it belonged, to the Jews who were innocent. The eminence of the author, who is a justice on the Israeli Supreme Court, will secure for this thesis a careful consideration.

pilgrimage feasts (Tos. *Sanhedrin* XI. 7). To carry out this provision in the case of Jesus it was necessary that he should be tried and condemned immediately after his arrest.[112] The objection that if Jesus was sentenced to death by the Sanhedrin for blasphemy he would have been stoned, when in fact he was crucified by the Roman procurator, is based upon the assumption that the Sanhedrin possessed the competence to execute a capital sentence. The evidence, however, is overwhelming that the power of the sword was the most jealously guarded prerogative in Roman provincial administration, even in a center like Alexandria where there was no question of the disloyalty of the people to Rome.[113] In Judea, where a spirit of revolt constantly simmered just beneath the surface, there can have been no concession on this sensitive point. *De jure* the competence of the Sanhedrin remained intact, but *de facto* the governor alone possessed the capital power. Jesus was sentenced by the Sanhedrin on the charge of blasphemy, but it was necessary to prepare a political charge *ad hoc* in order to secure the execution of the death sentence by the provincial praefect. The essential historicity of the Marcan account should be accepted.[114]

53 Jesus was led back into the town from Gethsemane to the residence of Caiaphas[115] where the Sanhedrin was assembled as a body in one of the upstairs rooms (cf. verse 66, "as Peter was below in the courtyard"). There is no evidence in the rabbinic literature or Josephus that the court used the palace of the high priest for its chambers, and it is now impossible to determine why this place was chosen in preference to the usual seat in one of the market halls.[116] The haste with which

---

112 J. Jeremias, *TWNT* V (Eng. Tr. 1967), pp. 899 f.

113 See especially A. N. Sherwin-White, *Roman Society and Roman Law in the New Testament* (Oxford, 1963), pp. 1-47; J. Blinzler, *op. cit.*, pp. 229-244; E. Lohse, *TWNT* VII (1964), pp. 862-864.

114 Cf. J. Blinzler, *op. cit.*, pp. 174-216; A. N. Sherwin-White, "The Trial of Jesus" in *Historicity and Chronology in the New Testament*, ed. D. Nineham (London, 1965), pp. 97-116; P. J. Verdam, "Sanhedrin and Gabbatha," *Free University Quarterly* 7 (1961), pp. 3-31.

115 On the tradition of Jn. 18:12 f., 19-24 that Jesus was led first before Annas ben Seth, the father-in-law of Caiaphas, see J. Blinzler, *op. cit.*, pp. 129-136. For a review of ancient tradition concerning the house of Caiaphas see C. Kopp, *op. cit.*, pp. 352-357.

116 Cf. P. Winter, "The Meeting Place of the Sanhedrin and Mark's Nocturnal Session," ZNW 50 (1959), pp. 221-225; J. Blinzler, *op. cit.*, pp. 166-170, Exkurs VI: "Der Versammlungsort des Synhedriums." The Mishnah speaks of "the chamber of

the Sanhedrin was assembled is consonant with the deliberations reported in Ch. 14:1 f., 10 f. and the necessity of reaching a binding verdict before daybreak. Moreover, it was normal to try persons immediately after arrest since Jewish criminal law made no provision for detention on remand.

The three categories of persons mentioned in verse 53 are precisely those which, according to Josephus, constituted the Sanhedrin of Jerusalem, the supreme Jewish court of law.[117] The council was composed of seventy members and the ruling high priest who presided over its deliberations (M. *Sanhedrin* I. 6; cf. Josephus, *Antiquities* IV. v. 4; *War* II. xx. 5; Tos. *Sukka* IV. 6). While Mark says that "all" of the Sanhedrin has assembled, his statement need not be taken quite literally (cf. Ch. 1:5); some few individuals may have been absent. His intention is to indicate clearly that the court met in plenary session. According to the Mishnah the presence of 23 members constituted a quorum.[118]

The high priest at this time was Joseph, surnamed Caiaphas (Josephus, *Antiquities* XVIII. ii. 2; iv. 3).[119] His ability as a diplomat and an administrator is suggested by his tenure of office over a period of nineteen years (A.D. 18-37) in an era when the average term of office was only four years.[120] He is associated in the record with the "chief priests," who included former holders of the high priestly office (presumably

---

hewn stone" in the Temple precincts as the seat of the court (M. *Sanhedrin* XI. 20), and it has been argued that since the Temple gates were locked at night (M. *Middoth* I. 1), access to the court chambers was barred. But on the night of the Passover the gates of the Temple forecourt were opened at midnight rather than the usual hour of daybreak (Josephus, *Antiquities* XIV. ii. 2).

117 Cf. A. F. J. Klijn, "Scribes, Pharisees, Highpriests and Elders in the New Testament," *Nov Test* 3 (1959), pp. 259-267; J. Spencer Kennard, Jr., "The Jewish Provincial Assembly," *ZNW* 53 (1962), pp. 25-51. See further H. Mantel, *Studies in the History of the Sanhedrin* (Cambridge, Mass., 1961).

118 Cf. M. Wolff, "De samenstelling en het karakter van het groote synedrion te Jeruzalem voor het jaar 70 n. Chr.," *Theologisch Tijdschrift* 51 (1917), pp. 299-320.

119 The surname "Caiaphas" may have stood for something like "inquisitor." Cf. J. Levy, *Wörterbuch über die Talmudin und Midrasch* IV (Berlin, 1924), p. 299b.

120 The nearest to this record was Ananias with twelve, and Annas with nine years. Cf. TB *Yoma* 8b: "And as the candidate paid money in order to become high priest, they [the procurators] were in the habit of depriving the high priest of office every twelve months." See further, J. Jeremias, *Jerusalem in the Time of Jesus* (Philadelphia, 1969), pp. 377 f., "Complete List of High Priests from 200 BC to AD 70" (based on Josephus, *Antiquities* XX, Ch. 10).

Annas, Ishmael ben Phiabi, Eleazar and Simon ben Kamithos), the commander of the Temple Guard, the steward of the Temple, and the three Temple treasurers.[121] The "elders" represented the most influential lay families in Jerusalem, and seem to have been primarily wealthy landowners.[122] The chief priests and the elders constituted the old ruling class in Jerusalem, with Sadducean leanings, who still held the balance of power in the Sanhedrin. The third group, the representatives of the scribes, consisted primarily of lawyers drawn from the middle classes who tended to be Pharisaic in their convictions.[123] If the Mishnah accurately preserves the arrangement of the court in the first century, the members sat in a semi-circle on elevated seats so that they all could see each other (M. *Sanhedrin* IV. 3a). To their right and left stood two court clerks who recorded the minutes of the transactions, while a seat for the accused and for the witnesses was placed in the center (M. *Sanhedrin* IV. 3b, 4).

54 At first sight, verse 54 appears to be abruptly introduced and disruptive to the account of the proceedings before the Sanhedrin. It would seem more appropriate in connection with verses 66-72. The reference to Peter, however, is dictated by Mark's concern to present two incidents which happened at the same time. Because the council session and the denial were concurrent events, he is not content to present them simply one after the other, but employs a literary device which is characteristic of his style. He records the hearing before the Sanhedrin prior to the account of Peter's denial, but by introducing the second incident at the beginning of the first he indicates that the episodes occurred simultaneously. In verse 66 the words "and while Peter was below in the courtyard" establish the link with the situation already described at this point. Following the narrative of the denial, Mark then resumes his account of the action of the Sanhedrin, specifying once more those taking part (Ch. 15:1). By the technique of anticipation and flashback the impression of consecutive occurrence is overcome.[124]

---

[121] *Ibid.*, pp. 160-181; E. M. Smallwood, "High Priests and Politics in Roman Palestine," *JThS* 13 (1962), pp. 14-34.

[122] J. Jeremias, *op. cit.*, pp. 221-232.

[123] *Ibid.*, pp. 233-267. That the balance of power lay with the Sadducean wing of the court, and that Jesus was condemned according to the Sadducean penal code, is demonstrated by J. Blinzler, *op. cit.*, pp. 216-229.

[124] Cf. E. von Dobschütz, "Zur Erzählerkunst des Markus," *ZNW* 27 (1928), pp. 193-198, esp. pp. 197 f.

When Peter came to the courtyard to find out what those assembled in the palace intended to do with their prisoner, he found the servants of the high priest crowding around a charcoal fire because of the chilly night air. Ordinarily these men would have gone to their homes by this hour, but the extraordinary meeting of the court accounted for their presence in the courtyard until daybreak.

55-56 The proceedings against Jesus began with the taking of evidence, which is essential to any proper hearing. In capital cases condemnation required the unanimous evidence of at least two witnesses (M. *Sanhedrin* IV. 1), a provision firmly rooted in pentateuchal law (Deut. 17:6; 19:15; Num. 35:30; Josephus, *Antiquities* IV. viii. 15). Since in Jewish judicial procedure the witnesses functioned as the prosecution, they gave their evidence individually and verbally in the presence of the judges and the accused. If their respective depositions differed one from the other even in trivial details, they were inadmissible as evidence.[125] The ready availability of witnesses for the prosecution suggests that they had been alerted that the arrest of Jesus could be expected momentarily and that they were to appear on call. A number were called and heard, but all that is recorded is that they failed to agree with each other and so invalidated their testimony. This detail indicates that the Sanhedrin adhered strictly to the legal standards for the hearing of witnesses. The one reproach to which the court was open, according to Mark's record, was that they assembled together, not with the intention of reaching a just verdict, but with a firm resolve to convict Jesus of a capital crime (Ch. 14:1, 55). This violation of the purpose and spirit of the law outweighed the regard, or disregard, of external legal forms.[126]

57-59 After the first group of witnesses had been dismissed, a substantial charge was levelled that Jesus had declared that he would destroy the Temple and in three days build another in its place. While this accusation is labelled "false," the term may refer to some detail of the charge or to some circumstance which rendered the witness in-

---

125 Cf. B. Cohen, "Evidence in Jewish Law," *Recueils de la Société J. Bodin* 16 (1965), pp. 103-115. Johanan ben Zakkai earned a reputation for his searching and clever interrogation of witnesses (M. *Makkoth* I. 4; *Sanhedrin* IV. 5; V. 1f.). See further Susanna and the Elders 36ff., 54ff.

126 See J. Blinzler, *op. cit.*, pp. 197-210.

competent.[127] In point of fact, Jesus had once said, within sight of the Jerusalem Temple, "if this temple be destroyed, in three days I will raise it up" (Jn. 2:19).[128] After Jesus' resurrection these cryptic words were understood by the disciples to refer to the temple of his body (Jn. 2:21 f.), but quite naturally those who were present heard a dire threat against the sanctuary. Moreover, if the text of verse 58 and of Jn. 2:19 preserves a verbatim report of what was said, Jesus' accusers gave to his words a form which emphasized the threat still more: "*I* will destroy this temple." The accusation was utterly serious, for throughout the Graeco-Roman world the destruction or desecration of places of worship was regarded as a capital offense.[129] When the prophet Jeremiah had simply announced the catastrophe that would overtake the Temple in Jerusalem he was seized and brought before the royal court as a criminal who deserved to die (Jer. 26:1-19; Josephus, *Antiquities* X. vi. 2). The mere threat of violence against the Temple might well seem to the Sanhedrin a crime meriting the death penalty (cf. Tos. *Sanhedrin* XIII. 5; TB *Rosh-Ha-Shanah* 17a; TJ *Berachoth* IX. 13b). If the verdict announced in verse 64 had been secured on the basis of this evidence, it would have represented gross injustice. Jesus certainly had no intention of destroying the sanctuary. He expected its destruction as the judgment of God upon an appalling sacrilege (Ch. 13:1 f., 14). But the testimony concerning the Temple definitely did not provide the basis for the final verdict. Mark states emphatically that in this instance also the witnesses differed in their evidence and were disqualified. While the accusation concerning the Temple did not influence the outcome of the trial decisively, it serves to clarify the taunt of Ch. 15:29,[130] and it may

---

[127] Cf. J. A. Kleist, "The Two False Witnesses (Mk. 14:55 ff.)," *CBQ* 9 (1947), pp. 321-323.

[128] For this rendering see K. Beyer, *Semitische Syntax im Neuen Testament* I 1 (Göttingen, 1962), p. 252. On the meaning of the passage see J. Jeremias, *Jesus als Weltvollender* (Göttingen, 1930), pp. 35-44; G. Schrenk, *TWNT* III (Eng. Tr. 1965), pp. 244-246; O. Michel, *TWNT* IV (Eng. Tr. 1966), pp. 883-885.

[129] J. Juster, *Les Juifs dans l'Empire Romain* I (Paris, 1914), pp. 459-469.

[130] Mark refers to the saying of Jesus recorded in Jn. 2:19 in Ch. 15:29, where it is clearly assumed that the reader has prior knowledge of these words from an earlier part of the Gospel. It is clear that Mark has taken the taunt concerning the Temple from the account of the proceedings before the Sanhedrin handed down by apostolic tradition. It is precisely because Ch. 14:53-65 contains verse 58, which clearly alludes to words Jesus had actually spoken, that the appearance before the Sanhedrin is proved to be authentic tradition and an integral part of Mark's Gospel.

have provided the clue that Jesus regarded himself as the Messiah (see below on verse 61).

60-61 Because the hearing of witnesses did not secure the desired result, Caiaphas, as the presiding justice, determined to interrogate Jesus himself. He arose and stepped into the middle of the assembly where the accused was seated. Jesus was required by law to answer the accusations brought against him, and his failure to do so frustrated the council. By his steadfast silence he deprived the court of exploiting, for its purposes, the evidence that had been given against him. This brought the proceedings to a deadlock, and prompted the high priest to seek a decision by direct means. Although disqualified as admissible evidence, the utterance about destroying the Temple and rebuilding another in its place was messianic in tone, because Judaism anticipated a renewal of the glory of the Temple when the Messiah should come.[131] Perhaps for that reason Caiaphas asked Jesus pointedly if he claimed to be the Messiah. In the formulation "the Messiah, the son of the Blessed One,"[132] the second clause stands in apposition to the first and has essentially the same meaning. In Jewish sources contemporary with the NT, "son of God" is understood solely in a messianic sense.[133] Jewish hopes were situated in a messianic figure who was a man.[134] The question of the high priest cannot have referred to Jesus' deity, but was limited to a single issue: do you claim to be the Messiah?

---

[131] Cf. M. Simon, "Retour du Christ et reconstruction du Temple dans la pensée chrétienne primitive" in *Aux sources de la tradition chrétienne (Mélanges M. Goguel)* (Paris, 1950), pp. 247-257; O. Betz, *What Do We Know About Jesus* (Philadelphia, 1968), pp. 87-92 (based on 4QFlorilegium i. 1-7); L. Gaston, *No Stone on Another* (Leiden, 1970), pp. 65-205; J. Jeremias, "Die Drei-Tage-Worte der Evangelien" in *Tradition und Glaube,* ed. G. Jeremias, H. W. Kuhn, H. Stegemann (Göttingen, 1971), pp. 221-229.

[132] The expression "Blessed One" is a periphrasis for God as in M. *Berachoth* VII. 3; TB *Berachoth* 50a; TJ *Berachoth* VII. 11c 4, 21, and appears to involve a contraction for the common expression "the Holy One, blessed be he."

[133] Ps. 2 and II Sam. 7:14 are interpreted messianically in 1QSa ii. 1 ff. and 4QFlorilegium. In 4QFlorilegium i. 10 f. the scroll reads "I will be to him as a father and he will be to me as a son. He is the shoot of David . . . ," providing evidence of a sonship being predicated of the Davidic Messiah. Cf. Ps. Sol. 17:27 with Ps. 2:8; Ps. Sol. 17:36; 18:6, 8 with Ps. 2:2. See further J. Blinzler, *op. cit.,* pp. 150 f. n. 45.

[134] Cf. Justin, *Dialogue with Trypho* 49:1, "we all await in the Messiah a man of men." Cf. S-B*K* III (1926), pp. 20-22.

In the Marcan account this question appears to provide the climax to the proceedings. The impression is inescapable that the success or failure of the conspiracy on the part of the Sanhedrin to secure Jesus' death depended upon the response which follows. If Jesus answered affirmatively, they had won their case; if he replied negatively, they must discover some new stratagem. This means that if Mark has described the course of the investigation correctly in its essentials, the council was prepared to regard the open and unequivocal claim of Jesus to be the Messiah a capital crime.[135] Judaism expected the Messiah to provide proof of his identity. A Messiah imprisoned, abandoned by his followers, and delivered helpless into the hands of his foes represented an impossible conception. Anyone who, in such circumstances, proclaimed himself to be the Messiah could not fail to be a blasphemer who dared to make a mockery of the promises given by God to his people.[136] Moreover, there is some rabbinic evidence that God alone had the right to announce and enthrone the Messiah, so that one who claimed the messianic dignity before God had crowned him could be regarded as having infringed the majesty of God.[137] For these reasons, Caiaphas' question is decisive, and demands a forthright "Yes" or "No."

62 It is evident from Mark's Gospel that Jesus had carefully avoided calling himself the Messiah (see on Ch. 8:29). This reserve was inherent in the tension between veiledness and open manifestation which is characteristic of the public ministry. It was not his desire to arouse the nationalistic and political hopes which clustered around the figure of the Messiah in popular thinking. Nevertheless, he knew himself to be God's anointed servant, and in spite of the paradoxical circumstances in which he found himself he refused to ignore the question or deny his identity. To the question whether he claimed to be the promised Messiah he replied clearly, "I am." That his reply was an affirmative reply, and not a pronouncing of the theophanic formula "I am he" is evident from the structure of verses 61-62. The question "Are you . . . ?" demands and receives the response "I am," which is then strengthened by the prophecy which follows.

---

[135] Cf. J. Blinzler, *op. cit.*, pp. 148-152; J. C. O'Neill, "The Silence of Jesus," *NTS* 15 (1969), pp. 165-167.

[136] Cf. J. Blinzler, *op. cit.*, pp. 155 f. n. 61.

[137] See the evidence discussed by J. C. O'Neill, *op. cit.*, p. 166.

The utterance of verse 62b brings together Ps. 110:1 and Dan. 7:13 (cf. Isa. 52:8), in a formulation describing the enthronement and parousia of the Son of Man,[138] while the context leaves no doubt that Son of Man is a self-designation. "Power" was a recognized circumlocution for God,[139] while "to sit at the right hand of" someone was a familiar idiom meaning to occupy the place of highest honor (see above on Ch. 10:37). Jesus thus spoke without reserve of his exaltation and coming as the eschatological Judge (see on Chs. 8:38; 13:26). This prophecy counters the objection which the affirmation that he is the Messiah immediately provoked, that his claim lacks all proof. The day will come, he affirms, when those who now judge him will see him with unmistakable clarity enthroned at God's side, invested with power and majesty, and assigned the task of the eschatological Judge. He will then be unveiled in a convincing manner as the Anointed of God.[140] The high priest and the Sanhedrin, as representatives of the people, had the responsibility to recognize the Messiah. Accordingly, they who have rejected him must see their decision overturned when the truth concerning Jesus' person and work is clearly revealed at the parousia, and he is disclosed in the position of supreme authority. There is evidence that contemporary Judaism also conceived of the Messiah as sitting at God's right hand and coming in the clouds of heaven.[141] The Sanhedrin would understand Jesus' words as an unqualified claim to messianic dignity. The prophecy and the clear response "I am" are mutually supportive.

---

138 For a defense of the authenticity of this logion see A. L. Moore, *op. cit.*, pp. 184-186; F. H. Borsch, "Mark xiv. 62 and I Enoch lxii. 5," *NTS* 14 (1968), pp. 565-567. See also J. Blinzler, *op. cit.*, p. 158, n. 66.

139 E.g. Mekilta of Rabbi Simon XIV. 21; Sifré on Num. 15:31. Cf. A. M. Goldberg, "Sitzend zur Rechten der Kraft. Zur Gottesbezeichnung *Gebura* in der frühen rabbinischen Literatur," *BZ* 8 (1964), pp. 284-293.

140 A. L. Moore, *op. cit.*, pp. 139-142.

141 The midrashic combination of Dan. 7:13 with Ps. 110:1 occurs in the Midrash on Psalms on Ps. 2:7 (i. 40, § 9) and on Ps. 18 (i. 261, § 29). In the first passage Ps. 2:7 is linked with texts from the Torah, the Writings and the Prophets: "And in one place in the Writings it says, 'The Eternal One said to my Lord, "Sit at my right hand"' (Ps. 110:1), and it says: 'The Eternal One said to me, "You are my Son"' (Ps. 2:7). And in another place it says, 'See, one came with the clouds of heaven, as a Son of Man' (Dan. 7:13)." See further E. Lövestam, "Die Frage des Hohenpriesters (Mark. 14, 61 par. Matt. 26, 63)," *Sv Ex Års* 26 (1961), pp. 93-107.

63-64 The pentateuchal law concerning blasphemy (Lev. 24:15-16) was very elastic in the first century. It covered the sins of "defaming" God and "piercing" his name. The Hebrew root of the essential verb in Lev. 24:15 means to undervalue someone and to say so. Applied to God it meant to dishonor him by diminishing his majesty or depriving him of rights to which he is entitled (cf. Ch. 2:7).[142] Only in the post-Christian period, through the deliberations at Jamnia and elsewhere, did "blasphemy" acquire the technical significance defined in the Mishnah: "The blasphemer is only guilty if he pronounces the name of God distinctly" (M. *Sanhedrin* VII. 5a). The Tannaim of a later generation supposed that the strictest possible interpretation of Lev. 24:10-17 was mandatory in order to safeguard the possible loss of an Israelite life by stoning. The exegetical procedure adopted was to read the several verses as if they controlled each other and mutually narrowed the application of the law. God's covenant name must be distinctly uttered and must be openly dishonored according to a recognized curse-formula. It may be accepted as certain that this narrow definition of blasphemy had no validity in the proceedings described in Ch. 14:53 ff.[143] The action of the high priest in tearing his garments, together with the explicit declaration "You have heard his blasphemy," indicate that Jesus' open avowal of his messiahship was regarded by Caiaphas and the court as an infringement of God's majesty and a diminishing of his honor. Under the circumstances in which Jesus asserted his claim God appeared to be mocked and was denied his right to enthrone the Messiah and declare his dignity.[144]

By tearing his garments, Caiaphas expressed symbolically the fact that he regarded Jesus' declaration as blasphemous. It is not necessary to infer that he tore the sacred and magnificent robes worn by the high

---

[142] D. W. Amram, *Leading Cases in the Bible* (Philadelphia, 1905), pp. 91 ff.; J. D. M. Derrett, *An Oriental Lawyer Looks at the Trial of Jesus and the Doctrine of Redemption* (London, 1966), pp. 59-61.

[143] *Loc. cit.;* D. Catchpole, "You Have Heard His Blasphemy," *The Tyndale House Bulletin,* No. 16 (1965), pp. 10 f. (where attention is called especially to Tos. *Sanhedrin* I. 2); J. Blinzler, *op. cit.,* pp. 216-229, Exkurs IX, "Zur Frage der Geltung des mischnischen Strafrechts in der Zeit Jesu."

[144] A number of commentators prefer to find the point of blasphemy in the affirmation that the court will see Jesus sitting at God's right hand, e.g. J. D. M. Derrett, *op. cit.,* p. 31; D. Catchpole, *op. cit.,* pp. 11-18; O. Linton, "The Trial of Jesus and the Interpretation of Psalm CX," *NTS* 7 (1960-61), pp. 260 f. The evidence in support of this conclusion is not conclusive, and the passage from the Midrash to Ps. 2:7 cited in n. 141 would appear to militate against it.

priest when officiating at one of the appointed feasts. There is nothing either in the circumstances of the night session or in the Marcan text which suggests that he was wearing his official robes. The significant element was the gesture of sorrow and indignation (cf. II Kings 18:37; 19:1, 4; Judith 14:19; M. *Sanhedrin* VII. 5, 6), which was as eloquent of his convictions as his call for a verdict when he specified the offense of blasphemy. The law of Moses prescribed death by stoning for blasphemy (Lev. 24:16). In the absence of any stated objection, a unanimous verdict was attained and Jesus was sentenced to death.

The statement that the Sanhedrin passed a formal death sentence has frequently been disputed on linguistic and historical grounds. It is argued that the council expressed a judicial opinion (i.e. they regarded him as deserving death) or that a writ of indictment was drawn up,[145] but that there can be no thought in the passage of an actual death sentence. Mark, however, unequivocally reports a death sentence, using accepted legal terminology when he says that "all condemned him as liable to death." As curious as this wording may sound, it means that a formal judgment took place and that a death sentence was handed down.[146] That Mark has a real death sentence in mind is confirmed by Ch. 10:33 where Jesus prophesies that the chief priests and scribes will "condemn" him to death, using the same terminology found in verse 64. In the absence of a court of appeal in Jewish criminal law, the sentence was valid. A capital sentence, however, could not be executed by the Jewish court under Roman provincial rule. Only the procurator possessed the power of life and death in terms of his imperial authority.[147] The session of the court thus ended with the formal decision to hand Jesus over to the Roman procurator with a carefully formulated charge which would secure the execution demanded by the court (see Ch. 15:1).

65 Once Jesus was condemned, it was necessary for the council to show that it could not condone his (apparently) abhorrent behavior. This was accomplished through the spitting and the administering of blows, which were conventional gestures of rejection and repudiation (cf. Job 30:10; Num. 12:14; Deut. 25:9; Isa. 50:6; M. *Berachoth* IX. 5b; TJ *Soṭah* II. 16d [37]). The detail that Jesus was blindfolded and

145 Representative of these two positions are E. Bickermann, *op. cit.*, pp. 169-199; P. Winter, *op. cit.*, pp. 227-234 respectively.

146 Cf. J. Blinzler, *op. cit.*, pp. 184-186.

147 See above, n. 113.

cuffed, with the demand to "prophesy," i.e. to say who it was that struck him, accurately preserves an old interpretation of Isa. 11:2-4, according to which the Messiah could judge by smell without the need of sight.[148] What is described in the text is a traditional test of messianic status, to which Jesus declined to submit. Since the indignities heaped upon Jesus were consistent with the court's understanding of his unqualified claim to be the Messiah, there is nothing improbable in the conduct reported by Mark. Verse 65 is thus integrally related to the larger account, the degrading treatment corresponding to the basis of the condemnation.[149]

11. Peter's Denial of Jesus. Ch. 14:66-72

66 And as Peter was beneath in the court, there cometh one of the maids of the high priest;
67 And seeing Peter warming himself, she looked upon him, and saith, Thou also wast with the Nazarene, even Jesus.
68 But he denied, saying, I neither know, nor understand what thou sayest: and he went out into the porch, and the cock crew.[150]

---

148 J. D. M. Derrett, *op. cit.*, p. 20; cf. S-B*K* I (1922), p. 641; II (1924), p. 439. The key text is TB *Sanhedrin* 93b, "He smells [a man] and judges, as it is written, 'and he shall not judge after the sight of his eyes, neither reprove after the hearing of his ears, yet with righteousness shall he judge the poor' (Isa. 11:3 f.)." The Tannaim judged that since the Messiah uses neither his eyes nor his ears, he must judge through the sense of smell. They therefore read Isa. 11:2 ("His delight is in the fear of the Lord") as if it read "his smell is through the fear of the Lord," i.e. they understood the Hebrew והריחן (his delight) to be derived from ריח (smell). The passage which immediately follows is of prime importance, for it concerns the messianic pretender Simon bar Kochba (A.D. 132-135): "Bar Koziba reigned two and a half years, and then said to the rabbis, 'I am the Messiah.' They answered, 'Of Messiah it is written that he smells and judges: let us see whether he [bar Koziba] can do so.' When they saw that he was unable to judge by the scent, they slew him." The situation is analogous to Ch. 14:61-65.

149 See further J. Blinzler, *op. cit.*, pp. 162-166; P. Benoit, "Les Outrages à Jésus Prophète," in *Neotestamentica et Patristica* (Leiden, 1962), pp. 92-110. For parallels in antiquity (Diodorus Siculus XXIV. 2; Pollux IX. 113, 129) see W. C. van Unnik, "Jesu Verhöhnung vor dem Synedrium (Mc. 14, 65 par.)," *ZNW* 29 (1930), pp. 310 f.

150 The last phrase has the support of Caesarean, Western and Byzantine witnesses but is omitted by א B L W Ψ 892 *l*$^{17, 76}$ *c* sy^{s} cop geo^{1} Diatessaron and finds no support in the parallel passages Mt. 26:71; Lk. 22:57, Jn. 18:25, where only one cock-crowing is mentioned. In the Bible Societies' edition of the Greek text the final clause is placed in brackets and assigned a D rating (of dubious textual

69 And the maid saw him, and began again to say to them that stood by, This is one of them.
70 But he again denied[151] it. And after a little while again they that stood by said to Peter, Of a truth thou art one of them; for thou art a Galilean.
71 But he began to curse, and to swear, I know not this man of whom ye speak.
72 And straightway the second time the cock crew. And Peter called to mind the word, how that Jesus said unto him, Before the cock crow twice, thou shalt deny me thrice. And when he thought thereon, he wept.[152]

66-68 The strand of narrative suspended in verse 54 is taken up at this point. The use of the literary technique of flashback indicates that the trial and interrogation of Jesus coincided, and is to be contrasted with the ordeal and interrogation of Peter (see on Ch. 14:54). The irony inherent in the situation is evident when the force of juxtaposing verse 65 and verses 66-72 is appreciated. At the precise time when the court attendants were heaping scorn and derision upon Jesus' claim to be the Messiah, the prophecy that Peter would deliberately deny him was being fulfilled. The most plausible source for this tradition is Peter himself, who must have authorized, if he did not actually construct, the version of the events.

According to Jn. 18:16, the servant girl who first recognized Peter was the portress. While it seems improbable that she had accompanied the auxiliary police to Gethsemane, from some prior occasion she was certain that she had seen Peter with Jesus. Her scornful observation, "You also were with this Nazarene, this Jesus," was calculated to embarrass and unsettle the one addressed. The reference to Jesus appears to be contemptuous, and it is possible that the expression "with this Nazarene" is intended to identify Peter as a disciple (see on Ch. 3:14).[153]

---

validity). Yet of the witnesses for the omission in verse 68 only ℵ L *c* Diatessaron omit ἐκ δευτέρου in verse 72. The omission is perhaps due to assimilation to the texts of Matthew and Luke.

151 The imperfect ἠρνεῖτο suggests repeated denials, possibly addressed to some of those who were present.

152 The meaning of ἐπιβαλὼν ἔκλαιεν is uncertain (cf. RSV: "he broke down and wept"). D Θ 565 latt sy cop^{sa} goth arm geo read ἤρξατο κλαίειν, "he began to weep," which may be a translation variant to the Semitic expression behind the text. See the important note in Bauer^4 2b (A-G, pp. 289 f.); Bl-D-F, § 308, (p. 162).

153 So J. M. Robinson, *The Problem of History in Mark* (Chicago, 1957), pp. 79 f.; R. P. Meye, *op. cit.*, p. 167.

He is one who had been "with Jesus," and who was known in terms of this relationship. But Peter denied the charge, using the form common in rabbinical law for a formal, legal denial (e.g. M. *Shebuoth* VIII. 3: "'Where is my ox?' He said to him, 'I do not know what you are saying'").[154] Peter's refusal to acknowledge his relationship to Jesus constitutes the fact of denial, behind which stands the solemn pronouncement of Ch. 14:30. Denial implies a previous relationship of obedience and fidelity. It can occur only when there has just been acknowledgment and commitment (cf. Chs. 8:29; 14:29, 31). Peter's unfaithfulness to the person of Jesus expressed anxiety for his own safety and the determination to seek approval from the bystanders rather than from the Lord. In an attempt to escape further notice he moved out to the forecourt. The crowing of the cock was so regular and common an occurrence it seemed to possess no significance for him.

69-72 Shifting his position from one part of the courtyard to another did not relieve Peter from attack. The portress not only singled him out for recognition but involved the others who were present in the situation. Her remark that Peter was "one of them" shows an awareness that Jesus had given leadership to a significant movement and had attracted a stable following of men who were nearly always with him. But Peter again failed to acknowledge his discipleship, presumably in the form employed in verse 68. His denials earned him only a brief respite, for the bystanders sensed his discomfort and refused to leave him alone. The Galileans are often mentioned in the Talmud because of their dialect (e.g. TB *'Erubin* 53b; *Megillah* 24b). They were unable to distinguish between the several guttural sounds that are so important an element in Semitic languages. Peter's speech showed him to be a Galilean and his presence among the Judeans in the courtyard invited the deduction that he was a follower of the heretic Galilean, Jesus of Nazareth.

The confident challenge, "Certainly you are one of them, for you are a Galilean," provoked Peter to maintain vehemently and formally that he had no knowledge of the Nazarene. The statement that he began to invoke a curse is intentionally left without an object in the Greek text to denote both that he cursed himself if he is lying and those present if

---

[154] The form is repeated in M. *Shebuoth* VIII. 6, and is reflected in the Testament of Joseph 13:1 f.: "'What is this that I hear concerning you, that you steal persons . . . and sell them for slaves?' But the merchant fell at his feet, and pleaded with him, saying, 'I beseech you, my Lord, I do not know what you are saying.'"

they insist on asserting that he is a disciple.[155] Peter's avoidance of the name of Jesus ("this man of whom you speak") is deliberate and exposes the Lord to the contempt envisioned in Ch. 8:38 ("ashamed of me and of my words").

Peter's emphatic denial was punctuated by the crowing of the cock a second time. It was the peculiar habit of the cock crowing, with comparative regularity, at three times during the period between midnight and 3:00 A.M. that accounts for the designation of the third watch of the night as "cock-crow" (cf. Ch. 13:35b). An early rabbinic tradition speaks of people setting out upon a night journey, departing at the first cock-crow, or the second, or the third (TB *Yoma* 21a, Baraitha). Observation over a period of twelve years in Jerusalem has confirmed that the cock crows at three distinct times, first about a half hour after midnight, a second time about an hour later, and a third time an hour after the second. Each crowing lasts from 3-5 minutes, after which all is quiet again.[156] Thus between the first crowing, noted in verse 69, and the second only an hour had passed, but Peter had been provoked to deny solemnly and emphatically his relationship to Jesus three times. He remembered Jesus' prophecy of his faithlessness and the circumstances in which it had been uttered (Ch. 14:27-31),[157] and was overwhelmed with grief. It was like awakening from an evil dream that had begun with the failure to stay awake in Gethsemane (cf. Ch. 14:37). Peter fled in shame from those who had witnessed his ignominious denial and wept tears of remorse.

The tradition of Peter's denial was undoubtedly included in the Gospel to provide a sober example to the Christian community in Rome. The fact that it is intimately tied to the account of Jesus before the Sanhedrin emphasizes the integrity of Jesus and his confession and the faithlessness of his disciple who refused to acknowledge his Lord. Preparation for this pointed contrast was provided in the account of the sleeping disciples in Gethsemane who failed in the disciplines of vigilance and

---

155 Cf. J. Behm, *TWNT* I (Eng. Tr. 1964), p. 355; J. Schneider, *TWNT* V (Eng. Tr. 1967), pp. 184 f.

156 H. Kosmala, "The Time of Cock-Crow," *Annual of the Swedish Theological Institute* 2 (1963), pp. 118-120; 6 (1968), pp. 132-134.

157 J. N. Birdsall, "τὸ ῥῆμα ὡς εἶπεν αὐτῷ ὁ Ἰησοῦς: Mk xiv. 72," *Nov Test* 2 (1958), pp. 272-275 has called attention to the subtle idiom expressed by the ὡς construction, according to which the ὡς can be used in place of a relative pronoun when the reference is greater than the mere existence of an antecedent. In verse 72 Mark indicates that Peter recalled not merely the words of Jesus but the situation in which they were directed to him.

prayer, in the reference to the futile attempt to defend Jesus with the sword, and to the distant and hesitant "following" of Peter. This was of primary significance to Mark's readers, whose faith was severely tested by the measures adopted in imperial Rome to stamp out an unwanted sect. The fact of Peter's denial constituted a solemn warning that a bold affirmation of fidelity did not guarantee faithfulness. It constituted a plea to hold fast to one's confession of Jesus. But it also provided a word of encouragement that one who failed his Lord through denial could be restored, for the episode recounted in Ch. 14:66-72 remains incomplete without the promise to Peter in Ch. 16:7 that he will experience forgiveness and restoration in Galilee.

CHAPTER 15

12. The Trial of Jesus before Pilate's Tribunal. Ch. 15:1-15

1 And straightway in the morning the chief priests with the elders and scribes, and the whole council, held a consultation,[1] and bound Jesus, and carried him away, and delivered him up to Pilate.
2 And Pilate asked him, Art thou the King of the Jews? And he answering saith unto him, Thou sayest.
3 And the chief priests accused him of many things.[2]
4 And Pilate again asked him, saying, Answerest thou nothing? behold how many things they accuse thee of.
5 But Jesus no more answered anything; insomuch that Pilate marvelled.
6 Now at the feast he used to release unto them one prisoner, whom they asked of him.
7 And there was one called Barabbas, lying bound with them that had made insurrection, men who in the insurrection had committed murder.
8 And the multitude went up[3] and began to ask him to do as he was wont to do unto them.
9 And Pilate answered them, saying, Will ye that I release unto you the King of the Jews?

---

1 Gr. συμβούλιον ποιήσαντες cannot mean "held a council meeting," but must carry the same nuance of "taking a decision" or "making a resolution" that this phrase has in Ch. 3:6; Mt. 12:14; 22:15; 27:7; 28:12. This συμβούλιον provides no support for holding that there was a second meeting of the Sanhedrin early in the morning. What is reported is the final phase of the meeting which took place in the palace of the high priest near the hour of midnight, Ch. 14:53-65 (see above on Ch. 14:54). Cf. A. N. Sherwin-White, *Roman Society and Roman Law in the New Testament* (Oxford, 1963), pp. 44 f.; G. Schneider, "Gab es eine vorsynoptische Szene 'Jesus vor dem Synhedrium'?" *Nov Test* 12 (1970), pp. 22-39.

2 In predominantly Caesarean witnesses (W Δ Θ pc *al a c* sy^s h geo aeth arm) the words αὐτὸς δὲ οὐδὲν ἀπεκρίνατο ("but he answered nothing") are added after πολλά ("many things"). Verse 4 seems to presuppose a statement such as this.

3 Gr. ἀναβάς is supported by the better witnesses (א* B D 892 latt cop); most other MSS, however, have ἀναβοήσας (the people "cried out"), and this variant reading, which presupposes the practice of demanding the release of a prisoner through acclamation, is held to be original by J. Colin, *Les villes libres de l'Orient gréco-romain et l'envoi au supplice par les acclamations populaires* (Bruxelles, 1965), pp. 13 f.

10 For he perceived that for envy the chief priests had delivered him up.
11 But the chief priests stirred up the multitude, that he should rather release Barabbas unto them.
12 And Pilate again answered and said unto them, What then shall I do unto him whom ye call the King of the Jews?
13 And they cried out again, Crucify him.
14 And Pilate said unto them, Why, what evil hath he done? But they cried out exceedingly, Crucify him.
15 And Pilate, wishing to content the multitude, released unto them Barabbas, and delivered Jesus, when he had scourged him, to be crucified.

In the narrative of Jesus' trial by the Roman prefect Pilate, Mark was not concerned to produce a detailed report of the proceedings but to sketch a course of events significant for the salvation of mankind. Analogous to the account in Ch. 14:53-65, the tradition clusters around the interrogation, condemnation and subsequent mockery of Jesus. Yet between the two narratives there are profound differences. While Jesus was prosecuted under the Jewish law and condemned for blasphemy by the Sanhedrin, he was tried before Pilate under the Roman law governing *lèse majesté* or high treason. Other details in the two accounts correspond to this fundamental distinction. Thus Jesus is mocked by the attendants of the Sanhedrin as a messianic prophet, while the rude treatment he received from the Roman soldiery showed contempt for his pretensions to kingship. What is of utmost significance to Mark is that both the Sanhedrin and the Roman governor consigned Jesus to die *as the Messiah,* and that this course of events conformed to the will of God expressed forcefully in the solemn passion prophecy of Ch. 10:33-34.

The account of Jesus' conduct before Roman authority was of primary importance to Mark's readers. Many of them would be compelled to stand before a pagan tribunal and would be subjected to the same indignities he suffered. They were to expect no preferential treatment. Jesus had clearly said that his followers would be "handed over" to governors and kings for his sake and would be held in contempt (Ch. 13:9-13). From this account of Jesus, who was "handed over" to the Roman military governor, the Church learned that it experienced nothing which was not already familiar to its Lord, "who in his testimony before Pontius Pilate made the good confession" (I Tim. 6:13). Understanding the meaning behind Jesus' humiliation from the context of the will of God, Christians could prepare themselves for their own passion narrative with faith and dignity.

1 The city of Jerusalem, together with the province of Judea which was under its jurisdiction, was designated "subject territory" in the time of the procurators.[4] This signified that matters of legislation, the administration of justice, and government were subject to the supervision of the Roman provincial authorities. Generally speaking, however, the Romans permitted even the subject territories to retain their own legislation, administration of justice, and local government, and there is considerable evidence that Jewish authorities in Judea were allowed a great measure of self-government. The Sanhedrin exercised not only civil jurisdiction according to Jewish law but also a certain degree of criminal jurisdiction. Under certain circumstances it could pronounce a death sentence, but there is no definite proof that it could legitimately execute capital sentences. The "right of the sword" was reserved to the Roman magistrate as sole bearer of the full imperial authority *(imperium)*. This was one of the most carefully guarded prerogatives of the Roman government and permitted no concessions.[5]

Consequently, the Sanhedrin had to surrender its prisoner to the Romans if the sentence of the court was to be carried out. The prefect could exercise the right of confirmation or he could reverse the death sentence passed by the Jewish council (cf. Jn. 19:10). Naturally, this alternative demanded that he acquaint himself independently with the subject of the conviction. In such a case a new trial had to be conducted before the Roman court, and the Sanhedrin would be required to convince the governor that Jesus had committed a capital offense under Roman law.[6] Since blasphemy was not one of the crimes for which Roman law provided punishment, and was a subject which did not

---

[4] See V. A. Tcherikover, "Was Jerusalem a *Polis?*" *Israel Exploration Journal* 14 (1964), pp. 61-78.

[5] See A. N. Sherwin-White, *op. cit.*, pp. 1-47; E. Lohse, *TWNT* VII (1964), pp. 862-864; P. Garnsey, "The Criminal Jurisdiction of Governors," *Journal of Roman Studies* 58 (1968), pp. 51-59; J. Blinzler, *Der Prozess Jesu*[4] (Regensburg, 1969), pp. 229-244.

[6] The fact that Jesus was delivered to Pilate, not as a blasphemer, in accordance with the judgment rendered in Ch. 14:64, but as "King of the Jews," is sufficient proof that the accusation against him had been formulated in terms of another law, and specifically one which proceeded with particular severity against *political* crimes. So J. Blinzler, *op. cit.*, pp. 247 f. n. 14.

concern the Roman judge, this charge played no part in the trial which followed. The incendiary charge of high treason, which the Roman court could not possibly dismiss, was substituted in its place.[7] This recasting of the indictment was necessarily one of the subjects of the resolution indicated by Mark in verse 1. This decision constituted the final action of the council and terminated its all-night session.

The official residence of the Judean procurators was Caesarea Maritima.[8] When the Roman officials came to Jerusalem on special occasions, particularly at the great Jewish festivals, they took up quarters in the palace of Herod, which was situated in the northwest of the city.[9] Josephus states explicitly that the procurator, Gessius Florus, lived there and held his court on the public square in front of the buildings (*War* II. xiv. 8, xv. 5). That this was true of Pilate as well may be deduced from the information that he had gilded votive tablets bearing Tiberius' name erected in the royal palace (Philo, *Legation to Gaius* 38). Mark locates the Roman trial of Jesus in "the praetorium" (Ch. 15:16), which in this context can only mean the official residence of the governor. While the question whether the praetorium of Pilate is to be situated in the fortress Antonia, which was located northwest of the Temple, or whether it was identical with the palace of Herod has been disputed, the weight of evidence favors the latter location.[10] Jesus was therefore bound and led through the city from the quarters of Caiaphas to the strongly fortified and handsomely equipped palace of the Herods, where he was accused of high treason before Pontius Pilate.

Pilate belonged to a special group of imperial administrators, consisting of men beneath the rank of senator, the so-called equestrian class or Roman "knights." These magistrates, who owned a moderate minimum of property, were used to govern relatively small areas that

---

7 *Ibid.*, pp. 248-250.

8 Cf. A. Reifenberg, "Caesarea. A Study in the Decline of a Town," *Israel Exploration Journal* 1 (1950-51), pp. 20-23, 27-29. For Pilate see Josephus, *Antiquities* XVIII. iii. 1; *War* II. ix. 2; Philo, *Legation to Gaius* 38.

9 C. Kopp, *The Holy Places of the Gospels* (New York, 1963), pp. 367-370. It was a Roman custom for the governors to take up residence in the palaces of the former rulers.

10 *Ibid.*, pp. 369 f. Cf. R. Eckardt, "Das Praetorium des Pilatus," *ZDPV* 34 (1911), pp. 39-48; P. Benoit, "Prétoire, Lithostraton et Gabbatha," *RB* 59 (1952), pp. 531-550; *idem*, "L'Antonia d'Hérode le Grand et le Forum Oriental d'Aelia Capitolina," *HTR* 64 (1971), pp. 135-167; M. Aline, *La fortresse Antonia à Jerusalem et la Question du Prétoire* (Jerusalem, 1955); J. Blinzler, *op. cit.*, Exkurs XI: "Wo lag des Praetorium des Pilatus?", pp. 256-259 with full bibliography.

required careful supervision. Their official title in the period prior to Claudius was not procurator but prefect *(praefectus)*.[11] So far as criminal and political jurisdiction was concerned, they possessed powers similar to those held by senatorial proconsuls and imperial legates.[12] Pilate came to Judea in the year A.D. 26 as the fifth of the provincial prefects and remained in office ten years. He showed himself a harsh administrator who despised the Jewish people and their particular sensitivities.[13]

The detail that Jesus was delivered to Pilate's forum early in the morning is a significant index of the historical accuracy of the tradition. It was necessary for the Sanhedrin to bring its business to Pilate as soon after dawn as possible because the working day of a Roman official began at the earliest hour of daylight. Legal trials in the Roman forum were customarily held shortly after sunrise, as Seneca noted in a wry comment: "All these thousands hurrying to the forum at the break of day–how base their cases, and how much baser are their advocates" (*On Anger* II. vii. 3). If the chief priests had delayed until morning to examine Jesus and then sought to bring him before the governor, they would have arrived too late and interrupted Pilate in the carefully organized leisure of a Roman gentleman.[14] That is a major reason why the Jewish court conducted its own proceedings throughout the night.

2 While the Sanhedrin was essentially a bench of judges, judgment in a Roman tribunal was the sole responsibilty of the imperial magistrate. Those who usually sat with him on the bench, the barristers and officials, had no judicial power, but served only as legal advisors. In the eastern provinces of the empire Greek was the language most commonly used in the administration of justice, and Josephus states that in Judea the procurators conducted their legal proceedings with the provincials through interpreters (*War* V. ix. 2; VI. ii. 1). The proceedings, which

---

11 When Tacitus, *Annals* XV. 44 calls Pilate "procurator," he is using a later term familiar to him. This is confirmed by a Latin inscription found in Caesarea in 1961 which mentions Pilate and calls him "[praef]ectus Iud[aea]e." See J. Vardaman, "A New Inscription which mentions Pilate as 'Prefect'," *JBL* 81 (1962), pp. 70 f.; E. Stauffer, *Die Pilatusinschrift von Caesarea* (Erlangen, 1966).

12 See A. N. Sherwin-White, *op. cit.*, pp. 5-23.

13 For a review of Pilate's career and a full bibliography, see J. Blinzler, *op. cit.*, pp. 260-273. Cf. H. Wansbrough, "Suffered Under Pontius Pilate," *Scripture* 18 (1966), pp. 84-93.

14 A. N. Sherwin-White, *op. cit.*, pp. 45 f.

were public on principle, were opened by an indictment on the part of the plaintiff and by a magisterial examination in which the principle of free assessment of testimony was exercised. The statements of the defendant and the evidence of witnesses were regarded as the chief source of proof. When all evidence had been taken this fact was declared by a herald. After consulting with his advisors, the magistrate announced his verdict from the judgment seat, and the sentence had to be executed immediately. [15]

The specialist in Roman law, A. N. Sherwin-White, has remarked that "in the hearing before Pilate, the Markan narrative fits the Roman framework well, considering that it was written with an entirely different purpose in mind." [16] Mark's account of the trial proceedings is actually of a very summary kind, and must be supplemented by details from the other Gospels and from known Roman legal procedure. [17] It must be assumed that when Jesus was handed over to the governor by court attendants that Pilate was informed either in writing or verbally of the accusations made against the prisoner. The first question addressed to Jesus, "Are you the king of the Jews?" indicates that the procurator had already been informed of such a charge when Jesus was delivered up at the praetorium. The chief accusation was that Jesus was guilty of high treason against the government because he wanted to make himself king of the Jews. The designation "king of the Jews" is a secularized form of "Messiah" which permitted Jesus' messianic claim to be transposed into a political key inviting the decisive intervention of Pilate. The Sanhedrin certainly recognized that the words "king of the Jews" conveyed to the Roman governor an understanding essentially different from the designation "Messiah" which Jesus had accepted (Ch. 14:62). The new formulation meant "a leader of the resistance," as shown by the remarks of Josephus concerning the riots which followed Herod's death: "as the several companies of the seditious met anyone to give them leadership, he was created king immediately, in order to do mischief to the public; they were in some small ways hurtful to the Romans ..." (*Antiquities* XVIII. x. 8). It must be considered highly ironical that having branded Jesus a blasphemer because he failed to correspond to the nationalistic messianic ideal, the council now wanted

---

15 *Ibid.*, pp. 14-22; J. Blinzler, *op. cit.*, pp. 251 f., 343 f.
16 *Op. cit.*, p. 24.
17 For a full treatment see J. Blinzler, *op. cit.*, pp. 277-346.

him condemned by the pagan tribunal on the plausible allegation that he made claims of a distinctly political character.

Jesus was the king of the Jews by virtue of his messiahship, but the implications in the secular designation were false. Therefore, he responded affirmatively to Pilate's question whether he was the king of the Jews, but with a reservation which hinted that his own conception of kingship did not correspond to that implied in the question.[18] If a concise, unreserved affirmation was implied in his response, Pilate would have declared the examination ended and passed sentence. The restrictive wording of Jesus' admission, however, made necessary an examination of the accusers for the purpose of obtaining further information.[19]

3-5 The chief priests seized the opportunity of substantiating their charges, but only the evangelist Luke provides the details. According to Lk. 23:2 the Sanhedrin urged the multiple charge that Jesus was inciting the populace to riot, that he was forbidding the payment of taxes to Caesar, and that he had royal pretensions. When Pilate remained unconvinced, they reintroduced their first impeachment that Jesus was stirring up the people with his teaching throughout Judea and Galilee (Lk. 23:5). Such multiple charges were common in criminal jurisdiction in the provinces during the period of the Flavian emperors.[20] While the report of these accusations is generalized in Mark, in practice there must have been only two or three spokesmen who alleged certain facts which Pilate must adjudicate.

After listening to the chief priests, Pilate challenged the accused to define his position, but to his astonishment Jesus refused to defend himself. Surrounded by unbelief and hostility, he manifested the exalted, sublime silence of the suffering servant of God (Isa. 53:7). Such silence was wholly unusual in the forum, and demonstrated a presence and a dignity which puzzled the prefect. Nevertheless, without a defense it would have been necessary for Pilate to have pronounced against Jesus.[21] To judge from early martyr trials, those who refused to defend themselves were given three opportunities to change their minds before sentence was passed. Roman magistrates were as reluctant to sentence

---

18 Cf. Bl-D-F § 441:3 (p. 227); J. Irmscher, "Σὺ λέγεις," *Studii Clasice* 2 (1960), pp. 151-158.

19 Already pointed out by M. Dibelius, "Herodes und Pilatus," *ZNW* 16 (1915), p. 117.

20 A. N. Sherwin-White, *op. cit.*, p. 35.

21 *Ibid.*, pp. 25 f.

an undefended man as one who was inadequately accused (cf. Acts 25:16). As it was, Pilate was disinclined to believe that Jesus was guilty. In order to understand this it is important to remember that the Gospels preserve only an excerpt from the trial, and it is obvious that Jesus' answer to the magistrate's initial question was necessarily fuller than the reserved admission reported in verse 2. At this point it is possible to supplement Mark's account with tradition peculiar to John alone (Jn. 18:33-38), where Jesus' explanation of the nature of his kingship indicates why Pilate became convinced that he was not a political offender.[22]

The theme of Jesus' silence is sustained throughout the Marcan passion narrative. From the time of his arrest until his death, he makes only two brief responses, one to Caiaphas and one to Pilate. He remains the passive one, in the conviction that the Son of Man *must* suffer and die (Ch. 8:31). Mark's reader senses in Jesus' passivity and silence that the sovereign Lord of history is accomplishing his mysterious purposes to which even the Son of Man must be submissive.

6 Pilate did not believe Jesus was guilty, but rather than pronouncing for acquittal he decided it would be politically expedient to deal with this case in terms of the paschal amnesty. Two forms of amnesty existed in Roman law, the *abolitio* or acquittal of a prisoner not yet condemned, and the *indulgentia,* or pardoning of one already condemned.[23] What Pilate intended in the case of Jesus, who at this stage of the proceedings had not yet been sentenced by the court, was clearly the first form. It was the governor's custom to release one prisoner upon popular request at the Feast of the Passover, and apparently he believed that the people would ask for Jesus. This mistaken conviction, with the consequences to which it led, becomes the focus of Mark's concern in the verses which follow.

The historicity of the paschal amnesty has been disputed often,[24]

---

[22] Cf. J. Blinzler, *op. cit.,* pp. 282 f. J. D. M. Derrett, *An Oriental Lawyer Looks at the Trial of Jesus and the Doctrine of Redemption* (London, 1966), p. 33 points out that for Pilate "to feel the pulse of public life he required a complicated system of precautions about which we know very little but which cannot for a moment be doubted. Pilate must have had informers, spies and advisers, and can have had more than an inkling of what was going on."

[23] Cf. W. Waldstein, *Untersuchung zum römischen Begnadigungsrecht. Abolitio-indulgentia-venia* (Vienna, 1964).

[24] Cf. P. Winter, *On the Trial of Jesus* (Berlin, 1961), pp. 91 f.: "The custom of *privilegium paschale* (the release of a prisoner at Passover) is nothing but a

primarily because Josephus offers no evidence that such a custom ever existed. There is, however, a parallel in Roman law which indicates that an imperial magistrate could pardon and acquit individual prisoners in response to the shouts of the populace. This practice is illustrated by a papyrus document which may be dated A.D. 85, reporting the trial of one Phibion, who had locked up his alleged creditor and certain women of his household. The magistrate, G. Septimius Vegetus, the governor of Egypt, said to the defendant: "You deserve to be scourged for having imprisoned, on your own responsibility, a decent man and his women, but I will deal more humanely with you and will give you to the populace."[25] Although there is no evidence here of a regular amnesty on a feast, the case is analogous to the one before Pilate: the governor released a criminal at the wish of the people, an action that was consistent with his imperial authority. Moreover, a provision in the Mishnah tractate *Pesachim* VIII 6a ("they may slaughter for one... whom they have promised to bring out of prison..."), which is judged to belong to the earliest strata of the Mishnah, implies that the custom of releasing one prisoner or several at the Feast of the Passover must actually have existed in Jerusalem in the first century.[26]

7-9 In quelling an uprising the Romans had seized the insurgent Barabbas, who was charged with murder, together with some of his

---

figment of the Gospel writer's imagination. No such custom existed." Cf. H. Z. Maccoby, "Jesus and Barabbas," *NTS* 16 (1969), pp. 55-60, who dismisses as unhistorical both the paschal privilege and the incident of Barabbas' release.

25 Papyrus Florentinus 61, 59 ff. on which see J. Blinzler, *op. cit.,* pp. 301-303 and especially n. 7 (p. 303). A. Steinwenter, "Il processo di Gesù," *Jus* n.s. 3 (1952), pp. 471-490 calls attention to an Ephesian inscription dated A.D 441 where Phlegethius, the proconsul of Asia, reminds the people of Smyrna that they deserve punishment, but adds, "because of the shouts of this illustrious metropolis of the Ephesians, and because their petitions ought not to be set aside, we release you." The action of these two Roman officials in the eastern empire at an interval of centuries shows that Pilate's action fell within his *imperium*. Cf. Acts 3:14.

26 See C. B. Cheval, "The Releasing of a Prisoner on the Eve of Passover in Ancient Jerusalem," *JBL* 60 (1941), pp. 273-278; J. Blinzler, *op. cit.,* pp. 317-320. Blinzler comments: "The fact that the Mishna considers, beside the case of the sick and aged, what one might think the wholly exceptional case of a prisoner promised release, permits one to conclude that the release of a Jewish prisoner shortly before the evening of the paschal meal, i.e. on the fourteenth of Nisan, was at least a frequent, but most probably a regular occurrence. Hence, the Mishna text actually represents a notable support for the NT account concerning the paschal amnesty" (p. 318).

accomplices. Nothing is known about this insurrection, although Mark speaks of it as well known. In the period of the procurators revolts and bloodshed were constant occurrences (cf. Lk. 13:1; Josephus, *Antiquities* XVIII. i. 1; iii. 2), and the redemptive associations of the pilgrimage feasts only added fuel to a resentment of the Roman presence that constantly smoldered. The leader of this revolt seems to have been a popular hero, and may have been a leading Zealot, but little is known of him or his deeds.[27] The surname Barabbas (Bar Abba, i.e. "son of Abba" or "son of the father") was not uncommon among the rabbis.[28] The fact that Barabbas is introduced prior to the reference to the petitioners in verse 8 suggests that the latter were supporters of the insurgent who came to the forum specifically to ask for his release.

In the course of the proceedings a substantial crowd came from the lower town to the praetorium to exercise the customary privilege of petition. Pilate apparently regarded their arrival as opportune. He could achieve his ends by guiding the amnesty negotiations along lines he had determined. Before listening to the people he seems to have presented as his own candidate for release "the king of the Jews." His offer of generosity was doubtlessly tinged with irony, but he believed that the people would fall in line with his proposal.[29]

10 Pilate's efforts to rescue Jesus were not dictated simply by motives of justice and humanity. On the contrary, the predominant motive of his actions was undoubtedly that anti-Semitic bias for which both Philo and

---

[27] For a review of fact and conjecture see J. Blinzler, *op. cit.*, pp. 308 f. nn. 25, 26; A. Bajšić, "Pilatus, Jesus und Barabbas," *Biblica* 48 (1967), pp. 7-28.

[28] S-B*K* I (1922), p. 1031.

[29] Pilate may have been the victim of a misunderstanding. According to the Caesarean text of Mt. 27:16 f. (Θ λ 700* sys pal arm geo² old MSS known to Origen [*In Matt. Comm. Ser.* 121]) the insurgent leader is called "Jesus Barabbas," a reading which may be correct (cf. NEB "Jesus Bar-Abbas"). If the insurgent was also named Jesus, Pilate may have mistaken the shouts of the crowd for the release of Jesus (Barabbas) as a demonstration in favor of Jesus of Nazareth. This would offer a cogent explanation why the case of Jesus became confused with the amnesty demonstration of the crowd. Cf. P. L. Couchoud-R. Stahl, "Jesus Barabbas," *Hibbert Journal* 25 (1927), pp. 26-42; H. A. Rigg, Jr., "Barabbas," *JBL* 64 (1945), pp. 428-432; R. Dunkerley, "Was Barabbas also Called Jesus?" *ExT* 74 (1963), pp. 126 f. (with a reply by R. C. Nevius, p. 255). K. H. Rengstorf, *TWNT* IV (Eng. Tr. 1967), p. 262 feels that what was involved was a sorry jest on the part of Pilate, who allowed the people to choose Jesus bar Abba or Jesus bar Joseph, both presented as Zealot leaders.

Josephus faulted him.[30] Because he despised the Jews, whom he regarded as an obstreperous and rebellious race, and seized every opportunity to let them see this, he inevitably adopted an attitude of resistance when he was asked to condemn the prisoner brought before him. He could not have failed to perceive that the insistence of the priests on the execution of Jesus was due to some hidden agenda. His suspicion of ulterior motives increased when he learned that the defendant was to be put to death as a political offender. It did not require any peculiar sagacity on Pilate's part to realize that the spokesmen for the Sanhedrin were not acting out of loyalty to Rome. They clearly wanted to be rid of someone troublesome to them and they intended to use the Roman magistrate as their henchman. Seen in this light, Pilate's reluctance to accede to the priests' demand is understandable and inevitable. His determination to evade their scheme was undoubtedly strengthened when in the course of his examination of the accused it became clear he was anything but a political agitator.

11 Pilate had failed to consider that the populace, who were incensed about a Roman presence in Jerusalem, would never align themselves with him if they were asked to choose between a solution he proposed and one supported by the leaders of the Sanhedrin. Moreover, it is probable that the crowd had already agreed to seek the release of the freedom fighter Barabbas, whose bold actions seem to have won popular support. In Judea it was customary to confront the Roman authorities with as large and boisterous a delegation as could be mustered (cf. Acts 24:1; Josephus, *Antiquities* XVIII. viii. 4). With the encouragement of the chief priests the noisy crowd emphatically rejected Pilate's offer and clamored for the release of Barabbas (cf. Acts 3:13 f.). This tragic decision is best explained by the fact that Jesus had been formally condemned by the Sanhedrin as a violator of the law who deserved to die. There was no reason for the people, who openly regarded Jesus as a threat to the release of their man, to dispute this sober fact as represented by the spokesmen for the Jewish court who urged them to persist in their acclamation of Barabbas. That alone seems to account for their calloused response when Pilate inquired what should be done with Jesus.[31]

---

[30] Cf. A. D. Doyle, "Pilate's Career and the Date of the Crucifixion," *JThS* 42 (1941), pp. 190-193; P. L. Maier, "Sejanus, Pilate and the Date of the Crucifixion," *Church History* 37 (1968), pp. 3-13.

[31] See J. Blinzler, *op. cit.*, pp. 309-311.

12-14 The rejection of his offer seems to have surprised the prefect, who continued to attempt to negotiate with the crowd. He consulted the will of the people with the ill-considered question, "What then do you want me to do with the king of the Jews?" If he had hoped that the populace would call for some milder form of punishment than that demanded by the chief priests he was mistaken. They promptly responded with the shrill yell, "Crucify him!" When the governor protested that no sufficient cause had been demonstrated and challenged the crowd to name the treasonable crime by which the Galilean had merited this punishment, the people contemptuously and persistently shouted their demand more loudly. The shouts of the crowd are probably to be categorized as "acclamations," in accordance with the legal provision for decision upon popular demand.[32] Both the leaders of the people and the inflamed crowd demanded not simply capital punishment, but the most ignominous form of death, crucifixion. Jesus must be declared guilty of high treason and punished with the full rigor of the law promulgated by the Emperor Augustus, the *lex Iulia maiestatis.*[33]

15 The tactical blunder of deferring to the riotous crowd in the matter of the paschal amnesty created the dangerous situation in which the point of control had passed from the magistrate to the excited people. On the ground of political expediency Pilate decided that he had no choice but to yield to the determined will of the now fanatical mob. In order to placate the people he released Barabbas and gave orders for Jesus to be scourged.[34]

---

[32] *Ibid.*, pp. 312 f. n. 38. The primary sources are Tacitus, *Annals* I. 44; Codex Theodosianus VI. ix. 2; IX. xlvii. 12; Maximius, *History of Augustus* XVI. 6. For examples of the proneness of Roman judges to yield before popular clamor see E. Bickermann, "*Utilitas crucis.* Observations sur les récits du procès de Jésus dans les Évangiles canoniques," *Revue de l'Histoire des Religions* 112 (1935), pp. 209 f.

[33] Cf. C. W. Wilton, "The Roman Law of Treason under the Early Principate," *Journal of Roman Studies* 45 (1955), pp. 73-81; E. Koestermann, "Die Majestätsprozesse unter Tiberius," *Historia* 4 (1955), pp. 72-106; R. S. Rogers, *Criminal Trials and Criminal Legislation under Tiberius* (Middletown, Conn., 1935). High treason was classed as a capital offense and was punishable by crucifixion, by consignment to the wild beasts in the arena, or by banishment to an island, according to the status of the delinquent. In the provinces of the empire the *crimen laesae maiestatis* was normally punished with crucifixion.

[34] E. Stauffer, *Jesus and His Story* (New York, 1960), pp. 131-134 finds the explanation for Pilate's apparent vacillation and indecisiveness in the execution

A Roman scourging was a terrifying punishment. The delinquent was stripped, bound to a post or a pillar, or sometimes simply thrown to ground, and was beaten by a number of guards until his flesh hung in bleeding shreds. The instrument indicated by the Marcan text, the dreaded *flagellum,* was a scourge consisting of leather thongs plaited with several pieces of bone or lead so as to form a chain. No maximum number of strokes was prescribed by Roman law, and men condemned to flagellation frequently collapsed and died from the flogging.[35] Josephus records that he himself had some of his opponents in Galilee scourged until their entrails were visible (*War* II. xxi. 5), while the procurator Albinus had the prophet Jesus bar Ḥanan scourged until his bones lay visible (*War* VI. v. 3). Although scourging was a customary preliminary to execution after a capital sentence (e.g. Josephus, *War* II. xiv. 9; V. xi. 1; VII. vi. 4; Livy XXXIII. 36), it was also inflicted as an independent punishment. According to Mark (cf. Lk. 23:16, 22; Jn. 19:1-4), the scourging ordered by Pilate preceded in time the sentence of crucifixion.[36] Not until the governor pronounced a death sentence could the scourging be regarded as a prelude to crucifixion. The text is most intelligible on the understanding that the flogging took place, not in the public square in front of the praetorium, but inside the building, since Mark explicitly states that the mocking of Jesus took place within the courtyard of the palace (verse 16). It is scarcely credible that Jesus should have been taken into the governor's residence after he had been scourged, since the mocking is a boisterous sequel to the scourging and was doubtless set in motion by the men responsible for its administration. The two phases of Jesus' humiliation presumably took place on the same site.

The statement that Pilate "delivered him to be crucified" may have been formulated to call to mind Isa. 53:6, 12 LXX, where the expression "delivered" is used in reference to the sufferings and death of the servant of the Lord. The early Christians were less interested in the

---

of his patron, the anti-Semite Sejanus, by Tiberius on Oct. 19, A.D. 31. This turn of events greatly endangered his own political standing. He could not afford to be charged with criminal leniency toward a subversive agitator accused of high treason. Cf. P. L. Maier, *op. cit.,* pp. 3-13.

[35] Cf. C. Schneider, *TWNT* IV (Eng. Tr. 1967), pp. 517-519.

[36] J. Blinzler, *op. cit.,* pp. 334-336, argues that the fact that the order that Jesus be scourged is a different act from the delivering to be crucified and, moreover, one which preceded it, indicates that the death sentence was passed only after the scourging had been administered.

question whether the decision of the prefect was a legal sentence than in the fact that his action marked the fulfilment of OT prophecy. Nevertheless, while the statement is imprecise, it is equivalent to the announcement of the death sentence and means "he condemned him to death by crucifixion."[37] The mode of death had to be specified under Roman law, and it may be assumed that Pilate used the conventional form, "You shall mount the cross" *(ibis in crucem)* or "I consign you to the cross" *(abi in crucem).*[38]

13. The Mocking of Jesus. Ch. 15:16-20

16 And the soldiers led him away within the court, which is the Praetorium;[39] and they call together the whole band.[40]
17 And they clothe him with purple, and platting a crown of thorns, they put it on him,
18 and they began to salute him, Hail, King of the Jews!

---

[37] So L. Wenger, *Die Quellen des römischen Rechts* (Vienna, 1953), p. 287 n. 11; J. Blinzler, *op. cit.*, pp. 333-343, 346-356. Josephus contains a passage which has been the occasion of sustained controversy because of the Christian interpolations it contains today, the so-called "Flavian Testimony." The studies of C. Martin and F. Scheidweiler are sufficient to establish the following text: καὶ αὐτὸν ἐνδείξει τῶν πρώτων ἀνδρῶν παρ' ἡμῖν σταυρῷ ἐπιτετιμηκότος Πιλάτου οὐκ ἐπαύσαντο [θορυβεῖν] οἱ τὸ πρῶτον ἀγαπήσαντες (*Antiquities* XVIII. iii. 3); "When Pilate, upon hearing him accused by men of the highest standing among us, had condemned him to be crucified, those who had in the first place come to love him did not cease [to provoke disorders]." This text asserts that Pilate condemned Jesus to the cross as the result of accusations prosecuted by the Jewish authorities. It thus confirms the Marcan record. See C. Martin, "Le *Testimonium Flavianum.* Vers une solution définitive?" *Revue Belge de Philologie et d'Histoire* 20 (1941), pp. 409-465; F. Scheidweiler, "Sind die Interpolationen im altrussischen Josephus wertlos?," *ZNW* 43 (1950-51), pp. 177 f.; *idem,* "Das *Testimonium Flavianum,*" *ZNW* 45 (1954), pp. 230-243; F. Dornseiff, "Zum *Testimonium Flavianum,*" *ZNW* 46 (1955), pp. 245-250. Cf. Tacitus, *Annals* XV. 44, who specifies that this happened when Tiberius was emperor.

[38] *Ibid.*, p. 339, citing Petronius, *Satires* CXXXVII. 9; Plautus, *Mostellaria* III. ii. 163 (§ 850).

[39] See above on Ch. 15:1.

[40] Gr. σπεῖρα ordinarily means a cohort, i.e. one-tenth of a Roman legion or 600 men. It may also designate a *maniple,* which consisted of two or three hundred men. It is important, however, in this context to understand that the reference is to an auxiliary cohort which had accompanied Pilate from Caesarea to Jerusalem and need not have been identical in numbers to the cohort normally stationed in the Antonia fortress in Jerusalem.

19 And they smote his head with a reed, and spat upon him, and bowing their knees worshipped him.
20 And when they had mocked him, they took off from him the purple, and put on him his garments. And they lead him out to crucify him.

16-19 The scourging of the Galilean who claimed to be king of the Jews caused a sensation among the detachment of soldiers quartered in the praetorium. They were auxiliary troops recruited from among the non-Jewish inhabitants of Palestine who were assigned to the military governor, and had accompanied him from Caesarea to Jerusalem to assist in the maintenance of public order. After the sentence had been carried out the soldiers, who knew from the trial of Jesus' admission, proceeded to make a mockery of his kingship by an uproarious masquerade.[41] Mark's description suggests a kind of grotesque vaudeville: Jesus, bruised and bleeding, is pushed among the coarse soldiers who gathered in the expectation of a few moments of entertainment. From their point of view the condemned man represented a welcome diversion from the tension that always mounted in Jerusalem during the festival season. In imitation of the purple robe and the gilded wreath of leaves which were the insignia of the Hellenistic vassal kings (cf. I Macc. 10:20, 62, 69; 11:58; 14:43 f.), they threw around Jesus' naked body a faded scarlet cloak (cf. Mt. 27:28) or some shabby purple rug, and pressed down on his head a wreath plaited from the branches of some available shrub such as acanthus or of palm-spines. This pretendant to the throne would be both a vassal prince and a figure of fun. The so-called crown of thorns was not meant primarily as a torture but was part of the mock royal attire, like the robe. It may well have been an improvised caricature of the radiate crown signifying divine kingship and frequently depicted

[41] Cf. R. Delbrueck, "Antiquarisches zu den Verspottungen Jesu," *ZNW* 41 (1942), pp. 124-145. The nearest parallels are the mocking of the imbecile Karabas in Alexandria in A.D. 38 to express contempt for Agrippa I (Philo, *Against Flaccus* VI, 36-39), the brutal action of Roman soldiers with the dethroned emperor Vitellius prior to his execution (Dio Cassius LXV. 20 f.), and a similar incident after the Jewish uprising of A.D. 115-117 reported in a fragmentary papyrus (see V. A. Tcherikover and A. Fuks, *Corpus Papyrorum Judaicarum* II [Cambridge, Mass., 1960], pp. 89, 94, 96 n. 7 for text, translation and commentary respectively on Papyrus Louvre 68, col. i. 1-14). The parallels show simply that a perverted sense of humor, which would indulge in such mockery as Mark reports, was not uncommon in this period.

on coins then in circulation.[42] When Jesus had been invested with the regalia of a vassal prince, the soldiers pretended to recognize his regal claim. The salutation "Hail, King of the Jews!" corresponds formally to the Roman acclamation "Ave, Caesar!", the vocative admitting the royal prerogative, while the bending of the knee before Jesus parodied an essential requisite of Hellenistic homage to the ruler. The act of spitting at him may be interpreted as a parody on the kiss of homage which was customary in the East. On the other hand, the buffeting and striking of the exhausted prisoner with rods and with the fist was mere brutality. The several elements of this rough farcical play throw into bold relief the royal pretensions of Jesus and the vulgar mentality of the soldiery, who regarded him only as an object of ridicule since he dared to rival the sovereignty of the divine emperor.

20 The soldiers then removed the mock regalia and gave Jesus back his own clothes. Normally those condemned to be crucified were led naked to the place of execution and were scourged on the way while carrying the cross-beam (cf. Dionysius of Halicarnassus VII. 69, "They accompanied him, beating his naked body with scourges"; Josephus, *Antiquities* XIX. iv. 5). Because Jesus had already been scourged, this custom was not followed. This fact also explains why the scourging which always precedes the Roman crucifixion was not administered. If it had been repeated, Jesus would have doubtless died by flagellation rather than by crucifixion. When he was clothed he was remanded to the execution squad consisting of four soldiers (Jn. 19:23) under the command of a centurion and was led out to be crucified.

14. The Crucifixion of Jesus. Ch. 15:21-32

21 And they compel one passing by, Simon of Cyrene, coming from the country, the father of Alexander and Rufus, to go with them, that he might bear his cross.

22 And they bring him unto the place Golgotha,[43] which is, being interpreted, the place of a skull.

---

[42] See H. St. J. Hart, "The Crown of Thorns in John XIX. 2-5," *JThS* n.s. 3 (1952), pp. 66-75; C. Bonner, "The Crown of Thorns," *HTR* 46 (1953), pp. 47 f.; W. Grundmann, *TWNT* VII (1964), pp. 615-622, 631 f.

[43] Gr. Γολγοθᾶ transliterates the Aramaic גֻּלְגֻּלְתָּא. In common pronunciation the second *lamed* was dropped.

23 And they offered him wine mingled with myrrh: but he received it not.
24 And they crucify him, and part his garments among them, casting lots upon them, what each should take.
25 And it was the third hour, and they crucified him.[44]
26 And the superscription of his accusation was written over, THE KING OF THE JEWS.
27 And with him they crucify two robbers; one on his right hand, and one on his left.[45]
29 And they that passed by railed on him, wagging their heads, and saying, Ha! thou that destroyest the temple, and buildest it in three days,
30 save thyself, and come down from the cross.
31 In like manner also the chief priests mocking him among themselves with the scribes said, He saved others; himself he cannot save.
32 Let the Christ, the King of Israel, now come down from the cross, that we may see and believe. And they that were crucified with him reproached him.

Death by crucifixion was one of the cruelest and most degrading forms of punishment ever conceived by human perversity, even in the eyes of the pagan world.[46] Josephus described it as "the most wretched of all ways of dying" (*War* VII. v. 4), and the shudder caused by the cross as an instrument of execution is still reflected in the English word "excruciating." Yet in the Roman provinces crucifixion was one of the customary means of preserving public order, and the history of turbulent Judea is punctuated by accounts of men being crucified. So unimportant was the crucifixion of Jesus of Nazareth from a Roman point of view

---

[44] The Western variant (D it), "they kept watch over him" is clearly secondary. It was an attempt to avoid the duplication of verse 24 and is modeled on Mt. 27:36.

[45] Caesarean and Byzantine authorities insert verse 28, "And the Scripture was fulfilled which says, 'He was reckoned with the transgressors'" (Isa. 53:12), apparently under the influence of Lk. 22:37. The omission of this verse is so strongly attested (א A B C D X Ψ *Lect* it *d k* sys cop Eusebian Canons Ammonius) that the Bible Societies' edition assigns it an "A" rating (the text is virtually certain).

[46] J. Blinzler, *op. cit.*, p. 367 cites Cicero, *Pro Rabirio* V. 16: "Even the mere word, cross, must remain far not only from the lips of the citizens of Rome, but also from their thoughts, their eyes, their ears." Elsewhere Cicero calls crucifixion the grossest, cruelest, or most hideous manner of execution (see *In Verrem* V. 64, 66).

that Tacitus, in his review of the troubles in Judea, comments, "Under Tiberius nothing happened" (*History* V. 9, *sub Tiberio quies*).

Jewish criminal law made no provision for crucifixion. The hanging on a gibbet, prescribed by law for idolaters and blasphemers who had been stoned, was not a form of capital punishment but of humiliation, since it followed death. The public exposure of an executed person branded him as one cursed by God, in accordance with the provision of Deut. 21:23 (LXX): "for he is accursed of God who hangs on a tree." These words were applied equally to one who was crucified. When the chief priests and the crowd demanded death by crucifixion for Jesus they expressed the conviction that he must take his last breath on the cross as one "accursed of God" (cf. Gal. 3:13).

In Christian perspective the cross of Christ is the focal point of the Gospel. Here God dealt definitively with the problem of human rebellion and made provision for the salvation of men. The unique character of Jesus' sufferings lies in the fact that he went to the cross in fulfilment of his mission to bear the burden of the divine judgment upon sin (see on Ch. 1:9-11; 10:38; 14:36; 15:34). The obedience he manifested in submitting to the will of God reversed a pattern of disobedience which began with Adam and has been confirmed in all subsequent human experience (cf. Rom. 5:12-21). In the cross of Christ the Christian finds that place where God identified himself with man the transgressor and overcame the alienation of men by taking upon himself the death and wrath merited by human rebellion. The account of Jesus' crucifixion thus became the centerpoint of the joyful tidings proclaimed by the Church, in the conviction that the message centering in the cross was empowered by God to overturn the note of offense and the objections of human cleverness and to bring men into the experience of redemption.

21 Jesus, together with two other condemned men, was conducted by a detachment of soldiers from the praetorium to the place of execution. The route followed normally led through busy streets in order to intimidate the people. It was customary for men condemned to die by crucifixion to carry the transverse beam of the cross (cf. Plutarch, *Moralia* 554 A: "Each of the condemned bore his own cross"). Jesus, however, had been so weakened by the scourging he had endured that he carried the beam only for a short distance. As the procession neared the city gate, the soldiers impressed a man who had just returned from the country to take the plank from Jesus and carry it to the site of execution. He was Simon of Cyrene, who appears to have been a diaspora Jew resident in Jerusalem. His full name served to distinguish him from other men of the same personal name. Mark alone mentions his two sons, Alexander and Rufus, who seem to have been well known to his readers. In Rom. 16:13 greetings are sent to a certain Rufus, and it is possible that he is identical with the man mentioned by Mark. Yet both names were in common use among Jews as well as Gentiles and permit no certain conclusion. A burial-cave used in the first century prior to the destruction of the Temple and belonging to a family of Cyrenian Jews was discovered by Israeli archeologists on the southwestern slope of the Kidron valley in November 1941. The intriguing possibility that this tomb was owned by Simon and his family is raised by an ossuary inscribed twice in Greek, "Alexander, son of Simon,"[47] although the similarity to Mark's record may be coincidental.

22 It was both Jewish and Roman practice to perform executions beyond the inhabited area of a town (cf. Lev. 24:14; Num. 15:35 f.; I Kings 21:13; Acts 7:58; Plautus, *Miles Gloriosus* II. iv. 6 f.). The place where Jesus was crucified lay outside, but near, the city wall (Jn. 19:20). Designated by the people Golgotha, "a skull," the Aramaic name suggests a round, bare hillock, while the reference to the mockery of those who passed by on the road presupposed that the hill was not very high. In the early second century Jewish Christians in Jerusalem venerated an unprepossessing end of a rocky slope outside the city as the site both of the crucifixion and of Adam's grave (Origen, *Comm. in Matt.* 27:32; PG XIII, col. 1777). The most probable site is near the present Church of the Holy Sepulchre in an area which lay outside the northern, or so-called second, wall.[48] While the course of this wall is uncertain, it seems to have extended from the Garden Gate at the eastern end of Herod's palace along a northerly direction, but then made a right-angled turn eastward, past Golgotha, but close to it on the eastern side, and on to the Antonia fortress.[49]

---

47 See N. Avigad, "A Depository of Inscribed Ossuaries in the Kidron Valley," *Israel Exploration Journal* 12 (1962), pp. 1-12.

48 Cf. C. Kopp, *op. cit.,* pp. 374-388; A. Parrot, *Golgotha and the Church of the Holy Sepulchre* (London, 1957); V. Corbo, "La basilica del S. Sepulcro a Gerusalemme," *Liber Annus* 19 (1969), pp. 65-144. The name Calvary comes from the Latin *Calvaria,* an elaboration of *calva,* "a skull."

49 So J. Simons, *Jerusalem in the Old Testament* (Leiden, 1952), pp. 282-343. The "third wall," which enclosed Golgotha, was not built until the time of Herod Agrippa I.

23 According to an old tradition, respected women of Jerusalem provided a narcotic drink to those condemned to death in order to decrease their sensitivity to the excruciating pain (TB *Sanhedrin* 43a). This humane practice was begun in response to the biblical injunction of Prov. 31:6-7: "Give strong drink to him who is perishing, and wine to those in bitter distress; let them drink and forget their poverty, and remember their misery no more." In the first century A.D. the army physician, Dioscorides Pedanius, who made an intensive study of almost 600 plants and 1,000 drugs, observed the narcotic properties of myrrh (*Materia Medica* I. lxiv. 3). When Jesus arrived at Golgotha he was offered, presumably by the women since this was a Jewish rather than a Roman custom,[50] wine mixed with myrrh, but he refused it, choosing to endure with full consciousness the sufferings appointed for him (cf. Ch. 10:38; 14:36).

24 The fact of Jesus' crucifixion is recorded with utmost restraint. The details were too familiar in the Roman world to require extended comment.[51] Normally, the delinquent was stripped, and after having been scourged, his outstretched arms were nailed or tied with cords to the cross-beam, which he himself had been forced to carry to the place of execution (cf. Artemidorus, *Oneirokritika* II. 56: "He who is nailed to the cross first carries it out"). The cross-piece was then lifted up with the body on it and fastened to an upright stake already sunk into the earth to which the feet were now nailed. The cross thus formed by the upright and the transverse beam was probably in the shape of a T. A block of wood fixed about midway up the post supported the body.

While the use of nails to fasten a body to the cross is not widely

---

[50] W. Michaelis, *TWNT* VII (1964), pp. 457-459 objects that TB *Sanhedrin* 43a is not a true parallel, since it speaks of wine mixed with frankincense. He prefers to think rather of a soldier's wine which the executioner offered to those who on the way had become exhausted, since in verse 23 "we are concerned with Roman soldiers, not Jewish women; and with wine mixed with myrrh, not frankincense." It seems probable, however, that the wine offered to those about to be crucified consisted of various ingredients, while the use of the indefinite plural is typically Marcan and need not have reference to the soldiers. For women at the site of the crucifixion see Ch. 15:40 f.

[51] For details see J. J. Collins, "The Archaeology of the Crucifixion," *CBQ* 1 (1939), pp. 154-159; E. Stauffer, *Jerusalem und Rom im Zeitalter Jesu Christi* (Bern, 1957), pp. 123-127; J. Schneider, *TWNT* VII (1964), pp. 572-584; J. Blinzler, *op. cit.*, Exkurs XVIII: "Zur Archäologie der Kreuzigung," pp. 375-381.

attested,[52] in June, 1968, a team of Israeli scholars discovered at Giv'at ha-Mivtar in northeastern Jerusalem a Jewish tomb which produced the first authenticated evidence of a crucifixion in antiquity. Among the remains in an ossuary were those of an individual whose lower calf bones had been broken and whose heel bones had been transfixed with a single iron nail.[53] The pottery and ossuaries found in the tomb establish a date in the first century A.D. prior to the mass crucifixions of A.D. 70, when tomb burials were no longer possible. Detailed study of the find showed that the feet of the victim had been nailed together between a cross of olive wood and a piece of pistacia or acacia wood with a 17-18 centimeter iron nail which had hit a knot and bent in the process.[54] Moreover, new light was shed on the position of the body on the cross:

> "the feet were joined almost parallel, both transfixed by the same nail at the heels, with the legs adjacent; the knees were doubled, the right one overlapping the left; the trunk was contorted; the upper limbs were stretched out, each stabbed by a nail in the forearm."[55]

The nature and date of these findings in the vicinity of Jerusalem provide concrete data on the manner in which Jesus was crucified.

The height of the cross varied. Normally it was not much higher than the stature of a man, so that the feet of the crucified nearly touched the ground. A high cross seems to have been used when there was the desire to make the victim visible for as wide a radius as possible. That the cross upon which Jesus was crucified was higher than normal may be deduced from the fact that the soldier who offered him a drink with a sponge soaked in vingar could not reach his mouth by hand, but had

---

[52] J. W. Hewitt, "The Use of Nails in the Crucifixion," *HTR* 25 (1932), pp. 29-45. Plautus, *Mostellaria* II. i. 12 f. states that the simple nailing of the four limbs was the normal procedure in crucifixions, but see below, n. 54. M. *Shabbath* VI. 10 mentions "the nail from the post of one who was crucified" as a healing amulet. Cf. Jn. 20:25.

[53] V. Tzaferis, "Jewish Tombs at and near Giv'at ha-Mivtar, Jerusalem," *Israel Exploration Journal* 20 (1970), pp. 18-32, especially p. 31.

[54] N. Haas, "Anthropological Observations on the Skeletal Remains from Giv'at ha-Mivtar," *Israel Exploration Journal* 20 (1970), pp. 49-59 and especially figure 6 (p. 56).

[55] *Ibid.*, p. 58. See Plate 24 for a drawing based on these findings.

to extend it with a reed (verse 36). A higher cross also gives point to the scornful challenge for Jesus to "come down" (verse 32).

Crucifixion was essentially death by exhaustion. The time required for death naturally depended on the physical condition of the victim as well as on the manner by which the body was affixed to the cross. When nails were used physical torment was heightened, but ordinarily it was less protracted because death was hastened by the loss of blood. When men had been tied to the gibbet they sometimes remained alive for several days. Yet the weight of the body hanging on the cross frequently caused such a state of exhaustion that death occurred in a matter of several hours. When it was desired to hasten the death of one who was crucified, his limbs were beaten with an iron club (cf. Jn. 19:31-33).

Men were ordinarily crucified naked (Artemidorus II. 61). Jewish sensitivities, however, dictated that men ought not to be publicly executed completely naked, and men condemned to stoning were permitted a loin-cloth (M. *Sanhedrin* VI. 3). Whether the Romans were considerate of Jewish feelings in this matter is unknown. Roman legal texts confirm that it was the accepted right of the executioner's squad to claim the minor possessions of an executed man.[56] In the case of Jesus this was limited to his clothing, which probably consisted of an under and outer garment, a belt, sandals, and possibly a head covering.[57] For these items the soldiers cast lots, oblivious to the fact that their gambling recalled the ancient lament of Ps. 22:18, "they divided my garments among them and for my raiment they cast lots." What is in the OT a poetic expression of defeat and impotence is in Mark's account a token of the powerlessness of Jesus in his humiliation.

25 The assertion that Jesus was crucified at "the third hour," that is, about nine o'clock in the morning, is problematic. Not only is this statement unreconcilable with Jn. 19:14, where it is said that Pilate pronounced his verdict "about the sixth hour" (noon), but it appears to be out of sequence in the Marcan context. Mark stated the fact of Jesus' crucifixion in verse 24a, and then proceeded to describe the division of

---

[56] See T. Mommsen, *Droit pénal romain* I (Paris, 1903), p. 280 n. 2, citing *Digest* XLVIII. iv. 11; xx. 6; Tacitus, *Annals* VI. 29. Cf. TB *Sanhedrin* 48b, "The property of those executed by the State belongs to the State."

[57] Cf. J. Repond, "Le costume de Jésus," *Biblica* 3 (1922), pp. 3-14; W. Michaelis, *TWNT* IV (Eng. Tr. 1967), p. 246.

Jesus' clothing by the soldiers following his execution. The reference to the fact of the crucifixion once more in verse 25 appears an unnecessary duplication of information just provided. If it was the evangelist's intention to specify the hour when Jesus was crucified he could have done so when the crucifixion was first reported, namely, in verse 24. In the place where the time reference now occurs, it conveys the impression of an afterthought. These considerations assume importance when it is observed that Matthew and Luke have accepted all Mark's indications of time in their respective narratives of Jesus' sufferings. Yet this verse has no parallel in either Gospel. The absence of a parallel in either Matthew or Luke can be satisfactorily explained only by the conjecture that the two evangelists did not find this verse in the copy of Mark used by them. This proposal is supported by the Gospel of Peter, whose author knew and used the canonical Gospel of Mark, which fails to indicate the hour when Jesus was crucified (Ch. 4:10), although the fact that the darkness began at midday (Ch. 5:15) and ended at the ninth hour (Ch. 6:22) is noted. This cumulative evidence suggests that verse 25, in spite of its firm textual support, is a gloss inserted by an early reviser who noticed that Mark had failed to state the hour when Jesus was nailed to the cross. Since he had no authoritative tradition at his disposal, he had to establish the hour of the crucifixion on his own authority. He chose the third hour because it appeared consistent with the three-hour interval presupposed in verse 33.[58] If this analysis is correct, verse 25 has no independent value for determining the hour when Jesus was placed on the cross. That there was an interval between the act of crucifixion and the darkening of the sky seems to be presupposed by the reference to the mocking of Jesus by those around the cross. But the duration of this interval cannot be determined from Mark's account.

26 On the way to the execution site a delinquent wore or had carried before him a wooden board whitened with chalk on which letters were

[58] This paragraph summarizes J. Blinzler, *op. cit.,* pp. 416-420. A. Mahoney, "A New Look at 'The Third Hour' of Mk 15, 25," *CBQ* 28 (1966), pp. 292-299 prefers to link the reference to the third hour with the preceding clause, and holds that the dividing of the garments probably took place at the time of the scourging, while Ch. 15:33 indicates noon as the hour of the crucifixion. This proposal fails to resolve the difficulties noted by Blinzler and is contradicted by verse 20 which speaks of the return of Jesus' clothing to him following the scourging and the mocking.

written in ink or burned in specifying his crime. After the execution this summary statement was fastened to the cross above the head of the crucified (cf. Juvenal, *Satires* VI. 230; Pliny the Younger, *Epistles* VI. x. 3; IX. xix. 3; Suetonius, *Life of Caligula* 32; *Life of Domitian* 10). The notice attached to the cross on which the tortured body of Jesus hung bore, in black or red letters on the white ground, the inscription "King of the Jews." [59] It declared that Jesus had been sentenced to death as politically subversive of the authority of imperial Rome. The wording was designed to convey a subtle insult to Jewish pretensions and to mock all attempts to assert the sovereignty of a subject territory. The detail concerning the inscription, which conforms to Roman penal procedure and must reflect eyewitness report, is a solid historical fact. [60] It provides the unimpeachable information that Jesus went to his death as the Messiah.

27 The cross upon which Jesus hung was situated between the crosses of two other men. The crime for which they had been convicted and executed may also have been high treason. Roman law distinguished between theft (*furtum*) and robbery (*rapina,* theft combined with violence), but neither of these crimes was regarded as a capital offense. [61] The term used by Mark to describe them can legitimately be translated "robbers" (see on Ch. 14:48), but it is more probable that it designates men guilty of insurrection (as in Jn. 18:40). In Josephus it is constantly used for the Zealots, who committed themselves to armed conflict against Roman rule on the principle that God alone was sovereign in Israel. Josephus' intention was to brand the Zealots as an illegal movement composed of a criminal constituency. He reports that the Romans crucified the Zealots they captured, which indicates that they were treated as serious political offenders. The execution of these men with Jesus, who was crucified in accordance with the law of high treason, suggests that they had been

---

[59] Cf. P. F. Regard, "Le titre de la croix d'après les Évangiles," *Revue Archéologique* 28 (1928), pp. 95-105; K. H. Rengstorf, *TWNT* IV (Eng. Tr. 1967), p. 262.

[60] Cf. P. Winter, "Marginal Notes on the Trial of Jesus II," *ZNW* 50 (1959), p. 251: "That Jesus died by crucifixion and that his cross bore an inscription stating the cause for which he had been sentenced, is the one solid and stable fact that should be made the starting point of any historical investigation dealing with the Gospel accounts of his trial." See further W. C. van Unnik, "Jesus the Christ," *NTS* 8 (1962), pp. 101-116.

[61] Cf. A. Berger, "Law and Procedure, Roman," *The Oxford Classical Dictionary* (Oxford, 1949), p. 490.

seized in connection with the insurrection mentioned in Ch. 15:7 and were tried and sentenced under the same statute.[62]

29-30 The crucifixion attracted a large crowd, a part of which indulged in derisive remarks to the crucified Messiah. The scornful allusion to the words of Jesus concerning the destruction of the Temple which had been introduced by witnesses in the proceedings at Caiaphas' palace (see Ch. 14:58) serves to identify the first group of mockers as members of the Sanhedrin or court attendants who may have been privileged to sit in on the hearings. The expression "shaking their heads" recalls the derision heaped upon the poor but righteous sufferer in the Psalms (Ps. 22:7; 109:25) and the reviling of Jerusalem in her hour of abject humiliation (Lam. 2:15; cf. Jer. 18:16). The contemptuous challenge for Jesus to rescue himself and come down from the cross is intelligible in the light of an early Jewish dictum preserved in Midrash Tannaim III. 23: "Before a man puts his trust in flesh and blood, (i.e. another man) and asks him to save him, let him (i.e. the other) save himself from death first."[63] Mockery is an expression of verbal violence which inevitably accompanies the raw acts of violence in martyrdom, as Judaism was reminded in a synagogue homily on the sufferings of the people of God: "The peoples of the world mock the martyred people of Israel and say, 'Where is your God? Why does he not save you?'" (Pesikta Rabbati 36).

31-32 By handing Jesus over to the Roman magistrate and successfully prosecuting their complaint, the chief priests and scribes brought to fruition a long-nurtured desire to destroy him (Ch. 3:6; 11:18; 12:12; 14:1f., 10f., 64; 15:1, 3, 11). Now they took the opportunity to congratulate themselves on their success. Though their words were not directly addressed to Jesus, the subject of their mockery was the powerlessness of the one nailed to the cross, and the inscription fastened to it. When they refer to others he had "saved" they undoubtedly think of Jesus' healing ministry, but Mark intends his readers to understand these words in their full Christian sense. Paradoxically, the scornful words of verse 31b expressed a profound truth. If Jesus was to fulfil

---

[62] So K. H. Rengstorf, *TWNT* IV (Eng. Tr. 1967), pp. 257-262; W. R. Wilson, *The Execution of Jesus: a Judicial, Literary and Historical Investigation* (New York, 1970), p. 110.

[63] Cited by M. Smith, *Tannaitic Parallels to the Gospels* (Philadelphia, 1951), p. 138. Cf. the polemic in TJ *Ta'anith* II. 1; Origen, *Against Celsus* II. 9.

his mission on behalf of men he could not save himself from the sufferings appointed by God (Ch. 8:31). When the Jewish leaders mocked Jesus' messianic claim they substituted for Pilate's wording "King of the Jews" another expression. "Israel" is the proper designation for the people of God and "the King of Israel" is the correct Palestinian form of the claim of Jesus.[64] There is cruel sarcasm in the challenge "come down now," which seeks to throw into bold relief Jesus' helplessness, while the addition "that we may see and believe" clothes their taunt in the garb of piety. The contempt shown for Jesus by those gathered about the cross may have encouraged the two others who were crucified to vent their rage upon him. In their eyes Jesus was a contemptible caricature of sovereignty, and they reproached him.

15. The Death of Jesus. Ch. 15:33-41

33 And when the sixth hour was come, there was darkness over
the whole land until the ninth hour.
34 And at the ninth hour Jesus cried with a loud voice, Eloi,
Eloi, lama sabachthani?[65] which is, being interpreted, My
God, my God, why hast thou forsaken me?[66]
35 And some of them that stood by, when they heard it, said,
Behold, he calleth Elijah.
36 And one ran, and filling a sponge full of vinegar, put it on
a reed, and gave him to drink, saying, Let be: let us see
whether Elijah cometh to take him down.
37 And Jesus uttered a loud voice, and gave up the ghost.[67]
38 And the veil of the temple was rent in two from the top to
the bottom.

---

[64] Cf. W. Gutbrod, *TWNT* III (Eng. Tr. 1965), pp. 360-362, 376.

[65] If Mark is using a Palestinian tradition, it is natural that he should transmit the saying in an Aramaic form, but it is more probable that the original form of the saying is preserved in D Θ *pc* itala and Mt. 27:46, which conforms to the Targum of Ps. 22:2, with the address in Hebrew and the question in Aramaic. Only this form explains why those standing near thought that Jesus was calling for Elijah. See J. Jeremias, *TWNT* II (Eng. Tr. 1964), p. 935 n. 62; T. Boman, "Das letzte Wort Jesu," *Stud Theol* 17 (1963), pp. 103-119.

[66] According to Codex D^{gr} $it^{c\,i}$ sy^{h} Porphyry and Greek MSS known to Macarius Magnes (I. 12), the text read ὠνείδισάς με: "why have you reproached me?" This variant presupposes that the darkness is to be interpreted as a curse sanction upon Jesus.

[67] Gr. ἐξέπνευσεν, "he expired." Mark describes a sudden, violent death.

39 And when the centurion, who stood by over against him, saw that he so gave up the ghost,[68] he said, Truly this man was the Son of God.[69]
40 And there were also women beholding from afar: among whom were both Mary Magdalene, and Mary the mother of James the less and of Joses, and Salome;
41 who, when he was in Galilee, followed him, and ministered unto him; and many other women that came up with him unto Jerusalem.

33 At noon, when the sun was at its zenith, it went into eclipse and remained darkened for three hours (cf. Lk. 23:45, "the sun's light failed"). This was a miraculous darkening and a cosmic sign. The objection that a solar eclipse is astronomically impossible at the time of the Passover fails to appreciate the significance of the event, for which there are numerous parallels.[70] Amos prophesied darkness at noon in the eschatological context of the Day of the Lord, where the darkness expresses "the mourning for an only son" (Amos 8:9 f.). Philo spoke of a supernatural eclipse of the sun or the moon as signifying "either the death of kings or the destruction of cities" (*De Providentia* II. 50). The darkening of the sun marks a critical moment in history and emphasizes the eschatological and cosmic dimensions of Jesus' sufferings upon the cross. This symbolic significance is already apparent in the Marcan time scheme: the darkness fills the interval between the crucifixion and

[68] There are four different readings in verse 39: (i) when the centurion saw "that he expired in this manner" (ℵ B L Ψ 892 2148 cop^bo); (ii) "that having cried out, he expired" (W Θ 565 sy^s arm geo Origen^lat); (iii) "that having cried out in this manner, he expired" (A C K X Δ Π λ φ *pm* it *aur ff*2, *l, n, q* vg sy p/h Augustine); (iv) "that he so cried out" (*k*). Apparently the first reading represents the oldest form of the text, which makes the confession of Jesus' dignity dependent solely upon Jesus' manner of death. So J. Blinzler, *op. cit.,* p. 373 n. 61. For a defense of the fourth variant as original see C. H. Turner, "Western Readings in the Second Half of St. Mark's Gospel," *JThS* 29 (1927-28), pp. 12 f.

[69] Gr. υἱὸς θεοῦ ἦν. E. C. Colwell, "A Definite Rule for the Use of the Article in the Greek New Testament," *JBL* 52 (1933), pp. 13, 21 showed that "definite predicate nouns which precede the verb usually lack the article" while "a definite predicate nominative has the article when it follows the verb." The translation "the Son of God" thus represents Mark's intention. Cf. R. G. Bratcher, "A Note on υἱὸς θεοῦ (Mark xv. 39)," *ExT* 68 (1956), pp. 27 f.; T. F. Glasson, "Mark xv. 39: The Son of God," *ExT* 80 (1969), p. 286.

[70] For rabbinic parallels see S-B*K* I (1922), pp. 1040-1042; for Hellenistic parallels cf. Virgil, *Georgics* I. 463 ff.; Diogenes Laertius IV. 64; Plutarch, *Pelopidas* 295A.

the moment of Jesus' death.[71] There is, however, another, more ominous aspect to the darkening. In the plague of darkness which preceded the first Passover, darkness over the land was the token that the curse of God rested upon it (Exod. 10:21 f.). The darkness that envelops Jesus in his death thus makes visible what the cry of dereliction declares, and throws into sharp relief the breadth and depth of the passion (cf. Gal. 3:13).

34 Crucifixions were marked by screams of rage and pain, wild curses and the shouts of indescribable despair by the unfortunate victim. The demeanor of Jesus during his death agony is not described by the evangelist. But about three o'clock in the afternoon Jesus cried out in a loud voice those shattering words borrowed from Ps. 22:1, "My God, my God, why have you forsaken me?" This is the only saying from the cross recorded by Mark, and it is one of the most difficult to interpret.

In Ps. 22 the initial cry is an urgent appeal for God to intervene on behalf of the righteous sufferer. Jesus, on the cross, was living out the situation described in this eschatological psalm of suffering. He instinctively expressed his feelings in biblical language, imploring the help of God in a confident invocation and an anguished plea. The form of his words probably reflected the Targum, where the address is in Hebrew but the searching question is in Aramaic.

Various expedients have been adopted to cushion the offense of this passionate outburst. It has been argued that, in accordance with Jewish practice, the citation of the first verse implies the entire psalm, which ends on a note of triumph and serenity, and that Jesus' words are an affirmation of faith that looks beyond the despair and tragedy of the cross.[72] Alternatively, it is urged that Jesus felt forsaken, but in actuality he was not.[73] Such explanations bear the marks of special pleading and are unsatisfactory. The sharp edge of this word must not be blunted. Jesus' cry of dereliction is the inevitable sequel to the horror which he experienced in the Garden of Gethsemane (see on Ch. 14:33-34, 36).

---

[71] Cf. H. Conzelmann, *TWNT* VII (1964), pp. 439 f. E. F. F. Bishop, *Jesus of Palestine* (London, 1955), p. 250 and G. R. Driver, "Two Problems in the New Testament," *JThS* 16 (1965), pp. 327-337 prefer to think in terms of an atmospheric darkening caused by a sudden spring sirocco, but the parallel in Lk. 23:44 f. militates against this interpretation.

[72] J. Blinzler, *op. cit.*, pp. 373 f. n. 64 cites many authors who support this point of view, which he shares. See also E. Stauffer, *op. cit.*, pp. 139 f.

[73] See V. Taylor, *The Gospel According to St. Mark* (London, 1952), p. 594.

It must be understood in the perspective of the holy wrath of God and the character of sin, which cuts the sinner off from God (cf. Isa. 59:2). In responding to the call to the wilderness and identifying himself completely with sinners, Jesus offered himself to bear the judgment of God upon human rebellion (see on Ch. 1:9-11). Now on the cross he who had lived wholly for the Father experienced the full alienation from God which the judgment he had assumed entailed. His cry expresses the profound horror of separation from God. "Cursed is everyone who hangs upon a cross" was a statement with which Jesus had long been familiar, and in the manner of his death Jesus was cut off from the Father (Deut. 21:23; Gal. 3:13; II Cor. 5:21). The darkness declared the same truth. The cry of dereliction expressed the unfathomable pain of real abandonment by the Father.[74] The sinless Son of God died the sinner's death and experienced the bitterness of desolation. This was the cost of providing "a ransom for the many" (Ch. 10:45). The cry has a ruthless authenticity which provides the assurance that the price of sin has been paid in full. Yet Jesus did not die renouncing God. Even in the inferno of his abandonment he did not surrender his faith in God but expressed his anguished prayer in a cry of affirmation, "My God, my God."

35-36 The plea "Eli, Eli" was misconstrued, or wilfully misinterpreted, as a cry for help to Elijah[75] by those standing around the cross. Presumably they were Jews or Palestinian recruits who were familiar with various strands of folk piety. Later Jewish sources illumine the popular belief that Elijah will come in times of critical need to protect the innocent and rescue the righteous.[76] On the call from Jesus a soldier soaked a sponge in a wine vinegar diluted with water and reached it up to his mouth on the end of a reed or a shaft. A sour wine vinegar is mentioned in the OT as a refreshing drink (Num. 6:13; Ruth 2:14), and in Greek and Roman literature as well it is a common beverage appreciated by laborers and soldiers because it relieved thirst more effectively than water and was inexpensive (e.g. Plutarch, *Cato Major* I. 13; Papyrus

---

[74] See H. C. Read, "The Cry of Dereliction," *ExT* 65 (1957), pp. 260-262; L. Morris, *The Cross in the New Testament* (Grand Rapids, 1965), pp. 42-49.

[75] T. Boman, *op. cit.*, pp. 116 f. suggests that Jesus cried out אֵלִי אַתָּה, "you are my God" (see Ps. 22:11), but the bystanders heard אֵלִיָּא תָּא, "Elijah, come!"

[76] S-B*K* IV (1928), pp. 773-777; J. Jeremias, *TWNT* II (Eng. Tr. 1964), pp. 930-935.

London 1245, 9). There are no examples of its use as a hostile gesture. The thought, then, is not of a corrosive vinegar offered as a cruel jest, but of the sour wine of the people. [77] While the words "let us see if Elijah will come" express a doubtful expectation, the offer of the sip of wine was intended to keep Jesus conscious for as long as possible.

37 Jesus maintained consciousness to his last breath; in the moment of death, an inarticulate cry burst from his throat. The strength of the cry indicates that he did not die the ordinary death of those crucified, who normally suffered long periods of complete exhaustion and unconsciousness before dying. [78] The stark realism of Mark's statement describes a sudden, violent death. Jesus' death differed from the common experience of men in two respects. It was the death which God caused him to die for us (cf. Chs. 8:31; 10:45; 14:24); and death was not his debt to sin but a reality to which he submitted. The meaning of his death becomes clear only from the perspective of the triumph of the resurrection which marked his vindication and demonstrated that death had no claim upon him.

38 The statement concerning the rending of the Temple veil is difficult. There were in fact two hangings in the Jerusalem Temple. An outer curtain separated the sanctuary from the forecourt (cf. Exod. 26:37; 38:18; Num. 3:26; Letter of Aristeas § 86), while the second, or inner, veil partitioned the Holy Place from the Holy of Holies to which the high priest alone was admitted on the Day of Atonement (cf. Exod. 26:31-35; 27:21; 30:6; Lev. 16:2, 12-15, 21, 23; 24:3; II Chron. 3:19; M. *Yoma* V. 1). It is not at once apparent whether Mark's reference is to the inner or the outer veil. A tearing of the exterior curtain would have the character of a public sign, comparable to the darkness that covered the land. The rending of the interior veil would be visible, presumably, only to a few priests and could have been concealed from public knowledge by the Jewish authorities. The detail "from top to

---

[77] See R. C. Fuller, "The Drink Offered to Christ at Calvary," *Scripture* 2 (1947), pp. 114 f.; J. Colin, "Il soldato della matrona di Efeso e l'aceto dei crucifissi," *Rivista Filologica* n.s. 31 (1953), pp. 97-128 (a study of Petronius, reporting a fact dating *ca.* A.D. 29-35); *idem,* "Essig," *Reallexikon für Antike und Christentum* VI (1965), pp. 635-646.

[78] Cf. J. Blinzler, *op. cit.,* pp. 381-384, Exkurs XIX: "Der Kreuztod in medizinischer Sicht," for a review of medical opinion concerning the death of Jesus.

bottom" suggests an actual and irreversible occurrence which coincided with the moment of Jesus' death. The reference then is to the magnificent curtain which in Herod's Temple hung before the entrance and was visible from the forecourt when the doors were opened during the day (cf. Mt. 27:51, 54). This conclusion is supported by the fact that Jewish and Jewish-Christian traditions, which are divergent but clearly refer to the same event, speak of an astonishing happening at the entrance to the sanctuary, not at the partition between the sanctuary and the Holy of Holies. [79] The early Church Fathers commonly interpreted the event as a warning sign of the impending destruction of the Temple, confirming the sober prophecy of Ch. 13:2. [80] That an intimate connection exists between the destruction of the Temple and the death of Jesus is established by the tradition preserved in Ch. 14:58 and the taunt of Ch. 15:29. The rending of the Temple veil is a public sign that the rejection of the Messiah by the leaders of the people discloses a failure in sensitivity to the divine purpose so serious that it seals the disaster of A.D. 70. Jesus' death and the destruction of the formal structures of Judaism are inseparably bound together.

39 The centurion who stood facing Jesus was the Roman officer who superintended the execution. [81] He had followed each stage of the crucifixion exactly, and knew that Jesus had not died the normal death of

---

[79] So O. Michel, *TWNT* IV (Eng. Tr. 1967), p. 885; A. Pelletier, "La Tradition synoptique du 'Voile déchiré' à lumière des réalités archéologiques," *RSR* 46 (1958), pp. 161-180. The key Jewish and Jewish Christian references (Josephus, *War* V. 3; TB *Yoma* 39b; TJ *Yoma* VI. 43c; Gospel of the Nazarenes [fragment 23], cited by Jerome, *Comm. in Matt.* 27:51 [MPL XXVI, 236 f.]; cf. Tacitus, *History* V. 13) are discussed by H. Montefiore, *Josephus and the New Testament* (London, 1962), pp. 16-22.

The rending of the inner veil would also have rich symbolic significance, pointing to the end of the repeated sacrifice for atonement and the establishment of a new way of access to God through the death of Jesus. Such associations are actually developed theologically in Heb. 6:19; 9:2 f., 6 f., 11 f.; 10:19 f. It is methodologically important, however, not to read Mark from the perspective of the author to the Hebrews. For the contrary point of view, that the word concerning the veil is symbolic rather than literal and has reference to Jesus' flesh which was pierced, see J. R. Michaels, "The Centurion's Confession and the Spear Thrust," *CBQ* 29 (1967), pp. 102-109.

[80] E.g. Tertullian, *Against Marcion* IV. 42; Chrysostom, *Homilies on Matthew* LXXXVIII. 2 (MPG LVIII, 826); cf. Gospel of the Hebrews § 52.

[81] For a review of the later tradition concerning the centurion see C. Schneider, "Der Hauptmann am Kreuz," *ZNW* 33 (1934), pp. 1-17.

crucified men (see above on verse 37). The strength which he possessed at the moment of death was so unusual the centurion spontaneously acknowledged Jesus' transcendent dignity. In Mark's account the reason for the exclamation is unmistakably the manner of Jesus' death, rather than any accompanying event.

By "Son of God" the centurion presumably meant that Jesus was a divine man or deified hero who accepted humiliation and death as an act of obedience to a higher mandate. It can be expected that his words reflect a religious point of view shaped by popular Hellenism. Mark, however, clearly intended his readers to recognize in the exclamation a genuine Christian confession, in the consciousness that these words are true in a higher sense than the centurion understood. In this light the centurion's words constitute an appropriate complement to the affirmation of Peter that Jesus is the Messiah in Ch. 8:29 and the triumphant climax to the Gospel in terms of the programmatic confession of Jesus in Ch. 1:1. It is probably significant that in the preface to the Gospel there is a rending of the sky and the proclamation that Jesus is the divine Son (Ch. 1:11) to which correspond the rending of the Temple veil and the confession that Jesus is Son of God in Ch. 15:38 f. The fact that the truth of Jesus' person was publicly declared, whether intentionally or unintentionally, by a Roman was undoubtedly important to the Christians in Rome. In contemporary practice the designation "Son of God" had been arrogated for the Roman ruler, who was worshipped in the state cult. Most effectively, therefore, Mark reports that the centurion proclaimed that the crucified Jesus (and not the emperor) is the Son of God. [82] His words provide a discerning Gentile response to the death of Jesus.

40-41 Contemporary testimony indicates that at the place of execution crucified men were often surrounded by relatives and friends (e.g. TJ *Giṭṭin* 48c; Tos. *Giṭṭin* VII. 1). Mark mentions certain Galilean women who had accompanied Jesus and assisted him in a material way. Their active service of love was a mark of true devotion to him. The related passage, Lk. 8:1-3, states that these women had experienced healing from Jesus, and specifies that Mary Magdalene had been released from severe demonic possession. She is distinguished from other women named Mary by the surname Magdalene, which designates her birth-

---

[82] P. H. Bligh, "A Note on Huios Theou in Mark 15:39," *ExT* 80 (1968), pp. 51-53.

place, Magdala, a fishing village on the western shore of the Sea of Galilee. Little is known concerning Mary, the mother of James and Joses, but her sons appear to have been well known in the early Church (cf. verse 21). According to Mt. 27:56 Salome was the wife of Zebedee and the mother of the disciples James and John. The significance of the presence of these women to Mark is that they were eyewitnesses to the primary events proclaimed in the gospel, the death (verses 40-41), burial (verse 47) and resurrection (Ch. 16:1) of Jesus. The details of what took place could be substantiated by their testimony.

16. The Burial of Jesus. Ch. 15:42-47

42 And when even was now come, because it was the Preparation,[83] that is, the day before the sabbath,
43 there came Joseph of Arimathaea, a councillor[84] of honorable estate, who also himself was looking for the kingdom of God; and he boldly went in unto Pilate, and asked for the body of Jesus.
44 And Pilate marvelled if he were already dead: and calling unto him the centurion, he asked him whether he had been any while[85] dead.
45 And when he learned it of the centurion, he granted the corpse to Joseph.
46 And he bought a linen cloth, and taking him down, wound him in the linen cloth, and laid him in a tomb which had been hewn out of a rock; and he rolled a stone against the door of the tomb.
47 And Mary Magdalene and Mary the mother of Joses beheld where he was laid.

42-43 In antiquity the execution of a condemned man did not mark the final moment of his humiliation. Roman law dictated the loss of all

---

[83] Gr. παρασκευή designates the day prior to a festival or the Sabbath. In this instance it means Friday, which ended with sunset.

[84] Gr. βουλευτής is not a technical expression used by Jewish writers, but appears to have been chosen by Mark with Gentile readers in mind to designate a member of the Sanhedrin.

[85] Gr. εἰ πάλαι. There is strong textual support (B D W Θ *pc* latt) for the reading εἰ ἤδη ("if already"). It is difficult to decide if this variant is original, or if it represents a transcriptional error because the copyist found this expression in the initial clause of the sentence.

honors in death, and even the right of burial was determined by magisterial decree. Writing of the age of Tiberius, Tacitus remarks that "people sentenced to death forfeited their property and were forbidden burial" (*Annals* VI. 29). Apparently the nature of the crime or the manner of execution played no significant role in this matter. It was not at all uncommon for a body to be left upon a cross either to rot or to be eaten by predatory birds or animals.[86] The release of a corpse for burial depended solely upon the generosity of the magistrate. In actual practice, if the relatives of a condemned man sought permission for burial, the body was normally given to them. Cicero had permitted the burial of confederates of Catiline in response to the request of their wives (Plutarch, *Antonius* 2; Cicero, *Orationes Philippicae* II. vii. 17), and Philo reports that before a great festival, like the emperor's birthday, the bodies of those who had been crucified were given to the relatives for proper burial (*Against Flaccus* X. § 83). From such examples of legal praxis as have been preserved in documents from this period the practice in Palestine under Tiberius can be estimated. In most instances the request of relatives for the body of one executed was honored. The major exception to this was that permission to bury one convicted of high treason was denied on principle.[87] Whenever such a request was granted the action represented a special dispensation by the imperial magistrate. Moreover, the famous jurist in the age of Trajan, Neratius Priscus, specified that there could be no ceremony nor public mourning in connection with the interment.[88]

The burial of the dead as an act of piety is attested in the OT and later Jewish sources (cf. II Sam. 21:12-14; Tobit. 1:17-19; 2:3-7; 12:12f.; Sirach 7:33; 38:16). Josephus says explicitly, "we consider it a duty to bury even enemies" (*War* III. viii. 5). Jewish law prescribed that those hung should be taken down and buried before sundown (Deut. 21:23; cf. M. *Sanhedrin* VI. 6; TB *Sanhedrin* 46b, Baraitha). Although cursed of God, a body was not to hang on a cross after dark lest there be a defiling of the land, and it was considered unthinkable that burial should be denied to anyone, not even a convicted criminal. An area far outside the city of Jerusalem had been consigned for the burial of executed criminals (Tos. *Sanhedrin* IX. 8f.; M. *Sanhedrin* VI. 7).

---

[86] C. Schneider, *TWNT* III (Eng. Tr. 1965), pp. 411f., citing Horace, *Epistles* I, 16, 48; Petronius, *Satura* 111.

[87] J. Blinzler, *op. cit.*, p. 386 n. 14, citing *Digest* XLVIII. xxiv. 1-2, xvi. 15, 3.

[88] *Ibid.*, p. 387 n. 16, citing *Digest* III. ii. 11, 2.

The request for the body of Jesus would normally have come from a member of his family or from his disciples (cf. Ch. 6:29). Mary, however, must have been emotionally exhausted by the course of events, and there is no evidence that Jesus' brothers or sisters were in the city. The disciples had fled. In the absence of those related to the crucified Messiah, Joseph of Arimathea, a much respected member of the Sanhedrin whose piety is clearly indicated by the statement that he was looking for the fulfilment of Israel's messianic hope, courageously asked permission to bury the body of Jesus. His surname indicates that he was originally from the village of Ramathaim-zophim (cf. I Sam. 1:1), about 20 miles northwest of Jerusalem (Eusebius, *Onomasticon* 32). His earnest expectation of the coming redemption had apparently attracted him to Jesus and his teaching concerning the Kingdom of God. His request was daring because it amounted to a confession of his commitment to the condemned and crucified Jesus.[89] As a member of the council undoubtedly he was familiar with the Roman regulations governing the disposal of a corpse. Despite the fact that Jesus had been crucified for high treason and that Joseph was unrelated to him, he boldly petitioned the prefect for the right of burial. The approach of the Sabbath, which began at sundown, lent urgency to his action if burial was to be completed within the time prescribed by pentateuchal law (Deut. 21:23).

44-45 Pilate regarded the request seriously. He was surprised, however, that Jesus was already dead. Since contemporary records show that crucified men often lived two or three days before dying, there was something extraordinary about the rapid death of Jesus. Mark alone mentions the detail that Pilate assured himself from the centurion responsible for the superintending of the execution that Jesus had been dead for some time. He then released the corpse for interment. The release of the body of one condemned of high treason, and especially to one who was not an immediate relative, was wholly unusual and confirms the tenor of the Gospel account of the Roman trial (Ch. 15:1-15). Only if Pilate had no reservations concerning Jesus' innocence of the charge of *lèse majesté,* but had pronounced sentence begrudgingly to placate the irate mob, would he have granted the request of the councillor.[90]

---

[89] *Ibid.,* pp. 392 f.

[90] *Loc. cit.*

46 The removal of the body from the cross, the purchase of linen cloth, and the actual burial are actions expressed of Joseph alone. The implication of the sentence, however, does not exclude the presence of others who assisted him (cf. Jn. 19:39-42). At least the removal of the body and the closing of the entrance to the tomb Joseph could not have accomplished alone. As an eminent person, he undoubtedly had servants who must have attended to many of the details required during the brief time between the granting of permission for burial and sunset. It seems necessary to read the entire verse in a causative sense, i.e. he caused the body to be taken down from the cross, linen cloth to be purchased, and the body prepared for burial. With servants to assist him, two hours was sufficient time for accomplishing all that was required.[91]

Once the body was removed from the cross, it was hastily prepared for interment. Mark speaks only of the tight wrapping of the corpse with fine linen. This detail indicates that the body of Jesus was accorded an honorable burial. While none of the Gospels speaks of the washing of the body, this was considered so important in Jewish practice that it was a permitted action on the Sabbath (M. *Shabbath* XXIII. 5; cf. Acts 9:37; TB *Moed Qaṭan* 28b). It is unlikely that Joseph took time to secure the linen cloth and yet left the corpse bloody. The statement that Jesus was buried according to the Jewish tradition (Jn. 19:40) furnishes presumptive evidence that the body was washed before it was wrapped tightly with linen.

The body was then carried a short distance to a tomb which had been cut from bedrock, where it was placed on a stone bench or a shelf cut into the rock parallel with the wall of the chamber.[92] The necessity for haste, because of the impending Sabbath, dictated that a grave near the place of execution be used (cf. Jn. 19:41 f.). The site traditionally identified as the tomb of Jesus and its immediate vicinity is now known to have been a cemetery in the first century.[93] As was frequently the case in Palestine, this cemetery utilized an abandoned quarry, where several centuries before stone-cutters had worked their way back into a

---

91 *Ibid.*, pp. 416-422, Exkurs XXI: "Die Stunde des Karfreitages."

92 R. H. Smith, "The Tomb of Jesus," *BA* 30 (1967), pp. 87 f. notes that this type of cutting was sometimes used in Jerusalem in this period, as the tombs of the Sanhedria attest. They were rare at this early date, however, and are found almost exclusively in the tombs of persons of high rank.

93 *Ibid.*, pp. 74-85; L. E. Cox Evans, "The Holy Sepulchre," *Palestine Exploration Quarterly* 100 (1968), pp. 112-136.

hillside, leaving a rugged scarp into which tombs were cut in the early Roman period. The façade cut into the hillside opened into an antechamber, at the back of which a rectangular doorway about two feet high led inside (cf. Jn. 20:5, 11, they "stooped to look inside"). Burial itself took place within an inner chamber. Ordinarily in this period such a tomb was sealed with a flat stone slab wedged into place to shut out animals or intruders. The Marcan account speaks of some sort of stone which could be rolled into place. This may have been only a boulder, but if the tomb was an exceptionally fine one, it may have had an elaborate disc-shaped stone, about a yard in diameter, like a millstone, which was placed in a wide slot cut into the rock. Since the groove into which the stone fitted sloped toward the doorway, it could be easily rolled into place; but to roll the stone aside would require the strength of several men. Only a few tombs with such rolling stones are known in Palestine, but all of them date from the period of Jesus. [94]

47 Two of the women who had been present when Jesus died (verse 42) were observers of his burial. This fact was significant since the burial assumed importance in the early proclamation of the gospel (I Cor. 15:4). As Jewish culture placed no value on the testimony of women (M. *Rosh Ha-Shanah* I. 8), [95] their presence on the scene in the Marcan account can only be explained as factual. The absence of any reference to an open expression of mourning suggests that the women followed the burial of their Lord with silent pain. Open manifestation of sorrow was unnecessary. Moreover, it was prohibited by law in this instance (see on verses 42-43). The detail that the women saw the place where Jesus' body was laid to rest is primarily important because it confirms the identity of the tomb specified in Ch. 16:5 with that in which Jesus' body was interred. The account of the burial thus finalizes the passion narrative and prepares for the report concerning the empty tomb and the resurrection of Jesus on Easter morning. [96]

---

[94] For the archeological details, see R. H. Smith, *op. cit.*, pp. 82-88.

[95] See further J. M. Baumgarten, "On the Testimony of Women in 1QSa," *JBL* 96 (1957), pp. 266-269.

[96] Cf. E. Dhanis, "L'ensevelissement de Jésus et la visite au tombeau dans l'évangile de saint Marc (Mc. XV. 40-XVI. 8)," *Gregorianum* 39 (1958), pp. 367-410.

CHAPTER 16

VIII. The Resurrection of Jesus. Ch. 16:1-8

1 And when the sabbath was past, Mary Magdalene, and Mary
the mother of James, and Salome,[1] bought spices, that they
might come and anoint him.
2 And very early on the first day of the week,[2] they came to the
tomb when the sun was risen.
3 And they were saying among themselves, Who shall roll us
away the stone from the door of the tomb?[3]

---

[1] The initial words καὶ διαγενομένου . . . καὶ Σαλώμη are omitted by Western authorities (D *d* [*k*] *n*). The force of the omission is to assign to the women mentioned in Ch. 15:47 the action of buying the spices. This reading is supported by C. H. Turner, "Western Readings in the Second Half of St. Mark's Gospel," *JThS* 29 (1927-28), pp. 13 f., who argues that the longer version arose under the influence of Mt. 28:1. The Western variant, however, may be explained as an attempt at simplification. The strong attestation for the fuller text (ℵ A B C K L W Δ Π Ψ λ φ *pl*) justifies the (A) rating (= virtually certain) assigned to the text by the editors of the Greek text issued by the Bible Societies.

[2] Gr. ἡ μιὰ τῶν σαββάτων. The use of the cardinal numeral for the ordinal is often explained as a Semitism. For a dissenting opinion see J. H. Moulton, *A Grammar of New Testament Greek*[3] (Edinburgh, 1908-1929), I, pp. 95 f., 237; II, p. 174.

[3] Codex Bobiensis (*k*) has here an extensive gloss which is interesting for its attempt to describe the resurrection: "Suddenly, at the third hour of the day, there was darkness over the whole earth, and angels descended from heaven, and rising in the splendor of the living God they ascended together with him, and immediately it was light." The only other early attempt to describe the resurrection occurs in the Gospel of Peter 35-44: "Now in the night when the Lord's day dawned, as the soldiers were keeping guard two by two in every watch, there came a great sound in the heaven, and they saw the heavens opened and two men descend, shining with a great light, and drawing near to the sepulchre. And that stone which had been set at the door rolled away of itself and went back to the side, and the sepulchre was opened and both of the young men entered in. When those soldiers saw that, they awakened the centurion and the elders . . . and they saw three men come out of the sepulchre, two of them sustaining the other, and a cross following them. And they saw that the heads of the two reached to heaven, but the head of the one who was led by them passed through the heavens. And they heard a voice out of the heavens saying, 'Have you preached to those who sleep?' And an answer was heard from the cross, 'Yes.'" For a discussion of these passages see L. Vaganay, *L'Évangile de Pierre* (Paris, 1930), pp. 287-303; W. L. Lane, "Apocrypha," *EC* I (1964), pp. 338 f.

4 And looking up, they see that the stone is rolled back: for it was exceedingly great.[4]
5 And entering into the tomb, they saw a young man sitting on the right side, arrayed in a white robe; and they were amazed.
6 And he saith unto them, Be not amazed: ye seek Jesus, the Nazarene, who hath been crucified: he is risen; he is not here: behold, the place where they laid him!
7 But go, tell his disciples and Peter, He goeth before you into Galilee: there shall ye see him, as he said unto you.[5]
8 And they went out, and fled from the tomb; for trembling and astonishment had come upon them: and they said nothing to any one; for they were afraid.[6]

Mark concludes his Gospel with this paragraph concerning the visit of the women to the tomb of Jesus and the dramatic announcement of his resurrection. Two aspects of the truth are emphasized. First, there is no difference between the crucifixion and the resurrection on the point

---

[4] Gr. ἦν γὰρ μέγας σφόδρα is located at the end of verse 3 in D Θ 565 *c d ff n* sys pal Eusebius. As the text now stands these words appear badly placed. Yet Mark tends to place an explanatory clause at the end of a sentence, rather than with the word or phrase it qualifies (see Ch. 1:16; 2:15; 12:12).

[5] The variant found in D *k* ("I am going before you to Galilee; there you will see me, even as I told you"), which implies that the speaker is the risen Lord, may have arisen from a conviction that Mark, like the other Gospels, must have reported a resurrection appearance. It is noteworthy that MS *k* lacks the longer ending with its resurrection appearances.

[6] Gr. ἐφοβοῦντο γάρ. The possibility of ending a sentence, or a paragraph, or even a work with γάρ, and of using ἐφοβοῦντο without a qualifying object or clause finds strong support in the texts gathered by R. H. Lightfoot, *The Gospel Message of St. Mark* (Oxford, 1950), pp. 80-97, 106-116; cf. N. B. Stonehouse, *The Witness of Matthew and Mark to Christ* (Philadelphia, 1944), pp. 86-118. A new instance of the final position of γάρ is known through the recent publication of the *Dyscolos* of Menander, lines 437 f.: ναὶ μὰ τὸν Δία, τὸ γοῦν πρόβατον μικροῦ τέθνηκε γάρ ("Yes by Zeus! In any case, the sheep nearly died" cited by F. W. Danker, "Menander and the New Testament," *NTS* 10 [1964], p. 366). It seems not to have been noticed that Musonius Rufus concludes his *Discourse* XII, περὶ 'Αφροδισίων (ed. O. Hense [Leipzig, 1905], p. 67, line 2) with γνώριμον γάρ ("for this is well known"). F. W. Danker, "Postscript to the Markan Secrecy Motif," *Con Th Mon* 38 (1967), pp. 24-27 emends the text of Mk. 16:8 to read ἐφοβοῦντο γὰρ φόβον μέγαν, proposing that the last two words were omitted by haplography. It seems better to recognize that Ch. 16:8 as it stands in the critical editions of the text is Mark's original and intended ending. Forms of φοβέομαι occur twelve times in Mark; in six of these instances the word is used absolutely (Ch. 5:5, 33, 36; 6:50; 9:6; 10:32).

of historicity or factuality. The resurrection of Jesus is an historical event. On a given date, in a defined place, the man Jesus, having been crucified and buried two days earlier, came forth from the tomb. Mark stresses the identity of the risen one with the crucified one (verse 6). Secondly, as an historical event, the resurrection of Jesus cannot be explained by categories open to human understanding. It possesses no givenness which is self-elucidating. The reality cannot be incorporated into our history as if it conformed to our experience. Apart from revelation, it remains merely a mysterious event in history, unable to impart understanding. History can declare only that Jesus' body disappeared, but this baffling fact fails to communicate the gospel. The event of Jesus' resurrection is open to understanding only through a word of revelation received in faith. The focus of Mark's account falls, therefore, upon the presence of the divine messenger and the disclosure of the truth (verses 5-6).

The mysterious activity of God in the resurrection was accompanied by specific, knowable phenomena which can confront human experience and are open to human judgment. The purpose of these phenomena is not to create faith, but to inform faith of certain consequences with regard to the event. In Mark's narrative the empty tomb indicates that the resurrection includes man's past, and points to the continuity of the past, the present and the future in the perspective of redemption. The empty tomb, however, derives its meaning from the fact of the resurrection of Jesus, even while it informs that event. [7]

Were it not for his resurrection, Jesus of Nazareth might have appeared as no more than a line in Josephus' *Antiquities of the Jews,* if he were mentioned at all. The witness of the four Gospels is unequivocal that following the crucifixion Jesus' disciples were scattered, their hopes

---

[7] Questions directed against the phenomena must be set aside as queries addressed to the thesis of divine revelation. If men argue for a closed continuum (i.e. such events are beyond man's history and improper to God's activity) it should be recognized that they are arguing against the proposition that God has the right to reveal himself in history. If God possesses the right to do so, he has the right to choose the means, the place and the circumstances. The purpose of revelation is finally to inform men of God. For a careful consideration of the historical questions see R. Russell, "Modern Exegesis and the Fact of the Resurrection," *Downside Review* 76 (1958), pp. 251-264, 329-343; D. P. Fuller, *Easter Faith and History* (Grand Rapids, 1965); *idem,* "The Resurrection of Jesus and the Historical Method," *Journal of Bible and Religion* 34 (1966), pp. 18-24. For a theology of the resurrection see F. X. Durrwell, *The Resurrection, A Biblical Study* (New York, 1966); W. Künneth, *The Theology of the Resurrection* (St. Louis, 1965).

shattered by the course of events. What halted the dissolution of the messianic movement centered in Jesus was the resurrection. It is the resurrection which creates "the good news concerning Jesus the Messiah, the Son of God" (Ch. 1:1).

The detailed reference to the women in Ch. 16:1 indicates that this unit of tradition existed at one time independent from the passion narrative. Whenever the Easter account was proclaimed, those to whom the word of revelation was first entrusted were specified.

1 At the conclusion of the Sabbath (i.e. after sunset on Saturday), the women who had witnessed the crucifixion and burial (see on Ch. 15:40, 47) purchased aromatic oils with which to anoint the body of Jesus. Spices were not used for mummification, which was not a Jewish custom, but to offset the odors from decomposition. It is not uncommon to find in Palestinian tombs dating to the first century such funerary objects as perfume bottles, ointment jars and other vessels of clay and glass designed to contain aromatic oils.[8] The desire of the women to "anoint" the body indicates that the oils were to be poured over the head. The preparations for returning to the tomb in performance of an act of piety show that the women had no expectation of an immediate resurrection of Jesus.[9] Since in the climate of Jerusalem deterioration would occur rapidly, the visit of the women with the intention of ministering to the corpse after two nights and a day must be viewed as an expression of intense devotion.

2 The temporal expressions designating the time when the women came to the tomb are problematic. Normally "very early" refers to the earlier part of the period 3:00-6:00 A.M., prior to sunrise (cf. Ch. 1:35), but the text states explicitly that the women went "when the sun had risen." This difficulty was early recognized and is reflected in the manuscript tradition where several expedients were adopted to relieve the apparent disparity in the text.[10] If the text originally included both temporal

---

8 R. H. Smith, "The Tomb of Jesus," *BA* 30 (1967), p. 89, fig. 8; cf. J. Blinzler, *Der Prozess Jesu*[4] (Regensburg, 1969), p. 399.

9 Cf. W. Michaelis, *TWNT* VII (1964), p. 458.

10 E.g. certain Western authorities (D *c ff n q* Augustine) read ἀνατελλόντος, "while the sun was rising"; λίαν πρωΐ ("very early") is omitted by *c*, λίαν by D W *k n* sys p pal arm, and πρωΐ by *q*. R. H. Lightfoot, *op. cit.*, p. 96, followed by G. Hebert, "The Resurrection Narrative in St. Mark's Gospel," *ScJTh* 15 (1962), p. 67, insists that ἀνατείλαντος τοῦ ἡλίου cannot be a note of time, but is an

clauses, the time of the women's visit was immediately after sunrise on the first day of the week.

3-4 Although the women had witnessed the burial of Jesus and the closing of the entrance to the sepulchre (Ch. 15:47), they had no knowledge of the official sealing of the tomb by the Sanhedrin nor of the posting of a guard (cf. Mt. 27:62-66). This is evident from the fragment of conversation preserved by Mark alone concerning the rolling back of the stone from the entrance to the tomb. While the setting in place of a large stone was a relatively easy task, once it had slipped into the groove cut in bedrock just before the entrance it could be removed only with great difficulty (see on Ch. 15:46). Mark's account is characterized by great restraint. The evangelist makes no attempt to explain how the stone was rolled back, but records simply that the women looked up and saw that it had been removed. That the tomb was empty is clearly implied, but this is not stated until the startling announcement of the divine messenger in verse 6.[11]

5 Inside the large opening in the façade of the tomb was an antechamber, at the back of which a rectangular doorway about two feet high led inside. Small low doorways between the antechamber and the burial chamber were standard features of Jewish tombs in this period. The inner chamber where the body had been laid was perhaps six or seven feet square, and about the same height.[12] When the women entered the burial chamber they were startled to see "a young man clothed

---

allusion to Mal. 4:2 LXX, which speaks of the rising of "the Sun of righteousness with healing in his wings." The point of Mark's reference, according to Hebert, is that the Sun has risen (i.e. Jesus), though the world is still in darkness.

[11] For a treatment of the text from a Hellenistic viewpoint appropriate to a θεῖος ἀνήρ Christology, see N. Q. Hamilton, "Resurrection Tradition and the Composition of Mark," *JBL* 84 (1965), pp. 415-421. Hamilton argues that Mark was the creator of the empty tomb narrative, and that the story concerns a "removal" rather than a "resurrection." In Hellenism a hero is recognized by the evidence of an empty grave. Hamilton contends that Mark composed the story of the empty tomb in part to satisfy Graeco-Roman expectations aroused by his Son of God Christology (Ch. 15:39). For a defense of the historicity of the Marcan account of the empty tomb see E. Stauffer, *Jesus and His Story* (New York, 1960), pp. 143-147; J. Daniélou, "The Empty Tomb," *Month* 39 (1968), pp. 215-222. See below, verses 5-6.

[12] See R. H. Smith, *op. cit.*, pp. 86-88, and especially fig. 6 for the reconstruction of Jesus' tomb proposed by L. H. Vincent.

in a white robe, sitting on the right side." Mark's language could designate a valiant young man (see on Ch. 14:51f.) or an angel. Careful study of the distinctive vocabulary has demonstrated that whenever the reference is to an angel, the text or the context makes the supernatural character of the young man explicit.[13] The feature which shows that the evangelist means an angel is the factor of revelation (verses 6-7). God often uses visible means to reveal himself, and the angel fits into this pattern. As frequently in the OT and the Jewish literature from the later period, the angel appears as the divine messenger.[14] This conclusion is supported by the detail of the white garment. In the color symbolism of the NT, white is primarily the heavenly color and is mentioned almost exclusively in eschatological or apocalyptic contexts.[15] In this instance the white clothes are not properly a description, but an indication of the dazzling character of their glory (cf. Ch. 9:3; Rev. 6:11; 7:9, 13). The presence of the angel underscores the eschatological character of the resurrection of Jesus and anticipates the parousia when the Son of Man will come in "the glory of the Father with the holy angels" (Ch. 8:38; cf. Ch. 13:26f.).

The response of the women to the angelic presence is described by a strong word which Mark alone among the NT writers uses (cf. Ch. 9:15). It introduces the note of dread which is woven into the theme until it becomes the dominant motif in verse 8. Confronted with the messenger of God, the women were terrified.

6 The action of God is not always self-evident. For this reason it is invariably accompanied by the word of revelation, interpreting the significance of an event (e.g. Exod. 15:1-18 interprets the flight from Egypt as the action of God). The emptiness of the tomb possessed no factual value in itself. It simply raised the question, What happened to the body? God, therefore, sent his messenger to disclose the fact of the resurrection. The announcement of the angel is the crystallization point for faith.

---

[13] H. Waetjen, "The Ending of Mark and the Gospel's Shift in Eschatology," *Annual of the Swedish Theological Institute* 4 (1965), pp. 114-116. Cf. Josephus, *Antiquities* V. viii. 2 where the word νεανίας is applied to the heavenly messenger who appeared to Manoah's wife with the glad tidings that she is to bear a son. Waetjen (p. 116) finds this the closest parallel to Mk. 16:5.

[14] See G. Kittel, *TWNT* I (Eng. Tr. 1964), pp. 76-83; P. Gaechter, "Die Engelerscheinungen in der Auferstehungsberichten," *Zeitschrift für katholische Theologie* 89 (1967), pp. 191-202.

[15] W. Michaelis, *TWNT* IV (Eng. Tr. 1967), pp. 244-266.

The women had been misguided in their seeking of Jesus.[16] They came to anoint the body of one who was dead, but Jesus was risen from the dead!

The reference to "Jesus of Nazareth, who was crucified" allows no equivocation concerning the subject of the emphatic statements, "he is risen, he is not here; see the place where they laid him."[17] The resurrection presupposes the death and burial of Jesus, and both of these events are specified in the angel's declaration. The statements which qualify the affirmation "he is risen" refer specifically to the shelf on which the body had been placed. They stress that the tomb in which Jesus had been laid on Friday afternoon was empty on Easter morning. This testimony is supported by primitive kerygmatic summaries preserved by Luke and Paul. The argument that David "died and was buried and his tomb is with us to this day" (Acts 2:29), which prepares for the proclamation of the resurrection of Jesus, implies a reference to the empty tomb of Jesus which could be examined as freely as the traditional tomb of David. Peter's formulation finds an echo in the gospel which Paul, in common with the Jerusalem apostles (I Cor. 15:11), preached, that Jesus "died . . . was buried . . . and the third day rose again" (I Cor. 15:3 f.). While no explicit reference is made to the tomb of Jesus, the sequence death, burial, resurrection demands that the tomb was empty. It is significant that early Jewish polemicists never sought to dispute this fact. The story of the theft of the body (cf. Mt. 28:15; Justin, *Dialogue with Trypho* 108) simply confirms that the tomb was in fact empty.[18] In the Gospel of Mark, however, the certainty of the resurrec-

---

16 R. H. Lightfoot, *op. cit.,* pp. 23 f. n. demonstrated that in Mark the verb ζητεῖν is always used in a derogatory sense. In Ch. 8:11 f.; 11:18 f.; 12:12; 14:1, 11, 55 the seeking has an evil intention, while in Chs. 3:22 and 16:6 it is being carried out in the wrong way and is unacceptable. Cf. G. Hebert, *op. cit.,* pp. 69 f.

17 The kerygmatic formulation of verse 6, and specifically the words "see the place where they laid him," has encouraged L. Schenke, *Auferstehungsverkündigung und leeres Grab. Eine traditionsgeschichtliche Untersuchung von Mk 16, 1-8* (Stuttgart, 1968), to associate the development of the tradition with the annual veneration of the tomb of Jesus by the Jerusalem Community at the time of Passover-Easter. For the veneration of tombs in Palestine see J. Jeremias, *Die Heiligengräber in Jesu Umwelt* (Göttingen, 1958).

18 For a discussion of the inscription from Nazareth summarizing an imperial edict directed against the theft of corpses and the desecration of graves see L. Wenger, *Die Quellen des römischen Rechts* (Rome, 1946), pp. 456 f.; E. Stauffer, *op. cit.,* pp. 146 f.

tion rests solely upon the word of revelation. The empty tomb possessed no evidential value apart from this norm of interpretation.[19]

The fact that women were the first to receive the announcement of the resurrection is significant in view of contemporary attitudes. Jewish law pronounced women ineligible as witnesses.[20] Early Christian tradition confirms that the reports of the women concerning the empty tomb and Jesus' resurrection were disregarded or considered embarrassing (cf. Lk. 24:11, 22-24; Mk. 16:11). That the news had first been delivered by women was inconvenient and troublesome to the Church, for their testimony lacked value as evidence. The primitive Community would not have invented this detail, which can be explained only on the ground that it was factual.

7 Having assured the women that Jesus was alive, the angel commissioned them to tell his followers that they would be reunited with him in Galilee. The expression "his disciples and Peter" corresponds to Ch. 1:36, "Simon and those with him." Peter is singled out because of his repeated and emphatic denial of Jesus (Ch. 14:66-72). He has not been mentioned by Mark since that shameful occasion, and his disloyalty might well be regarded as an extreme example of sin and blasphemy which disqualified him from participating in Jesus' triumph. Yet he had been forgiven (cf. Ch. 3:28). The summons to Galilee provided the assurance that Peter had not been rejected by the risen Lord.

The message that Jesus will precede his disciples to Galilee repeats the promise of Ch. 14:28. In the immediate context of the passage Jesus spoke of his violent death and prophesied that all of the disciples would fall away. When Peter vehemently protested his loyalty, Jesus announced that Peter would deny him three times that night. The one note of comfort was the assurance that after Jesus' resurrection the disciples would be regathered in Galilee. The fulfilment of the prophecy of failure and denial is to be redressed by the corresponding fulfilment of the promised restoration. Galilee is specified by Jesus, and by the angel, as the place where the disciples will encounter the Lord. The promise,

---

[19] Cf. W. Nauck, "Die Bedeutung des leeren Grabes für den Glauben an den Auferstandenen," *ZNW* 47 (1956), pp. 243-267.

[20] M. *Rosh Ha-Shanah* I. 8 speaks of the disqualification of women as witnesses as a matter of common knowledge. Cf. M. *Shebuoth* IV. 1, "The law about an oath of witness applies to men but not to women"; Josephus, *Antiquities* IV. viii. 15; Num. Rabba X, 159b; TJ *Yoma* VI. 2.

"there you will see him," implies a resurrection appearance to Peter and to the others (cf. I Cor. 15:5).[21]

8 The response of the women to the evidence of God's decisive intervention in raising Jesus from the dead is described in the categories of terror. They fled from the tomb, unable to control the dread which overwhelmed them and reduced them to silence. For a time they kept their experience to themselves because "they were afraid."[22] The prior use of words expressing terror and amazement in verses 5-6 has prepared for the forceful language of verse 8 and confirms that the cause of the women's fear is the presence and action of God at the tomb of Jesus. They recognized the significance of the empty tomb. This has important bearing on the interpretation of Mark's final comment, "for they were afraid." This statement finds its closest parallel in the transfiguration narrative, where Peter's brash proposal to build three tabernacles calls forth the remark, "for he did not know what to say, for they were exceedingly afraid" (Ch. 9:6). Those who are confronted with God's direct intervention in the historical process do not know how to react. Divine revelation lies beyond normal human experience, and there are no categories available to men which enable them to understand and respond appropriately. The first human response is overwhelming fear. It is probable that the fear experienced at the transfiguration and at the empty tomb was an anticipation of judgment. A devout Jew would understand the announcement that the resurrection had begun to signify that the end was at hand. The revelational context and the similarity of vocabulary in these two accounts confirm that the object of the women's

---

[21] For the contention of E. Lohmeyer, *Galiläa und Jerusalem* (Göttingen, 1936), pp. 10 ff.; *idem, Das Evangelium des Markus*[16] (Göttingen, 1963), pp. 355 f.; W. Marxsen, *Mark the Evangelist* (Nashville, 1969), pp. 75-92, that the reference is to the parousia of Jesus rather than to a resurrection appearance, see above on Ch. 14:28. For the fruitful suggestion that the promise of Ch. 1:17 ("I will make you fishers of men") finds its fulfilment through the meeting in Galilee see R. P. Meye, *Jesus and the Twelve* (Grand Rapids, 1968), pp. 83 f., 99-110.

[22] Cf. C. F. D. Moule, "St. Mark XVI. 8 Once More," *NTS* 2 (1955), pp. 58 f. J. Luzarraga, "Retraducción Semítica de *Phobeomai* en Mc 16, 8," *Biblica* 50 (1969), pp. 497-510, traces this final comment back to a Semitic source which used some form of the verb בהל, which can mean either "to be afraid" or "to hasten." He holds that the underlying sense was, "They went away in haste." This proposal lacks support from the text, for the departure with haste is covered already by ἔφυγον, while an adoption of Luzarraga's reading of the source leaves the silence of the women unexplained.

fear was divine revelation. Fear is the constant reaction to the disclosure of Jesus' transcendent dignity in the Gospel of Mark (cf. Chs. 4:41; 5:15, 33, 36; 6:50; 9:6, 32). In the light of this pervasive pattern, the silence and fear of the women are an indirect Christological affirmation.

Mark concluded his Gospel at this point. That verse 8 marks the ending to the Gospel in its present form is scarcely debated.[23] The contention that this is the original and intended ending, however, continues to be resisted.[24] The abrupt ending on the phrase "for they were afraid" has been regarded as evidence that the Gospel is incomplete or mutilated. It has been conjectured that the original ending reported a resurrection appearance to Peter and to all the disciples in Galilee, in harmony with the promise of verse 7 (cf. I Cor. 15:5, "he appeared to Cephas, and then to the Twelve"). A common feeling is that a Gospel would be terminated by a narrative reporting a resurrection appearance with a confession of faith by believers or by an expression of joy among those who have seen the risen Lord. All such proposals reflect a preconception of the form of a true Gospel. It is necessary to recognize that Mark was a theologian and historian in his own right, who has developed his conception throughout his work. Methodologically, it is imperative that the form be defined from the data offered by the Gospel in its totality.[25]

In point of fact, the present ending of Mark is thoroughly consistent with the motifs of astonishment and fear developed throughout the Gospel.[26] These motifs express the manner in which Mark understands the events of Jesus' life. In verse 8 the evangelist terminates his account of the good news concerning Jesus by sounding the note by which he has

---

[23] The most recent attempt to defend the authenticity of the longer ending (verses 9-20) was made by M. van der Valk, "Observations on Mark 16, 9-20 in Relation to St. Mark's Gospel," *Humanitas* n.s. 6-7 (1958), pp. 52-95. The article gives no consideration to the external evidence of manuscripts and is marred by speculative considerations which fail to support the author's conclusions.

[24] E.g. V. Taylor, *The Gospel According to St. Mark* (London, 1952), pp. 609 f.; C. E. B. Cranfield, *The Gospel According to Saint Mark*[2] (Cambridge, 1963), pp. 470 f.; B. M. Metzger, *The Text of the New Testament* (New York, 1964), pp. 226-229; E. Linnemann, "Der (wiedergefundene) Markusschluss," *ZThK* 66 (1969), pp. 255-287. For a response, especially to the article of Linnemann, see K. Aland, "Der wiedergefundene Markusschluss. Eine methodologische Bemerkung zur textkritischen Arbeit," *ZThK* 67 (1970), pp. 3-13.

[25] Rightly stressed by K. Tagawa, *Miracles et Évangile* (Paris, 1966), pp. 110-122.

[26] *Ibid.*, pp. 99-110.

characterized all aspects of Jesus' activity, his healings, miracles, teaching, the journey to Jerusalem. Astonishment and fear qualify the events of the life of Jesus. The account of the empty tomb is soul-shaking, and to convey this impression Mark describes in the most meaningful language the utter amazement and overwhelming feeling of the women. With his closing comment he wished to say that "the gospel of Jesus the Messiah" (Ch. 1:1) is an event beyond human comprehension and therefore awesome and frightening. In this case, contrary to general opinion, "for they were afraid" is the phrase most appropriate to the conclusion of the Gospel. The abruptness with which Mark concluded his account corresponds to the preface of the Gospel where the evangelist begins by confronting the reader with the fact of revelation in the person of John and Jesus (Ch. 1:1-13). The ending leaves the reader confronted by the witness of the empty tomb interpreted by the word of revelation. The focus upon human inadequacy, lack of understanding and weakness throws into bold relief the action of God and its meaning.[27]

---

[27] So N. B. Stonehouse, *op. cit.*, pp. 86-118; R. H. Lightfoot, *op. cit.*, pp. 80-97; K. Tagawa, *op. cit.*, pp. 110-122; R. P. Meye, "Mark 16:8–The Ending of Mark's Gospel," *Biblical Research,* 14 (1969), pp. 33-43, among others. K. Tagawa (pp. 112 f.) points out that astonishment is an absence of faith only when it is motivated by profane power. For the textual considerations which bear upon this question see the Additional Note on the Supplementary Endings of Mark.

Additional Note on Repentance in the Rabbinic Literature

The rabbis regarded the prophet Hosea as the great exponent of repentance in the Old Testament. Particularly the opening verses of Ch. 14 attracted their attention; it was this section (Hos. 14:2 ff.) which provided the reading from the prophets for the Sabbath of repentance between *Rosh Ha-Shanah* (the New Year) and *Yom Kippur* (the Day of Atonement). Here the rabbis found their full doctrine of repentance. Here, too, they found a Scriptural base for their view that prayer, confession, and repentance are God's chosen substitutes for sacrifice and burnt-offering, a view that became central after the destruction of the Temple made sacrifice impossible. The first two texts selected to illustrate the approach of rabbinic teachers are portions of sermons actually preached in a synagogue in the second or third century A.D. Their source is a collection of homilies delivered on the high feast and fast days of the Jews, the *Pesikta de Rab Kahana.* The occasion of both of these sermons was the Sabbath between *Rosh Ha-Shanah* and *Yom Kippur,* where the *Haftarah* reading began with Hos. 14:2.

> *Text 1:* "Good and upright is the Lord. Therefore, he will instruct sinners in the way" (Ps. 25:8). Men went and asked Wisdom: What shall be the punishment of the sinner? She answered: "Evil pursues sinners" (Prov. 13:21). They asked the Prophets: What shall be the punishment of the sinner? They answered: "The soul that sins shall surely die" (Ezek. 18:4). They asked the Torah: What shall be the punishment of the sinner? It said: "Let him bring a sin offering and he shall be atoned, as it is written, 'It shall be accepted for him to make a covering for him'" (Lev. 1:4). They asked God: What shall be the punishment of the sinner? He said: "Let him repent and he shall be atoned. For it is written: 'Good and upright is the Lord. Therefore, he will teach sinners in the way' (Ps. 25:8). My sons, what do I desire from you? 'Seek me and live!'" (Amos 5:4. R. Phineas said: Why is he good when he is upright? Why is he upright when he is good? Because he will teach sinners in the way. Because he teaches to them the way, that they should repent. Therefore, Hosea warned Israel and said: "Turn (repent), O Israel" (Hos. 14:2).
>
> "Parashoth Shubah," *Pesikta de Rab Kahana* 158b

R. Phineas exegetes Ps. 25:8 in the light of the rabbinic understanding of the Biblical phrase, "good and upright," qualities attributed to the Lord. These words may seem synonymous, but to the rabbis no expression in Scripture was superfluous or redundant; accordingly, they understood the expression, "good," to signify God as he exercised the "measure of mercy." The problem posed by Ps. 25:8 is to discern why God is described as "good" and "upright" at the same time. The answer is found in God's urging the sinner to repent, a gracious expression of his mercy given peculiar urgency in the light of his judgment. There should be observed in the text the rabbinic understanding that to reason (Wisdom), moral law (the Prophets), the ritual requirement (the Torah), repentance makes no sense. Repentance makes sense only with God, who acts in grace, even in those contexts where one would expect sheer judgment.

> *Text 2:* Israel said to God: Lord of the Worlds, if we repent, will you receive us? He said to them: I received the repentance of Cain, and will I not receive your repentance? God had decreed upon him a severe decree, as it is written: "When you till the ground it shall not any longer yield unto thee its strength; a fugitive and a wanderer shalt thou be in the earth" (Gen. 4:12). But when he repented, one half of the decree was removed from him. And how is it known that Cain repented? "And Cain said unto God: My affliction is greater than I can bear" (Gen. 4:13). And how is it known that one half of the decree was removed from him? "And Cain went from God and dwelt in the land of Nod, east of Eden" (Gen. 4:16). Do not read "in the land, a fugitive and a wanderer" (נע ונד) but "in the land of Nod" (נוד).
>
> What is meant by the expression, "He went up from before the Lord?" R. Judah said in the name of R. Eibu: He went up as one who threw the words (which he had heard) over his shoulder and tried to fool God. R. Berachiah said in the name of R. Eleazar bar Simeon: He went out as one who desecrated and cast away his Creator. But R. Huna said in the name of R. Hananiah bar Papa: He went out as one who was joyous, as it is written: "Behold, he comes forth to meet thee, and when he sees thee he will be glad in his heart" (Ex. 4:14). When he went out Adam met him, and he said to him: What has happened with respect to your judgment? Cain answered: I have repented and I have been released. Then Adam began to strike upon his face in amazement, and said:

> How great is the strength of repentance, and I did not know it. Then he said: "It is good to give thanks to God" (Ps. 92:2). R. Levi said: This psalm is by Adam, for it says "A Psalm, A Song for the Seventh Day."
>
> *Pesikta de Rab Kahana* 160a-163b

This text is a small portion of a long sermon which celebrates the repentance of the great sinners of the Old Testament; if God accepted their repentance, surely he will accept the repentance of Israel. Cain is followed by Ahab (I Kings 21:19 is compared with I Kings 21:27-29); by the men of Anathoth who sought to take Jeremiah's life (Jer. 11:21-23 is compared with Ezra 2:23); by the men of Nineveh (Jonah 3:4, 6-8 is compared with Jonah 3:10). The midrash then exegetes Joel 2:13, "Rend your hearts and not your garments, and turn unto the Lord your God," before returning to Manasseh, whose celebrated repentance called attention to itself (II Chron. 33:10 is compared with II Chron. 33:13). The point made is that Manasseh's repentance was conditional ("if you answer me, fine, but otherwise . . . "), and yet God accepted it. The last example is the repentance of Jeconiah (Jer. 22:24, 28, 30 are compared with Hag. 2:23; I Chron. 3:17). The homily concludes: "It happens in the world that if a man shoots an arrow, it may travel one field's length or more. But great is the power of repentance for it reaches unto the Throne of Glory, as it is written: 'Turn, O Israel, unto the Lord your God.'" Throughout the emphasis is that Israel has a gracious God who provides an opportunity for repentance.

In the exposition of Cain's repentance the different interpretative strands should be noted. The first strand plays on the similarity in sound between *nad,* "a fugitive," and *nod,* "Nod." God removed that half of the decree which said Cain would be a "wanderer." The next two rabbis address themselves to the question: Why was only half of the decree removed? Because Cain's repentance was not really sincere. The last rabbi represents a wholly distinct point of view from the previous two: repentance is a great mystery, understandable only in terms of grace and mercy. When a man repents, God releases him from his debt.

In the rabbinic literature there is nowhere a complete and precise definition of repentance in the abstract, though the practical implications of repentance are discussed repeatedly. The rabbis speak of the value of repentance, of its effects, of great types and exponents of repentance, but they do not describe it in theological language. The verb, *shub,* occurs only rarely in rabbinical literature, but the noun, *teshubah,* occurs very frequently. When a verbal form is used, the rabbis prefer the expression, "do repentance," to the verb, *shub*. This is in marked contrast to the Intertestamental literature, in which the noun, *teshubah,* occurs rarely. This indicates that the concept of *teshubah* has become crystallized and concretized to the point where it held a definite place in rabbinic thinking and was unmistakably clear to the common people. This process may be illustrated by the fifth of the "Eighteen Benedictions," which were to be recited daily by every devout Jew, and which were employed by Palestinian Jews prior to the destruction of the Temple in A.D. 70. The Palestinian recension represents the original form of the petition: its language is thoroughly biblical (compare Jer. 31:18; Lam. 5:21). The Babylonian recension is more developed and more concrete, reflecting an interpretation of the petition in keeping with rabbinic theology.

> *Text 3:* Fifth Petition (Palestinian Recension): "Return us, O Lord, unto Thee, and we shall return. Renew our days as before. Blessed art Thou, Who hast pleasure in repentance."
>
> Fifth Petition (Babylonian Recension): "Bring us back, our Father, to Thy Torah, and draw us near, Our King, to Thy service, and cause us to repent with perfect repentance before Thee. Blessed art Thou, O Lord, Who hast pleasure in repentance."

According to developed rabbinic thought, repentance *(teshubah)* was pre-existent to creation, being one of the seven great provisions made by the Lord before creation. Thus, long before man sinned, a remedy had been provided for that sin. Repentance is a healing gift (TB *Yoma* 86[a]), a shield against the punishment of God (*Pirqe Aboth* IV. 11). So great is its power, that the perfectly righteous cannot stand where the repentant sinner is able to stand (TB *Berachoth* 34[b]). So great is the power of repentance, and so universal is its need, that Enoch, Noah, Moses and all the prophets had as their greatest mission the preaching of repentance (*Pesikta Rabbati* 44). For the same reason, the rabbis represent the great sinners of the Old Testament as models of repentance, as in Text 2.

Paul Billerbeck writes on the rabbinic conception of *teshubah:* "The necessary components of repentance are (i) the recognition of the sin and an imploring of pardon with regret and remorse; (ii) the abandonment of the sin. When one of these elements is lacking, the repentance is not true, but deceitful; and if the man continues in this manner, finally the possibility of a genuine repentance will be withdrawn" (S-B*K* I [1922], p. 170). The accuracy of this statement may be seen from a *baraitha* (TB *Yoma* 86b) stating that God may forgive a second or third fall, but not a fourth; and from the principle that he who sins with the thought that he can always repent, inevitably loses out (M. *Yoma* VIII. 9). The element of deep contrition in repentance is brought out by the fact that the rabbis base their teaching on such poignant texts of grief as Jer. 8:5; 31:18; Ps. 51 and the book of Hosea.

In the rabbinical material there is frequent emphasis on the necessity for confession of sin. The efficacy of confession may be illustrated from a mishnaic text urging a criminal condemned to death to confess his sin.

> *Text 4:* When he was about ten cubits from the place of stoning, they used to say to him: "Make your confession," for such is the way of them that have been condemned to death to make confession, for everyone who makes confession has a share in the world to come. For so have we found it with Achan. Joshua said to him: "My son, give glory to the Lord, the God of Israel, and make confession with him, and tell me now what thou hast done. Do not hide it from me, and Achan answered Joshua and said, Truly, I have sinned against the Lord, the God of Israel, and thus and thus have I done" (Josh. 7:19). And how do we know that his confession made atonement for him? It is written, "And Joshua said, Why have you troubled us? The Lord shall trouble you this day" (Josh. 7:25) – "this day" you shall be troubled, but in the world to come you shall not be troubled. M. *Sanhedrin* VI. 2.

The exegesis turns on the expression, "this day." If Joshua had not meant to limit God's punishment of Achan to a single experience he would not have specified "this day." From this the rabbis reasoned that confession insures a place in the world to come. In a similar vein, all who were fatally ill were obliged to confess their sins (TB *Shabbath* 32a, *baraitha).* The Scriptural ground for such confession was found in Num. 5:6; Lev. 16:21; Ps. 51; 107:1; I Kings 8:47; Dan. 9:5; Prov. 28:13. Whether this confession had to be detailed and specific or general was a matter of dispute among the Tannaim of the second generation (TJ to *Yoma* VIII. 8).

One of the best sources for the rabbinic concept of repentance is the Mishnaic tractate *Yoma* and the liturgy it describes for the *Yom Kippur,* the Day of Atonement. Most of the material in *Yoma* antedates the destruction of the Temple.

Yom Kippur was a day of mourning for sin. The preparation for it began with the blowing of the *shofar* on New Year's Day, to warn the people to lift up their hearts and to return to God (Num. 29:1; Lev. 23:24). The prayers designated for use during the first ten days of the New Year are penitential in character, preparing the people for *Yom Kippur*. On the day itself, a man was forbidden to eat or drink, or to bathe and anoint himself. He could not wear sandals, nor enter into marriage (M. *Yoma* VIII. 1ff.). His disposition was to be one of profound sorrow for sin. The High Priest would read Lev. 3:16; 23:27-32 and recite by memory Num. 29:7-11, bringing before the people the history of the observance of the day, together with the exhortation to "afflict your souls" (Lev. 23:32).

Confession plays a central role in the liturgy of *Yom Kippur*. On this day the High Priest made three formal confessions. The first was made in his own name and in that of his family; after this confession, his family would concur in it by acknowledging the confession and blessing God's name (M. *Yoma* III. 8). The second confession was made in his name, in that of his family and in the name of the sons of Aaron, all of whom would then acknowledge the confession and bless God's name (M. *Yoma* IV. 2). Finally the High Priest made the great confession for all the people and the house of Israel (M. *Yoma* VI. 2). As soon as the people in the court heard the High Priest begin this confession, they bowed down, prostrating themselves, with their face to the courtyard, blessing God's name, and acknowledging the confession and their desire for repentance. The Palestinian Gemara to *Yoma* adds that in addition to the three public confessions of the High Priest, individuals were required to make a private, personal confession. The nature and character of this private confession does not seem to have been clearly specified, however (TJ to *Yoma* VIII. 9).

The relationship of national repentance to the coming of the messianic deliverance was a matter of debate toward the end of the first century A.D. The most famous debate was that between the Shammaite, R. Eliezer ben Hyrkanos, and the Hillelite, R. Jehoshua ben Ḥananya. R. Eliezer contended that Messiah could not come and would not come until Israel repented as a nation. His reasoning was based on a popular expectation that Messiah would come at the conclusion of Daniel's seventy week-years, which the rabbis calculated should fall on the ninth of Ab in the year A.D. 68. But instead of Messiah's coming and deliverance, on this date Titus burned the Temple! The explanation for this reversal in expectation was found in the allegation that Israel had not repented. R. Eliezer's reasoning was challenged by R. Jehoshua, who argued that when God's appointed time came the messianic end will take place regardless of the repentance of Israel. R. Jehoshua worked with a different set of figures, basing his calculations on the sabbatical scheme of seven millennia. According to this scheme, Messiah would come in the year A.D. 240, a date sufficiently far off in the future to allow Jehoshua to dispute the reasoning of his colleague. The debate is recorded several times in the sources, but the briefest account occurs in *Tanchuma* B. to Lev. בחקתי § 5 (ed. Buber, 56a).

> *Text 5:* R. Eliezer said: If Israel will repent, it will be redeemed. If Israel will not repent, it will not be redeemed, as it is written: "In returning and rest you shall be saved" (Isa. 30:15). R. Jehoshua said, Whether they return or not, as soon as the End is come, so soon will they be redeemed, as it is written: "I am the Lord. In its time I will hasten it" (Isa. 60:22). R. Eliezer said: God places over them an evil man like Haman, and he afflicts them, and as a result they will do repentance, as it is written: "For he will come like a rushing stream which the wind of the Lord drives *in that hour* [underlined words not in M.T.] and he will come to Zion as Redeemer, even to those in Jacob who turn from transgression..." (Isa. 59:19-20).

In an expanded form the debate may be found in TJ *Ta'anith* I, i, 63ª and TB *Sanhedrin* 97ᵇ (see S-B*K* I [1922], pp. 162 ff.). The main difference in the accounts centers in the Biblical texts cited to support these two positions. Anonymous statements supporting R. Eliezer's view that Israel would not experience the messianic redemption until the nation repented are found in TJ *Ta'an.* 1, 1, 64a; *Pesikta Rabbati* 33 (153ª); Num. R. VII (148ᶜ). Not until the third century A.D. was the opinion presented that if Israel repented for a single day the messianic deliverance would come. It is first attributed to Amoraim of the 3rd generation, Tanchuma ben Chijja and R. Levi (TJ *Ta'an.* 1, 1, 64a; *Pesikta* 163ᵇ; Midrash Canticles 5, 2, 118a).

By way of conclusion, in the rabbinic literature a development in the concept of repentance may be noted in three areas:

(1) The teaching on repentance becomes increasingly practical. This is seen in the wide discussion of the ancient models of repentance, as illustrated in Text 2. In the early Intertestamental period there is little appeal to the great penitents of the past, but gradually the number of appeals increases until the Tannaim have a whole galaxy of them. The

Tannaim constantly appeal to them to show what must be done in repentance, and to show that the rabbinic demand has been, and can be met.

(2) The teaching on repentance becomes more explicit, with attention being focused upon individual elements and requirements in true repentance, as seen in Texts 3 and 4. When these elements are assembled together they provide the raw materials for a fully developed theology of repentance.

(3) In this period there is a growing conviction that God himself will take a hand and force Israel to repent by bringing upon the people a period of "messianic woes." These consist of catastrophic reversals which will cause the people to return to God, and so shall serve as the birth-pangs of the Messiah, for they shall be followed by the messianic deliverance once Israel has repented. It is this conviction which informs R. Eliezer's viewpoint in Text 5.

Between Pharisaic teaching, and its consolidation in the rabbinic tradition, and the proclamation of first John the Baptist and then Jesus there is a difference in perspective which must be appreciated. The preaching of John and of Jesus belongs to the prophetic tradition in which there is a radical demand for a once-for-all commitment to God, a "turning" of one's whole self to the fulfilment of his will. The urgency in the summons to repentance is drawn from the eschatological context in which this summons is conveyed: there is no time for delay. In the Pharisaic and later rabbinic tradition repentance is conceived in terms of legal observance, while provision for forgiveness is made through such repeated practices as prayer, fasting and almsgiving. The source of this conception is found more in the priestly and legal traditions of Judaism. What is stressed is the repeatable character of repentance and its applicability and availability to all Israel at all times. In the Pharisaic tradition repentance is feasible and relevant, but there is rarely heard the distinctive note sounded in the preaching of John and of Jesus, that it is urgent because God has acted in a sovereign manner to bring near the Kingdom. In such a context the former pattern of repeated sin, repentance and restoration is inadequate. The great ultimate *teshubah* is now at hand, to be followed by the Kingdom. This emphasis belongs to the heart of the gospel, not to the rabbinic tradition.

ADDITIONAL NOTE ON THE SUPPLEMENTARY ENDINGS TO THE GOSPEL

The earliest Greek, versional and patristic evidence supports the conclusion that Mark ended his Gospel at Ch. 16:8. To the witness of the two earliest parchment codices, Vaticanus (B) and Sinaiticus (א), may be added minuscules 304 and 2386. The absence of Ch. 16:9-20 in the Old Latin MS *k*, the Sinaitic Syriac, several MSS of the Armenian version, the Adysh and Opiza MSS of the Georgian version, and a number of MSS of the Ethiopic version provide a wide range of support for the originality of the abrupt ending. Writing in the fourth century Eusebius remarked that "accurate" copies of Mark ended with verse 8, adding that Ch. 16:9-20 were missing from "almost all MSS" (*Quaestiones ad Marinum* 1 [MPG XXII, 937]), and the original form of the Eusebian sections makes no provision for numbering sections after Ch. 16:8. Jerome echoes this testimony when he says of the last twelve verses of Mark that "almost all the Greek codices do not have this concluding portion" (*Epistle* CXX. 3, *ad Hedibiam* [MPL XXII, 987]). Clement of Alexandria, Origen, Cyprian and Cyril of Jerusalem show no awareness of the existence of these verses. Moreover, a number of MSS which do contain them have scholia stating that older Greek copies lack them (e.g. 1, 20, 22, 137, 138, 1110, 1215, 1216, 1217, 1221, 1582), while in other witnesses the final section is marked with asterisks or obeli, the conventional signs used by scribes to mark off a spurious addition to a literary text. The evidence allows no other assumption than that from the beginning Mark circulated with the abrupt ending of Ch. 16:8. The fact that Matthew and Luke follow Mark until verse 8, but then diverge completely, lends further support to the supposition that the Gospel of Mark began its literary existence in this form.

The ending of the Gospel at Ch. 16:8, however, appeared too abrupt to some readers. The attempt to provide a more appropriate conclusion to the narrative affords the most plausible explanation for the origin of so-called shorter ending:

> "But they reported briefly to Peter and those with him all they had been told. And after this Jesus himself sent out by means of them, from east to west, the sacred and imperishable proclamation of eternal salvation."

From the language it is clear that these lines cannot have been written by Mark. The intention of this report is to round off verse 8a, and to indicate that the women obeyed the injunction of verse 7. As such, it stands in opposition to the statement in verse 8b that "they said nothing to anyone." This is made explicit in Codex Bobiensis (*k*), which is the only text which has the shorter ending alone. In joining the shorter ending to verse 8 the phrase "they said nothing to anyone" was omitted in this MS. The impression conveyed is that the women fled because they were afraid; nevertheless, they reported to Peter and to the others all they had been told.

This supplement to Mark's ending is found, in combination with Ch. 16:9-20, in several uncial MSS of the seventh, eighth, and ninth centuries (L Ψ 099 0112) as well as in a few minuscule or lectionary MSS (274^{mg} 579 $l^{961\ 1602}$) and in certain ancient versions (sy^{hmg} sa^{mss} bo^{mss} $aeth^{mss}$). Codex Vaticanus (B) also provides evidence for the existence of the shorter ending.[1]

In a recent study of the supplementary endings to Mark[2] K. Aland concluded that (1) the origin of the shorter ending is conceivable only with the hypothesis that the copy of Mark which lay before the author ended with Ch. 16:8, and that neither the longer conclusion nor any other continuation of the Gospel was then known. (2) The brevity and clumsiness of the shorter ending reflect either an early period of composition, a remote place of origin, or a very awkward author. It makes no attempt to create a link with Ch. 16:9-20, but arose evidently from the desire to round out the abrupt ending of Ch. 16:8. It should therefore be regarded as a parallel construction to Ch. 16:9-20. It is highly probable that the shorter and longer endings originated in completely separate areas. (3) There is strong authority for placing the shorter ending before the longer in the MS tradition.[3] (4) There are almost no patristic allusions to the shorter ending which assist one to assign a date

[1] After the conclusion of Mark in column 3 of folio 1303 (recto), a column is left free. This is a wholly singular phenomenon, for in Codex B a new book follows in the next column as soon as possible. The fact of a free column after the conclusion of Mark can be explained only from the supposition that the scribe knew a continuation after Ch. 16:8. Space calculations indicate that this can only have been the shorter ending. See T. Zahn, *Introduction to the New Testament* II (Edinburgh, 1909), p. 469.

[2] K. Aland, "Bemerkungen zum Schluss des Markusevangeliums," in *Neotestamentica et Semitica* (Edinburgh, 1969), pp. 157-180

[3] E.g. MS 274 has the shorter ending after Ch. 16:20, yet critical signs indicate an awareness that the shorter ending belongs after verse 8 and before the longer ending.

to its composition.[4] The only formulation in the shorter ending which appears to offer a clue is "the sacred and imperishable proclamation of eternal salvation," but for this phrase there are no really close parallels. The latest possible date for the composition of the shorter ending is the fourth century. Codex Bobbiensis (*k*) was transcribed in the fourth or fifth century, but it is based on a much earlier text. It shows paleographic marks of having been copied from a second-century papyrus.[5] Moreover, the narrow connection between MS *k* and the text of Cyprian (almost variant-free) suggests that the shorter ending was in existence at least as early as the beginning of the third century, and that in North Africa a relatively great number of MSS possessed the shorter ending.[6] Because the copy from which *k* was transcribed gives every appearance of going back to an earlier Greek text it is necessary to push the date back into the second century. This judgment is consistent with the increasingly established text-critical principle that all genuine textual alteration in normal cases goes back to the second century. There is no other explanation for the fact that although the longer ending was in existence at the latest by the middle of the second century, until the thirteenth century the shorter ending stands before the longer (e.g. L Ψ 099 0112 579 sy^{hmg} sa^{mss} bo^{mss} $aeth^{mss}$). This primacy of position is understandable only on the hypothesis of an early origin for the shorter ending. A date near the middle of the second century is probable.[7]

The fact that the shorter ending is now extant in only six Greek textual witnesses is not a counter-argument against its early origin. It is sobering to recall that the original abrupt ending is transmitted in only four Greek witnesses (ℵ B 304 2386 [lectionary?]). As soon as the longer ending became widespread it simply supplanted (as more valuable) the shorter as well as the abrupt ending. The formulation of the shorter ending stands as an erratic piece of tradition in the production of Christian writers, and it was soon displaced by the dominant tradition embodied in the longer ending.

---

[4] The only true parallel to the formula τοῖς περὶ τὸν Πέτρον comes from Ignatius, *To the Smyrneans* 3:2, ὅτε [ὁ 'Ιησοῦς] πρὸς τοὺς περὶ Πέτρον ἦλθεν, ἔφη αὐτοῖς κτλ.

[5] See B. M. Metzger, *The Text of the New Testament* (New York, 1964), p. 73.

[6] C. H. Turner, "Did Codex Vercellensis (*a*) Contain the Last Twelve Verses of St. Mark?" *JThS* 29 (1927-28), pp. 16-18 showed that MS *a* "must have had either the shorter ending or none at all." K. Aland, *op. cit.*, pp. 176 f. has now strengthened the case for this conclusion.

[7] K. Aland, *op. cit.*, pp. 169-178.

Unlike the shorter ending, the longer ending (Ch. 16:9-20) does not appear to have been compiled originally for the purpose of rounding off Mark. It actually interrupts the sequence of thought in Ch. 16:6-8, for it fails to relate the appearance of the risen Lord in Galilee, which was promised in Ch. 16:7. Instead of continuing the narrative it provides a list of appearances of the Lord which, in general, are brief extracts from the resurrection reports in Matthew, Luke and John. [8] Moreover, the transition from verse 8 to verse 9 is not smooth. While the subject in verse 8 is the women, the presumed subject in verse 9 is Jesus. The fact that the subject is understood in verse 9 suggests that the entire section was drawn from a context in which the subject was expressed. As it now stands, Ch. 16:9-20 is a mosaic which is clearly secondary in character, which serves to round off the kerygma of the primitive Church with a reference to Christ's ascension (Ch. 16:19). The tradition may have been composed originally as a catechetical summary of post-resurrection events. The development of a single theme, belief and unbelief, serves to unify the material theologically. The climax is provided by verse 14, where the disciples are rebuked for failing to believe, on the witness of others, the very message they will soon be urging their hearers to believe. [9]

Although the longer ending is found in the vast number of witnesses (A C D K L W X Δ Θ Π Ψ φ 28 33 274 565 700 892 1009 latt sy$^{c\ p\ h\ pal}$ cop^{pt}), the form, language and style of these verses militate against Marcan authorship. [10] The earliest definite witness to these verses as a part of Mark's Gospel is Irenaeus (*Adv. Haer.* III. x. 6), who cites

---

[8] Cf. verses 9 f. with Jn. 20:11-18; verses 12 f. with Lk. 24:13-35; verses 14 ff. with Lk. 24:25-29 and Jn. 20:19-29; verse 15 with Mt. 28:18-20; verse 19 with Lk. 24:50-53.

[9] Cf. F. Wagenaars, "Structura litteraria et momentum theologicum pericopae Mc 16, 9-20," *Verb Dom* 45 (1967), pp. 19-22.

[10] E.g. Mary Magdalene is introduced as the woman "from whom he had cast out seven demons" (cf. Lk. 8:2), as if she had not been mentioned already in Ch. 16:1. In verses 9-20 one finds neither Ἰησοῦς nor Χριστός, but the title Κύριος twice (Ch. 16:19-20). The vocabulary is marked by the presence of 17 non-Marcan words or words used in a non-Marcan sense: e.g. πρώτῃ in place of μιᾷ (cf. verse 2); ἐφάνη (verse 9); ἐκείνη (verse 10); πορεύεσθαι (verse 10, 12); θεᾶσθαι (verse 14); ἀπιστεῖν (verses 11, 16); μετὰ ταῦτα (verse 12); φανεροῦσθαι (verses 12, 14); ὕστερον (verse 14) in place of ἔσχατον (cf. Ch. 12:6, 22); πᾶσα ἡ κτίσις (verse 15); καλῶς ἔχειν (verse 18); ὁ μὲν οὖν κύριος (verse 19); συνεργεῖν (verse 20). Stylistically, Mark's usual transitions, εὐθύς, πάλιν are absent from verses 9-20; the use of καί is rare and no phrase begins with parataxis.

Ch. 16:9, although there is a possible echo of Ch. 16:20 in Justin (*Apology* XLV. 5). Justin's disciple Tatian included the longer ending in his *Diatessaron,* to judge from the Arabic version of this work. The evidence is sufficient to assert that the longer ending was in circulation by the middle of the second century, while its composition should be assigned to the first half of the second century.[11]

[11] In an attempt to marshall the patristic evidence for the Marcan endings K. Aland, *op. cit.,* p. 172 suggests that Hermas, *Similitudes* IX. xxv. 2 and Gospel of Peter 59 be compared with Ch. 16:10; and Epistle of the Apostles 2-3 be compared with Ch. 16:19.

An Armenian MS of the Gospels, copied A.D. 989, contains a brief rubric of two words in the space at the conclusion of the last line of verse 8 and before the last twelve verses, "of the Presbyter Ariston." That the reference is to Aristion, a contemporary of Papias and purportedly a disciple of the apostle John, is only an interesting conjecture. It is improbable, however, that an Armenian rubricator would have access to historically reliable information concerning the source of the longer ending at this late date. So also B. M. Metzger, *op. cit.,* p. 227; K. Aland, *op. cit.,* p. 172.

Additional Note on the Theology of the Freer Logion

An interesting addition to the longer ending of the Gospel has been preserved in the Freer Logion, a portion of which had been known through a Latin citation by Jerome. He commented that

> in certain exemplars and especially in the Greek manuscripts [of the Gospel] according to Mark, at the end of his Gospel, there is written: "Afterward, when the Eleven reclined at meal, Jesus appeared to them and upbraided [them for] their unbelief and hardness of heart because they had not believed those who had seen Him after His resurrection. And they made excuse, saying: 'This age of iniquity and unbelief is under Satan who, through unclean spirits, does not permit the true power of God to be apprehended. Therefore, reveal your righteousness, now.'"[1]

The Greek text of this fragment was supplied in a more complete form by a fifth-century uncial manuscript of the Gospels discovered in Egypt in 1906.[2] Appended to Mark 16:14 were sixteen lines of text containing the tradition preserved by Jerome with Jesus' response to his disciples. The addition is a unit of conversation which was inserted in the longer ending of Mark, apparently from a marginal gloss.[3] Its occurrence in

---

[1] *Dialogue against the Pelagians* II. 15 (P.L. XXIII, col. 576).

[2] Codex W, folio 184 recto, lines 9-24. For a photographic facsimile of the text see B. Botte, "Freer (Logion de)," *DB Suppl* III (1938), col. 528, fig. 351. For a transcription of the text, together with the principal conjectural emendations which have been proposed, see col. 525.

[3] The word of association which first attracted the gloss appears to be "unbelief," ἀπιστία, in Mark 16:14, "and he upbraided them for their unbelief (τὴν ἀπιστίαν αὐτῶν) . . . And they made excuse saying: 'This age of lawlessness and of unbelief (τῆς ἀπιστίας) . . . '" The opinion that the Freer Logion is a gloss has been challenged on the ground that without it the account passes very abruptly from reproof of the disciples' unbelief to the commission to proclaim the gospel to the world. The logion appears to supply the point of transition demanded by the context (so T. Zahn, *Geschichte des neutestamentlichen Kanons* II [Erlangen, 1896], p. 936; *Einleitung in das Neue Testament* II [Leipzig, 1900], p. 229, on the basis of Jerome's citation alone; H. B. Swete, *Zwei neue Evangelienfragmente* [Bonn, 1908], p. 10, who appealed to the ease with which such an obscure passage could be excised). The more moderate conclusion that the passage is a gloss derived from the same source which supplied verses 14-18, but which the original compiler of the longer ending had neglected, was suggested by A. Harnack, "Neues zum unechten Marcusschluss," *TLZ* 33 (1908), pp. 168-170, and was accepted with slight modification by H. Koch, "Der erweiterte Markusschluss und die kleinasiatischen Presbyter," *BZ* 6 (1908), pp. 266-278, and P. van Kasteren, "Het slot van

a single Greek manuscript suggests that it should be treated as an isolated logion embodying a local tradition.[4]

Jesus' response to the disciples merits attention for its modification of a more traditional eschatological scheme:

> And the Messiah said to them that the limit of the years of the authority of Satan has been fulfilled, but other terrible things are drawing near. And on behalf of those who have sinned, I was delivered to death, in order that they might turn to the truth and sin no more, in order that they might inherit the spiritual and incorruptible glory which is in heaven which consists in righteousness.[5]

The key sentence is the striking statement that "the limit of the years of the authority of Satan has been fulfilled, but other terrible things are drawing near." The disciples had claimed that this age, characterized by lawlessness[6] and unbelief, is under Satanic control.[7] Their proclama-

het Marcusevangelie," *Studien* 86 (1916), pp. 283-296; *idem,* "Nog een woord over het Marcusslot," *Studien* 87 (1917), pp. 484-490. Basic to this proposal is Zahn's original contention that the Freer Logion fills the hiatus between verses 14 and 15. Yet closer examination will show that if there is a hiatus between verses 14 and 15 in the longer ending, it is poorly overcome by this logion. The words of the disciples are scarcely directed to the charge of unbelief, but rather reflect on the difficulties they have encountered in their preaching. The unfortunate manner in which these words have been attached to the rebuke of Jesus is sufficient to expose an interpolation. Moreover, the hiatus is no less great between the response of Jesus in the logion and verse 15. The addition is an isolated logion embodying a local tradition. It probably owes its existence in the Freer MS to the intercalation of the text of the longer ending of Mark by some early reader of the Gospel whose attention was caught by the charge of unbelief. The contention that the entire text of the logion is a gloss is accepted by B. Botte, *op. cit.,* col. 526 f.; A. E. J. Rawlinson, *St. Mark*[5] (London, 1942), p. 248; V. Taylor, *The Gospel according to St. Mark* (London, 1952), p. 615; E. Schweizer, *The Good News According to Mark* (Richmond, 1970), pp. 375 f.; *et alia.*

[4] B. Botte, *op. cit.,* col. 526 f.

[5] καὶ ὁ χριστὸς ἐκείνοις προσέλεγεν ὅτι πεπλήρωται ὁ ὅρος τῶν ἐτῶν τῆς ἐξουσίας τοῦ σατανᾶ, ἀλλὰ ἐγγίζει ἄλλα δεινά· καὶ ὑπὲρ ὧν ἐγὼ ἁμαρτησάντων παρέδοθην εἰς θάνατον ἵνα ὑποστρέψωσιν εἰς τὴν ἀλήθειαν καὶ μηκέτι ἁμαρτήσωσιν, ἵνα τὴν ἐν τῷ οὐρανῷ πνευματικὴν καὶ ἄφθαρτον τῆς δικαιοσύνης δόξαν κληρονομήσωσιν.

[6] The judgment on the evil character of this age is thoroughly Palestinian: e.g., I Enoch 48:7, "this age of unrighteousness," II Enoch 66:6, "this age of pain"; cf. Gal. 1:4, "this present evil age." For lawlessness (ἀνομία) in the last days cf. Matt. 24:12; Didache 16:4; Hermas 8:3 and especially Barnabas 18:2, "This present time of lawlessness" (ὁ καιρὸς ὁ νῦν τῆς ἀνομίας), which closely parallels the Freer Logion.

[7] The exact expression, "the authority of Satan," is found in Acts 26:18, "that

tion of the truth had met both indifference and hostility. But in the age to come, when Satan's power has been broken, the truth will be recognized. They ask, therefore, for an immediate parousia ("therefore, reveal your righteousness now").[8] Their statements presuppose the traditional two-age concept of "this age" followed by "the age to come." This assumption governs their reflection on their own experience and their hope for the parousia.[9]

Jesus' answer cuts across this conception and modifies it significantly. He asserts that the limit of the years in which Satan was allowed to exercise authority has already come to an end.[10] But that does not mean that the age to come will immediately break into the time structure, bringing salvation in its fulness. On the contrary, "other terrible things" are drawing near.[11] The term translated "terrible things" does not occur elsewhere in the New Testament, but in the Apostolic Fathers it is found with the meaning "fearful" or "terrible" in association with punishment or torture.[12] In the Septuagint it occurs infrequently to describe deep personal anguish,[13] or severe affliction.[14] The two most interesting occurrences of the word are found in the Wisdom of Solomon. In a con-

---

they may turn from darkness to light and from the authority of Satan to God." Cf. Col. 1:18; Eph. 2:2; Lk. 4:6; 22:53; Rev. 13:2, 4, 5, 7, 12. See further, W. Foerster, *TWNT* II (Eng. Tr. 1964), pp. 567 f.

8 The appeal appears to be for the revelation of God's righteous judgment through the parousia of Christ, as in Acts 17:31; Rev. 19:11. So G. Schrenk, *TWNT* II (Eng. Tr. 1964), p. 198. For the association of righteousness with the Messiah see G. Schrenk, "The Messiah as the Righteous," *TWNT* II (Eng. Tr. 1964), pp. 186 f., and the passage cited there. The second occurrence of the term "righteousness" has a more distinctly Pauline character, "the glory to be inherited, which consists of righteousness." In this instance the term "righteousness" approximates in meaning "salvation."

9 This frame of mind was by no means unusual. It stands behind the implied request for an immediate restoration of the Kingdom in Acts 1:6, where "at this time" corresponds to "now" in the Freer Logion; in the early second century the author of Barnabas longed for that time "when there is no longer lawlessness, but all things have been made new by the Lord" (Barn. 15:7).

10 The closest parallel to "the limit of the years . . . has been fulfilled" is Mark 1:5, "the time has been fulfilled." For other examples see W. Bauer (A-G, p. 677). With the thought cf. Jn. 16:10.

11 Gr. ἄλλα δεινά.

12 I Clem. 6:2; II Clem. 17:7; M. Polyc. 2:4; Hermas, *Sim.* 6, 3, 3.

13 II Kings 1:9; Job 2:13; 33:15; Wisdom 18:17 ℵA; Sirach 38:16.

14 Wisdom 19:16; IV Maccabees 8:9, 15; 15:25.

text of judgment, the writer depicts the experience of the ungodly in the last day:

> When the ungodly shall come,
> When their deeds are reckoned up, with cowardly fear;
> And their lawless deeds shall convict them to their face,
> Then the righteous man shall stand in great boldness
> Before the face of them who afflicted him,
> Even those who reckoned his labors to be of no account.
> When they see this, they shall be troubled with terrible fear
> And they shall be amazed at his salvation.[15]

Here the term "terrible" is coupled with "fear," as in Job 33:15, to describe the horror that grips a man in anticipation of what is about to befall him. "Terrible fear" is merely a prelude to judgment. The author uses the term with this connotation later in his account to describe the dreams which troubled the Egyptians prior to the striking of the first-born by the Angel of Death. Their sleep was disturbed by "apparitions in terrible dreams" (Ch. 18:17). The terrible things they saw were an anticipation of the coming judgment. It is precisely in this sense that it seems best to interpret the reference in the Freer Logion; the term describes the fearful events which precede the judgment which accompanies the parousia of the Messiah. The "other terrible things" furnish a prelude to that judgment.[16] This is a distinctly Palestinian-Jewish concept, found in the rabbinic sources under the rubric "the birth-pangs of the Messiah."[17] Fearful persecutions and catastrophic reversals in men and nature precede the coming of the Days of the Messiah. If this interpretation of the expression is correct, the eschatological scheme reflected in the words of the risen Lord is intelligible and may be represented graphically.

---

15 Wisdom 4:20-5:2. The text of the key line runs ἰδόντες ταραχθήσονται φοβῷ δεινῷ.

16 In this connection the thesis of H. Koch, *op. cit.*, pp. 266-278, is interesting: he contends that the Logion is incomplete. After having alluded to his role as the Savior Jesus must have announced as well his role as judge. The context, however, would lead one to expect an explanation of the preliminary events, in the manner of Mark 13:6 and par.; M. *Soṭa* IX. 15; TB *Sanhedrin* 98b, *et al.*

17 חבלו של המשיח, see above on Ch. 13:8. Cf. S-B*K* IV (1928), pp. 977-986, "Die Vorzeichen der messianischen Zeit."

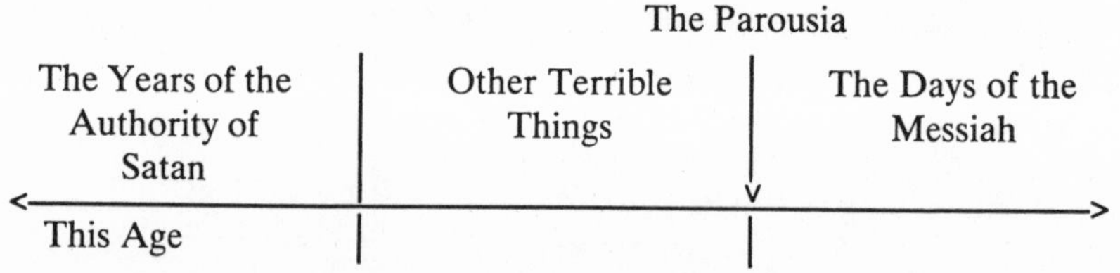

The twofold structure of "this age" and "the age-to-come" has been periodized to provide for a factor the disciples had not anticipated, the terrible things preceding the Days of the Messiah.[18]

The Freer Logion, with its periodization, is strikingly similar to Acts 3:19-21, where there is a reflection on the present times of refreshing and the yet future Days of the Messiah.[19] In the Freer Logion the disciples plead for the parousia of the Messiah, that is, for the time when the Messiah will display his vindicated righteousness. They recognize Jesus as the Messiah, but the world does not. As in Acts 3:19-21, the answer given is that the time for such a revelation has not yet come, and in both passages provision is built in for delay. More significant is the fact that both passages describe the final period as the Days of the Messiah. This is clearly stated in Acts 3:19-21, while in the Freer Logion it is demanded by the designation "the Messiah," as well as by the nuance in the expression "other terrible things." Moreover, both texts stress repentance as a condition for the in-breaking of the messianic era. The implication that the Days of the Messiah cannot come without the repentance of Israel is suggested in the Freer Logion as strongly as it is in Acts 3:19-21. Terrible things come upon those for whom the Messiah died to encourage the repentance which brings the inheritance of the elect community, the messianic era together with its glory.[20]

---

[18] The closest parallel to the thought, but not the vocabulary, of the Freer Logion at this point appears to be Barn. 4:9: "Wherefore let us pay heed in the last days, for the whole time of our life and faith will profit us nothing unless we resist, as becomes sons of God *in this present lawless time and in the offenses which are about to come* (νῦν ἐν τῷ ἀνόμῳ καιρῷ καὶ τοῖς μέλλουσιν σκανδάλοις), so that the Black One (ὁ μέλας) may have no opportunity of entry."

[19] On this passage see now W. L. Lane, "Times of Refreshment. A Study of Eschatological Periodization in Judaism and Christianity" (Diss. Harvard, 1962), pp. 142-181.

[20] That the text will bear the weight of such an interpretation is certain from the coordinating clauses introduced by the conjunction of purpose, ἵνα: ἄλλα δεινά· καὶ ὑπὲρ ὧν ἐγὼ ἁμαρτησάντων παρεδόθην εἰς θάνατον, ἵνα ὑποστρέψωσιν . . . ἵνα . . . κληρονομήσωσιν.

The cluster of primitive ideas found in Acts 3:19-21 is present in the Freer Logion as well, together with some significant differences. The nebulous concept of "the former days" which must be supplied for the Acts passage is here expressed under the rubric "the years of the authority of Satan," and it is stated explicitly that these years have been fulfilled. They now lie in the past. While Acts reflects upon the refreshment brought by the presence of the Holy Spirit, no attention is paid to this facet of the community's experience in the Freer Logion. Rather, the age between the former period and the Days of the Messiah is telescoped and presented in the perspective of the dramatic conflicts which usher in the final era.

Finally, the Freer Logion reflects on the experience of the community in the Days of the Messiah not in terms of restoration, as in Acts, but in the categories of a heavenly inheritance. [21] The Freer Logion and Acts 3:19-21 are independent witnesses to a tradition of the periodization of inherited eschatological hopes by the early Palestinian Church. [22]

---

21 Cf. I Peter 1:4, "unto an inheritance which is imperishable . . . kept in heaven for you." W. Bauer (A-G, p. 203) suggests Cleopatra, 146 f., ἐνέδυσεν αὐτοὺς θείαν δόξαν πνευματικήν in connection with this phrase of the Freer Logion.

22 It is difficult to assess the relative primitiveness of the Freer Logion. Apparently only T. Zahn, *Einleitung* II, p. 229; H. B. Swete, *op. cit.*, p. 10; and R. Dunkerley, *The Unwritten Gospel* (London, 1925), p. 197, were willing to plead for the authenticity of the logion. It is my opinion that it is not authentic, but reflects the thinking of the early Church; its relatively early character is reflected in its Palestinian language, its emphasis on the significance of repentance as a condition for the Days of the Messiah, its use of ὁ χριστός as a title of office, and its particular expression of periodization, which is without parallel in the extant literature. As to the date when the Logion was added to the margin of a MS of Mark, any guess is hazardous. C. R. Gregory, *Das Freerlogion* (Leipzig, 1908), pp. 64 f., suggested the first half of the second century as most probable on the basis of the style and vocabulary of the fragment, and because after A.D. 150 it became increasingly difficult to make additions to the Gospels. T. Zahn, *op. cit.*, pp. 230-232, followed by A. Harnack and H. Koch, alleged that the source of the Logion (as well as of vv. 14-18 for Zahn) was the tradition Papias had received from the Asiatic Presbyter Aristion. Zahn cites as confirmatory evidence a marginal gloss to Rufinus' translation of Eusebius, *Eccl. Hist.* III. xxxix. 9, which connects Aristion's name with the story taken from Papias that Justus Barsabbas (Acts 1:23) once drank a deadly poison, but was preserved from all harmful effects by the grace of the Lord. The story may have been circulated as an illustration of Mark 16:18, but as proof for the source of the Freer Logion it lacks persuasive demonstration. See further E. Helzle, *Der Schluss des Markusevangeliums (Mk. 16:9-20) und das Freer-Logion (Mk. 16:14 W), ihre Tendenzen und ihr gegenseitiges Verhältnis* (Dissertation Tübingen, 1959).

INDEXES

INDEX OF AUTHORS

INDEX OF PERSONS AND PLACES

SUBJECT INDEX

SCRIPTURE INDEX

OLD TESTAMENT

SCRIPTURE INDEX

NEW TESTAMENT